Competition Law –
Enforcement and Procedure

Competition Law – Enforcement and Procedure

Martin Smith MA, LLM, Solicitor
Partner, Simmons & Simmons, London

Butterworths
London, Edinburgh, Dublin
2001

United Kingdom	Butterworths, a Division of Reed Elsevier (UK) Ltd, Halsbury House, 35 Chancery Lane, LONDON WC2A 1EL and 4 Hill Street, EDINBURGH EH2 3JZ
Australia	Butterworths, a Division of Reed International Books Australia Pty Ltd, CHATSWOOD, New South Wales
Canada	Butterworths Canada Ltd, MARKHAM, Ontario
Hong Kong	Butterworths Hong Kong, a division of Reed Elsevier (Greater China) Ltd, HONG KONG
India	Butterworths India, NEW DELHI
Ireland	Butterworth (Ireland) Ltd, DUBLIN
Malaysia	Malayan Law Journal Sdn Bhd, KUALA LUMPUR
New Zealand	Butterworths of New Zealand Ltd, WELLINGTON
Singapore	Butterworths Asia, SINGAPORE
South Africa	Butterworths Publishers (Pty) Ltd, DURBAN
USA	Lexis Law Publishing, CHARLOTTESVILLE, Virginia

A CIP Catalogue record for this book is available from the British Library.

ISBN 0 406 903 808

ISBN 0-406-90380-8

9 780406 903808

Typeset by Phoenix Photosetting, Chatham, Kent
Printed and bound in Great Britain by Butler and Tanner Ltd, Frome, Somerset

Preface

When Butterworths suggested that Divisions X and XI of *Butterworths Competition Law*, which deal with the procedure by which EC and UK competition law are enforced by the regulatory authorities and national courts, be used as a basis for a standalone text, I was delighted. In the 9 years since *Butterworths Competition Law* was first published, the pace of change in the procedural and enforcement arena has been relentless. At the EC level, we have seen developments such as the European Commission Notices on enforcement by the national courts and national competition authorities and on leniency in cartel cases; the first individual fine for infringement of Articles 81 or 82, EC Treaty in excess of €100 million; the radical 1999 White Paper on Modernisation, with its proposal for abandonment of the Commission's monopoly over application of Article 81(3); and major European Court judgments on a range of issues relating to the rights of defence in competition cases, culminating in the 1000 page judgment in the *Cement* case earlier this year.

The pace of change at the UK level has been less frenetic but nonetheless the last few years have seen the enactment of the Competition Act 1998, a major and long-awaited piece of legislation which brings UK competition law broadly in line with EC law. The Office of Fair Trading has signalled its intention to apply the new regime with vigour. It remains to be seen how it will work in practice. We must also wait to see how the Competition Commission will apply its new appeal functions under the Act.

This year saw the repeal of the Restrictive Trade Practices Act 1976, the Resale Prices Act 1976 and the anti-competitive practice provisions of the Competition Act 1980. I suspect that few will rue the passing of the Restrictive Trade Practices Act, even though there was a certain intellectual charm about the many conundra which that Act threw up. This book does not deal with those three sets of statutory provisions (apart from covering briefly the scope to invoke the Restrictive Trade Practices Act in the context of agreements still in force today but containing provisions rendered unenforceable for want of being furnished to the Office of Fair Trading whilst the Act was still in force).

I should like to thank all those at Butterworths who have been involved in helping bring this book to fruition. My thanks go also to my secretary, Karen Thompson, who has committed the text to the printed page. Last, but very definitely not least, my thanks go to my wife, Helma, and our daughters, Philippa and Hannah, for putting up with the days and evenings sacrificed to the updating altar.

Looking forward, there is no reason to believe that the pace of change in respect of enforcement and procedural issues will let up: whither the EC modernisation initiative? What will be the impact of the Human Rights Act 1998 in relation to competition law enforcement in the UK? How will the Competition Act 1998 be applied in practice? How will the Competition Commission interpret its role under the Act? Only time will tell.

In order to keep this book to one volume, we have deliberately excluded any materials. There are a number of excellent and comprehensive sources for such materials, notably Butterworths own *Competition Law Handbook*.

The law is stated in this book as at 1 August 2000.

Martin Smith

November 2000

Contents

All references in bold are to paragraph numbers

Table of Statutes

References in this Table to *Statutes* are to Halsbury's Statutes of England (Fourth Edition) showing the volume and page at which the annotated text of the Act may be found.

References in the right-hand column are to paragraph numbers.

All references are to paragraph numbers

All references are to paragraph numbers

All references are to paragraph numbers

All references are to paragraph numbers

Foreign Enactments

UNITED STATES

All references are to paragraph numbers

Table of Statutory Instruments

References in the right-hand column are to paragraph numbers.

All references are to paragraph numbers

Table of European Communities Legislation

References in the right-hand column are to paragraph numbers.

Treaties

All references are to paragraph numbers

Secondary Legislation

DECISIONS

All references are to paragraph numbers

All references are to paragraph numbers

All references are to paragraph numbers

Commission Decision 91/299/EEC OJ [1991] L 152/21 . . 2.06, 8.55, 9.25, 9.30, 9.55
Commission Decision 91/300/EEC OJ [1991] L 152/40 . . 8.55, 9.30, 9.55
Commission Decision 91/329/EEC OJ [1991] L 178/31 . . . . 8.37
Commission Decision 91/335/EEC OJ [1991] L 185/23 . . . . 9.42
Commission Decision 91/532/EEC OJ [1991] L 287/39 . . 2.09, 9.42, 9.50
Commission Decision 91/562/EEC OJ [1991] L 306/22 . . . . . . 8.36, 8.44
Commission Decision 92/33/EEC OJ [1992] L 12/24 . . . . 8.37
Commission Decision 92/44/EEC OJ [1992] L 246/37 . . . . 8.60
Commission Decision 92/51/EEC OJ [1992] L 326/31 . . . . . . 8.60, 9.54
Commission Decision 92/154/EEC OJ [1992] L 66/1 . . . . 9.31
Commission Decision 92/157/EEC OJ [1992] L 68/19 . . . . 4.34
Commission Decision 92/163/EEC OJ [1992] L 72/1 . . . 2.06, 8.53, 8.55, 9.07, 9.56
Commission Decision 92/204/EEC OJ [1992] L 92/1 . . . . . . 9.54, 10.62
Commission Decision 92/212/EEC OJ [1992] L 95/50 . . . . 9.35, 9.54
Commission Decision 92/237/EEC OJ [1992] L 121/45 . . 6.61, 6.69, 9.87
Commission Decision 92/262/EEC OJ [1992] L 134/1 . . . . 9.32
Commission Decision 92/500/EEC OJ [1992] L 305/16 . . 6.54, 6.69, 9.87
Commission Decision 93/47/EEC OJ [1993] L 20/6 . . . . 6.69, 9.87
Commission Decision 93/49/EEC OJ [1993] L 20/14 . . . . 8.44
Commission Decision 93/50/EEC OJ [1993] L 20/23 . . . . 8.56
Commission Decision 93/82/EEC OJ [1993] L 34/20 . . . . 9.32
Commission Decision 93/252/EEC OJ [1993] L 116/21 . . . . 8.55
Council Decision 93/350/Euratom, ECSC, EEC OJ [1993] L 144/21 10.02
Commission Decision 93/406/EEC OJ [1993] L 183/19 . . . . 10.62
Commission Decision 93/554/EEC OJ [1993] L 272/28 . . . . 8.60
Commission Decision 94/19/EC OJ [1994] L 15/8 . . . . 8.28
Council Decision 94/149/ECSC, EC OJ [1994] L 66/29 . . . . . . 10.02
Commission Decision 94/215/ ECSC OJ [1994] L 116/1 . . . . 2.06, 8.52, 9.58
Commission Decision 94/272/EC OJ [1994] L 117/30 . . . . 8.29, 18.17
Commission Decision 94/384/EC OJ [1994] L 174/34 . . . . 8.40
Commission Decision 94/599/EC OJ [1994] L 239/14 . . . . 8.68, 9.57, 9.102
Commission Decision 94/601/EC OJ [1994] L 243/1 . . 2.06, 8.52, 8.54, 9.12, 9.58
Commission Decision 94/735/EC OJ [1994] L 294/31 . . . . . . 6.67, 6.70
Commission Decision 94/810/ECSC, EC OJ [1994] L 330/67 . . 7.32, 7.34, 7.44, 7.61
Commission Decision 94/815/EC OJ [1994] L 343/1 . . . 2.06, 8.52, 9.58
Commission Decision 94/985/EC OJ [1994] L 378/17 . . . . 9.31
Commission Decision 94/987/EC OJ [1994] L 378/45 . . . . 9.76
Commission Decision 95/477/EC OJ [1995] L 272/16 . . . . 9.19
Commission Decision 96/546/EC OJ [1996] L 239/23 . . . . 8.44
Commission Decision 97/84/EC OJ [1997] L 26/23 . . . . 9.48
Commission Decision 97/780/EC OJ [1997] L 318/1 . . . . 8.44
Commission Decision 98/273/EC OJ [1998] L 124/60 . . . . 2.06, 9.07, 9.56, 9.61, 9.90, 11.21
Commission Decision 98/531/EC OJ [1998] L 246/1 . . . . 5.13
Commission Decision 1999/210/EC OJ [1999] L 76/1 . . . . 2.12, 9.45, 9.51
Commission Decision 1999/60/EC OJ [1999] L 24/1 . . . . 9.61
Commission Decision 2000/12/EC OJ [2000] L 5/55 . . . . 9.31
Commission Decision 2000/74/EC OJ [2000] L 30/1 . . . . 9.68
Commission Decision 2000/117/EC OJ [2000] L 39/1 . . . . 9.25
Commission Decision 2000/146/EC OJ [2000] L 49/37 . . . . 6.21, 9.84

REGULATIONS

Council Regulation 17/62 OJ Sp Ed [1959–62] p 87 . . . . 4.06, 4.18, 4.29, 4.68, 4.73, 4.76, 5.17, 7.43, 7.61, 7.62, 8.72, 10.04, 10.25, 11.11, 11.14–11.16, 11.23, 11.40, 15.29, 15.107, 15.177, 15.179, 18.06, 18.08, 20.11, 20.12, 20.17
  preamble 4.11, 6.06, 9.53

All references are to paragraph numbers

All references are to paragraph numbers

Conventions and Agreements

All references are to paragraph numbers

Table of Cases and Commission Decisions

Judgments of the European Court of Justice and decisions of the EC Commission are listed below alphabetically. Judgments of the European Court of Justice are also listed numerically. The numerical Table follows the alphabetical.

References in the right-hand column are to paragraph numbers.

A

All references are to paragraph numbers

All references are to paragraph numbers

B

All references are to paragraph numbers

All references are to paragraph numbers

C

D

All references are to paragraph numbers

E

All references are to paragraph numbers

F

All references are to paragraph numbers

G

All references are to paragraph numbers

H

All references are to paragraph numbers

I

J

All references are to paragraph numbers

K

L

All references are to paragraph numbers

N

O

All references are to paragraph numbers

P

All references are to paragraph numbers

R

All references are to paragraph numbers

S

T

All references are to paragraph numbers

U

V

W

Y

Z

Decisions of the European Court of Justice are listed below numerically. These decisions are also included in the preceding alphabetical list.

All references are to paragraph numbers

All references are to paragraph numbers

All references are to paragraph numbers

All references are to paragraph numbers

All references are to paragraph numbers

Chapter 1 An Overview

A Introduction

1.01
The institutional structure which exists under EC and UK law differs so substantially that it is necessary to consider separately the enforcement and procedural aspects of the two systems. Accordingly, Chapters 3 to 12 deal with EC law and Chapters 13 to 16 deal with UK law. The one area in which the two are dealt with together is in the discussion of compliance programmes (Chapter 2). Chapters 17 to 20 deal with the enforcement of EC and UK law by the national courts.

1.02
The differences between the two systems have become less marked since the enactment of the Competition Act 1998 in the United Kingdom. Prior to the enactment of that statute, the Office of Fair Trading (the principal competition law enforcement agency in the United Kingdom) had far weaker powers of investigation than the European Commission has under Articles 81 and 82 of the EC Treaty. Also, the remedies under UK competition law were, prior to the 1998 Act, much weaker. In particular, there was only very limited scope under the Restrictive Trade Practices Act 1976 for the Office of Fair Trading to seek the imposition of financial penalties. That position has now been remedied by the 1998 Act, which empowers the Director General of Fair Trading to impose significant financial penalties for violation of either of the two new prohibitions introduced by that Act. The 1998 Act also makes significant changes to the institutional structures which operate in the United Kingdom. Nevertheless, there remain significant differences between the UK and EC institutional structures.

B Institutional Structure

1.03
One of the most striking features of UK competition law is the number of institutions which are involved in its application and enforcement. The principal institutions are the Office of Fair Trading, the Competition Commission and the Secretary of State for Trade and Industry. The head of the Office of Fair Trading, the Director General of Fair Trading (DGFT), performs a number of functions in the competition law field . He plays a key role in the enforcement of the Competition Act 1998[1], under which he has the power to:

(*a*) carry out investigations into alleged breaches of the so-called Chapter I prohibition (modelled on Article 81, EC Treaty) and Chapter II prohibition (modelled on Article 82, EC Treaty);
(*b*) require termination of infringements of either of those prohibitions;
(*c*) impose penalties of up to 10% of UK turnover in respect of such violations and
(*d*) grant exemption from the Chapter I prohibition.

Under the Fair Trading Act 1973 (FTA 1973) he can enquire into alleged monopoly situations and refer these for fuller investigation to the Competition Commission (CC); in relation to the investigation of mergers under the FTA 1973 he advises the Secretary of State whether a merger falling within the ambit of the Act should be referred to the CC.

1 See Chapter 15.

1.04
The CC carries out detailed investigations into alleged monopoly and merger situations under the FTA 1973. It has no power to choose what matters to investigate under the FTA 1973. This choice is made for it by the Secretary of State for Trade and Industry (in the field of mergers) and principally by the DGFT in the field of monopoly situations (although in relation to monopoly situations the Secretary of State has concurrent jurisdiction with the DGFT). In each of these cases, the role of the CC is to report and make recommendations to the Secretary of State. It has no power to take remedial action itself. The CC also plays a role in the regulatory framework established in relation to a number of privatised industries, notably telecommunications, gas, water and electricity. It also has an important role under the Broadcasting Act 1990.

1.05
The CC inherited the roles referred to in para **1.04** above, from its predecessor, the Monopolies and Mergers Commission. This transfer of power was brought about by the Competition Act 1998. That Act also conferred upon the CC the role of appeal from certain decisions of the DGFT under the CA 1998[1].

1 See para **15.210** ff.

1.06
Lastly, but by no means least, there is the Secretary of State for Trade and Industry himself. He plays a role in all the principal UK competition law statutes. This is perhaps most evident in the merger field. It is the Secretary of State alone (albeit after the receipt of advice from the DGFT) who decides whether a particular qualifying merger should be referred for investigation to the CC and it is the Secretary of State to whom the CC ultimately reports. The government is however, in the process of consulting on a proposal to depoliticise merger policy except in cases raising exceptional public interest issues (such as defence mergers).

1.07
In addition to the 'core' regulatory bodies referred to above[1], the spate of privatisation statutes in the latter half of the 1980s and early 1990s has led to the creation of a number of new institutions which have important functions in the competition law field, notably the Director Generals of Telecommunications, Electricity and Gas Supply, Water Supply, Gas for Northern Ireland and the Rail Regulator. The Independent Television Commission also has functions in this field under the Broadcasting Acts 1990–1996. The multiplicity of institutions which now perform one or more functions led one author[2] to describe UK competition law as a 'multicephalous beast'.

1 See paras **1.03–1.06**.
2 Whish *Competition Law* (3rd edn, 1993) p 25.

1.08
By contrast, the institutional structure in the context of EC competition law is much simpler. The European Commission (the Commission) is responsible for carrying out investigations in respect of, and subsequently taking action against, those undertakings found to have infringed the law. Its powers include the imposition of substantial penalties[1]. Indeed, the role of the Commission as both investigator, judge and jury has been the subject of much criticism in the past[2]. This criticism has led to certain important reforms[3] with a view to ensuring that the rights of the defence are respected, but not to any radical overhaul of the system; nor does such overhaul seem likely. In its 1990 Report on Competition Policy the Commission rejected the suggestion by the European Parliament that the Commission should, in its internal procedures, make a distinction between its investigatory, examinatory and decision-making functions[4].

1 See Chapter 9.
2 See eg the evidence to the *HL Select Committee on Competition and Practice in the EEC 8th Report* (HLP 1981–82).
3 Eg the creation of the post of hearing officer, see para **7.58**.
4 20th Report on Competition Policy (1990), para 89.

1.09
The activities of the Commission are controlled in two principal ways. The first is through the operation of the Advisory Committee on Restrictive Practices and Monopolies; this consists of officials from each of the Member States who consider and comment on drafts of all final decisions by the Commission in this field. The second major institutional check is the ability of undertakings which are the subject of decisions by the Commission to challenge such decisions before the European Court of Justice (in the first instance, such challenges are now heard by the Court of First Instance[1]).

1 See para **10.72** ff.

Chapter 2 Compliance Programmes

A Introduction

2.01
There is growing awareness both within and outside the EC of the existence of Articles 81 and 82 of the EC Treaty and of the consequences which can flow from engaging in prohibited conduct. This is certainly true of those industries in relation to which the European Commission has been particularly active in its enforcement of these Articles—for example, the chemicals[1] and automotive[2] industries—but it now extends much more widely. During the 1980s the Commission made a determined effort to increase the level of fines imposed in cases which it regarded as constituting serious violations of Articles 81 or 82[3]. This, together with the greater publicity which the Commission's activity in this field has attracted, has served to increase industry's awareness of the consequences which can flow from violating either of these provisions of the EC Treaty.

1 See eg Commission Decision (85/74/EEC) *Peroxygen Products* OJ [1985] L 35/1, [1985] 1 CMLR 481; Commission Decision (86/398/EEC) *Polypropylene Cartel* OJ [1986] L 230/1, [1988] 4 CMLR 347; Commission Decision (89/190/EEC) *PVC* OJ [1989] L 74/1, [1990] 4 CMLR 345 (this decision was annulled by the ECJ on procedural grounds: see para **8.66**); Commission Decision (89/191/EEC) *LdPE* OJ [1989] L 74/21, [1990] 4 CMLR 382 (also annulled on procedural grounds: see para **8.66**).
2 See eg Commission Decision (78/155/EEC) *BMW Belgium* OJ [1978] L 46/33, [1978] 2 CMLR 126; on appeal Case 32/78 *BMW v EC Commission* [1979] ECR 2435, [1980] 1 CMLR 370; Commission Decision (84/379/EEC) *BL* OJ [1984] L 207/11, [1984] 3 CMLR 92; on appeal Case 226/84 *British Leyland v EC Commission* [1986] ECR 3263, [1987] 1 CMLR 185; Commission Decision (82/628/EEC) *Ford* OJ [1982] L 256/20, [1982] 3 CMLR 267; on appeal *Ford v EC Commission* [1984] ECR 1129, [1984] 1 CMLR 649. In 1998 the Commission imposed on *Volkswagen* the highest fine yet imposed under Article 81, 102 million ECU: Commission Press Release 18/98/94, 28 January 1998.
3 Heralded by its decision in Commission Decision (80/256/EEC) *Pioneer* OJ [1980] L 60/21, [1980] 1 CMLR 457; on appeal Cases 100–103/80 *Musique Diffusion Française v EC Commission* [1983] ECR 1825, [1983] 3 CMLR 221.

2.02
This gradually increasing awareness of Articles 81 and 82 of the EC Treaty is now matched by a concerted attempt by the United Kingdom Office of Fair Trading to publicise the new powers of investigation and penal sanctions under the Competition Act 1998, which entered fully into force on 1 March 2000[1]. The OFT has embarked on a major programme designed to make business aware of the sanctions under the new Act.

1 See Chapter 15.

2.03
Whilst it is impossible to measure the current level of awareness of competition law within the EC, it is unlikely that it has yet reached the level which exists in the United States. This is hardly surprising. After all, United States anti-trust legislation has now been in existence for 100 years. Moreover, not only is there the risk of fines for violating the United States anti-trust laws, there is also the risk of treble damage actions by third parties. There is, in addition, a considerable difference between general awareness that a particular set of laws exist and the understanding that those laws might actually apply to the activities of one's own company. There are doubtless still many companies operating within the EC which believe that these laws are intended only to apply to the powerful multi-nationals. That this is not the case is shown by cases such as *Reuter/BASF*[1], *AOIP/Beyrard*[2] and *Royon v Meilland*[3]. The scope for competition law to bite on relatively small undertakings will be increased, so far as the United Kingdom is concerned, by the Competition Act 1998.

1 Commission Decision (76/743/EEC) OJ [1976] L 254/40, [1976] 2 CMLR D44.
2 Commission Decision (76/29/EEC) OJ [1976] L 6/8, [1976] 1 CMLR D14.
3 Commission Decision (85/561/EEC) OJ [1985] L 369/9, [1988] 4 CMLR 193.

2.04
With the increased awareness of EC competition law has come a growing interest, particularly on the part of larger companies, in the establishment of internal compliance programmes; that is to say, programmes designed to ensure that the company in question does not fall foul of the law. Compliance programmes of one form or another have been a feature of business life in the United States for many years and United States companies with substantial European operations have been at the forefront of the establishment of compliance programmes in Europe.

B Reasons for Establishing a Compliance Programme

1 REDUCING RISK OF VIOLATING THE LAW

2.05
The principal reason for establishing a compliance programme is to reduce, if not eliminate, the risk of violating the law. Although the consequences of engaging in conduct prohibited by EC and UK competition law are dealt with in detail elsewhere in this work, it may help to provide a brief summary in this chapter.

(1) EC Law

2.06
As far as EC law is concerned, the principal consequences flowing from violations of Articles 81 or 82 of the EC Treaty are as follows:

(1) The European Commission has power to impose substantial fines on the undertakings concerned. These can range from 1,000 to 1 million ECU or 10% of the undertaking's annual turnover (whichever is higher). In a number of decisions in recent years the Commission has imposed very large fines in cases which it regarded as serious infringements of the Treaty provisions. For example, a fine of 10 million ECU was imposed on *AKZO* in 1985 for alleged predatory pricing (this was reduced on appeal to 7.5 million ECU)[1]; in December 1990 the Commission imposed aggregate fines of 48 million ECU on three soda ash producers, including a fine of 30 million ECU on one company, Solvay[2]; in the 1991 *Tetra Pak* decision[3], the Commission imposed a record fine of 75 million ECU for alleged abuse of a dominant position; in 1994 the Commission imposed aggregate fines of nearly 500 million ECU in three alleged cartel cases[4]; and in 1998 it imposed a fine of 102 million ECU on *Volkswagen* for allegedly impeding parallel trade[5].

(2) Third parties claiming to have suffered loss as a result of infringements of Articles 81 and 82 can claim damages in national courts. Although such actions are still relatively rare, they are increasing and the Commission is keen to encourage these, as a means of increasing the level of enforcement within the Community whilst at the same time relieving it of some of the burden of enforcement. Although it is unlikely that the extent of private enforcement of Articles 81 and 82 will reach the levels reached under the United States anti-trust laws, the risk of private actions should not be underestimated;

(3) An agreement (or the relevant part of an agreement) prohibited under Article 81(1) is automatically void and unenforceable pursuant to Article 81(2), unless it is exempted under either an individual or block exemption pursuant to Article 81(3). Although there is no equivalent provision to Article 81(2) in Article 82 (which deals with abuses by dominant undertakings), it is open to a defendant in a national court to plead Article 82 by way of defence.

(4) The Commission has power to order an undertaking to cease conduct found to be in breach of Article 81 or 82; failure to comply entitles the Commission to impose daily penalty payments of between 50 and 1,000 ECU.

In addition, it should be borne in mind that the cost of defending oneself in proceedings brought by the Commission under Article 81 or 82 can be substantial (both in terms of the cost of engaging outside advisers and the management time, frequently at senior level, which is involved). Finally, there is the adverse publicity associated with Commission proceedings.

1 Commission Decision (85/609/EEC) *ECS/AKZO* OJ [1985] L 374/1, [1986] 3 CMLR 273; on appeal Case C-62/86 *AKZO Chemie BV v EC Commission* [1991] ECR I-3359, [1993] 5 CMLR 215, ECJ.

2 Commission Decision (91/297/EEC) *Soda-ash-Solvay/ICI* OJ [1991] L 152/1; Commission Decision (91/298/EEC) *Soda-ash-Solvay/CFK* OJ [1991] L 152/16; Commission Decision (91/299/EEC) *Soda-ash-Solvay* OJ [1991] L 152/21.

3 Commission Decision (92/163/EEC) OJ [1992] L 72/1, upheld by the CFI in Case T-83/91 *Tetra Pak International SA v EC Commission* [1994] ECR II-755 and confirmed by the ECJ in Case C-333/94P, [1996] ECR II-5951.

4 Commission Decision (94/215/ECSC) *Steel Beams* OJ [1994] L 116/1, [1994] 5 CMLR 353 (aggregate fines in excess of 100 million ECU); Commission Decision (94/601/EC)

Cartonboard OJ [1994] L 243/1, [1994] 5 CMLR 547 (aggregate fines in excess of 130 million ECU) and Commission Decision (94/815/EC) *Cement* OJ [1994] L 343/1 (aggregate fines in excess of 240 million ECU). Each of those decisions was subsequently the subject of multiple appeals in which the fines were significantly reduced in a number of cases (eg Case T-141/94 *Thyssen Stahl v EC Commission*, [1999] 4 CMLR 810 on appeal from the *Steel Beams* Decision) and in some instances annulled altogether (eg Joined Cases T-25/95–104/95 *Cimenteries CBR v EC Commission*, (the *Cement* case) [2000] 5 CMLR 204).

5 Commission Decision (98/273/EC) OJ [1998] L 124/60.

(2) United Kingdom Law

2.07

Until the enactment of the Competition Act 1998 the only circumstances in which fines could be imposed under UK restrictive trade practices law was where a company or person bound by a court order or undertaking under the Restrictive Trade Practices Act 1976 breached that order or undertaking, thereby committing contempt of court. Under the 1998 Act, however, the Director General of Fair Trading has been given the power to impose fines of up to 10% of UK turnover[1] for violation of the so-called Chapter I and Chapter II prohibitions, which mirror their EC counterparts (Articles 81 and 82 of the EC Treaty). As in the case of Articles 81 and 82 of the EC Treaty, third parties claiming to have suffered loss as a result of infringements of the Chapter I or Chapter II prohibitions can almost certainly bring private actions for damages[2]. Also, an agreement (or the relevant part of an agreement) prohibited under the Chapter I prohibition is automatically void and unenforceable, unless it is exempted under either an individual or block exemption (or parallel EC block exemption[3]). Similarly, it is open to a defendant in a national court to plead the Chapter II prohibition by way of a defence. As in the case of the European Commission, the DGFT has power to order an undertaking to cease conduct found to be in breach of the Chapter I or Chapter II prohibition[4].

1 See para **15.176** ff.
2 See para **15.16**.
3 See para **15.40** ff.
4 See para **15.163** ff.

2.08

As far as the monopoly provisions of the FTA 1973 are concerned, the Secretary of State has far-reaching powers to remedy conduct found by the Competition Commission to be against the public interest[1]. However, until such time the conduct in question is lawful. Moreover, even after an adverse finding third parties have no right to claim damages for any loss they may have suffered before that finding.

1 See para **14.77** ff.

2 FAVOURABLE ATTITUDE OF REGULATORY AUTHORITIES

2.09

However comprehensive a compliance programme may be, it cannot be guaranteed to eliminate entirely the risk of an infringement taking place.

However, if an infringement does occur in such circumstances one can expect the regulatory authorities to take the existence of the compliance programme into account in deciding whether a fine should be imposed (and, if so, what amount). As far as the Commission is concerned, it has had an opportunity to demonstrate its favourable view of compliance programmes on a number of occasions. In several cases[1] the establishment of a compliance programme has been noted as a mitigating factor when assessing fines.

1 See eg Commission Decision (82/853/EEC) *National Panasonic* OJ [1982] L 354/28, [1983] 1 CMLR 497; Commission Decision (88/86/EEC) *Fisher-Price/Quaker Oats Ltd–Toyco* OJ [1988] L 49/19, [1989] 4 CMLR 553; Commission Decision (88/138/EEC) *Eurofix-Bauco v Hilti* OJ [1988] L 65/19, [1988] 4 CMLR 677, upheld on appeal in Case T-30/89 *Hilti AG v EC Commission* [1992] 4 CMLR 16; Commission Decision (91/532/EEC) *Viho/Toshiba* OJ [1991] L 287/39.

2.10
These cases show that, although the Commission will view most favourably the situation in which a compliance programme is in place before there is any threat of Commission proceedings, even the belated initiation of a compliance programme will be regarded as a mitigating factor (provided, of course, the Commission can be persuaded that it is being established in good faith and not just as a means of obtaining a lower fine).

2.11
As far as the position under the new Competition Act 1998 is concerned, the DGFT has made it clear that he intends to take a more lenient attitude when a compliance programme has been in operation[1], similar to the attitude shown by the European Commission.

1 See para **15.190** ff.

2.12
If, however, a compliance programme has been established which is clearly ineffective, it is unlikely to be regarded as much, if any, of a mitigating factor. Indeed when a compliance programme has been introduced but subsequently has not been complied with, that is likely to be treated as an aggravating factor[1].

1 See, for example Commission Decision (1999/210/EC) *British Sugar* OJ [1999] L 76/1 at paras 208 and 209.

C Main Elements of a Compliance Programme

1 GENERAL

2.13
A compliance programme can be made up of a number of elements. There is no such thing as a standard programme. Each one needs to be tailored to the requirements of the undertaking concerned, having regard to factors

such as the type of business involved and the resources, both human and financial, available. The most important single element is a commitment to the success of the programme on the part of senior management within the organisation. Commercial pressure for business success may bring with it pressure to engage in activity which falls foul of EC or domestic competition law. For example, an undertaking which over the years has created for itself a dominant position in a particular market may be tempted to consolidate that position, in the face of competition from new entrants into the market, by a variety of unlawful means such as predatory pricing or offering fidelity rebates to key customers. Those involved in settling the market strategy of the company in question will be expected by senior management to 'deliver the goods', that is to say maintain or improve the company's market position. If that company introduces a compliance programme, the programme will only have a chance of succeeding if it has the full backing of senior management, so that pressure is not placed on the marketing personnel to achieve enhanced performance at all costs, even at the risk of violating the law.

2.14
A number of possible elements of the compliance programme are considered below, namely:

(*a*) the legal audit;
(*b*) training of personnel;
(*c*) document retention and destruction.

Before considering each of those elements in turn, something should be said about the make-up of the compliance team itself.

2 MAKE-UP OF THE COMPLIANCE TEAM

2.15
One of the key aspects of any compliance programme is ensuring that it is properly organised and supervised. Overall supervision should be carried out by someone within the company—ideally a senior in-house lawyer—as he will have a much better idea of the company's trading activities and the role played by various employees than someone from outside the company. However, depending on the knowledge of competition law possessed by the person who takes on this supervisory role, it may well be necessary to call upon the assistance of an outside lawyer, particularly when the programme is being established and an initial legal audit[1] is carried out. Moreover, the fact that communications with independent lawyers are protected from disclosure to the Commission in the context of proceedings brought by it under Articles 81 and 82 but that communications between employees and in-house lawyers are not[2] provides another reason for bringing in an outside lawyer, certainly if written reports on matters such as the state of compliance are to be made to management.

1 See para **2.17** ff.
2 See para **11.21**. It should be noted that legal privilege does extend to in-house lawyers under the Competition Act 1998: see para **15.151** ff.

2.16
Two other categories of personnel who can play an important role in the operation of a successful compliance programme are a senior executive of the company and the personnel manager. It is important that a senior executive be given specific responsibility for the programme because this demonstrates to employees the seriousness with which the company takes the matter of compliance. He can also provide a useful source of support for the in-house lawyer, who can sometimes come under intense pressure from his business colleagues to take what they regard as a 'more commercial attitude' in relation to conduct which may constitute a violation of Articles 85 and 86. The personnel manager can be of assistance in helping the in-house lawyer to ensure that the various internal memoranda of guidance and training sessions prepared by the lawyer concerned are prepared in a way which is likely to be understood by the employees to which they are aimed.

3 THE LEGAL AUDIT

2.17
Once a company has decided to implement a compliance programme and determined who within the company should take the responsibility for setting it up, the first step is to ascertain to what extent the company is already complying with the law—the so-called legal audit. This will typically involve reviewing company documentation (standard contracts, correspondence, internal memoranda, trade association minutes, etc), interviewing relevant personnel and subsequently preparing a report summarising the results of the audit.

2.18
In order to carry out the audit, it is necessary first for the lawyers responsible for carrying it out to make sure that they have a good grasp of the market(s) in which the company is operating, including, in particular, the identity of the principal competitors, customers and suppliers, the market share of the company and its competitors, the state of the relevant market (for example, whether it is in decline or buoyant), the importance of the company's technology, and so on.

2.19
Only if the lawyers undertaking the audit have a proper understanding of the market can they be expected to produce a meaningful report. In the course of developing some knowledge of the market, the lawyers should begin to develop an idea of which are the key departments within the company which should form the focus of the review and which are the key individuals to talk to.

(1) Discussions with Key Employees

2.20
Before reviewing relevant documentation, it is advisable to have preliminary discussions with the personnel most likely to be directly affected. There are

a number of reasons for doing this. Firstly, it will enable the personnel concerned to be given an understanding of what is involved and the purpose of the exercise; they will inevitably be suspicious of the motives of those conducting the audit and defensive, possibly even obstructive, in their attitude. It is vital that any wall of mistrust which may exist be broken down. Secondly, they will be able to provide guidance as to the documentation which is relevant and to identify other members of staff who may be able to help.

(2) Document Review

2.21
Having had discussions with key employees, the next stage is for the lawyer(s) undertaking the audit to review relevant documentation. Depending on the size of the company concerned, it will frequently be impossible to review every conceivable relevant document. In such circumstances, it will be necessary to focus on those files which are likely to be most relevant. These will be files containing, for example:

(*a*) copies of any standard form contracts with customers or suppliers;
(*b*) copies of other agreements, such as joint venture agreements, technology licence agreements and distribution agreements;
(*c*) agreements with competitors;
(*d*) market analyses, market share statistics, etc;
(*e*) minutes recording discussions with customers, suppliers or competitors;
(*f*) trade association documentation.

It will often be necessary to have follow-up meetings to discuss the documentation with the relevant personnel in order to clarify matters arising on the face of the documentation.

(3) The Audit Report

2.22
Having undertaken the review of documents and interviews with relevant personnel, the lawyers involved will be in a position to write a report summarising their findings. Although it is a key part of the programme (and may even determine whether or not the company wishes to put in place an ongoing compliance system), it will inevitably contain highly sensitive information, which if it came into the hands of the European Commission or the Office of Fair Trading might be extremely damaging. As is described in Chapter 6, the Commission has very broad powers of investigation, including on the spot investigations without prior warning, and the audit report will be a document to which the Commission or OFT is entitled to have access (assuming it relates to the subject-matter of the investigation[1]), unless it is protected from disclosure on grounds of legal privilege.

1 The Commission and the OFT cannot simply go on a 'fishing expedition': see para **6.45** and para **15.132** ff.

2.23
As is described at paras **11.14–11.30**, the European Court of Justice has held[1] that communications between a company and its lawyers are protected from disclosure if two conditions are satisfied. Firstly, the communications must have been prepared for the purpose of the defence of the company in relation to the particular matter at issue; secondly, the communications must be with an independent lawyer. As far as the first condition is concerned, it is not entirely clear whether an audit report (even one prepared by an independent lawyer) is protected: by its very nature, it covers a range of activities carried on by the company, rather than any particular agreement or activity, and there must be some doubt as to whether this type of document is covered by the court's judgment. Even assuming that an audit report does in principle fall within the scope of the *AM & S*[1] judgment, that case makes it quite clear that in order to qualify it must have been written by an independent lawyer entitled to practise in a Member State. This is a strong reason for involving an outside lawyer in the audit.

1 Case 155/79 *AM & S Europe Ltd v EC Commission* [1982] ECR 1575, [1982] 2 CMLR 264.

2.24
The report itself should summarise the findings of the audit, identify particular high-risk areas of activity and recommend what further action should be undertaken by way of an ongoing programme designed to ensure that the risk of violating Articles 81 and 82 is reduced as far as possible. If the audit has revealed documents which may indicate the existence of an infringement of Article 81 or 82 on the part of the company, the question obviously arises as to what the company should do with such documents; this is considered at para **2.27**.

4 TRAINING OF PERSONNEL

(1) Initial Training

2.25
If a company decides that it wishes to institute a system of on-going compliance monitoring, the first step is to issue guidelines to relevant personnel. These should be provided to all senior members of staff as well as to any staff who have dealings with competitors, customers or suppliers. Although the type of guidelines which are appropriate will vary from case to case, a number of general points can be made:

(1) As these are likely to be the first guidelines on the subject, they should begin with a clear statement from a senior member of the company's management as to why the company regards compliance with the competition laws as a matter of importance.
(2) The guidelines should be clear and succinct. If they are not, one cannot expect employees to read through them to the end, let alone take heed of them.

(3) It is unwise to include too much detail in the guidelines. Although competition law is complex, the purpose of the guidelines is to make the employee aware of situations in which problems can arise, rather than to turn him into an expert on the subject. If the guidelines read like a textbook, they are likely to achieve nothing. They should therefore be confined to making a few basic points, including examples of conduct which is prohibited, making it clear that if the employee has any doubts about any particular point he should not hesitate to consult a member of the compliance team.

(2) On-Going Training

2.26
For those employees involved in activities which are most likely to give rise to conduct which may amount to an infringement of the competition laws (for example, the marketing personnel) it is useful to follow up the written guidelines with periodic oral training sessions. This often enables the message to be put across more vividly than does the written word and it also enables the employees concerned to put questions to the lawyer conducting the training.

5 DOCUMENT RETENTION AND DESTRUCTION

(1) Dealing With Incriminating Documents Already In Existence

2.27
A legal audit of the type described at paras **2.17–2.24** may well reveal the existence of one or more documents which provide evidence of infringements of Article 81 or 82 (or corresponding national law). For example, correspondence may come to light which reveals that the company has stipulated to its distributors in various Member States that they are not to sell the goods which they buy from the company in other Member States; alternatively, trade association minutes may come to light which evidence collusion with regard to pricing. However incriminating the evidence may be, it is extremely dangerous to destroy any of the documents in question. This is because if the Commission (or in the UK, the OFT) does eventually investigate the conduct to which the documents in question relate, it is most unlikely that those documents (or at the very least the fact that they once existed) will not come to light. There are a number of obvious ways in which this can happen. Firstly, a number of copies of the document will probably have been made and will be in various files and it is likely to be impossible to ensure that every copy is destroyed; secondly, there may still exist drafts of the document (for example, draft agreements) and these can be as damaging as the final document itself; thirdly, the document may well be referred to in other documents: nothing is guaranteed to arouse suspicion more in the minds of the Commission investigator than to find a letter referred to in later correspondence mysteriously missing; fourthly, copies of the document may well be held by third parties.

2.28
The safer course of action is to leave the document in the file, accompanied by a note which provides some explanation of the situation and which may serve to limit the potential damage caused by the document itself if it ever comes into the hands of the Commission or the OFT. For example, there may be an innocent explanation for a document which on its face appears to provide evidence of an infringement; alternatively, the infringement revealed by the document may have been an isolated incident. Steps should be taken to ensure that it does not happen again and details of these steps should be put on file with the document itself. In addition the company may wish to consider bringing the matter to the attention of the Commission or the OFT in order to take advantage of the leniency programmes for so called 'whistle blowers' which are being actively promoted by both regulators[1].

1 See para **9.44** ff (EC) and para **15.193** ff (UK).

(2) Preventing Further Incriminating Documents from Coming into Existence

2.29
Once an incriminating document is in existence, the damage is effectively done and the action described at para **2.27** is very much in the nature of damage limitation. Applying the maxim that 'prevention is better than cure', it is obviously far better to take such steps as are practicable to ensure that the risk of further damaging documents coming into existence is reduced as far as possible. In order to achieve this it is desirable to introduce procedures with regard to who is authorised to sign particular documentation. Ideally, all documents would be vetted in advance by the company's in-house lawyer or another member of the compliance team. However, many companies would cease to function if every single document had to be cleared by a lawyer, particularly bearing in mind that a huge range of documents are capable of evidencing an infringement of domestic or EC competition laws, from a note of a telephone conversation or secretarial shorthand right through to a multi-party joint venture agreement. One approach which may be practical is a combination of training of personnel (see paras **2.25–2.26**) and the establishment of procedures for ensuring that all agreements are vetted in advance by the legal department (other than standard documentation which has previously been prepared by the legal department).

(3) Systematic Document Retention and Destruction

2.30
Although the ad hoc destruction of incriminating documents is a very dangerous strategy, there is nothing in principle to prevent a company operating a systematic destruction programme. Indeed, bearing in mind the large amounts of paper which can build up over the years in any sizeable

organisation, there may be compelling practical reasons for establishing such a programme. There are, however, several important considerations which should be borne in mind.

2.31
Firstly, the programme should not discriminate according to whether or not the document in question provides evidence of some illegal practice. In principle, all documents of a certain age should be included. Secondly, in establishing a document programme the opportunity should be taken to review the way in which files are maintained. For example, it may be advisable to keep all legal advice received from independent lawyers on a separate file[1]. Thirdly, it is important to ensure that the company complies with any applicable national or EC law requirements as to the length of time for which particular documents should be retained. This third point is considered below.

1 Because of the position in relation to legal privilege under EC law: see para **2.15**.

(a) EC Law

2.32
Although EC law does not expressly require that documents be kept in existence for a particular length of time, Regulation 2988/74[1] does lay down limitation periods regarding the enforcement of Articles 81 and 82 and the imposition of sanctions and these need to be borne in mind when carrying out the destruction of documents. The scope of Regulation 2988/74 is described at para **9.96** ff; in brief the position is that there is a limitation period of five years (three years in certain circumstances), but the period only begins to run from the date on which the infringement in question comes to an end[2].

1 Council Regulation (EEC) 2988/74, OJ [1974] L 319/1.
2 See para **9.99**.

(b) UK Law

2.33
There are a variety of statutory provisions which require particular classes of document to be retained for minimum periods. The most significant of these are as follows. Firstly, the Companies Acts 1985 and 1989 lay down various obligations in relation to companies formed and registered in the UK. For example, they must keep their statutory books available for inspection throughout their life[1]; they are also required to keep accounting records sufficient to show and explain their transactions: these must be kept by public companies for six years and by private companies for three years and must cover day-to-day entries of sums received and expended and an indication of what entries relate to, details of assets and liabilities of the company and, where the company's business involves dealings in goods, statements of all stocktakings, statements of stock held by the company at the end of each financial year, and (except in the case of goods sold by way

of ordinary retail trade) details of all goods sold and purchased, identifying the goods and the buyers or sellers[2]. Secondly, under rules made pursuant to the VAT Act 1994, persons subject to value added tax are required to keep business records including orders, delivery notes and books of account for at least six years.

1 Companies Act 1985, s 383.
2 Companies Act 1985, ss 221–2.

2.34
In addition, there are a number of other statutory provisions which tend to influence the document retention policy of companies, although they do not impose any specific obligation to retain documents for minimum periods. For example, under the Taxes Management Act 1970, HM Inspectors of Taxes have the power to require taxpayers to produce documents which may be relevant to their tax liability[1]. Tax assessments can normally be made up to six years after the end of a chargeable period, although in the case of fraudulent or negligent conduct the Inland Revenue has a right to go back twenty years. As a matter of good practice, the Institute of Chartered Secretaries and Administrators therefore recommends that taxation records be kept permanently, so that a company can respond to a notice to produce and can contest allegations of fraudulent conduct. Under the Taxation of Chargeable Gains Act 1992 one is allowed, in computing any capital gain, to deduct costs of acquisition, incidental costs of acquisition and costs of enhancement. These costs need to be supported by documentary evidence. Such evidence should therefore be retained until the asset (usually shares or land) is disposed of. The provisions of the Limitation Act 1980, relating to the time limits within which proceedings must be commenced, have an obvious influence on document retention policy. The documentary evidence needed to support any legal claim will need to be retained for at least the period provided for under the Act for bringing legal action of that type[2].

1 Taxes Management Act 1970, s 20.
2 Eg three years in actions for damages for personal injury and six years in actions on a simple contract, for damages recoverable under statute (unless the statute otherwise provides) and in actions for tortious damages.

2.35
There are in addition a number of statutory provisions which make it illegal to destroy company documents (quite apart from the statutory retention provisions referred to at para **2.27**). For example, the Companies Act 1985[1] provides that an officer of a company carrying on business in Great Britain who destroys or is privy to the destruction of a document affecting or relating to the company's property or affairs is guilty of an offence unless he proves that he had no intention to conceal the state of affairs of the company or to defeat the law. The phrase 'document affecting or relating to a company's property or affairs' is a very broad description and could include correspondence, internal memoranda and notes of meetings. However, if the destruction takes place during the course of an organised programme designed to reduce the amount of outdated paperwork being held by the company, it should be relatively easy to establish that there was

no intention to conceal the state of affairs of the company or to defeat the law.

1 Companies Act 1985, s 450(1), (2) as amended by the Companies Act 1989, s 66.

2.36

Similarly, the destruction of evidence can amount to perversion of the course of justice. This common law offence is committed by doing an act which has a tendency and is intended to pervert or obstruct the administration of public justice. The administration of justice includes both civil and criminal proceedings and the offence may be committed even if proceedings have not been started, provided that they are imminent or an investigation which might bring about proceedings is in progress. An intention to pervert the course of justice is required for an offence to be established, although it is enough that a person knows that his act will cause a perversion of justice even though that is not his purpose.

2.37

A company which is involved in civil litigation will normally be obliged at a certain stage in proceedings to make discovery of (ie disclose) all relevant documents in its possession. Failure to make proper discovery (which would include destroying documents after an obligation to make discovery had arisen or failure to disclose documents which had been destroyed) is a civil contempt of court for which the most serious penalty is imprisonment.

2.38

Finally, under the Competition Act 1998, it is an offence for a person who intentionally or recklessly is required to furnish any documents or information under the Act to destroy any document which he is required to produce[1]. Where an offence committed by a body corporate is proved to have been committed with the consent of, or to be attributable to the neglect on the part of any officer of the company, that person as well as the body corporate is liable to be proceeded against and punished accordingly[2].

1 See para **15.157**.
2 See para **15.158**.

Chapter 3 Introduction to Chapters 4–12

3.01
Articles 81 and 82 of the EC Treaty are enforceable by the European Commission which has the power, inter alia, to impose fines and penalties and to order undertakings to terminate infringements. This is in addition to direct enforceability at the instigation of private parties in national courts of Member States. The issue of enforceability of Articles 81 and 82 by private parties in national courts is dealt with in Chapters 17 to 20. Chapters 4 to 11 deal with the role and powers of the Commission in the enforcement of Articles 81 and 82. Chapter 12 considers the scope for national competition authorities to apply Articles 81 and 82 directly themselves.

3.02
On 28 April 1999 the Commission published a White Paper entitled 'Modernisation of the Rules implementing Articles 81 and 82 of the EC Treaty'[1]. The White Paper proposes a radical change in the way EC competition law should be applied, notably:

— by abolishing the Article 81(3) notification system and replacing it by a 'directly applicable' Article 81(3);
— by surrendering the Commission's monopoly over exemption, allowing national authorities and courts to apply Article 81(3); and
— by giving the Commission greater powers to control agreements *ex post facto*.

This is a radical set of proposals which have already stimulated considerable debate and this debate is set to continue.

1 Commission Programme No 99/027.

3.03
The following subjects are covered in Chapters 4 to 10:

(*a*) the initiation of a Commission investigation, which can flow from the *notification* of an agreement, the filing of a *complaint* by a third party or independent Commission action based on information coming to its attention through its own enquiries (for example, from newspapers, trade journals or sectoral investigations);
(*b*) the nature and conduct of a *Commission investigation* and the rights of those being investigated and of third parties;
(*c*) the *decisions* which the Commission has the power to make;
(*d*) the scope for the imposition by the Commission of *fines*; and

(*e*) *judicial review* of Commission decisions by the European Court of Justice and the newly-constituted Court of First Instance.

3.04
Chapter 11 considers a number of fundamental Community law principles which have particular relevance in the context of the enforcement of Articles 81 and 82, in particular the scope of legal privilege, the principle of proportionality, the protection afforded to commercially sensitive business information and the extent to which undertakings are entitled to protection from self-incrimination.

3.05
Chapters 4 to 12 are broken down as follows:

Chapter 4–Notification
Chapter 5–Complaints
Chapter 6–Investigations by the Commission
Chapter 7–Commission Proceedings
Chapter 8–Decisions of the Commission
Chapter 9–Fines and Penalties
Chapter 10–Judicial Review: EC
Chapter 11–EC Law Principles of General Application
Chapter 12–Enforcement by National Authorities

Chapter 4 Notification

A Reasons for Notification

4.01
As noted in para **3.02**, the European Commission published a White Paper on 28 April 1999 on the 'Modernisation of the Rules implementing Articles 81 and 82 of the EC Treaty'. The impetus for the radical proposals contained in the White Paper is that the Commission wishes to establish a procedural framework which will allow it to focus on the most serious threats to competition and which will allow de-centralised application of the competition rules. As part of this, the Commission wishes to end the system of notification and exemption, giving parallel competence to grant exemptions under Article 81(3) to national competition authorities and courts. It is too early to know what reforms these proposals will ultimately lead to. Chapter 4 deals with the law as it stands today. However, it is noteworthy that the opportunity has already been taken to make one significant move in the direction of reducing the notification burden, by extending Article 4(2) of Regulation 17/62[1] to all so-called vertical agreements. These can now be exempted by the Commission pursuant to Article 81(3) without the need for notification[2].

1 Council Regulation (EEC) 17/62, OJ Sp Ed [1959–62] p 87, as amended by Council Regulation (EC) 1216/1999 OJ [1999] L 148/5.
2 See para **4.11** ff.

4.02
Although the term 'notification' is frequently used somewhat loosely, a distinction must be drawn between an 'application for negative clearance' and a 'notification'. The purpose of an application for negative clearance is to seek confirmation from the Commission that a particular agreement or practice falls outside the ambit of Articles 81 and 82 of the EC Treaty altogether. A notification is the means by which an undertaking seeks a decision by the Commission that an agreement which falls or may fall within Article 81(1) nevertheless satisfies the criteria for an individual exemption which are set out in Article 81(3)[1]. The applicant for an exemption has the right to obtain from the Commission a decision on the substance of his request for exemption[2]. In practice, undertakings which decide to submit an agreement to the Commission almost invariably apply in the alternative for negative clearance and an individual exemption and the same form is used for each purpose. Notification is not of relevance under Article 82, for which there is no equivalent to Article 81(3), but applications for negative clearance can be made in order to seek confirmation that Article 82 does not apply[3].

1 See *Butterworths Competition Law* Division 1.

2 Commission's draft Notice on co-operation between national competition authorities and the Commission, OJ [1996] C 262/5, citing Case T-23/90 *Peugeot v EC Commission* [1991] ECR II-653 at para 47.
3 See eg Commission Decision (90/363/EEC) *Metaleurop SA* OJ [1990] L 179/41.

4.03
In addition to agreements stricto sensu, Article 81 applies to decisions of associations of undertakings and concerted practices. For the sake of clarity, reference in the remainder of this chapter will be confined to agreements. However, the same principles regarding notification apply also to decisions and concerted practices; this is also true of conduct the subject of an application for negative clearance under Article 82.

4.04
By virtue of Article 81(2), agreements prohibited by Article 81(1) are automatically void. Moreover, third parties claiming to have suffered damage from the operation of such an agreement may seek damages or an injunction in a national court[1]. The grant by the Commission of an exemption under Article 81(3) removes those consequences, rendering the agreement in question valid and enforceable as a matter of Community law for the duration of the exemption. Accordingly, the principal purpose of notification is to obtain the legal security which an exemption confers.

1 See Chapter 19.

4.05
The other principal benefit of notification is that it immunises the parties to the agreement from the risk of fines in respect of the operation of that agreement. That immunity generally operates from the date of notification[1] (although it usually operates from an earlier date in relation to so-called 'old agreements' and 'accession agreements'[2]). Several qualifications should, however, be noted. Firstly, the immunity from fines only applies in relation to activities falling within the scope of the notification[3]. Secondly, art 15(6) of Regulation 17/62 specifically provides that the immunity from fines which flows from notification does not have effect where 'the Commission has informed the undertakings concerned that after preliminary examination it is of opinion that Article 81(1) of the Treaty applies and that application of Article 81(3) is not justified'. For example, a notified distribution agreement containing an absolute export ban is very likely to be dealt with in this way. In practice, it is rarely necessary for the Commission to invoke this procedure, largely because parties notifying agreements are well advised to exclude any provision which is likely to cause the Commission to apply art 15(6). Where the Commission does apply this provision, it must issue a reasoned decision and provide the parties concerned with an opportunity to be heard[4]. Thirdly, the benefit of immunity from fines under Article 81(1) only applies if an agreement is notified for exemption under Article 81(3): application for negative clearance alone does not confer this benefit[5]. This is a practical reason for making a combined application for negative clearance and an exemption.

1 Council Regulation (EEC) 17/62, art 15(5)(a), OJ Sp Ed [1959–62] p 87.
2 Council Regulation (EEC) 17/62, arts 15(5)(b) and 25(3).

3 Council Regulation (EEC) 17/62, art 15(5)(a).
4 Case 8–11/66 *Cimenteries v EC Commission* [1967] ECR 75, [1967] CMLR 77. Article 15(6) is considered in more detail at paras **8.29–8.31**.
5 Commission Decision (85/79/EEC) *John Deere & Co* OJ [1985] L 35/58, [1985] 2 CMLR 554.

B Old Agreements, Accession Agreements and New Agreements

4.06
A complication which arises in the context of notification is that the governing regulation, Regulation 17/62, lays down two sets of rules, namely:

(*a*) transitional rules for agreements which came into existence before 13 March 1962, the date on which Regulation 17/62 itself came into force (so-called 'old agreements') and agreements which were brought within Article 81(1) only because of the accession of new Member States in, respectively, 1973, 1981 and 1986 (so-called 'accession agreements'); and
(*b*) general rules for all other agreements (so-called 'new agreements').

The remainder of this chapter will focus primarily on the position of new agreements. However, the transitional rules are still of relevance and it is therefore necessary to consider also the treatment of old agreements and accession agreements.

C The Notification of New Agreements

1 INTRODUCTION

4.07
New agreements comprise all agreements other than old and accession agreements; or, to put it less obliquely, they comprise all those agreements which have come into existence since 13 March 1962, *except* (*a*) those which were already in existence on 1 January 1973 and fell within Article 85(1) (now Article 81(1)) solely as a result of the accession of the United Kingdom, Ireland and Denmark; (*b*) those which were already in existence on 1 January 1981 and fell within Article 85(1) (now Article 81(1)) solely as a result of the accession of Greece; and (*c*) those which were already in existence on 1 January 1986 and fell within Article 85(1) (now Article 81(1)) solely as a result of the accession of Spain and Portugal.

4.08
New agreements themselves fall into two categories from the point of view of notification. Agreements which fall within art 4(2) of Regulation 17/62[1] do *not* require to be notified in order to obtain an exemption under

Article 81(3), although it is always open to the parties to notify such agreements. The position regarding these agreements is considered at paras **4.11–4.23**. In relation to agreements not falling within art 4(2) of Regulation 17/62, the principal benefits of notification have already been referred to at paras **4.04–4.05**, namely immunity from fines and the potential for obtaining an exemption under Article 81(3).

1 Council Regulation (EEC) 17/62, OJ Sp Ed [1959–62] p 87.

4.09
The procedure for the filing of an application for negative clearance/notification with the Commission is set out at paras **4.29–4.57**. Paragraph **4.58** summarises subsequent developments following the initial filing of the notification/application, leading to the possible grant/refusal of an exemption or, more commonly, the issue of a so-called 'comfort letter'[1].

1 See para **8.72** ff.

4.10
Very few formal exemption decisions are taken annually by the Commission (three in 1995[1]). Moreover, it was until recently unusual for an exemption to be obtained in much less than two years (an example of a case in which an exemption was obtained extremely quickly is *Olivetti/Canon*[2], where the agreement was notified in April 1987 and exempted in December 1987). Accordingly, an important practical issue which arises is the legal enforceability (or otherwise) in a national court of an agreement which has been notified but in relation to which an exemption has neither been granted nor refused by the Commission. This issue is considered at paras **18.13–18.14**. The Commission is aware that its procedures for dealing with notifications are too slow and announced in 1992 its intention to try to speed up those procedures, initially in relation to structural joint ventures of a 'co-operative' nature[3].

1 25th Report on Competition Policy (1995) at p 305.
2 Commission Decision (88/88/EEC) OJ [1988] L 52/51.
3 See para **4.59**.

2 NEW AGREEMENTS FALLING WITHIN ARTICLE 4(2) OF REGULATION 17/62

4.11
A class of agreements, set out in art 4(2) of Regulation 17/62, can be exempted by the Commission pursuant to Article 81(3) *without* the need for notification. The types of agreement to which art 4(2) applies (see paras **4.14–4.22**) are those which, in the language of the preamble to Regulation 17/62, 'have special features which may make them less prejudicial to the development of the Common Market'. The rationale for treating them more leniently from the point of view of the requirement to notify was simply that it was a means of reducing the Commission's administrative burden, faced with the possibility of thousands of agreements being notified to it each year. Indeed, the ECJ has held that art 4(2):

'must be interpreted with reference to the structure of Article 4 and its aim of simplifying administrative procedure'[1].

The class of agreement covered by Article 4(2) was extended in 1999 to cover all so-called vertical agreements[2].

1 Cases 240–242, 261–262, 268–269/82 *Stichting Sigarettenindustrie v EC Commission* [1985] ECR 3831, [1987] 3 CMLR 661.
2 See para **4.18**.

(1) Status of Article 4(2) Agreements

4.12
The practical consequence of removing from article 4(2) agreements the need to notify in order to obtain an individual exemption under Article 81(3) is that if in fact the Commission considers such an agreement and decides to grant an exemption in relation to it, that exemption can take effect from the date of the agreement[1] (the way in which such an agreement is likely to come to the attention of the Commission, in the absence of notification, is through a complaint by a third party or a report in a newspaper or trade journal). There is, however, nothing to prevent parties to an article 4(2) agreement from notifying that agreement to the Commission. Moreover, Regulation 17/62 does not contain any provision preventing parties to an unnotified article 4(2) agreement from being fined by the Commission: indeed, the power of the Commission to impose fines in such circumstances was expressly upheld by the ECJ in *SSI*[2]. Nevertheless, the very basis on which the categories of agreement covered by art 4(2) of Regulation 17/62 were formulated (namely that they are likely to be less prejudicial to the development of the Common Market) means that it will be rare for the parties to an agreement falling within art 4(2) to be fined.

1 Council Regulation (EEC) 17/62, art 6(2), OJ Sp Ed [1959–62] p 87.
2 Cases 240–242, 261–262, 268–269/82 *Stichting Sigarettenindustrie v EC Commission* [1985] ECR 3831, [1987] 3 CMLR 661.

4.13
Paragraph **4.12** summarises the position of article 4(2) agreements vis-a-vis the Commission. As far as the position between the parties/third parties in national courts is concerned, the position is likely to be little different from that of a new agreement not falling within art 4(2) but which has been notified to the Commission[1].

1 See paras **18.13–18.14**.

(2) Scope of Article 4(2)

4.14
Article 4(2) applies to four categories of agreement. These are considered in turn below.

(a) Domestic Agreements

4.15
The first category of article 4(2) agreements is one to which the only parties are undertakings from one Member State and the agreement in question does not relate either to imports or exports between Member States. Even if only one of a large number of parties is from a different Member State, art 4(2) is inapplicable[1]. The same is true if one party is from a non-Member State[2]. Indeed, the Commission takes the view that this is also the case even where the parties are all from one Member State but one party has a parent company in another Member State[3].

1 Case 209–215, 218/78 *Van Landewyck v EC Commission* [1980] ECR 3125, [1981] 3 CMLR 134.
2 Case 22/71 *Béguelin Import v GL Import Export* [1971] ECR 949, [1972] CMLR 81.
3 Commission Decision (79/934/EEC) *BP Kemi* OJ [1979] L 286/32, [1979] 3 CMLR 684.

4.16
As far as the requirement that the agreement should not 'relate either to imports or to exports between Member States' is concerned, the existing case law renders the legal position somewhat unclear. The position following two judgments of the ECJ in the 1970s in the *Bilger*[1] and *Fonderies Roubaix*[2] cases was that local exclusive supply arrangements can fall within art 4(2) even if the goods in question have at some stage been imported into the Member State concerned and/or the effect of the exclusivity is to prevent the distributor from acquiring the goods in question from another Member State. However, later cases (for example, the *IAZ*[3] and *SSI*[4] cases) make it clear that the application in any given case of this limb of art 4(2) will in fact require careful analysis. The *IAZ*[5] case concerned an agreement between two trade associations, an association of water boards and an association of electricity boards, all Belgian, regarding the running of an agreement for the supply of conformity labels concerning washing machines in a way which discriminated against parallel imports. In relation to art 4(2), the ECJ said that:

> '... the purpose of the agreement is ... appreciably to restrict parallel imports ... and it thus tends to isolate the Belgian market ... the agreement therefore concerns imports to an extent which cannot be regarded as negligible. Accordingly, it cannot be granted exemption from the requirement of notification prescribed by Article 4(2) of Regulation 17'[6].

This was cited with approval by the Advocate General in *SSI*[7], where he expressed the view that price agreements or agreements to limit sales which relate in part to imported goods were agreements which 'related' to imports between Member States within the meaning of art 4(2). The ECJ did not deal with this issue in its judgment.

1 Case 43/69 *Bilger v Jehle* [1970] ECR 127, [1974] 1 CMLR 382.
2 Case 63/75 *Fonderies Roubaix v Fonderies Roux* [1976] ECR 111, [1976] 1 CMLR 538.
3 Cases 96–102, 104–5, 108 and 110/82 *IAZ International Belgium NV v EC Commission* [1983] ECR 3369, [1984] 3 CMLR 276.
4 Cases 240–242, 261–262, 268–269/82 *Stichting Sigarettenindustrie v EC Commission* [1985] ECR 3831, [1987] 3 CMLR 661.
5 See n 3 above.

6 [1983] ECR 3369 at 3413, [1984] 3 CMLR 276 at 308–9.
7 See n 4 above.

4.17
In *MELDOC*[1] the Commission decided that the agreement in question related to imports (and was therefore outside art 4(2)) because one of the main purposes of the agreement was to protect the Dutch market from imports. The Commission took a similar view in *Roofing Felt*[2].

1 Commission Decision (86/596/EEC) OJ [1986] L 348/50, [1989] 4 CMLR 853.
2 Commission Decision (86/399/EEC) OJ [1986] L 232/15, [1991] 4 CMLR 130 (appeal dismissed by the ECJ in Case 246/86 *Belasco v EC Commission* [1991] 4 CMLR 96).

(b) Vertical agreements

4.18
The second category of agreement exempt from notification is one which is entered into by two or more undertakings, each operating, for the purposes of the agreement, at a different level of the production or distribution chain, and relating to the conditions under which the parties may purchase, sell or resell certain goods or services (so-called 'vertical agreements'). This category replaced a previous, much narrower category, and was introduced by amendment to Regulation 17/62 in 1999[1]. The amendment followed the publication in January 1997 of a Green Paper on Vertical Restraints which led to reform of the then current block exemption regime in relation to vertical agreements. A new block exemption[2] for vertical agreements was adopted by the Commission in December 1999, applicable from 1 June 2000.

1 Council Regulation (EC) 1216/1999, OJ [1999] L 148/5.
2 Commission Regulation (EC) 2790/1999, OJ [1999] L 336/21.

4.19
The introduction of this broader category of agreement covered by Article 4(2) of Regulation 17.62 was designed to achieve a situation in which those vertical agreements which do not benefit from the new block exemption are nevertheless capable of individual exemption under Article 81(3), EC Treaty retrospective to the date on which the agreement came into force (rather than only retrospective to the date of notification). The aim is to remove the incentive to notify vertical agreements which are likely to benefit from Article 81(3).

4.20
In its Guidelines[1] in relation to the new block exemption regulation[2] relating to vertical agreements, the Commission confirms its view that the extension of Article 4(2) of Regulation 17.62 to all vertical agreements removes the need for precautionary notifications in respect of such agreements. If, for example, a contractual dispute arises between the parties an undertaking can still notify and gain exemption retrospective to the date of entry into force of the agreement. The Guidelines[3] indicate that a notifying party will not be required to explain to the Commission why the agreement

was not notified earlier and that any notification will be reviewed on its merits. The Commission expresses the hope that this change 'should eliminate artificial litigation before national courts and thus strengthen the civil enforceability of contracts'.

1 Draft Guidelines on Vertical Restraints were published on 24 September 1999, OJ [1999] C 270/12. These Guidelines have now been finalised but have not yet been published in the Official Journal.
2 See para **4.18**.
3 *Guidelines* at para 63.

(c) *Intellectual Property Rights*

4.21
The third category of agreement covered by art 4(2) must again have no more than two undertakings party to it and the agreement must only:

> 'impose restrictions on the exercise of the rights of the assignee or user of industrial property rights—in particular patents, utility models, designs or trade marks—or of the person entitled under a contract to the assignment, or grant, of the right to use a method of manufacture or knowledge relating to the use and application of industrial processes'.

This provision is of only limited application, for two principal reasons. Firstly, it does not apply to any restrictions imposed on the assignor/licensor of the industrial property right, only to restrictions on the assignee/licensee. An exclusive patent licence, for example, would not be able to benefit from this provision (because the licensor would be unable to practise the patent himself, by virtue of the exclusivity granted). This probably also applies even to a sole licence (that is to say, a licence where the licensor agrees not to license third parties, though retaining the right to practise the patent himself). The provision would also be inapplicable if the licensor accepted any other type of restriction (for example, a non-competition covenant).

4.22
The second limitation is that the restrictions on the assignee/licensee must all fall within the 'rights' of the patent, design, etc. Accordingly, the following provisions have been held to fall outside the scope of this provision:

(*a*) no-challenge clause[1];
(*b*) tie-in obligation, requiring the licensee to purchase certain products not covered by the industrial property right[2];
(*c*) obligation on the licensee to affix notices about the licence on the finished product[3].

Any other restriction, not strictly falling within the subject matter of the rights granted, would share the same fate.

1 Case 193/83 *Windsurfing International Inc v EC Commission* [1986] ECR 611, [1986] 3 CMLR 489.
2 See n 1 above.
3 See n 1 above.

(d) Research and Development

4.23
The final category of agreement covered by art 4(2) is that which has as its sole object:

(*a*) the development or uniform application of standards or types; or
(*b*) joint research and development; or
(*c*) specialisation in the manufacture of products, including agreements necessary for the achievement thereof:

- where the products which are the object of specialisation do not, in a substantial part of the Common Market, represent more than 15% of the volume of business done in identical products or those considered by consumers to be similar by reason of their characteristics, price and use; *and*
- where the total annual turnover of the participating undertakings does not exceed 200 million ECU.

This provision is of relatively narrow scope. In particular, the requirement that one of the objects referred to in (*a*)–(*c*) above be the *sole* object of the agreement is a particularly limiting factor. More importantly, the adoption of block exemptions in the fields of research and development[1] and specialisation[2], with the legal certainty which they confer, has greatly reduced the usefulness of this provision of art 4(2).

1 Commission Regulation (EEC) 418/85, OJ [1985] L 53/5.
2 Commission Regulation (EEC) 417/85, OJ [1985] L 53/1.

D Treatment of Old Agreements and Accession Agreements

1 OLD AGREEMENTS

4.24
In respect of old agreements (ie those in existence on 13 March 1962, the date on which Regulation 17/62 came into force), art 5(1) of Regulation 17/62 provides that any agreement not falling within art 4(2) had to be notified before 1 November 1962 (or, in the case of purely bilateral agreements, before 1 February 1963). The benefit of an exemption granted in respect of such an agreement notified before those dates can be back-dated to the date of the agreement, rather than merely the date of notification[1].

1 Council Regulation (EEC) 17/62, art 6(2), OJ Sp Ed [1959–62] p 87.

4.25
Old agreements notified within the time limits specified at para **4.24** (or exempted from notification by virtue of being article 4(2) agreements) benefit from the doctrine of provisional validity, a doctrine developed by the ECJ and set out in a number of judgments, for example, *de Bloos*[1]. The

application of this doctrine, which affects the enforceability of old agreements in national courts, is described at paras **18.06–18.09**.

1 Case 59/77 *Etablissements de Bloos v Bouyer* [1977] ECR 2359, [1978] 1 CMLR 511.

2 ACCESSION AGREEMENTS FALLING OUTSIDE ARTICLE 4(2)

4.26

Regulation 17/62, art 25 contains somewhat similar transitional provisions in relation to accession agreements to those relating to old agreements. As noted at para **4.07**, relevant accession dates so far are 1 January 1973 (in respect of the United Kingdom, Denmark and Ireland), 1 January 1981 (in respect of Greece) and 1 January 1986 (in respect of Spain and Portugal).

4.27

Under art 25(2) of Regulation 17/62, accession agreements (other than those falling within art 4(2)[1]) were required to be notified within six months from the date of accession, ie by 30 June 1973, 1981 or 1986 as the case may be. The effect of notifying by those dates was as follows:

(1) The agreements in question were immune from fines in respect of the period prior to notification (art 25(3) of Regulation 17/62).
(2) An exemption in relation to such an agreement can be back-dated by the Commission to the relevant date of accession, rather than the date of notification (arts 6(2) and 25(1) of Regulation 17/62).
(3) The doctrine of provisional validity almost certainly applies pending a decision by the Commission under Article 81(3)[2].

1 See para **4.28**.
2 See para **18.07**.

3 ACCESSION AGREEMENTS FALLING WITHIN ARTICLE 4(2)

4.28

The position of an article 4(2)[1] accession agreement notified within the six month period following the relevant date of accession[2] is the same as that of an accession agreement not falling within art 4(2) but notified by that date. That is to say, fines cannot be imposed for acts committed prior to notification and the benefit of an exemption can be back-dated to the relevant date of accession. Conversely, article 4(2) accession agreements not notified by the relevant date can be made the subject of a fine, although this is a remote possibility (for the reason set out at para **4.12**). However, in accordance with the general principle applicable to article 4(2) agreements, accession agreements falling within art 4(2) can be made the subject of an exemption even if they have not been notified (and in such a case the exemption would be back-dated to the relevant date of accession).

1 See para **4.28** ff.
2 See para **4.07**.

E Notification Procedure

1 INFORMAL PRELIMINARY APPROACH TO THE EUROPEAN COMMISSION

4.29

It is open to any undertaking contemplating entering into and notifying a particular agreement to have informal discussions with European Commission officials prior to doing so, with a view to ascertaining the Commission's likely attitude[1]. Although this can sometimes be a useful exercise, the view obtained from Commission officials at that stage does not in any way bind the Commission. Early discussion with the Commission is frequently essential in relation to proposed joint ventures, particularly if there is any possibility of the joint venture being regarded as a concentration and falling within the scope of the Merger Control Regulation[2].

1 This is expressly contemplated in Commission Regulation (EC) 3385/94 on the form, content and other details of applications and notifications provided for in Council Regulation No 17, OJ [1994] L 377/28.
2 Council Regulation (EEC) 4064/89, OJ [1990] L 257/14.

2 REGULATION 27/62

4.30

Under art 24 of Regulation 17/62[1], the Commission has power to adopt implementing provisions concerning the form, content and other details of applications for negative clearance (made pursuant to art 2 of Regulation 17/62) and of notifications (made pursuant to arts 4 and 5 of Regulation 17/62). These implementing provisions are set out in Regulation 3385/94, which came into force on 1 March 1995[2].

1 Council Regulation (EEC) 17/62, OJ Sp Ed [1959–62] p 87.
2 Commission Regulation (EC) 3385/94, OJ [1994] L 377/28 which replaced Commission Regulation (EEC) 27/62, OJ Sp Ed [1959–62] p 132 (as amended by Commission Regulation (EEC) 2526/85 and Commission Regulation (EC) 3666/93, OJ [1993] L 336/1).

4.31

Regulation 3385/94[1] requires all such applications to be submitted in the manner prescribed by Form A/B. The text of Form A/B, which was revised in 1985, 1993 (the latter revision to reflect the coming into force of the Agreement on the European Economic Area) and 1994, is annexed to Regulation 3385/94, together with a Note which sets out the information which the Commission requires[2]. Copies of Form A/B can be obtained from the Commission's Information Offices in each Member State. Form A/B is not a form to be filled in. Undertakings are simply required to provide the information requested in it, and annex the requisite supporting documentation.

1 Article 2.
2 See paras **4.39–4.46**.

4.32
Any undertaking which is party to the agreement in question may submit an application/notification to the Commission[1]. If the application/notification is submitted by only some of the undertakings concerned, they are required to notify the others of what they are doing[1]. If an application/notification is to be signed by a representative of an undertaking or association of undertakings, that representative is required to provide the Commission with written proof of his authority to act (usually in the form of a board minute or letter of authority)[2]. If, as is frequently the case, a joint application/notification is submitted, Regulation 3385/94 suggests that a joint representative be appointed[3] (although this is not obligatory[4], it is common practice).

1 Commission Regulation (EC) 3385/94, art 1(1).
2 See n 1 above, art 1(3).
3 See n 1 above, art 1(4).
4 Introduction to Form A/B, Section G.

3 DOCUMENTATION TO BE SUPPLIED TO THE COMMISSION

4.33
Seventeen copies of each application/notification are required to be submitted to the Commission[1], together with three copies of the requisite supporting documentation. Under the previous version of Form A/B, it was only necessary to provide three copies of the agreement(s). The new Form A/B does not make it entirely clear how many copies have to be provided. However, it appears that the Commission is satisfied if three copies are supplied, as before (ie the same number as for supporting documentation). The three sets of supporting documentation which are required comprise:

(*a*) the annual reports and accounts of the parties for the last three years;
(*b*) the most recent in-house or external long-term market studies or planning documents for the purpose of assessing or analysing the affected markets with respect to competitive conditions, competitors (actual or potential) and market conditions. The author is required to be identified; and
(*c*) reports and analyses which have been prepared by or for any officer or director for the purpose of evaluating or analysing the notified agreement(s).

This is a much more extensive requirement for supporting documentation than was the case under the previous version of Form A/B. Supporting documentation can be provided in either original or copy form but copies must be certified as true copies of the originals[2]. Applications/notifications must be submitted in one of the official languages of the Community[3] (or, when applications/notifications are made pursuant to Articles 53 and 54 of the EEA Agreement[4], one of the official languages of the EFTA States or the working language of the EFTA Surveillance Authority, which is English) but supporting documents must be submitted in their original language. If the original language is not one of the official languages of the Community, a translation into an official language must be provided[5].

1 Commission Regulation (EC) 3385/94, art 2(2).
2 See n 1 above, art 2(3).
3 Commission Regulation (EC) 3385/94, art 2(4).
4 See n 3 above, art 2(5).
5 See n 3 above, art 2(5).

4 EFFECTIVE DATE OF SUBMISSION OF APPLICATIONS/NOTIFICATIONS

4.34

Subject to the qualification noted in para **4.35** the date of submission of an application/notification is the date on which it is received by the Commission; however, if it is sent by registered post, it is deemed to have been received by the Commission on the date shown on the postmark of the place of posting[1]. The principal significance of establishing the precise date of submission is that the effective date of an exemption decision pursuant to Article 81(3) cannot, with the exception of old agreements and accession agreements, be earlier than the date of notification[2].

1 Commission Regulation (EC) 3385/94, art 4(1).
2 See Commission Decision (92/157/EEC) *UK Agricultural Tractor Registration Exchange* OJ [1992] L 68/19, at para 59.

4.35

If the Commission considers that the information (including supporting documentation) contained in the application/notification is incomplete in a material respect it is required to inform the applicant/notifying party of this in writing without delay and fix an appropriate time limit for the completion of the information. In such cases, the application/notification only becomes effective on the date on which the complete information is received by the Commission[1]. If the Commission has not, within one month following the date on which the application/notification has been received by it, indicated to the applicant/notifying party that it considers the application/notification to be incomplete in a material respect, it is deemed to have become effective on the date of its receipt by the Commission[2]. This was not specifically provided for in Regulation 27/62[3], the predecessor Regulation to Regulation 3385/94.

1 Commission Regulation (EC) 3385/94, art 4(2).
2 Ibid art 4(5).
3 Commission Regulation (EEC) 27/62, OJ Sp Ed [1959–62] p 132 (as most recently amended by Commission Regulation (EC) 3666/93, OJ [1993] L 336/1).

5 FORM A/B

4.36

The requirement to submit applications/notifications in the manner prescribed by Form A/B is not merely a matter of convenience; the ECJ has held that failure to observe this requirement removes any possibility of an exemption[1]. The strictness of the position is illustrated by the *Distillers*[2] case. In that case, the Commission had formally requested Distillers to provide it with particulars of new terms of business which had been introduced by the company. These terms and conditions amended terms and conditions which had been notified by the company two years earlier. Although the revised set of terms and conditions were not supplied to the Commission under cover of Form A/B, the Commission did not at any stage in its discussions with the company ask that they be supplied under cover of that Form; moreover, the Commission even used the same reference number as it had used in relation to the original notification. Nevertheless, the ECJ held that the fact that the new terms and conditions had not been submitted to the Commission under Form A/B meant that they had not been duly notified and could not therefore be the subject of an exemption under Article 81(3).

1 Case 30/78 *Distillers v EC Commission* [1980] ECR 2229, [1980] 3 CMLR 121; Case 209–215, 218/78 *Van Landewyck v EC Commission* [1980] ECR 3125, [1981] 3 CMLR 134; see also Commission Decision (84/405/EEC) *Zinc Producer Group* OJ [1984] L 220/27, [1985] 2 CMLR 108.
2 See n 1 above.

4.37
On the other hand, in *Metro II*[1], the ECJ held that a formal notification using Form A/B is not necessary where the undertaking concerned is merely seeking an extension of an existing exemption. According to the judgment of the ECJ, this is the case even where the agreement has undergone substantial amendment since the date of the original notification, provided that the amended version does not differ 'in principle'. In such circumstances, it is open to the undertakings concerned to provide details of the agreement, identifying the relevant amendments, by some other means, for example a letter. However, if one is in any doubt in such circumstances as to whether or not to use Form A/B, the prudent course in the light of the *Distillers*[2] judgment must be to use the Form.

1 Case 75/84 *Metro–SB–Grossmärkte GmbH v EC Commission (Metro II)* [1986] ECR 3021, [1987] 1 CMLR 118.
2 Case 30/78 *Distillers v EC Commission* [1980] ECR 2229, [1980] 3 CMLR 121.

6 CONTENTS OF FORM A/B

4.38
The information requested in the new Form A/B which is annexed to Regulation 3385/94[1], which came into effect on 1 March 1995[2], is more extensive than was required under the previous Form A/B. There are two general points to note in this context. Firstly, more extensive information is required in relation to structural joint ventures for which accelerated treatment is claimed than is required in all other cases. As noted in para **4.59**, and as is pointed out in Form A/B, the Commission announced in 1992 that it had adopted new internal administrative rules that provided that certain applications/notifications, namely those of co-operative joint ventures[3] which are structural in nature, would be dealt with within fixed

(though non-binding) deadlines. In such cases, the Commission endeavours, within two months of receipt of a complete notification, to inform the parties in writing of the results of the initial analysis of the case and, as appropriate, the nature and probable length of the administrative procedure in which they intend to engage. The Commission's letter is likely to take one of three forms[4].

1 Commission Regulation (EC) 3385/94, OJ [1994] L 377/28.
2 Ibid art 6.
3 The new system is modelled in part on the experience acquired by the Commission in applying the Merger Regulation and is intended to ensure that the time frame within which it reaches a decision in relation to co-operative joint ventures of a structural nature is not significantly different from that which applies under the Merger Regulation. The need for such administrative rules was lessened in 1997 when the Merger Regulation was amended to extend to all so-called full-function joint ventures—see *Butterworths Competition Law* Division VII, para [759] ff.
4 See para **4.59**.

4.39
Secondly, Commission Regulation 3385/94 specifically provides[1] (unlike its predecessor[2]) that the Commission may dispense with the obligation to provide any particular information (including documents) required by Form A/B where the Commission considers that such information is not necessary for the examination of the case. In one of the recitals to the Regulation, it is expressly stated that the Commission will, in appropriate cases, give the parties (if they request) an opportunity to discuss the intended agreement informally and in strict confidence. That could be used as an occasion to raise with the Commission the question of what information request it may be possible to dispense with (as is frequently the case under the Merger Regulation procedure).

1 Article 3(3).
2 Commission Regulation (EEC) 27/62, OJ Sp Ed [1959–62] p 132 (as most recently amended by Commission Regulation (EC) 3666/93, OJ [1993] L 336/1).

4.40
Turning to Form A/B itself, the first part, the Introduction, is in eleven sections. This is followed by a so-called 'Operational Part' which specifies the information which has to be provided to the Commission. The matters covered by the Introduction are as follows:

(1) Section A provides a very brief summary of the purpose and scope of the competition rules contained in the EC Treaty and the EEA Agreement.
(2) Section B summarises the situations in which an application/notification should be made to the European Commission and those in which it should be made to the EFTA Surveillance Authority under the EEA Agreement[1].
(3) Section C states the purpose of Form A/B itself.
(4) Section D explains that there is a rather different information requirement in relation to agreements concerning the creation of a co-operative joint venture of a structural character, where the parties wish to benefit from an accelerated procedure[2], from that which applies to other agreements.

(5) Section E emphasises that, in order to be valid, an application/notification must be complete[3]. It specifically notes two qualifications to the requirement for completeness. First, if the information or documents required are not reasonably available to the notifying party, the Commission will accept that an application/notification is complete and valid, notwithstanding the failure to provide such information, provided a reason for the unavailability of the information is given and best estimates for the missing data are provided. Secondly, it is only information which is relevant and necessary which is required and Section E notes the Commission's power to dispense with the obligation to provide certain information[4]. As noted in para **4.35**, the Commission must inform the applicant/notifying party within one month from receipt of the application/notification if it considers it to be incomplete in a material respect, otherwise the application/notification is deemed to be complete and valid.

(6) Section F emphasises the need for accurate information and makes reference to the power which the Commission has to impose fines of up to 5,000 ECU where, intentionally or negligently, the applicant/notifying party intentionally or negligently supplies incorrect or misleading information[5].

(7) Section G explains that any party to the relevant agreement, decision or concerted practice can file the relevant application/notification. Alternatively, this can be done by all the parties acting together.

(8) Section H explains how to submit the application/notification, including giving details of the address to which it should be sent.

(9) Section I deals with the important issue of confidentiality[6]. It points out that, if an undertaking believes that its interests would be harmed if any of the information it is asked to supply were to be published or otherwise divulged to other undertakings, it should put all such information in a separate annex with each page clearly marked 'Business Secrets'. It should also give reasons for the request for confidentiality.

(10) Section J summarises the subsequent procedure post-application/notification. This may involve requests for further information from either party or third parties[7].

(11) Section K defines some of the terms used in the Operational Part of Form A/B.

1 As to the EEA Agreement generally, see *Butterworths Competition Law* Division XIII.
2 The accelerated procedure is described in para **4.59**.
3 See too Commission Regulation (EC) 3385/94, art 3(1).
4 Ibid art 3(3).
5 See paras **9.82–9.83**.
6 As to which generally see para **11.02** ff.
7 See further para **4.58**.

4.41

The information which has to be provided to the Commission is set out in the Operational Part of Form A/B. This is in four Chapters. The information requested in Chapters I and IV is common to all applications/notifications. The information requested in relation to co-operative joint ventures of a structural nature for which the benefit of the accelerated procedure[1] is requested is set out in Chapter III. In all other cases, it is the information requested in Chapter II which has to be provided. Chapter II contains a more limited range of questions on the relevant market(s), and the position of the parties in relation to the market(s), than does Chapter III.

1 As to the accelerated procedure, see generally para **4.59**.

4.42
Any person seeking to complete Form A/B should clearly have regard to the full text of the Operational Part of the Form. However, in summary, the principal areas on which information is required are as follows.

4.43
Chapter I requires information concerning the parties, their respective groups and the agreement. For example, it is necessary to provide details of the worldwide turnover of any group to which any of the parties belong. The applicant/notifying party is required to indicate whether he would be satisfied with a comfort letter, rather than a formal decision by the Commission[1]. If it considers that a comfort letter would be an inappropriate way to dispose of the matter, it has to give its reasons for this view. It is also necessary to provide details of those provisions obtained in the agreement which the applicant/notifying party considers may restrict the parties in their freedom to take independent commercial decisions. It is also required to indicate between which Member States of the EC/EEA trade may be affected by the arrangements. Lastly, Chapter I requests a non-confidential summary of the nature and objectives of the agreement, suggesting as a guideline that this summary should not exceed 100 words. This is a new requirement introduced in the revised Form A/B attached to Regulation 3385/94. It is designed to assist the Commission in speeding up its processing of notified agreements: shortly following receipt of the notification, the Commission may choose to publish a notice inviting third party comments on the agreement in question and the short summary provided in the application/notification assists it in preparing such a notice[2]. It is therefore important to ensure the short summary does not contain any business secrets or other confidential information.

1 As to comfort letters generally, see para **8.72** ff.
2 Such a notice should be distinguished from a formal notice published pursuant to art 19(3) of Council Regulation 17/62, as to which see para **8.71**.

4.44
Chapter II is applicable to all applications/notifications *other* than those relating to structural joint ventures for which accelerated treatment is claimed (in relation to which Chapter III sets out the information which is required[1]). Chapter II requires the applicant/notifying party to explain the definition of the relevant product and geographic market(s) which in its opinion should form the basis of the Commission's analysis of the notification. Reasons for the definitions adopted are required to be given. Details of any companies within the same group as any of the parties to the agreement and who are active in the same or neighbouring product markets also have to be provided. Other information which is requested includes: the market shares of the parties (including any relevant group companies) on the

relevant geographic market during the previous three years and, where different, the corresponding market shares in the EEA as a whole, the EC as a whole, the territory of the EFTA States as a whole, each EC Member State and each EFTA Member State, again for the previous three years; in relation to any relevant markets in which the parties have a combined market share exceeding 15%, details of the five main competitors and five main customers of each of the parties (in each case with contact details, where possible); again in relation to relevant markets in which the parties have a combined market share exceeding 15%, the various factors influencing entry into the market in both product and geographic terms, together with any new undertakings who have in fact entered the relevant market during the last three years (again, where possible, with contact details).

1 See para **4.45**.

4.45

Chapter III sets out the (more detailed) information which has to be provided in relation to structural joint ventures for which accelerated treatment is claimed, and operates in place of Chapter II. The principal respects in which Chapter III is more demanding than Chapter II are as follows:

(*a*) Chapter III requires greater detail on what the applicant/notifying party considers to be close economic substitutes for the products/services affected by the agreement in question;
(*b*) more detailed information is required in respect of the geographic market definition;
(*c*) as far as companies within the same group as any of the parties to the agreement are concerned, information additional to that required by Chapter II includes details of their activities in markets upstream and/or downstream of those included in the relevant product market(s);
(*d*) similarly, more detailed information is required concerning the position of competitors and customers on the relevant product market(s). The threshold for the requirement to supply this information is where the parties (in respect of any relevant product market(s)) have a combined market share exceeding 10% in the EEA as a whole, the EC as a whole, the territory of the EFTA States as a whole, any EC Member State or any EFTA Member State. This contrasts with the 15% threshold in Chapter II;
(*e*) the same difference between the information thresholds laid down in Chapters II and III applies in relation to information on market entry and potential competition.

4.46

Chapter IV applies, like Chapter I, to all applications/notifications. It requires the applicant/notifying party to give reasons why, if it is applying for negative clearance, it believes that Article 81(1) or 82 of the EC Treaty[1], as the case may be, is inapplicable. If an exemption under Article 81(3)[2] is requested, again reasons for the application for exemption have to be provided. Chapter IV also sets out the supporting documentation which is required[3]. Finally, it states the form of declaration which has to be signed by, or on behalf of, the applicant/notifying party, to the effect that, to the best of their knowledge and belief, the information given in the application/notification is correct, that complete copies of the supporting documentation have been supplied, that all estimates are identified as such and are their best estimates of the underlying facts and that all the opinions expressed are sincere.

1 The corresponding provisions of the EEA Agreement are Articles 53(1) and 54.
2 The corresponding provision of the EEA Agreement is Article 53(3).
3 See para **4.33**.

7 COMPLETE AND ACCURATE INFORMATION

4.47
Regulation 3385/94[1] provides that all applications/notifications must contain the information requested in Form A/B. Article 15 of Regulation 17/62 empowers the Commission to impose fines (of between 100 and 5,000 ECU) on undertakings which, intentionally or negligently, supply incorrect or misleading information in such an application/notification. The Commission has made it clear that in its view notification only makes an agreement or particular course of conduct eligible for exemption if it has been sufficiently clearly described in the notification[2]. Moreover, as has been noted earlier[3], notification only provides the applicant with immunity from fines in respect of acts which fall within the limits of the activity described in the Application[4].

1 Commission Regulation (EC) 3385/94, art 3(1), OJ [1994] L 377/28.
2 Commission Decision (85/206/EEC) *Aluminium Imports from Eastern Europe* OJ [1985] L 92/7, [1987] 3 CMLR 813.
3 See para **4.05**.
4 Council Regulation (EEC) 17/62, art 15(5)(a), OJ Sp Ed [1959–62] p 87. See eg Case 28/77 *Tepea v EC Commission* [1978] ECR 1391, [1978] 3 CMLR 392.

4.48
In *Sperry New Holland*[1] a UK distribution agreement containing an export ban had been notified. The notification made no reference to it. Indeed, the existence of the export ban was implicitly denied because the notification claimed that trade between Member States was not affected and that Regulation 67/67[2] applied. Nevertheless, the Commission chose not to take this point and therefore decided not to impose a fine for this infringement. On the other hand, the Commission dismissed the claim that notification of the UK agreement provided immunity from fines for other agreements, albeit on similar terms.

1 Commission Decision (85/617/EEC) *W Burns Tractors Ltd v Sperry New Holland* OJ [1985] L 376/21, [1988] 4 CMLR 306.
2 The predecessor of Commission Regulation (EEC) 1983/83, OJ [1983] L 173/1, now itself superseded by Commission Regulation (EC) 2790/1999, OJ [1999] L 336/21.

4.49
It is fair to say that in the *Eldi*[1] case the ECJ did not take a particularly formalistic approach, holding that where the complete text of an agreement

had been notified it was not fatal to the notification that the completed Form A/B itself did not identify all the restrictions contained in the agreement, *provided* that the information supplied related 'fairly to the provisions which at the time were considered the most important'. Although there is nothing to suggest that this statement is not still good law today (and indeed it represents a welcome and practical approach to a difficult issue), it should be borne in mind that the judgment was delivered at a time when the information required in Form A/B was set out with far less specificity than is the case today.

1 Case 106/79 *VBBB v Eldi Records* [1980] ECR 1137, [1980] 3 CMLR 719.

8 STANDARD FORM CONTRACTS

4.50
It is frequently the case that an undertaking will enter into a standard form contract with a number of parties, in one or more Member States. Any agreements which are in the same terms as the standard form benefit from the notification with effect from the date of notification of the standard form, irrespective of whether or not they were entered into prior to notification[1]. If, however, an undertaking merely notifies an agreement, without holding it out as being a standard form contract, that notification is unlikely to be sufficient to cover other agreements in similar form[2].

1 Case 48/72 *Brasserie de Haecht v Wilkin* [1973] ECR 77, [1973] CMLR 287.
2 Commission Decision (85/617/EEC) *W Burns Tractors Ltd v Sperry New Holland* OJ [1985] L 376/21, [1988] 4 CMLR 306.

9 EXCHANGES BETWEEN THE COMMISSION AND NATIONAL COMPETITION AUTHORITIES

4.51
Under art 10(1) of Council Regulation 17/62 the Commission is obliged to transmit to the competent authorities of the Member States a copy of applications for negative clearance[1] and notifications for the purpose of seeking an individual exemption[2]. The question arises as to what use the competent authorities may make of that information. Article 20(2) of Regulation 17 provides that (like the Commission itself) the competent authorities of Member States are under an obligation not to disclose information acquired by them as a result of application of the Regulation and of the kind covered by the obligation of professional secrecy[3]. As far as the scope of the term 'professional secrecy' is concerned, reference should be made to paras **11.05–11.06**. Assuming a particular category of information is covered by the obligation of professional secrecy, the obligation not to disclose it provided for in art 20(2) appears to be absolute. This does not, however, appear to prevent actual *use* of the information by the relevant competent authority provided that, in so doing, it does not disclose the information to a third party—this may, in practice, be a considerable obstacle.

1 Under Council Regulation 17/62, art 2.
2 Under Council Regulation 17/62, art 4.

3 It should be noted that Regulation 17/62, art 20(1) states that information acquired as a result of the application of arts 11–14 shall be used only for the purpose of the relevant request or investigation. This does not on its face appear to apply to information supplied in an application for negative clearance pursuant to art 2 or notification seeking an individual exemption pursuant to art 4.

4.52
The question of what use can be made by competent authorities of Member States of information forwarded to them by the Commission and contained in an application for negative clearance (or notification for an individual exemption) was put to the ECJ in a reference[1] by the Spanish Tribunal for the Defence of Competition[2]. The Court held that the effect of Article 287 (formerly Article 214) of the EC Treaty[3], coupled with art 20 of Regulation 17/62, was that the national authority could not use information obtained by the Commission under arts 11–14 of Regulation 17/62, or information contained in notifications under arts 2, 4 or 5 of that Regulation, as a means of proof in the enforcement of either national or EC competition law. The Commission had argued that national authorities should be able to use such information in the enforcement of EC competition law but not national competition law (no doubt in the hope of increasing the enforcement of EC competition law by national courts/authorities[4]). The Court did, however, indicate[5] that such information could be taken into account by the national authorities in deciding whether to open their own procedure. On the other hand, the CFI went on to say[6] that the national authority could only make use of documentation supplied by the Commission 'on condition that the proof of their existence must be established not by documents or information obtained by the Commission but by proof obtained in accordance with national law and having regard to the rights of defence inherent in their national law'.

1 This is pursuant to the EC Treaty, Article 234 (formerly 177). See paras **10.67–10.69**.
2 Case C-67/91 *Dirección Géneral de Defensa de la Competencia v Asociación Espanola de Banca Privada* [1992] ECR-I 4785.
3 See para **11.03**.
4 See paras **17.07–17.08**.
5 See n 2 above, at para 39.
6 See n 2 above, at para 43.

4.53
In *Postbank*[1] the Commission had authorised the use in national court proceedings of a version of the statement of objections which it had previously forwarded to the complainant in parallel administrative proceedings commenced by the Commission. The applicant alleged that this constituted an infringement of art 20(1) of Regulation 17/62, which prohibits the use of information acquired under arts 11–14 for a purpose other than that for which it was sought. The CFI rejected the applicant's case, holding that:

— the principle of 'sincere co-operation' inherent in Article 5 of the EC Treaty required the Commission to give active assistance to any national judicial authority dealing with an infringement of community rules;
— such co-operation between the Commission and the national courts fell outside the scope of Regulation 17/62, which governed only relations between the Commission and the authorities of the Member States;

— any other interpretation would undermine the rights of litigants deriving from the direct effect of Articles 81 and 82 of EC Treaty in relations between individuals, which the national courts must safeguard.

The Court dismissed the argument that access by the national court to the statement of objections would undermine the rights of the defence in those national court proceedings: it was for the national court to guarantee, on the basis of national rules of procedure, that the rights of defence of undertakings were protected (the Court noted that the national court could, inter alia, take account of the provisional nature of the statement of objections and of the possibility of suspending the national proceedings pending adoption by the Commission of a final decision). However, the CFI held that Article 287 (formerly Article 214) of the Treaty and art 20(2) of Regulation 17/62 did require the Commission to ensure that the entitlement of the undertakings concerned to protection of confidential information was not undermined by or during the transmission of the documents to the national courts (for example, by informing the latter of the documents or passages of documents which contained confidential information on business secrets: it was then for the national court to take steps to guarantee protection of the confidentiality of such information or business secrets).

1 Case T-353/94 *Postbank NV v EC Commission* [1996] All ER (EC) 817, CFI.

10 AMENDMENTS/RENEWALS OF AGREEMENTS

4.54
Regulation 3385/94[1] does not specifically require details of renewals of, or variations to, an agreement which is the subject of an application/notification to be supplied to the Commission. On the other hand, it is prudent to inform the Commission of any amendments, if they are likely to be material to the evaluation carried out by the Commission. The judgment of the ECJ in *Distillers*[2] suggests that the Commission cannot take account of any such amendment unless it has been formally notified (ie as prescribed by Form A/B). However, it is debatable whether the rationale of the *Distillers* judgment extends to every amendment to the agreement or is confined to those which are material; it may be that minor changes to the agreement which do not have any impact on the analysis under Articles 81 and 82 can be provided to the Commission under cover of a letter.

1 Commission Regulation (EC) 3385/94, OJ [1994] L 377/28.
2 Case 30/78 *Distillers v EC Commission* [1980] ECR 2229, [1980] 3 CMLR 121.

11 THE STATUS OF CONFIDENTIAL INFORMATION

4.55
It will be apparent from paras **4.40–4.46** that a considerable amount of information of a potentially confidential nature has to be supplied to the Commission as part of the notification exercise. The position of confidential

business information as a matter of Community law in the context of Articles 81 and 82 is described in Chapter 11[1]. However, in the specific context of notification it should be noted that Form A/B sets out the Commission's suggestion for the way in which to deal with information which the applicant claims to be confidential. It recommends that, if the applicant believes that its interests would be harmed if certain information were to be published or otherwise divulged to other parties, it should be included in a separate annex with each page clearly marked 'Business Secrets'.

1 At paras **11.02–11.13**.

12 PUBLICITY

4.56
Agreements which are the subject of an application/notification to the Commission are not placed on a public register. However, art 19(3) of Regulation 17/62[1] requires the Commission, before giving negative clearance or taking a decision under Article 81(3), to publish a summary of the relevant application/notification, in order to enable interested third parties to submit their observations within a fixed time limit[2]. The same procedure is now applied before the Commission issues a formal comfort letter[3]. In publishing such a summary the Commission is required by art 19(3) to have regard to the legitimate interest of undertakings in the protection of their business secrets[4]. Under the revised version of Form A/B which came into force on 1 March 1995[5], the applicant/notifying party is required to provide a short, non-confidential summary of the nature and objectives of the notified agreement, ideally not exceeding 100 words. The purpose of this is to provide the Commission with a ready basis for preparing and publishing, shortly following receipt of the application/notification, an informal preliminary notice, in order to elicit any third party comments[6]. The Commission does not publish such a notice in all cases.

1 Council Regulation (EEC) 17/62, OJ Sp Ed [1959–62] p 87.
2 See para **8.71**.
3 See para **8.78**.
4 For a discussion as to the way in which the Commission balances the need for publicity with the need to respect an undertaking's legitimate interest in the protection of its business secrets: see para **11.07** ff.
5 Ie the version annexed to Commission Regulation (EC) 3385/94, OJ [1994] L 377/28.
6 Such a notice should be contrasted with an article 19(3) notice, which is more detailed and gives an indication of the Commission's likely approach in the case in question.

13 TO NOTIFY OR NOT TO NOTIFY?

4.57
The decision whether or not to notify is not one to be taken lightly. It should not be regarded as a 'mere filing'; it can have far-reaching ramifications for the undertaking(s) concerned. Considerations to be borne in mind include:

4.57 *Notification*

(1) The benefits of notification have already been described earlier in this chapter: notification (though not merely an application for negative clearance) provides immunity from fines[1]; except in relation to the class of agreements covered by art 4(2) of Regulation 17/62[2], it is only a notified agreement which can ultimately benefit from an individual exemption under Article 81(3). Given the broad application of Article 81(1) by the Commission, this is a very significant factor. The extension of art 4(2) to include all vertical agreements, on the other hand, has reduced the incentive for precautionary notifications in respect of that class of agreement (see para **4.18**).

(2) Notification enables the parties to an agreement to put the case for the agreement the way in which they want to put it; this is far easier than in the situation where they are on the defensive as a result of the commencement of an investigation by the Commission. This is a particularly important aspect in relation to any agreement or arrangement which is likely to attract publicity.

(3) Even a late notification, ie one made some time after the agreement has come into operation, may be worthwhile: although it does not provide immunity from fines for the period prior to notification, it may serve to mitigate any possible fines for that period. A particular situation where this might arise would be where there is a change of ownership of an undertaking party to a potentially restrictive agreement. Following the normal type of document audit which the new owners are likely to carry out (either as part of the disclosure exercise before making the purchase or following the purchase), one or more 'dubious' agreements may be unearthed. Consideration should be given at that stage either to terminating such agreements or, if they may well be justifiable, late notification should be considered as the Commission may well be sympathetic in such a situation.

(4) On the other hand, the submission of an application/notification does, as already noted, require the applicant(s) to submit a considerable amount of information, much of it of a sensitive nature and, although the Commission is required to have regard to the commercial sensitivity of such information, it may decide that the importance of disclosing the information in question overrides its commercial sensitivity (unless it amounts to a 'business secret'). In addition, during the course of the procedure following the notification a considerable amount of further information, beyond that supplied in the original notification, may be requested by the Commission.

(5) During the course of proceedings following the initial notification, the Commission is very likely to enquire about other related arrangements to which one or more of the undertakings may be party within the Community. Undertakings should therefore be very wary of falling into the situation where a different approach to the issue of notification is taken in relation to one set of agreements from that in relation to another set of similar agreements. This can frequently arise where a number of undertakings within a group of companies enter into similar arrangements in different Member States, perhaps using different legal advisers who may take different views in relation to the notification issue.

(6) Although it should constitute the least important factor, the cost element is of no little importance these days: preparation of a comprehensive application/notification can require a considerable amount of time on the part of both the commercial/marketing representatives of the undertakings concerned and their in-house and/or outside legal advisers.

1 See para **4.05**.
2 See para **4.11** ff.

F Procedure Following Notification

4.58
The notification of an agreement can lead to a variety of steps being taken by the Commission. Each of these is described elsewhere in this work. In brief, the various possible outcomes are as follows:

(*a*) the issuance by the Commission of a 'comfort letter', which can be of a formal or informal nature[1];
(*b*) the taking of a formal decision by the Commission, granting or refusing either negative clearance under Article 81(1) or an individual exemption pursuant to Article 81(3);
(*c*) the granting of an exemption pursuant to the opposition procedure laid down in a number of the more recent block exemptions[2];
(*d*) the taking of a decision under art 15(6) of Regulation 17/62–an interim measure not often taken by the Commission but one which removes the immunity from fines provided by the notification[3];
(*e*) no action at all: it is not infrequently the case that undertakings notifying an agreement to the Commission hear nothing from the Commission for several years, or at all. This largely reflects the fact that the Commission only has limited resources at its disposal and must necessarily set priorities in such circumstances. Whilst this eventuality is clearly less satisfactory than a formal favourable decision, or the issuance of a comfort letter, this position will sometimes be reasonably acceptable to the parties: the notification itself will have protected them from fines but, of course, the enforceability of the potentially restrictive provisions (and indeed possibly the agreement as a whole) is still likely to be in doubt in such circumstances. If in such a case one party decides to resort to litigation in a national court (perhaps seeking the recovery of royalties under a licence agreement), the parties should press the Commission to reach an early decision.

1 See para **8.72** ff.
2 See para **4.63** ff.
3 See para **8.29** ff.

4.59
The slowness of Commission procedures for dealing with notifications under Article 81 has been brought into sharp focus by the contrasting speed with which the Commission has shown itself able to deal with cases under

the Merger Control Regulation[1]. In its 22nd Report on Competition Policy (1992) the Commission accepted that its procedures for dealing with Articles 85 and 86 cases (now Articles 81 and 82) were too time-consuming[2]. Against this background, at the end of 1992 the Commission announced a new system for dealing with structural joint ventures which are 'co-operative' in nature (and therefore fell outside the scope of the Merger Control Regulation)[3]. This new system came into operation on 1 January 1993. It is modelled in part on the experience acquired by the Commission in applying the Merger Control Regulation. It envisages that within two months of receiving all the necessary information from the parties concerned the Commission will inform them in writing whether the notified agreement raises significant concerns. The Commission's letter is likely to take one of three forms[4]:

(*a*) in cases not posing any problems, the Commission will send a comfort letter, confirming that the agreement is compatible with Article 81(1) or (3);
(*b*) if the Commission believes that it is necessary to close the case by means of a formal decision rather than merely a comfort letter, the Commission will inform the undertakings concerned of its intention to adopt a decision either granting or rejecting exemption;
(*c*) if the Commission has serious doubts as to the compatibility of the agreement with the competition rules, it will send a letter giving notice of an in-depth examination; that examination may ultimately result in a decision either prohibiting or exempting the agreement in question (and the exemption may itself be subject to conditions or obligations in the normal way).

Where the Commission's letter indicates that a formal decision will have to be taken, it will inform the parties of the proposed date for such a decision. The Commission indicated[4] that, once it had had an opportunity to see how the new system was working, it would consider whether it could be extended to other categories of agreement[5].

1 Council Regulation (EEC) 4064/89, OJ [1990] L 257/14.
2 Commission's 22nd Report on Competition Policy (1992), at para 123.
3 Under amendments made to the Merger Regulation in 1997, co-operative joint ventures now fall within the scope of that Regulation, provided they are full-function: see *Butterworths Competition Law* Division VII, para [759] ff.
4 See n 2 above, para 124.
5 See para **4.62**.

4.60
An early example of this new system in action was the Commission's decision authorising (by means of a comfort letter) the creation of a co-operative joint venture between Philips Electronics, Thomson Consumer Electronics and SAGEM. This was originally notified under the Merger Control Regulation but the Commission decided that the joint venture was co-operative in nature and therefore needed to be considered under Article 81[1].

1 'Europe' 1 May 1993.

4.61
The new system described in para **4.59** for dealing with structural joint ventures of a co-operative nature was accompanied by a parallel Commission move in 1992 to increase greater transparency into the decision-making process. This involves the Commission publishing a notice informing third parties of a notification and requiring them to submit comments, usually within ten days. This enables comments to be received at the beginning of the Commission's investigation, thereby enabling it to speed up the procedure[1]. The first case in which this was done was *Carlsberg-Tetley*[2]. The published notices take a very similar form to those published under the Merger Control Regulation[3], summarising very briefly the nature of the joint venture and the business activities of the undertakings concerned[4].

1 Commission's 22nd Report on Competition Policy (1992), para 116.
2 OJ [1992] C 97/21; subsequent examples include *Unilever/BSN* OJ [1992] C 111/10; *Menasha/Solidur* OJ [1993] C 134/3; *France Telecom/Deutsche Bundespost Telecom* OJ [1993] C 175/11; and *Alenia/Honeywell* OJ [1993] C 171/3.
3 Council Regulation (EEC) 4064/89, OJ [1990] L 257/14: see Division VII.
4 See also para **4.56**.

4.62
The accelerated procedure described above is summarised in the revised version of Form A/B which came into force on 1 March 1995[1]. It makes it clear that the accelerated procedure is based entirely on the principle of self-discipline: that is to say, the two-month deadline is not legally binding on the Commission, although the Commission confirms its intention to do its best to abide by it. In its Twenty-fourth Report on Competition Policy (1994)[2], the Commission indicated that, of eighteen structural co-operative joint ventures notified to it, ten were dealt with within the two-month deadline. In its twenty-fifth Report on Competition Policy (1995), the Commission indicated that, of fifteen structural co-operative joint ventures notified to it, seven were dealt with within the two-months deadline (of the other eight, the deadline did not apply for a variety of reasons: accelerated procedure not applicable (three), notification not complete (two), administrative delay (two), suspension of procedure (one))[3]. As far as the extension of the accelerated procedure to other forms of agreement between undertakings is concerned, Form A/B merely reiterates that the Commission reserves the right to do so.

1 Commission Regulation (EC) 3385/94, art 6, OJ [1994] L 377/28.
2 24th Report on Competition Policy (1994), p 631.
3 25th Report on Competition Policy (1995), p 307.

G Opposition Procedure

1 BACKGROUND

4.63
Only the European Commission is empowered to grant exemptions under Article 81(3). In order to be eligible for an individual exemption an

agreement must, with limited exemptions[1], be notified to the Commission[2]. There are, however, now a number of block exemptions which afford automatic exemption to various types of agreement which fulfil specific conditions, without the need to notify. Each block exemption sets out in detail those restrictions which can be included in the particular type of agreement concerned without losing the benefit of the exemption (often known as white-listed clauses) and those which cannot (often known as black-listed clauses).

1 See para **4.11** ff.
2 As regards the notification procedure generally, see paras **4.29–4.57**.

4.64
Even though the lists of white and black clauses in some of the block exemptions are detailed, they are not comprehensive. Accordingly, agreements can contain provisions which are arguably restrictive but which are neither white-listed nor black-listed. Such agreements require to be exempted on an individual basis, following notification to the Commission. In order to deal with such cases on an expedited and simplified basis, the Commission introduced an opposition procedure in a number of block exemptions, namely:

(*a*) Regulation 417/85–specialisation agreements[1];
(*b*) Regulation 418/85–research and development agreements[2];
(*c*) Regulation 4087/88–franchise agreements[3];
(*d*) Regulation 240/96–technology transfer agreements[4].

1 Commission Regulation (EEC) 417/85, art 4, OJ [1985] L 53/1.
2 Commission Regulation (EEC) 418/85, art 7, OJ [1985] L 53/5.
3 Commission Regulation (EEC) 4087/88, art 6, OJ [1988] L 359/46.
4 Commission Regulation (EC) 240/96, art 4, OJ [1996] L 31/2.

4.65
In outline, the opposition procedure operates as follows. It applies where an agreement contains restrictions which are neither expressly permitted nor expressly prohibited by the relevant block exemption (by way of variation, the opposition procedure which applies in Regulation 417/85, the specialisation regulation, is based on the turnover limitation set out in the Regulation). If such an agreement is notified to the Commission and the Commission does not oppose exemption within six months[1], the block exemption automatically applies.

1 Four months in the case of the technology transfer regulation, Commission Regulation (EC) 240/96, OJ [1996] L 31/2.

4.66
The recitals to the first block exemption to include an opposition procedure—that dealing with patent licences—expressly referred to the procedure as providing a simplified means of achieving legal certainty[1]. However, doubts have been expressed about the 'vires' of the opposition procedure[2]; that is to say, whether it is permissible under the relevant enabling Regulations[3]. The latter require each block exemption to specify the restrictions which must not be contained in an agreement, as well as those which

must, 'or the other conditions which must be satisfied'. By definition, the opposition procedure applies to unidentified restrictions (namely those which are neither white nor black-listed). On the other hand it can be argued that the reference to other conditions being satisfied encompasses the procedure under the block exemptions whereby an agreement is notified to the Commission and exempted automatically if the Commission does not oppose it.

1 Commission Regulation (EEC) 2349/84, 14th recital (now replaced by the technology transfer regulation, Commission Regulation (EC) 240/96, OJ [1996] L 31/2).
2 Eg Venit 'The Commission's opposition procedure—between the Scylla of ultra vires and the Charybdis of Perfume: legal consequences and tactical considerations' (1985) CML Rev 167; Korah *Research and Development and the EEC competition rules: Regulationn 418/85* (1986) ch 7; Korah *Franchising and the EEC competition rules: Regulation 4087/88* (1989) ch 7.
3 Council Regulation (EEC) 19/65, OJ Sp Ed [1965–66] p 35 (in relation to Commission Regulations (EEC) 2349-84, 4087/88 and 556/89); Council Regulation (EEC) 2821/71, OJ Sp Ed [1971] III p 1032 (in relation to Commission Regulations (EEC) 417/85 and 418/85).

4.67
In a departure from the approach in previous block exemptions, the technology transfer regulation[1], adopted in 1996, specifies certain types of restriction which fall within the opposition procedure.

1 Commission Regulation (EC) 240/96, art 4(2), OJ [1996] L 312/2.

4.68
The other main argument regarding the vires of the opposition procedure is based on the fact that it does not incorporate the safeguards protecting complainants which are laid down in Regulation 17/62[1] in the context of the grant of individual exemption under Article 81(3) (for example, the need to publish an article 19(3) notice[2]). This is indeed a difficult issue; in essence one has to balance the desirability of simplifying the exemption procedure in relation to agreements which do not contain black-listed clauses against the erosion of the right of complainants and other third parties to be heard. The ECJ has not been called upon to express a view on this issue.

1 Council Regulation (EEC) 17/62, OJ Sp Ed [1959–62] p 87.
2 See para **8.71**.

2 OPERATION OF THE OPPOSITION PROCEDURE

(1) Requirement to Notify

4.69
In order to be capable of benefiting from the opposition procedure, an agreement must be notified in accordance with Regulation 3385/94[1], providing the information prescribed by Form A/B[2]. Each of the block exemptions requires express reference to be made to the opposition procedure and Form A/B itself contains a question asking whether the opposition procedure is being relied upon. The block exemptions also require the

information furnished with the notification to be 'complete and in accordance with the facts'. This is reinforced in Form A/B. This states that:

> 'Where an undertaking is claiming the benefit of a group exemption by recourse to an opposition procedure the period within which the Commission must oppose the exemption by category only applies from the date that a valid [ie complete] notification is received'.

1 Commission Regulation (EC) 3385/94, OJ [1994] L 377/28.
2 See para **4.36** ff.

4.70
As has been noted at paras **4.41–4.46** Form A/B sets out the information which has to be provided to the Commission when notifying an agreement. In the context of the opposition procedure, two specific aspects should be noted. Firstly, Form A/B requires that undertakings claiming the benefit of the opposition procedure should identify the restrictions which exceed those automatically exempted by the relevant block exemption. Secondly, it requires that such restrictions be justified (in the context of Article 81(3)).

(2) Effect of Notification

4.71
The way in which the opposition procedure operates gives rise to the question whether the exemption only takes effect from the end of the six-month[1] period following notification or whether it takes effect immediately but with the possibility of being lost if the Commission opposes. In the former case, the exemption could operate either retroactively or not. Each of the block exemptions concerned is regrettably silent on this aspect. There is, however, a provision which stipulates that if the Commission makes an opposition but subsequently withdraws it because the undertakings concerned have shown that the conditions of Article 81(3) are fulfilled, the exemption applies from the date of notification. It would seem therefore that, where no opposition is made, the effective date of the opposition is also the date of notification. However, it remains unclear whether this only operates with retroactive effect or whether the exemption operates automatically from the date of notification, with the possibility of being withdrawn subsequently.

1 Four months in the case of the technology transfer regulation, Commission Regulation (EC) 240/96, OJ [1996] L 31/2.

(3) Opposition from the Commission

4.72
The Commission can oppose an exemption at any time within a period of six months[1]. Each of the block exemptions concerned stipulates that the period of six months runs from the date on which the notification is received by the Commission, except that where the notification is made by registered post the period runs from the date shown on the postmark of the place of posting. The grounds on which the Commission can oppose are not set out in the various block exemption regulations and there would seem

therefore to be no constraints on the Commission in that regard. If an agreement does not qualify for the opposition procedure (for example, because it contains black-listed clauses), the Commission would not need to oppose (although it will usually notify the undertakings concerned that the agreement is not eligible for the opposition procedure).

1 Four months in the case of the technology transfer regulation, Commission Regulation (EC) 240/96, OJ [1996] L 31/2.

4.73

If the Commission opposes exemption, the undertakings which have submitted the notification would seem to be in a similar position to the one in which they would have been if they had merely applied for an individual exemption. That is to say, they will need to satisfy the Commission that it should withdraw its opposition. Various possibilities arise. Firstly, the opposition could be withdrawn because the undertakings concerned have shown that the conditions of Article 81(3) are fulfilled. Secondly, the opposition could be withdrawn for some other reason (for example, the undertakings concerned may satisfy the Commission that a provision which the Commission originally regarded as a restriction within the meaning of Article 81(1) is not). Thirdly, the opposition could be withdrawn because the undertakings concerned have amended the agreement so that the conditions of Article 81(3) are fulfilled or by removing certain restrictions altogether. Fourthly, each of the block exemptions provides that if the Commission opposes the exemption and its opposition is not withdrawn, 'the effects of the notification shall be governed by the provisions of Regulation 17'. This means that a notification made for the purpose of invoking the opposition procedure can be treated as a notification for the purpose of Regulation 17/62, bringing with it immunity from fines and the possibility of obtaining an individual exemption. However, it would seem that in order to be eligible for such treatment from the date of notification (as opposed to the date on which the opposition is withdrawn) the undertakings concerned must notify in the alternative for an individual exemption.

4.74

The Commission is required to oppose exemption if it receives a request to do so from a Member State within three months[1] of the forwarding to it of the notification. Such a request has to be justified on the basis of considerations relating to the competition rules of the Treaty. If the Commission's opposition is based on a request from a Member State, it can be withdrawn only after consultation with the Advisory Committee on Restrictive Practices and Dominant Positions.

1 Two months in the case of the technology transfer regulation, Commission Regulation (EC) 240/96, OJ [1996] L 31/2.

(4) Confidentiality

4.75

Each of the block exemptions which contains an opposition procedure[1] sets out rules concerning the confidentiality of information provided to the

Commission which are broadly similar to those set out in Regulation 17/62, art 20[2]. Both the Commission and the Member States are required to refrain from disclosing information acquired by them pursuant to the Regulation and which is of a kind which is covered by the obligation of professional secrecy. In addition, information acquired pursuant to the operation of the opposition procedure can only be used for the purposes of the relevant block exemption regulation (this is broader than the corresponding provision in Regulation 17/62[3], which only applies to information obtained by use of the Commission's formal investigatory powers).

1 See para **4.64**.
2 See para **11.03**.
3 Council Regulation (EEC) 17/62, art 20(1), OJ Sp Ed [1959–62] p 87.

(5) Position of Third Parties

4.76
The opposition procedure provides little protection to third party complainants. In particular, the procedure provides no means by which the fact that an application has been received is made public. This contrasts with the position prevailing under Regulation 17/62 and Regulation 2842/98[1] where the Commission proposes to grant an individual exemption. It may very well be, for example, that the six-month[2] period will expire without a potential third party complainant even being aware that the application has been made.

1 Commission Regulation (EC) 2842/98, OJ [1998] L 354/18. See para **8.65**.
2 Four months in the case of the technology transfer regulation, Commission Regulation (EC) 240/96, OJ [1996] L 31/2.

(6) Judicial Review

4.77
The opposition procedure raises a number of issues in the context of judicial review of acts (or failures to act) on the part of the Commission. The relevant provisions of the EC Treaty are Articles 230[1] and 232[2]. Article 230 provides for decisions of the Commission to be challenged where they are addressed to the undertaking concerned or are of direct and individual concern to it. Article 232 allows for actions to be brought against the Commission in certain circumstances for failure to act. In the context of Article 230, it should be borne in mind that the ECJ has distinguished in the *IBM*[3] case between a final decision by the Commission (which is susceptible to challenge) and procedural steps along the way (which are not; for example, in *IBM*[4], the issuance of the Statement of Objections).

1 See para **10.09** ff.
2 See para **10.48** ff.
3 Case 60/81 *IBM v EC Commission* [1981] ECR 2639, [1981] 3 CMLR 635.
4 See n 3 above.

4.78
Against that background, the position in relation to the opposition procedure would appear to be as follows (although there is as yet no guidance from the ECJ or the Court of First Instance (CFI): firstly, it is most unlikely that the raising of an opposition itself is capable of challenge under Article 230 being merely a step along the way to a final decision by the Commission (for example, the granting of an individual exemption). Secondly, a complainant is almost certainly unable to challenge a failure to oppose, because the making of an opposition is not an act addressed to the complainant within the meaning of Article 232. Thirdly, if the Commission withdraws an opposition, it may be that a party to the agreement or a third party who can show 'sufficient interest' may be able to challenge this (on the basis that withdrawal of opposition has similar effects to the grant of an individual exemption under Article 81(3)).

Chapter 5 Complaints

A Introduction

5.01
One means by which the Commission may become aware of an agreement, namely the submission of an application/notification for negative clearance/exemption, has already been described[1]. The second means by which this can occur is through the filing of a complaint by a third party (for example, a disgruntled customer who has been unable to obtain particular products from a potential supplier because of a restrictive agreement to which that supplier is a party).

1 See Chapter 4.

5.02
This chapter describes the procedure for the making of such a complaint and the rights of the complainant in such circumstances. The rights of the undertaking complained against (for example, to know the substance of the case against it) are considered in Chapter 7[1].

1 At paras **7.12–7.13**.

B Who May Complain

5.03
Under Regulation 17/62[1], art 3(2), Member States and natural or legal persons claiming a 'legitimate interest' are entitled to make an application to the Commission for a finding that one or more undertaking is infringing Article 81 or 82 of the EC Treaty and seeking a decision requiring such undertaking(s) to bring the infringement to an end. There is not as yet a definitive statement by the ECJ as to what constitutes a legitimate interest. Article 3 makes no distinction between the parties to the agreement in question and third parties. It may very well be that one of the parties to the agreement itself will wish to lodge a complaint, claiming a violation of Article 81 or Article 82. It is difficult to imagine that a party to the agreement would not have a legitimate interest. As far as third parties are concerned, the phrase 'legitimate interest' probably requires the complainant to show that it stands to be affected by the agreement or conduct in question.

1 Council Regulation (EEC) 17/62, OJ Sp Ed [1959–62] p 87.

5.04
The following list provides examples of cases where a complainant has been found (either by the ECJ or the Commission) to have a legitimate interest. It is by no means an exhaustive list:

(*a*) a distributor bound by an export ban[1];
(*b*) a retailer who is unable to buy products from another Member State because of an export ban[2];
(*c*) a licensee bound by restrictive provisions in a licence agreement[3];
(*d*) a person subject to a refusal of supply by a dominant supplier[4];
(*e*) a supplier which is the victim of predatory pricing by a dominant supplier[5];
(*f*) the target of a take-over bid[6];
(*g*) a supplier claiming to be adversely affected by a merger of two rival suppliers operating in the same market[7].

1 Case 30/78 *Distillers v EC Commission* [1980] ECR 2229, [1980] 3 CMLR 121.
2 Case 792/79R *Camera Care v EC Commission* [1980] ECR 119, [1980] 1 CMLR 334.
3 Commission Decision (85/561/EEC) *Royan v Meilland (Breeders' Rights: Roses)* OJ [1985] L 369/9, [1988] 4 CMLR 193.
4 Commission Decision (73/457/EEC) *Zoja v CSC/ICI* OJ [1972] L 299/51, [1973] CMLR D50; on appeal Cases 6, 7/73 *Commercial Solvents v EC Commission* [1974] ECR 223, [1974] 1 CMLR 309.
5 Commission Decision (85/609/EEC) *ECS/AKZO* OJ [1985] L 374/1, [1986] 3 CMLR 273.
6 Case 6/72 *Europemballage and Continental Can v EC Commission* [1973] ECR 215, [1973] CMLR 199.
7 Cases 142/84 and 156/84 *British American Tobacco Co and Reynolds v EC Commission* [1987] ECR 4487, [1988] 4 CMLR 24.

5.05
The CFI has held[1] that an association of undertakings (in the case concerned, it was an association representing a number of discotheque operators) may claim a legitimate interest in lodging a complaint even if it is not directly concerned (as an undertaking operating in the relevant market) by the conduct complained of, provided that first, it is entitled to represent the interests of its members and secondly, the conduct complained of is liable adversely to affect the interest of those members.

1 Case T-114/92 *BEMIM v EC Commission* [1995] ECR II-147, at para 28.

5.06
A somewhat unusual example of a case in which the Commission had to consider if the complainant had a legitimate interest is that of *BP/TGWU*[1]. The Transport and General Workers Union lodged a complaint against the closure of an oil refinery, which it alleged was the result of a concerted practice between BP and Texaco. The Commission considered the union interest obvious (although it found no evidence of a concerted practice). The Commission did not, however, consider that the union had a legitimate interest in an allegedly anti-competitive oil-processing arrangement between BP and Texaco and that part of the complaint was found to be inadmissible.

1 16th Report on Competition Policy (1986), point 43.

C Form and Contents of Complaint

5.07
The Commission has prepared a form (Form C) for use by complainants and copies of Form C are available from the Commission's Information Offices. It is not obligatory to use Form C when filing a complaint (compare here the position in relation to Form A/B in relation to applications for negative clearance or an individual exemption[1]). A letter setting out the salient facts will suffice. It is, however, advisable to use Form C or, at the very least, to provide as much as possible of the information requested in Form C. After all, the purpose of filing a complaint is to arouse the Commission's interest in a matter about which it may know very little, if anything. In such circumstances, the more professional and authoritative the complaint can be made to look, the better. If the complaint is signed by a representative, written proof of the latter's authority to act must be produced[2]. The Commission published a separate standard complaint form[3] which can be used, for example, in relation to a complaint against a Member State.

1 See para **4.31**.
2 This was laid down in Commission Regulation (EEC) 27/62, art 1(2), OJ Sp Ed [1959–62] p 132. Regulation 27/62 was repealed by Commission Regulation (EC) 3385/94, art 5, OJ [1994] L 377/28, and this latter Regulation does not deal with complaints at all. Nevertheless, it would be prudent to provide written proof of authority to act.
3 OJ [1989] C 26/6.

5.08
The information which Form C requests is as follows:

Information regarding Parties concerned

The person filing the complaint is required to provide the name and address of the undertaking on whose behalf it is filed and proof of the representative's authority to act must be supplied.

Details of the Alleged Infringement

The complainant is required to indicate what agreements/practices of which complaint is made have, as their object or effect, the prevention, restriction or distortion of competition or constitute an abuse of a dominant position within the Common Market. Similarly, a statement must be made as to the extent to which trade between Member States may be affected.

Existence of Legitimate Interest

The need for the complainant to have a legitimate interest has already been explained[1]. A statement to this effect can usually be quite short.

Evidence

The names and addresses of any persons able to testify to the facts set out (and, in particular, persons affected by the alleged infringement) should be provided. For example, a customer claiming to be the victim of a refusal to supply may choose to provide details of other customers who have been treated in the same way.

Other Information

Finally, Form C asks for all copies of documentation relating to the complaint. This might include copies of agreements, correspondence, terms of business, notes of meetings and so on. It is obviously of considerable assistance to the Commission if the complainant indicates what remedy it believes would be appropriate to bring the alleged infringement to an end. If, as will frequently be the case, the complainant believes that the Commission should take interim measures[2], this should be expressly stated in the complaint and reasons why interim measures are believed to be appropriate should be provided.

1 See para **5.03**.
2 See para **8.05** ff.

D Timing of Complaint

5.09
There is no stipulated time period within which a complaint should be made. However, if the complainant seeks the adoption by the Commission of interim measures, it is vital that the complaint be made speedily, in view of the fact that one of the factors which the Commission will take into account in deciding whether to adopt interim measures is the urgency of the situation[1]. In much the same way as is the case in relation to interlocutory injunctions applied for under English law, the Commission may well refuse interim measures if it believes that the complainant has acted in a dilatory fashion.

1 See para **8.11**.

E Considerations to be Taken into Account when Deciding Whether to File a Complaint or Bring Proceedings in a National Court

1 INTRODUCTION

5.10
A person who believes he is suffering damage as a result of an agreement or conduct in violation of Article 81 or 82 has two options. He can either file a complaint with the European Commission or commence proceedings in a national court of a Member State (or do both[1]). The bringing of proceedings in a national court of a Member State is dealt with in Chapters 17–21. The purpose of this section is to consider the advantages and disadvantages

of filing a complaint with the Commission, as opposed to commencing proceedings in a national court. The section sets out some general considerations, before going on to deal specifically with the situation where the aggrieved person seeks speedy relief (interim measures in EC law parlance, or an interlocutory injunction to use English law terminology).

1 See eg Commission Decision (83/462/EEC) *ECS/AKZO* [1983] OJ L 252/13, [1983] 3 CMLR 694.

5.11

First, the current thrust of the Commission's policy in this regard should be noted. In its 1993 Notice on the application of Articles 85 and 86 (now Articles 81 and 82) of the EC Treaty by national courts[1] the Commission points out that it only has limited administrative resources and it is therefore necessary for it to establish priorities[2]. The Notice goes on to indicate that the Commission intends to concentrate on matters having 'particular political, economical or legal significance for the Community', stating that complaints which lack these features should be handled by national courts or national authorities[3]. If the complainant can secure adequate protection of his rights before a national court, the Commission considers that there would not normally be sufficient Community interest to justify it dealing with the matter[4]. During the course of consultation leading up to the adoption of this Notice, the Commission's view that it is entitled to establish priorities in deciding how to utilise its finite resources received support from the CFI in its judgment in *Automec II*[5]. There, the CFI examined the Commission's obligations when it receives a complaint under art 3 of Regulation 17/62[6]. The Court held that:

> '. . . for an institution performing a public-service task, the power to take all the organisational measures necessary for the fulfilment of that task, including settling priorities in the framework laid down by law, where those priorities have not been settled by the legislature, is an inherent part of the administration . . . the fact that the Commission allocates different degrees of priority to the matters referred to it in the field of competition is compatible with its obligations under Community law'[7].

1 OJ [1993] C 39/6. The Notice does not apply to the transport sector or to the competition rules laid down in the ECSC Treaty: para 45.
2 Notice, para 13.
3 Notice, para 14.
4 Notice, para 15.
5 Case T-24/90 *Automec v EC Commission* [1992] 5 CMLR 431.
6 Council Regulation (EEC) 17/62, OJ Sp Ed [1959–62] p 87.
7 See n 5 above, at para 77.

5.12

The CFI stated that its role is to verify whether the Commission has given proper reasons for closing the file on a complaint on the basis of its power to accord different degrees of priority to different matters. It was legitimate for the Commission to refer to the Community interest in order for it to decide its priorities. However, the CFI made it clear that the Commission could not simply cite the Community interest in a vacuum; it must set out the legal and factual considerations which had led it to conclude that there is insufficient Community interest in the particular case in point[1]. The CFI identified a number of factors to which the Commission had to have particular regard, namely the importance of the alleged infringement to the functioning of the Common Market; the probability of being able to establish the existence of the infringement; and the extent of the investigative measures necessary in order to fulfil successfully its task of ensuring compliance with Articles 81 and 82. In *Ufex*2, the ECJ emphasised the flexibility inherent in the phrase 'Community interest'. In rejecting the argument that this created legal uncertainty, the court ruled that the number of criteria of assessment which the Commission may refer to should not be limited, nor conversely should it be required to have recourse specifically to certain criteria (ie those referred to in *Automec II*). One aspect which weighed heavily with both the Commission and the CFI in the *Automec II*[3] case was the fact that the contractual interpretation of the distribution arrangements in question was already before the Italian courts and there was no reason why the Article 81 aspects should not be brought before the national courts as well. However, the principles laid down by the CFI are of more general application and the judgment is relied on heavily in the Commission's 1993 Notice.

1 Case T-24/90 *Automec v EC Commission* [1992] 5 CMLR 431 at para 85.
2 Case C-119/97P *Ufex v EC Commission* [2000] 4 CMLR 268.
3 See n 1 above.

5.13
The desire to encourage de-centralisation of the application of Articles 81 and 82 can be seen as an example of subsidiarity, the concept which has been much in vogue since being formally enshrined in the Maastricht Treaty[1]. It is still too early to know to what extent the 1993 Notice[2], the CFI's judgment in *Automec II*[3] and the doctrine of subsidiarity will change the current imbalance between the enforcement of Articles 81 and 82 by the Commission and their application in national courts. One important factor which acts as a deterrent to the bringing of national proceedings, at least in cases where the agreement in question has been notified to the Commission[4], is that the Commission alone is competent to grant individual exemptions under Article 81(3). The significance of this will cease if the Commission's 1999 White Paper proposal to end the system of notification and exemption is proceeded with[5]. In *Van den Bergh Foods Ltd*[6] the Commission rejected the argument by a company found to have infringed Articles 81 and 82 that the Commission should not have proceeded with the case but rather should have left the matter to be dealt with at the national level.

1 Article 3(*b*) of the EC Treaty provides that '. . . in areas which do not fall within [the Community's] exclusive competence, the Community shall take action, in accordance with the principle of subsidiarity, only if and so far as the objectives of the proposed action cannot be sufficiently achieved by the Member States and can therefore, by reason of the scale or effects of the proposed action, be better achieved by the Community'.
2 Notice on co-operation between national courts and the Commission in applying Articles 81 and 82 of the EC Treaty.
3 Case T-24/90 *Automec v EC Commission* [1992] 5 CMLR 431.
4 As to notification generally, see para **4.02** ff.
5 See para **4.01**.
6 Commission Decision (98/531/EC) OJ [1998] L 246/1 at paras 274–280.

5.14

In *Tremblay*[1], the CFI upheld the Commission's view that there was insufficient Community interest to justify it making a decision on the issues raised and that these should instead be dealt with by the national courts (in that case the French courts in respect of complaints against SACEM, the performing rights society for the French music business). The Court noted that the rights of a complainant could not be regarded as sufficiently protected before a national court if that court were not reasonably able, in view of the complexity of the case, to gather the factual information necessary in order to determine whether the practices in question constituted an infringement of Article 81 or 82[2]. The Court did not consider that to be the case. It did, however, partially annul the Commission's decision to reject the applicant's complaint, in so far as it raised an allegation of market partitioning between SACEM and the copyright-management societies in the other Member States, because it was not satisfied that the Commission's rejection had adequately addressed this issue.

1 Case T-5/93 *Tremblay v EC Commission* [1995] ECR II-185 (upheld by the ECJ in Case C-91/ 95P [1996] ECR I-5547; see too Case T-114/92 *BEMIM v EC Commission* [1995] ECR II-147.
2 See n 1 above *Tremblay*, para 68.

5.15

The *BEUC*[1] case illustrates the role played by the CFI in verifying whether the Commission has given proper reasons for closing the file on a complaint on the basis of 'Community interest'[2]. In that case, the Court reviewed in detail the basis on which the Commission had reached its decision to reject a complaint concerning an agreement concluded between the British Society of Motor Manufacturers and Traders and the Japan Automobile Manufacturers Association regarding the export of Japanese cars to the United Kingdom. The Court annulled the decision of the Commission which had rejected the complaint[3].

1 Case T-37/92 *BEUC and NCC v EC Commission* [1994] ECR II-285.
2 See para **5.12**.
3 See also Case T-198/98 *Micro Leader Business v EC Commission* [2000] All ER (EC) 361.

2 GENERAL CONSIDERATIONS

5.16

The principal advantages of complaining to the European Commission are:

(*a*) this route is likely to be cheaper for the complainant; if the Commission can be persuaded to take the matter up itself it will be responsible for handling the case;
(*b*) the investigatory powers of the Commission[1], particularly the power to undertake dawn raids under art 14(3) of Regulation 17/62[2], are more likely to yield valuable evidence than the discovery process under English law, particularly if it is believed that relevant documentation is held in more than one country within the Common Market;
(*c*) the defendant in proceedings in a national court in the United Kingdom will be able to invoke the privilege against self-incrimination[3];

the protection against self-incrimination afforded to an undertaking investigated by the Commission is substantially weaker[4];

(*d*) whereas the claimant in proceedings before a national court will have to establish a causal nexus between the loss which it has suffered and the alleged infringement of Article 81 or 82, the Commission is not so constrained in its consideration of the conduct of the undertaking being investigated; its task is to ascertain whether or not the undertaking complained against has acted in violation of the relevant Treaty provision, rather than whether the violation has caused loss to one particular third party;

(*e*) a cease and desist order or interim measures decision by the Commission is likely to apply throughout the Community, whereas a permanent or temporary injunction by a national court is likely to have little effect outside the Member State in which the court is located;

(*f*) if it is felt likely on the facts of a particular case that a national court would in any event be likely to stay proceedings pending a decision by the Commission[5], it may be better to begin by filing a complaint with the Commission, with the possibility of subsequently commencing an action for damages in a national court; although the Commission decision would not be determinative of matters before the national court it would be likely to be persuasive[6].

1 See Chapter 6.
2 Council Regulation (EEC) 17/62, OJ Sp Ed [1959–62] p 87.
3 Civil Evidence Act 1968, s 14; see also *Rio Tinto Zinc v Westinghouse Electric Corpn* [1978] AC 547, [1978] 1 All ER 434, HL.
4 See paras **6.74–6.76**.
5 See paras **18.13–18.14**.
6 In Commission Decision (88/491/EEC) *Bloemenveilingen Aalsmeer* [1988] OJ L 262/27, [1989] 4 CMLR 500, the Commission took a final decision even though the infringement of Article 81(1) had come to an end, partly in order to assist potential plaintiffs in a national court.

5.17

The principal advantages of commencing proceedings in a national court are:

(*a*) a national court can almost certainly award damages[1]; the Commission cannot;

(*b*) it is always open to the claimant to abandon his claim, albeit at the risk of being liable for a portion of the defendant's costs; conversely, if the Commission decides to take up a complaint filed with it the complainant loses control over matters;

(*c*) national courts in the United Kingdom and in certain other countries are able to grant injunctions ex parte (ie without prior notice to the defendant). In view of the Commission's obligation to maintain the essential safeguards guaranteed by Regulation 17/62[2], in particular the right of the party complained against to be heard, it seems unlikely that the Commission has power to order interim measures on an ex parte basis;

(*d*) the Commission does not have power to award legal costs to a successful complainant;

(*e*) the claimant may wish to assert other causes of action in addition to an alleged violation of Article 81 or 82 (for example, a claim based on domestic competition law and/or other domestic claims, such as breach of contract[3]). Whereas all these causes of action can be asserted in a national court, the Commission is empowered to deal only with claims based on Articles 81 and 82.

1 See paras **19.31–19.34**.
2 See paras **11.31–11.33**.
3 See, eg, *Shearson Lehman Hutton Inc v Maclaine Watson & Co Ltd* [1989] 3 CMLR 429.

3 INTERIM MEASURES v INTERLOCUTORY RELIEF

5.18
In addition to the general considerations outlined at paras **5.16–5.17**, there are a number of specific points which need to be borne in mind where the potential complainant/plaintiff is suffering severe damage which requires a speedy remedy (for example, as a result of a refusal to supply by a dominant undertaking). Here the respective merits of a complaint to the European Commission, seeking interim measures[1], and an application to the High Court for interlocutory relief[2] need to be considered. Factors to be borne in mind include:

(1) The availability of ex parte relief from a national court, a remedy which it appears is not available to the Commission[3].
(2) The fact that the standard of proof of the alleged infringement required by the Commission (a reasonably strong prima facie case) appears to be rather stricter than the test applicable under English law (there must be a serious question to be tried[4]).
(3) The need under Community law to establish serious and irreparable harm; in *La Cinq*[5] the Commission considered that such harm was limited to harm that could not be remedied by any final decision (this would have included a damages award by a national court). The CFI rejected this view, holding that the reference to harm should be viewed only in the context of final decisions of the Commission.
(4) In both situations, there is a need to apply promptly: failure to do so is likely to make it fatal to both a claim for interim measures from the Commission and interlocutory relief from a national court.
(5) An English court will usually order a party in favour of whom interlocutory relief is granted to give a cross-undertaking in damages; although no express reference was made to such an undertaking by the ECJ in its judgment in the *Camera Care*[6] case (the ECJ's first judgment in relation to interim measures), the Commission has subsequently indicated that it may require such an undertaking in appropriate circumstances. No such undertaking was given in the *ECS/AKZO*[7] case, nor in the more recent *Brass Band Instruments Ltd v Boosey and Hawkes*[8] case (although in the latter the Commission obtained an undertaking from the complainant that it would deal fairly with Boosey and Hawkes and not denigrate it or use it as a loss leader).

(6) The Commission indicated in a statement following the *Camera Care*[9] case that, on any application for interim measures, it will always consider whether the matter should more appropriately be dealt with by a national court, the implication being that if it believes this to be the case this will be a ground on which it would reject the application. A complainant should therefore bear this in mind before applying for interim measures.

(7) One can normally expect the process[10] leading up to the adoption of interim measures to take longer than that for an interlocutory injunction.

1 See para **8.05** ff.
2 See paras **19.25–19.29**.
3 See para **8.17**.
4 As to the position under English law, see *American Cyanamid v Ethicon* [1975] AC 396, [1975] 1 All ER 504, HL and subsequent case law.
5 Case T-44/90 *La Cinq SA v EC Commission* [1992] 4 CMLR 449.
6 Case 792/79R *Camera Care v EC Commission* [1980] ECR 119, [1980] 1 CMLR 334.
7 [1983] OJ L 252/13, [1983] 3 CMLR 694.
8 [1987] OJ L 286/36, [1988] 4 CMLR 67.
9 See n 5 above.
10 See paras **8.17–8.19**.

F Rights of Complainant

1 COMMISSION'S DUTY TO INVESTIGATE

5.19

The ECJ has held[1] that the Commission has a positive duty to consider a complaint submitted to it. This is bolstered by the fact that, under art 6 of Regulation 2842/98[2], a complainant is entitled to be informed of the reasons why its complaint is being rejected (assuming that is the case). If the Commission fails to do this (ie fails either to initiate proceedings against the undertaking complained of or to reject the complaint), the complainant could almost certainly successfully bring proceedings against the Commission under Article 232 of the EC Treaty[3]. Before reaching a view on the substance of a complaint, the Commission almost invariably seeks further information from the complainant and will often also seek the views of the party complained of (as it did, for example, in the *CICCE*[4] case, where it issued the complainant with a request for information under Regulation 17/62, art 11[5]). Ultimately, the Commission will need to decide whether to initiate formal proceedings by issuing a Statement of Objections[6] or whether to reject the complaint[7].

1 Case 210/81 *Demo–Studio Schmidt v EC Commission* [1983] ECR 3045, [1984] 1 CMLR 63 applied in Case 298/83 *CICCE v EC Commission* [1985] ECR 1105, [1986] 1 CMLR 486.
2 Commission Regulation (EC) 2842/98, OJ [1998] L 354/18. See para **5.28**.
3 See paras **5.28, 10.51**.
4 See n 1 above.
5 Council Regulation (EEC) 17/62, OJ Sp Ed [1959–62] p 87. See para **6.12** ff.
6 See para **7.12** ff.
7 See paras **5.28–5.30**.

2 CONFIDENTIAL INFORMATION

5.20

As noted at para **5.19**, the Commission will frequently wish to put the substance of the complainant's allegations to the undertaking complained of before deciding whether or not to initiate formal proceedings. It is not unusual for the Commission to pass a copy of the complaint to the undertaking complained of. It is therefore important that if the complainant regards any particular information contained in the complaint as constituting business secrets it should identify that information as being confidential and request that it not be disclosed to third parties[1].

1 With regard to the treatment of business secrets, see paras **11.07–11.10**.

5.21

The ECJ ruled in the celebrated *Stanley Adams*[1] case that where a person supplies information to the Commission voluntarily, accompanied by a specific request that his identity be kept secret, the Commission must comply with that condition, failing which it will be liable for damages under Article 288 of the EC Treaty.

1 Case 145/83, 53/84 *Adams v EC Commission* [1986] QB 138, [1985] ECR 3539.

5.22

Following that case the Commission issued internal instructions in the light of the ECJ's judgment as to how its officials should deal with information which comes into its possession regarding possible infringements of Articles 81 and 82. These instructions were as follows:

In circumstances where the identity of the person providing the information is known to the Commission: here the documents may be shown or returned to the undertaking concerned only after the person providing the information has been warned of the various risks which this may entail for him (which will, as in the *Stanley Adams*[1] case itself, usually be dependent on the national laws involved—the problems of Mr Adams centred around the Swiss laws on industrial espionage) and on the strict condition that he has authorised the Commission to do so.

Where the identity of the person providing the information has not been revealed to the Commission: here the documents will not be shown or returned to the undertaking in question until after a detailed examination by the Commission staff of their importance to the investigation, the risk that they might be traced back to the person concerned and the possibility that he might be subjected to legal proceedings.

1 Case 145/83, 53/84 *Adams v EC Commission* [1986] QB 138, [1985] ECR 3539.

3 RIGHT OF THE COMPLAINANT TO BE HEARD

5.23

Assuming the Commission decides to initiate proceedings against an undertaking, the position regarding the right of the complainant to be heard in such proceedings is as follows. Under art 19(2) of Regulation 17/62[1], the Commission *may* hear any natural or legal persons whom it considers necessary to hear and this may well include the complainant. Article 19(2) goes on to provide that applications to be heard on the part of any such natural or legal person *must* be granted, if that person can show a 'sufficient interest'. It seems inconceivable that a complainant (ie someone who has a legitimate interest within the meaning of art 3(2)(b) of Regulation 17/62)[2] does not have a sufficient interest such that he has a right to be heard during the proceedings pursuant to art 19(2). Indeed, art 7 of Commission Regulation 2842/98 makes it clear that a complainant will be given an opportunity to make known its views in writing, having been provided with a non-confidential version of the Commission's statement of objections. The Commission may (but is not obliged to do so) give the complainant the opportunity to express its views orally, if it has so requested[3].

1 Council Regulation (EEC) 17/62, OJ Sp Ed [1959–62] p 87.
2 See para **5.03**.
3 See also Case 43/85 *ANCIDES v EC Commission* [1987] ECR 3131.

5.24
Any other natural or legal person having a sufficient interest (within the meaning of art 19(2) of Regulation 17/62) must be given the opportunity by the Commission of making known its views in writing within a time limit fixed by the Commission. Such a person may also be given the opportunity to make known its views orally[1]. However, in both cases the right to be heard only applies if the complainant actually applies to be heard[2].

1 Commission Regulation (EC) 2842/98, art 9, OJ [1998] L 354/18.
2 Case 43/85 *ANCIDES v EC Commission* [1987] ECR 3131, [1988] 4 CMLR 821.

5.25
In order to comment meaningfully during the course of the proceedings, the complainant will wish to have some knowledge of the views being expressed by the undertaking(s) complained of. Present practice, as set out in the Commission's Thirteenth Report on Competition Policy[1], is that the complainant is provided with the substance of the replies and observations regarding the complaint. As far as the complainant's access to commercially sensitive information is concerned, the position is as set out at paras **11.02** ff: in essence, the Commission must never disclose the business secrets of one undertaking to another but other information or documents of the kind covered by the concept of 'professional secrecy' may be communicated to another undertaking (including the complainant) if the Commission believes this is necessary for the proper conduct of the investigation[2].

1 At para 74.
2 Case 53/85 *AKZO Chemie BV v EC Commission* [1986] ECR 1965, [1987] 1 CMLR 231. See too Joined Cases 142, 156/84 *BAT and Reynolds v EC Commission* [1987] ECR 4487, [1988] 4 CMLR 24.

5.26
The CFI re-confirmed in the *Matra Hachette*[1] case that the rights of third parties (such as complainants), as laid down by art 19 of Council Regulation 17/62, are limited to the right to participate in the administra-

tive procedure and that the requirement for full disclosure by the Commission applies only to undertakings which may be the subject of an infringement decision under Article 81 or 82. In particular, the CFI dismissed the applicant's contention that third parties could claim a right of access to the file compiled by the Commission on the same basis as the undertakings under investigation[2].

1 Case T-17/93 *Matra Hachette SA v EC Commission* [1994] ECR II-595.
2 Ibid at para 34. As far as the issue of access to the Commission's file generally is concerned, see para **7.27** ff.

5.27
Although it is for the Commission to assess whether or not a particular document contains business secrets, the ECJ held in the *AKZO*[1] case that the Commission must follow a set procedure: firstly, provide the undertaking in question with an opportunity to express its views; secondly, notify it of the reasons for a decision that a document does not contain business secrets and thirdly, give that undertaking an opportunity to bring an action before the ECJ for review before implementing the decision. It has been suggested[2] that the procedural steps laid down by the ECJ may enable a 'fractious defendant' to hold up the Commission's administrative procedure and that, in order to avoid this, the Commission 'may prefer in future cases to do without the complainant's input on the evidence'.

1 Case 53/85 *AKZO Chemie BV v EC Commission* [1986] ECR 1965, [1987] 1 CMLR 231.
2 Joshua 'Information in EEC Competition Law Procedures' (1986) EL Rev 409 at 422.

G Rejection of Complaint

5.28
If the Commission decides, following a complaint, that, on the basis of the information available to it, there are insufficient grounds for granting the complainant's application, it is required to inform the complainant and to fix a time limit within which the complainant may submit any further comments in writing[1]. If the Commission fails to do this the complainant could commence proceedings against the Commission under Article 232 of the EC Treaty for failure to act, ie failure to state its views on the substance of the complaint pursuant to art 6 of Regulation 2842/98[2]. Assuming an article 6 letter is issued by the Commission, that does not amount to a 'decision' which can be challenged before the ECJ under Article 230 of the Treaty. This is because art 6 expressly envisages that the complainant will wish to make further comments, on the basis of which the Commission may well wish to review the provisional view expressed in the article 6 letter[3].

1 Commission Regulation (EEC) 99/63, art 6, OJ Sp Ed [1963–64] p 47.
2 See para **10.51**. As in Case T-74/92 *Ladbroke Racing (Deutschland) GmbH v EC Commission* [1995] ECR II-115, CFI.
3 See the judgment of the Court of First Instance, dismissing an application as inadmissible, in Case T-64/89 *Automec Srl v EC Commission* [1991] 4 CMLR 177 (*Automec I*); see also Case T-28/90 *Asia Motor France SA v EC Commission* [1992] 5 CMLR 431 and Case T-186/94 *Guérin Automobiles v EC Commission*, [1995] ECR II-1753.

5.29

Once the complainant has submitted any comments in response to the article 6 letter (and assuming that these further comments do not cause the Commission to change its provisional view), the Commission's practice is usually to issue a definitive letter, stating that it still rejects the complaint[1]. Such a definitive letter constitutes a decision which the complainant can appeal to the ECJ under Article 230[2]. The Commission may in fact decide to go one step further and take a formal decision rejecting the complaint. However, this is not strictly necessary because a definitive letter of rejection following the initial article 6 letter is sufficient for the complainant to be able to commence Article 230 proceedings. In *BEUC*[3] the CFI rejected the Commission's contention that a complaint was inadmissible because the contested decision took the form of a letter signed by a Director in DGIV rather than the Commissioner responsible for competition matters. In the CFI's words 'to accept such an argument would render article 3 of Regulation 17/62 wholly ineffective'[4]. The Commission's rejection of a complaint must be reasoned with sufficient precision and detail to enable the CFI to review the Commission's use of its discretion to define priorities[5]. Accordingly, the Commission must set out the facts justifying the decision and the legal considerations on the basis of which it was adopted[6].

1 15th Report on Competition Policy (1985), para 1. See *Dealing with the Commission* (1997) European Commission at para 7.3.
2 Joined Cases 142, 156/84 *BAT and Reynolds v EC Commission* [1987] ECR 4487, [1988] 4 CMLR 24; see too Case 210/81 *Demo-Studio Schmidt v EC Commission* [1983] ECR 3045, [1984] 1 CMLR 63; Case 298/83 *CICCE v EC Commission* [1985] ECR 1105, [1986] 1 CMLR 486; Case T-7/92 *Asia Motors France v EC Commission (No 2)* [1994] 4 CMLR 30; Case C-39/93P *SFEI v EC Commission* [1994] ECR I-2681, ECJ, and 15th Report on Competition Policy (1985), para 127.
3 Case T-37/92 *BEUC and NCC v EC Commission* [1994] ECR II-285.
4 See n 3 above, at para 38.
5 Case C-19/93P *Rendo v EC Commission* [1995] ECR I-3319 at para 27.
6 Joined Cases 142, 156/84 *BAT and Reynolds v EC Commission* [1987] ECR 4487 and Case C-119/97P *Ufex v EC Commission* [2000] 4 CMLR 268.

5.30

The ECJ made it clear in the *Guérin Automobiles* case[1] that the Commission is required either to initiate a procedure against the person to whom a complaint relates or to take a definitive decision rejecting the complaint, once the complainant has submitted its observations on the letter sent under article 6 of Regulation 2842/98. The ECJ went on in that case to make it clear that, in accordance with the principles of good administration, the Commission's decision must be adopted within a reasonable time after receipt of the complainant's observations. Where the court finds that the Commission has failed to comply with this obligation it will confine itself to declaring that there has been an unlawful failure to act in violation of Article 232 of the EC Treaty. It has no jurisdiction to issue directions to the Commission, requiring the latter to take the measures required within a stipulated period[2]. The issue decided upon in the *Guérin Automobiles* case should be distinguished from the question whether the complainant is entitled to obtain a decision from the Commission on the existence of the alleged infringement. The ECJ has held that it is not[3]. If the Commission rejects a complaint on the ground that there has been no infringement of Article 81 or Article 82, it is under a duty to set out in its decision the facts and considerations on which that decision is based[4].

1 C-282/95P *Guérin Automobiles v EC Commission* [1997] ECR 1-1503.
2 Case T-127/98 *UPS Europe v EC Commission* [1999] All ER (EC) 794.
3 Case 125/78 *GEMA v EC Commission* [1979] ECR 3173, [1980] 2 CMLR 177. See also para **10.49**.
4 Case T-387/94 *Asia Motors France v EC Commission* [1996] ECR II-961 upheld on appeal in Case C-401/96P *Somaco v EC Commission* [1998] ECR I-2587. For a case in which the Commission's decision rejecting a complaint was annulled, see Case T-504/93 *Tiercé Ladbroke SA v EC Commission* [1997] ECR II-923.

5.31

In *Koelman*[1] the ECJ held that a decision to reject a complaint is not a definitive ruling on the question whether or not there is an infringement of Article 81(1), EC Treaty and accordingly it has the same legal status as a comfort letter[2]. The court held that it followed therefore that the assessments made by the Commission in a decision rejecting a complaint do not prevent a national court which is asked to rule upon the Article 81(1) issue declaring the agreement in question to be void under Article 81(2). The fact that, unlike in the case of comfort letters, the Commission's assessments are contained in a challengeable measure did not affect that conclusion[3].

1 Case C-59/96P *Koelman v EC Commission* [1997] ECR I-4809.
2 In relation to comfort letters generally, see para **8.72** ff.
3 Case T-575/93 *Koelman v EC Commission* [1996] ECR II-1 at para 42, upheld on appeal in Case C-59/96P *Koelman v EC Commission* [1997] ECR I-4809.

5.32

If, rather than rejecting the complaint, the Commission adopts a decision (in relation to the undertaking complained of) which implicitly rejects the complaint, the complainant is entitled to challenge that decision under Article 230[1].

1 Case 26/76 *Metro v EC Commission* [1977] ECR 1875, [1978] 2 CMLR 1: see also para **10.18**.

5.33

The Commission is entitled to reject a complaint when it considers that the case does not display a sufficient Community interest to justify further investigation[1]. This reflects the fact that article 3 of Regulation 17/62 does not confer upon a person who lodges an application under that article the right to obtain a decision from the Commission as to the existence or otherwise of an infringement of Articles 81 or 82, EC Treaty[2]. In *Ufex*[3], the ECJ ruled that, in deciding to discontinue consideration of a complaint against alleged anti-competitive practices on the ground of lack of Community interest, the Commission cannot rely solely on the fact that practices alleged to be contrary to the EC Treaty have ceased, without having ascertained that their anti-competitive effects no longer continue.

1 See para **5.11** ff and Case T-114/92 *BEMIM v EC Commission* [1995] ECR II-147 at para 80.
2 Ibid at para 62.
3 Case C-119/97P *Ufex v EC Commission* [2000] 4 CMLR 268.

H The Complainant and Defamation

5.34
In *Hasselblad (GB) Ltd v Orbinson*[1] the English Court of Appeal was required to consider whether defamation proceedings could be brought against a person who had supplied evidence to the European Commission in support of a complaint made against the plaintiffs. The defendant argued that the Commission's procedure was quasi-judicial and that accordingly the letter in question was the subject of absolute privilege. The Court of Appeal rejected this argument but nevertheless found in favour of the defendant on the ground that the public interest required that the letter could not form the basis of a libel action; otherwise, the Commission would be frustrated in the performance of the duty imposed on it of enforcing compliance with Articles 81 and 82.

1 [1985] QB 475, [1985] 1 All ER 173, [1984] 3 CMLR 679. This was the first case in which the European Commission itself had been invited to address an English court.

Chapter 6 Investigations by the Commission

A Introduction

6.01
The Commission obtains information concerning potential violations of Articles 81 and 82 of the EC Treaty from a wide variety of sources. The parties to a particular agreement may decide to apply for negative clearance and/or seek an individual exemption[1]; a party to an agreement or a third party may decide to file a complaint with the Commission[2]; information may come to the attention of the Commission informally, through reading newspapers, trade journals, etc; the Commission also has power under Regulation 17/62[3] to conduct inquiries into any sector of the economy in which there is reason to believe that competition is being restricted or distorted: this is a rarely used procedure, although the Commission launched such an inquiry in 1989 in relation to the EC beer industry[4]. In addition, the Commission has two important, formal powers to obtain information. These are laid down in arts 11 and 14 of Regulation 17/62. Article 11 gives the Commission power to 'obtain all necessary information from the governments and competent authorities of the Member States and from undertakings and associations of undertakings'; art 14 authorises the Commission to 'undertake all necessary investigations into undertakings and associations of undertakings'. The scope of these two articles will be considered in turn.

1 See para **4.01** ff.
2 See para **5.01** ff.
3 Council Regulation (EEC) 17/62, art 12, OJ Sp Ed [1959–62] p 87.
4 Culminating with a press release, summarising the Commission's findings.

B Article 11 Requests for Information

1 INTRODUCTION

6.02
Article 11(1) of Regulation 17/62 gives the Commission power, in carrying out the duties assigned to it by Article 85, to obtain all 'necessary information' from undertakings and associations of undertakings. The only guidance which art 11 itself provides as to the determination of what constitutes 'necessary information' is the reference to Articles 83 and 85 of the EC Treaty. Article 83 is the provision which empowers the European Council,

acting on a proposal from the Commission, to adopt appropriate regulations or directives to give effect to the principles set out in Articles 81 and 82; Article 85 imposes a general duty on the Commission to ensure the application of the principles laid down in Articles 81 and 82. In essence, therefore, the Commission has power to obtain from undertakings such information as is necessary to enable it to enforce Articles 81 and 82. In the *SEP* case[1] the CFI held that the requirement that information requested be 'necessary' was satisfied if there was a relationship between the request for information and the presumed infringement of Article 81 or 82. It dismissed the argument that the Commission had violated the principle of proportionality[2], although it held that the principle did apply in the context of art 11.

1 Case T-39/90 *SEP v EC Commission* [1992] 5 CMLR 33. Upheld by the ECJ in Case C-36/92P *SEP v EC Commission* [1994] ECR I-1911.
2 As to this principle generally, see para **11.49** ff.

6.03
At the same time as it sends a request for information to an undertaking or association of undertakings, the Commission is required to forward a copy of the request to the competent authority of the Member State in whose territory the seat of the undertaking or association of undertakings is situated (that is to say, the Office of Fair Trading in the case of the United Kingdom).

2 WHICH UNDERTAKINGS CAN BE THE SUBJECT OF AN ARTICLE 11 REQUEST?

6.04
Article 11(1) of Regulation 17/62 refers to undertakings and associations of undertakings and these terms should be interpreted in the same way as they are when used in Article 81 of the EC Treaty. There is nothing in art 11 to suggest that the only undertakings which can be the subject of such a request are those which the Commission believes have committed infringements of Article 81 or 82 and the Commission certainly considers that it has power to request information from other undertakings. Third parties who might be asked to provide information in this way would include, for example, customers or competitors of the allegedly infringing undertaking. An undertaking which has filed a complaint with the Commission alleging an infringement of Article 81 or 82 could also be the subject of an article 11 request, asking it to provide further information[1].

1 It is evident from the ECJ's judgment (point 5) in Case 298/83 *CICCE v EC Commission* [1985] ECR 1105, [1986] 1 CMLR 486 that this happened in that case.

6.05
It may well be that the tentacles of art 11 extend even further, ie beyond what one might call 'trade witnesses' (ie competitors, customers, etc) to professionals such as accountants, lawyers and bankers. Firms of solicitors and accountants almost certainly constitute undertakings for the purpose of

Articles 81 and 82 (and therefore fall within the scope of art 11). To the extent that the information requested does not concern a client, a lawyer would not be able to pray in aid the lawyer/client relationship. Even where the information requested concerns a client it is by no means certain that a professional adviser would be able to refuse to supply the information requested. The mere fact that the information is confidential would not be a sufficient defence because the Commission is bound in any event to keep secret information governed by the obligation of professional secrecy[1]. As far as lawyers are concerned, they may be able to rely on the principle of attorney/client privilege[2].

1 EC Treaty, Article 287; Council Regulation (EEC) 17/62, art 20(2), OJ Sp Ed [1959–62] p 87.
2 See para **11.14** ff.

6.06
It is not clear whether the Commission has power to request information under art 11 from undertakings located outside the Community. If the undertaking has a branch within the Community, the request can be served on that branch. Similarly, if the undertaking has a wholly-owned subsidiary within the Community it would appear that the request could be served on the subsidiary (by analogy with the *Dyestuffs* case[1]). Where the undertaking concerned has no presence whatsoever within the Community, it is submitted that the better view is that art 11 does not apply to it (for example, the recitals to Regulation 17/62 refer to the need for the Commission to have power to obtain information 'throughout the Common Market'). This is not to say that the Commission does not have power to make a simple request for information from such an undertaking, albeit without legal sanction for failure to comply, and the undertaking concerned will frequently wish to reply.

1 Case 48/69 *ICI v EC Commission* [1972] ECR 619, [1972] CMLR 557.

3 SCOPE OF AN ARTICLE 11 REQUEST—'NECESSARY' INFORMATION

6.07
The only guidance which art 11 itself provides as to the meaning of the phrase 'necessary information' is its reference to Articles 83 and 85 of the EC Treaty[1]. The Commission itself considers that information is 'necessary' if it is required in order to enable it to establish the applicability of Articles 81 and 82[2]. However, the request itself must state the purpose for which it is being made[3] and it is not therefore legitimate for the Commission to embark on a 'fishing expedition'. If an undertaking refuses to supply information requested of it on the grounds that the undertaking does not believe that the information is necessary for the Commission's purpose, the Commission is likely to make a formal decision[4] requiring that information (pursuant to art 11(5) of Regulation 17/62[5]); ie it, rather than the undertaking, decides what is necessary (always subject, of course, to possible review by the CFI). In *SEP v EC Commission*[6] the CFI held that the term 'necessary information' in art 11(1) must be interpreted by reference to the

purposes for which the powers of investigation in question were conferred upon the Commission. It went on to state that 'the requirement for a correlation between the request for information and the presumed infringement is met if, at this stage of the procedure, the request can be legitimately considered to be related to the presumed infringement'[7]. This interpretation was upheld by the ECJ[8].

1 See para **6.02** and the CFI decision in the *SEP* case referred to in para **6.02**.
2 As in Commission Decision (78/516/EEC) *RAI/UNITEL* OJ [1978] L 157/39, [1978] 3 CMLR 306.
3 Council Regulation (EEC) 17/62, art 11(3).
4 See n 2 above.
5 See para **6.12**.
6 Case T-39/90 [1992] 5 CMLR 33.
7 Ibid at para 29.
8 Case C-36/92P *SEP v EC Commission*, [1994] ECR I-1911.

4 SELF-INCRIMINATION

6.08
The extent to which undertakings who receive an article 11(3) request, or are the subject of an article 11(5) decision, can benefit from any privilege against self-incrimination is considered at paras **6.74–6.76**.

5 INFORMAL AND FORMAL REQUESTS FOR INFORMATION

6.09
Article 11 sets out a two-stage process by which the Commission can request information. An informal request can be made pursuant to art 11(3); if, but only if, an undertaking fails to comply with such a request does the Commission have the power to issue a formal decision, requiring the information to be supplied (art 11(5)).

(1) Article 11(3) Request

6.10
An article 11(3) request usually takes the form of a letter. The Commission is required to state the legal basis and purpose of the request and it must also expressly state the penalties which can be incurred for supplying incorrect information. Although art 11(3) does not specifically require the Commission to stipulate a period of time within which a response should be made, it invariably does fix such a time limit (and indeed it can only go on to take a formal decision under art 11(5) if the undertaking concerned has not supplied the information requested pursuant to art 11(3) within the specified time limit). It is not unusual for the Commission to stipulate a tight timetable for replying and the undertaking concerned will frequently need to seek an extension; if so, it is wise not to delay the request for an extension until too close to the date fixed for a reply.

6.11
No penalties flow from a refusal by an undertaking to supply information requested pursuant to art 11(3). However, if it does so the Commission will almost certainly take a decision under art 11(5) and fines can be imposed for failure to comply with that decision[1]. More often than not, undertakings do choose to respond to the article 11(3) request and great care should be taken in the preparation of such a reply in view of the penalties which can be imposed for supplying incorrect information[2].

1 See para **6.19–6.20**.
2 See paras **6.20–6.22**.

(2) Article 11(5) Decision

6.12
If an undertaking fails to supply the information requested by the Commission pursuant to art 11(3) within the time limit which has been fixed, or supplies incomplete information, the Commission is under a duty to make a decision requiring the information to be supplied (art 11(5))[1]. Such a decision must specify the information required, fix an appropriate time limit within which it is to be supplied and indicate the penalties which can be imposed for failing to comply. The undertaking concerned does not have any right to be heard by the Commission before the latter takes a decision pursuant to art 11(5)[2]. Although all decisions of the Commission must state the reasons on which they are based[3], it is probably sufficient in the context of an article 11(5) decision for the Commission merely to state the purpose for which the information is requested (and, of course, the purpose must in any event have been stated in the original article 11(3) request)[4].

1 It is sufficient if the failure is merely passive in nature; it does not have to be wilful: Case T-46/92 *Scottish Football Association v EC Commission* [1994] ECR II-1039 at para 31.
2 By analogy with the ruling of the ECJ in Case 136/79 *National Panasonic (UK) Ltd v EC Commission* [1980] ECR 2033, [1980] 3 CMLR 169. That case concerned Council Regulation (EEC) 17/62, art 14, OJ Sp Ed [1959–62] p 87, but the reasoning of the ECJ is equally applicable to art 11.
3 EC Treaty, Article 253.
4 The applicant unsuccessfully challenged an article 11(5) decision in Case T-46/92 *Scottish Football Association v EC Commission* [1994] ECR II-1039 and Case T-34/93 *Société Générale v EC Commission* [1995] ECR II-545.

6.13
Article 11(5) decisions do not have to be published by the Commission[1] but they almost invariably are[2].

1 Council Regulation (EEC) 17/62, art 21, OJ Sp Ed [1959–62] p 87.
2 Eg Commission Decision (76/593/EEC) *CSV* OJ [1976] L 192/27; Commission Decision (78/ 516/EEC) *RAI/UNITEL* OJ [1978] L 157/39, [1978] 3 CMLR 306; Commission Decision (82/175/EEC) *Fire Insurance* OJ [1982] L 80/36, [1982] 2 CMLR 159; Commission Decision (83/205/EEC) *Deutsche Castrol* OJ [1983] L 114/26, [1983] 3 CMLR 165; Commission Decision (85/121/EEC) *Olympic Airways* OJ [1985] L 46/51, [1985] 1 CMLR 730.

6.14
In the *Orkem*[1] and *Solvay*[2] cases, the undertakings concerned appealed to the ECJ against article 11(5) decisions. One of the grounds on which they

relied was that, because each article 11(5) decision contained precise charges relating to alleged participation in infringements of Article 81, they in fact constituted Statements of Objections and, as such, they should have been given an opportunity to express their views. The ECJ dismissed this argument, holding that, by referring to its suspicion of the existence of agreements contrary to Article 81(1) as the reason for its request for information, the Commission had merely fulfilled its obligation (under Regulation 17/62, art 11(3)) to state the purpose of its request.

1 Case 374/87 *Orkem v EC Commission* [1989] ECR 3283, [1991] 4 CMLR 502.
2 Case 27/88 *Solvay & Cie v EC Commission* [1989] ECR 3355, [1991] 4 CMLR 502.

(3) Notification of Member States

6.15
Copies of article 11(3) requests and article 11(5) decisions must be forwarded to the competent authority of the Member State in whose territory the seat of the undertaking or association of undertakings is situated[1]. Article 11 does not stipulate that the replies to those requests/decisions must be forwarded to the competent authority concerned. However, art 10(1) obliges the Commission to transmit to the competent authorities of the Member States 'copies of the most important documents lodged with the Commission for the purposes of establishing the existence of infringement of Articles 81 or 82 of the Treaty'. The reply to an article 11 request or decision may well fall within this category of documents. Two questions arise: first, to what use can a competent authority of a Member State put information contained in such a reply, transmitted to it by the Commission (for example, can it make use of such information in the context of domestic competition law proceedings)? This issue is considered at paras **6.16–6.17**. Secondly, to what extent is art 10(1) qualified in the context of business secrets? This issue is considered at para **6.18**.

1 Council Regulation (EEC) 17/62, art 11(2) and (6).

6.16
In order to answer this question, the starting point is Council Regulation 17/62, art 20. Article 20(1) of this provides that information acquired as a result of the application of art 11 is to be used only for the purpose of the relevant request or investigation. More generally, art 20(2) provides that neither the Commission nor the competent authorities of the Member States are to disclose information acquired by them as a result of the application of Regulation 17/62 and of the kind covered by the obligation of professional secrecy. Although art 20(1) does not expressly refer to the competent authorities of Member States it would seem wrong, in principle, for Member States to have any greater freedom than the Commission in the use of information acquired by the Commission pursuant to art 11. The position, as far as information obtained pursuant to art 11 is concerned, would seem to be that the competent authorities of the Member States are not free to make use of any information obtained by the Commission, except to the extent that they do so with a view to

aiding the Commission in its investigation; ie in relation to article 11 replies, art 20(1) governs the situation and one does not need to go on to consider art 20(2).

6.17
This issue was raised directly with the ECJ under an Article 234 reference[1] by the Spanish Tribunal for the Defence of Competition[2]. In this case, the Tribunal has asked the following questions:

(1) May the national authority responsible for the application in a Member State of Articles 81 and 82 use information obtained by the European Commission pursuant to art 11 of Council Regulation 17/62 in proceedings for the imposition of a penalty conducted solely under Articles 81 and 82?
(2) May the authority use this information in proceedings for the imposition of a penalty conducted under both Community competition law and national competition law?
(3) May the authority use this information in proceedings for the imposition of a penalty conducted solely under national competition law?
(4) May the authority use this information in proceedings for the authorisation of practices restrictive of competition conducted solely under its national law?

The ECJ held that the effect of Article 287 of the EC Treaty[3], coupled with art 20 of Regulation 17/62, was that the national authority could not use information obtained by the Commission under arts 11–14 of Regulation 17/62, or information contained in notifications under arts 2, 4 or 5 of that Regulation, as a means of proof in the enforcement of either national or EC competition law. The Commission had argued that national authorities should be able to use such information in the enforcement of EC competition law but not national competition law (no doubt in the hope of increasing the enforcement of EC competition law by national courts/ authorities[4]). The Court did, however, indicate[5] that such information could be taken into account by the national authorities in deciding whether to open their own procedure. On the other hand, the CFI went on to say[6] that the national authority could only make use of documentation supplied by the Commission 'on condition that the proof of their existence must be established not by documents or information obtained by the Commission but by proof obtained in accordance with national law'. This situation in reverse (ie the extent to which documents revealed during the course of proceedings in the High Court can be disclosed to the Commission to assist it in parallel proceedings) was decided by the High Court, which ruled in favour of disclosure[7].

1 For Article 234 references generally, see paras **10.67–10.69**.
2 Case C-67/91 *Dirección Géneral de Defensa de la Competencia v Asociación Espanola de Banca Privada* [1992] ECR I-4785, ECJ.
3 See para **11.03**.
4 See paras **17.07–17.08**.
5 See n 2 above, at para 39.
6 See n 2 above, at para 43.
7 *Apple Corpn Ltd v Apple Computer Inc* [1992] 1 CMLR 969; see para **20.10**.

6.18
In *SEP v EC Commission*[1], the ECJ was required (on appeal from the CFI) to consider the complex inter-relationship between arts 10, 11 and 20 of Regulation 17/62. That case concerned an article 11(5) decision of the Commission, which required disclosure of a particular contract. SEP was concerned that disclosure, via the Commission, to the competent Dutch authorities would seriously damage its negotiating position in future gas supply negotiations with the Dutch government. The CFI held that art 20 provided an adequate safeguard to SEP, by prohibiting national officials not only from disclosing the contents of the contract in question but also from 'using the information contained in it in order to establish the commercial policy pursued by certain public undertakings'[2]. On appeal, the ECJ cited its judgment in the *Spanish Banks* case[3], noting that the procedural safeguard contained in art 20 did not go so far as to call for the information transmitted actually to be ignored by the national authorities (they were not, as the ECJ put it in *SEP*[4], required to suffer 'acute amnesia'). Article 20 did not therefore prevent the use of the information in question in connection with the determination of the commercial policy of Gasunie (the Dutch monopoly supplier of natural gas in which the Dutch state had a 50% holding), with the possible consequence that damage might be caused to SEP. The ECJ therefore held that the CFI had committed an error of law. However, the ECJ did not go on to uphold the appeal. Instead, it ruled that art 10 of Regulation 17/62[5] did not automatically oblige the Commission to transmit the contract in question to the Dutch authorities. In particular, art 10 has to be interpreted in the light of the general principle of the right of undertakings to the protection of their business secrets[6]. It held that, if the Commission wishes to transmit a document to the competent national authorities (notwithstanding a claim that in the particular circumstances of the case that document is of a confidential nature with respect to those authorities), it must adopt a properly reasoned decision amenable to judicial review by means of an action for annulment[7] (the ECJ cited by way of analogy its approach to the situation where an undertaking against which proceedings have been commenced under Article 81 or 82 seeks to prevent disclosure by the Commission to a third party which has submitted a complaint against that undertaking of documents which the undertaking claims to be of a confidential nature[8]).

1 Case C-36/92-P *SEP v EC Commission* [1994] ECR I-1911, ECJ.
2 Case T-39/90 *SEP v EC Commission* [1991] ECR II-1497 at para 56.
3 Case C-67-91 *Dirección General de Defensa de la Competencia v Asociación Espanola de Banca Privada* [1992] ECR I-4785.
4 See n 1 above, at para 29.
5 See para **6.15**.
6 See the EC Treaty, Article 287; see also para **11.03** ff.
7 See n 1 above, at para 39.
8 See Case 53/85 *AKZO Chemie v EC Commission* [1986] ECR 1965; see also paras **11.07–11.08**.

6 PENALTIES FOR FAILING TO SUPPLY INFORMATION AT ALL OR FOR SUPPLYING INCOMPLETE INFORMATION

(1) Penalties for Failing to Supply Information at all

6.19
As noted above[1], no penalties can be imposed on an undertaking which refuses to supply information pursuant to an article 11(3) request. The only sanction is the making by the Commission of a decision pursuant to art 11(5). If the undertaking fails to comply with that decision, two types of fine can be imposed. Firstly, the Commission may impose fines of between 100 and 5,000 ECU for the failure to supply the information requested within the time limit fixed[2]. Secondly, the Commission can impose periodic penalty payments of between 50 and 1,000 ECU per day (calculated from a date appointed by the Commission) in order to compel the undertaking to supply complete and correct information[3]. These penalties can be imposed either together or in the alternative. However, before either is imposed, the undertaking concerned must be given the opportunity to be heard[4].

1 See para **6.11**.
2 Under Council Regulation (EEC) 17/62, art 15(1)(b), OJ Sp Ed [1959–62] p 87.
3 Under ibid art 16(1)(c).
4 Council Regulation (EEC) 17/62, art 19(1).

(2) Penalties for Supplying Incorrect or Incomplete Information

6.20
If an undertaking provides the Commission with incorrect information, either in response to a request made pursuant to art 11(3) or a decision made pursuant to art 11(5), the Commission can impose on that undertaking fines ranging from 100 to 5,000 ECU[1]. In respect of this penalty, no distinction is drawn between incorrect information supplied pursuant to an article 11(3) request and that supplied pursuant to an article 11(5) decision. The supply of incorrect information in response to an article 11(5) decision can be made the subject of periodic penalty payments, ranging from 50 to 1,000 ECU per day, calculated from a date appointed by the Commission[2]. These periodic penalty payments cannot, however, be levied in relation to an incorrect response to an article 11(3) request.

1 Under Council Regulation (EEC) 17/62, art 15(1)(b).
2 Under ibid art 16(1)(c).

6.21
The Commission's interpretation of what it regards as constituting 'incorrect information' is set out in its decision in *Telos*[1]:

> 'Any statement is incorrect which gives a distorted picture of the true facts asked for, and which departs significantly from reality on major points. Where a statement is thus false or so incomplete that the reply taken in its entirety is likely to

mislead the Commission about the true facts, it constitutes incorrect information within the meaning of Article 15(1)(b)'.

The Commission has imposed fines under art 15(1)(b) of Regulation 17/62 for the supply of incorrect information in a number of cases[2].

1 Commission Decision (82/124/EEC) OJ [1982] L 58/19, [1982] 1 CMLR 267.
2 Eg in *Telos* itself; also Commission Decision (82/53/EEC) *Comptoir Commercial d'Importation* OJ [1982] L 27/31, [1982] 1 CMLR 440; Commission Decision (85/506/EEC) *Peugeot* OJ [1986] L 295/19, [1989] 4 CMLR 371 and Commission Decision (2000/146/EC) *Anheuser-Busch Incorporated-Scottish & Newcastle* OJ [2000] L 49/37. See, too, Commission Decision (91/55/EEC) *Secrétema* OJ [1991] L 35/23.

6.22
The fine of between 100 and 5,000 ECU which can be imposed under art 15(1)(b) is in relation to each request. If, as is frequently the case, the Commission requests information from an undertaking on several occasions in relation to the same matter it will be a question of fact in each case as to whether they amount to a single 'request' under art 15(1)(b). In *Peugeot*[1] the Commission sent two letters (one over four months after the other) requesting information but was prepared to accept that they amounted to a single request 'because they put a series of questions in a single context and because the second letter made reference to the first'[2].

1 Commission Decision (85/506/EEC) OJ [1986] L 295/19, [1989] 4 CMLR 371.
2 Para 53 of the Commission's Decision.

7 FOREIGN LAW AS A DEFENCE TO A FAILURE TO COMPLY

6.23
The Commission's decision in *CSV*[1] provides an interesting example of the possible tension between the Commission's investigative powers and a foreign law, in that case the Swiss criminal code. The Commission made an article 11(5) decision which required CSV, a Dutch joint selling agency, to supply information concerning exports outside the Community. This required CSV to disclose information concerning a Swiss company and CSV was concerned that such disclosure could violate the Swiss criminal code. It accordingly asked that the Commission take a formal decision under art 11(5) requiring it to supply such information so that, if necessary, CSV could raise this as a defence to criminal charges in Switzerland. Because CSV refused to comply with the article 11(3) request, the Commission had no alternative but to make a decision under art 11(5). However, it indicated that it did not believe that the position under Swiss law meant that CSV was justified in its refusal to comply with the article 11(3) request: the information in question was within the Community and the Commission believed it had a right to call for it.

1 Commission Decision (76/593/EEC) OJ [1976] L 192/27.

8 WHAT AMOUNTS TO INFORMATION UNDER ARTICLE 11?

6.24
Article 11 is entitled 'Requests for Information' and, unlike art 14, does not refer to documentation at all but only to information. There are, however, a number of article 11(5) decisions in which the Commission has required documents to be supplied[1]. The ECJ has now confirmed[2] that the Commission is entitled to require the disclosure of documents (even in a case where the Commission has already carried out an article 14 investigation).

1 Eg Commission Decision (76/593/EEC) *CSV* OJ [1976] L 192/27; Commission Decision (78/ 516/EEC) *RAI/UNITEL* OJ [1978] L 157/39, [1978] 3 CMLR 306.
2 Case 374/87 *Orkem v EC Commission* [1989] ECR 3283, [1991] 4 CMLR 502 and Case 27/88 *Solvay & Cie v EC Commission* [1989] ECR 3355, [1991] 4 CMLR 502.

9 POWER TO OBTAIN INFORMATION FROM MEMBER STATES

6.25
For completeness, it should be noted that art 11(1) of Regulation 17/62[1] gives the Commission power to obtain all necessary information (in carrying out its duties under Article 81 and under provisions adopted under Article 83 of the EC Treaty) from the governments and competent authorities of the Member States. The designated competent authority in the UK is the Secretary of State[2]. However, in practice, the UK authority which acts as competent authority for the purposes of Regulation 17/62 is the Office of Fair Trading.

1 Council Regulation (EEC) 17/62, OJ Sp Ed [1959–62] p 87.
2 European Communities (Designation) Order 1973, SI 1973/1889.

10 RELATIONSHIP BETWEEN ARTICLES 11 AND 14

6.26
The power of the Commission to undertake on-the-spot investigations under Regulation 17/62, art 14 is considered at paras **6.27–6.73**. Articles 11 and 14 are entirely independent of each other. In cases in which the Commission exercises its powers under art 14 it frequently uses its article 11 powers at a later stage in order to obtain further information. In the *Orkem*[1] and *Solvay*[2] cases the ECJ confirmed that the Commission had the right to do this, rejecting the claim that the article 11 power had to be exercised prior to the power under art 14.

1 Case 374/87 *Orkem v EC Commission* [1989] ECR 3283, [1991] 4 CMLR 502.
2 Case 27/88 *Solvay & Cie v EC Commission* [1989] ECR 3355, [1991] 4 CMLR 502.

C Article 14 Investigations

1 INTRODUCTION

6.27
Article 14 of Regulation 17/62 empowers the Commission, in carrying out the duties assigned to it by Article 85 and by provisions adopted under Article 83 of the EC Treaty, to undertake all necessary[1] investigations into undertakings and associations of undertakings. The Commission considers that, as between itself and the undertaking in question, it is for the Commission to decide what investigation is 'necessary'[2]. This is subject to the right to appeal the Commission's view of what is 'necessary' to the ECJ.

1 As to the meaning of the term 'necessary', see para **6.02** in relation to Council Regulation (EEC) 17/62, art 11, OJ Sp Ed [1959–62] p 87.
2 Commission Decision (82/756/EEC) *FNICF* OJ [1982] L 319/12, [1983] 1 CMLR 575.

6.28
Article 14 provides for two types of investigation. The first is an investigation under authorisation pursuant to art 14(2); the Commission officials carrying out such an investigation are required to produce a written authorisation (or 'mandate'). The second type of investigation is an investigation pursuant to a Commission decision under art 14(3). Each of these will be considered in more detail below. At this stage, however, it should be noted that the two types of investigation do not represent a two-stage process. That is to say, the Commission can proceed immediately to investigate by decision pursuant to art 14(3), without first carrying out an investigation by authorisation[1]. Moreover, the procedure under art 14 is entirely separate from that under art 11[2]. Accordingly, the Commission can proceed under arts 14(2) or 14(3) without proceeding first under arts 11(3) or 11(5).

1 Case 136/79 *National Panasonic (UK) Ltd v EC Commission* [1980] ECR 2033, [1980] 3 CMLR 169.
2 For a description of the article 11 procedure, see paras **6.02–6.25**.

6.29
The crucial distinction between an investigation carried out under art 14(2) and one carried out pursuant to art 14(3) is that the undertaking being investigated is not required to submit to an article 14(2) investigation. It is, however, under a duty to submit to an article 14(3) investigation and if it refuses to do so penalties can be imposed for failure to comply. Accordingly, the article 14(3) procedure tends to be used where the Commission suspects that the undertaking concerned is unlikely to be co-operative. It also tends to be used where the Commission wishes to investigate several undertakings simultaneously.

6.30
Under art 13(2) of Regulation 17/62 the Commission can request the competent authorities of the Member States (in the case of the UK, the Office of Fair Trading) to undertake an article 14 investigation on its behalf. This power was exercised in the UK for the first time in 1992[1]. In his 1992

Annual Report the Director General of Fair Trading stated that he regarded this as an important development in the context of subsidiarity and indicated that he anticipated that more use would be made of art 13 in future cases[2].

1 *Annual Report of the Director General of Fair Trading* (1992) at p 35.
2 *Annual Report of the Director General of Fair Trading* (1992) at p 36.

2 RESPONSIBILITY WITHIN THE COMMISSION FOR AUTHORISING ARTICLE 14 INVESTIGATIONS

6.31
Decisions under art 14(3)[1] are usually adopted under the delegation procedure provided for in a Commission decision of 5 November 1980. That decision permitted the member of the Commission responsible for competition matters to adopt, in the name and on behalf of the Commission, a decision under art 14. In the *AZKO*[2] case the applicants contested this delegation of internal authority, contending that it did not accord with the principle of collective responsibility laid down in Article 17 of the 1965 Merger Treaty (the Treaty establishing a single Council and a single Commission of the European Communities). The ECJ held that the decision of 5 November 1980 did not infringe the principle of collective responsibility and accordingly rejected this argument. In the later *Dow Chemical Ibérica*[3] case, it was argued that a contested article 14(3) decision was vitiated by a breach of an essential procedural requirement, in that it was not signed by the body which had adopted it. The ECJ rejected this argument, observing that no provision laid down a rule that the copy of the decision served on the undertaking had to be signed by the member of the Commission to whom power had been delegated. In any event, it was common ground that the contested decision had been duly certified as authentic by the signature of the Secretary General of the Commission.

1 See para **6.36** ff.
2 Case 5/85 *AKZO Chemie BV and AKZO Chemie UK Ltd v EC Commission* [1986] ECR 2585, [1987] 3 CMLR 716.
3 Joined Cases 97–99/87 *Dow Chemical Ibérica SA v EC Commission* [1989] ECR 3165, [1991] 4 CMLR 410.

3 ARTICLE 14(2) INVESTIGATIONS

6.32
Article 14(2) is in the following terms:

> 'The officials of the Commission authorised for the purpose of these investigations shall exercise their powers upon production of an authorisation in writing specifying the subject matter and purpose of the investigation and the penalties provided for in Article 15(1)(c) in cases where production of the required books or other business records is incomplete. In good time before the investigation, the Commission shall inform the competent authority of the Member State in whose territory the same is to be made of the investigation and of the identity of the authorised officials'.

The powers of the officials concerned when conducting the investigation are described at para **6.45** ff.

6.33
The authorisation identifies the relevant Commission officials and briefly describes the purpose of the investigation (as is required by the terms of art 14(2) itself). The Commission official(s) should be asked to produce a staff card for the purpose of confirming their identification.

6.34
In an effort to clarify the article 14(2) procedure for the benefit of undertakings being investigated, the Commission published an explanatory note in 1982; there is a very similar explanatory note in relation to art 14(3). Paragraph 2 of the note relating to art 14(2) states that the Commission officials will, if requested, provide explanations regarding the subject matter and purpose of the proposed investigation and also on procedural matters, particularly confidentiality. This opportunity should always be taken advantage of by the undertaking concerned, particularly with a view to ascertaining as precisely as possible the exact parameters of the investigation. The explanatory note goes on to confirm that an article 14(2) authorisation—unlike a Commission decision under art 14(3)—does not oblige the undertaking to submit to the investigation.

6.35
One issue which has been much debated, and which is dealt with in the explanatory note, is the extent to which the undertaking may have access to legal advice during the course of the investigation. This issue is, of course, of just as great a significance in the context of an article 14(3) investigation and is dealt with later in this chapter[1].

1 See para **6.69** ff.

4 ARTICLE 14(3) INVESTIGATIONS

6.36
Article 14(3) is in the following terms:

> 'Undertakings and associations of undertakings shall submit to investigations ordered by decision of the Commission. The decision shall specify the subject matter and purpose of the investigation, appoint the date upon which it is to begin and indicate the penalties provided for in Article 15(1)(c) and Article 16(1)(d) and the right to have the decision reviewed by the Court of Justice'.

A number of general points should be noted. Firstly, before taking a decision under art 14(3) the Commission is required to consult with the competent authority of the Member State in whose territory the investigation is to be carried out[1]. The ECJ confirmed in *AKZO*[2] that this consultation can be carried out informally (in that case the UK authorities were contacted by telephone and no minute of the conversation was drawn up). Secondly, as noted earlier[3], the Commission can proceed immediately to a decision under art 14(3) without first carrying out an investigation pursuant to a simple authorisation under art 14(2). The Commission is not required to give any reasons as to why it is availing itself of the article 14(3) procedure, although it usually proceeds on this basis where it suspects that the undertaking concerned may not be willing to co-operate with the Commission officials or may contemplate destroying or concealing relevant evidence. Thirdly, an article 14(3) decision is required to specify the subject-matter and purpose of the investigation. Under Article 253 (formerly Article 190) of the EC Treaty, an article 14(3) decision (like any other decision of the Commission) must state the reasons on which it is based. However, the judgment of the ECJ in the *National Panasonic*[4] case makes it clear that an article 14(3) decision will be adequately reasoned (for the purpose of Article 253 of the EC Treaty) if it contains all the 'essential constituents' specified in art 14(3), that is to say if it:

(*a*) specifies the subject matter and purpose of the investigation;
(*b*) appoints the date on which the investigation is to begin;
(*c*) indicates the penalties for refusing to submit to an investigation and/or providing information in incomplete form;
(*d*) indicates the right of the undertaking concerned to have the decision reviewed by the ECJ.

This was confirmed by the ECJ in *Hoechst*[5] and *Dow Benelux*[6]. In the *Dow Benelux*[7] case the undertaking went even further in its appeal, arguing that the Commission had to show that it had reasonable evidence before launching an article 14 investigation. The ECJ readily dismissed this.

1 Council Regulation (EEC) 17/62, art 14(4), OJ Sp Ed [1959–62] p 87.
2 Case 5/85 *AKZO Chemie BV and AKZO Chemie UK Ltd v EC Commission* [1986] ECR 2585, [1987] 3 CMLR 716.
3 See para **6.28**.
4 Case 136/79 *National Panasonic (UK) Ltd v EC Commission* [1980] ECR 2033, [1980] 3 CMLR 169.
5 Cases 46/87, 227/88 *Hoechst v EC Commission* [1989] ECR 2859, [1991] 4 CMLR 410.
6 Case 85/87 *Dow Benelux NV v EC Commission* [1989] ECR 3137, [1991] 4 CMLR 410.
7 See n 6 above.

6.37
In *AKZO*[1], the applicants sought to rely on an alleged absence of reasons in a slightly different context. They had refused to submit to an article 14(2) investigation and, in so doing, had sent the Commission a letter justifying their refusal. The applicants claimed that the Commission should, in taking the article 14(3) decision, have responded to the points made in their letter. The ECJ rejected this argument, taking a pragmatic approach: if the Commission had decided to act under art 14(3) immediately, there would have been no opportunity for the applicants to have submitted their views in any event.

1 Case 5/85 *AZKO Chemie BV and AKZO Chemie UK Ltd v EC Commission* [1986] ECR 2585, [1987] 3 CMLR 716.

6.38
As in the case of art 14(2), the Commission issued in 1982 an explanatory note concerning authorisations to investigate an execution of a Commission decision under art 14(3). It is in very similar terms to the text of the note

relating to art 14(2). However, the following specific points should be noted. Firstly, it reminds the undertaking to whom the decision is addressed that undertakings are legally obliged to submit to investigations ordered by decision under art 14(3) (this is not the position under art 14(2)[1]). Secondly, the note expressly states that the investigating officials 'cannot be required to enlarge upon the subject matter as set out in the decision or to justify in any way the taking of the decision'. This is in contrast with the explanatory note to art 14(2), which states that Commission officials are obliged, upon the undertaking's request, to provide explanations regarding the subject matter and purpose of the investigation. The reason for this distinction is quite simply that the purpose and subject matter of an article 14(3) decision are required to be set out in the decision itself. A number of other aspects of the explanatory note, which are of equal relevance in the context of article 14(2) investigations, are considered later in this chapter[2].

1 See para **6.34**.
2 See para **6.73**.

6.39
When the Commission decides to resort to use of an article 14(3) decision, the first the undertaking in question will frequently know of it is when the Commission officials arrive at the door of the undertaking's premises (so-called 'dawn raids'). Occasionally, Commission officials will undertake simultaneous dawn raids on a number of undertakings in different parts of the Community[1].

1 As in Commission Decision (86/398/EEC) *Polypropylene* OJ [1986] L 230/1, [1988] 4 CMLR 347, where the Commission carried out simultaneous investigations without prior warning at the premises of ten undertakings.

6.40
In the *National Panasonic*[1] case the company argued that the principle of proportionality[2] implied that an article 14(3) decision, without first the making of an article 14(2) request, could only be justified if the situation was 'very grave' and there was the 'greatest urgency' and the need for 'complete secrecy'. The ECJ rejected this, holding that the Commission's choice between the use of art 14(2) and art 14(3) depended on the need for an appropriate inquiry, having regard to the special features of the case[1]. In identifying the special features of a particular case, the Commission has a large measure of discretion.

1 Case 136/79 *National Panasonic (UK) Ltd v EC Commission* [1980] ECR 2033, [1980] 3 CMLR 169.
2 See paras **11.49–11.50**.

5 REVIEW BY THE EUROPEAN COURT OF JUSTICE

6.41
Article 14(3) of Regulation 17/62 expressly states that the Commission's decision to investigate must specify the right to have that decision reviewed by the ECJ (now the CFI). That appeal can be made at any time within two

months of the decision[1]. The mere making of the appeal does not cause the Commission's decision to be suspended but it is open to the undertaking concerned to apply for a stay of execution of the decision under Article 242 of the EC Treaty[2]. In the *Hoechst*[3] case, in which the company took the unprecedented step of refusing to admit the Commission's inspectors, the company attempted to obtain a suspension of the Commission's article 14(3) decision and its decision to impose a daily fine of 1,000 ECU (this fine had been imposed because of the company's refusal to submit to the investigation[4]). Hoechst argued that the Commission's decision was so lacking in legality and constitutionality that the company would inevitably suffer grave and irreparable damage. Without pre-judging the substance of the case, the President of the court had no doubt that Hoechst had not established a need for interim relief. He pointed out that if the article 14(3) decision was subsequently annulled by the ECJ, the Commission could make no use of the papers which it had obtained in execution of that decision. Similarly, if the decision to impose a daily fine was overturned by the court, the amount of the fine would have to be repaid. This emphasises the difficulty which an undertaking is likely to have if it seeks to persuade the Court to suspend an article 14(3) decision under Article 242 of the EC Treaty.

1 EC Treaty, Article 230. For Article 230 generally, see para **10.09** ff.
2 See para **10.57** ff.
3 Case 46/87R *Hoechst v EC Commission* [1987] ECR 1549, [1988] 4 CMLR 430. See also Case 85/87R *Dow Chemical Nederland v EC Commission* [1987] ECR 4367, [1988] 4 CMLR 439.
4 See para **6.65**.

6 USE WHICH CAN BE MADE OF INFORMATION OBTAINED UNDER ARTICLE 14

6.42

Under Regulation 17/62, art 20(1)[1], information acquired as a result of an investigation carried out under art 14 must be used by the Commission only 'for the purpose of the relevant investigation'. In *Dow Benelux*[2], the applicant disputed the Commission's article 14(3) decision to investigate, arguing that the decision had been based on information obtained during an earlier investigation involving an alleged cartel operating in a different product market. Accordingly, so the company argued, the Commission had made use of information in breach of art 20(1). The ECJ emphasised that the purpose of art 20 was to preserve professional secrecy and that this did not prevent the Commission from opening an investigation in order to verify or add to information which it happened to obtain during an earlier investigation, if that information indicated the existence of conduct contrary to Article 81 or 82. Such a prohibition would, the ECJ held, go beyond what was necessary to observe professional secrecy and the right to a fair hearing and would impede the Commission in carrying out its duty to enforce those Treaty provisions. This ruling has serious implications for companies operating in a number of separate, though closely-related, product sectors. Frequently, internal company documentation may deal with more than one product sector. The ECJ's judgment upholds the right of the Commission to make use of information contained in such a document and relating to one product sector even if its original access to that document came about as a result of its investigation of another product sector.

1 Council Regulation (EEC) 17/62, OJ Sp Ed [1959–62] p 87.
2 Case 85/87 *Dow Benelux NV v EC Commission* [1989] ECR 3137, [1991] 4 CMLR 410.

6.43
It is well established that documents found at one undertaking which incriminate another may constitute evidence against the latter as well as against the creator of the document[1].

1 Cases 40–48, etc/73 *Suiker Unie v EC Commission* [1975] ECR 1663, para 164 and *Soda-ash—Solvay/CFK* OJ [1991] L152/16, para 9.

6.44
A separate question which arises is whether the information which emerges from an art 14 investigation is likely to be made available to the competent authorities of the Member States and, if so, what use those competent authorities may make of it (for example, whether they are free to use it in the context of enforcement of domestic competition law). It is submitted that the position should be no different to that relating to article 11 requests for information: see para **6.15**.

7 POWERS OF THE COMMISSION'S INSPECTORS

(1) In General

6.45
As is clear from the text of art 14(2) and 14(3) themselves, the Commission authorisation or Commission decision (as the case may be) must specify the subject matter and purpose of the investigation and any undertaking being investigated should make sure that the Commission officials involved keep within the parameters. As in the case of art 11, it is not appropriate for the Commission to use an article 14 investigation as a 'fishing expedition'. Pursuant to art 14(1), Commission officials conducting an investigation under either art 14(2) or art 14(3) are empowered:

(*a*) to examine the undertaking's books and other business record;
(*b*) to take copies of or extracts from the books and business records;
(*c*) to ask for oral explanations on the spot;
(*d*) to enter any premises, land and means of transport undertakings.

Although it is almost invariably the case that undertakings which are the subject of an article 14 investigation are suspected of engaging in infringements of Articles 81 and/or 82, there is no reason in principle why other undertakings should not be susceptible of an investigation under art 14 (if the Commission believes that they may hold relevant evidence).

6.46

Before considering each of the four powers of the Commission referred to at para **6.45**, there are a number of general principles laid down by the ECJ which should be noted. The powers of the Commission as set out in art 14 (and, in particular, the power to carry out on-the-spot investigations without prior notification of the undertaking concerned) do not infringe any rights derived from Article 8 of the European Convention on Human Rights: in the *National Panasonic*[1] case, the ECJ was asked to consider the applicability of Article 8, under which 'everyone has to right to respect for his private and family life, his home and his correspondence'. In dismissing the applicant's argument, the ECJ pointed out that Article 8 itself acknowledges (in sub-paragraph (2)) that interference with these rights by public authorities is permissible to the extent to which it is 'in accordance with the law and is necessary in a democratic society in the interests of national security, public safety or the economic well-being of the country, for the prevention of disorder or crime, for the protection of health or morals, or for the protection of the rights and freedom of others'. The ECJ pointed out that the function of Articles 81 and 82 was to prevent competition from being distorted to the detriment of the public interest, individual undertakings and consumers and in these circumstances the powers given to the Commission by Regulation 17/62 did not infringe any basic human rights.

1 Case 136/79 *National Panasonic (UK) Ltd v EC Commission* [1980] ECR 2033, [1983] 3 CMLR 169.

6.47

More recently, in the *Dow*[1] and *Hoechst*[2] cases, the ECJ observed, with regard to the fundamental right to the inviolability of the home, that, although recognition of that right clearly existed in Community law with regard to private dwellings, the same was not true with regard to commercial premises, because there were significant differences between the legal systems of the Member States in relation to the nature and degree of protection against intervention by the public authorities granted to commercial premises. Nevertheless, the ECJ pointed out that all the legal systems of the Member States provided protection against arbitrary or disproportionate intervention by public authorities in connection with the activities of any person, whether a natural or a legal person. It would be unwise to interpret the ECJ's distinction between private dwellings and commercial premises as inviting undertakings to arrange for sensitive documentation to be removed from their premises. As is noted at para **6.68**, the Commission can impose fines on undertakings which supply their books or other records to it in incomplete form[3].

1 Case 85/87 *Dow Benelux v EC Commission* [1989] ECR 3137, [1991] 4 CMLR 410 and Joined Cases 97-99/87 *Dow Chemical Ibérica v EC Commission* [1989] ECR 3165, [1991] 4 CMLR 410.
2 Cases 46/87, 227/88 *Hoechst v EC Commission* [1989] ECR 2859, [1991] 4 CMLR 410.
3 Council Regulation (EEC) 17/62, art 15 (1)(c), OJ Sp Ed [1959-62] p 87.

6.48

With regard to the right to a fair hearing before a decision is taken against an undertaking[1], the ECJ has drawn a distinction between the investigative procedure provided for in art 14 (whose object is to enable the Commission to gather the necessary information in order to ascertain whether there is a violation of Article 81 or 82) and the substantive proceedings following the issuance of a Statement of Objections[2]. This distinction was most recently confirmed by the ECJ in the *Dow*[3] and Hoechst[4] cases. However, in these recent cases the ECJ made it clear that, although certain rights of the defence only applied during the contentious phase of the procedure, other rights had to be respected at all times, ie also during investigations, and in this context it referred specifically to the right to be legally represented[5] and the privileged nature of correspondence between lawyer and client[6].

1 See paras **11.31–11.33**.
2 Case 136/79 *National Panasonic UK Ltd v EC Commission* [1980] ECR 2033, [1983] 3 CMLR 169.
3 Case 85/87 *Dow Benelux v EC Commission* [1989] ECR 3137, [1991] 4 CMLR 410; Joined Cases 97-99/87 *Dow Chemical Ibérica v EC Commission* [1989] ECR 3165, [1991] 4 CMLR 410.
4 Cases 46/87, 227/88 *Hoechst v EC Commission* [1989] ECR 2859, [1991] 4 CMLR 410.
5 See para **6.69** ff.
6 See para **11.14** ff.

(2) Examination of Books and other Business Records

6.49

This is a broad phrase and there would appear to be no reason in principle why it should not be interpreted as extending, for example, to documentation held on computer disc, rather than in hard copy form. The broad power of the Commission to demand to see documentation which may reveal an infringement of Article 81 or 82 is one of the reasons why the issue of document retention (and more generally compliance programmes) has become topical in recent years[1]. As to whether the Commission has a general power of search under art 14, reference should be made to para **6.60**.

1 Compliance programmes are considered at para **2.01** ff.

6.50

The Commission takes the view that art 14(1) requires the undertaking being investigated to go further than merely announcing to the Commission officials that all their records are at their disposal:

> '... the obligation on undertakings to supply all documents required by Commission inspectors must be understood to mean not merely giving access to all files, but actually producing the specific documents required'[1].

1 Commission Decision (80/334/EEC) *Fabbrica Pisana* OJ [1980] L 75/30, [1980] 2 CMLR 354.

6.51

The Commission decided in *FNICF*[1] that the undertaking's representative handling the investigation cannot refuse to produce documents to the Commission investigators merely on the ground that he cannot disclose them without the authority of a more senior officer of the undertaking.

1 Commission Decision (82/756/EEC) OJ [1982] L 319/12, [1983] 1 CMLR 575.

6.52

In a gesture of even-handedness, the final paragraph of the Commission's explanatory notes to article 14(2) authorisations and article 14(3) decisions states that:

> 'In addition to the documents requested by the Commission officials, the undertaking is entitled to draw attention to other documents or information where it considers this necessary for the purpose of protecting its legitimate interest in a complete and objective clarification of the matters raised, provided that the investigation is not thereby unduly delayed'.

(3) Taking Copies of or Extracts from the Books and Business Records of the Undertaking

6.53

The same explanatory notes make it clear that where an undertaking makes available photocopies of documents at the request of the Commission officials the Commission will, on request, reimburse the cost of the photocopies. Although it is not entirely clear whether or not an undertaking is under a duty to make photocopying facilities available (the alternative being for the Commission to take longhand notes), it is usual for the undertaking concerned to do so. Moreover, in doing so it can look after its own interests, by taking extra photocopies so as to enable it to have an exact record of what copies the Commission officials take away. In addition, the undertaking is entitled to request a signed inventory of the copies.

6.54

In *CSM*[1] the company failed to comply fully with an article 14(3) decision which empowered Commission officials to examine certain business records and to take copies of those records. It refused to allow the officials to take copies of certain documents on the first day of the investigation, although it did allow the Commission officials to take copies of some of these documents during the second day of the investigation. The Commission decided that this did not alter the fact that the company had committed a breach of its obligations under art 14(3); in its view any other interpretation would jeopardise the effectiveness of the investigation (although the fact that the company had allowed copies of certain of the documents to be taken on the second day of the investigation was taken into account in assessing the fine: see para **9.87**).

1 Commission Decision (92/500/EEC) OJ [1992] L 305/16.

(4) Oral on-the-spot Explanations

6.55

It is a moot point whether this limb of art 14(1) of Regulation 17/62[1] enables the Commission officials to ask wide-ranging questions (albeit still within the subject matter of the investigation) or is limited to enabling the officials to seek clarification of matters arising out of the books and business records to which they are given access. The scope of this limb of art 14(1) was considered by the ECJ in the *National Panasonic*[2] case but it did not rule decisively on the point. The issue there arose in the context of the relationship between arts 11 and 14, the argument being that it is art 11 (rather than art 14) which empowers the Commission to obtain all necessary information. Accordingly, art 11 contains certain in-built protections for the undertaking under investigation, namely that the request must be put in writing and the undertaking should have a period of time within which to reply. If art 14(1)(c) in fact allows the Commission to put wide-ranging questions to the undertaking during the course of an on-the-spot enquiry, this would appear to undermine the safeguards built into art 11.

1 Council Regulation (EEC) 17/62, OJ Sp Ed [1959–62] p 87.
2 Case 136/79 *National Panasonic (UK) Ltd v EC Commission* [1980] ECR 2033, [1980] 3 CMLR 169.

6.56

Although the point has not been finally resolved by the ECJ, it is submitted that art 14(1)(c) allows the Commission to seek explanations of matters arising directly out of the books and records which are made available to it and, in so doing, to ask questions about the conduct of the undertaking in question as revealed by those documents; but that it does not extend so far as to enable the Commission officials to ask questions about alleged behaviour of the undertaking which is not revealed on the face of those documents. Against that it can be pointed out that arts 11 and 14 are independent means of investigation and that a narrow interpretation of art 14 might impede the Commission's enforcement of Articles 81 and 82.

6.57

As far as the identity of the person who should give the answers to the on-the-spot questions is concerned, the position is that the responsibility to comply with Regulation 17/62 rests with the undertaking concerned rather than with any individual employee. It must be in the interests of the undertaking to ensure that the Commission officials are seen by someone who is able to answer the questions as correctly and completely as possible. If an undertaking chooses to put forward as its representative someone who is unable to provide any of the oral explanations for which the Commission officials ask, there must be a risk that the undertaking could be regarded as having refused to submit to the investigation (and possibly being fined as a result under art 15 of Regulation 17/62[1]).

1 See para **6.65**.

6.58

If the Commission officials take a note of explanations given to them it is not open to the undertaking concerned to seek, through judicial remedy, annulment of that report[1]. This reflects the basic legal principle that an act is challengeable only if it is an act definitively laying down the position of the institution on the conclusion of a procedure, and not an intermediate step intended to pave the way for a final decision[2].

1 Case T-9/97 *Elf Atochem v EC Commission* [1997] 5 CMLR 844 at paras 18–26.
2 See, for example, Case 60/81 *IBM v EC Commission* [1981] ECR 2639.

(5) Entry onto any Premises, Land and Means of Transport of Undertakings

6.59
This part of art 14(1) provides the Commission officials with the necessary power to enable them to carry out the investigative work envisaged by the earlier limbs of art 14(1). It does not, however, empower the Commission officials to make a forceable entry. If they are refused entry, the appropriate remedy in the first instance is for the Commission to invoke the provisions of art 14(6) of Regulation 17/62. That paragraph provides that:

> 'Where an undertaking opposes an investigation ordered pursuant to this Article, the Member State concerned shall afford the necessary assistance to the officials authorised by the Commission to enable them to make their investigation'.

Some guidance has now been provided as to the operation of this provision in the ECJ's judgment in the *Hoechst*[1] case. In that case, the company refused to submit to an article 14(3) investigation. The Commission, with the assistance of the German Bundeskartellamt (the domestic competition law authority), attempted to obtain a search warrant from a German court but was unsuccessful. Indeed, Hoechst obtained an injunction against the search measures from an administrative tribunal in Frankfurt. Hoechst's refusal to comply with the article 14(3) decision led to a further Commission decision imposing periodic penalty payments[2] and subsequently a final decision imposing a fine for the refusal to submit to the investigation[3].

1 Cases 46/87, 227/88 *Hoechst v EC Commission* [1989] ECR 2859, [1991] 4 CMLR 410.
2 See para **6.65**.
3 See para **6.65**.

6.60
The ECJ ruled in *Hoechst*[1] that art 14 did not entitle the Commission to enter premises forceably or break into filing cabinets. That is to say, there is no automatic power of entry and search. Where an undertaking refuses to admit the Commission investigators to its premises the Commission has to elicit the assistance of the competent national authority and has to comply with the procedural guarantees laid down by national law. However, the national authorities in turn are obliged (by art 14(6)) to provide all necessary assistance to the Commission and the ECJ made it quite clear that the national authority had no right to substitute its own assessment as to the need for the investigation for that of the Commission. Its role was confined to verifying the authenticity of the decision ordering the investigation and considering whether the particular enforcement measures envisaged were arbitrary or excessive in relation to the purpose of the investigation.

1 Cases 46/87, 227/88 *Hoechst v EC Commission* [1989] ECR 2859, [1991] 4 CMLR 410.

6.61
The judgment of the ECJ in *Hoechst*[1] does not make particularly clear the nature of the obligations of Member States under art 14(6) of Regulation 17/62. Until the enactment of the Competition Act 1998[2], enforcement of the Commission's investigatory powers in the United Kingdom was by way

of an application to the High Court for an injunction, failure to comply with such an injunction amounting to contempt of court. For an example of a case in which this occurred, see the Commission's decision in *Ukwal*[3]. The Advocate General in the *Hoechst* case suggested that such a procedure might not fulfil the requirements of art 14(6) but the court itself chose not to comment.

1 Cases 46/87, 227/88 *Hoechst v EC Commission* [1989] ECR 2859, [1991] 4 CMLR 410.
2 See Chapter 15.
3 Commission Decision (92/237/EEC) OJ [1992] L 121/45, taken under the corresponding provisions of Council Regulation (EEC) 4056/86 (maritime transport).

6.62
The Competition Act 1998 introduced specific powers for the Director General of Fair Trading (DGFT) to assist the European Commission in relation to investigations under article 14. The reason such provisions were finally introduced in the 1998 Act was that the powers which that Act gives to the DGFT to investigate possible breaches of UK competition law[1] highlight the fact that no similar express powers had previously existed by way of compliance with the United Kingdom's obligations under art 14(6) of Regulation 17/62.

1 See para **15.130** ff.

6.63
The powers are contained in the Competition Act 1998, ss 61–65. In essence, the DGFT is given power to enter premises with a warrant, using reasonable force as necessary, in the event of obstruction of:

(*a*) a European Commission investigation which the DGFT is assisting (a so-called 'Commission investigation'[1]); or
(*b*) an investigation being carried out by the DGFT under EC law at the request of the European Commission (a so-called 'Director's investigation'[2]); or
(*c*) a Director's investigation carried out by the DGFT in connection with a Commission investigation (a so-called 'Director's special investigation')[3].

1 See the Competition Act 1998 (Commission Investigation and Director's Investigation) Order 1999 (SI 1999/3027), para 2.
2 Ibid, para 3.
3 CA 1998, s 61.

6.64
The powers themselves are very similar to those in the case of investigations carried out by warrant under s28 of the Competition Act 1998[1].

1 CA 1998, ss 62 and 63. As to those powers generally under the CA 1998, see para **15.145** ff.

6.65
Under s 65 of the Competition Act 1998 a person is guilty of a criminal offence if he intentionally obstructs any person in the exercise of his powers under a warrant issued under ss 62 or 63. Such offences are punishable, on

summary conviction, by a fine and, on conviction on indictment, by a fine, imprisonment for a term not exceeding two years or both[1].

1 CA 1998, s 65.

6.66
The powers given to the DGFT to assist in European Commission investigations should not be confused with the question of direct enforcement by the DGFT of Articles 81 and 82, EC Treaty. As explained in para **12.01**, no such power has yet been given by the United Kingdom Government to the DGFT, although it is a power that has been given to the competition authorities in a number of Member States.

6.67
In *Akzo Chemicals BV*[1] the article 14(3) decision identified the company by reference to two of its offices in the Netherlands. The company argued that the Commission officials were not therefore entitled to carry out the investigation at a third Dutch office of the company. The Commission rejected this contention, holding that the reference to the two offices was solely to identify the company to which the decision was addressed; the operative part of the decision referred to *all* the company's business premises and the scope of the decision was therefore broad enough to encompass any premises of the company.

1 Commission Decision (94/735/EC), OJ [1994] L 294/31.

8 PENALTIES IN RELATION TO ARTICLE 14 INVESTIGATIONS

6.68
The position regarding fines in relation to article 14 investigations is as follows:

(*a*) the Commission has no power to impose fines on an undertaking which refuses to submit to an investigation by way of authorisation, rather than decision (ie an article 14(2) investigation as opposed to an article 14(3) investigation); the appropriate remedy for the Commission in such circumstances is to take a decision under art 14(3);

(*b*) if an undertaking does submit to an article 14(2) investigation, fines of between 100 and 5,000 ECU may be imposed by the Commission under art 15(1)(c) where, intentionally or negligently, an undertaking produces the required books or other business records in incomplete form;

(*c*) if an undertaking refuses to submit to an investigation ordered by a decision pursuant to article 14(3), the Commission may impose fines ranging between 100 and 5,000 ECU under art 15(1)(c); the Commission may also, under art 16(1)(d), impose fines of between 50 and 1,000 ECU per day, for each day during which the undertaking refuses to submit to the investigation (beginning from a date stipulated by the Commission).

The undertaking has a right to be heard by the Commission before any fines are imposed (art 19(1) of Regulation 17/62[1]).

1 Council Regulation (EEC) 17/62, OJ Sp Ed [1959–62] p 87.

6.69
In *CSM*[1] the Commission imposed a fine of 3,000 ECU on a company for failing to allow copies of certain documents to be taken. In two other decisions taken in 1992, the Commission imposed fines of 5,000 ECU[2] and 4,000 ECU[3] respectively for failure to submit to an investigation ordered under art 18(3) of Council Regulation 4056/86[4]. In the first of these two cases, there was an absolute refusal to comply, thereby forcing the Commission to obtain an order from the English High Court. The maximum permissible fine was therefore imposed. In the second of these two cases, the refusal was temporary, in that the Secretary-General of the maritime conference concerned forced the Commission to delay its investigation by 24 hours in order to allow him to return to his office in Marseille from Paris.

1 Commission Decision (92/500/EEC) OJ [1992] L 305/16.
2 Commission Decision (92/237/EEC) *Ukwal* OJ [1992] L 121/45.
3 Commission Decision (93/47/EEC) *Mewac* OJ [1993] L 20/6.
4 For Council Regulation (EEC) 4056/86 generally, see *Butterworths Competition Law* Division IX, para [382] ff.

6.70
In *Akzo Chemicals BV*[1] the Commission imposed the maximum fine of 5,000 ECU for failure fully to submit to the Commission's investigation, by firstly, denying that the company had offices at a particular location[2] and secondly, refusing access to the office of a particular person in the organisation. In this context, the Commission held that offices which are occupied in the name of another member of the corporate group of the business concerned may be inspected if the executives of the business to which the investigation relates have offices there.

1 Commission Decision (94/735/EC), OJ [1994] L 294/31.
2 See para **6.62**.

9 ACCESS TO LEGAL ADVICE

6.71
The Commission cannot object to an undertaking having its legal advisers present during the course of an on-the-spot investigation, whether conducted under art 14(2) or art 14(3), and the importance of access to legal advice during the investigative stage was underlined in the recent *Dow*[1] and *Hoechst*[2] cases. However, as has already been made clear, an article 14 investigation can take place without notice and a vexed issue is the extent to which, in such circumstances, the undertaking concerned can ask for the investigation to be delayed until the arrival of its legal adviser. The judgment of the ECJ in the *National Panasonic*[3] case makes it clear that the undertaking is not in such circumstances entitled to delay the commencement of the investigation. In that case, the officials concerned were not prepared to

delay the commencement of the investigation until the undertaking's solicitor had arrived and insisted on beginning the investigation less than an hour after they had arrived at the premises. The ECJ held that no fundamental right of the undertaking had been infringed.

1 Case 85/87 *Dow Benelux v EC Commission* [1989] ECR 3137, [1991] 4 CMLR 410 and Joined Cases 97–99/87 *Dow Chemical Ibérica v EC Commission* [1989] ECR 3165, [1991] 4 CMLR 410.

2 Cases 46/87, 227/88 *Hoechst v EC Commission* [1989] ECR 2859, [1991] 4 CMLR 410.

3 Case 136/79 *National Panasonic (UK) v EC Commission* [1980] ECR 2033, [1980] 3 CMLR 169.

6.72

The Commission's practice on the matter is set out in its explanatory notes to art 14(2) and (3). The notes confirm the right of the undertaking to consult a legal adviser during the investigation but state that the presence of a lawyer 'is not a legal condition for the validity of the investigation, nor must it unduly delay or impede it. Any delay pending a lawyer's arrival must be kept to the strict minimum'. The notes also make it clear that even a minimal delay will only be countenanced if two conditions are satisfied. Firstly, the management of the undertaking must undertake to ensure that the business records remain in the place and state they were in when the Commission officials arrived. Secondly, the officials should not be hindered from entering into and remaining in occupation of offices of their choice. These conditions highlight the Commission's overriding concern that any delay might provide an opportunity for evidence to be tampered with. Finally, the explanatory notes make it clear that if the undertaking has an in-house legal department there is to be no delay whilst awaiting the arrival of an external legal adviser.

10 PRACTICAL CONSIDERATIONS

6.73

Article 14 investigations can take place with little or no warning. The purpose of this paragraph is to set out a number of practical considerations for any undertaking which has the misfortune of being subjected to such an investigation. This paragraph focuses on investigations ordered by decision under art 14(3), no prior warning being given to the undertaking concerned. However, the various points referred to below apply equally to investigations carried out by mandate under art 14(2), with the obvious difference that because some warning (usually a few days) is given, the undertaking will be able to make some advance preparation (for example, ensuring that relevant senior personnel and legal advisers are available). On no account, however, should the period between the date of notification of the inspection and the date on which it takes place be used to destroy incriminating documents—this will only rebound on the undertaking at a later stage[1]. The principal practical considerations to be borne in mind are as follows:

(1) Once an undertaking submits itself to an investigation (and, in relation to an article 14(3) investigation, it is obliged to do so[2]), it must

co-operate fully with the Commission inspectors. There are, for example, penalties for supplying incomplete books or records. Moreover, if the undertaking is totally unco-operative there is a danger that the inspectors will regard this as a refusal to submit to the investigation which, if it has been ordered by decision, could lead to the undertaking being fined[3].

(2) Once the Commission inspectors have identified themselves, the undertaking should ensure that they show their written authorisation under art 14(2) or, as the case may be, the text of the article 14(3) decision. These details should be carefully noted, particularly the exact scope of the investigation. This is the only way the undertaking can judge whether or not the inspectors are entitled to see a particular file or document.

(3) If there is any doubt as to the scope of the investigation, the undertaking should ask the inspectors to elaborate. This is expressly envisaged by the Commission's explanatory note relating to article 14(2) investigations[4] but not by the explanatory note relating to article 14(3) decisions[5]; indeed the latter note expressly states that the inspectors 'cannot be required to enlarge upon the subject matter as set out in the decision'[6].

(4) Although the undertaking is free to decide who should deal with the inspectors, it is wise to ensure that one or more executives are available who have sufficient knowledge and authority to ensure that the inspectors are shown the documents they wish to see and to answer questions relating to them. They may take advice and instructions from colleagues before answering.

(5) It is not sufficient simply to inform the inspectors that they are free to inspect the company's files. The inspectors normally make specific requests for documents on certain subjects and the company must do its best to produce those documents[7], provided they are within the scope of the investigation and provided they are not legally privileged (see (8) below).

(6) The inspectors are entitled to take copies of or extracts from relevant documents. The undertaking may request a signed inventory of the copies and extracts taken by the Commission officials during the investigation and this should certainly be done. If the undertaking makes available photocopies of documents at the request of the Commission inspectors, the Commission can be asked to reimburse the cost of the photocopies. It is advisable for the undertaking to keep a copy of every photocopy made for the Commission.

(7) The Commission accepts that even on an unannounced inspection the company may consult its lawyers provided that this does not 'unduly' delay the investigation. In practice, where an investigation is being conducted without warning an undertaking can expect the inspectors to wait for about an hour until the lawyers arrive. The intervening period could be used to deal with uncontroversial matters such as describing the company's internal organisation and identifying the executives who are to deal with the inspectors' enquiries. If the undertaking has an in-house legal adviser, the Commission is less willing to accept any delay in the investigation.

(8) The undertaking is entitled to withhold from the Commission inspectors communications to or from its independent (but not in-house) legal advisers; the Commission inspectors are, however, entitled to be given a sufficient indication of the contents of such communications (address of addressee, date, heading, etc) to satisfy themselves that the claim for privilege is genuine[8].

(9) As noted at para **6.55**, it is not entirely clear whether the Commission inspectors are entitled to ask wide-ranging questions (albeit still within the subject matter of the investigation) or whether they are confined to asking questions arising out of the books and business records to which they are given access. The undertaking's representatives should attempt to answer relevant and reasonable questions honestly but should beware of being led into making gratuitous comments. A competent shorthand typist should ideally be present to record the questions and answers; the explanatory notes relating to both art 14(2)[9] and art 14(3)[10] provide that, where the undertaking gives oral explanations on the spot at the request of the Commission inspectors, the explanations may be minuted at the request of the undertaking and the undertaking is entitled to receive a copy of the Commission's minutes. These should obviously be checked in due course to ensure that they are consistent with the undertaking's own note of what has been said.

(10) Similarly, both explanatory notes specifically provide that the undertaking is entitled to draw attention to other documents or information if it considers this necessary for the purpose of protecting its legitimate interest in a complete and objective clarification of the matters raised, provided that the investigation is not thereby delayed. The undertaking and its legal advisers should consider whether it wishes to avail itself of this opportunity; alternatively, it may decide to do this by means of a follow-up letter to the Commission.

1 See para **2.27** ff.
2 See para **6.29**.
3 Council Regulation (EEC) 17/62, art 15(1)(c), OJ Sp Ed [1959–62] p 87.
4 See para **6.38**.
5 See n 4 above.
6 The reason for this distinction is discussed at para **6.38**.
7 Commission Decision (80/334/EEC) *Fabbrica Pisana* OJ [1980] L 75/30, [1980] 2 CMLR 354 and see para **6.50**.
8 The issue of legal privilege is considered at para **11.14** ff.
9 See n 4 above.
10 See n 4 above.

D Self-Incrimination

6.74
In the *Orkem*[1] and *Solvay*[2] cases, the ECJ was required to consider, in the context of Regulation 17/62, art 11[3], whether an undertaking to whom questions had been put could claim privilege from self-incrimination. The Commission had sent a list of questions to both companies and some, but

not all, of the questions would have required the companies to admit to the very infringements which the Commission was seeking to establish. The ECJ noted that the national laws of Member States recognised no general principle affording privilege against self-incrimination, except in the field of criminal law. Nevertheless, it was prepared to annul the Commission's decision, in so far as it contained questions which would have required the companies to admit infringements of Article 81.

1 Case 374/87 *Orkem v EC Commission* [1989] ECR 3283, [1991] 4 CMLR 502.
2 Case 27/88 *Solvay & Cie v EC Commission* [1989] ECR 3355, [1991] 4 CMLR 502.
3 See para **6.02** ff.

6.75
The ECJ has therefore established a privilege against self-incrimination. However, it held that the Commission could legitimately require the companies concerned to furnish copies of all documents in their possession relating to the alleged concerted practices, even if those documents might serve to establish (either in relation to the undertaking concerned or another undertaking) the existence of practices infringing Article 81. The ECJ therefore appears to have drawn a distinction between the production of documents and the answering of questions which might serve to incriminate the undertaking concerned[1].

1 See also Case T-34/93 *Société Générale v EC Commission* [1995] ECR II-545, at paras 72–74.

6.76
It remains to be seen to what extent the principle of privilege from self-incrimination (as laid down in the *Orkem*[1] and *Solvay*[2] cases) applies to article 14 investigations. There is no reason in principle why it should not.

1 Case 374/87 *Orkem v EC Commission* [1989] ECR 3283, [1991] 4 CMLR 502.
2 Case 27/88 *Solvay & Cie v EC Commission* [1989] ECR 3355, [1991] 4 CMLR 502.

6.77
In the *Orkem*[1] and *Solvay*[2] cases the ECJ cited the fact that Article 6 of the European Convention on the Protection of Human Rights and Fundamental Freedoms[3] did not uphold a general privilege against self-incrimination. The European Court of Human Rights has since held, in the *Funke*[4] case, that Article 6(1) of the Convention contains an unconditional right to remain silent. It remains to be seen to what extent that judgment will influence future case law under Articles 81 and 82[5].

1 Case 374/87 *Orkem v EC Commission* [1989] ECR 3283, [1991] 4 CMLR 502, ECJ.
2 Case 27/88 *Solvay & Cie v EC Commission* [1989] ECR 3355, [1991] 4 CMLR 502, ECJ.
3 Case 82/1991/334/407 *Funke/France* (1993) 16 EHRR 297, [1993] 1 CMLR 897.
4 4 November 1950.
5 Overbeek 'The Right to Remain Silent in Competition Investigations; the Funke decision of the Court of Human Rights makes revision of the ECJ's case law necessary' [1994] 3 ECLR 127.

E Legal Professional Privilege

6.78
The extent to which an undertaking may withhold from Commission officials communications between it and its legal advisers is dealt with at para **6.02** ff.

Chapter 7 Commission Proceedings

A Introduction

7.01
On the basis of information coming to the Commission's attention from the sources described in Chapters 5 and 6[1], the Commission may choose to commence proceedings against one or more undertakings for alleged violation of Articles 81 and/or 82. The purpose of this chapter is to describe those proceedings, from their commencement through to the adoption of one or more different types of decision. The various possible decisions themselves are described in Chapter 8, as is the scope for the informal settlement (as between the Commission and the undertaking(s) concerned) of proceedings commenced by the Commission: in practice, this is an extremely important aspect of the enforcement of Articles 81 and 82.

1 For example, a complaint under Council Regulation (EEC) 17/62, art 3, OJ Sp Ed [1959–62] p 87 (see Chapter 5); or a notification (see Chapter 4).

7.02
Before considering in some detail the various stages in the Commission's proceedings, a number of preliminary points should be noted. Although the Commission has the power to impose substantial fines on undertakings found to be in breach of Articles 81 and 82[1], its procedure is administrative rather than judicial[2]. Undertakings challenging the Commission's procedures leading up to an adverse finding frequently cite the European Convention on Human Rights[3]. In this context, the ECJ has held that the Commission, when exercising its powers to enforce Articles 81 and 82, is not acting as a 'tribunal' within the meaning of Article 6 of the Convention[4].

1 See Chapter 9.
2 Case 45/69 *Boehringer Mannheim v EC Commission* [1970] ECR 769, [1972] CMLR D121.
3 See, eg Case 136/79 *National Panasonic (UK) Ltd v EC Commission* [1980] ECR 2033, [1980] 3 CMLR 169; Case 5/85 *AKZO Chemie BV and AKZO Chemie UK Ltd v EC Commission* [1986] ECR 2585, [1987] 3 CMLR 716; Cases 46/87 and 227/88 *Hoechst v EC Commission* [1989] ECR 2859, [1991] 4 CMLR 410, ECJ.
4 Case 100–103/80 *Musique Diffusion Française v EC Commission* [1983] ECR 1825, [1983] 3 CMLR 221; Article 6 provides that 'in determination of his civil rights . . . everyone is entitled to a fair and public hearing within a reasonable time by an independent and impartial tribunal established by law'. As to the relevance of fundamental rights in the context of Articles 81 and 82, see para **11.34** ff.

7.03
The Commission is responsible for the proceedings from their inception through to the adoption of the final decision. It is involved in the gathering

of evidence (for example, by exercising its powers under arts 11 and 14 of Regulation 17/62[1]), it acts as prosecutor in bringing proceedings against one or more undertakings on the basis of the evidence gathered and it is also the body which decides what sanction should be imposed upon the undertakings in the event that an infringement is established. The running by the Commission of every stage of the proceedings has been the subject of much criticism over the years[2]. Until 1985 there was an internal division of responsibility within the Commission between those officials charged with carrying out the investigation and those involved in the decision-making process. In *Shell*[3] the applicant argued that the abandonment of this division of responsibility removed the impartiality inherent under the previous procedure (indeed, it argued that its position had been particularly prejudiced because the change in internal responsibility within the Commission took place during the course of the procedure leading up to the decision in its own case). While recognising the importance of the rights of the defence, the CFI held that these did not require the Commission to adopt an internal organisation which precluded the same official from acting as both investigator and rapporteur in the same case[4]. In its 1993 Report[5], the House of Lords Select Committee on the European Communities rejected the suggestion that there should be a structural separation of the three functions, namely detection, prosecution and decision-making. What is in the Select Committee's opinion essential is that the procedure should be transparent and that there should be the possibility of independent judicial control to guarantee this. The Select Committee therefore recommended[6] that the CFI's role be extended in this regard.

1 See Chapter 6.
2 Eg, evidence to the *HL Select Committee on Competition and Practice in the EEC 8th Report* (HL Paper (1981–82)) and the *HL Select Committee on Enforcement of Community Competition Rules 1st Report* (HL Paper (1993–94)).
3 Case T-11/89 *Shell International Chemical Co Ltd v EC Commission* [1992] ECR II-757.
4 Ibid at para 40.
5 *HL Select Committee on Enforcement of Community Competition Rules 1st Report* (HL Paper (1993–94)).
6 Ibid at para 160.

7.04

Although the procedure for the enforcement of Articles 81 and 82 by the Commission is administrative in nature, Regulation 17/62 lays down a number of important procedural safeguards designed to protect undertakings. These will be considered during the course of the examination of the various stages of the procedure, but include in particular the right to be heard before the Commission takes a decision against an undertaking[1]. Failure to respect the rights of defence of an undertaking against which Article 81 or 82 proceedings are brought may provide that undertaking with grounds for challenging the Commission's decision: the grounds of appeal under Article 230 of the EC Treaty (the Article under which appeals can be made against decisions of the Commission) include 'infringement of an essential procedural requirement, infringement of the Treaty or of any rule relating to its application, or misuse of powers'[2].

1 Council Regulation (EEC) 17/62, art 19.

2 For one Commission official's view on a range of procedural issues (albeit expressed in a personal capacity) see Joshua 'Proof in Contested Competition Cases: A comparison with the Rules of Evidence in Common Law' 12 EL Rev 315 (October 1987).

7.05
If a party involved in Commission proceedings believes that its rights of defence have been violated its only effective legal recourse is to raise this issue after the Commission has taken its *final* decision, ie by bringing an action for annulment under Article 230 of the EC Treaty before the CFI. That is to say, there is no effective means of raising this issue during the course of the Commission proceedings. This is demonstrated by the *Cimenteries*[1] case. There, a number of companies against whom the Commission has issued a Statement of Objections[2] asked the CFI to annul a Commission decision (in the form of a letter) in which the Commission had refused to communicate to each of the applicants the complete Statement of Objections. The CFI held that refusal of access to part of the Statement of Objections produced in principle only limited effects, characteristic of a preparatory measure forming part of a preliminary administrative procedure. This was very much in line with previous case law of the ECJ[3] but nevertheless demonstrates the lack of a means to raise this type of issue at the interlocutory stage.

1 Joined Cases T-10–12, T-15/92 *Cimenteries CBR SA v EC Commission* [1993] 4 CMLR 259, CFI.
2 As to the Statement of Objections generally, see para **7.12** ff.
3 See Case 60/81 *IBM v EC Commission* [1981] ECR 2639, [1981] 3 CMLR 635.

7.06
Notwithstanding the right to be 'heard', the Commission's procedure is primarily written, rather than oral. Regulation 2842/98, art 5[1] does provide a specific right for an undertaking to put forward its arguments orally if it can show a sufficient interest or if the Commission proposes to impose on it a fine or periodic penalty payment; however, the basic right to be heard is largely exercised by means of written, rather than oral, submissions. Although undertakings will usually exercise their right to be heard orally, it is unusual for such hearings to last more than a day.

1 Commission Regulation (EC) 2842/98, OJ [1998] L 354/18. This superseded the previous Regulation dealing with such matters, Commission Regulation (EEC) 99/63, OJ Sp Ed [1963–64] p 47.

7.07
In *Baustahlgewebe*[1], the applicant contended that the procedure before the CFI had breached the principle that proceedings must be disposed of within a reasonable time. In that case, proceedings commenced in October 1989 and the judgment of the CFI was delivered in April 1995. The ECJ held that, notwithstanding the relative complexity of the case, the proceedings before the CFI had not satisfied the requirements concerning completion within a reasonable time. However, it did not believe that the length of the proceedings had affected their outcome in any way and it decided that a sum of ECU 50,000 (out of an original fine of ECU 3 million) constituted reasonable satisfaction for the excessive duration of the proceedings.

1 Case C-185/95P *Baustahlgewebe v EC Commission* [1998] ECR I-8417, at paras 47 and 141.

B Initiation of Procedure

1 THE COMMISSION'S USUAL PRACTICE

7.08
The usual way in which proceedings are commenced by the Commission is by the Commissioner responsible for competition matters signing a short document to that effect. Although the undertaking(s) concerned will normally be informed of the fact in due course, there is no legal obligation on the Commission to do so and the way in which an undertaking usually becomes aware that proceedings have been commenced is through receipt from the Commission of a Statement of Objections[1]. It is clear from the judgment of the ECJ in the *Dyestuffs*[2] case that it is the Statement of Objections rather than the notification that proceedings have been initiated which is the crucial document from the point of view of ensuring that the undertaking's rights of defence are not infringed.

1 As to the Statement of Objections generally, see para **7.12** ff.
2 Case 48/69 *ICI v EC Commission* [1972] ECR 619, [1972] CMLR 557.

2 SIGNIFICANCE OF THE INITIATION OF A PROCEDURE

7.09
Notwithstanding the fact that it is the Statement of Objections (rather than the fact that a procedure has been opened) which is the crucial first stage from the point of view of the undertaking's rights of defence[1], the determination of the precise date on which proceedings have been initiated does have some significance. Firstly, the commencement of proceedings by the Commission is one of the actions which serves to interrupt the limitation period which applies under Council Regulation 2988/74[2], the Regulation which sets out the periods of time within which the Commission must impose fines and penalties and enforce the collection of fines and penalties. As far as the commencement of the proceedings by the Commission is concerned, the relevant date for interrupting the limitation period is the date on which the fact that proceedings have been commenced is notified to at least one of the undertakings (or association of undertakings) which have participated in the infringement[3].

1 See para **7.08**.
2 See para **9.100**.
3 Council Regulation (EEC) 2988/74, art 2, OJ [1974] L 319/1.

7.10
Secondly, initiation of a procedure by the Commission serves to remove from the competent authorities of the Member States (though not the

ordinary courts)[1] the power to take action under Article 81 or 82. Article 9(3) of Regulation 17/62[2] provides that:

> 'As long as the Commission has not initiated any procedure under Articles 2, 3 or 6, the authorities of the Member States shall remain competent to apply Article 85(1) [now Article 81(1)] and Article 86 [now Article 82] in accordance with Article 88 [now Article 84] of the Treaty'.

The significance of art 9(3) of Regulation 17/62 is considered elsewhere in this work[3]. One of the leading judgments of the ECJ under art 9(3), *Brasserie de Haecht v Wilkin-Janssen*[4], provides some guidance on what can amount to the initiation of a procedure. The ECJ indicated that the simple acknowledgment by the Commission of its receipt of an application for negative clearance or notification for exemption does not amount to an initiation of a procedure. Similarly, in another judgment the ECJ has held that a letter from the Commission informing an undertaking that it has closed its file on a particular case does not amount to the initiation of a procedure[5].

1 See para **18.02**.
2 Council Regulation (EEC) 17/62, OJ Sp Ed [1959–62] p 87.
3 See para **18.02**.
4 Case 48/72 [1973] ECR 77, [1973] CMLR 287.
5 Cases 253/78, 1–3/79 *Procureur de la République v Giry and Guerlain* [1980] ECR 2327, [1981] 2 CMLR 99.

7.11
Notwithstanding the two important legal consequences which flow from the initiation of a procedure[1], the ECJ has made it clear that the initiation of a procedure does not amount to a 'decision' which can be challenged under Article 230 of the EC Treaty[2].

1 See paras **7.09–7.10**.
2 Case 60/81 *IBM v EC Commission* [1981] ECR 2639, [1981] 3 CMLR 635.

C The Commission's Statement of Objections

1 PURPOSE

7.12
Article 19(1) of Regulation 17/62[1] requires the Commission to give the undertakings concerned the opportunity of being heard on any matters to which the Commission has taken objection, before the Commission takes any decision adverse to that undertaking (other than a decision to request information under art 11(5) or a decision to undertake an on-the-spot investigation under art 14(3)). This basic right to be heard is elaborated upon in Regulation 2842/98[2].

1 Council Regulation (EEC) 17/62, OJ Sp Ed [1959–62] p 87.
2 Commission Regulation (EC) 2842/98, OJ [1998] L 354/18.

7.13
Under art 3(1) of Regulation 2842/98, the Commission is obliged to inform undertakings (and associations of undertakings) in writing of the objections raised against them. These objections are contained in a document which is known as a 'Statement of Objections'. The purpose of the Statement of Objections is to make known to the undertaking concerned the nature of the case which is being made against it and it sets out, in separate sections, the facts and legal analysis upon which it is based. An important corollary of this is that the Commission cannot, when ultimately adopting a decision adverse to the undertaking(s) concerned, rely on any matters on which it has not provided an opportunity for comment[1]: art 2(2) of Regulation 2842/98 provides that:

> 'the Commission shall in its decisions deal only with objections in respect of which the parties have been afforded the opportunity of making their views known'.

1 See Case 85/76 *Hoffman-La Roche v EC Commission* [1979] ECR 461 at point 14; Joined Cases C-89/55 etc *Ahlström v EC Commission* [1993] 4 CMLR 407 at point 135.

2 STATUS OF STATEMENT OF OBJECTIONS

7.14
The Statement of Objections is no more than one step in the process leading ultimately to a Commission decision and, as such, its issuance is not a 'decision' which can be challenged before the ECJ under Article 230 of the EC Treaty[1].

1 Case 60/81 *IBM v EC Commission* [1981] ECR 2639, [1981] 3 CMLR 635. See Joined Cases T-10-12/92, T-15/92 *Cimenteries v EC Commission* [1993] 4 CMLR 259.

3 SERVICE OF STATEMENT OF OBJECTIONS

7.15
The Statement of Objections must be addressed to each undertaking against which objections are raised, or to an agent appointed by them[1]. In *FRUBO*[2] the ECJ dismissed an appeal by two trade associations based on the fact that the Statement of Objections had been served on their members but not on the associations themselves. There is an alternative procedure available to the Commission, although one which is rarely, if ever, used: under art 3(2) of Regulation 2842/98 the Commission may choose to inform the undertakings concerned by giving notice in the Official Journal of the European Communities, if from the circumstances of the case this appears appropriate (in particular, where notice is to be given to a number of undertakings but no joint agent has been appointed). It is not, however, open to the Commission to impose a fine or a periodic penalty payment on undertakings if the objections are only notified to them through the Official Journal, rather than being sent to them direct[3].

1 Commission Regulation (EC) 2842/98, art 3(1), OJ [1998] L 354/18.
2 Case 71/74 *FRUBO v EC Commission* [1975] ECR 563, [1975] 2 CMLR 123.
3 Commission Regulation (EC) 2842/98, art 3(3).

7.16

If the undertaking in question is outside the Community, the Statement of Objections is usually sent direct to it and the ECJ has held this to be good service[1]. If the undertaking has a branch or subsidiary within the Community, service can probably be effected on the branch or subsidiary.

1 Case 48/69 *ICI v EC Commission* [1972] ECR 619, [1972] CMLR 557.

4 CONTENTS OF STATEMENT OF OBJECTIONS

7.17

The contents of the Statement of Objections necessarily reflect the fact that the Commission must in its ultimate decision only deal with such objections as have been put to the undertakings concerned, thereby enabling them to comment[1]. It is usually in three sections: the first sets out the facts upon which the Commission is relying; the second sets out the legal analysis upon which the Commission is proposing to rely; the third summarises the proposed remedy which the Commission is contemplating adopting (for example, the imposition of fines). Although the Commission is obliged to set out all the essential elements[2] of the case made against the undertaking(s) concerned, it does not have to cite every single fact upon which reliance may ultimately be placed. In the *Dyestuffs*[3] case, the ECJ said that:

> 'To safeguard the rights of the defence in administrative proceedings it suffices that undertakings be informed of the essential factual elements on which the objections are based'.

As an example of an essential factual element, in *AEG-Telefunken*[4] the ECJ said that specific instances of alleged anti-competitive conduct must be referred to in the Statement of Objections or, alternatively, communicated to the defendant undertaking in 'sufficient' time for it to comment.

1 Commission Regulation (EC) 2842/98, art 2(2) OJ [1998] L 354/18. See, in the context of an adverse decision following a request for the application of Article 81(3), Case T-66/89 *Publishers' Association v EC Commission (No 2)* [1992] 5 CMLR 120 at para 64.
2 Cases 100–103/80 *Musique Diffusion Française v EC Commission* [1983] ECR 1825, [1983] 3 CMLR 221.
3 Case 48/69 *ICI v EC Commission* [1972] ECR 619, [1972] CMLR 557.
4 Case 107/82 *AEG-Telefunken v EC Commission* [1983] ECR 3151, [1984] 3 CMLR 325.

7.18

In *Shell*[1] the CFI held that by not informing the company that certain documents would be used in the decision, the Commission prevented it from putting forward its view of the probative value of such documents. They were not therefore admissible in evidence against that company. It went on to hold that documents which were inadmissible in evidence against the company could nevertheless be used by it as evidence in its favour[2]. However, where a company chooses to append documents to its own reply to a Statement of Objections those documents can be used against it in support of the allegations already made against it[3].

1 Case T-11/89 *Shell International Chemical Co Ltd v EC Commission* [1992] ECR II-757, at para 55.

2 Ibid at para 57.
3 See n 1 above, at para 59.

7.19

In *BPB de Eendracht*[1], the CFI held that the statement of objections must be framed in terms that are sufficiently clear, albeit concise, to enable the persons concerned properly to identify the conduct to which the Commission objected[2]. The applicant alleged that the Commission had failed to identify the behaviour of the individual producers in the statement of objections as the only objections in respect of the applicant were those set out in the individual particulars annexed to the statement of objections[3]. The CFI rejected this argument as it was expressly stated in the preliminary note to the individual particulars addressed to the applicant that 'these individual particulars must be read in conjunction with the main statement of objections'[4].

1 Case T-311/94 *BPB de Eendracht NV v EC Commission* [1998] ECR II-1129.
2 Ibid, at para 10.
3 Ibid, at para 41.
4 Ibid, at para 52.

7.20

In *Cimenteries CBR SA v EC Commission*[1], the CFI was asked during the course of the administrative procedure to annul a Commission decision (in the form of a letter) in which the Commission had refused to communicate to each of the applicants the complete Statement of Objections. In that case, the Commission had begun proceedings against 76 undertakings or associations of undertakings in the cement industry. Although the Statement of Objections took the form of a single document, the full text was not communicated to each of the undertakings and associations of undertakings concerned. A number of chapters concerned conduct at an international level and this was communicated to all those concerned. However, those chapters which dealt with conduct at national level were sent only to the undertakings and associations of undertakings established in the Member State in question. Having cited the *IBM*[2] case[3], the CFI held that refusal of access to part of the Statement of Objections produced in principle only limited effects, characteristic of a preparatory measure forming part of a preliminary administrative procedure. Only measures immediately and irreversibly affecting the legal situation of the undertakings concerned would be of such a nature as to justify, before completion of the administrative procedure, the admissibility of an action for annulment[4]. The application for annulment was therefore rejected.

1 Joined Cases T-10–12, T-15/92 [1992] ECR II-2667.
2 Case 60/81 *IBM v EC Commission* [1981] ECR 2639, [1981] 3 CMLR 635.
3 See para **7.14**.
4 See n 1 above, at para 42.

7.21

As far as the question of fines is concerned, the Statement of Objections does not have to provide details of the level of fines which the Commission is contemplating. It does, however, have to state the duration of the alleged infringement of Articles 81 and/or 82, having regard to the fact that duration of the infringement is one of the two factors (along with gravity of the infringement) to which the Commission is obliged to have regard when fixing the fine[1]. In the *Pioneer*[2] case, for example, the Commission's decision, which imposed a fine, referred to a longer period of infringement than did the Statement of Objections; on appeal, the ECJ held that the fine had to be reviewed, having regard to the shorter period referred to in the Statement of Objections.

1 Council Regulation (EEC) 17/62, art 15, OJ Sp Ed [1959–62] p 87.
2 Case 100–103/80 *Musique Diffusion Française v EC Commission* [1983] ECR 1825, [1983] 3 CMLR 221.

7.22

When serving the Statement of Objections, the Commission is required to fix a time limit within which the undertakings concerned may inform the Commission of their views[1]. In fixing this time limit, the Commission is required to have regard both to the time required for the preparation of comments and to the urgency of the case; the time limit must not in any event be less than two weeks and may be extended[2]. It has been known for the time for a reply fixed by the Commission to be as long as six months[3], although this is unusual. In its Twenty-third Report on Competition Policy (1993) the Commission stated that it had decided to standardise the deadlines for replying to Statements of Objections[4]. In cases of 'average importance' it indicated that generally a period of two months will be granted; in complicated cases, the period will be three months. An extra two weeks will automatically be allowed when these periods fall at Christmas or Easter and an extra one month will be granted automatically when the periods include all or part of the month of August. These periods will not normally be extended (any application for an extension will be dealt with by the hearing officer[5]). In the case of expedited procedures (for example, applications for interim measures) only the minimum period of two weeks is likely to be granted (without any extension).

1 Commission Regulation (EC) 2842/98, art 3(4), OJ [1998] L 354/18. For a case in which a decision was annulled because of a failure to comply with this requirement, see Joined Cases T-39/92 and T-40/92 *Groupement des Cartes Bancaires and Europay International v EC Commission* [1994] ECR II-49, at paras 57–61.
2 Commission Regulation (EC) 2842/98, art 14.
3 Case 60/81 *IBM v EC Commission* [1981] ECR 2639, [1981] 3 CMLR 635.
4 At para 207.
5 See para **7.61**.

7.23

If a cogent reason can be given as to why an extension is sought, so much the better.

7.24

The addressee of a statement of objections will be required by the Commission to state (by a date set by the Commission) whether any parts of the statement of objections contains business secrets or other confidential material. If an addressee does not do so by that date, the Commission will assume that the objections do not contain such information[1]. The significance of this is that the Commission is likely to provide a non-confidential version of the statement of objections to any third party complainant[2].

1 Commission Regulation (EC) 2842/98, art 3(5), OJ [1998] L 354/18.
2 Ibid, para 7.

5 SUPPLEMENTARY STATEMENT OF OBJECTIONS

7.25
It is not unusual for the Commission to send a supplementary Statement of Objections to the undertaking(s) concerned during the course of proceedings; indeed, it is necessarily obliged to do so if it contemplates relying in its final decision on matters not covered in the original Statement of Objections[1]. In *Eurocheque International*[2] a supplementary Statement of Objections, which was formally notified to one of the undertakings concerned, was merely copied to the other 'by way of information', without any period of time being stipulated within which the latter was to inform the Commission of its views in accordance with art 2(4) of Regulation 99/63[3]. The CFI decided that it could not rule out the possibility that the procedure (which culminated in the imposition of a fine of 1 million ECU) might have had a different result if the Commission had properly notified the supplementary Statement of Objections and prescribed a time limit for a response. Accordingly, it ruled that the undertaking's rights of defence had been infringed and the relevant part of the decision was annulled (including the imposition of the fine).

1 Case 48/69 *ICI v EC Commission* [1972] ECR 619, [1972] CMLR 557.
2 Joined Cases T-39/92 and T-40/92 *Groupement des Cartes Bancaires and Europay International v EC Commission* [1994] ECR II-49, at paras 57–61.
3 See para **7.62**. This Regulation was the predecessor to Regulation 2842/98.

6 SUPPORTING DOCUMENTS ACCOMPANYING STATEMENT OF OBJECTIONS

7.26
If the Commission intends to rely on certain documents, it must supply those to the undertaking concerned so that it can comment on them[1]. This applies even if the documents in question had originally come from the undertaking itself, because the undertaking must be able to assess and comment on the weight to which the Commission is giving such documents[2]. However, if the undertaking concerned accompanies its reply to the Commission's Statement of Objections with certain documents, those documents constitute evidence which can subsequently be relied upon by the Commission against that undertaking (ie even though they were not referred to in the Statement of Objections)[3]. This is on the basis that the Commission must take into account the factors emerging during the course of the administrative procedure (in order either to abandon such objections as have been shown to have been unfounded or to supplement those objections). The Commission is not obliged to provide translations of documents annexed to the Statement of Objections[4].

1 Cases 100–103/80 *Musique Diffusion Française v EC Commission* [1983] ECR 1825, [1983] 3 CMLR 221; Case 107/82 *AEG-Telefunken v EC Commission* [1983] ECR 3151, [1984] 3 CMLR 325; Case C-62/86 *AKZO Chemie v EC Commission* [1991] ECR I-3359 at para 21; Case T-11/89 *Shell International Chemical Co Ltd v EC Commission* [1992] ECR II-757 at para 55.
2 Case 107/82 *AEG-Telefunken*, n 1 above.
3 Case T-11/89 *Shell International Chemical Co Ltd v EC Commission* [1992] ECR II-757 at paras 59 and 60.
4 Joined Cases T-25-95–104-95 *Cimenteries v EC Commission* [2000] 5 CMLR 204.

D Access to Commission's File

7.27
The issue of the extent to which an undertaking against which Article 81/82 proceedings are brought by the Commission should have access to the Commission's file has provoked considerable debate. Moreover, it is an issue which brings into conflict the right of the 'defendant' undertaking to be heard on the one hand and the right of third parties to ensure that information confidential to them is not disclosed to the 'defendant' undertaking. The strict legal position, as originally enunciated by the ECJ, contrasted with the somewhat more open approach to access adopted by the Commission since 1982. Each aspect will be considered in turn. The court's own approach has become more favourable to defendant undertakings in recent years. The Commission set out its internal rules of procedure, in the light of the case law and its own practice to date, in a Notice issued in 1997[1].

1 OJ [1997] C 23/3.

1 THE STRICT LEGAL POSITION

7.28
The ECJ ruled as long ago as 1966 that there was no legal right of access to the Commission's entire file. In that case[1] the ECJ held that the right of the undertaking concerned was adequately protected if it was informed of the facts upon which the complaints against it were based; it was not necessary in the court's view for the entire contents of the Commission's file to be communicated. On the other hand, it was clear from the judgment of the ECJ in *Hoffmann-La Roche v EC Commission*[2] that the undertaking concerned must be given the opportunity to make known its views '. . . on the documents used by the Commission to support its claim that there has been an infringement of . . . the Treaty'. Accordingly, if the Commission based a particular decision in whole or part on documents which are not disclosed to the undertaking concerned, the ECJ could be expected on appeal to ignore those documents in deciding whether the decision itself was valid[3].

1 Cases 56, 58/64 *Consten & Grundig v EC Commission* [1966] ECR 299, [1966] CMLR 418; see also Joined Cases 43, 63/82 *VBVB v VBBB* [1984] ECR 19, [1985] 1 CMLR 27 and Case C-62/86 *AKZO Chemie BV v EC Commission* [1991] ECR I-3359, [1993] 5 CMLR 215, ECJ.

2 Case 85/76 [1979] ECR 461, [1979] 3 CMLR 211 at para 11.
3 Case 107/82 *AEG-Telefunken v EC Commission* [1983] ECR 3151, [1984] 3 CMLR 325.

7.29
The dividing line drawn by the ECJ in terms of the need for disclosure accordingly focused on whether or not the particular document in question had been relied on by the Commission in reaching its decision. This was far from satisfactory from the point of view of the undertaking alleged to have infringed Article 81 or 82, as it may well be that the Commission has on its file documentation which would in fact help it in its defence but on which the Commission does not intend to rely. In *Solvay*[1] the CFI accepted this, invoking what it called 'the general principle of equality of arms'. It held that it was not for the Commission to decide on its own whether documents seized during an investigation were exculpatory or not. It held that the principle of equality of arms and its corollary in competition cases, namely the principle that the information available to the Commission and the defence should be the same, required that the applicant should be able to assess the value of documents emanating from a third party and which the Commission chose not to annex to the Statement of Objections. It did not accept that the Commission could base its outright refusal to make disclosure on the grounds of confidentiality. This approach was reconfirmed in the landmark 1,000 page judgment in 2000 in 'the *Cement* case'[2], in which the CFI confirmed that the Commission is obliged to disclose the entire investigatory file, apart from business secrets of third parties, other confidential information and internal Commission documents.

1 Case T-30/91 *Solvay SA v EC Commission* [1995] All ER (EC) 600, CFI. See also Case T-36/91 *ICI plc v EC Commission* [1995] All ER (EC) 600, CFI.
2 Joined Cases T-25-95–104-95 *Cimenteries v EC Commission* [2000] 5 CMLR 204.

7.30
The mere fact that the Commission has not given an undertaking proper access to the file does not of itself warrant annulment of the subsequent decision: it is necessary to consider whether the undertaking's ability to defend itself has been affected by the conditions on which it has had access to the Commission's file. In *LVM*[1] the CFI held that:

> 'it is sufficient for a finding of infringement of defence rights for it to be established that non-disclosure of the documents in question might have influenced the course of the procedure and the content of the decision to the applicant's detriment . . . if that were so, the administrative procedure would be defective and the decision would have to be annulled'.

1 Joined Cases T-305/94–T-335/94 *LVM v EC Commission* [1999] 5 CMLR 303, citing the *Solvay* case. See also the *Cement* case referred to in para **7.29** at para 156.

2 COMMISSION PRACTICE

7.31
In its Twelfth Report on Competition Policy (1982) the Commission announced its intention[1] to 'go beyond the requirements laid down by the ECJ and improve the exercise of the rights of defence in the course of

administrative procedures', by permitting the undertakings involved in a procedure to inspect the Commission's file on their case. The practice set out by the Commission was as follows. The undertaking against which proceedings are brought would be provided with a list of the contents of the Commission's file, in the form of an annex to the Statement of Objections. The annex would indicate to which of these documents (or parts thereof) the undertaking was allowed to have access and it was entitled to 'consult' these at the Commission, requesting photocopies if only a few documents were involved. The Commission made it clear[2] that certain documents were not accessible to the undertaking concerned, namely:

(*a*) documents or parts thereof containing other undertakings' business secrets;
(*b*) internal Commission documents, such as notes, drafts or other working papers;
(*c*) any other confidential information, such as documents enabling complainants to be identified where they wished to remain anonymous, and information disclosed to the Commission subject to an obligation of confidentiality.

If the undertaking concerned makes a request to consult a document which falls into one of these three non-accessible categories, the Commission may provide it with a non-confidential summary, if that is practical. The CFI has made it clear that, having announced its intention to go beyond the requirements laid down by the ECJ, the Commission must not depart from the rules which it has chosen to impose on itself[3]. It therefore has an obligation to make available to the undertakings involved in Article 81 proceedings all documents, whether in their favour or otherwise, which it has obtained during the course of the investigation, except where business secrets of third parties, the internal documents of the Commission or other confidential information are involved[4]. The Commission is not entitled to rely on a document which it has not, on grounds of confidentiality, released to the undertaking against whom the proceedings are brought. For example, in *AEG-Telefunken*[5] the ECJ decided that the Commission was wrong to have placed reliance, in reaching its final decision, on a document which it did not release to the defendant undertaking on the grounds of professional secrecy.

1 At para 34.
2 12th Report on Competition Policy (1982), at para 35.
3 Case T-7/89 *SA Hercules Chemicals NV v EC Commission* [1991] ECR II-1711, [1992] 4 CMLR 84, upheld on appeal in Case C-51/92P *Hercules v EC Commission* [1999] 5 CMLR 976.
4 Ibid at para 54.
5 Case 107/82 *AEG-Telefunken v EC Commission* [1983] ECR 3151, [1984] 3 CMLR 325.

7.32

In its 1997 Notice[1] the Commission states that, where business secrets provide evidence of an infringement or tend to exonerate a firm, the Commission must reconcile the interest in the protection of sensitive information, the public interest in having the infringement of the competition rules terminated and the rights of the defence. It goes on to say that this calls for an assessment of:

- — the relevance of the information to determine whether or not an infringement has been committed;
- — its probative value;
- — whether it is indispensable;
- — the degree of sensitivity involved;
- — the seriousness of the infringement.

The Notice states that if an undertaking maintains the view that a document contains business secrets/is confidential to it and refuses to provide a non-confidential version, the Commission's hearing officer[2] will, if necessary, implement a procedure leading to a decision pursuant to the Commission Decision which lays down the terms of reference of hearing officers[3]. That Decision requires the Commission to give the undertaking concerned at least a week's notice prior to disclosing the information. This provides the undertaking concerned with the opportunity to challenge the decision before the CFI[4].

1 OJ [1997] C 23/3.
2 As to the role of the hearing officer generally, see para **7.58** ff.
3 Commission Decision 94/810/ECSC, EC on the terms of reference of hearing officers in competition procedures before the Commission, OJ [1994] L 330/67.
4 See paras **11.07–11.08**.

7.33
The 1997 Notice[1] sets out the Commission's current practical arrangements for access to the file. The Commission's Statement of Objections will in future be accompanied only by the evidence and documents on which the objections are based. This represents a reversal of its previously announced practice[2], under which copies of all documents to which access is being given were sent with the Statement of Objections. Undertakings are therefore now invited to examine the relevant files at the Commission's premises (which was its original practice). However, the 1997 Notice indicates that if the file is not too bulky, the undertaking will be given the option of being sent all accessible documents (apart from those already with the Statement of Objections) or of consulting the file on the Commission's premises. Any request for access made prior to submission of the Statement of Objections will in principle be inadmissible.

1 OJ [1997] C 23/3.
2 23rd Report on Competition Policy at para 205.

7.34
The Commission has also now given a formal role to the hearing officer in relation to any dispute which arises between the Commission and an undertaking regarding access to the Commission's file: if, on the basis of the list of documents in the Commission's file sent together with the Statement of Objections, and with its own knowledge of the case, the undertaking has reasonable grounds to believe that it should receive additional documents, the hearing officer will examine such a request and decide on its merits[1]. This was a change recommended by the House of Lords Select Committee in its 1993 Report[2]. However, the Select Committee also recommended[3] that the hearing officer's decision should be capable of review on an interlocutory basis by the CFI. This is not possible at present[4].

1 Commission Decision 94/810/ECSC, EC on the terms of reference of hearing officers in competition procedures before the Commission, OJ [1994] L 330/67.
2 *HL Select Committee Report on Enforcement of Community Competition Rules 1st Report* (HL Paper (1993–94)).
3 Ibid at para 112.
4 See paras **7.42–7.43**.

7.35
In *BPB Industries*[1] the Commission refused access to, inter alia, a third party's answer to a Commission request for information and certain correspondence with third party undertakings. The CFI decided that this refusal of access did not affect the legality of the Commission's decision, noting that:

> 'An undertaking to which a Statement of Objections has been addressed, and which occupies a dominant position in the market, may, for that very reason, adopt retaliatory measures against a competing undertaking, a supplier or a customer, who has collaborated in the investigation carried out by the Commission'[2].

1 Case T-65/89 *BPB Industries plc and British Gypsum Ltd v EC Commission* [1993] 5 CMLR 32, upheld by the ECJ in Case C-310/93P [1995] ECR I-865.
2 Ibid at para 33.

7.36
One issue which has arisen is whether an undertaking against which proceedings are brought is entitled to have sight of the replies of other undertakings. This was a proposition arising out of the Commission's decision in *Polypropylene*[1]. In *Hercules*[2] the CFI concluded that it was unnecessary to examine whether the Commission's refusal to allow Hercules sight of other undertakings' replies to the Commission's statement of objections constituted an infringement of the rights of the defence. On appeal, the ECJ[3] avoided opining on this issue, simply holding that Hercules had failed to establish that those replies in fact contained evidence of use for its defence.

1 Commission Decision (86/398/EEC) OJ [1986] L230/1.
2 Case T-7/89 *Hercules v EC Commission* [1991] ECR II-1711.
3 Case C-51/92P *Hercules v EC Commission* [1999] 5 CMLR 976.

7.37
In *PVC*[1], a number of the undertakings against which proceedings had been commenced made a joint approach to the Commission and, on the basis of reciprocal waivers of confidentiality, requested that the Commission permit each to inspect the documents obtained by the Commission from all the others. The Commission's response was that if they wished to do this, it would have no objection to them arranging this amongst themselves. However, the Commission noted that[2]:

> 'It should be pointed out that any waiver by undertakings of confidentiality for their internal business documents is subject to the overriding public interest in ensuring that competitors are not informed of each other's commercial activities and intentions in such a way that competition between them is restricted'.

Such exchanges should therefore be undertaken with care.

1 Commission Decision (89/190/EEC) OJ [1989] L 74/1, [1990] 4 CMLR 345 (annulled on procedural grounds: see para **8.65**).
2 At para 27.

7.38

The position of one particular type of internal document, namely reports prepared by Commission inspectors following an article 14 inspection visit, was clarified in the Commission's Thirteenth Report on Competition Policy (1983)[1]. There the Commission makes it clear that reports drawn up after an inspection visit and which contain a purely factual account are accessible to the undertaking which was subject to the investigation; however, the report in which the inspectors assess their visit is considered to be an internal Commission document and not accessible. The Thirteenth Report also makes it clear[1] that access to the Commission's file is not offered until the undertaking concerned has received the Statement of Objections. This is frequently the first time the undertaking concerned has any knowledge of the fact that proceedings are being brought in any event (although there may be advance notice of the likelihood of proceedings, for example, if the Commission seeks information under art 11 or carries out an on-the-spot investigation under art 14).

1 At para 74(b).

7.39

In *AKZO*[1] the applicant argued that the Commission's decision was procedurally flawed because it had not allowed the company access to the reports of Commission inspectors drawn up after an article 14 visit, even though these reports might have contained matters which could have helped the company in its defence. AKZO specifically argued that the Commission had failed to follow the policy outlined in its own Reports on Competition Policy[2]. The ECJ dismissed AKZO's claim summarily[3], merely citing its previous jurisprudence on the issue of access to the Commission's file[4].

1 Case C-62/86 *AKZO Chemie BV v EC Commission* [1991] ECR I-3359, [1993] 5 CMLR 215, ECJ.
2 See para **7.38**.
3 ECJ judgment in Case C-62/86 *AKZO Chemie BV v EC Commission* [1991] ECR I-3359 at paras 15–17.
4 See para **7.28**.

7.40

An application was made for sight of part of the Commission's internal file in *BAT and Reynolds v EC Commission*[1]. Reynolds argued that the Commission had given no valid reasons for an apparent change of assessment of the case and suggested that the reason for this change was pressure exerted by an adviser to Philip Morris who had previously been a Vice President of the Commission. The ECJ emphasised the preparatory nature of a Statement of Objections, the factual and legal assessments in it being purely provisional. The contention that there was a contradiction between its assessment of one set of agreements and of another set of agreements involving the same case did not 'constitute a reason for suspecting the existence of covert reasons extraneous to Community law'. As far as access to the Commission internal documents was concerned, the court was very clear:

'... examinations by the court of the Commission's internal file with a view to verifying whether the Commission decision was influenced by factors other than those indicated in the statement of the reasons on which the decision is based or stated by the Commission during the proceedings before the court would constitute an exceptional measure of enquiry. Such a measure would pre-suppose that the circumstances surrounding the decision in question give rise to serious doubts as to the real reasons and in particular to suspicions that those reasons were extraneous to the objectives of Community law and hence amounted to a misuse of powers'[2].

1 Joined Cases 142, 156/84 *BAT Co Ltd and RJ Reynolds Industries Inc v EC Commission* [1986] ECR 1899, [1987] 2 CMLR 551.
2 Point 11 of the judgment.

7.41

In *ICI v EC Commission*[1], the applicant sought discovery of certain Commission documents including documents relating to press releases which seemed to indicate reasons for the Commission's final decision[2] different from those set out in the preamble to the decision itself. Citing the *BAT* case[3], the ECJ observed that an examination of internal Commission documents, with a view to verifying whether the Commission's decision had been influenced by factors other than those indicated in the statement of the reasons on which the decision is based, would constitute an exceptional measure of enquiry. It again said that there would need to be circumstances surrounding the decision which gave rise to serious doubts as to the real reasons lying behind it and, in particular, to suspicions that those reasons were extraneous to the objectives of Community law and amounted to a misuse of powers. The applicant had not made any submission of this nature and accordingly the court dismissed the application.

1 Case 212/86 [1987] 2 CMLR 500.
2 Commission Decision (86/398/EEC) *Polypropylene* OJ [1986] L 230/1, [1988] 4 CMLR 347.
3 Joined Cases 142, 156/84 *BAT and Reynolds Industries v EC Commission* [1986] ECR 1899, [1987] 2 CMLR 551.

7.42

In *Cimenteries*[1] a number of applicants applied to the CFI for annulment of a decision (in the form of a letter) by the Commission in which the latter had refused to grant them access to the complete file. In that case the applications to the CFI were made during the course of the administrative procedure, indeed before they had replied to the allegations set out in the Statement of Objections. The CFI held that Commission measures refusing access to the file produced in principle only limited effects, characteristic of a preparatory measure forming part of a preliminary administrative procedure. Only measures immediately and irreversibly affecting the legal situation of the undertakings concerned would be of such a nature as to justify, before completion of the administrative procedure, the admissibility of an action for annulment. This effectively means that for all practical purposes a challenge of this nature can only be made after the adoption by the Commission of its final decision in any particular case.

1 Joined Cases T-10–12, T-15/92 *Cimenteries CBR SA v EC Commission* [1992] ECR II-2667, [1993] 4 CMLR 259.

7.43

In its 1993 Report[1] the House of Lords Select Committee on the European Communities recommended that there should be a possibility of appeal to a judge of the CFI from rulings by the hearing officer, including rulings on access to the file. Its recommendation was that this should be dealt with under an expedited procedure similar to that employed for requests for interim measures. The Report recognises that this would require amendment of Regulation 17/62[2] so as to avoid the limitation on admissibility established in the *Cimenteries*[3] case.

1 *HL Select Committee Report on Enforcement of Community Competition Rules 1st Report* (HL Paper (1993–94)), at para 129.
2 Council Regulation (EEC) 17/62, OJ Sp Ed [1959–62] p 87.
3 Joined Cases T-10-12/92, T-15/92 *Cimenteries CBR SA v EC Commission* [1992] ECR II-2667, [1993] 4 CMLR 259, CFI.

7.44

As far as access to the file is concerned, the position of complaints is weaker than that of undertakings under investigation. In *Matra Hachette*[1], the CFI ruled that third parties (such as a complainant) cannot claim a right of access to the file compiled by the Commission on the same basis as the undertakings under investigation[2]. In its 1997 Notice[3] the Commission states, however, that a complainant who has been informed of the intention to reject his complaint may request access to those documents on which the Commission based its position. If the complainant considers that the Commission holds documents which fall into this category but have not been disclosed to it, it may draw this matter to the attention of the Commission's hearing officer[4] and ask for a reasoned decision in response to that request.

1 Case T-17/93 *Matra Hachette SA v EC Commission* [1994] ECR II-595.
2 See para **5.26**.
3 OJ [1997] C 23/3.
4 Commission Decision 94/810/ECSC, EC, OJ [1994] L 330/67.

E The Right of Reply

1 GENERAL

7.45

The right of an undertaking against which the Commission proposes to take a decision to be heard is a basic Community law principle[1] and is also enshrined in the context of Articles 81 and 82 of the EC Treaty in Regulation 17/62, art 19(1)[2]. This provides that, before any of the following types of decision are taken, the undertakings concerned must be given the opportunity of being heard on the matters to which the Commission has taken objection:

(*a*) negative clearance;
(*b*) termination of infringements (including interim measures[3]);
(*c*) individual exemptions under Article 81(3);

(*d*) renewal, revocation or amendment of an exemption under Article 81(3);
(*e*) the imposition of a fine;
(*f*) the imposition of a periodic penalty payment.

1 See para **14.13** ff.
2 Council Regulation (EEC) 17/62, OJ Sp Ed [1959–62] p 87.
3 See para **8.05** ff.

7.46
As has been noted previously[1], the undertaking concerned does not have a right to be heard before the Commission takes a decision requiring information to be supplied (under art 11 of Regulation 17/62) or a decision ordering an on-the-spot investigation (under art 14 of Regulation 17/62). By way of contrast, the ECJ has held that before the Commission takes a decision pursuant to art 15(6)[2] of Regulation 17/62 (removing the protection of fines in relation to a notified agreement) the undertaking does have a right to be heard[3].

1 See para **7.12**.
2 See para **8.29** ff.
3 Cases 8–11/66 *Cimenteries v EC Commission* [1967] ECR 75, [1967] CMLR 77.

7.47
Although the right referred to in art 19 of Regulation 17/62 is a right to be 'heard', the Commission's procedure is in fact largely a written procedure, although oral hearings do also take place. The right of reply in, respectively, writing and oral hearing is considered separately below.

7.48
In *Tetra Pak*[1], the CFI rejected the applicant's contention that the right to be heard included the right to express its views on the level of fine proposed to be imposed by the Commission. The CFI pointed out that the applicant's right under art 19(1) of Regulation 17/62[2] was a right to be heard 'on the matters to which the Commission has taken objection', not on the amount of the fine proposed. The protection afforded to the applicant regarding the amount of the fine lay in the CFI's unlimited jurisdiction under Article 172 of the EC Treaty[3] to review the fine imposed.

1 Case T-83/91 *Tetra Pak International SA v EC Commission* [1994] ECR II-755, upheld by the ECJ in Case C-333/94P *Tetra Pak International SA v EC Commission* [1996] ECR I-5951.
2 Council Regulation (EEC) 17/62, OJ Sp Ed [1959–62] p 87.
3 See paras **10.05–10.07**.

2 WHO HAS A RIGHT OF REPLY?

(1) The Undertaking Against Which Proceedings are Brought

7.49
It is quite clear from art 19(1) of Regulation 17/62[1] that any undertaking against which proceedings are brought has a right to be heard on all matters

to which the Commission has taken objection before any of the decisions listed at para **7.45** are taken. This right is exercised first and foremost in writing: art 4 of Regulation 2842/98[2] provides that the undertaking against which the Statement of Objections is directed *shall*, within a time limit stipulated by the Commission, make known its views in writing concerning those objections. As far as the oral reply is concerned, the relevant article of Regulation 2842/98 (art 5) gives the parties against whom the objections are made the right to attend an oral hearing.

1 Council Regulation (EEC) 17/62, OJ Sp Ed [1959–62] p 87.
2 Commission Regulation (EC) 2842/98, OJ [1998] L 354/18.

(2) Third Parties

7.50
The right to be heard set out in art 19(1) of Regulation 17/62 is limited in scope to the 'undertaking concerned'. This phrase has been interpreted by the ECJ as being limited to the undertakings against which proceedings are brought and does not extend to third parties[1]. The position of third parties is dealt with in art 19(2), which provides that if the Commission considers it necessary it may also hear natural or legal persons other than the undertaking which is the subject of the proceedings. Applications to be heard on the part of such persons must be granted if they show a 'sufficient interest'[2]. The scope of the phrase 'sufficient interest' has not been judicially defined by the ECJ. However, a person entitled to file a complaint with the Commission under art 3 of Regulation 17/62[3] would seem clearly to have a sufficient interest and indeed the term almost certainly extends rather more broadly than this.

1 Case 43/85 *ANCIDES v EC Commission* [1987] ECR 3131, [1988] 4 CMLR 821.
2 Council Regulation (EEC) 17/62, art 19(2), OJ Sp Ed [1959–62] p 87.
3 See Chapter 5.

7.51
Article 7 of Regulation 2842/98[1] makes it clear that where the Commission issues a statement of objections relating to an issue in respect of which it has received a complaint it should provide the complainant with a copy of the non-confidential version of the statement of objections and set a date by which the complainant may make known its views in writing. Under art 8 of Regulation 2842/98, the Commission may (but is not obliged to do so) afford to the complainant the opportunity of orally expressing its views (if it has requested that opportunity at the time it submitted its written comments).

1 Commission Regulation (EC) 2842/98, OJ [1998] L 354/18.

7.52
As far as third parties are concerned (ie those other than the person(s) to whom the statement of objections is addressed and a complainant), if those parties apply to be heard and show a sufficient interest they have an opportunity to make known their views in writing; the Commission may (but is not obliged to do so) invite such parties to develop their arguments at the

oral hearing of the parties against which objections have been raised if they have made such a request in their written observations.

7.53
If a third party does not ask to be heard, the Commission cannot be subsequently criticised for failing to give that third party the opportunity to express its views orally[1].

1 Case 43/85 *ANCIDES v EC Commission* [1987] ECR 3131.

3 THE WRITTEN REPLY

(1) Contents

7.54
The undertaking which is the subject of the Commission's proceedings should take the opportunity of replying in writing to respond to every aspect of the case put against it (ie factual, economic and legal). Before finally signing off on the written reply, an undertaking finding itself in such a position is well advised to dissect the Statement of Objections on a sentence by sentence basis, ensuring that it has commented on everything on which it wishes to comment. This is crucial, because it may be that if the undertaking fails to reject a particular assertion at this stage of the proceedings it will be unable to do so later on. In the *Distillers*[1] case, the Advocate General said:

> 'It would indeed be very odd if, for instance, the court were now to hold that the Decision was void in so far as it declared that the price terms were caught by Article 85(1) [now Article 81(1)], when, in the administrative proceedings, DCL (quite rightly in my opinion) accepted that they were'.

1 Case 30/78 *Distillers v EC Commission* [1980] ECR 2229, [1980] 3 CMLR 121.

7.55
Regulation 2842/98, art 4[1] states specifically that the undertaking may, in its written comments, set out all matters relevant to its defence and that it may also attach any relevant documents in proof of the facts set out. This might include copies of agreements, correspondence and so on. Article 4 also suggests that the undertaking concerned may wish to put forward the names of third parties who are in a position to corroborate its evidence (for example, suppliers, customers, etc).

1 Commission Regulation (EC) 2842/98 L 354/18.

(2) Time Limit for Written Reply

7.56
At the time the Commission serves the Statement of Objections, it is required to fix a time limit within which the undertaking concerned should inform the Commission of its views[1]. In fixing the time limit, the Commission is required to have regard both to the time required for

preparation of comments and to the urgency of the case; in any event, the time limit must not be less than two weeks and may be extended[2]. In practice, the period usually given is approximately two months and can be longer in complex cases[3]. If the undertaking concerned wishes to apply for an extension, it is certainly wise to do so at the earliest opportunity, rather than wait until shortly before the initial time period expires.

1 Commission Regulation (EC) 2842/98, art 3(5), OJ [1998] L 354/18.
2 Commission Regulation (EEC) 99/63, art 11.
3 Case 60/81 *IBM v EC Commission* [1981] ECR 2639, [1981] 3 CMLR 635 (over six months).

4 THE ORAL HEARING

(1) General

7.57

The circumstances in which the undertaking against which proceedings are brought and third parties may be heard orally, either as a matter of right or at the discretion of the Commission, are described at paras **7.49–7.52**. As far as the conduct of the hearing is concerned, the following basic procedural points should be noted:

(1) *Timing*: It is not unusual for the Commission to give fairly short notice of the proposed date of the hearing (sometimes as short as a couple of weeks) but it will, of course, frequently be known from an earlier date that a hearing will in due course be taking place (because the person concerned will have indicated its wish to be heard orally when submitting its written comments[1]). If the proposed date is not convenient for some reason, the Commission should be contacted as a matter of urgency with a view to ascertaining whether an alternative date would be possible.

(2) *Legal Representation*: Under Regulation 2842/98, art 12, persons attending must appear either in person or be represented by legal representatives or by representatives authorised by their constitution. Article 12 also provides that persons heard by the Commission may be assisted by their legal adviser or 'other qualified persons admitted by the hearing officer'. The effect of this appears to be that, although an independent legal adviser can be present at the hearing in order to assist the undertaking concerned to present its case, that adviser cannot appear in the capacity of *representative* of the undertaking, unless he is permanently employed by it. That is to say, the undertaking cannot appear solely through its independent legal adviser.

(3) *Other persons who may be present*: Other persons who may be present at a hearing fall into two categories. Firstly, the competent authorities of each Member State (in the case of the United Kingdom, the Office of Fair Trading) must be notified of the hearing and may (and usually do) appoint an official to take part in the hearing[2]. Their involvement in the hearing is described at para **7.66**. Secondly, although hearings are private[3], art 12(3) of Regulation 2842/98 provides that persons can be heard either separately or in the presence of other persons summoned

to attend; in the latter case, the Commission is required to have regard to the legitimate interest of the various undertakings in the protection of their business secrets. In practice, the Commission prefers wherever possible to have various of the undertakings concerned present at one and the same hearing. For example, if two undertakings are alleged to be party to an agreement which infringes Article 81, the Commission will usually hear them together, although it will frequently hear each of them separately for part of the hearing in order to enable confidential matters to be dealt with. Similarly, the Commission will sometimes have the undertaking which is subject to the proceedings and a complainant present at the same hearing.

(4) *Record of the Hearing*: the statements made by each person at the hearing are recorded on tape. The recording is made available to each such person on request, by means of a copy from which business secrets and other confidential information are deleted[4].

(5) *Procedure at the hearing*: The procedure which is typically followed at the hearing is outlined at paras **7.65–7.67**.

(6) *Duration of the hearing*: The hearing does not usually last longer than one day (although this is not an inflexible rule and a longer hearing may be unavoidable in complex cases). The shortness of the hearing underlines the fact that the Commission's procedure is primarily a written one. In the words of the Commission:

> 'The Commission's administrative procedure takes place mainly in writing and this must remain so on account of the complicated nature of the cases it examines. The oral hearing is the place to clarify certain matters which have not been settled during the written procedure and to emphasise the main lines of the case'[5].

1 See para **7.49**.
2 Commission Regulation (EC) 2842/98, art 11(2), OJ [1998] L 354/18.
3 See n 2 above, art 12(3).
4 Ibid, art 12(4).
5 11th Report on Competition Policy (1981), para 26.

5 THE HEARING OFFICER

(1) Background to the Creation of the Position of Hearing Officer

7.58

The Commission's procedure in competition cases (and particularly its role as investigator, prosecutor and judge) has from time to time, especially in the early 1980s, been the subject of considerable criticism[1]. Mindful of these criticisms, the Commission decided to create the post of Hearing Officer with effect from 1 September 1982; the functions of the hearing officer are described below. When announcing this proposal in its Eleventh Report on Competition Policy (1981)[2], the Commission claimed that:

> 'This would provide an even better guarantee that the Commission, when stating its views on an individual case as a decision-making authority, would be fully informed of all features of the case whether favourable or unfavourable to the

undertakings. It must, however, be kept in mind that the Commission's procedure relating to restrictive practices and abuse of a dominant position is administrative and not judicial; it must not be turned into a trial'.

The Commission rejected as being incompatible with the institutional scheme of the Treaty the suggestion made in some quarters that autonomous administrative law judges should be introduced, similar to the way in which they are appointed to the Federal Trade Commission in the United States (the Commission also indicated that it believed that this would only serve to make procedures in individual cases even more complicated and prolonged). It also rejected the proposal of the European Parliament[3] that the ECJ or the Commission itself should appoint persons independent of the Directorate-General for Competition who would take part in investigations and deal with certain procedural problems.

1 See, eg *HL Select Committee on Competition Procedure 8th Report* (HL Paper (1981–82)).
2 At paras 26 and 27.
3 Resolution on the 10th Report on Competition Policy, at para 10.

(2) Status and Role of the Hearing Officer

7.59
The announcement of the post of hearing officer was made in the Commission's Twelfth Report on Competition Policy (1982). Although he is part of the Directorate-General for Competition, he is not part of the various operational Directorates; in an effort to ensure his independence in the performance of his duties, he has direct right of access to the Commissioner responsible for competition policy. The principal functions of the hearing officer were described by the Commission when creating the post[1], namely:

(*a*) to ensure that the hearing is properly conducted and to contribute to the objectiveness of the hearing itself and of any subsequent decision;
(*b*) to ensure that the rights of the defence are respected, while taking account of the need for effective application of the competition rules;
(*c*) to ensure that in preparing its draft decisions, the Commission takes due account of all the relevant facts, whether favourable or unfavourable to the parties concerned;
(*d*) to organise preparations for the hearing, fixing the date, duration and place;
(*e*) to let the undertakings concerned know in advance the particular matters on which they are to set forth their points of view (this is similar to the procedure followed by the UK Monopolies and Mergers Commission);
(*f*) to take responsibility for the hearing itself, deciding, for example, whether to hear the persons concerned separately or in the presence of other persons;
(*g*) to ensure that the essential content of the statements made by each person are recorded in the minutes;
(*h*) to report to the Director General for Competition on developments at the hearing and on his views as to how the procedure subsequent to the

hearing should be handled; he may, if he feels it appropriate, refer his observations direct to the Commissioner responsible for competition matters.

1 12th Report on Competition Policy (1982), at para 36.

7.60
The Commission took stock of the impact of the creation of the post of hearing officer in its Eighteenth Report on Competition Policy (1988)[1], by which time the hearing officer had presided over more than 50 hearings. The Commission's assessment was as follows: firstly, the hearing officer makes frequent use of his right to supply in advance a list of the matters that are to be discussed, thereby enabling the hearing to focus on the key questions; secondly, it believes that the hearing officer has helped to clear up complaints by undertakings that they have not had sufficient opportunity of being heard. The Commission's general conclusion at that stage was that 'the post of hearing officer has proved its worth and it will continue to play a useful part in the Commission's procedures'.

1 At para 44.

7.61
The Commission further assessed the role of the hearing officer in its Twenty-third Report on Competition Policy (1993)[1] and announced that it intended to extend significantly his role, to cover the following areas:

(1) *Deadline for reply to the Statement of Objections*: If an undertaking considers that the deadline imposed on it is too short, the hearing officer will decide whether an extension should be granted.
(2) *Access to relevant information*: The hearing officer will act as arbiter in the event of a dispute between the Commission and the undertaking regarding the latter's access to the Commission's file[2].
(3) *Right of third parties to be heard*: The hearing officer will now be given the right to decide whether third parties should be allowed to intervene (under Regulation 17/62[3], natural or legal persons proving sufficient interest have the right to be heard[4]).
(4) *Hearings*: The hearing officer will have the task of deciding who is to be allowed to speak at hearings[5].
(5) *Business secrets and other confidential information*: The hearing officer will have the task of deciding which items of information supplied by an undertaking and contained in the Commission's file can be communicated to other undertakings (or indeed published), in accordance with the procedure laid down by the ECJ in *AKZO*[6].

These points are reflected in the revised terms of reference of the Hearing Officer published in December 1994[7].

1 At para 205.
2 See para **7.32**.
3 Council Regulation (EEC) 17/62, OJ Sp Ed [1959–62] p 87.
4 See para **7.51**.
5 As to hearings generally, see para **7.57**.
6 Case 53/85 [1986] ECR 1965; see para **11.08**.
7 OJ [1994] L 330/67, [1995] 4 CMLR 115.

7.62
In its 1993 Report the House of Lords Select Committee on the European Communities recommended[1] that rulings of the hearing officer should be capable of speedy review (on an interlocutory basis) by a judge of the CFI (or alternatively that the hearing officer's ruling should be referred to the Commissioner responsible for competition matters, whose decision in turn should be appealable to a judge of the CFI: it favoured the former). This recommendation is not favoured by the Commission and would require an amendment to Regulation 17/62[2] in the light of ECJ/CFI case law on admissibility[3].

1 *HL Select Committee Report on Enforcement of Competition Rules 1st Report* (HL Paper (1993–94)) at para 112.
2 Council Regulation (EEC) 17/62, OJ Sp Ed [1959–62] p 87.
3 See, for example, Joined Cases T-10–12/92, T-15/92 *Cimenteries CBR SA v EC Commission* [1992] ECR II-2667, [1993] 4 CMLR 259.

7.63
If for some reason the hearing officer is not available for a particular case, the Director General of DGIV is entitled to designate another official (not one involved in the case in question) to carry out the hearing officer's duties. Evidence to the House of Lords Select Committee on the European Communities[1] indicated that arrangements do not always work as well where the official hearing officer has to be substituted in this ad hoc way. The Select Committee recommended that there should be more hearing officers, with adequate support staff[2]. There are, in any event, now already two official hearing officers; one of these is appointed to deal with cases arising under the Merger Control Regulation[3] but he is entitled to handle Article 81 and 82 cases as well.

1 *HL Select Committee Report on Enforcement of Competition Rules 1st Report* (HL Paper (1993–94)); see, for example, evidence of the Joint Working Party on Competition Law of the Law Societies and Bar of the United Kingdom.
2 See n 1 above, at para 149.
3 See *Butterworths Competition Law* Division VII.

7.64
In *ICI v Commission*[1], the company requested the ECJ, pursuant to art 91 of its Rules of Procedure, to order the Commission to produce the report of the hearing officer. The company based its application, inter alia, on the fact that there was a substantial divergence between the content of the Commission's decision against the company and statements made by the hearing officer at the hearing. Citing art 7 of the Terms of Reference of the Hearing Officer[2], which makes it clear that his findings are no more than an opinion, the ECJ held that his report was not a decisive factor and accordingly the application was dismissed[3]. The Court of First Instance has held[4] that there is no obligation on the Commission to communicate the report of the hearing officer to the Advisory Committee[5].

1 Case 212/86 [1987] 2 CMLR 500. See also Case T-2/89 *Petrofina v EC Commission* [1991] ECR II-1087, CFI.
2 13th Report on Competition Policy (1983), pp 273–4: see para **7.59**.
3 See also Case T-13/89 *ICI v EC Commission* [1992] ECR II-1021. In its 1993 Report reviewing the enforcement of Articles 81 and 82 the House of Lords recommended that the hearing officer's report should be sent to the parties: *HL Select Committee on Enforcement of Community Competition Rules 1st Report* (HL Paper 1993–94)), para 111.

4 Case T-2/89 *Petrofina v EC Commission* [1991] ECR II-1087, CFI and Case T-7/89 *Hercules v EC Commission* [1992] 4 CMLR 84 at para 303.
5 See para **7.69**.

6 A TYPICAL PROCEDURE AT THE HEARING

7.65
Following a brief summary by the Commission case officer in charge of the case—the 'rapporteur'—(which, though brief in nature, may provide some indication of those aspects of the case on which the Commission is placing particular emphasis), the undertaking concerned is invited to make a presentation. Although this can cover as broad a range of matters as the undertaking wishes, it should avoid merely re-stating what has already been said in writing. Undertakings do not give evidence on oath and there are no rules of evidence. The presentation is simultaneously translated into the other Community languages. The likely length of the presentation is something which it can be useful to discuss with the hearing officer in advance. If the hearing is scheduled to last only for a full day it would be wise to ensure that its initial presentation does not last longer than half a day.

7.66
Following the undertaking's presentation, questions can be put by the Commission officials and by the representatives of the Member States. These questions do not need to be confined to matters covered in the undertaking's oral presentation but can cover any aspect of the case. The purpose of the hearing is to enable the undertaking to be heard (ie to supplement its written submissions orally)[1], rather than to enable the Commission to conduct a form of cross-examination. There appears therefore to be no reason in principle why the undertaking should answer the questions put to it (and no penalties flow from a refusal to do so). On the other hand, blanket refusal to answer questions does not present a very good impression and indeed more often than not the questions raise matters which the undertaking would not in any event wish to leave unanswered. If a question raises a matter which cannot be answered on the spot, the undertaking is perfectly within its rights to offer an answer in writing after the hearing.

1 Commission Regulation (EC) 2842/98, OJ [1998] L 354/18.

7.67
Finally, the undertaking is entitled to make a few concluding remarks, which may either have been prepared in advance or which may touch on matters which have arisen during the course of the hearing.

F Procedure Following the Oral Hearing

7.68
The oral hearing does not constitute the last stage in exchanges between the Commission and the undertaking(s) against which proceedings are

commenced before the Commission adopts a decision. New facts or documents may come to the attention of the Commission at any stage and, if it wishes to rely on these, it must (in accordance with its basic duty to afford the undertaking a right to be heard) enable the undertaking to comment. Moreover, the undertaking is always at liberty to put certain proposals to the Commission by way of settlement of the proceedings (for example, suggested changes to an agreement which allegedly infringes Article 81). In fact, a large number of proceedings are settled without a formal decision being taken. Settlement of proceedings, together with the associated issue of 'plea-bargaining', is considered at para **8.72** ff.

7.69

The next formal step in the proceedings following the oral hearing is for the Commission to consult the Advisory Committee on Restrictive Practices and Monopolies. This must be consulted before the Commission takes any adverse decision under Article 81 or 82[1], a decision granting negative clearance or an individual exemption under Article 81(3)[2], or a decision imposing fines[3] or periodic penalty payments[4]. It must also be consulted before the Commission takes any decision concerning the renewal, amendment or revocation of a decision pursuant to Article 81(3)[5]. It was suggested by the Advocate General in *ACF Chemiefarma*[6] and *Ford*[7] that failure to consult the Advisory Committee properly (or at all) may serve to render void the Commission's decision.

1 Council Regulation (EEC) 17/62, art 10, OJ Sp Ed [1959–62] p 87.
2 See n 1 above.
3 See n 1 above, arts 10 and 15(3).
4 See n 1 above, arts 10 and 16(3).
5 See n 1 above, art 10(3).
6 Case 41/69 *ACF Chemiefarma v EC Commission* [1970] ECR 661 at 710.
7 Cases 228, 229/82 *Ford of Europe Inc v EC Commission* [1984] ECR 1129 at 1172–4.

7.70

The Advisory Committee is composed of officials competent in the matter of restrictive practices and monopolies and each Member State must appoint an official to represent it who, if prevented from attending, can be replaced by another official[1].

1 Council Regulation (EEC) 17/62, art 10(4).

7.71

Consultation takes place at a joint meeting convened by the Commission on not less than 14 days' notice; the notice must be accompanied by a summary of the case, together with an indication of the most important documents and preliminary draft decision[1]. The opinion delivered by the Advisory Committee following such a consultation is not vitiated because some of its members are not present[2].

1 Council Regulation (EEC) 17/62, art 10(5).
2 Council Regulation (EEC) 17/62, art 10(6).

7.72

In the *RTE* case[1] the applicant claimed that the failure of the Commission to provide the Advisory Committee with a copy of the minutes of the oral hearing held by the Commission constituted an infringement of an essential procedural requirement and accordingly justified annulment of the Commission's Article 82 decision. The applicant claimed that the approved minutes of the hearing were amongst the 'most important' documents in the case within the meaning of art 10(5) of Council Regulation 17/62. The CFI accepted (at para 22) that the minutes of the hearing are, in principle, among the most important documents and should therefore be sent to the Advisory Committee. However, it held that this was not an essential procedural requirement unless, in the case in point, the absence of the minutes would cause the Committee to be misled in a material respect. On the facts, the CFI was satisfied that there was no additional information contained in the minutes which might have affected the outcome of the Committee's deliberations.

1 Case T-69/89 *Radio Telefis Eireann v EC Commission* [1991] 4 CMLR 586 (upheld on appeal in Joined Cases C-241/91P and C-242/92P *RTE and ITP v EC Commission* [1995] ECR I-743 (this issue was not raised on appeal)).

7.73
In the *RTE* case[1] the applicant maintained that the meeting of the Advisory Committee had been held less than 14 days after despatch of the convening notice, contrary to art 10(5) of Council Regulation 17/62. The CFI concluded that there was no evidence to substantiate the applicant's claim. It went on to say that in any event the fourteen day notice period constituted a purely internal procedural rule. It cited earlier ECJ jurisprudence[2] to the effect that a failure to comply with an internal procedural rule does not render the final decision unlawful unless it is sufficiently substantial and had a harmful effect on the legal and factual situation of the party alleging the irregularity (see para 27 of the judgment).

1 Case T-69/89 *Radio Telefis Eireann v EC Commission* [1991] 4 CMLR 586 (upheld on appeal in Joined Cases C-241/91P and C-242/92P *RTE and ITP v EC Commission* [1995] ECR I-743 (this issue was not raised on appeal)).
2 Case 51/69 *Farbenfabriken Bayer v EC Commission* [1972] ECR 745, paras 16–17; Case 41/69 *ACF Chemifarma NV v EC Commission* [1970] ECR 661, paras 48–52; Case 277/84 *Jänsch v EC Commission* [1987] ECR 4923, para 11.

7.74
A report of the outcome of the consultative proceedings is required to be annexed to the Commission's draft decision but it is not required to be made public[1]. The ECJ has held that a failure by the Commission to disclose the opinion to the undertaking against which proceedings are brought does not infringe that undertaking's right to be heard[2].

1 Council Regulation (EEC) 17/62, art 10(6).
2 Cases 100–103/80 *Musique Diffusion Française v EC Commission* [1983] ECR 1825, [1983] 3 CMLR 221.

Chapter 8 Decisions of the Commission

A Introduction

8.01
The purpose of this chapter is to describe the various types of decision which the Commission is empowered to take once it has completed the procedures which have been described in Chapter 7 of this Division. This chapter deals with both the provisional decisions which can be adopted by the Commission and with final decisions. The topic of fines and penalties is considered separately in Chapter 9.

8.02
Many proceedings commenced by the Commission under Articles 81 and 82 come to an end informally, without a formal decision ever being taken by the Commission. This important area of practice, and the legal considerations which relate to it, is also considered in this chapter.

8.03
The various types of Commission decision which will be dealt with in this chapter are as follows:

Provisional Decisions

(*a*) interim measures;
(*b*) provisional decision under art 15(6) of Regulation 17/62[1].

Final Decisions

(*a*) negative clearance under Article 81(1);
(*b*) individual exemption under Article 81(3);
(*c*) termination of infringement.

This chapter does not deal with the operation of the 'opposition procedure' laid down in a number of recent block exemptions[2]. That topic is discussed in Chapter 4.

1 Council Regulation (EEC) 17/62, OJ Sp Ed [1959–62] p 87.
2 The block exemptions relating to specialisation agreements (Commission Regulation (EEC) 417/85, OJ [1985] L 53/1: research and development agreements (Commission Regulation (EEC) 418/85, OJ [1985] L 53/5: franchise agreements (Commission Regulation (EEC) 4087/88, OJ [1988] L 359/46: and technology transfer licences (Commission Regulation (EC) 240/96, OJ [1996] L 31/2).

8.04
One other category of decision—namely decisions to require information under art 11 of Regulation 17/62 and to undertake on-the-spot investigations under art 14 of Regulation 17/62)—is essentially procedural in nature. Article 11 and article 14 decisions are considered separately in Chapter 6.

B Interim Measures

1 BACKGROUND

8.05
Nothing in Regulation 17/62 (the regulation which deals with the various types of decision which the Commission can take) expressly gives the Commission power to adopt so-called 'interim measures', ie an interim decision designed to maintain the status quo pending a final decision. Indeed, the text of art 3 of Regulation 17/62 (which deals with termination of infringements) appears to suggest that the only type of decision which the Commission can take is a final decision in the event that an infringement of Article 81 or Article 82 is established.

8.06
However, in its judgment in *Camera Care v EC Commission*[1], the ECJ decided that the Commission does have power under art 3(1) of Regulation 1762 to take interim measures if they are:

> '. . . indispensable for the effective exercise of [the Commission's] functions and, in particular, for ensuring the effectiveness of any decisions requiring undertakings to bring to an end infringements which it has found to exist'.

1 Case 792/79R [1980] ECR 119, [1980] 1 CMLR 334.

8.07
Consideration will now be given, in turn, to the circumstances in which interim measures can be ordered, the nature of the measures which can be ordered, the procedure adopted by the Commission and the right of appeal.

2 CIRCUMSTANCES IN WHICH INTERIM MEASURES CAN BE ORDERED

8.08
The principal criteria which have to be established in order for interim measures to be taken are:

(*a*) a prima facie case of infringement of Articles 81 and/or 82;
(*b*) urgency;
(*c*) a serious risk of irreparable harm to the party seeking them, or to the public interest.

Finally, the measures must be temporary and must not exceed what is necessary in the case in question.

(1) Prima Facie Case of Infringement

8.09
Although art 3(1) of Regulation 17/62[1] (from which the ECJ has derived the power for the Commission to grant interim measures) refers to the finding of an infringement of Article 81 or Article 82, it would defeat the purpose of interim measures if the Commission was required, as a pre-condition for adopting them, to have made a final determination on the issue of infringement. Accordingly, the requirement is that a prima facie case of infringement be shown before interim measures can be taken[2]. This requirement was immediately echoed by the Commission in a statement made to the parties involved in the *Camera Care* case prior to the oral hearing taking place.

1 Council Regulation (EEC) 17/62, OJ Sp Ed [1959–62] p 87.
2 Case 792/79R *Camera Care v EC Commission* [1980] ECR 119, [1980] 1 CMLR 334; Cases 228, 229/182R *Ford v EC Commission* [1982] ECR 3091, [1982] 3 CMLR 673.

8.10
In the *Peugeot* case[1], involving an interpretation of Regulation 123/85[2] (the motor vehicle block exemption), the Court of First Instance upheld the interim measures taken by the Commission, holding that the Commission is not required to establish definitively that an agreement between a manufacturer and its dealers does not fall within the ambit of the Regulation before adopting a decision ordering its interim suspension. In the *La Cinq* case[3], the CFI annulled a decision of the Commission, in which it had refused to grant interim relief to a complainant. The Commission rejected the application on the basis, inter alia, that there had been no 'clear and flagrant' breach of Article 81 or 82. The CFI ruled that the Commission had thereby applied a stricter test than the prima facie test laid down by the ECJ in the *Camera Care*[4] case.

1 Case T-23/90 *Peugeot v EC Commission* [1991] ECR II-653, [1993] 5 CMLR 540, CFI.
2 Commission Regulation (EEC) 123/85, OJ [1985] L 15/16.
3 Case T-44/90 *La Cinq SA v EC Commission* [1992] 4 CMLR 449.
4 Case 792/79R *Camera Care v EC Commission* [1980] ECR 119, [1980] 1 CMLR 334.

(2) Urgency

8.11
The second criterion laid down by the ECJ in the *Camera Care*[1] case was that the interim measures should only be taken in cases proved to be urgent 'in order to avoid a situation likely to cause serious and irreparable damage to the parties seeking their adoption, or which is intolerable for the public interest'[2]. The assessment of urgency is a question of degree but it should be noted that the Commission statement made following the court's judgment in the *Camera Care* case[3] states that 'unreasonable delay by a complainant seeking interim measures may be grounds for rejecting the application if this is otherwise appropriate'.

1 Case 792/79R *Camera Care v EC Commission* [1980] ECR 119, [1980] 1 CMLR 334.
2 See n 1 above, at para 19.
3 See n 1 above.

(3) Serious and Irreparable Damage/Intolerable for the Public Interest

8.12
The third criterion is stated in the alternative: either the person applying for interim measures to be adopted must show that, without such measures, it is likely to suffer serious and irreparable damage, or interim measures must be necessary to avoid a situation 'which is intolerable for the public interest'. The assessment of serious and irreparable damage is largely a question of fact and degree in any given case[1]. In the *La Cinq*[2] case, the CFI annulled a decision by the Commission not to grant interim measures. In applying the serious and irreparable harm test, the Commission had taken into account whether the harm in question could be remedied by *any* final decision (ie including a decision of a national court to award damages). The CFI held that the Commission should confine itself to looking at whether the harm in question could be remedied by a final decision of the Commission. As far as the alternative criterion of intolerability for the public interest is concerned, this probably needs to be assessed primarily in the context of the Community's competition policy: in *Camera Care*[3] the ECJ said that interim measures may be suitable:

> 'When the practice of certain undertakings in competition matters has the effect of injuring the interests of some Member States, causing damage to other undertakings, or of unacceptably jeopardising the Community's competition policy'.

1 See para **8.28** for examples of cases in which interim measures have been adopted. The Commission's decision in *Ecosystem SA v Peugeot SA* [1990] 4 CMLR 449 was upheld by the CFI in Case T-23/90 *Peugeot SA v EC Commission* [1991] ECR II-653, [1993] 5 CMLR 540, CFI. For a case in which interim measures were refused, see *Goldstein v General Medical Council* [1994] 4 CMLR 492.
2 Case T-44/90 *La Cinq SA v EC Commission* [1992] 4 CMLR 449.
3 Case 792/79R *Camera Care v EC Commission* [1980] ECR 119, [1980] 1 CMLR 334, at para 14.

8.13
Although this is again a question of degree, the word 'intolerable' suggests something major and it cannot be the case, for example, that any infringement of Article 81 or 82 would 'unacceptably jeopardise the Community's competition policy'.

3 OTHER RELEVANT FACTORS

8.14
In addition to satisfying itself that the criteria described at paras **8.08–8.13** are satisfied, the Commission must ensure that the legitimate interests of the undertaking against which the measures are to be taken are properly taken into account. In this context, the ECJ has mentioned[1] three aspects:

(*a*) the need for the measures in question to be only 'temporary and conservatory' in nature;

(*b*) the need to apply the essential procedural safeguards in Regulation 17/62 (in particular, the right to be heard pursuant to art 19 of Regulation 17/62);
(*c*) the requirement that the measures be in such a form that they can be made the subject of an appeal to the ECJ.

Each of these aspects is considered in turn below.

1 Case 792/79R *Camera Care v EC Commission* [1980] ECR 119, [1980] 1 CMLR 334.

(1) Nature of the Measures

8.15

The measures must be temporary and conservatory in nature[1]. This is somewhat analogous to the doctrine of proportionality[2], in that the requirement is essentially that the measures taken go no further than is necessary. In determining what is necessary, it is submitted that the Commission should primarily have regard to ensuring that the measures go sufficiently far (but no further) as to ensure that any final order which it may wish to make has a real effect (ie is not merely a pyrrhic victory): the cause of competition law would not be greatly advanced in a case where the Commission ultimately orders a dominant undertaking to resume supplies of products to a customer from whom it has been found to have unlawfully withheld them if, through failing to adopt interim measures, the continuing refusal to supply up to the date of the final Commission decision in fact puts the customer out of business. Indeed, in *BBI/Boosey and Hawkes*[3], the Commission stated that it intended to make an order which would, as far as possible, ensure that the applicants were not put out of business pending the final outcome of the administrative procedure by the very means of which the applicants complained.

1 Case 792/79R *Camera Care v EC Commission* [1980] ECR 119, [1980] 1 CMLR 334.
2 This doctrine is considered at para **11.49**.
3 Commission Decision (87/500/EEC) OJ [1987] L 286/36, [1988] 4 CMLR 67.

8.16

In *Ecosystem SA v Peugeot SA*[1] the measures adopted were designed to re-establish the freedom of Peugeot dealers to respond positively to the orders of Ecosystem. However, an annual ceiling was set, reflecting the volume of Peugeot vehicles for which Ecosystem had acted as agent in the twelve month period prior to the intervention by Peugeot. In this case the company argued before the CFI that the Commission had failed to keep the interim measures which it had ordered within the framework of the final decision which it could order under art 3 of Regulation 17/62. It cited the decision of the ECJ in *Ford*[2], in which the ECJ had laid down this principle. On the facts of the case, the CFI was satisfied that the Commission had not violated the principle laid down in the *Ford*[2] case and accordingly the company's claim was rejected.

1 [1990] 4 CMLR 449 at 461–2, upheld on appeal in Case T-23/90 *Peugeot v EC Commission* [1991] ECR II-653, [1993] 5 CMLR 540, CFI.
2 Cases 228, 229/82 *Ford v EC Commission* [1984] ECR 1129, [1984] 1 CMLR 649, paras 19–21.

(2) Commission Procedure

8.17
Nowithstanding the inherent urgency of any application for interim measures, the ECJ made it clear in the *Camera Care*[1] case that the Commission is under a duty to maintain the essential safeguards guaranteed by Regulation 17/62, particularly art 19 (right to be heard). This means, in particular, that:

(1) Commission proceedings must be formally initiated and, if this is at the request of a third party, that third party must file a complaint.
(2) A Statement of Objections[2] must be served and the undertaking against which proceedings are brought must be allowed to reply, if appropriate orally as well as in writing.
(3) Although the extent to which Commission Regulation 2842/98, art 14[3] applies is not entirely clear, it is probably the case that the time limit for reply given to the undertaking against which interim measures may be ordered should not be less than the two weeks referred to in art 14 of Regulation 2842/98; in its Twenty-third Report on Competition Policy (1993) the Commission said that it will only grant the minimum period of two weeks provided for in art 14, with no possibility of any extension[4].
(4) Liaison should take place with the competent authorities of the Member States pursuant to art 10 of Regulation 17/62 and according to Advocate General Slynn in the *Ford*[5] case the Advisory Committee on Restrictive Practices and Monopolies should be consulted by the Commission.
(5) In view of these various procedures (and particularly the basic right to be heard), it would seem that the Commission cannot adopt measures in an ex parte fashion[6].

1 Case 792/79R *Camera Care v EC Commission* [1980] ECR 119, [1980] 1 CMLR 334.
2 See para **7.12** ff.
3 See para **7.22**.
4 At para 207.
5 Cases 228, 229/82R *Ford v EC Commission* [1982] ECR 3091, [1982] 3 CMLR 673.
6 Compare applications for interlocutory injunctions under English law.

8.18
It is interesting to note the timetable of events (including an appeal to the Court of First Instance) in the 1990 decision in the *Ecosystem/Peugeot* case[1]. The chronology of principal events was as follows:

(1) *Mid-April 1989*: Complaint submitted by Ecosystem to Commission.
(2) *Late April 1989*: Commission request for information from Peugeot under Regulation 17/62, art 11.
(3) *May/June 1989*: Peugeot replies to request for information.
(4) *July 1989*: Commission sends Peugeot initial statement of position.
(5) *September 1989*: Commission requests, and Peugeot refuses, voluntary restoration of supplies to Ecosystem.
(6) *December 1989*: Two statements of objection sent to Peugeot, one dealing with the interim measures issue and one with the substantive issues.

(7) *January 1990*: Commission hearing with Peugeot.
(8) *March 1990*: Interim measures decision.
(9) *April 1990*: Proceedings brought by Peugeot before CFI.
(10) *May 1990*: Hearings before CFI.
(11) *May 1990*: Order of the President of the CFI.

1 *Ecosystem SA v Peugeot SA* [1990] 4 CMLR 449; upheld on appeal in Case T-23/90 *Peugeot v EC Commission* [1991] ECR II-653, [1993] 5 CMLR 540, CFI.

8.19

It can be seen from the chronology set out at para **8.18** that it took nearly a year from the date of Ecosystem's original complaint before the Commission adopted its interim measures decision. This is in fact an unusually long period. For example, it appears that in *ECS/AKZO*[1] the period between the request for interim measures and the decision to grant them was about two months. Even this is, however, a longer period than one would normally expect it to take to obtain interim relief in an English court.

1 Commission Decision (83/462/EEC) OJ [1983] L 252/13, [1983] 3 CMLR 694.

(3) The Commission's Decision and its Appeal to the Court of First Instance

8.20

According to the ECJ in the *Camera Care*[1] case, the Commission's decision must be in such a form as to be capable of appeal to the ECJ (now the CFI). This applies to both the grant and the refusal of interim measures[2]. Although no substantive fine can be imposed on the undertaking concerned at the interim measures stage pursuant to Regulation 17/62, art 15[3] (because no final determination as to the infringement or otherwise of Article 81 or 82 is at that stage made), it seems that the Commission can impose a periodic penalty payment under art 16(1)(a) of Regulation 17/62 as a means of compelling compliance with the interim measures decision (as it did, for example, in *BBI/Boosey and Hawkes*[4] and *Ecosystem*[5]).

1 Case 792/79R *Camera Care v EC Commission* [1980] ECR 119, [1980] 1 CMLR 334.
2 For a successful challenge to a refusal to grant interim measures, see Case T-44/90 *La Cinq SA v EC Commission* [1992] 4 CMLR 449.
3 Council Regulation (EEC) 17/62, OJ Sp Ed [1959–62] p 87.
4 Commission Decision (87/500/EEC) OJ [1987] L 286/36, [1988] 4 CMLR 67.
5 *Ecosystem SA v Peugeot SA* [1990] 4 CMLR 449.

8.21

The Court is prepared in appropriate cases to order interim suspension (under Article 243 of the EC Treaty) of a Commission decision which is itself an interim measures decision[1]. A recent case in which it refused to do so is *Peugeot*[2].

1 Cases 228, 229/82R *Ford v EC Commission* [1982] ECR 3091, [1982] 3 CMLR 673. As to Article 243 generally, see para **10.57** ff.
2 Case T-23/90R *Peugeot v EC Commission* [1990] 4 CMLR 674. See too Cases T-24/92R and T-28/92R *Langnese–Iglo GmbH and Schöller Lebensmittel GmbH & Co KG v EC Commission* OJ [1992] C 199/8, 10, in which the CFI ordered partial suspension of an interim measures decision.

4 ADDITIONAL CONSIDERATIONS

8.22
The Commission's statement issued following the ECJ's judgment in the *Camera Care* case[1] refers to the following additional considerations:

(1) It expressly states that complainants should consider whether a similar remedy is available from a national court before applying to the Commission for interim measures—particularly if the national procedures are cheaper or the likely order more easily policed.
(2) The Commission normally acts primarily on the evidence put before it by the parties and does not consider itself bound to investigate the facts fully (for example, by using its powers under arts 11 or 14 of Regulation 17/62[2]) before deciding whether to adopt interim measures.
(3) The Commission's decision to grant or refuse interim measures does not affect in any way its later definitive decision as to whether an infringement of the EC Treaty has occurred.

1 Case 792/79R *Camera Care v EC Commission* [1980] ECR 119, [1980] 1 CMLR 334.
2 See Chapter 6.

5 DURATION

8.23
In its statement referred to at para **8.22**, the Commission indicated that, in any given case, it may either set a particular time limit by which the matter should be reviewed again, or may order interim measures to remain in force until a final decision by the Commission[1]. It expressly acknowledged that any party concerned can ask for the interim measures to be reviewed in the event of a change of circumstances. In *BBI/Boosey and Hawkes*[2] the interim measures were expressly limited in time.

1 It adopted the latter course in *Ecosystem SA v Peugeot SA* [1990] 4 CMLR 449; upheld on appeal in Case T-23/90 *Peugeot v EC Commission* [1991] ECR II-653, [1993] 5 CMLR 540, CFI.
2 Commission Decision (87/500/EEC) OJ [1987] L 286/36, [1988] 4 CMLR 67.

6 ROLE OF THE COMPLAINANT

(1) General

8.24
More often than not the Commission will be considering whether to adopt interim measures against the background of a complaint by a third party. In such circumstances, the Commission's statement on interim measures[1] makes it clear that an application for interim measures will not be accepted if it is not accompanied or preceded by a formal complaint under art 3 of Regulation 17/62[2], unless the Commission has already opened formal proceedings. In addition, unreasonable delay by a complainant in seeking interim measures may provide grounds for rejecting the application. In

practice, many complaints are accompanied by a request for interim measures; if they are to have any real prospect of success they should address all the factors referred to at paras **8.08–8.13** (as well as the three criteria described at para **8.22**).

1 Referred to in para **8.22**.
2 See Chapter 5.

8.25
There seems to be no reason in principle why the Commission should not adopt interim measures at its own instigation (ie without a complaint being filed with it). Certainly, this is the view of the Commission (as expressed in its statement[1] previously referred to) and this does seem inherent in the fact that the third criterion which the Commission must consider in deciding whether to adopt interim measures is, in the alternative, the question whether there is serious and irreparable damage to a particular undertaking or, of relevance in this context, the threat of a situation which is intolerable for the public interest[2].

1 See para **8.22**.
2 See para **8.12**.

(2) Cross-Undertaking by the Complainant

8.26
In the Commission's statement[1] on interim measures, it indicated that it would in appropriate cases:

> 'order the party requesting interim measures to give a suitable bond or guarantee to indemnify the party against which interim measures are ordered against any loss resulting from the interim measures if the latter party is finally found not to have infringed the Treaty'.

This possibility was not expressly referred to in the *Camera Care*[2] case but it was mentioned by the ECJ in a similar context in a case under the ECSC Treaty[3]. In principle, the Commission would appear correct in assuming that there is no difference in this context between the EC Treaty and the ECSC Treaty.

1 See para **8.22**.
2 Case 792/79R *Camera Care v EC Commission* [1980] ECR 119, [1980] 1 CMLR 334.
3 Cases 109, 114/75 *National Carbonising v EC Commission* [1977] ECR 381.

8.27
There may be cases in which, as a condition of granting interim measures at the request of a complainant, the Commission requires undertakings from the complainant itself. For example, in *BBI/Boosey and Hawkes*[1] the Commission ordered the resumption of supplies of musical instruments. However, the complainants undertook to deal fairly with B&H instruments and in particular not publicly to denigrate them or use them as a bait or loss-leader. The Commission expressly reserved the right to amend or cancel the interim measures if this undertaking was broken.

1 Commission Decision (87/500/EEC) OJ [1987] L 286/36, [1988] 4 CMLR 67.

7 CASES IN WHICH INTERIM MEASURES HAVE BEEN ADOPTED

8.28
There have so far been relatively few cases in which the Commission has adopted interim measures. The principal cases to date are: *Ford*[1], *ECS/AKZO*[2], *BBI/Boosey and Hawkes*[3], *Ecosystem*[4], *Sealink*[5], *Langnese–Iglo/ Scholler–Mars*[6] and *Morlaix (Port of Roscoff)*[7]. In addition, there are a number of cases in which the Commission has been willing to accept undertakings in lieu of ordering interim measures[8]. In the *La Cinq* case[9] the CFI annulled the Commission's refusal to grant interim relief, for the reasons described in paras **8.10** and **8.12**. In *Sea Containers/Stena Sealink*[10] the Commission concluded that there was a prima facie case for ordering interim measures but decided not to do so in circumstances where the undertaking against which the complaint had been made an offer to the complainant which the Commission considered remedied the situation.

1 Commission Decision (82/628/EEC) *Ford Werke* OJ [1982] L 256/20, [1982] 3 CMLR 267 (annulled on appeal in Cases 228, 229/82 *Ford of Europe Inc and Ford Werke AG v EC Commission* [1984] ECR 1129, [1984] 1 CMLR 649).
2 Commission Decision (83/462/EEC) OJ [1983] L 252/13, [1983] 3 CMLR 694.
3 Commission Decision (87/500/EEC) OJ [1987] L 286/36, [1988] 4 CMLR 67.
4 [1990] 4 CMLR 449; upheld on appeal by the Court of First Instance in Case T-23/90 *Peugeot v EC Commission* [1991] ECR II-653.
5 EC Commission Press Release IP(92) 478, 11 June 1992.
6 'Europe' 3 April 1992, partially upheld on appeal in Cases T-24/92R and T-28/92R *Langnese–Iglo GmbH and Schöller Lebensmittel GmbH & Co KG v EC Commission* OJ [1992] C 199/8, 10.
7 Reported as *Irish Continental Group v CCI Morlaix* [1995] 5 CMLR 177.
8 Eg *Hilti* [1985] 3 CMLR 619 (undertaking subsequently broken, a factor taken into account in the Commission's later decision imposing a heavy fine: Commission Decision (88/138/ EEC) *Eurofix-Bauco v Hilti* OJ [1988] L 65/19, [1988] 4 CMLR 677); *Napier Brown v British Sugar* [1986] 3 CMLR 594; *Irish Distillers Group v GC & C Brands Ltd* [1988] 4 CMLR 840.
9 Case T-44/90 *La Cinq SA v EC Commission* [1992] 4 CMLR 449.
10 Commission Decision (94/19/EC) OJ [1994] L 15/8.

C Provisional Decisions under Article 15(6) of Regulation 17/62

8.29
The protection from fines for the infringement of Article 81 which is conferred by notification of an agreement to the Commission (as provided for in art 15(5) of Regulation 17/62) is considered in Chapter 4[1]. Article 15(6) provides that this immunity does not apply:

> 'where the Commission has informed the undertakings concerned that after preliminary examination it is of the opinion that Article 85(1) [now Article 81(1)] of the Treaty applies and that application of Article 85(3) [now Article 81(3)] is not justified'.

It is rare for this power to be used[2]. This is probably due in large part to the fact that an undertaking notifying an agreement to the Commission would be wise to exclude from that agreement any provision which is so clearly unlikely to benefit from Article 81(3) exemption as to merit the application of this procedure. In *Vichy*[3] the CFI rejected the applicant's argument that the article 15(6) decision was discriminatory (as between Vichy and its competitors), stating that it merely put the company back in the position it would have been in had it failed to notify its arrangements and did not put it at a disadvantage in relation to its competitors.

1 At para **4.05**.

2 Six cases in which it has been used are: Case 8–11/66 *Cimenteries v EC Commission* [1967] ECR 75, [1967] CMLR 77; Commission Decision (75/297/EEC) *Sirdar/Phildar* OJ [1975] L 125/27, [1975] 1 CMLR D93; Commission Decision (75/570/EEC) *Bronbemaling and Heidemaatschappij* OJ [1975] L 249/27, [1975] 2 CMLR D67; Commission Decision (78/571/EEC) *SNPE/LEL* OJ [1978] L 191/41, [1978] 2 CMLR 758; Commission Decision (91/153/EEC) *Vichy* OJ [1991] L 75/57 (upheld on appeal in Case T-19/91 *Société d'Hygiène Dermatologique de Vichy v EC Commission* [1992] ECR II-415 and Commission Decision (94/272/EC) *SCK/FNK* OJ [1994] L 117/30. A Statement of Objections prior to an article 15(6) decision was issued in Commission Decision (85/615/EEC) *Protection and Indemnity Clubs Agreement* OJ [1985] L 376/2, [1989] 4 CMLR 178 but the matter was not pursued. In addition, it appears from the Commission's decision in Commission Decision (89/113/EEC) *Decca Navigator System* OJ [1989] L 43/27 that an article 15(6) decision was taken but not pursued.

3 Case T-19/91 *Société d'Hygiene dermatologique de Vichy v EC Commission* [1992] ECR II-415.

1 STATUS OF ARTICLE 15(6) DECISIONS

8.30

The ECJ has made it clear[1] that an opinion reached by the Commission pursuant to art 15(6) amounts to a decision. As such, it falls within Article 189 of the EC Treaty and therefore must be properly reasoned. As a decision, it is an act which is subject to judicial review under Article 173 of the EC Treaty[2]. In a recent case[3], proceedings were commenced against the Commission on the ground that it had infringed Article 175 of the Treaty[4] for failing to apply art 15(6) against the parties to an agreement to which the applicant was not a party.

1 Case 8–11/66 *Cimenteries v EEC Commission* [1967] ECR 75, [1967] CMLR 77.

2 As to Article 173 generally, see para **10.09** ff.

3 Case T-3/90 *Prodifarma v EC Commission* OJ [1991] ECR II-1.

4 Ie alleged failure to act: as to Article 175 generally, see para **10.48** ff.

2 PROCEDURE TO BE FOLLOWED BY THE COMMISSION

8.31

An article 15(6) decision falls within the scope of art 19(1) of Regulation 17/62[1] and accordingly the undertaking(s) concerned must be given the opportunity of being heard on the matters to which the Commission has taken objection. It is quite clear that the right can be exercised in writing; it is less clear whether there is also a right to an oral hearing. There would seem to be no reason in principle why Regulation 99/63[2] (which sets out certain procedures governing the hearings provided for in art 19 of Regulation 17/62) should not apply to article 15(6) decisions, in which case the undertaking against which it is proposed to take an article 15(6) decision should have a right to an oral hearing[3]. Indeed, the Commission decisions in *Sirdar/Phildar*[4], *Bronbemaling*[5] and *SNPE/LEL*[6] all expressly refer not only to art 19(1) of Regulation 17/62 but also Regulation 99/63. Equally, however, the undertakings do not appear to have had oral hearings in any of those cases and on the face of it that could well amount to a procedural irregularity providing scope for challenge of the decision before the ECJ.

1 Council Regulation (EEC) 17/62, OJ Sp Ed [1959–62] p 87.
2 Commission Regulation (EC) 2842/98, OJ [1998] L 354/18, which superseded Commission Regulation (EEC) 99/63, OJ Sp Ed [1963–64] p 47.
3 Commission Regulation (EEC) 99/63, art 7.
4 Commission Decision (75/297/EEC) OJ [1975] L 125/27, [1975] 1 CMLR D 93.
5 Commission Decision (75/570/EEC) OJ [1975] L 249/27, [1975] 2 CMLR D 67.
6 Commission Decision (78/571/EEC) OJ [1978] L 191/41, [1978] 2 CMLR 758.

D Final Decisions

1 NEGATIVE CLEARANCE

8.32
The first type of final decision envisaged by Regulation 17/62 is negative clearance: art 2 of Regulation 17/62 provides that:

> 'upon application by the undertakings or associations of undertakings concerned, the Commission may certify that, on the basis of the facts in its possession, there are no grounds under Article 85(1) [now Article 81(1)] or Article 86 [now Article 82] of the Treaty for action on its part in respect of an agreement, a decision or practice'.

Although a decision granting negative clearance amounts to a 'clean bill of health' as far as the Commission is concerned, there are a number of qualifications which should be noted:

(1) As far as the application for negative clearance itself is concerned, this does not (as has been explained elsewhere in this Division[1]) of itself confer immunity from fines under Article 81(1)[2]. This contrasts with the position in relation to a notification under Article 81(1), which *does* (subject to art 15(6)[3]) confer such immunity.
(2) The Commission can review a decision to grant negative clearance at a later date (for example, if there is a change of circumstances or if the Commission becomes aware of facts which had not been disclosed to it).
(3) A decision granting negative clearance does not appear, strictly speaking, to be binding on a national court[4], although it is likely to be regarded as being of persuasive value.
(4) A decision granting negative clearance does not stop a national court or tribunal from applying national competition law to the agreement.

1 See para **4.05**.
2 Commission Decision (85/79/EEC) *Deere* OJ [1985] L 35/58, [1985] 2 CMLR 554.
3 See para **8.29** ff.
4 Opinion of Advocate General Reischl in Case 37/79 *Marty v Lauder* [1980] ECR 2481 at 2507.

8.33
A number of general procedural aspects relating to decisions adopted by the Commission (be they negative clearance, the grant of an individual exemption or the termination of an infringement) are described at para **8.65**. Two particular points should, however, be noted in the context of negative clearance. Firstly, a decision granting negative clearance must state the reasons on which it is based[1]. Secondly, before the Commission grants negative clearance it is required (as is also the case before it grants an individual exemption pursuant to Article 81(3)) to publish a summary of the relevant application for negative clearance and to invite all interested third parties to submit their observations within a period of not less than one month[2]. In doing so, the Commission must have regard to the legitimate interest of undertakings in the protection of their business secrets[3].

1 EC Treaty, Article 190.
2 Council Regulation (EEC) 17/62, art 19(3), OJ Sp Ed [1959–62] p 87.
3 See para **11.07** ff.

E Individual Exemption under Article 81(3)

1 GENERAL

8.34
The second possible decision by the Commission is a decision granting individual exemption under Article 81(3). In order for an agreement to qualify for individual exemption it must (subject to certain exceptions[1]) have previously been notified[2] to the Commission. Successful challenge under Article 230[3] to the grant of an Article 81(3) exemption is relatively rare. The Commission's exemption decision in the *Metropole*[5] case was annulled on the ground that the Commission erred in law in its interpretation of Article 81(3).

1 See para **4.11** ff.
2 See Chapter 4.
3 See para **10.09**.
4 Joined Cases T-528/93, 542, 543, 546/93 *Métropole v EC Commission* [1996] ECR II-649.

(1) Date from which Exemption Runs

8.35
A decision of the Commission granting individual exemption pursuant to Article 81(3) must state the date from which the decision takes effect[1]. The basic position is that the specified date cannot be earlier than the date of notification[1]. This is, however, subject to the following exceptions:

(1) *Agreements falling within article 4(2) of Regulation 17/62*[2]: In respect of a relatively narrow class of agreements, to which art 4(2) applies, the Commission may (although it is not obliged to do so) back date the effective date of an individual exemption granted in respect of such an agreement to a date earlier than the date of notification[3].
(2) *'Old' Agreements*[4]: In respect of agreements which were in existence on 13 March 1962, the date of entry into force of Regulation 17/62 (so-called 'old' agreements), the exemption can be back-dated, provided that the agreement in question was notified before 1 November 1962[5] unless they were agreements of the type falling within art 4(2) of Regulation 17/62 (see (1) above).
(3) *Accession Agreements*[6]: The position of accession agreements is considered elsewhere in this Division. In essence, any exemption granted in relation to an accession agreement can be back-dated to the relevant accession date, provided that it was notified to the Commission within six months of accession. In relation to accession agreements falling within art 4(2), the Commission has jurisdiction to grant an exemption under Article 81(3), effective from the relevant date of accession, even if the agreement has not been notified[7].
(4) *Article 7 of Regulation 17/62*: In relation to old agreements and accession agreements which were notified within the stipulated time limits[8], if they did not satisfy the requirements of Article 81(3) when they were notified but the undertakings concerned have subsequently ceased to give effect to them, or have modified them in such a way that they no longer fall within the prohibition contained in Article 81(1) (or satisfy the requirements of Article 81(3)), the prohibition contained in Article 81(1) is only to apply for a period fixed by the Commission. This power is intended to give recognition to the principle of legal certainty[9]. Article 7 was applied in *Zanussi*[10] (in the context of negative clearance) and the *Society of Motor Manufacturers and Traders Ltd*[11] case (in the context of an exemption under Article 81(3)).

1 Council Regulation (EEC) 17/62, art 6(1), OJ Sp Ed [1959–62] p 87.
2 See para **4.11** ff.
3 See n 1 above, art 6(2).
4 See para **4.24**.
5 See n 1 above, art 6(2).
6 See paras **4.26–4.28**.
7 See n 1 above, arts 6(2) and 25.
8 See paras **4.26–4.28**.
9 Case 48/72 *Brasserie de Haecht v Wilkin-Janssen* [1973] ECR 77, [1973] CMLR 287.
10 Commission Decision (78/922/EEC) OJ [1978] L 322/26, [1979] 1 CMLR 81.
11 Commission Decision (83/666/EEC) OJ [1983] L 376/1, [1984] 1 CMLR 611.

8.36

It is not always the case that the Commission backdates an exemption to the date of notification. For example, in *Computerland*[1] the company's standard franchise agreement as first notified did not qualify for exemption. It was subsequently amended to take account of Commission objections and the Commission accordingly backdated the exemption to the date on which the franchisees were informed of the amended terms of the agreement.

1 Commission Decision (87/407/EEC) OJ [1987] L 222/12, [1989] 4 CMLR 259. See also Commission Decision (90/535/EEC) *Cekacan* OJ [1990] L 299/64; Commission Decision (91/128/EEC) *Sippa* OJ [1991] L 60/19 and Commission Decision (91/562/EEC) *Eirpage* OJ [1991] L 306/22.

(2) Duration and Revocation

8.37

An individual exemption granted pursuant to Article 81(3) must be issued for a specified period[1]. There is no standard period which the Commission tends to apply and each case will necessarily depend very much on its own facts. However, in principle it would be reasonable to expect the Commission to make the duration of the exemption sufficiently long to enable the parties to achieve the aims of the agreement. Generally, periods of exemption have tended to be between five and ten years[2]. However, on occasion they have run for as long as 15 years[3], and occasionally 20[4]. The duration of an exemption is frequently of considerable concern to the parties involved, particularly if the agreements require them to invest a large amount of capital expenditure (for example, in relation to a joint venture). It should be noted that it is possible to apply for an exemption to be renewed and this has occurred in a number of cases[5]. In *Yves Saint Laurent Parfums*[6] the Commission expressly stated in its decision that it was granting an exemption for only six years in order to enable it to re-examine the effects of the company's distribution system on competition at the end of a 'relatively short period'.

1 Council Regulation (EEC) 17/62, art 8(1).
2 Eg Commission Decision (90/46/EEC) *Alcatel Espace/ANT Nachrichtentechnik* OJ [1990] L 32/19, [1991] 4 CMLR 208 (ten and a half years from date of notification); Commission Decision (91/128/EEC) *Sippa* OJ [1991] L 60/19 (ten years from date agreement brought into line with Commission objections).
3 Commission Decision (83/668/EEC) *VW/MAN* OJ [1983] L 376/11, [1984] 1 CMLR 621; Commission Decision (86/405/EEC) *Optical Fibres* OJ [1986] L 236/30; Commission Decision (89/96/EEC) *EMO* OJ [1989] L 37/11 (a case involving the renewal of an existing exemption); Commission Decision (89/95/EEC) *Uniform Eurocheques* OJ [1989] L 36/16; Commission Decision (88/541/EEC) *BBC Brown Boveri* OJ [1988] L 301/68, [1989] 4 CMLR 610; Commission Decision (91/329/EEC) *Scottish Nuclear, Nuclear Energy Agreement* OJ [1991] L 178/31.
4 As in Commission Decision (88/563/EEC) *Delta Chemie/DDD* OJ [1988] L 309/34, [1989] 4 CMLR 535.
5 See para **8.45** ff.
6 Commission Decision (92/33/EEC) OJ [1992] L 12/24.

8.38

Regulation 17/62, art 8(3) gives the Commission power to revoke or amend an Article 81(3) exemption where:

(*a*) there has been a change in any of the facts which were basic to the making of the decision;
(*b*) the parties commit a breach of any obligation attached to the decision;
(*c*) the decision is based on incorrect information or was induced by deceit;
(*d*) the parties abuse the exemption from the provisions of Article 81(1) of the Treaty granted to them by the decision.

In the last three of these four situations, the Commission's decision can be revoked with retroactive effect. The conditions in art 8(3) do not require to be satisfied where the Commission decides to withdraw the benefit of block exemption (as opposed to an individual exemption) since there is, in such cases, no formal decision to revoke[1].

1 Case T-7/93 *Langnese-Iglo GmbH v EC Commission*, [1995] ECR II-1533, upheld on appeal in Case 279/95P *Langnese-Iglo GmbH v EC Commission* [1998] ECR I-5609.

8.39
There is as yet no reported Commission decision revoking an exemption pursuant to art 8(3) of Regulation 17/62 and the Commission is only likely to exercise its powers in a particularly serious case. As far as the first ground is concerned, it should be noted that it is not just any change in the factual situation which triggers the Commission's power but only a change in any of the facts which were 'basic' to the original decision. Equally, it would appear from the plain wording of this ground that it is not limited to circumstances within the control of one or more of the parties: for example, there may be relevant changes in the structure of the market during the term of the exemption which serve to increase the anti-competitive effect of the agreement in question. However, at the end of the day it is submitted that it would not be in the interests of legal certainty for the Commission to invoke this 'change of circumstance' ground except in extreme cases and the lack of any decisions so far under art 8(3) may suggest that the Commission also takes this view.

8.40
The revocation or amendment of an Article 81(3) exemption is itself a decision of the Commission and, as such, falls within art 19(1) of Regulation 17/62. Accordingly, before taking the decision the Commission must give the undertakings concerned the opportunity of being heard on the matters to which the Commission has taken objection[1]. In addition, the Advisory Committee on Restrictive Practices and Monopolies must also be consulted, pursuant to art 10(3) of Regulation 17/62. Finally, any such decision must be published[2] and can be the subject of an appeal under Article 230 of the EC Treaty. In *Bayer/BP*[3] the Commission decided to relax a condition attached to the original Article 81(3) exemption decision[4].

1 Council Regulation (EEC) 17/62, art 19(1).
2 Council Regulation (EEC) 17/62, art 21(1).
3 Commission Decision (94/384/EC) OJ [1994] L 174/34.
4 Commission Decision (88/330/EEC) OJ [1988] L 150/35, [1989] 4 CMLR 24.

(3) Conditions Attached to Exemption

8.41
A decision granting an individual exemption under Article 81(3) can have 'conditions and obligations' attached to it[1]. This power is frequently exercised by the Commission. A common type of requirement is one whereby

the parties must submit periodic reports regarding the operation of the agreement[2]. A variety of other types of requirement have been imposed by the Commission in particular cases (see para **8.44**).

1 Council Regulation (EEC) 17/62, art 8(1), OJ Sp Ed [1959–62] p 87.
2 For recent examples, see Commission Decision (90/46/EEC) *Alcatel Espace/ANT Nachrichtentechnik* OJ [1990] L 32/19, [1991] 4 CMLR 208; Commission Decision (88/88/ EEC) *Olivetti/Canon* OJ [1988] L 52/51; Commission Decision (91/38/EEC) *KSB/Goulds/ Lowara/ITT* OJ [1991] L 19/25.

8.42
A distinction must be drawn between the reference to 'conditions' and the reference to 'obligations' in art 8(1) of Regulation 17/62. If a conditional exemption is granted and the parties fail to comply with the condition, the benefit of the exemption is automatically lost, with the result that the restrictions contained in the agreement are rendered null and void (pursuant to Article 81(2) of the EC Treaty). On the other hand, if an exemption is made subject to one or more obligations and the parties break those obligations the benefit of the exemption is not automatically lost. Rather, the Commission has power to impose fines on the parties concerned for breach of the obligation[1] or the Commission can revoke or amend the exemption decision as a result of the breach of obligation[2].

1 Council Regulation (EEC) 17/62, art 15(2)(b).
2 Council Regulation (EEC) 17/62, art 8(3)(b).

8.43
As far as the type of condition or obligation which may be imposed is concerned, the ECJ has not delivered a clear statement. However, in *Transocean Marine Paint Association v EC Commission*[1] the Advocate General suggested that there were two limitations on the Commission's powers. Firstly, the condition/obligation should be 'relevant to competition' in the Common Market and secondly, the requirement should not be oppressive, ie disproportionate to the value which the Commission could expect to obtain from it.

1 Case 17/74 [1974] ECR 1063, [1974] 2 CMLR 459.

8.44
Examples of conditions and obligations which have been imposed by the Commission when granting individual exemptions under Article 81(3) include:

(*a*) the requirement to be informed of any arbitration award[1];
(*b*) the obligation to notify the Commission of any amendments to the agreement[2];
(*c*) reporting obligations designed to inform the Commission of any new shareholding links or interlocking directorships between any of the undertakings concerned[3];
(*d*) the obligation to notify the Commission of any refusal to allow an undertaking to participate in, for example, the activities of a trade association[4];

(*e*) express reservation of the right to ask the parties to supply any information which the Commission deems necessary to check that competition is not being restricted more than the decision allows[5];

(*f*) a condition that the parties to a joint venture not exchange information concerning prices, marketing plans or any other competitive information[6];

(*g*) the obligation to make available to the Commission at a specified time, during the term of the exemption, information to enable the Commission to assess developments in the relevant market[7].

The Commission's decision[8] regarding the joint venture between France Telecom and Deutsche Telekom contained a detailed set of conditions.

1 Eg Commission Decision (77/781/EEC) *GEC-Weir* OJ [1977] L 327/26, [1978] 1 CMLR D42.
2 Eg Commission Decision (83/668/EEC) *VW/MAN* OJ [1983] L 376/11, [1984] 1 CMLR 621; Commission Decision (88/635/EEC) *Transocean Marine Paint Association (No 5)* OJ [1988] L 351/40, [1989] 4 CMLR 621; Commission Decision (90/46/EEC) *Alcatel Espace/ANT Nachrichtentechnik* OJ [1990] L 32/19, [1991] 4 CMLR 208; Commission Decision (91/562/ EEC) *Eirpage* OJ [1991] L 306/22.
3 As in Commission Decision (77/543/EEC) *De Laval/Stork* OJ [1977] L 215/11, [1977] 2 CMLR D69; *Transocean Marine Paint Association*, see n 2 above.
4 Eg Commission Decision (86/499/EEC) *VIFKA* OJ [1986] L 291/46; Commission Decision (89/96/EEC) *EMO* OJ [1989] L 37/11; Commission Decision (89/408/EEC) *National Sulphuric Acid Association* OJ [1989] L 190/22.
5 As in Commission Decision (87/3/EEC) *ENI/Montedison* OJ [1987] L 5/13, [1988] 4 CMLR 444.
6 As in Commission Decision (86/405/EEC) *Optical Fibres* OJ [1986] L 236/30; see also Commission Decision (93/49/EEC) *Ford/Volkswagen* OJ [1993] L 20/14.
7 Commission Decision (91/562/EEC) *Eirpage* OJ [1991] L 306/22.
8 Commission Decision (96/546/EC) *Atlas* OJ [1996] L 239/23. See also Commission Decision (97/780/EC) *Unisource* OJ [1997] L 318/1.

(4) Renewal of Exemption

8.45

Under art 8(2) of Regulation 17/62 a decision granting an individual exemption under Article 81(3) may, on application, be renewed if the requirements of Article 81(3) continue to be satisfied. This has occurred in a number of cases[1]. Alternatively, upon expiry of an existing exemption, the Commission might decide to take no further action pursuant to Articles 81 and 82 (by effectively issuing a form of comfort letter[2]). This is what happened in *Enichem/ICI (EVC)*[3]. In that case, the Commission had originally adopted a decision[4] granting an exemption for a period of five years. in view of the impending expiry of the exemption in March 1991 the parties approached the Commission with a view to putting their jointly owned company, EVC, on a permanent basis. In the light of the information provided, the Commission published an article 19(3) notice[5], indicating that it proposed to inform the parties that there appeared to be no need for further action on its part pursuant to Article 81 or 82.

1 Recent examples include Commission Decision (89/408/EEC) *National Sulphuric Acid Association* OJ [1989] L 190/22; Commission Decision (89/96/EEC) *EMO* OJ [1989] L 37/11 (where the extension, in relation to a trade exhibition's rules, was for 15 years);

Commission Decision (88/635/EEC) *Transocean Marine Paint Association (No 5)* OJ [1988] L 351/40, [1989] 4 CMLR 621.
2 As to comfort letters generally, see para **8.72** ff.
3 [1991] 4 CMLR 327.
4 Commission Decision (88/87/EEC) *Enichem/ICI* OJ [1988] L 50/18, [1989] 4 CMLR 54.
5 See n 3 above.

8.46
There is no special form which needs to be filled in when the parties to an exempted agreement apply for the exemption to be renewed. In particular, the ECJ has held that it is not necessary to use Form A/B, even if minor amendments have been made to the agreement in the intervening period[1]. When deciding whether to renew an exemption the Commission has to satisfy itself that the four conditions laid down in Article 81(3)[2] continue to be satisfied and therefore an undertaking applying for a renewal should set out in its application the reasons why it believes this to be the case. In most cases, the applicant is likely to place continued reliance on the arguments which it used when obtaining the original exemption and, of course, on the Commission's own reasoning for granting the original exemption (as set out in the exemption decision). However, if market conditions have changed during the period of the exemption, thereby rendering the agreement even less potentially restrictive, these factors should be set out in the application. For example, a number of new entrants may have come on to the market or there may be a new range of closely substitutable products for the products which are the subject matter of the exemption.

1 Case 75/84 *Metro-SB-Grossmärkte GmbH v EC Commission* [1986] ECR 3021, [1987] 1 CMLR 118.
2 See *Butterworths Competition Law*, Division I.

8.47
To all intents and purposes, the renewal of an exemption is in itself the grant of an exemption and accordingly the same procedural requirements apply as in the case of the original exemption. That is to say, the undertakings concerned have the right to be heard before the decision is taken[1]; the Commission may hear other natural or legal persons (and indeed must hear them if they are able to show a sufficient interest[2]); before taking the decision the Commission must publish a summary of the relevant application and invite interested third parties to submit their observations[3]; the Advisory Committee on Restrictive Practices and Monopolies must be consulted; and finally, the decision itself must be published pursuant to art 21(1) of Regulation 17/62.

1 Council Regulation (EEC) 17/62, art 19(1), OJ Sp Ed [1959–62] p 87.
2 See n 1 above, art 19(2).
3 See n 1 above, art 19(3).

2 SHORT-FORM EXEMPTION

8.48
Faced with the large number of pending applications in the early 1980s (almost 4,000 in 1981[1]), the Commission announced in its Eleventh Report

on Competition Policy (1981)[2] the intention to introduce 'simplified' (ie short-form) exemption decisions, in order to solve in particular 'the problem of the numerous cases having common features'. The first example of a case handled in this way is *BP/Kellogg*[3], a decision only three pages in length. However, no further short-form exemptions have been granted.

1 11th Report on Competition Policy (1981), para 69.
2 Paragraph 15.
3 Commission Decision (85/560/EEC) OJ [1985] L 369/6, [1986] 2 CMLR 619.

F Termination of Infringements

1 GENERAL

8.49
Article 3(1) of Regulation 17/62[1] provides that:

> 'where the Commission, upon application or upon its own initiative, finds that there is infringement of Article 85 [now Article 81] or Article 86 [now Article 82] of the Treaty, it may by decision require the undertakings or associations of undertakings concerned to bring such infringement to an end'.

Such a decision can also impose a fine and/or a periodic penalty payment[2].

1 Council Regulation (EEC) 17/62, OJ [1959–62] p 87.
2 See Chapter 9.

8.50
As has already been noted[1], in its decision finding an infringement the Commission must deal only with those objections which have been raised against the undertakings concerned in the Statement of Objections[2]. This is an important procedural protection. If this requirement has not been satisfied, it may provide grounds for challenging all or part of the decision before the ECJ (initially the Court of First Instance) under Article 230 of the EC Treaty.

1 See para **7.13**.
2 Commission Regulation (EEC) 99/63, art 4, OJ Sp Ed [1963–64] p 47.

8.51
A decision finding that an infringement of Articles 81 and/or 82 has been committed is typically structured as follows: the first part of the decision sets out the relevant facts, including details of the parties and a description of the market and the agreements or conduct in question; the second part of the decision provides the Commission's legal assessment, considering, in turn, the different limbs of Articles 81(1), 81(3) and/or 82 (as appropriate). If the agreement has been validly notified, this part of the decision will consider the four limbs of Article 81(3). If the agreement has not been validly notified, the decision will then address the issue of whether or not fines and/or periodic penalty payments should be imposed; finally, the operative part of the decision (the so-called 'dispositif') sets out the decision of

the Commission. This is usually very brief, merely identifying the undertakings concerned, the restrictions or conduct which constitute an infringement of Articles 81 and/or 82 and the order which the Commission has decided to make (together with details of any fine or periodic penalty payment).

8.52

There is nothing to prevent one decision dealing with infringements by a number of undertakings, even if not all the undertakings concerned have participated in all the infringements. Indeed, this is frequently the case, particularly in cartel cases[1]. All that is necessary is that each of the undertakings to which the decision is addressed is able to ascertain which of the infringements it has been found to have participated in, together with the reasons for that finding.

1 Eg Commission Decision (94/215/ECSC) *Steel Beams* OJ [1994] L 116/1, [1994] 5 CMLR 353; Commission Decision (94/601/EC) *Cartonboard* OJ [1994] L 243/1, [1994] 5 CMLR 547 and Commission Decision (94/815/EC) *Cement* OJ [1994] L 343/1.

2 TYPES OF ORDER WHICH CAN BE MADE

(1) General

8.53

Decisions requiring undertakings to terminate infringements of Article 81 or 82 usually come into immediate effect, although occasionally their operative stage is deferred for a short period of time[1]. Although art 3(1) of Regulation 17/62 appears to contemplate only decisions bringing to an end existing infringements of Article 81 or 82, the Commission has interpreted this as giving it the power to require the undertakings concerned to desist from doing anything similar thereto. For example, in *Eurofix-Bauco v Hilti*[2] the Commission decision required Hilti to refrain from adopting measures 'having an equivalent effect' to those found to have amounted to abusive conduct under Article 82[3]. The remedy ordered must, however, be limited to that which is necessary to ensure compliance with Article 81 or 82 of the EC Treaty as the case may be[4].

1 As in Commission Decision (82/861/EEC) *British Telecommunications* OJ [1982] L 360/36, [1983] 1 CMLR 457. In Commission Decision (91/50/EEC) *IJsselcentrale* OJ [1991] L 28/32 the Commission allowed the parties three months in which to make proposals for the ending of the infringement.

2 Commission Decision (88/138/EEC) OJ [1988] L 65/19, [1988] 4 CMLR 677, upheld on appeal in Case T-30/89 *Hilti AG v EC Commission* [1992] 4 CMLR 16 (subsequently upheld by ECJ, [1994] ECR I-667). See also Commission Decision (92/163/EEC) *Tetra Pak II* OJ [1992] L 72/1.

3 See also Commission Decision (85/617/EEC) *Burns Tractors Ltd v Sperry New Holland* OJ [1985] L 376/21, [1988] 4 CMLR 306; Commission Decision (87/409/EEC) *Sandoz* OJ [1987] L 222/28; Commission Decision (89/93/EEC) *Italian Flat Glass* OJ [1989] L 33/44; Commission Decision (89/190/EEC) *PVC* OJ [1989] L 74/1 (a decision subsequently annulled on procedural grounds: see para **8.66**); Commission Decision (89/515/EEC) *Welded Steel Mesh* OJ [1989] L 260/1.

4 Case C-62/86 *AKZO Chemie BV v EC Commission* [1991] ECR I-3359, [1993] 5 CMLR 215, ECJ.

8.54

In *Cartonboard*[1], the Commission decision prohibited future information exchanges between the parties to the alleged cartel. A number of the undertakings the subject of the decision contended before the CFI that this prohibition was too broad in nature[2]. The CFI concluded that, in part, the prohibition on future information exchange exceeded what was necessary in order to bring the conduct the subject of the decision in line with what was lawful because it sought to prevent the exchange of purely statistical information which was not in, or capable of being put into, the form of individual information. The CFI held that it was not apparent from the decision that the Commission considered the exchange of statistical data to be in itself an infringement of Article 81, EC Treaty[3].

1 Commission Decision 94/601/EC, OJ [1994] L 243/1.
2 See, for example, Case T-347/94 *Mayr-Melnhof v EC Commission* [1998] ECR II-1751.
3 Ibid, at paras 177-194.

8.55

The classic type of infringement decision involves what is sometimes known as a 'cease and desist order'; that is to say, a decision requiring the undertaking concerned to refrain from doing something[1]. Infringement decisions can, however, also take the form of a requirement for the undertakings concerned to do something positive. This can include relatively innocuous obligations such as an obligation to inform certain third parties that a particular infringement has been brought to an end[2] or a requirement to report back on certain matters periodically to the Commission (as in *ECS/AKZO*)[3]. More significant *positive* measures which have been ordered by the Commission include:

(*a*) a requirement that a dominant undertaking, which has abused its position by refusing to continue supplies to an existing customer, resume supplies within 30 days[4];
(*b*) a requirement that, where two parties have merged in contravention of Article 82, divestiture take place over a period of time[5];
(*c*) a requirement that broadcasting organisations supply each other and third parties with advance weekly programme listings: *Magill TV Guide*[6]. In that case, the Commission's decision required the broadcasting organisation to put to it proposals for achieving this result within two months (a partial stay of this decision was subsequently ordered[7] by the President of the ECJ, pending the outcome of an appeal to the ECJ);
(*d*) a requirement that a dominant undertaking abandon its system of fidelity rebates and replace it with a system under which rebates reflect cost savings[8];
(*e*) a requirement that a dominant undertaking not practise predatory or discriminatory pricing[9];
(*f*) a requirement that the parties to an agreement notify third parties who had concluded contracts with one of the contracting parties that they are free to renegotiate or terminate those contracts[10].

1 As in Commission Decision (82/367/EEC) *Hasselblad* OJ [1982] L 161/18, [1982] 2 CMLR 233; on appeal Case 86/82 *Hasselblad v EC Commission* [1984] ECR 883, [1984] 1 CMLR 559; Commission Decision (91/50/EEC) *IJsselcentral* OJ [1991] L 28/32,

[1992] 5 CMLR 154; Commission Decision (92/163/EEC) *Tetra Pak II* OJ [1992] L 72/1.
2 See n 1 above.
3 Commission Decision (85/609/EEC) OJ [1985] L 374/1, [1986] 3 CMLR 273; upheld on this point on appeal in Case C-62/86 *AKZO Chemie BV v EC Commission* [1991] ECR I-3359, [1993] 5 CMLR 215, ECJ.
4 Cases 6, 7/73 *Commercial Solvents v EC Commission* [1974] ECR 223, [1974] 1 CMLR 309.
5 Case 6/72 *Europemballage and Continental Can v EC Commission* [1973] ECR 215, [1973] CMLR 199: although the Commission decision was set aside, the ECJ endorsed this type of remedial action. In Commission Decision (93/252/EEC) *Warner-Lambert/Gillette, BIC/Gillette* OJ [1993] L 116/21, the Commission found that Gillette had abused a dominant position by participating in the buy-out of the European Wilkinson-Sword business. This took the form of an equity and creditor interest in the buy-out vehicle. The Commission ordered Gillette to bring this infringement to an end by disposing of those interests within a stipulated period (failing which Gillette was required to appoint an independent third party to do so).
6 Commission Decision (89/205/EEC) OJ [1989] L 78/43, [1989] 4 CMLR 757; upheld on appeal, Joined Cases C-241 and 242/91P *RTE and ITP v EC Commission* [1995] ECR I-743, ECJ.
7 Cases 76–77/89R, 91/89R *Radio Telefis Eireann v EC Commission* [1989] ECR 1141, [1989] 4 CMLR 749.
8 Commission Decision (91/299/EEC) *Soda-ash-Solvay* OJ [1991] L 152/21; Commission Decision (91/300/EEC) *Soda-ash-ICI* OJ [1991] L 152/40.
9 Commission Decision (92/163/EEC) *Tetra Pak II* OJ [1992] L 72/1.
10 Commission Decision (93/50/EEC) *Astra* OJ [1993] L 20/23.

8.56
In the *Magill* case referred to at para **8.55** one of the grounds of appeal was that the Commission had infringed art 3(1) of Regulation 17/62. The applicant alleged that the Commission did not merely require RTE to bring the infringement to an end but laid down the precise manner in which that was to be brought about, by requiring it to grant compulsory licences of protected works (thereby depriving it, as the holder of an intellectual property right, of the very substance of that right). The ECJ rejected the claim and held[1] that the constituent elements of the infringement justified the measures imposed by the Commission.

1 Joined Cases C-241 and 242/91P *RTE and ITP v EC Commission* [1995] ECR I-743, ECJ.

8.57
The pricing practices of dominant undertakings have frequently been the subject of Commission investigation. It has not, however, yet been established by the ECJ whether the Commission has the power positively to control the prices of a dominant undertaking[1]. There would seem in principle to be no reason why its powers do not extend to some form of price control. Indeed, in its interim measures decision in *ECS/AKZO*[2], a case involving alleged predatory pricing, the Commission did impose minimum prices.

1 Compare the powers of the Secretary of State under the UK Fair Trading Act 1973, Sch 8, see para **14.82**.
2 Commission Decision (83/462/EEC) OJ [1983] L 252/13, [1983] 3 CMLR 694.

8.58
In *Automec II*[1] the applicant challenged in the CFI the Commission's refusal, under Article 81(1), to grant an injunction requiring BMW Italia

(the operator of a selective distribution system) to fulfil the applicant's orders and to authorise the applicant to use certain BMW trade marks. The reason for its demands was that Automec considered that it met all the requisite conditions for inclusion in the BMW distribution network. In ruling in favour of the Commission, the CFI held that the Commission does not have the power, in the framework of its powers to put an end to infringements of Article 81(1), to order one party to enter into a contractual relationship with another, where other means exist for ending the infringement in question. It was the Court's view that, if an infringement was found to exist, this should be brought to an end by BMW Italia giving up or altering the distribution system. Under these circumstances, 'the Commission undoubtedly has power to find the existence of the infringement and order the parties concerned to end it, but it is not for the Commission to impose upon the parties its own choice among the different potential courses of action which all conform to the Treaty'[2].

1 Case T-24/90 *Automec Srl v EC Commission* [1992] 5 CMLR 431.
2 Ibid at para 52.

8.59
In the so-called *Ice-Cream* case[1], the Commission decided that certain exclusive purchasing agreements infringed Article 81(1). The decision went on to prohibit the applicant from concluding agreements of this kind for a further period of five years. The Court concluded that this prohibition went further than was permissible under art 3 of Regulation 17/62. It noted that Commission Regulation 1984/83[2] made available to undertakings a block exemption for certain exclusive purchasing agreements and that that block exemption expressly conferred on the Commission the power to withdraw the benefit of the block exemption in individual cases. However, the Court concluded that the block exemption did not give any legal basis for its benefit to be withheld from *future* agreements.

1 Case T-7/93 *Langnese-Iglo v EC Commission* [1995] ECR II-1533, upheld on appeal to the ECJ in Case C-279/95P *Langnese-Iglo v EC Commission* [1998] ECR I-5609.
2 Commission Regulation (EEC) 1984/83, OJ [1983] L 173/5.

(2) Declaratory Decisions

8.60
If, by the time of the Commission decision, the infringement in question has come to an end, the Commission nevertheless has power to issue a declaratory decision to the effect that the agreement/conduct in question constituted an infringement[1]. Recent decisions in which the Commission has done this include *Decca Navigator System*[2]; *Tetra Pak I*[3]; *British Dental Trade Association*[4]; *Belgian Roofing Felt*[5], *Bayer Dental*[6], *Scottish Salmon Board*[7], *Distribution of package tours during the 1990 World Cup*[8] and *Zera/Montedison–Hinkens Stähler*[9]. Conversely, the Commission decided not to do this in *Konica*[10].

1 Case 7/82 *GVL v EC Commission* [1983] ECR 483, [1983] 3 CMLR 645.
2 Commission Decision (89/113/EEC) OJ [1989] L 43/27.
3 Commission Decision (88/501/EEC) OJ [1988] L 272/27, [1990] 4 CMLR 47.

4 Commission Decision (88/477/EEC) OJ [1988] L 233/15.
5 Commission Decision (86/399/EEC) OJ [1986] L 232/15, [1991] 4 CMLR 130, upheld on appeal Case 246/86 *Belasco v EC Commission* [1991] 4 CMLR 96.
6 Commission Decision (90/645/EEC) OJ [1990] L 351/46.
7 Commission Decision (92/44/EEC) OJ [1992] L 246/37.
8 Commission Decision (92/51/EEC) OJ [1992] L 326/31.
9 Commission Decision (93/554/EEC) OJ [1993] L 272/28.
10 Commission Decision (88/172/EEC) OJ [1988] L 78/34, [1988] 4 CMLR 848.

8.61

In *Napier Brown–British Sugar*[1] the Commission did not take a decision under art 3 because British Sugar had adopted a comprehensive compliance programme and shown 'exemplary behaviour' since the issuance of the Statement of Objections. The Commission also noted that the complainant had concurred with the Commission's view that an article 3 decision was not necessary.

1 Commission Decision (88/518/EEC) OJ [1988] L 284/41.

8.62

One specific reason why the Commission may choose to take an article 3 decision, even where an infringement has come to an end, is to help a national court. For example, in *Florimex*[1], the Commission was aware that parallel proceedings before a Dutch court had been stayed pending the outcome of the Commission investigation. The Commission felt it necessary to take a decision stating the existence of an infringement in order to enable the stay to be ended.

1 Commission Decision (88/491/EEC) *Bloemenveilingen Aalsmeer* OJ [1988] L 262/27, [1989] 4 CMLR 500.

3 RECOMMENDATIONS FOR TERMINATION OF INFRINGEMENT

8.63

Under art 3(3) of Regulation 17/62, the Commission has power, before taking a decision requiring an infringement to be brought to an end, to address to the undertakings concerned 'recommendations' for termination of the infringement. This provides the Commission with a mechanism for closing a procedure without the need for a formal decision: although art 3(3) refers to the making of recommendations *before* the taking of a formal termination decision, it would appear that an art 3(3) recommendation can be issued *in place of* such a decision. However, in practice, the Commission hardly ever makes use of art 3(3). An article 3(3) recommendation has no binding force[1]; it cannot be challenged under Article 230 of the EC Treaty (which expressly excludes from its ambit recommendations of the Commission); the Commission has no obligation to publish recommendations under art 3(3)[2].

1 EC Treaty, Article 189.
2 Council Regulation (EEC) 17/62, art 21(1), OJ Sp Ed [1959–62] p 87.

8.64
Of far greater practical significance than article 3(3) recommendations is the practice of the Commission of settling cases before it on an informal basis, sometimes on the basis of undertakings offered to it by the parties involved. The informal settlement of Article 81 and 82 cases is dealt with at paras **8.72–8.89**.

G Procedural Aspects Relating to Final Decisions of the Commission

8.65
This paragraph summarises briefly a number of the important procedural aspects relating to Commission decisions granting negative clearance (under art 2 of Regulation 17/62) and individual exemption (under arts 6 and 8 of Regulation 17/62), or ordering termination of an infringement (under art 3 of Regulation 17/62). A number of these procedural aspects are dealt with in more detail elsewhere in this Division. The principal points to note are as follows:

(1) Under Regulation 17/62, art 19(1) the undertakings concerned (ie those to whom the particular decision is addressed) have the right to be heard on any matters to which the Commission takes objection; this includes the right to an oral hearing: art 8 of Regulation 2842/98[1].
(2) The Commission must, if it issues a statement of objections in relation to a matter in respect of which it has received a complaint, provide the complainant with the opportunity to make know its views in writing and may (but is not obliged to do so) give the complainant the opportunity to express it views orally2.
(3) The Commission may also hear other natural or legal persons and must hear them if they show a 'sufficient interest'[3]: art 19(2) of Regulation 17/62; persons showing a sufficient interest may be given the opportunity to make known their views orally: art 9 of Regulation 2842/98.
(4) Article 253 of the EC Treaty applies to each of the three types of decision, ie the Commission must state the reasons on which the decision is based. In the words of the ECJ, the decision must:

> 'allow the Court to exercise its power of review as to the legality of the decision and must provide the person concerned with the information necessary to enable him to decide whether or not the decision is well founded'[4].

(5) Any natural or legal person to whom the decision is addressed may appeal it to the Court of First Instance, as may any other person to whom the decision is of 'direct and individual concern'[5].
(6) Pursuant to Article 254 of the EC Treaty all three types of decision must be notified to the persons to whom they are addressed and they take effect upon the date of notification (which is relevant for the purpose of assessing the time within which an appeal must be lodged under Article 230 of the EC Treaty).
(7) Under Regulation 17/62, art 21(1), all three types of decision must be published. This is done in the Official Journal 'L' series. The publication

is required to state the names of the parties and the main content of the decision but the Commission is required to have regard to the legitimate interest of undertakings in the protection of their business secrets[6]. The issue of confidentiality is considered in more detail in Chapter 11; the date of publication is of relevance in the context of assessing the period within which an appeal can be lodged by a third party under Article 230 of the Treaty[7].

(8) Finally, the 'Article 19(3) procedure' applies where the Commission intends to grant negative clearance or to take a decision in application of Article 81(3) (but *not* where it intends to require an infringement to be terminated pursuant to art 3 of Regulation 17/62). Under art 19(3) of Regulation 17/62, the Commission is required to publish a summary of the relevant application/notification and to invite all interested third parties to submit their observations within a time limit fixed by it, being not less than one month[8].

In *Tetra Pak*[9], the CFI held that the length of the Commission's investigation (filing of the complaint in 1983 leading to despatch of the Statement of Objections in 1988) did not constitute an infringement of the principle of good administration, since it was attributable to the scale of difficulty of the investigation.

1 Commission Regulation (EC) 2842/98, OJ [1998] L 354/18.
2 Ibid, paras 7 and 8.
3 As to the meaning of 'sufficient interest', see para **7.50**.
4 Case 42/84 *Remia v EC Commission* [1985] ECR 2545, [1987] 1 CMLR 1; Case T-44/90 *La Cinq v EC Commission* [1992] ECR II-1, [1992] 4 CMLR 449.
5 EC Treaty, Article 230: see Chapter 10.
6 Council Regulation (EEC) 17/62, art 21(2), OJ Sp Ed [1959–62] p 87.
7 See para **10.09** ff.
8 Examples include *Moosehead/Whitbread* [1989] 4 CMLR 970n; *KSB/Goulds/Lowara/ ITT* [1990] 4 CMLR 248n; *ECR 900* [1990] 4 CMLR 256n; *Comasso* [1990] 4 CMLR 259n; *Sippa* [1991] 4 CMLR 86; *Yves Saint Laurent* [1991] 4 CMLR 163; *Jahrhundertvertrag* OJ [1991] C 116/6; *Ford/Volkswagen* OJ [1991] C 182/8; *Assurpol* OJ [1991] C 188/7.
9 Case T-83/91 *Tetra Pak v EC Commission* [1994] ECR II-755.

8.66

The Commission has internal rules regarding the way in which final decisions are formally adopted as acts of the Commission. The *PVC*[1] case raised a number of issues regarding the way in which the Commission adopts decisions. The applicant companies submitted that the Commission's decision, as notified to them, appeared to differ on several points from the decision formally adopted by the Commissioners at their meeting; in particular, its typographical appearance indicated that vital passages had been added or corrected. Some of the applicants had also concluded that the decision had not been adopted in two of the languages which were binding, namely Dutch and Italian, since only drafts in English, French and German had been submitted to the college of Commissioners. The ECJ, citing its judgment in the *Battery Hens*[2] case, held that only simple corrections of spelling and grammar may be made to the text of a decision after its formal adoption by the college of Commissioners, any further alteration being the exclusive province of the college[3]. The ECJ rejected the Commission's contention that in the decision-making process the college of

Commissioners could confine itself to making clear its intention to take certain action, without having to become involved in the drafting and finalisation of the act giving effect to its intention[4]. As far as the language of the decision was concerned, the ECJ noted that under art 12 of the Commission's Rules of Procedure, a Commission measure must be authenticated in the language(s) in which it is binding. The Court said that this was not (as the Commission claimed) a mere formality for archival purposes but was intended to guarantee legal certainty; authentication of acts referred to in the first paragraph of art 12 therefore constituted an essential procedural requirement within the meaning of Article 230 of the EC Treaty, breach of which gave rise to an action for annulment[5]. The ECJ therefore annulled the decision, without going on to consider various other pleas which had been raised by the applicants. A Commission decision in a subsequent case was challenged on similar grounds but the challenge was rejected on the facts[6].

1 Case C-137/92-P *Commission v BASF AG* [1994] ECR I-2555. See too Joined Cases T-80/89–T-112/89 *BASF v EC Commission (LdPE)*, [1995] ECR II-729.
2 Case 131/86 *United Kingdom v EC Council* [1988] ECR 905, [1988] 2 CMLR 364.
3 See n 1 above, at para 68.
4 The ECJ contrasted (at para 71 of its judgment) the position in relation to decisions ordering undertakings to submit to an investigation which, as a form of preparatory enquiry, could be regarded as straightforward measures of management: see para **6.31**.
5 See n 1 above, *Commission v BASF AG* at para 76.
6 Case T-29/92 *VSPOB v EC Commission* [1995] ECR II-289, CFI.

8.67

In *PVC*[1] the CFI concluded that the procedural defects were of such importance as to render the decision non-existent. Whilst recognising that an administrative measure is presumed valid until it is properly repealed or withdrawn by the institution which adopted it[2], the Court concluded that in this case the 'particularly serious and manifest defects'[3] had the effect that the decision was non-existent. However, on appeal the ECJ overturned[4] the CFI's judgment on this point, holding that such a finding is 'reserved for quite extreme situations'[5].

1 Joined Cases T-79, 84–86, 89, 91–92, 94, 96, 98, 102 and 104/89 *BASF AG v EC Commission* [1992] ECR II-315, [1992] 4 CMLR 357.
2 Case 15/85 *Consorzo Cooperative d'Abruzzo v EC Commission* [1987] ECR 1005, [1988] 1 CMLR 841.
3 Joined Cases T-79, 84–86, 89, 91–92, 94, 96, 98, 102 and 104/89 *BASF AG v EC Commission* [1992] 4 CMLR 357 at para 100.
4 Case C-137/92P *EC Commission v BASF AG* [1994] ECR I-2555, at points 44–54. In his opinion delivered on 29 June 1993, the Advocate General had noted that the doctrine of non- existence had been applied only once prior to the CFI's judgment in the *PVC* case: Joined Cases 1, 14/57 *Société des Usines à Tubes de la Sarre v High Authority* [1957/8] ECR 105. A survey of the ECJ's case law on the doctrine is provided by the Advocate General at paras 73–79 of his opinion in the *PVC* case.
5 See also Case T-29/92 *VSPOB v EC Commission* [1995] ECR II-289 and Joined Cases T-133 and 204/95 *IECC v EC Commission* [1998] 5 CMLR 992.

8.68

Following the ECJ's judgment in *PVC*[1] in June 1994, the Commission adopted a new decision[2] in the case the following month. That decision was appealed to the CFI in the *LVM* case[3]. A number of arguments were raised by the applicants:

(1) They contended that the principle of *res judicata* applied and that the Commission could not adopt the new decision without infringing that principle in the light of the ECJ's judgment in *PVC*. The CFI dismissed that argument, holding that the ECJ judgment of June 1994 had been based on a procedural impropriety (regarding authentication of the original 1998 decision) and that the court had not found it necessary to examine the other pleas raised by the applicants. The principal of *res judicata* had legal force only in relation to those points of fact or law which were actually or necessarily determined in the first case[4].

(2) It was argued that the Commission had infringed the *non bis in idem* principle by adopting a new decision after the court had annulled the original 1998 decision (ie the Commission had initiated proceedings twice in respect of the same alleged offence). Again, the CFI dismissed this argument, noting that when the ECJ had annulled the 1998 decision in its judgment of June 1994 it had not ruled on any of the substantive pleas raised by the applicants. Consequently, by adopting its second decision the Commission was merely remedying the formal defect found by the court[5].

(3) The applicants claimed that the Commission had infringed the general principle of Community law that decisions following administrative proceedings relating to competition policy must be adopted within a reasonable time. The CFI accepted that such a principle existed but found that it had not been violated[6].

(4) The applicants argued that the annulment of the 1998 decision by the ECJ in its June 1994 judgment meant that the new decision could not be taken without the Commission conducting a fresh administrative procedure; ie the 1994 judgment had automatically invalidated the whole adversarial administrative procedure which had preceded it. The CFI rejected this argument, stating that it was clear that the validity of the preparatory measures taken prior to the adoption of the 1998 decision had not been called into question by the annulment of that decision by the ECJ. That annulment was on account of a procedural defect affecting only the manner in which it was finally adopted by the Commission and that defect did not affect the validity of the measures preparatory to that decision (statement of objections, oral hearing, etc)[7].

(5) As a result, the CFI also rejected the argument that the Commission should have conducted a new oral hearing. Since the applicants did not deny that the text of the new decision contained no new objection compared with the text of the original 1998 decision, the Commission was entitled to adopt the new decision without holding a fresh hearing[8].

1 See para **8.67**.
2 Commission Decision (94/599/EC) *PVC* OJ [1994] L 239/14.
3 Joined Cases T-305/94–T-335/94, *LVM v EC Commission* [1999] 5 CMLR 303.
4 Ibid at paras 77–84.
5 Ibid at paras 95–98.
6 Ibid at paras 120–136. See Case C-185/95P *Baustahlgewebe v EC Commission* [1998] ECR I-8417 at paras 47 and 141.
7 *LVM*, at paras 183–193.
8 *LVM*, at paras 246–252.

8.69
In *Norsk Hydro*[1], the applicant had sought a declaration of invalidity and/or annulment of the Commission's decision in the *PVC*[2] case. The CFI dismissed the application as being out of time and therefore inadmissible[3]. The applicant subsequently sought revision of that decision on the basis of the CFI's own subsequent decision that the Commission's original decision was non-existent. The applicant argued that, as a non-existent measure, there was no applicable time limit for bringing proceedings. In the event, the ECJ decided on appeal[4] that the original Commission decision was not non-existent and accordingly the CFI dismissed Norsk Hydro's application for revision of the original order.

1 Case T-106/89R *Norsk Hydro A/S v EC Commission* [1994] ECR II-419. See also Case C-195/ 91P *Bayer AG v EC Commission* [1994] ECR I-5619.
2 Commission Decision (89/190/EEC) OJ [1989] L 74/1.
3 See n 1 above.
4 See para **8.67**.

8.70
In the *John Deere* case[1], the applicant claimed that it had reason to doubt whether the infringement decision taken against it had been authenticated in compliance with the requirements of art 12 of the Commission's Rules of Procedure (as invoked in the *PVC*[2] case). The CFI noted that no evidence had been placed before it to call into question the validity of the decision and it therefore saw no reason to overturn the presumption of validity enjoyed by Community measures.

1 Case T-35/92 *John Deere Ltd v EC Commission* [1994] ECR II-957, CFI. See also, arising from the same Commission decision, Case T-34/92 *Fiatagri UK Ltd and New Holland Ford Ltd v EC Commission* [1994] ECR II-905, CFI. Also, Case T-43/92 *Dunlop Slazenger International Ltd v EC Commission* [1994] ECR II-441.
2 Case C-137/92P *Commission v BASF AG* [1994] ECR I-2555.

8.71
In *Solvay*[1] the question of authentication was again raised. In that case, the Commission had failed to follow the sequence of events laid down in its own Rules of Procedure: the authentication of the contested decision was carried out after notification of the decision to the applicant, rather than the other way round. The CFI held that this amounted to an infringement of an essential procedural requirement and the Commission's decisions, imposing fines in aggregate of 23 million ECU on Solvay, were annulled in their entirety.

1 Cases T-31, 32/91 *Solvay SA v EC Commission* [1995] ECR II-1821, 1825, CFI. See also Case T-37/91 *ICI plc v EC Commission* [1995] ECR II-1901, CFI.

H Settlements/Undertakings and Comfort Letters in Lieu of a Formal Decision

1 INTRODUCTION

8.72

This chapter has so far focused on the formal decisions which can be taken by the Commission pursuant to Regulation 17/62, in application of its powers under Articles 81 and 82. In addition, however, a large number of cases are settled each year in a variety of informal ways, each of which falls short of a formal decision by the Commission[1]. The table[2] below puts this in context:

Year	*Full Decision*	*Informal Closure of File*[3]
1990	13	864
1991	21	814
1992	34	1,090
1993	14	734
1994	33	525
1995	14	419
1996	21	365
1997	27	490
1998	42	539
1999	68	514

1 See generally Waelbroeck 'New Forms of Settlement of Antitrust Cases and Procedural Safeguards: Is Regulation 17 falling into disuse?' (1986) 11 EL Rev 268.
2 Source: Annual Reports on Competition Policy.
3 These figures include closures by comfort letter and cases where the agreements had either been altered to conform with the competition rules, terminated or expired.

8.73

The informal settlement or closing of cases can take place in a number of ways and the terminology can sometimes be confusing. In this section the following classifications will be used:

(1) *'Comfort Letters'*: These are the administrative letters referred to at para **8.72**. More often than not, they arise in the context of an agreement submitted to the Commission by way of an application for negative clearance and/or a notification seeking individual exemption under Article 81(3). Indeed, Form A/B itself specifically asks the undertakings submitting an application/notification whether they would be satisfied with a comfort letter. Comfort letters can be issued in a variety of circumstances: for example, the Commission may regard the agreement in question as falling outside Article 81(1) altogether, as falling within the scope of a relevant block exemption or as satisfying the conditions set out in Article 81(3). The form of such a letter can vary: in 1982 the Commission up-graded the comfort letter procedure, in the light of the lack of legal security which such letters confer (see paras **8.75–8.76**).

(2) *Settlement and Suspension of Cases*: The Commission distinguishes between comfort letters and so-called 'informal settlements' and in turn between the settlement and suspension of proceedings[1]. However, it is not entirely clear what is meant by the terms 'settlement' and 'suspension' respectively. It has been suggested by one commentator[2] that a settlement of proceedings involves the undertaking concerned giving some form of undertaking regarding its future conduct. This happened in the celebrated *IBM*[3] case. However, the Commission clearly regards that case as a suspension, not a settlement[4]. The characteristics of that case which made it a suspension rather than a settlement were that the Commission reserved the right to re-open the case (either by terminating the suspension or by initiating a new proceeding in respect of IBM's conduct), whilst IBM for its part reserved the right to terminate the undertaking which it gave on giving one year's notice (taking effect at any time after 1 January 1990).

1 15th Competition Policy Report (1985), para 1.
2 Van Bael 'The Antitrust Settlement Practice of the EC Commission' (1986) CML Rev 61.
3 14th Competition Policy Report (1984) at paras 94–95; see also Bull EC 10–1984 (Documentation Section).
4 See n 3 above.

2 ADVANTAGES AND DISADVANTAGES

8.74
Both advantages and disadvantages (from the point of view of the undertaking concerned) can arise from the informal termination of Commission proceedings (whether by comfort letter, settlement or suspension). The principal advantages are that:

(1) Informal termination avoids the need for the Commission to go through the somewhat cumbersome procedures leading up to a final decision. This can be of benefit not only to the Commission but also to the parties concerned, in that there is likely to be a saving of cost and management time, as well as a shortening of the whole process.
(2) Because no formal decision is involved, there is no obligation on the Commission to publish[1]. However, there can be no guarantee that the Commission will not publish and indeed the Commission has stated[2] that its policy is to issue press releases in cases raising points of law or involving firms with significant economic power. In the *IBM*[3] case the Commission took the unusual step of publishing the entire undertaking. In fact, very few informal terminations of proceedings are published but one should not automatically assume that this will be the case.

The principal disadvantage is the uncertain legal status of the various types of informal termination of proceedings. This aspect is considered at paras **8.76–8.83**.

1 Ie Council Regulation (EEC) 17/62, art 21(1), OJ Sp Ed [1959–62] p 87 does not apply.
2 6th Report on Competition Policy at p 11.
3 Bull EC 10–1984 (Documentation Section).

3 LEGAL STATUS OF COMFORT LETTERS

8.75

The legal status of the standard type of comfort letter, indicating that the Commission intends to take no further action on a particular case[1], was considered by the ECJ in the *Perfumes* cases[2]. There, the Commission had sent a comfort letter to the undertakings party to certain agreements, indicating that it intended to take no action under Article 81(1) and was closing the case. The agreements subsequently came to be litigated in a national court and, on a reference under Article 177[3], the ECJ was asked to advise the national court on the status of the comfort letters. The principal points which emerged from the judgments in the *Perfumes*[4] cases are as follows:

(1) The comfort letters only amounted to an expression of the Commission's views (as opposed to constituting a formal decision) and, as such, the national court was entitled to come to a different view on the applicability of Article 81(1).

(2) The national court is, however, required to have regard to the comfort letter in reaching its own decision[5].

(3) The comfort letter did not fetter the national court in any way in its application of the relevant national competition law; it should be noted, however, that in the *Perfumes*[6] cases the comfort letters in question indicated that the Commission's view was that the agreements were outside Article 81 altogether and accordingly no real question of conflict between Community and national law could arise; in relation to a comfort letter expressing the view that an agreement merits exemption under Article 81(3), the position may be more complicated.

(4) With regard to the issue whether a comfort letter is binding on the Commission itself, the Advocate General in the *Perfumes*[7] cases expressed the view that the Commission could only later change its view (and re-open the proceedings) if there was a material change of circumstances or the Commission's finding was reached on the basis of incorrect information. The Court itself did not, however, express a view on this. In the so-called *Ice-Cream* case[8], the Commission had sent a comfort letter in 1985, indicating that certain notified supply agreements were compatible with EC competition rules but reserving the right to re-open the procedure if there was any appreciable change affecting certain matters of law or fact on which its assessment has been based. In a decision in 1992, the Commission concluded (following a complaint made by Mars) that the agreements in question infringed Article 81. The applicant argued that, by virtue of the principle of the protection of legitimate expectations[9], the Commission was required to maintain the position adopted in its comfort letter. The Court rejected this argument on the ground that new factors had arisen which justified a more detailed and precise analysis of the conditions of access to the market than that undertaken when the comfort letter was issued. Although cases such as this are rare, it illustrates the uncertain legal status of comfort letters.

(5) The issuance of a comfort letter withdraws any benefit of provisional validity which the agreement in question may have; this is, of course,

only relevant to 'old agreements' and 'accession agreements', as new agreements cannot benefit from the doctrine of provisional validity[10].

1 Which may be because the Commission regards the agreement as falling outside Article 81(1) completely or as meriting exemption under Article 83(3).
2 Cases 253/78 *Procureur de la République v Giry and Guerlain* [1980] ECR 2327, [1981] 2 CMLR 99.
3 Now Article 234. In relation to Article 234, see paras **10.67–10.69**.
4 See n 2 above.
5 See too the Commission Notice on co-operation between national courts and the Commission in applying Articles 81 and 82 of the EEC Treaty, paras 20, 25(a), OJ [1993] C 39/5.
6 See n 2 above.
7 See n 2 above.
8 Case T-7/93 *Langnese-Iglo v EC Commission* [1995] ECR II-1533.
9 See para **11.47**.
10 See para **18.07**.

8.76

For the sake of completeness, one other point should be noted, namely that the issuance of a comfort letter does not in any way affect the immunity from fines which is afforded by art 15(5) of Regulation 17/62[1] to agreements which have been notified to the Commission[2]. This is because a comfort letter does not constitute a 'decision in application of Article 81(3)' within the meaning of art 15(5)(a).

1 Council Regulation (EEC) 17/62, OJ Sp Ed [1959–62] p 87.
2 See para **4.05**.

8.77

The conclusions of the ECJ in the *Perfumes*[1] cases went a long way to undermining any reliance which undertakings might wish to place on comfort letters sent to them. Aware of this, and keen to pursue its policy of closing cases by means of comfort letters, the Commission announced in its Eleventh Report on Competition Policy (1981)[2] that it intended to 'increase the legal value of these letters', by prior publication of a notice in the Official Journal, thereby giving interested third parties the opportunity to submit comments. The Commission subsequently issued two formal notices[3] regarding its proposed 'up-graded' comfort letter procedure as a means of closing both cases of application for negative clearance and exemption. The procedure involved in relation to the issuance of these more formal comfort letters is set out at para **8.78**. The extent, if any, to which the new procedure changes the analysis adopted by the ECJ in the *Perfumes*[4] cases is unclear. All that one probably can say is that the fact that the Commission's intention to issue a formal comfort letter in a given case is made public (thereby giving third parties the opportunity to comment) may cause a national court before which the agreements subsequently come to be litigated to give greater credence to the views of the Commission as expressed in the comfort letter.

1 Cases 253/78 *Procureur de la République v Giry and Guerlain* [1980] ECR 2327, [1981] 2 CMLR 99.
2 At para 15.
3 OJ [1982] C 343/4, [1984] 1 CMLR 38–in relation to negative clearance—and OJ [1983] C 295/6, [1984] 1 CMLR 128 in relation to exemptions.
4 See n 1 above.

8.78

The procedure adopted in relation to this more formal type of comfort letter is as follows. Firstly, the Commission publishes the essential content of the agreements in question (pursuant to art 19(3) of Regulation 17/62[1]) in order to give interested third parties an opportunity to comment. Secondly, the Commission consults the Advisory Committee on Restrictive Practices and Dominant Positions[2], though since 1998 such consultation only takes place when the published notice gives rise to comments which might change the Commission's positive stance or when a member state requests it[3].

1 Council Regulation (EEC) 17/62, OJ Sp Ed [1959–62] p 87.
2 12th Report on Competition Policy (1982) at para 30.
3 29th Report on Competition Policy (1999) at para 40.

8.79

In its Fifteenth (1985) and Sixteenth (1986) Reports on Competition Policy the Commission included a note of the cases in which it had used this new comfort letter procedure during the previous year. Only two cases were identified in the 1985 Report[1], and one in the 1986 Report[2]. The 1987–89 Reports do not identify any such cases separately at the back. However, several cases in which this procedure has been used recently are identified in the main body of the Report[3].

1 *BBC/Grenfell/Holt* OJ [1984] C 209/3, [1984] 3 CMLR 162n; *VFA/Sauer* OJ [1985] C 68/2, [1985] 1 CMLR 663n.
2 *ICL/Fujitsu* OJ [1986] C 210/3.
3 In the 18th Report (1988): *EMC/DSM (LVM)* OJ [1988] C 18/3; *FIEC/CEETB* OJ [1988] C 52/2. In the 19th Report (1989): *Finnpap* OJ [1989] C 45/4; *Fluke/Philips* OJ [1989] C 188/2; *AMB/La Fondiaria* OJ [1989] C 210/4.

8.80

Analysis of those cases in which the 'upgraded' comfort letter procedure was used in the first eight months of 1991 shows the different types of approach which the Commission can adopt. In three cases[1] the Commission's article 19(3) notice stated that there appeared to be no need for action on its part under Article 81 or 82. In one of these three cases[2] the Commission specifically cited its 1982 Notice regarding applications for negative clearance[3]. In another case[4] the Commission indicated that it proposed to take a 'favourable position' in relation to a joint venture agreement. In that case the notice expressly states that while the agreement in question could possibly contain some restrictions on competition contrary to Article 81(1), it would, in any event, merit exemption pursuant to Article 81(3). A similar approach was adopted in one other case in 1991[5]. In this latter case the article 19(3) notice expressly refers to the Commission's 1983 Notice regarding applications for individual exemption[6].

1 *Stora-Feldmühle* OJ [1991] C 33/11; *Application of Unie Van Elektrotechnische Ondernemers* [1991] 4 CMLR 487; *Tepar* OJ [1991] 4 CMLR 860.
2 *Retel*, see n 1 above.
3 OJ [1982] C 343/4, [1984] 1 CMLR 38; see para **8.77**.
4 *Philips/Matsushita—D2B* OJ [1991] C 220/2; see more recently *Eleco-MiTek* OJ [1991] C 285/8.
5 *Fiat/Hitachi* OJ [1991] C 206/3.
6 OJ [1983] C 295/6, [1984] 1 CMLR 128; see para **8.77**.

8.81
This upgraded comfort letter procedure should not be confused with the separate procedure which the Commission introduced in 1992 for dealing with so-called structural joint ventures of a co-operative nature (which fall to be dealt with under Article 81 rather than the Merger Control Regulation[1]). Under that separate procedure[2], the Commission publishes a notice very shortly after receiving a notification, informing third parties of the notification and requesting them to submit comments, usually within ten days. This is designed to introduce greater transparency into the decision-making process, whilst at the same time enabling the Commission to deal with this type of joint venture as rapidly as possible (its stated aim[2] being to indicate to the parties within two months of notification whether it is possible to close the file by means of a comfort letter).

1 Council Regulation (EEC) 4064/89, OJ [1990] L 257/14.
2 See paras **4.59–4.61**.

8.82
One of the difficulties presented by a comfort letter which indicates that an agreement probably or possibly violates Article 81(1) but which indicates that the Commission takes a favourable view[1] under Article 81(3) (though short of issuing a formal decision to that effect) is that it places a national court before which the agreement comes to be litigated in something of a quandary. Only the Commission is entitled to grant an individual exemption[2] and in such a case it would, by definition, not have done so. The difficulties which national courts have with comfort letters are well illustrated by the words of M Barnes QC, sitting as Deputy Judge of the High Court in *Inntrepreneur Estates Ltd v Mason*[3]:

> 'It is not entirely easy to know what comfort letters are, or what letters amount to comfort letters but . . . it seems to me that even on the basis that the letters in question are comfort letters, there is a real argument as to the effect of such comfort letters in Community law'[4].

1 As in *Infonet* OJ [1992] C 7/3.
2 Council Regulation (EEC) 17/62, art 9(1), OJ Sp Ed [1959–62] p 87.
3 [1993] 2 CMLR 293.
4 Ibid at points 49 and 54.

4 LEGAL STATUS OF SETTLEMENTS/ SUSPENSIONS

8.83
There is no reason to suppose that settlements or suspensions of Commission procedures confer any greater legal certainty than comfort letters on the undertakings concerned. Indeed, in the *IBM*[1] case the undertaking given by the company not only expressly preserved the right of the Commission to re-open proceedings or initiate new proceedings (and also gave the company the right to withdraw from the undertakings after a certain date), but it also was given on what amounted to a 'without prejudice' basis[2], stating expressly that:

'this undertaking is made without prejudice and may not be used in any way by IBM or the Commission in this or any other proceeding and does not constitute in any way an admission by IBM or the Commission. It is fundamental to this undertaking that it should not be enforceable by any other natural or legal person or any national authority or agency. IBM understands and asks the Commission to confirm that the Commission will rely exclusively upon Articles 85 and 86 [now Articles 81 and 82] of the Treaty and not upon this undertaking in this or any other proceeding'.

1 14th Competition Policy Report (1984) at paras 94–95; see also Bull EC 10–1984 (Documentation Section).
2 See also the *Microsoft* undertaking referred to in para **8.85**.

5 THE POSSIBILITY OF GIVING UNDERTAKINGS

8.84

The possibility of the Commission being able to accept undertakings as to future conduct from one or more parties to a Commission proceeding is a means by which the Commission could speed up its procedures, enabling it to gain some concessions without being forced to take its procedures all the way through to a final decision and, as a consequence, without having to produce a reasoned decision which could withstand the test of scrutiny by the ECJ on an appeal under Article 230. The *IBM*[1] case already referred to is itself a highly-publicised case where detailed undertakings as to future conduct were given by IBM in return for a suspension of the Commission proceedings. Other recent examples are the giving of undertakings in lieu of interim measures in the *Hilti*[2] and *British Sugar*[3] cases. In neither of these cases did the undertakings involve suspension of the Commission's proceedings (unlike the *IBM*[4] case); rather they were in place of interim measures. In both cases final decisions were eventually taken, both involving fines[5].

1 See para **8.83**.
2 15th Report on Competition Policy (1985), para 49.
3 16th Report on Competition Policy (1986), para 74.
4 See n 1 above.
5 Commission Decision (88/138/EEC) *Eurofix–Bauco/Hilti* OJ [1988] L 65/19, [1988] 4 CMLR 677, upheld on appeal in Case C-53/92P *Hilti AG v EC Commission* [1994] ECR I-667, ECJ; Commission Decision (88/518/EEC) *Napier Brown–British Sugar* OJ [1988] L 284/41.

8.85

In *Microsoft*[1], the company gave an undertaking to the Commission and at the same time entered into a consent decree with the United States Department of Justice, in each case as a means of settling the investigations by both sets of regulators of alleged anti-competitive trading practices. The undertaking to the Commission is expressed to remain in force for six and a half years or until the entry into effect of a Commission decision with respect to the subject matter of the undertaking (whichever is earlier). As in the *IBM*[2] case, the undertaking was given on a 'without prejudice' basis. The Commission has subsequently made it clear in its Twenty-fourth Report on Competition Policy[3] that it is prepared to accept undertakings in Article 82 cases and that it will normally issue final decisions only where fines are justified, where the parties contest the Commission's findings or where a novel point of wider interest is involved. The Commission noted[4] that in the *Deutsche Bahn*[5] case, it had issued a final decision because the company had not only contested the case but also because fines were deemed appropriate.

1 [1994] 5 CMLR 133.
2 See para **8.83**.
3 24th Report on Competition Policy (1994), para 211.
4 Ibid para 214.
5 *Deutsche Bahn-Hov SVZ/MCN* OJ [1994] L 104/34.

8.86

In *Wood Pulp*[1], certain (but not all) of the producers against which proceedings had been brought agreed in future to omit all forms of exchange of individualised data on pulp prices and to abandon their system of regular quarterly price announcements; those producers also undertook to 'sell and invoice at least half the wood pulp sold to European countries in the local currency of the buyer'. The fines imposed on those producers who gave undertakings were accordingly reduced by the Commission; the fines on the other producers were not. Most of the companies involved appealed the Commission's decision to the ECJ seeking, inter alia, the annulment of the undertakings which had been given. The Commission asked the Court to declare the claim inadmissible, arguing that the undertakings constituted unilateral acts by the companies concerned and that they could therefore not be the subject of an action for annulment under Article 230 of the EC Treaty[2]. The ECJ rejected[3] the Commission's argument, holding that the obligations contained in the undertakings should be regarded in the same way as orders requiring an infringement to be brought to an end under art 3 of Regulation 17/62[4]. That is to say, the Court took the view that, in giving the undertakings, the companies had merely assented, for their own reasons, to a decision which the Commission was empowered to adopt under art 3. The Court went on to annul that part of the undertakings which sought to remedy findings of infringement which were not upheld by the Court.

1 Commission Decision (85/202/EEC) OJ [1985] L 85/1, [1985] 3 CMLR 474.
2 For Article 230 generally, see para **10.09** ff.
3 In Cases C-89, 104, 114, 116–117, 125–129/85 *A Ahlström Oy v EC Commission* [1993] 4 CMLR 407 at para 181.
4 For art 3 of Council Regulation (EEC) 17/62 generally, see para **8.49** ff.

6 CONSEQUENCES OF INFORMAL PROCEDURES FOR THE DEVELOPMENT OF THE LAW

8.87

In any given case, an undertaking against which proceedings are brought by the Commission may well decide that it is in its best interests for a case to be settled informally, most frequently by altering or even abandoning the agreements concerned. The statistics set out at para **8.72** serve to show that the vast majority of proceedings commenced by the Commission are in fact closed in this way. Although the Commission does not have to publish details of such cases[1], it frequently does so if it believes that the case gives rise to an interesting point of law or involves a substantial undertaking. Recent examples include *EC Community v Société Belge des Automobiles Citroën*[2], where the Commission closed its investigation into the policy of Citroen's Belgian subsidiary of limiting special discounts granted through its dealer network in Belgium and Luxembourg to buyers living in those countries, on the company agreeing to make these discounts available to any Community consumer; see also *Macron Fire Protection Ltd v Angus Fire Armour Ltd*[3], involving an alleged abuse of a dominant position. The Commission closed its file when Angus agreed to 'avoid unfair pricing' and make a 'substantial ex gratia' payment to Macron in full and final settlement of all claims for alleged breach of Article 82. The Commission itself has stated that one purpose of publishing such cases is to provide guidance to national courts in their application of Articles 81 and 82. This is not without its dangers, as it means that Community law in this field is being developed, in part at least, through cases in which not only does the legal principle involved not come to be tested in the ECJ, but the full procedures of the Commission itself have themselves been curtailed (albeit with the agreement of the undertaking concerned).

1 Council Regulation (EEC) 17/62, art 21(1), OJ Sp Ed [1959–62] p 87.
2 Commission press release IP (88) 778 of 6 December 1988, [1989] 4 CMLR 338n.
3 Commission press release IP (87) 340 of 30 July 1987, [1987] 3 CMLR 715.

8.88
Moreover, as Van Bael has pointed out[1], the Commission does not always appear consistent in the approach which it adopts to seemingly similar cases. He cites as an example the cases involving *Fiat*[2] and *Alfa Romeo*[3] on the one hand and *British Leyland*[4] on the other. Fiat and Alfa Romeo settled matters with the Commission by agreeing to instruct their dealers to stop discouraging purchases of right-hand drive cars on the Continent. In similar circumstances, British Leyland was fined.

1 Van Bael 'The Antitrust Settlement Practice of the EC Commission' (1986) CML Rev 61 at 67.
2 14th Competition Policy Report (1984), paras 70–71.
3 See n 2 above, para 72.
4 Commission Decision (84/379/EEC) *British Leyland* OJ [1984] L 207/11, [1984] 3 CMLR 92.

8.89
A novel approach was adopted by the Commission in the *Rover Group*[1] case. Between 1986 and 1990 Rover Group operated a particular discount system. The Commission considered that this was a clear breach of EC competition rules. Rover Group terminated the practice and notified its new discount arrangements to the Commission. It also informed its dealers that the previous discounting policy had been abandoned and undertook to reimburse dealers any margin which had been withheld from them. In addition, after discussions with the Commission, Rover Group agreed to contribute £1 million to the funding of two projects designed to benefit consumers who purchased motor vehicles in the United Kingdom. The Commission decided not to initiate official proceedings.

1 23rd Report on Competition Policy (1993), at para 228.

Chapter 9 Fines and Penalties

A Introduction

9.01

In addition to its power to issue decisions requiring undertakings to bring to an end infringements of Articles 81 and/or 82[1], the Commission has power to impose fines and periodic penalty payments on undertakings pursuant to arts 15 and 16 respectively of Regulation 17/62[2].

1 See Chapter 8.
2 Council Regulation (EEC) 17/62, OJ Sp Ed [1959–62] p 87.

9.02

This chapter considers in turn the following matters:

(*a*) the power of the Commission to impose fines on undertakings which, either intentionally or negligently, infringe Article 81(1) or Article 82 or commit a breach of an obligation imposed pursuant to art 8(1) of Regulation 17/62 in connection with the grant of an exemption under Article 81(3);

(*b*) the power of the Commission to impose on undertakings fines for certain procedural infringements, principally relating to the supply to the Commission of incorrect or misleading information, the supply of books or other business records in incomplete form during the course of a Commission investigation or the refusal to submit to an investigation which has been ordered by a Commission decision;

(*c*) the power of the Commission to impose periodic penalty payments which can be linked either to a substantive infringement of Article 81 or 82 or to a procedural infringement; and

(*d*) the relevant limitation periods in respect of the Commission's powers to impose fines and penalties and to enforce the collection of fines and penalties.

It should be noted that there is nothing to prevent the Commission imposing both a fine and a periodic penalty payment. This is because their functions are essentially different. Fines imposed under art 15 of Regulation 17/62 relate to infringements (whether substantive or procedural) which have already taken place at the date of the decision (albeit that they may still be continuing at that date). Periodic penalty payments imposed under art 16 of Regulation 17/62 are essentially directed to future action on the part of the undertaking concerned, namely to put an end to a substantive or procedural infringement.

1 PERSONS WHO MAY BE THE SUBJECT OF FINES OR PERIODIC PENALTY PAYMENTS

9.03
Fines and periodic penalty payments can only be imposed on 'undertakings'. This means, for example, that fines cannot be imposed on the directors or other officers of the undertaking concerned. This does not, of course, mean that an individual can never be the subject of a fine or a periodic penalty payment: if an individual constitutes an undertaking for the purposes of Articles 81 and 82 (as was the case, for example, in *Reuter/BASF*[1] and *AOIP/Beyrard*[2]), he may be fined in the same way as a large multinational group can be fined.

1 Commission Decision (76/743/EEC) OJ [1976] L 254/40, [1976] 2 CMLR D44.
2 Commission Decision (76/29/EEC) OJ [1976] L6/8, [1976] 1 CMLR D14.

2 PROCEDURAL PROTECTIONS

9.04
Before an undertaking is the subject of a fine or a periodic penalty payment, it must be given the opportunity to be heard on all the matters to which the Commission takes objection[1]. As well as putting forward its arguments in writing, the undertaking also has a right to be heard orally[2]. In addition, arts 15 and 16 of Regulation 17/62 expressly provide that the Commission must, before imposing a fine or a periodic penalty payment, consult the Advisory Committee on Restrictive Practices and Monopolies pursuant to art 10 of Regulation 17/62[3]. The fact that the name used to identify the addressee of a decision is not an existing company in law does not invalidate a fining decision if it is clear to the real addressee that it is to be identified by the name used: in the *Compagnie Maritime Belge*[4] case, a conflation of the names of the parent company and the subsidiary was sufficiently clear to indicate that the parent company was the addressee.

1 Council Regulation (EEC) 17/62, art 19(1), OJ Sp Ed [1959–62] p 87. However, it has no right to be heard on the amount of fine which the Commission proposes to impose: Case T-83/91 *Tetra Pak International SA v EC Commission* [1994] ECR II-755, CFI (upheld in Case C-333/94P *Tetra Pak International SA v EC Commission,* [1996] ECR I-5951.
2 Commission Regulation (EC) 2842/98, OJ [1998] L 354/18: see paras **7.49**–**7.50**.
3 See para **7.69**.
4 Joined Cases T-24/93, T-25/93, T-28/93 *Compagnie Maritime Belge v EC Commission* [1996] ECR II-1201, at para 36.

B Fines for Substantive Infringements

1 BASIC REQUIREMENTS

9.05
Under Regulation 17/62, art 15(2) the Commission has power to impose on undertakings fines of between 1,000 and 1 million ECU, or a sum in excess

thereof but not exceeding 10% of the turnover in the preceding business year of each of the undertakings participating in the infringements, where, either intentionally or negligently:

(*a*) they infringe Article 81(1) or Article 82 of the EC Treaty; or
(*b*) they commit a breach of any obligation imposed pursuant to Regulation 17, art 8(1).

By far the more important of the two circumstances in which fines can be imposed is (*a*) above—infringement of Article 81(1) or Article 82–and this chapter concentrates on that situation. Brief reference to art 8(1) of Regulation 17/62 (that is, breach of an obligation imposed in a decision granting exemption under Article 81(3)) is made later in this chapter[1]. In fixing the amount of the fine, regard must be had to the gravity and to the duration of the infringement[2].

1 See para **9.79**.
2 Council Regulation (EEC) 17/62, art 15(2), OJ Sp Ed [1959–62] p 87: see para **9.23** ff.

2 NATURE AND PURPOSE OF FINES

9.06
In the *Pioneer*[1] case the ECJ stated the general purpose of fines:

> '. . . the Commission's power to impose fines on undertakings which, intentionally or negligently, commit an infringement of the provisions of Article 85(1) or 86 [now Article 81(1) or 82] of the Treaty is one of the means conferred on the Commission in order to enable it to carry out the task of supervision conferred on it by Community law. That task certainly includes the duty to investigate and punish individual infringements, but it also encompasses the duty to pursue a general policy designed to apply, in competition matters, the principles laid down by the Treaty and to guide the conduct of undertakings in the light of those principles'.

This two-fold purpose of fines (ie to punish individual infringements and deter other undertakings from committing similar infringements) was echoed by the Commission in its Thirteenth Report on Competition Policy (1983):

> 'The purpose of the fines is two-fold: to impose a pecuniary sanction on the undertaking for the infringment and prevent a repetition of the offence, and to make the prohibition in the Treaty more effective[2].'

As far as the nature of the fines is concerned, art 15(4) of Regulation 17/62 expressly provides that they are not of a criminal law nature.

1 Cases 100–103/80 *Musique Diffusion Française v EC Commission* [1983] ECR 1825, [1983] 3 CMLR 221 (para 105 of judgment).
2 At para 62.

9.07
The *Pioneer*[1] case represents something of a turning point in the Commission's fining policy. In its decision[2] in that case, it expressed the intention to reinforce the deterrent effect of fines by raising their general level in cases of serious infringements (such as export bans, market

partitioning and horizontal and vertical price-fixing and, as far as dominant undertakings are concerned, refusals to supply, price discrimination, exclusive or preferential long-term supply agreements and loyalty rebates). In its subsequent judgment in that case, the ECJ endorsed the power of the Commission to review its fining policy from time to time, stating that:

> '. . . the fact that the Commission, in the past, imposed fines of a certain level for certain types of infringement does not mean that it is estopped from raising that level . . . if that is necessary to ensure the implementation of Community competition policy[3]'.

The Commission's 1991 decision in *Tetra Pak II*[4], together with a subsequent speech on policy by Sir Leon Brittan, then Vice President of the EC Commission responsible for Competition Policy and Financial Institutions[5], heralded a tougher approach to fining policy. In its Twenty-First Report on Competition Policy[6] the Commission stated that, in assessing the fine, the financial benefit which companies infringing the competition rules have derived from their infringement would become an increasingly important consideration:

> 'Wherever the Commission can ascertain the level of this ill-gotten gain, even if it cannot do so precisely, the calculation of the fine may have this as its starting-point. When appropriate, that amount could then be increased or decreased in the light of the other circumstances of the case, including the need to introduce an element of deterrence or penalty[6]'.

The toughening stance of the Commission was borne out by its three 1994 decisions[7] imposing aggregate fines of nearly 500 million ECU in three alleged cartel cases and a 1998 decision imposing the highest fine to date on a single company, a fine of 102 million ECU imposed on *Volkswagen*[8].

1 Cases 100–103/80 *Musique Diffusion Française v EC Commission* [1983] ECR 1825, [1983] 3 CMLR 221.
2 Commission Decision (80/256/EEC) OJ [1980] L 60/21, [1980] 1 CMLR 457; see also 13th Report on Competition Policy at para 63.
3 [1983] ECR 1825, [1983] 3 CMLR 221 at para 109.
4 Commission Decision (92/163/EEC) OJ [1992] L 72/1, upheld by the CFI in Case T-83/91 *Tetra Pak International SA v EC Commission* [1994] ECR II-755, upheld by the ECJ in Case C-333/94P *Tetra Pak International SA v EC Commission* [1996] ECR I-5951; see also para **9.57**.
5 'Competition Policy and Procedures', a speech on 16 September 1991 at the Centre for European Policy Studies.
6 1991, at para 139.
7 See para **9.58**.
8 Commission Decision (98/273/EC) OJ [1998] L 124/60, largely upheld on appeal on Case T-62/98 *Volkwagen v EC Commission* (6 July 2000, unreported).

9.08
The frequency and severity of fining decisions should, however, be put in perspective. In 1989 fines were imposed for substantive infringements of Article 81 or 82 in two cases; in 1990 the figure was two, in 1991, three and in 1992, eight. In 1998 the number was five and in 1999, three. The most severe fines are imposed in cases involving clear violations of the competition rules (for example, horizontal price cartels and export bans in supply agreements).

3 UNDERTAKINGS WHICH CAN BE FINED

9.09
There is usually no problem in ascertaining which undertaking should be fined—it is the undertaking which has committed the infringement. However, two particular situations require comment, that of parent and subsidiary and successor companies. The position of trade associations should also be noted.

(1) Parent and Subsidiary

9.10
It is not always clear in any given case which undertaking the Commission will fine where the relevant infringement has been committed by an undertaking within a group of companies. If the infringement has been committed by a subsidiary, acting completely autonomously, the fine is usually imposed on that undertaking alone[1]. Conversely, if the infringement has been committed by the subsidiary but acting together with the parent and/or under the control of the parent, the fine is likely to be imposed on the parent[2] (or sometimes even jointly and severally on both of them). In one of its most recent fining decisions, *PVC*[3], the Commission stated its policy as follows[4]:

> 'Although the concept of an undertaking as the subject of EEC competition rules does not depend upon company law, for the purposes of enforcement it is always necessary to identify an entity possessing legal personality. There might be considerable difficulties with regard to collection of a fine under Article 192 of the Treaty if the decision were not addressed to a legal entity. In the case of a large industrial group it is therefore normal to address any decision to the group holding company or headquarters company, although the undertaking itself consists of the unit formed by the parent and all its subsidiaries'.

The Commission made similar statements in its decisions in *LdPE*[5] and *Welded Steel Mesh*[6].

1 See eg Commission Decision (82/853/EEC) *National Panasonic* OJ [1982] L 354/28, [1983] 1 CMLR 497.
2 As in Commission Decision (85/79/EEC) *Deere* OJ [1985] L 35/58, [1985] 2 CMLR 554. See also Joined Cases T-24/93, 25/93, 28/93 *Compagnie Maritime Belge v EC Commission* [1996] ECR II-1201 at para 35.
3 Commission Decision (89/190/EEC) OJ [1989] L 74/1, [1990] 4 CMLR 345; subsequently annulled on procedural grounds: see para **8.66**.
4 See n 3 above, at para 45.
5 Commission Decision (89/191/EEC) OJ [1989] L 74/21, [1990] 4 CMLR 382 (subsequently annulled on procedural grounds: see para **8.66**).
6 Commission Decision (89/515/EEC) OJ [1989] L 260/1, [1991] 4 CMLR 13.

(2) Successor Companies

9.11
As a result of the acquisition or merging of two or more businesses, a situation can arise where the legal entity which originally committed an

infringement under Article 81 or 82 no longer exists by the time the Commission seeks to impose a fine for that infringement. This happened in the *Sugar*[1] case, where four co-operatives which had violated Article 81 had by the time of the Commission's decision been dissolved, their rights and liabilities being assumed by a new company. The ECJ had no difficulty in upholding the notion that in such circumstances the new company could be fined in respect of the conduct of the four dissolved co-operatives. The critical factor is not whether the legal entity which committed the infringement is still in existence but whether the underlying undertaking exists in some shape or form (and indeed to hold otherwise would provide a ready means of evading liability for infringement of Articles 81 and 82)[2]. Recent cases in which the Commission has applied this principle are *Welded Steel Mesh*[3]; *PVC*[4] and *LdPE*[5].

1 Case 40/73 *Suiker Unie v EC Commission* [1975] ECR 1663, [1976] 1 CMLR 295.
2 Compare the position under the UK RTPA 1976 in the context of fines for contempt of court.
3 Commission Decision (89/515/EEC) OJ 1989 L 260/1, [1991] 4 CMLR 13.
4 Commission Decision (89/190/EEC) OJ [1989] L 74/1, [1990] 3 CMLR 345; subsequently annulled on procedural grounds: see para **8.66**.
5 Commission Decision (89/191/EEC) OJ [1989] L 74/21, [1990] 4 CMLR 382.

9.12
In *Metsä-Serla v EC Commission*[1], the CFI was asked to consider whether an undertaking which has not been specifically and formally held liable for an infringement may be declared jointly and severally liable with another undertaking for payment of a fine imposed on that other undertaking, which has committed and been penalised for the infringement. The Commission in its decision in *Cartonboard*[2] had concluded that the Finnish Board Mills Board Association (Finnboard) had participated in a cartel. The Commission imposed a fine of ECU 20 million on Finnboard. In addition, it considered that each of the four applicant companies should be jointly and severally liable with Finnboard for that part of the total fine which approximated to the proportion of the Cartonboard sales made on its behalf by Finnboard. The CFI noted that Article 15(2) of Regulation 17/62 did not expressly state whether an undertaking not specifically and formally held liable for an infringement could be declared jointly and severally liable with another undertaking which had. The CFI concluded that it was legally possible for joint and several liability to arise, provided that the Commission demonstrates, in its decision, that the infringement could also have been found to have been committed by the undertaking held jointly and severally liable. In the circumstances of the case in question, the CFI held that the economic and legal links between Finnboard and each of the applicants were such that, in marketing cartonboard, Finnboard merely acted as an auxiliary organ of each of those companies. In practice therefore, Finnboard formed an economic unit with each of the cartonboard-producing member companies and the Commission was entitled, instead of imposing a fine directly on each of the applicant companies, to decide to hold each of them jointly and severally liable with Finnboard for payment of part of the fine imposed[3].

1 Joined Cases T-339/94 – 342/94 [1998] ECR II-1727.
2 Commission Decision 94/601/EC, OJ [1994] L 243/1.
3 Judgment of the CFI at paras 42–59.

9.13

Conversely, where the legal person responsible for the operation of the undertaking when the infringement was committed still exists, responsibility for the undertaking's infringement from that legal person, even though the assets and personnel which contributed to the commission of the infringement have been transferred to a third party[1].

1 T-6/89 *Enichem Anic v EC Commission* [1991] ECR II-1623 at paras 236–238, cited in Case T-327/94 *SCA Holding v EC Commission* [1998] ECR II-1373.

9.14

In *All Weather Sports*[1], the CFI made it clear that 'for a Commission decision, which in its statement of reasons merely identifies as the party committing an infringement the legal entity which existed prior to the date of the purchase of its assets, lawfully to be able to impute liability for that infringement to the purchaser of the undertaking, there must be no dispute as to the identity of the legal entity which is the legal successor of the party committing the infringement, or as to the reality of the continuance by that entity of the activity, carried on by the undertaking in question, which gave rise to the proceedings'[2]. In that case, the CFI held that the Commission's reasoning had been inadequate and annulled its decision (which had included the imposition of an 150,000 ECU fine).

1 Case T-38/92 *All Weather Sports Benelux BV v EC Commission* [1995] 4 CMLR 43.
2 See n 1 above, at para 30.

(3) Trade Associations

9.15

The Commission can impose fines on associations of undertakings and, when doing so, can take account of the turnover of an association's members[1]. However, if the entity fined is properly characterised as an undertaking in its own right (rather than an association of undertakings), the Commission cannot take account of the turnover of the firms it represents[2]. In guidelines submitted to the Commission in 1997[3], Competition Commissioner Karel van Miert stated that, in cases involving associations of undertakings, fines should as far as possible be imposed on the individual undertakings belonging to the association. If this is not possible (because, for example, the association has a very large number of members), the guidelines state the fine imposed on the association should equate to the total of individual fines which might have been imposed on each member.

1 Joined Cases T-213/95 and T-18/96 *SCK and FNK v EC Commission* [1997] ECR II-1739.
2 See n 1 above.
3 See para **9.59**.

4 REQUIREMENT THAT THE INFRINGEMENT BE COMMITTED INTENTIONALLY OR NEGLIGENTLY

9.16

In order to impose a fine under art 15 of Regulation 17/62[1], the Commission must be satisfied that the infringement has been committed either intentionally or negligently. The dividing line between what is intentional and what is negligent is not entirely clear. The formulations used by the Commission in individual decisions tend to vary: sometimes it refers to an intentional infringement, sometimes to a negligent infringement and sometimes it refers to both in the alternative. If a Commission decision refers only to an intentional infringement and on appeal the ECJ is satisfied that in fact the undertaking was only negligent it is likely that the ECJ would reduce the fine, but probably not annul the whole decision. The safest formulation for the Commission to adopt is probably along the lines of 'intentional or at least negligent'[2].

1 Council Regulation (EEC) 17/62, OJ Sp Ed [1959–62] p 87.
2 As in Commission Decision (85/618/EEC) *Siemens/Fanuc* OJ [1985] L 376/29, [1988] 4 CMLR 945.

9.17

In *Sandoz*[1], the company issued invoices bearing the words 'exports prohibited'. It claimed that this had been a 'mere oversight'. The Commission was clearly sceptical but said that even if it were true it would represent a 'grave form of negligence'. The ECJ subsequently[2] upheld the decision but reduced the fine from 800,000 ECU to 500,000 ECU because the company had co-operated with the Commission.

1 Commission Decision (87/409/EEC) OJ [1987] L 222/28.
2 Case C-277/87 *Sandoz Prodotti Farmaceutici SpA v EC Commission* [1990] ECR I-45.

9.18

The question whether the undertaking found to have committed an infringement of Article 81 or 82 acted intentionally or negligently is not only an issue which determines whether the Commission has any power to impose a fine at all; in addition, this issue will usually be a factor taken into account by the Commission in deciding what *level* of fine should be imposed.

9.19

In determining whether an undertaking has acted intentionally (for the purpose of establishing whether the Commission has any power to impose a fine at all), the Commission will look to see whether the undertaking knew that the agreement or conduct in question was likely to restrict competition (in the context of Article 81) or amount to an abuse (within the meaning of Article 82). Actual evidence of such awareness will frequently not be available but in cases of blatant infringements of the EC Treaty provisions (for example, an absolute export ban imposed upon a distributor), awareness of the restrictive nature of the agreement will be assumed. In this context, it is not necessary to show also that the undertaking was aware that the action in question amounts to an infringement of Article 81 or 82 (ie ignorance of the law is no defence)[1]. Conversely, if there is evidence on file that the undertaking was aware that the conduct in question did infringe Article 81 or 82, that would certainly be taken into account in assessing whether the infringement was intentional. The knowledge or otherwise on the part of the undertaking of whether or not the agreement/conduct in question violates Article 81 or 82 will also be one of the factors taken into account by the Commission in assessing the *amount* of the fine.

1 Case 19/77 *Miller v EC Commission* [1978] ECR 131, [1978] 2 CMLR 334. See also Case 246/86 *Belasco v EC Commission* [1991] 4 CMLR 96 at 125 and Commission Decision (95/ 477/EC) *BASF Lacke & Farben AG/Accinauto* OJ [1995] L 272/16, at para 103.

9.20

The alternative requirement of negligence probably means that the Commission must be satisfied that the undertaking in question ought to have known that a particular agreement/conduct was restrictive of competition or abusive (as the case may be). Although ignorance of the law is not a defence[1], it may be possible for the undertaking in question to show that it has not been negligent in a case where the Commission has chosen to condemn a particular practice or agreement for the first time. For example, in its decision in *Vegetable Parchment*[2], a case concerning the practice of exchanging information, the Commission said that:

> 'The practice by members of the GVPA of mutually informing each other on their own export quantities and on the level of their prices is an infringement which has not necessarily been committed intentionally. At the time in question the rules of competition of the EEC Treaty had not been sufficiently developed by decisions of the Commission in this field. The conditions for imposing a fine under Article 15(2) of Regulation 17/62 are accordingly not fulfilled'.

At the very least, the fact that a particular decision condemns a certain type of provision or practice for the first time is likely to lead the Commission to impose either no fine or a nominal fine, even if it believes that it has the power to impose a fine[3].

1 Case 19/77 *Miller v EC Commission* [1978] ECR 131, [1978] 2 CMLR 334.
2 Commission Decision (78/252/EEC) OJ [1978] L 70/54, [1978] 1 CMLR 534.
3 See para **9.31**.

5 AMOUNT OF FINE

9.21

The minimum fine which can be imposed for an infringement of Article 81(1) or Article 82 is 1,000 ECU. The maximum fine is either 1 million ECU or 10% of turnover for the preceding year of each of the undertakings participating in the infringement (whichever is the higher). It is not clear from art 15 of Regulation 17/62 whether the turnover in question is total worldwide turnover, total Community turnover or total turnover in only that part of the Community affected by the infringement; similarly, it does not make it clear whether it is turnover in all products (or services) or only in those within the scope of the infringement. This point was clarified by the ECJ in the *Pioneer*[1] case, where it held that it is total worldwide turnover in all products (or services) which is relevant in the context of assessing the upper limit. The reason given by the ECJ for this is that the upper limit is intended to 'prevent fines from being disproportionate in relation to the size of the undertaking' and it felt that it was only the total turnover which could provide this indication. However, turnover in the relevant products will nearly always be relevant in assessing the gravity of the infringement[2].

1 Cases 100–103/80 *Musique Diffusion Française v EC Commission* [1983] ECR 1825, [1983] 3 CMLR 221. See also Case C-279/87 *Tipp-Ex v EC Commission* [1990] ECR I-261 and Case T-13/89 *ICI v EC Commission* [1992] ECR II-1021.
2 See para **9.38**.

9.22
In *Eurocheque International*[1] the Groupement des Cartes Bancaires contended that, as an association of undertakings endowed with a legal personality distinct from that of its members, the maximum fine which could be imposed upon it was 1 million ECU, because it did not carry on any of the activities characteristic of those pursued by the undertakings which were members (the Commission had imposed a fine of 5 million ECU). The CFI dismissed the Groupement's assertion and held that the upper fining limit was 10% of the total turnover of its members[2].

1 Joined Cases T-39/92 and T-40/92 *Groupement des Cartes Bancaires and Europay International v EC Commission* [1994] ECR II-49.
2 See n 1 above, at paras 136–141.

6 GRAVITY AND DURATION OF THE INFRINGEMENT

9.23
Article 15(2) of Regulation 17/62[1] specifically requires the Commission to have regard to the gravity and duration of the infringement in assessing the fine. In *Pioneer*[2], the ECJ held that, in assessing gravity, the Commission must have regard to a large number of factors, the significance of each of which will necessarily vary from case to case. It provided a non-exhaustive list of relevant factors, namely: the volume and value of the goods in respect of which the infringement is committed, the size and economic power of the undertaking and the influence which the undertaking is able to exert on the market. In considering the issue of gravity, the Commission does not have to have regard to whether the infringement was intentional, as opposed to merely negligent: the concept of gravity embodied in the second paragraph of art 15(2) is distinct from the 'intentional or negligent' test[3] embodied in the first paragraph[4].

1 Council Regulation (EEC) 17/62, OJ Sp Ed [1959–62] p 87.
2 Case 100–103/80 *Musique Diffusion Française v EC Commission* [1983] ECR 1825, [1983] 3 CMLR 221 (para 120 of the judgment).
3 See para **9.16** ff.
4 Case C-137/95P *SPO v EC Commission* [1996] ECR I-1611 at paras 53–57.

9.24
Although linking the duration of a particular infringement to the level of a fine is far from a precise art, the *Pioneer*[1] case itself demonstrates the significance of establishing clearly the duration of the infringement. In that case, the ECJ decided that the Commission should only have had regard to a shorter period than that referred to in its decision, because only the shorter

period had been referred to in the Statement of Objections (and accordingly the undertaking's right to be heard had been violated)[2]. This was a factor which it took into account in deciding whether to order a reduction of the fine[3]. If the Commission errs with regard to the duration of the infringement, it does not necessarily follow that the court will reduce the fine by an amount proportionate to the reduction in the period of infringement. The court has unlimited jurisdiction to set the amount of the fine[4].

1 Cases 100–103/80 *Musique Diffusion Française v EC Commission* [1983] ECR 1825, [1983] 3 CMLR 221.
2 See para **7.21**.
3 See also Case T-43/92 *Dunlop Slazenger International Ltd v EC Commission* [1994] ECR II-441 (fine reduced from 5 million to 3 million ECU).
4 Case T-62/98 *Volkswagen v EC Commission* (6 July 2000, unreported).

7 RELEVANT FACTORS IN ASSESSING THE FINE

9.25

Various factors to which the Commission commonly has regard in deciding what level of fine to impose are set out below. The list is not exhaustive; this can be seen from the recent *PVC*[1] case, where the Commission regarded as a mitigating factor the fact that most of the undertakings had already been the subject of substantial fines for participating in a polypropylene cartel[2]. This is a somewhat curious form of mitigation. In the *Solvay*[3] case the Commission took into account, in assessing the amount of the fine, the fact that, in negotiations which it had previously had with the company, it accepted certain features of Solvay's distribution arrangements which were eventually condemned in its final decision. Although it required Solvay to abandon the provisions in question, it did not take them into account in assessing the level of fine. In *FEG and TU*[4] the Commission reduced the fine, having regard to the fact that the administrative proceedings had been very long drawn-out and that it had partially been to blame for this.

1 Commission Decision (89/190/EEC) OJ [1989] L 74/1, subsequently annulled on procedural grounds: see para **8.66**; see also Commission Decision (89/191/EEC) *LdPE* OJ [1989] L 74/21, also subsequently annulled on procedural grounds: see para **8.66**.
2 Commission Decision (86/398/EEC) *Polypropylene* OJ [1986] L 230/1, [1988] 4 CMLR 347.
3 Commission Decision (91/299/EEC) *Soda-ash-Solvay* OJ [1991] L 152/21 at para 71, subsequently annulled on procedural grounds.
4 Commission Decision (2000/117/EC) OJ [2000] L 39/1 at para 152.

9.26

The CFI made it clear in the *Tetra Pak*[1] case that the Commission is not required to break down the amount of fine imposed on an undertaking between the various aspects of the undertaking's behaviour which have given rise to the fine (in that case, Tetra Pak had been found guilty of various infringements of Article 82). The Court indicated that it was sufficient for the Commission merely to specify in the fining decision its criteria for setting the general level of the fine imposed: it did not need to state specifically how it took into account each factor mentioned among those criteria which contributed to setting the general level of the fine.

1 Case T-83/91 *Tetra Pak International SA v EC Commission* [1994] ECR II-755 (at para 236), upheld by the ECJ in Case C-333/94P *Tetra Pak International v EC Commission* [1996] ECR I-5951.

9.27
Where the Commission takes a decision against a number of undertakings (such as in a cartel case), the CFI is willing to review the decision in order to ascertain whether the Commission has been consistent in the treatment of a mitigating factor to undertakings to which the same mitigating factor applies: in *Usines Gustave Boël*[1], the CFI reduced the fine imposed by a fifth on this account. Conversely, an applicant cannot rely on the fact that no fine was imposed on another undertaking. In *Van Megen Sports*[2], the CFI held that an applicant may not rely on that fact in order himself to escape from a penalty imposed through breach of Article 81 when the other undertaking's circumstances are not even the subject of proceedings before the court.

1 Case T-142/89 *Usines Gustave Boël SA v EC Commission* [1995] ECR II-867, CFI.
2 Case T-49/95 *Van Megen Sports v EC Commission* [1996] ECR II-1799 at para 56.

9.28
The factors below are not set out in order of importance. Moreover, some of the factors will tend towards an increase in the fine and some will tend towards a decrease. These factors should now be read in the light of the guidelines submitted to the Commission by Commissioner van Miert in 1997[1].

1 See para **9.59**.

(1) Seriousness of the Infringement

9.29
The nature of the infringement is probably the single most important factor in determining the amount of the fine. The Commission indicated in its Thirteenth Report on Competition Policy (1983)[1] its intention to raise the general level of fines for 'serious infringements' (citing, in relation to Article 81, export bans, market partitioning and horizontal and vertical price-fixing and, in relation to Article 82, refusals to supply, price discrimination, exclusive or preferential long-term supply agreements and loyalty rebates).

1 At para 63.

(2) Repetition of Infringement

9.30
The fact that the same undertaking has previously infringed Article 81 or 82 is likely to be an exacerbating factor[1]. Against that, however, the fact that the undertaking concerned has previously been the subject of heavy fines appears to have been a mitigating factor in at least two recent cartel cases[2]. The CFI has held[3] that the absence of any previous infringement is not something which the Commission has to take into account as a mitigating factor.

1 See eg Commission Decision (89/93/EEC) *Italian Flat Glass* OJ [1989] L 33/44 at para 84; *Soda-ash-Solvay/ICI* OJ [1991] L 152/1 at para 65; *Soda-ash-Solvay/CFK* OJ [1991] L 152/16 at para 19; *Soda-ash-Solvay* OJ [1991] L 152/21 at para 71; *Soda-ash-ICI* OJ [1991] L 152/40 at para 70. The fact that this can be treated as an aggravating factor was upheld by the CFI in Case T-7/89 *SA Hercules Chemicals NV v EC Commission* [1991] ECR II-1711 at para 348, upheld on appeal in Case C-51/92P *Hercules v EC Commission* [1999] 5 CMLR 976.

2 Commission Decision (89/190/EEC) *PVC* OJ [1989] L 74/1 at para 52, subsequently annulled on procedural grounds: see para **8.66**; Commission Decision (89/191/EEC) *LdPE* OJ [1989] L 74/21 at para 64.

3 Case T-7/89 SA *Hercules Chemicals NV v EC Commission* [1992] 4 CMLR 84 at para 348.

(3) New Type of Infringement

9.31

The fine may be relatively modest (or there may be no fine at all) where a particular type of agreement or conduct is being condemned for the first time as violating Articles 81 and/or 82[1]. In *Italian Flat Glass*[2] the same conduct was condemned under Articles 81 and 82 but fines were imposed only in respect of the Article 81 infringement; this was because the Article 82 infringement was based on the new concept of 'collective dominance'[3]. Similarly, in *Napier Brown-British Sugar*[4], the Commission chose not to impose a fine in respect of one particular abuse, because it was the first time that such a practice had been condemned under Article 82. Fines were, however, imposed for other abuses. It is interesting to note that fines have not so far been imposed in relation to research and development agreements, production joint ventures and specialization agreements; this is probably attributable to the fact that it is frequently very difficult in such cases to determine whether or not a particular agreement is caught by Article 81. In the *Peugeot*[5] case, the Commission decided not to impose a fine in relation to a refusal of supplies within a distribution system because the law in that area had not, at the time of the infringement, been clarified (it was subsequently clarified in the *Ford*[6] case). This was one of the factors taken into account by the ECJ in reducing the fine in *AKZO*[7], a predatory pricing case, from 10 million ECU to 7.5 million ECU. In *1998 Football World Cup*[8] a 'symbolic' fine of 1000 EUR was imposed on the organisers of the 1998 World Cup in France.

1 See eg Commission Decision (82/897/EEC) *Toltecs/Dorcet* OJ [1982] L 379/19, [1983] 1 CMLR 412; on appeal Case 35/83 *BAT v EC Commission* [1985] ECR 363, [1985] 2 CMLR 470–non-use of trade mark; Commission Decision (88/477/EEC) *British Dental Trade Association* OJ [1988] L 233/15–first fine for exhibition policy; Commission Decision (87/1/ EEC) *Fatty Acids* OJ [1987] L 3/17, [1989] 4 CMLR 445–first fine for exchange of information agreement; Commission Decision (89/113/EEC) *Decca Navigator System* OJ [1989] L 43/27; Commission Decision (94/985/EC) *Far Eastern Freight Conference* OJ [1994] L 378/17–first decision applying Council Regulation (EEC) 1017/68 to members of a liner shipping conference.

2 Commission Decision (89/93/EEC) OJ [1989] L 33/34, [1990] 4 CMLR 535.

3 See *Butterworths Competition Law* Division VI.

4 Commission Decision (88/518/EEC) OJ [1988] L 284/41.

5 Commission Decision (85/506/EEC) OJ [1986] L 295/19, [1989] 4 CMLR 371. See also Commission Decision (92/154/EEC) *Eco System/Peugeot* OJ [1992] L 66/1, in which the Commission stated the 'explanatory' nature of its decision, in the context of Commission Regulation (EEC) 123/85, OJ [1985] L 15/16, made it unnecessary to impose fines.

6 Cases 25, 26/84 *Ford v EC Commission* [1985] ECR 2725, [1985] 3 CMLR 528, ECJ.
7 Case C-62/86 *AKZO Chemie BV v EC Commission* [1991] ECR I-3359.
8 Commission Decision (2000/12/EC) [2000] OJ L 5/55.

9.32
The Commission's decision in *French-West African shipowners' committees*[1] was the first application of Council Regulation 4056/86[2] for the purpose of imposing a fine for infringement of Articles 81 and 82. In its decision in that case the Commission expressly noted that it was 'customary' to show moderation in determining the amount of the fine, in order to take account of the fact that the parties concerned may not have been fully aware of their obligations under the competition rules or may have under-estimated the gravity of the infringements being committed. However, on the facts, the Commission concluded that this rationale did not apply in that case, on the basis that the Commission was satisfied that the members of the shipowners' committees concerned were fully aware of the application of the competition rules to their activities. The fact that this was the first application of Regulation 4056/86 was not therefore regarded as a mitigating factor[3].

1 Commission Decision (92/262/EEC) OJ [1992] L 134/1, at para 74(g).
2 OJ [1986] L 378/4; this Regulation applies Articles 81 and 82 to maritime transport services: for the application of the Regulation generally, see *Butterworths Competition Law*, Division IX.
3 See too Commission Decision (93/82/EEC) *Cewal* OJ [1993] L 34/20, upheld in Joined Cases T-24/93, 25/93, 26/93 and 28/93 *Compagnie Maritime Belge v EC Commission* [1996] ECR II-1201.

(4) Receipt or otherwise of Legal Advice

9.33
If the Commission obtains evidence that the undertaking was aware that the agreement or conduct in question infringed Article 81 or 82, this is likely to be an aggravating factor in relation to the level of fine[1]. This was shown by the *London European-Sabena*[2] case, in which the company had received advice from a member of its legal department that its behaviour could lead to penalties under Article 82. This was taken into account by the Commission in reaching the conclusion that the infringement had been deliberate. This case also underlines the fact that, whilst some communications between an undertaking and a legal adviser are privileged, many are not[3].

1 This was suggested by the Advocate General in Case 32/78 *BMW v EC Commission* [1979] ECR 2435, at 2495, [1980] 1 CMLR 370 at 392.
2 Commission Decision (88/589/EEC) OJ [1988] L 317/47.
3 The question of legal privilege is considered at para **11.14** ff.

(5) Size of the Undertaking's Market Share and Other Market-Related Factors

9.34
The larger the market share of the undertaking concerned, the more serious will be regarded the infringement and therefore the fine is likely to be higher

than it might otherwise have been because the likely effect on the market will be that much greater. For example, in *Moët et Chandon*[1], the Commission noted in the context of assessing the gravity of the infringement that the undertaking had a 'very substantial share of the United Kingdom market' (40%). However, one practical difficulty which one has in assessing the relevance of market share to the size of the fine in any particular case is that Commission decisions under Articles 81 and 82 usually exclude the market share information (in order to protect business secrets in accordance with art 21(2) of Regulation 17/62[2]).

1 Commission Decision (82/203/EEC) OJ [1982] L 94/7, [1982] 2 CMLR 166.
2 Council Regulation (EEC) 17/62, OJ Sp Ed [1959–62] p 87. See para **8.65**.

(6) Level of Profit made from the Infringement

9.35
The profits which the Commission considers that the undertaking may have made from the infringement (for example, by being able to charge higher prices as a result of an export ban) are a material factor in the assessment of the fine, although it will in many cases be difficult, if not impossible, to assess accurately the profit element arising from the particular transgression. A case in which the Commission attempted to carry out the exercise was *Kawasaki*[1]. More recently, the Commission estimated the profit element in *Eurocheque: Helsinki Agreement*[2].In that case, it concluded that '. . . the Helsinki Agreement must have earned the French banking sector approximately ECU 5 million in commissions from traders. This is income deriving from an agreement which is illegal by virtue of Article 81'. Whether coincidental or not, the fine imposed on the French bank grouping was the same amount, 5 million ECU.

1 Commission Decision (79/68/EEC) OJ [1979] L 16/9, [1979] 1 CMLR 448.
2 Commission Decision (92/212/EEC) OJ [1992] L 95/50, at paras 80–81.

(7) Profitability of the Undertaking or Sector Concerned

9.36
The ability (or otherwise) of an undertaking to pay a fine is a factor which the Commission may take into account and there are a number of cases in which the depressed state of a particular industry has led to the imposition of a lower fine[1]. In *Tipp-Ex*[2] the company argued that the fine imposed on it by the Commission (400,000 ECU) should be reduced because the Commission had failed to take into account the fact that the level of fine would threaten the company's competitive position. The company was not able to substantiate this assertion and the ECJ readily dismissed it. One factor to which the Commission does *not* have regard is whether or not the fine is tax deductible in the country in which the undertaking is resident[3].

1 Eg Commission Decision (84/405/EEC) *Zinc Producer Group* OJ [1984] L 220/27, [1985] 2 CMLR 108; Commission Decision (86/596/EEC) *MELDOC* OJ [1986] L 348/50, [1989] 4 CMLR 853; Commission Decision (89/515/EEC) *Welded Steel Mesh* OJ [1989] L 260/1, [1991] 4 CMLR 13.

2 Case C-279/87 *Tipp-Ex v EC Commission* [1990] ECR I-261.
3 Case 44/69 *Bucher v EC Commission* [1970] ECR 733.

9.37
In *Fiskeby Board*[1], the CFI rejected the argument that the fact that an undertaking was loss making during the period of an infringement should constitute a mitigating circumstance. The CFI noted the ECJ judgment in *IAZ*[2] that recognition of this as a mitigating circumstance would be tantamount to conferring an unjustified competitive advantage on undertakings least well adapted to the conditions of the market.

1 Case T-319/94 *Fiskeby Board v EC Commission* [1998] ECR II-1331.
2 Joined Cases 96/82 to 102/82, 104/82, 105/82, 108/82 and 110/82 *IAZ v EC Commission* [1983] ECR 3369 at para 55.

(8) Turnover in the Products Affected

9.38
As has already been noted at para **9.21**, the total worldwide turnover of the undertaking in all products is relevant in assessing the maximum fine which could be levied (1 million ECU or 10% of annual turnover, whichever is higher). However, it is equally clear[1] that the turnover of the undertaking in the products or services covered by the agreement is relevant; for example, if the relevant goods or services only represent a small fraction of the undertaking's total turnover, this will be a factor which will tend to lead to a lower fine. As in the case of market share figures, turnover figures are frequently excluded from published decisions on grounds of confidentiality and it is therefore difficult to ascertain any particular trends in fining policy in this regard.

1 Cases 100–103/80 *Musique Diffusion Française v EC Commission* [1983] ECR 1825, [1983] 3 CMLR 221; see also Case 246/86 *Belasco v EC Commission* [1991] 4 CMLR 96.

9.39
In *Parker Pen*[1], the CFI noted that the Commission's decision did not take into account the fact that the turnover accounted for by the product to which the infringement related was relatively low in comparison with the turnover from the company's total sales. It accordingly reduced the fine imposed from 700,000 ECU to 400,000 ECU.

1 Case T-77/92 *Parker Pen Ltd v EC Commission* [1994] ECR II-549, CFI.

(9) Extent of Culpability

9.40
In assessing the level of fines in cases where a number of undertakings are involved, the Commission has regard to the relative culpability of each of them[1].

1 See eg Commission Decision (86/596/EEC) *MELDOC* OJ [1986] L 348/50, [1989] 4 CMLR 853 at paras 80–81; Commission Decision (87/406/EEC) *Tipp-Ex* OJ [1987] L 222/1, [1989] 4 CMLR 425 at paras 76–79.

(10) Undertaking Acting under Pressure

9.41
Although it is no defence to Article 81 proceedings that the undertaking acted under economic pressure, this is certainly a factor which is likely (all other things being equal) to serve to reduce the fine, though not necessarily to eliminate it altogether[1].

1 Commission Decision (88/86/EEC) *Fisher-Price/Quaker Oats-Toyco* OJ [1988] L 49/19, [1989] 4 CMLR 553 at para 26; Commission Decision (86/399/EEC) *Belgian roofing felt* OJ [1986] L 232/15, [1991] 4 CMLR 130; on appeal Case 246/86 *Belasco v EC Commission* [1991] 4 CMLR 96; Commission Decision (87/406/EEC) *Tipp-Ex* OJ [1987] L 222/1, [1989] 4 CMLR 425; on appeal Case C-279/87 *Tipp-Ex v EC Commission* [1990] ECR I-261.

(11) Co-operation with the Commission

9.42
If the undertaking takes prompt action to bring the infringement to an end after the Commission has commenced its investigation, this is a mitigating factor in the assessment of a fine[1]. The Commission has frequently made reference in its decisions to the existence or otherwise of co-operation on the part of the undertaking concerned[2]. Conversely, in *Bayo-n-ox*[3] the Commission noted as an exacerbating factor the fact that Bayer had written to its customers, suggesting how they should reply to a Regulation 17/62, article 11[4] request for information sent to them by the Commission. The Commission considered that this obstructed its enquiries.

1 In Case C-277/87 *Sandoz Prodotti Farmaceutici SpA v EC Commission* [1990] ECR I-45, the ECJ reduced a fine from 800,000 to 500,000 ECU on this basis. See also Commission Decision (91/335/EEC) *Gosme/Martell DMP* OJ [1991] L 185/23.
2 See eg Commission Decision (85/618/EEC) *Siemens/Fanuc* OJ [1985] L 376/29, [1988] 4 CMLR 945; Commission Decision (84/282/EEC) *Polistil/Arbois* OJ [1984] L 136/9, [1983] 2 CMLR 594; Commission Decision (84/405/EEC) *Zinc Producer Group* OJ [1984] L 220/27, [1985] 2 CMLR 108; Commission Decision (88/587/EEC) *Hudson's Bay* OJ [1988] L 316/43, [1989] 4 CMLR 340; Commission Decision (89/113/EEC) *Decca Navigator System* OJ [1989] L 43/27; Commission Decision (91/532/EEC) *Viho/Toshiba* OJ [1991] L 287/39.
3 Commission Decision (90/38/EEC) OJ [1990] L 21/71.
4 Council Regulation (EEC) 17/62, OJ Sp Ed [1959–62] p 87.

9.43
In *Polypropylene*[1] the fine imposed on ICI was reduced on account of its cooperation in the investigation but the reduction involved was less than 10%. Before the CFI the company argued that the Commission had given insufficient weight to the company's level of cooperation in assessing the fine. The Court held that, 'having regard to the very detailed reply given by the applicant to the request for information, which concerned not only its own activities but also those of all the undertakings concerned, and without which it would have been much more difficult for the Commission to establish and bring to an end the infringement which is the subject of the Decision, greater account than that taken by the Commission should be taken of the applicant's cooperation'[2]. The Court reduced the fine imposed on ICI (originally set at 10 million ECU) by 1 million ECU.

1 Commission Decision (86/398/EEC) *Polypropylene* OJ [1986] L 230/1, [1988] 4 CMLR 347.
2 Case T-13/89 *ICI v EC Commission* [1992] ECR II-1021 at paras 393 and 394.

9.44

In *Mayr-Melnhof*[1], the applicant argued that it had, in effect, had its fine increased by 50% because it challenged some of the Commission's allegations. It contended that it therefore received a heavier penalty because it did not waive its rights of defence. It was conceded on the part of the Commission that it had informed the undertakings concerned that co-operation on their part would be taken into account when it calculated the fine. The CFI held that, since it regarded the general level of fines imposed by the Commission as justified, the Commission had in fact *reduced* the amount of fines imposed on the undertakings which had co-operated during the investigation, rather than *increasing* the amount of fines imposed on those which had not. The court went on to state that the fact that the Commission had held out the possibility of reduced fines if the undertakings concerned were to admit most or all of the factual allegations did not in itself constitute illegitimate pressure on those undertakings.

1 Case T-347/945 *Mayr-Melnhof v EC Commission* [1998] ECR II-1751.

9.45

In 1996 the Commission adopted a Notice[1] concerning the non-imposition or mitigation of fines in cases where undertakings co-operate in the preliminary investigation or proceedings in respect of an infringement. The Notice addresses specifically what it refers to as 'secret cartels' between enterprises aimed at fixing prices, production or sales quotas, sharing markets or banning imports or exports. It proposes the following treatment of undertakings which co-operate with the Commission and is designed to encourage them to come forward to reveal the existence of a secret cartel. In relation to co-operation taking place prior to publication of the notice on 18 July 1996, the notice is applied by analogy[2].

1 OJ [1996] C 207/4.
2 Commission Decision (1999/210/EC) *British Sugar* [1999] OJ L 76/1 at para 212.

9.46

The Notice states that an enterprise will benefit from a reduction of at least 75% of the fine (or even from total exemption from the fine) that would have otherwise been imposed if it satisfies the following conditions:

(*a*) it informs the Commission about the secret cartel before it has undertaken an investigation, ordered by decision, of the enterprises involved, provided that the Commission does not already have sufficient information to establish the existence of the alleged cartel;
(*b*) it is the first to adduce decisive evidence of the cartel's existence;
(*c*) it puts an end to its involvement in the illegal activity no later than the time at which it discloses the cartel;
(*d*) it provides the Commission with all the relevant information and all the documents and evidence available to it regarding the cartel and maintains continuous and complete co-operation throughout the investigation; and

(*e*) it has not compelled another enterprise to take part in the cartel and has not acted as an instigator or played a determining role in the illegal activity.

9.47
The Notice states that enterprises which satisfy all but the first of the five conditions identified in para **9.46**, and disclose the secret cartel after the Commission has undertaken an investigation ordered by decision on the premises of parties to the cartel and which has failed to provide sufficient grounds for initiating the procedure leading to a decision, will benefit from a reduction of 50% to 75% of the fine.

9.48
Where an enterprise co-operates with the Commission, but without having met all the conditions set out in para **9.46**, the Notice states that it will benefit from a reduction of 10% to 50% of the fine that would otherwise have been imposed. The first decision in which the Commission made reference to the Notice was the *Ferry Operators* case[1]. There, the Commission acknowledged that one of the undertakings had provided a full and frank reply to the Commission's request for information following its unannounced investigation. However, it considered that a reduction of the fine would not be appropriate, given that the co-operation came only after the Commission's investigation had brought the infringement to light and that the undertaking concerned had been found to be one of the principal organisers of the concerted practice.

1 Commission Decision (97/84/EC) *Ferry Operators–Currency Surcharges* OJ [1997] L 26/23.

9.49
The Notice makes it clear that the Commission will only decide whether or not to reduce or waive a fine once the administrative procedure has been completed (ie at the time it adopts its final decision). Nevertheless, the Notice expressly recognises that it will create legitimate expectations on which enterprises may rely when disclosing the existence of an alleged cartel. At the same time, it also notes that leniency in respect of fines cannot protect an enterprise from the civil law consequences of its participation in an illegal agreement. Finally, the Notice states that if an enterprise which has benefited from a reduction in a fine for not substantially contesting the facts then contests them for the first time in annulment proceedings before the CFI, the Commission will normally ask the Court to increase the fine imposed on the enterprise[1].

1 Under Article 229 of the EC Treaty, the Court is entitled to increase the fine imposed: see para **10.05**.

(12) Implementation of Compliance Programme

9.50
The operation by undertakings operating within the Community of internal compliance programmes has assumed increasing importance in recent years[1]. In the context of fines, the establishment by an undertaking of a

compliance programme following initiation of proceedings by the Commission under Article 81 has been held by the Commission to constitute a mitigating factor[2]. In *Eurofix-Bauco v Hilti*[3], the Commission regarded as factors mitigating an otherwise serious infringement of Article 82 the initiation by Hilti of a compliance programme and the fact that Hilti offered an undertaking in response to proceedings for interim measures. Nevertheless, a fine of 6 million ECU was still imposed in that case[4].

1 See Chapter 2.
2 Commission Decision (82/853/EEC) *National Panasonic* OJ [1982] L 354/28, [1983] 1 CMLR 497; Commission Decision (88/86/EEC) *Fisher Price/Quaker Oats Ltd-Toyco* OJ [1988] L 49/19, [1989] 4 CMLR 553; Commission Decision (88/518/EEC) *Napier Brown-British Sugar* OJ [1988] L 284/41.
3 Commission Decision (88/138/EEC) OJ [1988] L 65/19, [1988] 4 CMLR 677. See also Commission Decision (91/532/EEC) *Viho/Toshiba* OJ [1991] L 287/39.
4 Upheld on appeal in Case T-30/89 *Hilti AG v EC Commission* [1992] 4 CMLR 16, CFI and subsequently by the ECJ in Case C-53/92P, [1994] ECR I-667.

9.51
Where a compliance programme has been introduced but subsequently has not been complied with, that is likely to be treated by the Commission as an aggravating factor[1].

1 Commission Decision (1999/210/EC) *British Sugar* OJ [1999] L 76/1 at paras 208 and 209.

9.52
In *Fiskeby Board*[1] the CFI held that the Commission is not obliged in every case to take the implementation of a compliance programme into consideration as a mitigating factor.

1 Case T-319/94 *Fiskeby Board v EC Commission* [1998] ECR II-1331.

(13) Article 4(2) Agreements

9.53
Certain agreements (so-called 'article 4(2) agreements') can be the subject of an individual exemption by the Commission under Article 81(3) without having previously been notified[1]. Even though the reason these agreements do not have to be notified in order to be capable of being exempted is that 'they have special features which may make them less prejudicial to the development of the Community Market'[2], the ECJ decided in *SSI v EC Commission*[3] that this does not prevent them being the subject of fines. However, undertakings are rarely likely to be fined for operating an article 4(2) agreement.

1 See para **4.11** ff.
2 According to the preamble to Council Regulation (EEC) 17/62, OJ Sp Ed [1959–62] p 87.
3 Cases 240/82, etc [1985] ECR 3831, [1987] 3 CMLR 661.

(14) First fine for business sector concerned

9.54
If the Commission is imposing fines for the first time in relation to a particular business sector, this fact is likely to be cited as a mitigating factor: see,

for example, *Building and Construction Industry in the Netherlands*[1] (construction sector), *Eurocheque: Helsinki Agreement*[2] (banking sector) and *Distribution of package tours during the 1990 World Cup*[3] (distribution of tickets for a sporting event). However, as in the case of all mitigating factors, it is impossible to tell from the Commission's decisions what effect this aspect has had on the level of fine. For example, in the construction case aggregate fines of over 23 million ECU were imposed on 28 undertakings.

1 Commission Decision (92/204/EEC) OJ [1992] L 92/1, at para 141.
2 Commission Decision (92/212/EEC) OJ [1992] L 95/50, at para 90.
3 Commission Decision (92/51/EEC) OJ [1992] L 326/31, [1994] 5 CMLR 253.

8 GENERAL SCALE OF FINES IN RECENT YEARS

9.55
As will be clear from the foregoing section, the decision by the Commission as to what level of fines should be imposed in any given case is not a precise art. A whole range of factors can have a bearing and the relative significance of each of the factors necessarily varies from case to case. However, a few general observations can be made. Although the maximum possible fine is 10% of total worldwide turnover there is no case to date in which the Commission has imposed a fine of that magnitude. Indeed, a fine as high as 5% of total worldwide turnover would be considered high. Until the *Tetra Pak II*[1] case, the highest fines imposed on a single undertaking in one case were those imposed on AKZO in 1985, for alleged predatory pricing in contravention of Article 82 (10 million ECU, reduced to 7.5 million ECU on appeal to the ECJ)[2], those on Montedipe (11 million ECU upheld on appeal to the CFI) and ICI (10 million ECU, reduced to 9 million ECU on appeal to the CFI) for alleged participation in the polypropylene cartel[3] and those on Solvay (30 million ECU) and ICI (17 million ECU) for alleged participation in a market sharing agreement in the soda-ash market and abusive conduct in contravention of Article 82 (in relation to their respective rebate arrangements with customers)[4]. The decisions imposing fines in both the *Solvay* and *ICI* cases were annulled by the CFI on procedural grounds[5].

1 See para **9.56**.
2 Commission Decision (85/609/EEC) *ECS/AKZO* OJ [1985] L 374/1, [1986] 3 CMLR 273; on appeal Case C-62/86 *AKZO Chemie BV v EC Commission* [1991] ECR I-3359, ECJ.
3 Commission Decision (86/398/EEC) *Polypropylene* OJ [1986] L 230/1, [1988] 4 CMLR 347; on appeal Cases T-14/89 and T-13/89 *Montedipe v EC Commission* [1992] ECR II-1155, CFI and *ICI v EC Commission* [1992] ECR II-1021, CFI.
4 Commission Decision (91/297/EEC) *Soda-ash-Solvay/ICI* OJ [1991] L 152/1; Commission Decision (91/298/EEC) *Soda-ash-Solvay/CFK* OJ [1991] L 152/16; Commission Decision (91/299/EEC) *Soda-ash-Solvay* OJ [1991] L 152/21 and Commission Decision (91/300/EEC) *Soda-ash-ICI* OJ [1991] L 152/40.
5 Cases T-30-32, 36, 37/91 *Solvay v EC Commission* [1995] ECR II-1775, 1821, 1825, *ICI v EC Commission* [1995] ECR II-1847, 1901, CFI: see para **8.71**.

9.56
In *Tetra Pak II*[1] the Swiss-based packaging group was fined a record 75 million ECU for alleged abuse of a dominant position, including the use of

restrictive contracts and discriminatory and predatory pricing. The Commission emphasised the duration of the alleged infringement (some 15 years), the diversity of the abuses involved and the fact that trade in all Member States was affected. This fine represents a very substantial increase on the previous highest level of fine. Nevertheless, it was upheld by the CFI[2] which pointed out that the fine corresponded to 2.5% of the company's total turnover (compared with a maximum possible fine of 10%[3]). In *VW*[4], the Commission imposed a fine of 102 million ECU on the company for allegedly forcing its Italian concessionaires, on a systematic basis, to refuse to sell Volkswagen and Audi motor cars to foreign purchasers, notably German and Austrian customers.

1 Commission Decision (92/163/EEC) OJ [1992] L 72/1.
2 Case T-83/91 *Tetra Pak International SA v EC Commission* [1994] ECR II-755, upheld by the ECJ in Case C-333/94P *Tetra Pak International SA v EC Commission*, [1996] ECR I-5951.
3 Council Regulation (EEC) 17/62, art 15(2), OJ Sp Ed [1959–62] p 87.
4 Commission Decision (98/273/EC) OJ [1998] L 124/60, fine reduced to 90 million euros in Case T-62/98 *Volkswagen v EC Commission* (6 July 2000, unreported).

9.57

Large fines have, in aggregate, been imposed by the Commission in several of the celebrated cartel cases, in particular, *Polypropylene*[1] (in which the total aggregate fines were just under 60 million ECU), *PVC*[2] (in which the total aggregate fines exceeded 23 million ECU) and *LdPE*[3] (aggregate fines of 37 million ECU). The following statistics give some idea of recent overall trends in fining policy. During the three years from 1987 to 1989 there were fifteen Commission decisions imposing fines for substantive infringements of Article 81 or 82. The lowest fine during that period was 10,000 ECU, imposed on a distributor in the *Tipp-Ex*[4] case. The highest individual fines were imposed on two of the participants in the *Polypropylene*[5] cartel (Montedipe: 11 million ECU; ICI: 10 million ECU). That case was followed by the *Soda Ash* decisions referred to at para **9.55** and the *Tetra Pak II* decision referred to at para **9.56**. In a speech in September 1991[6], Sir Leon Brittan, then Vice President of the European Commission responsible for Competition Policy and Financial Institutions, expressed regret that some firms seem to regard fines under Articles 81 and 82 as 'just another overhead'. In the wake of the *Tetra Pak II* decision referred to at para **9.56**, that speech heralded a tougher approach on the part of the Commission in relation to fines.

1 Commission Decision (86/398/EEC) OJ [1986] L 230/1, [1988] 4 CMLR 347. The fines imposed on the companies involved in this case were reduced, on appeal to the CFI, by a small amount (less than 10% in aggregate) in relation to certain of the companies and not reduced at all in other cases: Cases T-1/89 *Rhône-Poulenc SA v EC Commission* [1991] ECR II-867, CFI; T-2/89 *Petrofina SA v EC Commission* [1991] ECR II-1087, CFI and T-3/89 *Atochem SA v EC Commission* [1991] ECR II-1177, CFI; Cases T-4/89 *BASF AG v EC Commission* [1992] ECR II-1591, CFI; T-6/89 *Enichem Anic SpA v EC Commission* [1992] ECR II-1623 and T-8/89 *DSM NV v EC Commission* [1992] ECR II-2399; Case T-7/89 *SA Hercules Chemicals NV v EC Commission* [1992] 4 CMLR 84; Cases T-9/89 *Hüls AG v EC Commission* [1992] ECR II-499; T-10/89 *Hoechst AG v EC Commission* [1992] ECR II-629; T-11/89 *Shell International Chemical Co Ltd v EC Commission* [1992] ECR II-757; T-12/89 *Solvay v EC Commission* [1992] ECR II-907; T-13/89 *ICI plc v EC Commission* [1992] ECR II-1021; T-14/89 *Montedipe SpA v EC Commission* [1992] ECR II-1155 and T-15/89 *Chemie Linz AG v EC Commission* [1992] ECR II-1275.

2 Commission Decision (89/190/EEC) OJ [1989] L 74/1, [1990] 4 CMLR 345, a decision subsequently annulled by the ECJ on procedural grounds: see para **8.66**, but replaced by a new decision, Commission Decision (94/599/EC) *PVC* OJ [1994] L 239/14, upheld on appeal in Joined Cases T-305/94–T-335/94 *LVM v EC Commission* [1999] 5 CMLR 303.
3 Commission Decision (89/191/EEC) OJ [1989] L 74/21, [1990] 4 CMLR 382, a decision subsequently annulled by the CFI on procedural grounds: see para **8.66**.
4 Commission Decision (87/406/EEC) OJ [1987] L 222/1.
5 See n 1 above.
6 'Competition Policy and Procedures', a speech on 16 September 1991 at the Centre for European Policy Studies.

9.58
In 1994 the Commission imposed aggregate fines of nearly 500 million ECU in three alleged cartel cases[1]. Each of those decisions was subsequently the subject of multiple appeals in which the fines were significantly reduced in a number of cases[2] and in some instances annulled all together[3].

1 Commission Decision (94/215/ECSC) *Steel Beams* OJ [1994] L 116/1, [1994] 5 CMLR 353 (aggregate fines in excess of 100 million ECU); Commission Decision (94/601/EC) *Cartonboard* OJ [1994] L 243/1, [1994] 5 CMLR 547 (aggregate fines in excess of 130 million ECU), and Commission Decision (94/815/EC) *Cement* OJ [1994] L 343/1 (aggregate fines in excess of 240 million ECU).
2 See, for example, Case T-141/94 *Thyssen Stahl v EC Commission* [1994] 4 CMLR 810 (on appeal from the *Steel Beams* decision) and Case T-347/94 *Mayr-Melnhof v EC Commission* [1998] ECR II-1751.
3 Joined Cases T-25/95–T-25/95–T-104/95, *Cimenteries CBR v EC Commission* [2000] 5 CMLR 204.

9.59
In 1997 Competition Commissioner Karel van Miert presented the Commission with guidelines[1] designed to clarify the method used in calculating fines imposed under Articles 81 and 82. These state that a 'base sum' be determined by reference to the duration and gravity of the infringement, without reference at that stage to the turnover of the undertaking(s) concerned. The amount will then be raised (or lowered) if aggravating (or mitigating) circumstances exist.

1 OJ [1998] C 9/3.

9.60
As far as gravity is concerned, the guidelines distinguish between minor infringements (likely fines between 1,000 and 1 million ECU), serious infringements (likely fines between 1 million and 20 million ECU) and very serious infringements (fines above 20 million ECU). In relation to duration, the guidelines distinguish short-term (less than one year), medium-term (one to five years) and long-term (more than five years) infringements. Short-term infringements will not involve any increase in the base fine calculated by reference to gravity. Medium-term infringements will suffer an increase of up to 50%. Long-term infringements will suffer an increase of up to 10% per year for the duration of the infringement. The guidelines specifically state that the increase for long-term infringements is intended to represent a 'considerable strengthening of the existing practice with a view to imposing effective sanctions'.

9.61
Aggravating circumstances cited in the guidelines are:

— repeated infringements;
— refusal to co-operate with the Commission's investigation;
— role of leader in or initiator of the infringement[1];
— retaliatory measures taken against other undertakings;
— need to increase the penalty in order to exceed the amount of improper gains made where these can be calculated.

Mitigating circumstances which are cited are:

— passive role;
— non-application in full of the illegal agreement;
— termination of the infringement as soon as the Commission intervenes;
— reasonable doubt whether the conduct is an infringement;
— infringement is negligent rather than intentional;
— co-operation with the Commission.

The guidelines undoubtedly sent a tough message, one reinforced by the *VW*[2] decision adopted only a month later. In that case, the Commission took as a base sum the figure of 50 million ECU, which it then increased by 10% per annum for each year of the infringement. It is less clear whether they do, as they claim, provide clear guidance on the method by which fines will be calculated.

1 See, for example, Commission Decision (1999/60/EC) *Pre-Insulated Pipe Cartel* OJ [1999] L 24/1.
2 Commission Decision (98/273/EC) OJ [1998] L 124/60.

9 ATTITUDE OF THE EUROPEAN COURT OF JUSTICE TO FINING LEVELS

9.62
In the *Pioneer* case[1] the ECJ endorsed a number of key elements of the Commission's fining policy, confirming, in particular, that the Commission can:

(*a*) from time to time review (ie increase) the general level of fines in relation to a particular type of infringement, if that is necessary to ensure the implementation of Community competition policy[2];
(*b*) have regard to the relevant undertaking's total worldwide turnover in all products (or services) for the purpose of considering the level of fine which was appropriate, whilst stressing that the Commission should only treat this as one of the relevant factors and should, in particular, also have regard to the undertaking's turnover in the particular products (or services) concerned in the market affected;
(*c*) have regard to the deterrent effect of fines.

1 Cases 100–103/80 *Musique Diffusion Française v EC Commission* [1983] ECR 1825, [1983] 3 CMLR 221.
2 See more recently Case T-347/94 *Mayr-Melnhof v EC Commission* [1998] ECR II-1751 at para 259.

9.63

In *Trefilunion*[1], the CFI held that it is desirable for undertakings to be able to determine in detail the method of calculation of the fine imposed upon them, without being obliged, in order to do so, to bring court proceedings against the Commission decision. In *KNP BT*[2], the CFI developed this proposition further, holding that the Commission must, if it systematically took into account certain basic factors in order to fix the amount of fines, set out those factors in the body of the decision in order to enable the addressees of the decision to verify that the level of fine is correct and to assess whether there has been any discrimination between undertakings in relation to the level of fine.

1 Case T-148/89 *Trefilunion v EC Commission* [1995] ECR II-1063 at para 142.
2 Case T-309/94 *KNP BT v EC Commission* [1998] ECR II-1007.

10 RELEVANCE OF PARALLEL PROCEEDINGS UNDER NATIONAL LAW IN THE CONTEXT OF FINES

9.64

It is not unusual for an agreement or conduct to amount to an infringement of Article 81 or 82 and at the same time to fall foul of the restrictive practices legislation in a particular Member State (or, perhaps more rarely, a non-Member State). In the context of fines, the risk is that an undertaking could be the subject of fines imposed both by the Commission and by national authorities (so-called double jeopardy).

9.65

This issue was considered by the ECJ in two of its early judgments, *Wilhelm v Bundeskartellamt*[1] and *Boehringer Mannheim v EC Commission*[2]. From these judgments the following propositions can be drawn:

(1) If an agreement or conduct is made the subject of a fine in a Member State the Commission is required, in later proceedings, to 'take account' of that fine in deciding what level of fine it should itself impose in relation to the same agreement or conduct[1].
(2) Where the earlier fine has been imposed by the authority of a non-Member State, the basic principle appears to be the same, with the important qualification that the Commission may well be able more readily to reach the view that there is not a sufficient 'identity' between the subject matter of the fine imposed in the non-Member State and that which it is imposing (for example, a fine imposed in the United States of America (as was the case in the *Boehringer Mannheim*[2] case itself) is likely to be assessed by reference to its effects on the United States market rather than the Community market).

In *Welded Steel Mesh*[3] the Commission took account of fines imposed by the French authorities in 1985 in respect of acts which were within the same 'organisational framework' as the agreements condemned by the Commission.

1 Case 14/68 [1969] ECR 1, [1969] CMLR 100.
2 Case 45/69 [1970] ECR 769, [1972] CMLR D121.
3 Commission Decision (89/515/EEC) OJ [1989] L 260/1, [1991] 4 CMLR 13, upheld in Case T-141/89 *Trefileurope v EC Commission* [1995] ECR II-791, CFI, at para 191.

9.66

In *Sotralentz*[1], one of the grounds of appeal was that the Commission had imposed a fine 115 times higher than that imposed by the French competition authorities. The CFI rejected this ground of appeal, holding that the Commission was entitled to reach its own conclusions on the basis of the evidence before it, and that it could not be bound by the conclusions of the French authorities in their application of the corresponding national law. It went on to state that any similarity there may be between the legislation of a Member State in the field of competition and the rules laid down in Articles 81 and 82 cannot serve to restrict the Commission's freedom of action in applying those Articles.

1 Case T-149/89 *Sotralentz v EC Commission* [1995] ECR II-1127, CFI, at para 78.

9.67

The *Wilhelm*[1] and *Boehringer Mannheim*[2] cases only dealt with the double jeopardy which can arise from two sets of fines; there is nothing in either judgment to suggest that this principle applies where the sanction applied under national law takes the form of a successful claim for damages by an injured third party, rather than a fine imposed by a public body. Secondly, those two cases dealt with the situation where the Commission sanction was imposed *after* the national law sanction; where the position is reversed, the question whether the national authority should have regard to the sanction imposed by the Commission would appear to be a matter of national law.

1 Case 14/68 *Wilhelm v Bundeskartellamt* [1969] ECR 1, [1969] CMLR 100.
2 Case 45/69 *Boehringer Mannheim v EC Commission* [1970] ECR 769, [1972] CMLR D 121.

11 PAYMENT OF FINES

9.68

The level of fine is stated in euros (previously the ECU). The amount used to be stated in both ECU and a national currency but it is now only stated in euros. It used to be the practice for Commission decisions to indicate that payment could either be made in ECU or in a relevant national currency[1]. This is no longer a practice adopted by the Commission[2]. The decision also states into which bank account the payment should be made and stipulates the date by which it should be made: this is usually three months from the date of notification of the decision, subject to possible suspension of the payment pending an appeal to the ECJ[3]. If payment is not made within that period, interest is payable[4]. The Commission's usual formulation is:

> '[After expiry of the three month period], interest shall automatically be payable at the rate applied by the European Central Bank to its repo operations on the first working day of the month in which this Decision is adopted plus 3.5 percentage points, namely X%[5].

1 See, for example: Commission Decision (89/515/EEC) *Welded Steel Mesh* OJ [1989] L 260/1, [1991] 4 CMLR 13; Commission Decision (89/190/EEC) *PVC* OJ [1989] L 74/1, a decision subsequently annulled on procedural grounds: see para **8.66**; Commission Decision (89/191/EEC) *LdPE* OJ [1989] L 74/21; Commission Decision (89/93/EEC) *Italian Flat Glass* OJ [1989] L 33/44; Commission Decision (89/22/EEC) *BPB Industries* OJ [1989] L 10/50. This was not, however, the case in the *Bayo-n-ox* decision: Commission Decision (90/38/EEC) OJ [1990] L 21/71.

2 See for example, Commission Decision (2000/74/EC) *Virgin/British Airways* OJ [2000] L 30/1.

3 See para **10.59**.

4 The right of the Commission to charge interest was confirmed by the ECJ in Case 107/82 *AEG-Telefunken v EC Commission* [1983] ECR 3151, [1984] 3 CMLR 325 (at paras 139–143 of the judgment).

5 As in the case referred to in n 2 above. This level of interest was unsuccessfully challenged in Joined Cases T-24/93, 25/93, 28/93 *Compagnie Maritime Belge v EC Commission* [1996] ECR II-1201.

9.69

If the undertaking concerned is in serious financial difficulty, the Commission may be willing to accept payment by instalments[1].

1 Commission Decision (75/77/EEC) *French and Taiwanese Mushroom Packers* OJ [1975] L 29/26, [1975] 1 CMLR D 83.

9.70

If an undertaking, the subject of a fine, decides to appeal the Commission's decision to the ECJ, the Commission's practice, which has been upheld by the ECJ[1], is to allow payment to be deferred pending the outcome of the appeal, provided that the undertaking agrees to pay interest if the appeal fails and provides bank guarantees in the meantime.

1 Case 107/82R *AEG-Telefunken v EC Commission* [1982] ECR 1549; Case 86/82R *Hasselblad v EC Commission* [1982] ECR 1555. See too, in the context of the ECSC Treaty, Case 263/82R *Klöckner-Werke v EC Commission* [1982] ECR 3995 and Case 392/85R *Finsider v EC Commission* [1986] ECR 959.

9.71

The CFI has made it clear[1] that, when the Court exercises its power under Article 229 to reduce a fine imposed by the Commission, it is doing precisely that, rather than setting a wholly new fine. In that case, the original fine (imposed in 1992) was 5 million ECU. In 1994, the CFI reduced this on appeal to 2 million ECU. The applicant argued that interest payable on the 2 million ECU fine should be calculated from the date of the 1994 judgment of the CFI rather than from the date of the 1992 decision of the Commission. This argument was rejected.

1 Case T-275/94 *Groupement des Cartes Bancaires 'CB' v EC Commission* [1995] ECR II-2169.

9.72

It is open to an undertaking which seeks the annulment of a decision imposing a fine to apply to the Court of First Instance for interim relief under Articles 185 and 186[1], suspending the Commission's decision. However, such an order is only likely to be made in exceptional circumstances, for example if the undertaking is likely to have difficulty obtaining a bank guarantee or if the cost of the guarantee could jeopardise its activities to such an extent as to risk causing it grave and irreparable damage[2]. In *SCK and FNK*[3] the applicants, two trade associations, claimed that the provision of a bank guarantee, with its associated expenses, would inevitably result in their dissolution, given their respective assets. The President of the CFI held that, on the facts, the risk of serious and irreparable harm had to be assessed having regard to the size and economic power of the undertakings which were members of the associations—ie it was not appropriate to look at the associations in isolation. This was upheld by the President of the ECJ[4].

1 For Articles 185 and 186 generally, see paras **10.57–10.66**.
2 Case 213/86R *Montedipe SpA v EC Commission* [1986] ECR 2623 at 2629. See also Case T- 295/94R *Buchmann v EC Commission* [1994] ECR II-1265 and Case T-301/94R *Laakmann Karton v EC Commission* [1994] ECR II-1279.
3 Case T-18/96R *SCK and FNK v EC Commission* [1996] ECR II-407.
4 Case C-268/96P(R) [1996] ECR I-4971.

9.73
In *Siderúrgica Aristrain Madrid v EC Commission*[1] (involving Article 65 of the ECSC Treaty), the Commission had agreed, following its fining decision, to apportion one of the fines between two group companies, rather than imposing the whole of it on one of them. In those circumstances, the President of the CFI decided that it was no longer justified for the Commission to require from the applicant a security covering the whole of the fine and he accordingly ordered the amount of the security to be reduced by half.

1 Case T-156/94R [1994] ECR II-715.

9.74
In *Parker Pen*[1], the company claimed reimbursement of its expenses incurred in providing security for payment of an 700,000 ECU fine which had been imposed on it (the fine was reduced by the CFI to 400,000 ECU). It claimed that these expenses had been necessarily incurred by it for the purpose of the proceedings and were therefore recoverable under the CFI's Rules of Procedure. The Court ruled that the application was inadmissible because it did not indicate the pleas in law on which the company based its claim. Moreover, it considered that the expenses incurred by the company in the case in providing a bank guarantee for the fine could not be regarded as expenses incurred for the purposes of the proceedings.

1 Case T-77/92 *Parker Pen Ltd v EC Commission* [1994] ECR II-549 at paras 99 and 101, CFI. See too Case T-43/92 *Dunlop Slazenger International Ltd v EC Commission* [1994] ECR II-441.

9.75
If an undertaking pays part of the fine, the Commission is entitled to apply that part-payment first against interest and then against principal, thereby obliging it to pay interest on the remainder of the sum. The fact that the company making the part-payment states, when doing so, that it is to be applied in full against paying off the principal sum due does not change the position[1].

1 Case T-275/94 *Groupement des Cartes Bancaires 'CB' v EC Commission* [1995] ECR II-2169.

12 LIABILITY FOR PAYMENT WHERE MORE THAN TWO UNDERTAKINGS ARE FINED

9.76
In principle, fines are imposed on individual undertakings and where one decision imposes fines on a number of undertakings (for example, in a cartel case such as *Polypropylene*[1] or *PVC*[2]) each undertaking is only responsible for payment of its own fine (ie there is no joint and several liability). However, where a parent company and a subsidiary company are fined the Commission has in the past made the two undertakings jointly and severally liable[3].

1 Commission Decision (86/398/EEC) OJ [1986] L 230/1.
2 Commission Decision (89/190/EEC) OJ [1989] L 74/1, subsequently annulled on procedural grounds: see para **8.66** but replaced by a new decision, see para **8.67**.
3 Cases 6, 7/73 *Commercial Solvents v EC Commission* [1974] ECR 223, [1974] 1 CMLR 309; Case 22/78 *Hugin v EC Commission* [1979] ECR 1869, [1979] 3 CMLR 345; Commission Decision (94/987/EC) *Tretorn* OJ [1994] L 378/45 upheld on appeal (without challenge on this point) in Case T-49/95 *Van Megen Sports v EC Commission* [1996] ECR II-1799.

13 ENFORCEMENT

9.77
Under Article 256 of the EC Treaty, decisions of the Commission imposing a pecuniary obligation are enforceable; enforcement is governed by the rules of civil procedure applicable in the state of the territory in which it is carried out. Article 256 requires each Member State to designate the relevant national authority for the purpose of enforcement.

9.78
In the case of the United Kingdom, Commission decisions can be registered in the High Court (the Court of Session in Scotland), following which they can be enforced as if they were judgments or orders of that court[1].

1 European Communities (Enforcement of Community Judgments) Order, SI 1972/1590.

14 FINE FOR BREACH OF AN OBLIGATION IMPOSED PURSUANT TO ARTICLE 8(1) OF REGULATION 17/62

9.79
Article 15(2) of Regulation 17/62[1] empowers the Commission to impose fines on undertakings which, either intentionally or negligently, commit a breach of any obligation imposed pursuant to art 8(1) of Regulation 17/62. Article 8(1) gives the Commission power to grant an individual exemption under Article 81(3) of the EC Treaty subject to specified conditions and obligations[2]. This is a power which the Commission frequently exercises when granting individual exemptions. However, there is as yet no decision

in which the Commission has imposed fines under art 15(2) for breach of any obligations imposed, although the principles outlined above in the context of art 15(2)(a) (fines for infringement of Article 81 or 82) would be applicable. It should be noted that art 15(2)(b) only refers to breaches of *obligations* imposed in decisions granting individual exemption and does not refer to breaches of *conditions* imposed in such decisions.

1 Council Regulation (EEC) 17/62, OJ Sp Ed [1959–62] p 87.
2 See para **8.41** ff.

C Fines for Procedural Infringements

9.80
Under art 15(1) of Regulation 17/62 the Commission may by decision impose on undertakings fines of from 100–5,000 ECU where, intentionally or negligently:

(*a*) they supply incorrect or misleading information in an application for negative clearance or in a notification[1]; or
(*b*) they supply incorrect information in response to a request made pursuant to art 11(3) or (5) or art 12 or do not supply information within the time limit fixed by a decision taken under art 11(5) of Regulation 17/62[2]; or
(*c*) they produce the required books or other business records in incomplete form during investigations under art 13 or 14, or refuse to submit to an investigation ordered by decision issued in implementation of art 14(3) of Regulation 17/62[3].

1 See paras **9.82–9.83**.
2 See para **9.84**.
3 See paras **9.85–9.86**.

9.81
The three limbs of art 15(1) cover different factual situations and the power to fine in each case is considered in turn below. The Advisory Committee must be consulted before any fine is imposed[1].

1 As to the Advisory Committee generally, see paras **7.69–7.72**.

1 SUPPLY OF INCORRECT OR MISLEADING INFORMATION IN AN APPLICATION FOR NEGATIVE CLEARANCE OR IN A NOTIFICATION

9.82
The importance of ensuring the accuracy of information supplied to the Commission when providing the information prescribed by Form A/B, the form which is used when making applications for negative clearance or submitting notifications for individual exemption under Article 81(3) of the EC Treaty, has already been emphasised in Chapter 4. The supply of

incorrect or misleading information could, in certain circumstances, invalidate the application/notification and accordingly render void any decision taken by the Commission in pursuance thereof. In addition, art 15(1)(a) of Regulation 17/62 gives the Commission power to impose fines in such circumstances, if the supply of the incorrect or misleading information has been done intentionally or negligently. The fines are, however, of a relatively modest nature (up to a maximum of 5,000 ECU).

9.83
A case in which the Commission imposed the maximum fine possible under art 15(1)(a) is *Theal/Watts*[1], which was upheld by the ECJ[2]. That case related to the notification of an oral exclusive distribution agreement where the parties failed to refer to an arrangement which they had concerning the exclusive use of trade marks, the consequence of the overall arrangement being to lead to a partitioning of markets within the Common Market. In holding that the undertaking concerned had acted either intentionally or at least negligently, the court expressly referred to the fact that the text of Form A/B which was then in operation asked parties notifying agreements to indicate whether they involved, inter alia, a sharing of markets or a restriction of freedom to purchase from or sell to third parties.

1 Commission Decision (77/129/EEC) OJ [1977] L 39/19, [1977] 1 CMLR D44.
2 Case 28/77 *Tepea v EC Commission* [1978] ECR 1391, [1978] 3 CMLR 392.

2 SUPPLY OF INCORRECT INFORMATION IN RESPONSE TO REQUESTS UNDER ARTICLE 11 OR 12 OF REGULATION 17/62[1] OR FAILURE TO RESPOND AT ALL TO AN ARTICLE 11(5) DECISION

9.84
The powers of the Commission to request information from undertakings are described in Chapter 6. If the Commission merely writes to an undertaking seeking information pursuant to art 11(3), the position is that the undertaking is not obliged to reply. However, if it does reply, and in so doing supplies incorrect information, a fine can be imposed under this limb of art 15 (similarly in relation to a sectoral inquiry under art 12)[1]. If the Commission issues a decision, requiring an undertaking to supply information pursuant to art 11(5), the undertaking is under an obligation to do so[2]. Non-compliance with such a decision renders the undertaking liable to a fine under this limb of art 15(1) but to date there is no decision in which the Commission has been forced to do this. Unlike art 15(1)(a), which refers to the supply of incorrect or misleading information, art 15(1)(b) only refers to the supply of incorrect information. However, it is not clear what, if any, significance should be attributed to this.

1 Commission Decision (82/124/EEC) *Telos* OJ [1982] L 58/19, [1982] 1 CMLR 267; Commission Decision (82/260/EEC) *National Panasonic (Belgium) NV* OJ [1982] L 113/18, [1982] 2 CMLR 410; Commission Decision (82/465/EEC) *National Panasonic (France) SA* OJ [1982] L 211/32, [1982] 3 CMLR 623; Commission Decision (82/53/EEC) *Comptoir Commercial d'Importation* OJ [1982] L 27/31, [1982] 1 CMLR 440; Commission Decision (85/506/EEC) *Peugeot* OJ [1986] L 295/19, [1989] 4 CMLR 371.

Commission Decision (2000/146/EC) *Anheuser-Busch Inc/Scottish & Newcastle* OJ [2000] L 49/37. See also Commission Decision (91/55/EEC) *Secrétama* OJ [1991] L 35/23, imposing the maximum fine of 5,000 ECU under the corresponding provision of Council Regulation (EEC) 4056/86, OJ [1986] L 378/4 (maritime transport).
2 See para **6.12**.

3 PRODUCTION OF INCOMPLETE BOOKS OR OTHER BUSINESS RECORDS DURING ARTICLE 13 OR 14 INVESTIGATIONS, OR REFUSAL TO SUBMIT TO AN ARTICLE 14(3) INVESTIGATION

9.85
Article 13 of Regulation 17/62 empowers Member State representatives to undertake article 14 investigations at the request of the Commission. Article 14 investigations are dealt with in Chapter 6. They can be of two kinds, either an investigation under authorisation[1] or an investigation by decision[2]. In the former case, the undertaking concerned is not obliged to submit to the investigation but, if it does so, it risks being fined under art 15(1)(c) if it produces its books or other business records in incomplete form. This happened in two cases arising out of the Commission's investigation of the glass market in Italy[3]. In each of those cases specific categories of documentation were requested by the Commission inspectors but were withheld by the undertakings. Similarly, in *FNICF*[4] a trade association was fined for its refusal to produce minutes or records of meetings of its management bodies. In all of these cases the maximum fine was imposed.

1 See para **6.32** ff.
2 See para **6.36** ff.
3 Commission Decision (80/334/EEC) *Fabbrica Pisana* OJ [1980] L 75/30, [1980] 2 CMLR 354; Commission Decision (80/335/EEC) *Fabbrica Lastre di Vetro Rietro Sciarra* OJ [1980] L 75/35, [1980] 2 CMLR 362.
4 Commission Decision (82/756/EEC) OJ [1982] L 319/12, [1983] 1 CMLR 575.

9.86
Article 15(1)(c) of Regulation 17/62 also covers the situation where an undertaking refuses to submit to an investigation ordered by decision under art 14(3) of Regulation 17/62. Article 15(1)(c) does not specifically deal with the situation where, during an on-the-spot investigation under art 14, the undertaking concerned provides incorrect or misleading information (it only refers to the production in incomplete form of the required books or other business records). In cases where the undertaking refuses outright to answer any (or most) of the questions put to it during such an investigation, it may well be that this would be held to constitute a refusal to submit to the investigation (which, if it had been ordered under art 14(3), would enable the Commission to impose a fine under art 15(1)(c)). Subject to that, it would appear that no fine can be imposed under art 15(1)(c) where incorrect or misleading information is provided during such an investigation (nor, by definition, where the undertaking agrees voluntarily to submit to an investigation carried out under investigation, as opposed to decision, but supplies incomplete answers to questions during the course of that investigation). Nevertheless, this should not be taken as

encouragement to provide incorrect or misleading information and the greatest care should always be taken to ensure that all information provided is accurate.

9.87
The Commission took three decisions in 1992 involving partial or total failure to comply with a decision ordering an investigation. In *CSM*[1] the Commission imposed a fine of 3,000 ECU because the company had prevented Commission officials who were undertaking an article 14(3) investigation from taking copies of certain documents on the first day of the investigation. In setting the amount of the fine, the Commission took account of the fact that, on the second day of the investigation, the company (at its own initiative) allowed the Commission officials to take copies of certain of these documents; the infringement was therefore to that extent only temporary and in the Commission's view negligent rather than deliberate. The other two decisions were taken under the corresponding provisions of Council Regulation 4056/96 (maritime transport). In *Ukwal*[2], an association of undertakings with offices in the UK refused to submit to an investigation ordered under art 18(3) of Regulation 4056/86[3] arguing, inter alia, that it had no legal personality and that some of its members were based outside the Community. The Commission held this to be a serious infringement because it prevented the Commission from carrying out simultaneous investigations of the same matter on the premises of different maritime conferences and it imposed a maximum fine of 5,000 ECU (the investigation took place a day later after the Commission had obtained a High Court order against Ukwal). In *Mewac*[4], involving a parallel investigation, the Commission imposed a fine of 4,000 ECU, where the Secretary-General of another conference forced the Commission to delay its investigation 24 hours to allow time for him to return to Marseille from Paris.

1 Commission Decision (92/500/EEC) OJ [1992] L 305/16.
2 Commission Decision (92/237/EEC) OJ [1992] L 121/45.
3 Article 18(3) corresponds to art 14(3) of Council Regulation (EEC) 17/62.
4 Commission Decision (93/47/EEC) OJ [1993] L 20/6.

D Periodic Penalty Payments

9.88
Regulation 17/62, art 16(1) gives the Commission power to impose on undertakings periodic penalty payments ranging from 50 to 1,000 ECU per day (calculated from a date appointed in the decision) in order to compel them:

(*a*) to put an end to an infringement of Article 81 or 82 of the Treaty;
(*b*) to refrain from any act prohibited under art 8(3) of Regulation 17/62;
(*c*) to supply complete and correct information which it has requested by decision taken pursuant to art 11(5) of Regulation 17/62[1]; or
(*d*) to submit to an investigation which it has ordered by decision taken pursuant to art 14(3) of Regulation 17/62.

Each of these situations is considered in turn below; some general points should, however, be noted. Firstly, under art 16(2) the Commission may, where the undertaking concerned satisfies the obligation which it was the purpose of the periodic penalty payment to enforce, fix the total amount of the periodic penalty payment at a lower level than that which would arise under the original decision. Secondly, the Advisory Committee must be consulted before any periodic penalty payment is imposed[2]. The ECJ has held in the *Hoechst*[3] case that this does not apply to the initial decision imposing the periodic penalty payment, because that is provisional in nature, but only to the final decision definitively fixing the amount payable. In *Dalmine*[4], the CFI held that because the initial decision was provisional in nature it did not therefore produce binding legal effects and was not a measure which could be challenged under Article 230, EC Treaty[5].

1 As it did in Commission Decision (91/213/EEC) *Baccarat* OJ [1991] L 97/16.
2 Council Regulation (EEC) 17/62, art 16(3), OJ Sp Ed [1959–62] p 87. As to the Advisory Committee generally, see para **7.69** ff.
3 Joined Cases 46/87, 227/88 *Hoechst AG v EC Commission* [1989] ECR 2859, [1991] 4 CMLR 410, see para **9.95**.
4 Case T-596/97 *Dalmine v EC Commission* [1998] ECR II-2383 at para 31.
5 In relation to Article 230 generally, see para **10.09** ff.

1 PERIODIC PENALTY PAYMENTS TO COMPEL UNDERTAKINGS TO TERMINATE AN INFRINGEMENT OF ARTICLES 81 AND 82

9.89
Article 16(1)(a) of Regulation 17/62 provides that a periodic penalty payment intended to compel an undertaking to terminate an infringement of Article 81 or 82 can only be imposed if the Commission has taken a decision (under art 3 of Regulation 17/62) requiring the infringement to be terminated. There is nothing in principle to prevent the Commission from imposing a periodic penalty payment in addition to a fine (under art 15) in respect of the existing infringement.

9.90
The Commission imposes a periodic penalty payment to compel compliance with an article 3 decision in one of two ways. Either it makes it clear to the undertaking concerned that it intends to impose periodic penalty payments if the order is not complied with (as in *Hasselblad*[1]) or it states the amount and effective date of the penalty in the original article 3 decision itself (as in *United Brands*[2]). Whichever route it adopts a further decision must be taken by the Commission before the undertaking is legally obliged to pay the penalty[3].

1 Commission Decision (82/367/EEC) OJ [1982] L 161/18, [1982] 2 CMLR 233; on appeal Case 86/82 *Hasselblad v EC Commission* [1984] ECR 883, [1984] 1 CMLR 559.
2 Commission Decision (76/353/EEC) *Chiquita* OJ [1976] L 95/1, [1976] 1 CMLR D28; on appeal Case 27/76 *United Brands v EC Commission* [1978] ECR 207, [1978] 1 CMLR 429 and [1978] ECR 345, [1978] 3 CMLR 83. See too Commission Decision (98/273/EC) *VW* OJ [1998] L 124/60.
3 Cases 228, 229/82 *Ford v EC Commission* [1984] ECR 1129, at 1173, [1984] 1 CMLR 649.

9.91

It has been the Commission's practice to date to impose periodic penalty payments to compel compliance with an order for interim measures[1].

1 Commission Decision (82/628/EEC) *Ford Werke AG* OJ [1982] L 256/20, [1982] 3 CMLR 267; Commission Decision (83/462/EEC) *ECS/AKZO* OJ [1983] L 252/13, [1983] 3 CMLR 694; Commission Decision (87/500/EEC) *BBI/Boosey and Hawkes* OJ [1987] L 286/36, [1988] 4 CMLR 67; *Ecosystem SA v Peugeot SA* [1990] 4 CMLR 449.

2 PERIODIC PENALTY PAYMENTS TO COMPEL UNDERTAKINGS TO REFRAIN FROM ANY ACT PROHIBITED UNDER ARTICLE 8(3) OF REGULATION 17/62

9.92

Article 8(3) of Regulation 17/62 enables the Commission to prohibit specified acts in certain circumstances in connection with an exemption granted under Article 81(3)[1]. There is not as yet any decision of the Commission imposing fines in such circumstances.

1 See para **8.38** ff.

3 PERIODIC PENALTY PAYMENTS TO COMPEL UNDERTAKINGS TO SUPPLY COMPLETE AND CORRECT INFORMATION REQUESTED BY THE COMMISSION PURSUANT TO ARTICLE 11(5) OF REGULATION 17/62

9.93

It is rare for the Commission to have to resort to this sanction but it has been exercised in at least two cases[1].

1 Commission Decision (76/593/EEC) *CSV* OJ [1976] L 192/27; Commission Decision (91/213/EEC) *Baccarat* OJ [1991] L 97/16.

4 PERIODIC PENALTY PAYMENTS TO COMPEL UNDERTAKINGS TO SUBMIT TO AN ARTICLE 14(3) INVESTIGATION

9.94

A periodic penalty payment was imposed on the German company Hoechst in 1987 for refusing to submit to an article 14(3) decision. The Commission decision imposed a payment of 1,000 ECU for each day of delay. The company sought annulment of this decision (and of the underlying article 14(3) decision) and also applied to the ECJ for interim measures, suspending the operation of the decision[1]. The President of the ECJ rejected the application for interim measures, on the basis that the company had established neither a prima facie case nor urgency[2]. The Commission eventually carried out the investigation about a month later and adopted a further decision, definitively fixing the amount of the periodic penalty payment at 55,000 ECU (representing 55 days' delay). The company also appealed against that decision.

1 As to interim measures applications generally, see paras **10.57–10.66**.
2 Case 46/87R *Hoechst AG v EC Commission* [1987] ECR 1549, [1988] 4 CMLR 430.

9.95
In its judgment in the *Hoechst* case the ECJ found against the company in relation to the decisions imposing and subsequently fixing the definitive amount of the periodic penalty payment[1]. In so doing, the ECJ held as follows: firstly, it was not necessary for the Commission to consult the Advisory Committee[2] *before* adopting the decision to impose the periodic penalty payment, because that decision was provisional. Such consultation only had to take place before the final decision was taken (ie fixing the payment at 55,000 ECU)[3]. Secondly, the Commission was entitled, in determining the final amount payable, not to exclude the time during which the company had been pursuing its unsuccessful claim for interim measures (ie suspension of the Commission's original decision) before the ECJ[4]. Thirdly, the court rejected the argument that the amount of the penalty payment was disproportionate, having regard to the fact that the company was invoking what it saw as its constitutional rights[5].

1 Joined Cases 46/87, 227/88 *Hoechst AG v EC Commission* [1989] ECR 2859.
2 As to the Advisory Committee generally, see para **7.69** ff.
3 Paragraphs 49–58 of the judgment.
4 Paragraphs 60–61 of the judgment.
5 Paragraphs 62–64 of the judgment.

E Limitation Periods Relating to the Imposition and Enforcement of Fines and Periodic Penalty Payments

9.96
In the interests of legal certainty[1], the EC Council in 1974 adopted Regulation 2988/74 'concerning limitation periods in proceedings and the enforcement of sanctions under the rules of the European Economic Community relating to transport and competition'. The Regulation came into force on 1 January 1975[2] but was made applicable also to infringements committed before the date of entry into force[3]. Undertakings threatened with fines, particularly in cartel cases, frequently seek to rely on it, usually without success[4]. The Regulation sets out limitation periods in relation to two situations, firstly, the Commission's power to *impose* fines or penalties and secondly, its power to *enforce* decisions imposing fines, penalties or periodic penalty payments. Each of these aspects is considered in turn below.

1 Preamble to Council Regulation (EEC) 2988/74, OJ [1974] L 319/1.
2 Article 8.
3 Article 7.

4 See, for example, Commission Decision (89/515/EEC) *Welded Steel Mesh* OJ [1989] L 260/1, [1991] 4 CMLR 13 , subsequently upheld on this issue in the various appeals against the decision, eg, Case T-145/89 *Baustahlgewebe v EC Commission* [1995] ECR II-987, upheld on appeal in Case C-185/95 *Baustahlgewebe v EC Commission* [1998] ECR I-8417.

9.97

Regulation 2988/74 deals only with the imposition and enforcement of fines and other pecuniary sanctions. It does *not* prevent the Commission from taking action as such. That is to say, it may still declare that an infringement has taken place; nor is there anything in the Regulation which appears to prevent the Commission from ordering action remedying the infringement.

1 LIMITATION PERIOD REGARDING THE IMPOSITION OF FINES AND PENALTIES

9.98

The period after which the Commission can no longer impose fines or penalties is as follows[1]:

(*a*) three years in the case of infringements of provisions concerning applications or notifications, requests for information[2] or the carrying out of investigations[3]; and
(*b*) five years in the case of all other infringements (ie substantive infringements of Articles 81 and/or 82).

1 Council Regulation (EEC) 2988/74, art 1, OJ [1974] L 319/1.
2 Under Council Regulation (EEC) 17/62, art 11, OJ Sp Ed [1959–62] p 87.
3 Under Council Regulation (EEC) 17/62, art 14.

9.99

Time begins to run on the day on which the infringement is committed. However, in the case of continuing or repeated infringements (which will usually be the case), time does not begin to run until the day on which the infringement ceases[1]. For example, in *Toltecs/Dorcet*[2] the Commission held that the earliest date for termination of the infringement was when BAT declared at the oral hearing that it attached no further importance to the continuation of the agreement in question.

1 Council Regulation (EEC) 2988/74, art 1(2). This provision was relied upon by the CFI in Case T-11/89 *Shell International Chemical Co Ltd v EC Commission* [1992] ECR II-757 at 891.
2 Commission Decision (82/897/EEC) OJ [1982] L 379/19, [1983] 1 CMLR 412.

9.100

Under art 2 of Regulation 2988/74, any action taken by the Commission (or by a Member State acting at the request of the Commission) for the purpose of the preliminary investigation or proceedings in respect of an infringement interrupts the limitation period. The date on which the interruption takes effect is that on which the action in question is notified to at least one of the undertakings which has participated in the infringement. Article 2 provides a non-exhaustive list of the actions which will serve to interrupt the limitation period, namely:

(*a*) written requests for information[1] or a Commission decision requiring information[2];
(*b*) written authorisations to carry out investigations[3], or a Commission decision ordering an investigation[4];
(*c*) the commencement of proceedings by the Commission[5]; and
(*d*) notification of the Commission's Statement of Objections.

1 Under Council Regulation (EEC) 17/62, art 11(3).
2 Under Council Regulation (EEC) 17/62, art 11(5).
3 Under Council Regulation (EEC) 17/62, art 14(2).
4 Under Council Regulation (EEC) 17/62, art 14(3); see eg Commission Decision (83/546/EEC) *Cast Iron and Steel Rolls* OJ [1983] L 317/1, [1984] 1 CMLR 694 at para 68.
5 See para **7.09**.

9.101
Each interruption starts time running afresh[1]. However, interruptions cannot extend the limitation period for longer than twice what it would otherwise have been (effectively six years in the case of procedural infringements and ten years in other cases).

1 Council Regulation (EEC) 2988/74, art 2(3).

9.102
The limitation period is suspended for as long as the decision of the Commission is the subject of proceedings pending before the ECJ[1].

1 Council Regulation (EEC) 2988/74, art 3; see also 4th Report on Competition Policy (1974) at para 49. For a case in which this was relevant, see Commission Decision (94/599/EC) *PVC* OJ [1994] L 239/14, at paras 56–58.

2 LIMITATION PERIOD IN RELATION TO THE ENFORCEMENT OF FINES, PENALTIES AND PERIODIC PENALTIES

9.103
The power of the Commission to enforce decisions imposing fines, penalties or periodic penalties is subject to a limitation period of five years, time beginning to run on the day on which the decision in question becomes final[1]. Again, there is provision for the limitation period to be interrupted. In the context of enforcement of sanctions, the relevant interrupting events are:

(*a*) notification of a decision varying the original amount of the fine, penalty or periodic penalty payment or refusing an application for variation;
(*b*) any action of the Commission (or a Member State acting at the request of the Commission) for the purpose of enforcing payment of the fine, penalty or periodic penalty.

Each interruption starts time running afresh; there is no 'long-stop' provision of the type referred to at para **9.101**.

1 Council Regulation (EEC) 2988/74, art 4, OJ [1974] L 319/1.

9.104
The limitation period for the enforcement of sanctions is suspended for as long as time to pay is granted to the undertaking or enforcement of payment is suspended pursuant to a decision of the ECJ.

Chapter 10 Judicial Review: EC

A Introduction

10.01
Various provisions of the EC Treaty provide scope for judicial challenge, by both Member States and natural and legal persons, against the acts of the Council of the European Union and the European Commission. These provisions are of general application and accordingly apply in relation to action (and inaction) by the European Commission under Articles 81 and 82 of the EC Treaty. This chapter describes the grounds on which the acts and omissions of the Commission under Articles 81 and 82 can be made the subject of judicial challenge.

10.02
Until September 1989 judicial review of Commission actions under Articles 85 (now Article 81) and 86 (now Article 82) was undertaken by the European Court of Justice of the European Communities (ECJ). However, since that date a new court 'attached to' the ECJ has been in operation, the Court of First Instance of the European Communities (CFI). The creation of the CFI was made possible by the Single European Act[1], which was signed in Luxembourg on 17 February 1986 and came into force, following ratification by the Member States, on 1 July 1987. The Single European Act inserted a new Article into the Treaty of Rome, Article 168*a* (now Article 225) (and corresponding wording in the ECSC[2] and Euratom[3] Treaties), empowering the Council of the European Union to establish the CFI. The CFI has jurisdiction to hear and determine at first instance certain classes of action or proceeding brought by natural or legal persons[4]. The Council was given power to determine the classes of action which were to be within the scope of the CFI. Amongst those actions over which jurisdiction was initially given to the CFI[5] were actions by natural or legal persons against a Community institution relating to the implementation of the EC competition rules applicable to undertakings (ie Articles 85 and 86 (now Articles 81 and 82)). Its jurisdiction was subsequently extended[6] to all actions brought by natural or legal persons under Articles 230[7] and 232[8] (with the exception of dumping and subsidy cases, where this extension will require a further decision by the Council). In the remainder of this chapter the term 'Court' connotes the ECJ and the CFI collectively.

1 OJ [1987] L 169/1.
2 Article 32*d*.
3 Article 140*a*.
4 EC Treaty, Article 168*a*; ECSC Treaty, Article 32*d*; Euratom Treaty, Article 140*a*.
5 Council Decision 88/591/ECSC, EEC, Euratom, adopted on 24 October 1988: published (in corrected form) OJ [1989] C 215/1, [1989] 3 CMLR 458.

6 Council Decision (93/350/Euratom, ECSC, EEC), adopted on 8 June 1993, OJ [1993] L 144/21. See too Council Decision (94/149/ECSC, EC) adopted on 7 March 1994, OJ [1994] L 66/29.
7 See para **10.09** ff.
8 See para **10.48** ff.

10.03
The background to the establishment of the CFI, its jurisdiction, relationship with the ECJ and procedures applicable before it, are summarised at paras **10.72–10.105**[1]. Firstly, however, this chapter describes the grounds on which the actions (or inactions) of the European Commission in relation to Articles 81 and 82 can be judicially reviewed.

1 On the CFI generally, see Millett *The Court of First Instance of the European Communities* (1990); *HL Select Committee on the European Communities 5th Report* (HL Paper 1987–88) 'A European Court of First Instance'; Schermers 'The European Court of First Instance' (1988) CML Rev 541; Kennedy 'The essential minimum: the establishment of the Court of First Instance' (1989) 14 EL Rev 7.

10.04
The principal Articles of the EC Treaty under which judicial control is exercised over the European Commission in relation to Articles 81 and 82 are as follows:

(*a*) Article 229, under which the Court has unlimited jurisdiction in relation to penalties (including fines) provided for in regulations made by the Council of the European Union (for example, Regulation 17/62[1]);
(*b*) Article 230, under which the Court is empowered to review the legality of acts of the Council and the Commission;
(*c*) Article 232, under which the Court has power to declare an infringement by the Council or the Commission by virtue of a failure to act;
(*d*) Articles 242 and 243, under which the Court may grant interim relief.

For completeness, brief reference is made in paras **10.67–10.70** to two other important Treaty provisions, namely Article 234 (dealing with preliminary rulings on references from national courts) and Article 288 (dealing with actions for damages against the Community).

1 Council Regulation (EEC) 17/62, OJ Sp Ed [1959–62] p 87.

B Article 229: Actions in Relation to Penalties

10.05
Article 229 (formerly Article 172) provides that regulations made by the Council of the European Union may give the Court unlimited jurisdiction in relation to the penalties provided for in such regulations. In pursuance of this, art 17 of Regulation 17/62 (the principal regulation implementing Articles 81 and 82 of the EC Treaty) provides the Court with unlimited jurisdiction to review decisions in which the Commission has fixed a fine or periodic penalty payment. It may cancel, reduce or increase the fine or periodic penalty payment imposed[1].

1 A corresponding provision is contained in the regulations which lay down rules for the application of Articles 81 and 82 in the fields of maritime and air transport: Council Regulation (EEC) 4056/86, art 21, OJ [1986] L 378/4 (maritime transport) and Council Regulation (EEC) 3975/87, art 14, OJ [1987] L 374/1 (air transport).

10.06

Notwithstanding the reference to unlimited jurisdiction contained in Article 229, it would appear that applicants for judicial review under this Article should invoke one or other of the grounds set out in Article 230, the EC Treaty provision which enables actions to be brought for the annulment of Commission decisions[1]. In practice, in cases in which the Commission imposes a fine or periodic penalty payment, application to the Court is almost invariably made under both Articles.

1 In relation to Article 230, see paras **10.09–10.47**.

10.07

On an application under Article 229, the Court can consider all relevant questions of law and fact. The Court has not infrequently reduced the level of fines imposed, for example where it has found that the duration of the infringement has not been as long as was held by the Commission[1] or by striking out one of the alleged infringements[2]. Although it has power to increase fines, the Court has not yet done so.

1 Eg Cases 100–103/80 *Musique Diffusion Française v EC Commission* [1983] ECR 1825, [1983] 3 CMLR 221.

2 Eg Case 27/76 *United Brands v EC Commission* [1978] ECR 207, [1978] 1 CMLR 429; Case 193/83 *Windsurfing International v EC Commission* [1986] ECR 611, [1986] 3 CMLR 489.

10.08

The CFI has made it clear[1] that, when the Court exercises its power under Article 229 to reduce a fine imposed by the Commission, it is doing precisely that, rather than setting a wholly new fine. In that case, the original fine (imposed in 1992) was 5 million ECU. In 1994 the CFI reduced this on appeal to 2 million ECU. The applicant argued that interest payable on the 2 million ECU fine should be calculated from the date of the 1994 judgment of the CFI rather than from the date of the 1992 decision of the Commission. This argument was rejected.

1 Case T-275/94 *Groupement des Cartes Bancaires 'CB' v EC Commission* [1995] ECR II-2169.

C Article 230: Action for Annulment

10.09

Article 230 (formerly Article 173) empowers the Court to review the legality of acts of the Commission on one or more of the following grounds:

(*a*) lack of competence;
(*b*) infringement of an essential procedural requirement;
(*c*) infringement of the EC Treaty or of any rule of law relating to its application;
(*d*) misuse of powers.

Member States may bring actions under Article 230 as of right[1]. A natural or legal person may only bring such an action against a decision addressed to him or against a decision which, although in the form of a regulation or decision addressed to another person, is of 'direct and individual concern' to the former[2].

1 See eg Case 41/83 *Italy v EC Commission* [1985] ECR 873, [1985] 2 CMLR 368, an action which arose out of Commission Decision (82/861/EEC) *British Telecommunications* OJ [1982] L 360/36, [1983] 1 CMLR 457.
2 See para **10.18** ff.

1 COMMISSION ACTS REVIEWABLE UNDER ARTICLE 230

10.10
Where an action is brought by a natural or legal person, he must establish that the act in question constitutes a decision of the type contemplated by Article 230. There will usually be no difficulty in establishing this. Indeed, Regulation 17/62[1] specifically provides that certain Commission acts are to take the form of decisions, thereby enabling them to be the subject of judicial review under Article 230: for example, orders to terminate infringements under art 3 of Regulation 17/62, orders imposing fines under art 15 or periodic penalty payments under art 16, decisions granting an Article 81(3) exemption under art 6, decisions ordering information to be provided under art 11(5) and decisions ordering an undertaking to submit to an investigation under art 14(3).

1 Council Regulation (EEC) 17/62, OJ Sp Ed [1959–62] p 87.

10.11
Cases do, however, arise in which there is more difficulty in deciding whether a particular act amounts to a decision. For example, in *IBM v EC Commission*[1], the ECJ had to decide whether the initiation of a procedure[2] and issuance of a Statement of Objections[3] amounted to decisions capable of review by the ECJ. It decided that they did not as they only amounted to interim acts during the administrative procedure leading up to the taking of a decision. The ECJ provided the following guidance:

> 'In the case of acts or decisions adopted by a procedure involving several stages, in particular where they are the culmination of an internal procedure, it is clear from the case law that in principle an act is open to review only if it is a measure definitively laying down the position of the Commission or the Council on the conclusion of that procedure, and not a provisional measure intended to pave the way for the final decision'[4].

1 Case 60/81 [1981] ECR 2639, [1981] 3 CMLR 635.
2 See para **7.08** ff.
3 See para **7.12** ff.
4 [1981] ECR 2639 at 2652. See, in the context of the merger control regulation (Commission Regulation (EEC) 4064/89, OJ [1989] L 395/1), Case T-52/96R *Sogecable v EC Commission* [1996] ECR II-797.

10.12
In *Air France*[1], the CFI was required to consider an action for annulment of a decision taken by the Commission in which it stated that the proposed concentration between British Airways and Dan Air was not considered to have a Community dimension under the EC Merger Regulation. The decision in question took the form of a statement by the spokesman for the Commissioner responsible for competition matters which was reported by the Europe press agency but was otherwise not documented. The Commission contended that the statement in question was not in the nature of a decision because, inter alia, it was not addressed to any particular person but simply amounted to an expression of an opinion on the interpretation of the Merger Regulation[2] and because it had only been made orally. Whilst accepting that the contested act was in an unusual form, the CFI rejected the Commission's contention.

1 Case T-3/93 *Air France v EC Commission* [1994] ECR II-121.
2 Council Regulation (EEC) 4064/89, OJ [1990] L 257/14.

10.13
In addition to those acts which are expressly required by Regulation 17/62 to take the form of decisions[1], other Commission acts have been held by the ECJ to amount to decisions within the meaning of Article 230. These include, in particular:

(*a*) a notice issued under art 15(6) of Regulation 17/62[2];
(*b*) a decision ordering[3] or refusing[4] interim measures;
(*c*) a letter formally rejecting a complaint made under art 3 of Regulation 17/62[5];
(*d*) a decision to disclose confidential documents[6].

Conversely, the Court of First Instance has held that a letter from the Commission indicating that it considers that an agreement notified to it falls within Article 81(1) (and is unlikely to benefit from an exemption under Article 81(3)), but which is phrased in a way which indicates that the Commission is still examining the matter, does not amount to a decision capable of being challenged under Article 230[7]. Moreover, suggestions in the letter as to the sort of changes to the agreement which the Commission would probably need to see to make an exemption decision possible were held not to be equivalent to conditions of an exemption decision within the meaning of art 8(1) of Regulation 17/62[8].

1 See para **10.10**.
2 Cases 8-11/66 *Cimenteries v EC Commission* [1967] ECR 75, [1967] CMLR 77: see para **8.29** ff.
3 Cases 228, 229/82 *Ford v EC Commission* [1984] ECR 1129, [1984] 1 CMLR 649: see para **8.05** ff.
4 Case 792/79R *Camera Care v EC Commission* [1980] ECR 119, [1980] 1 CMLR 334.
5 Joined Cases 142, 156/84 *BAT and Reynolds v EC Commission* [1987] ECR 4487; Case 298/83 *CICCE v EC Commission* [1985] ECR 1105, [1986] 1 CMLR 486: see para **5.28** ff.
6 Case 53/85 *AKZO v EC Commission* [1986] ECR 1965, [1987] 1 CMLR 231: see para **11.07** ff.
7 Case T-113/89 *Nefarma v EC Commission* [1990] ECR II-797, CFI.
8 As to art 8(1) generally, see paras **8.41–8.44**.

10.14
In contrast with the formal rejection of a complaint, which is a reviewable decision[1], it appears that a so-called article 6 letter does not amount to a reviewable decision[2]: this was the view of the Advocate-General in the *CICCE*[3] case, his reasoning being that art 6 of Commission Regulation 99/63[4] (now art 6 of Commission Regulation 2842/98[5]) specifically requires the Commission to provide the complainant with a further opportunity to submit comments on its view that there are insufficient grounds for ordering termination of the alleged infringement; by definition therefore the letter does not mark the culmination of the administrative procedure because it expressly contemplates further comments being made to, and considered by, the Commission. This appears now to have been confirmed by the CFI in *Automec Srl v EC Commission*[6].

1 Joined Cases 142, 156/84 *BAT and Reynolds v EC Commission* [1987] ECR 4487; Case 298/83 *CICCE v EC Commission* [1985] ECR 1105, [1986] 1 CMLR 486 and Case C-39/93P *SFEI v EC Commission* [1994] ECR I-2681, ECJ.
2 Ie a letter under Commission Regulation 99/63, art 6, indicating that the Commission does not believe there are grounds for granting the complainant's application, but inviting it to submit further comments. See para **5.28** ff.
3 See n 1 above.
4 Commission Regulation (EEC) 99/63, OJ Sp Ed [1963–64] p 47.
5 Commission Regulation (EC) 2842/98, OJ [1998] L 354/18.
6 Case T-64/89 [1990] ECR II-367.

10.15
In *Rendo*[1], the ECJ held that, where the Commission terminates (wholly or in part) an investigation initiated upon a complaint, such termination necessarily amounts to a measure producing legal effects which the complainant can challenge under Article 230.

1 Case C-19/93P *Rendo v EC Commission* [1995] ECR I-3319, at para 28.

10.16
In the *Wood Pulp*[1] case, a number of applicants who challenged a decision adopted by the Commission[2] sought, inter alia, the annulment of an undertaking which had been annexed to that decision. In giving that undertaking, all but one of the applicants seeking annulment had committed themselves to certain future conduct, as a result of which those companies which gave the undertaking obtained a substantial reduction in the fine imposed by the Commission. The Commission asked the ECJ to declare the applicants' claim inadmissible, on the basis that the undertaking which they had given constituted a unilateral act and could not therefore be the subject of an action for annulment under Article 230. The ECJ rejected this, holding that the obligations imposed on the applicants by the undertaking should be regarded in the same way as orders requiring an infringement to be brought to an end (as provided for by art 3 of Regulation 17/62[3]). The Court held that in giving the undertaking the applicants had merely assented, for their own reasons, to a decision which the Commission was empowered to adopt unilaterally. The effect of this was that the Court annulled those parts of the undertaking which imposed obligations which resulted from findings of infringement made by the Commission but which the Court in its judgment declared void[4].

1 Joined Cases C-89/85, C-104/85, C-114/85, C-116, 117/85 and C-125-129/85 *A Ahlström Oy v EC Commission* [1993] ECR I-1307.
2 Commission Decision (85/202/EEC) OJ [1985] L 85/1, [1985] 3 CMLR 474.
3 Council Regulation (EEC) 17/62, OJ Sp Ed [1959–62] p 87.
4 See n 1 above, at paras 178–185.

10.17
It is as yet unclear whether *formal* comfort letters[1] issued by the Commission amount to decisions capable of review under Article 230. In the *Perfumes*[2] cases the ECJ decided that comfort letters did not amount to decisions under arts 2 or 6 of Regulation 17/62 because they were not published under arts 19 and 21. Subsequently, with a view to giving comfort letters greater legal certainty, the Commission introduced a procedure under which more formal comfort letters are issued following publication of a summary of the main contents of the agreement in question in the Official Journal[3]. It is possible, though unlikely, that the position is different in relation to such formal comfort letters.

1 See para **8.77** ff.
2 Cases 253/78 etc *Procureur de la République v Giry and Guerlain* [1980] ECR 2327, [1981] 2 CMLR 99.
3 See para **8.78**.

2 NATURAL OR LEGAL PERSONS WHO CAN BRING ACTIONS UNDER ARTICLE 230

10.18
Any natural or legal person may commence proceedings against:

(*a*) a decision addressed to him; or
(*b*) a decision which, although in the form of a regulation or a decision addressed to another person, is of direct and individual concern to him.

It is not difficult to ascertain whether a decision is addressed to a particular person. As far as the second category is concerned, the crucial question is whether the applicant can satisfy the Court that the decision in question is of direct and individual concern to him. A complainant who has a legitimate interest[1] under art 3(2)(b) of Regulation 17/62 is certainly entitled to bring an action under Article 230[2]. Indeed, the ECJ went further in *Metro II*[3], indicating that a person could be directly and individually concerned even if it had not formally been a complainant under art 3 of Regulation 17/62. It repeated the formulation set out in previous judgments in other contexts:

> '... persons other than those to whom a decision is addressed may claim to be concerned within the meaning of Article 173(2) only if that decision affects them by reason of certain attributes which are peculiar to them, or by reason of circumstances in which they are differentiated from all other persons, and by virtue of these factors distinguishes them individually just as in the case of the person addressed'[4].

In *Métropole Television*[5], the CFI ruled that a failure to participate in the Commission's administrative procedure did not affect the applicant's right to take action under Article 173 (now Article 230). However, in *Kruidvat*[6], the ECJ held that a decision granting exemption to a selective distribution system cannot be regarded as being of individual concern to an undertaking in competition with the authorised distributors, in circumstances where that undertaking had not filed a complaint, nor participated in the administrative procedure, nor applied to the supplier for admission to the selective distribution network, since it was in a situation which could not be distinguished from that of numerous other economic operators on the market.

1 See para **5.03** ff.
2 Case 26/76 *Metro v EC Commission* [1977] ECR 1875, [1978] 2 CMLR 1.
3 Case 75/84 [1986] ECR 3021, [1987] 1 CMLR 118.
4 At para 20 of the judgment. See also Joined Cases T-528/93, 542/93, 543/93 and 546/93 *Métropole Télevision v EC Commission*, [1996] ECR II-649 in which the CFI ruled that a failure to participate in the Commission's administrative procedure did not affect the applicant's right to take action under Article 230.
5 Joined Cases T-528/93, 542/93 and 546/93 *Métropole Télevision v EC Commission* [1996] ECR II-649.
6 Case C-70/97P *Kruidvat v EC Commission* [1998] ECR I-7183.

10.19

In *Dutch Banks*[1] the Commission had granted a request for negative clearance in respect of an agreement between a number of Dutch banking associations. In its reasoning, the Commission stated that the agreement restricted competition, but that there was no appreciable effect on trade between Member States. The applicant associations appealed against those grounds of the decision finding a restriction of competition, but did not question the operative part of the decision (ie the grant of negative clearance). The CFI ruled that the application was inadmissible. The CFI cited[2] previous case law[3] for the proposition that an action under Article 230 of the EC Treaty can only be brought against an act which gives cause for complaint. In this case, the CFI considered that the Commission's grant of negative clearance gave satisfaction to the applicants and was not, by its very nature, capable of altering their legal position or giving them cause for complaint (it contrasted the position of a third party whose economic interests may well be affected by a grant of negative clearance and who could, if he showed a sufficient interest, bring an action for annulment). The CFI was not persuaded by the argument that a national court might in the future reach a different conclusion from the Commission on the issue of effect between Member States, but still take account of the Commission's position regarding the alleged restriction of competition.

1 Case T-138/89 *Nederlandse Bankiersvereniging and Nederlandse Vereniging van Banken v EC Commission* [1992] ECR II-2181.
2 See n 1 above, at para 31.
3 Case 60/81 *IBM v EC Commission* [1981] ECR 2639, [1981] 3 CMLR 635.

3 GROUNDS OF ANNULMENT

10.20

The four grounds of annulment set out in Article 230 tend to merge with one another. They do not differ greatly from the grounds on which judicial review of administrative action is available under English law[1]. However, Article 230 is in practice invoked much more frequently than is judicial review of the decisions of the competition authorities in the United Kingdom and the ECJ has accordingly played a much greater role in the development of EC competition law in the last few years than have the English courts in the development of UK competition law. There have now been a number of important judgments of the CFI in the competition law field which indicate that the CFI is willing to examine in detail the evidence on which the Commission has relied in particular cases for a finding of infringement of Article 81 or 82. One of the clearest examples of this so far is the *Italian Flat Glass*[2] case. There, it emerged from enquiries carried out by the CFI that when the Commission prepared documentary evidence with a view to communicating this to the undertakings concerned, certain relevant passages were deliberately deleted or omitted, even though they did not contain business secrets. In particular, nine words were deleted from a particular hand-written note, a deletion which in the view of the Court completely changed the tenor of the note in question. The judgment indicates that the Commission had tried 'in vain' to supply an objectively justifiable reason for the deletion of the words in question. As a result, the Court concluded that it was 'incumbent on it . . . to check meticulously the nature and import of the evidence taken into consideration by the Commission in the decision'[3].

1 See Chapter 17.
2 Joined Cases T-68/89 and T-77, 78/89 *Societá Italiano Vetro SpA v EC Commission* [1992] ECR II-1403, [1992] 5 CMLR 302.
3 Ibid at para 95.

10.21
In *Hilti*[1] the CFI rejected the Commission's argument that an applicant for annulment under Article 230 could not invoke arguments which it had not put forward during the administrative proceedings leading up to the Commission decision in question.

1 Case T-30/89 *Hilti AG v EC Commission* [1992] 4 CMLR 16.

(1) Lack of Competence

10.22
The powers of the Commission are set out in the EC Treaty itself and in implementing regulations. If it takes action in excess of those powers, that action can be annulled for lack of competence. Actions brought under this limb of Article 230 can involve alleged lack of either procedural or substantive competence. A case in the former category is *AKZO v EC Commission*[1], in which AKZO unsuccessfully argued that there was no power to delegate to the Commissioner responsible for competition matters the power to take decisions under art 14(3) of Regulation 17/62[2]. An illustration of alleged lack of substantive competence concerns the vexed issue of the extraterritorial application of Articles 81 and 82. This issue was raised in the *Dyestuffs*[3], *Continental Can*[4] and *Commercial Solvents*[5] cases; the alleged lack of competence was rejected in all three cases for the

reasons explained in Division XII. More recently, the issue was again brought before the Court (and the applicants' arguments again rejected) in the *Wood Pulp*[6] case.

1 Case 5/85 *AKZO v EC Commission* [1986] ECR 2585, [1987] 3 CMLR 716.
2 Ie a decision ordering inspections, see para **6.31** ff.
3 Case 48/69 *ICI v EC Commission* [1972] ECR 619, [1972] CMLR 557.
4 Case 6/72 *Europemballage and Continental Can v EC Commission* [1973] ECR 215, [1973] CMLR 199.
5 Cases 6, 7/73 *Commercial Solvents v EC Commission* [1974] ECR 223, [1974] 1 CMLR 309.
6 Joined Cases 89/85 etc *A Ahlström Oy v EC Commission* [1993] ECR I-1307.

(2) Infringement of an Essential Procedural Requirement

10.23

This is one of the most frequently invoked grounds of appeal, often with at least partial success. However, not every procedural irregularity will justify annulment. Rather, the Court must be satisfied that the decision reached by the Commission might have been different but for the irregularity[1]. Examples of irregularities which the Court has not considered sufficient to justify annulment are:

(*a*) delay in communicating the minutes of an oral hearing[2];
(*b*) issuance of a Statement of Objections to a trade association but not to its members[3];
(*c*) absence of some of the Commission's officials from part of an oral hearing[4].

1 Eg Case 30/78 *Distillers Co Ltd v EC Commission* [1980] ECR 2229 at 2265, [1980] 3 CMLR 121 at 167; see also Advocate General Warner in that case at pp 2290, 154, respectively.
2 Case 48/69 *ICI v EC Commission* [1972] ECR 619, [1972] CMLR 557.
3 Case 71/74 *FRUBO v EC Commission* [1975] ECR 563, [1975] 2 CMLR 123.
4 Joined Cases 43, 63/82 *VBVB v VBBB* [1984] ECR 19, [1985] 1 CMLR 27.

10.24

Other specific issues which have arisen in cases to date include those identified at paras **10.25–10.30**.

(*a*) *Consultation*

10.25

Under Regulation 17/62[1], the Commission is required to consult the Advisory Committee before taking certain decisions[2]; failure to do so would probably justify annulment[3].

1 Council Regulation (EEC) 17/62, OJ Sp Ed [1959–62] p 87.
2 See para **7.69** ff.
3 See Advocate General Gand in Case 41/69 *ACF Chemiefarma v EC Commission* [1970] ECR 661 at points 68/69; see also Advocate General Warner in Case 30/78 *Distillers Co Ltd v EC Commission* [1980] ECR 2229, [1980] 3 CMLR 121.

(b) Right to be heard

10.26
The right to be heard is a fundamental requirement of Community law[1]. Failure to afford this right is capable of vitiating a Commission decision in whole or part[2]. If, however, the Court believes that the failure related to an aspect of the case of relative insignificance, annulment of the entire decision is unlikely to follow.

1 See Chapter 11.
2 As in Cases 100–103/80 *Musique Diffusion Française v EC Commission* [1983] ECR 1825, [1983] 3 CMLR 221.

(c) Reasoning

10.27
Article 253 of the EEC Treaty requires decisions to be reasoned. In *Remia*[1] the ECJ said that 'the statement of the reasons on which a decision adversely affecting a person is based must allow the Court to exercise its power of review as to the legality of the decision and must provide the person concerned with the information necessary to enable him to decide whether or not the decision is well founded'. In *Cimenteries*[2] the Commission took action under art 15(6)[3] of Regulation 17/62. It considered that this did not amount to a decision and gave no reasons for its action. The ECJ disagreed and accordingly decided that the lack of reasoning meant that the decision must be annulled. The extent of reasoning required varies from case to case. Where a case breaks new legal ground, for example, the decision will need to be more fully reasoned than might otherwise be the case[4]. In general, however, the Commission does not have to cover every single legal and factual argument put forward by the undertakings in its decision[5], although it will clearly risk annulment if it omits to deal with any central issues raised by the parties.

1 Case 42/84 *Remia BV v EC Commission* [1985] ECR 2545, [1987] 1 CMLR 1, point 26; see also Case T-44/90 *La Cinq v EC Commission* [1992] ECR II-1, [1992] 4 CMLR 449, and Case C-360/92P *Publishers' Association v EC Commission* [1995] ECR I-23.
2 Cases 8–11/66 *Cimenteries v EC Commission* [1967] ECR 75, [1967] CMLR 77.
3 See para **8.29** ff.
4 Case 73/74 *Papiers Peints v EC Commission* [1975] ECR 1491, [1976] 1 CMLR 589.
5 See *Remia*, n 1 above; see also Joined Cases 43, 63/82 *VBVB v VBBB* [1984] ECR 19, [1985] 1 CMLR 27; Joined Cases 142, 156/84 *British American Tobacco Co v EC Commission* [1987] ECR 4487, [1988] 4 CMLR 24; Case 246/86 *Belasco v EC Commission* [1991] 4 CMLR 96; Joined Cases C-241 and 242/91P *RTE and ITP v EC Commission* [1995] ECR I-743.

10.28
In *Hilti*[1] the applicant referred, in annulment proceedings before the CFI, to a press release issued by the Commission shortly after its decision in the case. Hilti claimed that the contents of the press release indicated that the Commission had taken into account factors which were not relied upon on the face of the decision itself. The CFI dismissed Hilti's argument, holding that there was nothing in the press release to indicate that the contested decision was based on considerations other than those set out on its face[2].

1 Case T-30/89 *Hilti AG v EC Commission* [1991] ECR II-1439.
2 Ibid para 136.

10.29
In *Asia Motors France*[1] the Commission rejected a complaint filed with it under art 3 of Regulation 17/62. On review, the CFI held that the Commission's decision was 'flawed by a manifest error of assessment of the facts which has led the Commission to commit an error in law regarding the applicability of art 85 to the conduct of the enterprises in question'[2]. Accordingly, the Commission's decision was annulled.

1 Case T-7/92 *Asia Motors France v EC Commission* [1993] ECR II-669.
2 See n 1 above, at para 55.

(d) Burden of Proof

10.30
The burden of establishing an infringement of Article 81 or 82 rests with the Commission. If its decision does not adequately establish the facts on which the finding of infringement is based, this will provide grounds for annulment. For example, in *Continental Can*[1] the ECJ annulled the Commission's decision because it 'had not, as a matter of law, sufficiently shown the facts and the assessments on which it is based'[2]. The Court is willing, if necessary, to examine the facts upon which the Commission's decision is based in some detail. Since its establishment in 1989[3], the CFI has shown itself very willing to do this and, in particular, to examine in detail the evidence upon which the Commission has based a finding of a cartel or concerted practice between competitors[4]. At the same time, however, if a complex economic assessment is involved (as will frequently be the case) it is reluctant to intervene; thus, in the *Remia*[5] case the ECJ said:

> 'Although as a general rule the Court undertakes a comprehensive review of the question whether or not the conditions for the application of Article 85(1) [now Article 81(1)] are met, it is clear that in determining the possible duration of a non-competition clause incorporated in an agreement for the transfer of an undertaking the Commission has to appraise complex economic matters. The Court must therefore limit its review of such an appraisal to verifying whether the relevant procedural rules have been complied with, whether the statement of the reasons for the decision is adequate, whether the facts have been accurately stated and whether there has been any manifest error of appraisal or a misuse of powers'[6].

1 Case 6/72 *Europemballage and Continental Can v EC Commission* [1973] ECR 215, [1973] CMLR 199; see too Case 40/73 *Suiker Unie v EC Commission* [1975] ECR 1663, [1976] 1 CMLR 295.
2 See *Continental Can*, n 1 above, at 249.
3 See para **10.02**.
4 See eg Cases T-68/89 and T-77, 78/89 *Societá Italiano Vetro SpA v EC Commission* [1992] ECR II-1403, [1992] 5 CMLR 302; see also para **10.20**.
5 Case 42/84 *Remia BV v EC Commission* [1985] ECR 2545, [1987] 1 CMLR 1.
6 At point 34 of the judgment. See too Joined Cases T-39/92 and T-40/92 *Groupement des Cartes Bancaires and Europay International v EC Commission*, [1994] ECR II-49, at point 109.

10.31

In *Hilti*[1] (an Article 82 case), the company argued that, by requiring it to demonstrate that the relevant market was the one for which it contended, the CFI had taken a wrong approach to the burden of proof. The company believed that the Commission's decision was based on suppositions/inferences and it was therefore sufficient for Hilti merely to demonstrate that the facts established by the Commission could be interpreted differently. The ECJ concluded that the Commission decision was based on precise factual evidence, not mere supposition, and dismissed Hilti's plea.

1 Case C-53/92P *Hilti AG v EC Commission* [1994] ECR I-667 at 704–7.

10.32

In *Anic*[1], the applicant in a cartel case argued that the CFI[2] had erred in law in holding that, once Anic's participation in the regular meetings of polypropylene producers had been proved, it could not assert that it had not subscribed to the price initiatives which had been decided upon. Anic contended that that involved a reversal of the burden of proof. The ECJ, in upholding the CFI's judgment on this point, held that it was entitled to find, without unduly reversing the burden of proof, that since the Commission had been able to establish that Anic had participated in the meetings at which price initiatives had been decided upon, planned and monitored, it was for Anic to adduce evidence that it had not subscribed to those initiatives.

1 Case C-49/92 P *EC Commission v Anic*, judgment dated 8 July 1999, at paras 93–96.
2 Case T-6/89 *Enichem Anic v EC Commission* [1991] ECR II-1623.

(3) Infringement of the EC Treaty or of any Rule of Law relating to its Application

10.33

Interpreted in the broadest way, this ground embraces the other three grounds set out in Article 230. For example, where a decision is annulled for lack of reasoning this could be characterised as either breach of an essential procedural requirement or as an infringement of the EC Treaty (namely Article 253). Decisions can be annulled under this limb of Article 230 if the Commission has made an error of law[1]. Such cases are relatively rare. More often, annulment is based on the Court's view that the facts as established by the Commission do not support the finding of law—effectively lack of adequate evidence[2].

1 See eg Case 4/73 *Suiker Unie v EC Commission* [1975] ECR 1663, [1976] 1 CMLR 295; see also Case T-7/92 *Asia Motors France v EC Commission* [1993] ECR II-669 and Joined Cases T-528/93, 542/93, 543/93 and 546/93 *Métropole v EC Commission* [1996] ECR II-649.
2 As in Joined Cases T-79/95 and 80/95 *SNCF and British Rail v EC Commission* [1996] ECR II-1491.

10.34

In addition, there are a number of principles of Community law which, being of general application, are of relevance in cases under Articles 81 and

82[1]. Breach of such general principles would be likely to provide the basis of an action for annulment under Article 230.

1 See Chapter 11.

10.35
In the *RTE* case[1] the applicant argued that the Commission's decision to prescribe the granting of compulsory licences in respect of TV programme listings was incompatible with the Berne Convention (Article 9(1) of which confers on the author of a literary or artistic work the exclusive right of reproducing the protected work). The claim was dismissed.

1 Joined Cases C-241 and 242/91P *RTE and ITP v EC Commission* [1995] ECR I-743.

10.36
In *Parker Pen*[1] the applicant had been fined 700,000 ECU for including an export ban in an agreement with a distributor. On appeal to the CFI, it contended, inter alia, that the Commission had no interest in bringing proceedings against it, relying on the principle upheld in the *Automec*[2] case that the Commission is not required to reach a decision on a complaint if it does not believe that there is sufficient Community interest to justify doing so (for example, if it believes that it would be more appropriate for the matter to be dealt with by a national court). The Commission argued that although it may reject a complaint in cases with limited economic impact or little legal significance, it is not legally obliged to do so. The CFI held that the Commission made correct use of its discretion and did not commit an error of law.

1 Case T-77/92 *Parker Pen Ltd v EC Commission* [1994] ECR II-549, CFI.
2 Case T-24/90 *Automec Srl v EC Commission* [1992] ECR II-2223. See also para **5.10**.

(4) Misuse of Powers

10.37
A decision can in principle be annulled if the Commission exercises its powers for an illegitimate purpose. However, a decision is vitiated by misuse of powers only if it appears, on the basis of objective, relevant and consistent evidence, that it was adopted with the exclusive or main purpose of achieving ends other than those stated[1]. No decision under Article 81 or 82 has yet been successfully challenged on this ground, although it has been pleaded in a number of cases[2].

1 See Case C-84/94 *United Kingdom v EU Council* [1996] ECR I-5755 (at para 69) and Joined Cases T-133 and 204/95 *IECC v EC Commission* [1998] ECR II-3645 at para 188.
2 Eg Case 5/85 *AKZO v EC Commission* [1986] ECR 2585, [1987] 3 CMLR 716.

4 REMEDIES AND PROCEDURE UNDER ARTICLE 230

(1) Remedies

10.38
Under Article 231 of the EC Treaty, a decision successfully challenged under Article 230 is void. Annulment can be either total or partial; partial annulment would be ordered if the relevant part of the decision is capable of separation from the remainder and provided that the effect of severing the offending part in this way would not produce an unjust result. An example of how partial annulment operates in practice is provided by the *Transocean Marine Paint* case[1]. There, the Commission had granted an individual exemption under Article 81(3) subject to a reporting condition. The condition was imposed in breach of a fundamental procedural requirement. It would have been a curious result for this to have rendered the entire decision void (ie including the exemption itself) and accordingly the ECJ annulled only the condition. At the same time, however, the ECJ recognised the purpose underlying the condition and remitted the matter to the Commission to make a fresh decision, this time without breaking any fundamental procedural requirements. It is not the CFI's role to remake a contested decision; to do so could, in the view of the Court, 'disturb the inter-institutional balance established by the Treaty and would risk prejudicing the rights of defence'[2].

1 Case 17/74 *Transocean Marine Paint v EC Commission* [1974] ECR 1063, [1974]2 CMLR 459.
2 Cases T-68/69 and T-77, 78/89 *Societá Italiano Vetro SpA v EC Commission* [1992] ECR II- 1403, [1992] 5 CMLR 302 at para 319.

10.39
In *Viho Europe*[1], the applicant sought annulment of the Commission's rejection of its complaint made under Article 81. In addition to annulment, it requested the Court to make two positive orders against Parker Pen, including an order requiring it to supply the applicant at the same prices and terms as it applied to its independent exclusive distributors or subsidiaries in the various Member States. The CFI reaffirmed consistent ECJ case law that it has no jurisdiction to issue directions to the Commission, or indeed any other Community institution, in connection with an action for annulment under Article 230.

1 Case T-102/92 *Viho Europe BV v EC Commission* [1995] ECR II-17.

(2) Time Limits

10.40
Article 230, third paragraph, requires proceedings under Article 230 to be instituted within two months of publication of the decision in question or of its notification to the undertaking concerned. If both events occur, as will frequently be the case, it is unclear whether it is the earlier or later date

which is critical, although it is almost certainly the earlier date. It is usually the case that the date of notification precedes publication in the Official Journal of the European Communities. In order to cover all eventualities, Article 230, third paragraph, provides that if the decision is neither published nor notified to the undertaking concerned, the relevant date is the date on which the decision comes to the knowledge of that undertaking.

10.41

Under the detailed rules of procedure which are laid down, the two-month period begins to run from the day following the date of receipt of notification of the decision (or, if the relevant date is the date of publication, 15 days after publication in the Official Journal)[1]. Short extensions exist to allow for distance from Luxembourg, the seat of the ECJ and the CFI, and public holidays[2]. In one of the early rulings of the CFI[3], it held that the time limits must be interpreted strictly. In the case in question the applicant was out of time by two days and the CFI declared the application inadmissible.

1 CFI Rules of Procedure, art 102(1).

2 EEC Treaty Protocol on the Statute of the Court of Justice of the EEC, Article 42; CFI Rules of Procedure, arts 101(2) and 102(2). See also the ECJ's Rules of Procedure, Annexes I and II, OJ [1991] L 176/7.

3 Case T-125/89 *Filtrona Española v EC Commission* [1990] ECR II-393; see also Case T-106/89 REV *Norsk Hydro v EC Commission* [1994] ECR II-419.

10.42

In *Bayer*[1] the company put forward three defences to the Commission's claim that Bayer's appeal against an Article 81 decision was out of time. Firstly, it argued that there had been an irregularity on the part of the Commission in the notification of the decision to the company; secondly, the company argued that there had been an excusable error on its part; thirdly, it invoked the concept of force majeure. All three arguments were rejected.

1 Case T-12/90 *Bayer AG v EC Commission* [1991] ECR II-219, upheld by the ECJ in Case C-195/91P *Bayer AG v EC Commission* [1994] ECR I-5619.

(3) Interventions

10.43

Article 37 of the Protocol on the Statute of the European Court of Justice of the EEC gives Member States the general right to intervene in cases before the Court, including therefore cases brought under Article 230. Third parties, however, can only intervene if they can establish an interest in the result of the case. Persons who have filed a complaint under art 3 of Regulation 17/62[1] have been held to have such an interest[2]. Similarly, consumer organisations have also been allowed to intervene in a number of cases[3]. The intervener must support one or other of the submissions made by the principal party; that is to say, it cannot raise wholly new claims. It can, however, make different arguments in support of a particular submission.

1 Council Regulation (EEC) 17/62, OJ Sp Ed [1959–62] p 87. See Chapter 5.

2 As in Cases 6, 7/73 *Commercial Solvents v EC Commission* [1974] ECR 223, [1974] 1 CMLR 309; Case 792/79R *Camera Care v EC Commission* [1980] ECR 119, [1980] 1 CMLR 334. See too Case T-66/94 *Auditel v EC Commission* [1995] ECR II-239, CFI.
3 As in Cases 25, 26/84 *Ford v EC Commission* [1985] ECR 2725, [1985] 3 CMLR 528.

10.44
Applications to intervene must be made within three months of publication of the notice of commencement of proceedings in the Official Journal[1]. If the CFI[2] refuses the application to intervene, the applicant may appeal to the ECJ within two weeks of notification of the refusal.

1 CFI Rules of Procedure, art 115(1).
2 As to the CFI generally, see paras **10.72–10.91**.

10.45
The CFI's Rules of Procedure provide[1] that the President of the CFI shall, where necessary, prescribe a time limit within which the parties may reply to the intervener's statement[2].

1 Article 116(5).
2 Contrast the ECJ's own Rules of Procedure, which, until recently, did not give the principal parties the right of reply to the intervener's arguments; the inequity of this situation was commented on by Millett in his book *The Court of First Instance of the European Communities* (1990) p 54. This has now been put right in the ECJ's revised Rules of Procedure (art 93(6)), OJ [1991] L 176/7.

(4) Effect of Judgment on Third Parties Who do not Bring an Action for Annulment

10.46
In *AssiDomän Kraft Products*[1], the CFI was faced with the situation where the Commission decision in the celebrated *Wood Pulp* case[2], which had imposed fines on a large number of undertakings, was partially annulled by the ECJ on the application of 26 out of 43 original addressees[3]. Nine Swedish addressees who had not brought an action for annulment subsequently asked the Commission to reconsider their position in the light of the ECJ's judgment and to refund to them the fines which they had paid. The Commission rejected this request and the Swedish addressees challenged that rejection. The CFI ruled in essence as follows:

— the original fining decision, though published as a single decision, should be treated as a bundle of individual decisions and the partial annulment did not therefore take effect *erga omnes* but only vis-a-vis the applicants who had challenged the decision;
— however, the findings of the ECJ had the potential to raise serious doubts as to the legality of the decision vis-a-vis the Swedish addressees and the Commission was required, pursuant to Article 176 (now Article 233) of the EC Treaty, to review the legality of its decision in relation to the Swedish addressees in the light of the ECJ judgment;
— if the Commission were to conclude that its findings in relation to the Swedish addressees were unlawful, it would be authorised—indeed required—to refund the fines which they had paid; however, it was not

for the Court to issue directions to the Commission requiring it to refund the fines.

On appeal, however, the ECJ rejected the CFI's interpretation of Article 176, holding that the Commission was not required to review its decision in relation to the Swedish addressees[4].

1 Case T-227/95 *AssiDomän Kraft Products AB v EC Commission* [1997] All ER (EC) 769, CFI.
2 Commission Decision (85/202/EEC) *Wood Pulp* [1985] 3 CMLR 474.
3 In Case C-89 etc *Ahlström v EC Commission* [1993] ECR I-1307, [1994] 4 CMLR 407.
4 Case C-310/97P *EC Commission v AssiDomän Kraft Products* [1999] All ER (EC) 737.

5 PROCEDURE BEFORE THE COURT OF FIRST INSTANCE AND THE EUROPEAN COURT OF JUSTICE

10.47
An outline of the procedure before the CFI and the ECJ is set out at paras **10.84–10.105**.

D Article 232: Action for Failure to Act

1 GENERAL

10.48
Article 232 (formerly Article 175) provides for actions to be brought against the Commission for failure to act, where such failure amounts to an infringement of the EC Treaty. Such actions can be commenced by a Member State, provided the Commission has first been called on to act and has not 'defined its position' within two months thereafter. Natural or legal persons can also invoke Article 232 if the Commission has failed to address to them any act other than a recommendation or an opinion. Before actions can be brought under Article 232 the person must, as in the case of Member States, first call upon the Commission to define its position and the Commission must fail to do so within two months. If the Commission does define its position, but does so by refusing to take the action requested, recourse cannot be had to Article 232. Rather, the appropriate remedy is to seek annulment of the Commission's decision under Article 230[1]. However, as is noted below[2], it appears that the Commission can define its position sufficient to be immune from action under Article 232 but without taking a decision which can be challenged under Article 230.

1 See para **10.09** ff.
2 See para **10.55**.

10.49
The wording of Article 232 specifically requires that the failure to act must constitute an infringement of the EC Treaty. If it does not,

Article 232 cannot be invoked. In the context of Articles 81 and 82, this raises the question whether the parties to an agreement are entitled to make use of Article 232 to require the Commission to decide whether to grant negative clearance under art 2 of Regulation 17/62 or to grant or renew an individual exemption (under Article 81(3)) pursuant to arts 4, 6 or 8 of Regulation 17/62). There is no decision of the ECJ directly on the point. In *GEMA v EC Commission*[1], the ECJ decided that a *complainant* could not require the Commission to take a final decision as to whether or not a particular infringement existed. One of the reasons for this is that the act to which Article 232 relates must be one which, if taken, would be directed to the person bringing the proceedings and not to a third party; this aspect of *GEMA*[2] is considered below[3]. The second reason was that the relevant provision of Regulation 17/62 (art 3) is in permissive rather than mandatory terms ('the Commission ... may by decision require the undertakings ... concerned to bring such infringement to an end').

1 Case 125/78 *GEMA v EC Commission* [1979] ECR 3173, [1980] 2 CMLR 177.
2 See n 1 above.
3 See para **10.51**.

10.50
By analogy, the ECJ's judgment suggests that the parties to an agreement cannot require the Commission to decide whether to grant negative clearance or an individual exemption because the relevant provisions of Regulation 17/62 are, like art 3, permissive, not mandatory. On the other hand, the grant or refusal of individual exemption, in particular, is an act of crucial importance bearing in mind that only the Commission has power to grant exemptions[1] and having regard to the broad interpretation of Article 81(1) which tends to be adopted by the Commission in relation to various categories of business agreement (for example, joint ventures[2]). It would be undesirable if the Commission could not be required to decide whether or not to grant an individual exemption[3].

1 Council Regulation (EEC) 17/62, art 9, OJ Sp Ed [1959–62] p 87.
2 See *Butterworths Competition Law* Division III.
3 See also Bellamy and Child *Common Market Law of Competition* (4th edn, 1993) at p 797, and Kerse *EEC Anti-Trust Procedure* (3rd edn, 1994) at p 345.

10.51
In order to invoke Article 232, the applicant must show that the Commission has failed to address an act *to that person*, as opposed to a third party. In the *GEMA*[1] case the ECJ held that a complainant could not require the Commission to take a decision finding an infringement because such a decision would, by definition, be addressed to a third party and not to the complainant (if the Commission does decide to take a decision, the complainant is, however, entitled to challenge that decision under Article 230: see para **10.18**). However, a complainant is entitled to receive a letter under art 6 of Regulation 99/63[2], indicating that there are insufficient grounds for granting the application requested by it and could invoke Article 232 to achieve this[3]. A complainant can also invoke Article 232 to obtain a final decision rejecting its application, after the

Commission had heard any further representations which the applicant chose to make[4].

1 Case 125/78 *GEMA v EC Commission* [1979] ECR 3173, [1980] 2 CMLR 177; see also Case 246/81 *Bethell v EC Commission* [1982] ECR 2277, [1982] 3 CMLR 300.
2 Commission Regulation (EEC) 99/63, OJ Sp Ed [1963–64] p 47. See para **5.28**.
3 See *GEMA*, n 1 above.
4 See para **5.30**.

10.52
If the Commission takes a decision, albeit different from the one requested, that is sufficient to prevent a successful action under Article 232[1]. In *Asia Motor France*[2] the CFI rejected the applicant's claim under Article 232. In that case, after the action was commenced the Commission had sent the applicants, who had filed a complaint under Article 81, a communication pursuant to art 6 of Regulation 99/63[3], informing them that it did not envisage taking action on the complaint. Subsequently, the Commission had notified the applicants of its decision finally rejecting their complaint. Even though the CFI acknowledged that the Commission's final decision had come after a considerable delay, it concluded that the action under Article 232 had become devoid of purpose[4].

1 Case 8/71 *Deutscher Komponistenverband v EC Commission* [1971] ECR 705, [1973] CMLR 902. See also Case T-387/94 *Asia Motor France v EC Commission* [1996] 5 CMLR 537, CFI.
2 Case T-28/90 *Asia Motor France SA v EC Commission* [1992] 5 CMLR 431.
3 Commission Regulation (EEC) 99/63, OJ Sp Ed [1963–64] p 47 (since superseded by Commission Regulation (EC) 2842/98, OJ [1998] L 354/18.
4 See too Case T-32/93 *Ladbroke Racing Ltd v EC Commission* [1994] ECR II-1015, at para 22; Case C-282/95P *Guérin Automobiles v EC Commission* [1997] ECR I-1503 and Case T-38/96 *Guérin Automobiles v EC Commission* [1997] ECR II-1223.

10.53
In the *Ladbroke Racing* case[1], the CFI was required to consider the relationship between Article 232 and Article 86 (formerly Article 90). Ladbroke had requested the Commission to exercise its powers under Article 86(3) against the French government, arising from the enactment and maintenance of certain French legislation relating to racecourse companies. Ladbroke argued that a request that an infringement of Article 86 be brought to an end should be treated in the same way as a request that an infringement of Articles 81 and 82 by private undertakings be brought to an end. The Court rejected this request, ruling that Ladbroke was not 'directly and individually concerned' by the measure which the Commission had allegedly failed to adopt. The Court also relied on the fact that, when the Commission does decide to take action under Article 86(3), that action can take the form of a decision or a directive, a legislative measure of general scope addressed to the Member States, the adoption of which cannot be required by individuals[2].

1 Case T-32/93 *Ladbroke Racing Ltd v EC Commission* [1994] ECR II-1015.
2 See also Case T-84/94 *BdB v EC Commission*, order of the CFI [1995] ECR II-101.

2 CONSEQUENCE OF FAILURE TO ACT UNDER ARTICLE 232

10.54
Judgments of the Court under Article 232 are essentially declaratory. They do not order the Commission to take action. Rather, the need for action follows from the declaration itself and from Article 233 of the EC Treaty, which provides that institutions whose failure to act are declared contrary to the Treaty 'shall be required to take the necessary measures to comply with the judgments of the Court of Justice'[1].

1 See, for example, Case T-74/92 *Ladbroke Racing (Deutschland) GmbH v EC Commission* [1995] ECR II-115.

3 RELATIONSHIP BETWEEN ARTICLES 230 AND 232

10.55
One might have thought that Articles 230 and 232 provide a complete code, the former providing for judicial review of acts by the Commission and the latter for failure to act. More often than not, this will indeed be the case. However, it is possible for the Commission to define its position in a way which satisfies the requirements of Article 232 but does not constitute an act capable of annulment under Article 230[1]. In *Asia Motor France*[2] the CFI made it clear that an action for failure to act under Article 232 cannot subsequently be converted into an action for annulment under Article 230.

1 Case 48/65 *Lütticke v EC Commission* [1966] ECR 19, [1966] CMLR 378. This is not the case under the ECSC Treaty.
2 Case T-28/90 *Asia Motor France SA v EC Commission* [1992] ECR II-2285.

4 TIME LIMIT FOR ACTION

10.56
If the Commission fails to act within two months of being called upon to do so, action can be brought under Article 232 within a further period of two months. As in the case of Article 230[1], there is provision in the CFI's Rules of Procedure for short extensions to take account of distance from Luxembourg and public holidays. There is, however, nothing in Article 232 which stipulates a time limit within which the request to act itself must be made. Indeed in *GEMA*[2] there was a four-year gap between the date when GEMA was notified of the Statement of Objections and the date when it requested the Commission to act under Article 232. However, in a case under the corresponding provision of the ECSC Treaty[3], the ECJ held that an unreasonably long delay made the action inadmissible[4].

1 See para **10.41**.
2 Case 125/78 *GEMA v EC Commission* [1979] ECR 3173, [1980] 2 CMLR 177.
3 Article 35.
4 Case 59/70 *Netherlands v EC Commission* [1971] ECR 639.

E Articles 242 and 243: Interim Relief

10.57
Article 242 (formerly Article 185) of the EC Treaty provides that the bringing of proceedings before the ECJ (and now before the CFI) does not of itself serve to suspend the operation of the decision to which the action relates. For example, if the Commission orders the termination of an infringement of Article 81, an appeal to the Court does not automatically suspend the operation of that decision. However, Article 242 goes on to give the Court power, if it considers that circumstances so require, to order the suspension of the decision pending outcome of the judicial review. In addition, Article 243 (formerly Article 186) provides that the Court may, in any case before it, prescribe any 'necessary interim measures'. Article 243 applies only to cases which are already before the Court; that is to say, interim relief can only be granted if there is already a main action before it (for example, an action for annulment under Article 230)[1] and that main action must relate to the same subject matter[2].

1 See, for example, Case T-88/94R *SCPA v EC Commission* [1994] ECR II-263, CFI.
2 Case T-235/95R *Goldstein v EC Commission* [1996] 5 CMLR 106.

1 TYPICAL SITUATIONS IN WHICH INTERIM RELIEF IS APPLIED FOR

10.58
There are two typical situations in which interim relief is applied for in competition cases. The first is where the Commission has imposed fines which are the subject matter of an appeal; the second is where the parties appeal a Commission decision ordering termination of an infringement, involving either an order to do something or an order to cease doing something. Each of these situations is considered in turn below.

(1) Fines

10.59
Commission decisions normally stipulate that any fines imposed are payable within three months[1]. However, the Commission is usually willing not to enforce this pending any appeal, provided that the undertaking concerned agrees to pay interest if the appeal fails and puts up a bank guarantee covering principal and interest[2]. The payment of interest was upheld in *AEG-Telefunken v EC Commission*[3] and Commission decisions now expressly stipulate the interest payable[4].

1 See para **9.68**.
2 A practice upheld by the President of the ECJ in Case 107/82R *AEG–Telefunken v EC Commission* [1982] ECR 1549 and Case 86/82R *Hasselblad v EC Commission* [1982] ECR 1555.
3 Case 107/82 [1983] ECR 3151, [1984] 3 CMLR 325.
4 See para **9.68**.

10.60
In *Montedipe SpA v EC Commission*[1] the President of the ECJ confirmed the ECJ's attitude to applications to suspend decisions imposing fines. The company had been required to provide a bank guarantee for a fine of 11 million ECU (plus interest). The company's argument that the cost of producing a bank guarantee for the period until the appeal was heard amounted to a disguised and substantial fine was dismissed, as was the contention that the size of the Montedison Group (of which Montedipe was part) was itself sufficient to guarantee payment of the fine, without the need for a bank guarantee (Montedison had in fact offered to provide its own guarantee). The President of the ECJ ruled that it would only be in exceptional cases that such an application would be granted, such as difficulty in obtaining a bank guarantee or the risk that the cost of the guarantee could jeopardise the undertaking's activities to such an extent as to cause it serious and irreparable damage[2]. It is for the applicant to prove that it cannot await the outcome of the main proceedings without suffering such damage[3].

1 Case 213/86R [1986] ECR 2623.
2 See also Case T-295/94R *Buchmann v EC Commission* [1994] ECR II-1265 and Case T-301/ 94R *Laakmann Karton v EC Commission* [1994] ECR II-1279.
3 Case T-104/95R *Tsimenta Chalkidos v EC Commission*, [1995] ECR II-2235.

(2) Termination of Infringement

10.61
The conditions which have to be satisfied before the Court will be prepared to suspend a Commission decision pending an appeal were set out succinctly by the President of the ECJ in the *IBM*[1] case. He said:

> 'It is clear from the consistent case law of the Court that measures cannot be considered unless the factual and legal grounds relied on to obtain them establish a prima facie case for granting them. In addition there must be urgency in the sense that it is necessary for the measures to be issued and to take effect before the decision of the Court on the substance of the case in order to avoid serious and irreparable damage to the party seeking them; finally they must be provisional in the sense that they do not prejudice the decision on the substance of the case'[2].

In cases of extreme urgency the Court is prepared to suspend the Commission decision immediately for a short period, pending argument on whether it should remain suspended[3].

1 Cases 60, 190/81R *IBM Corpn v EC Commission* [1981] ECR 1857, [1981] 3 CMLR 93.
2 Ibid at point 4.
3 Cases 228, 229/82R *Ford v EC Commission* [1982] ECR 3091, [1982] 3 CMLR 673.

10.62
The ECJ has been willing to order interim relief in a number of competition cases. For example, in *VBVB and VBBB v EC Commission*[1], it was persuaded that if the agreement in question had been terminated (as the Commission decision required) and the appeal eventually succeeded, the agreement could not have been reinstated. Relief in part was ordered more recently in

Publishers' Association v EC Commission[2], an appeal from the Commission's decision in *Net Book Agreements*[3], in *Radio Telefis Eireann v EC Commission*[4], an appeal from the Commission decision in *Magill TV Guide*[5], in *Langnese-Iglo v EC Commission*[6], an appeal from the Commission decision in *Langnese-Iglo*[7], in the *Atlantic Container Line* case[8] and in the *Van den Bergh Foods* case[9]. In *Bayer*[10], an Article 81 parallel import case, the Court suspended that part of the decision which required Bayer to send a circular to wholesalers 'stating that exports are permitted within the Community and will not cause any penalty to be incurred'. Conversely, the ECJ was not satisfied that serious and irreparable damage would flow in either the *Continental Can*[11] or *AKZO*[12] cases. The Court is prepared in appropriate cases to order interim suspension of a Commission decision even if that decision itself is an interim measures decision, ie a case in which the Commission decided that immediate action on its part was called for[13].

1 Cases 43, 63/82R [1982] ECR 1241.
2 Case 56/89R [1989] 2 All ER 1059, [1989] 4 CMLR 816.
3 Commission Decision (89/44/EEC) OJ [1989] L 22/12, [1989] 4 CMLR 825.
4 Cases 76–77/89R, 91/89R [1989] 4 CMLR 749.
5 Commission Decision (89/205/EEC) OJ [1989] L 78/43, [1989] 4 CMLR 757.
6 Case T-7/93R [1993] ECR II-131. See also Case T-29/92R *VSPOB v EC Commission* [1992] ECR II-2161, an appeal from Commission Decision (92/204/EEC) *Building and Construction Industry in the Netherlands* OJ [1992] L 92/1.
7 Commission Decision (93/406/EEC) OJ [1993] L 183/19.
8 Case C-149/95P(R) *EC Commission v Atlantic Container Line AB* [1995] All ER (EC) 853.
9 Case T-65/98R *Van den Bergh Foods v EC Commission* [1998] ECR II-2641.
10 Case T-41/96R *Bayer v EC Commission* [1997] ECR II-381.
11 Case 6/72R *Europemballage and Continental Can v EC Commission* [1972] ECR 157, [1972] CMLR 690.
12 Case 62/86R *AKZO v EC Commission* [1987] 1 CMLR 225.
13 Cases 228, 229/82R *Ford v EC Commission* [1982] ECR 3091, [1982] 3 CMLR 673. However, the President of the CFI was not prepared to order interim suspension of a Commission interim measures decision in Case T-23/90R *Peugeot v EC Commission* [1990] ECR II-195. The CFI ordered partial suspension of an interim measures decision in Cases T-24/92R and T-28/92R *Langnese-Iglo GmbH and Scholler Lebensmittel GmbH & Co KG v EC Commission* [1992] ECR II-1839.

10.63

Applications for interim relief can be made in relation to procedural as well as substantive decisions (for example, Commission decisions under art 11 or 14 of Regulation 17/62). However, it is only likely to be in exceptional cases that interim relief is ordered in relation to procedural decisions[1]. In *SEP v EC Commission*[2] the Dutch association of electricity producers, SEP, requested the President of the CFI to suspend the effects of a Commission decision based on art 11(5) of Regulation 17/62. SEP was concerned about the Commission's request for information regarding a particular gas contract. Under art 10 of Regulation 17/62 the Commission is required to supply national authorities with copies of the most important documents obtained by it during the course of proceedings. SEP argued that disclosure of this contract would cause it serious and irreparable damage, because the Dutch government would become aware of the terms of the contract, thereby impairing SEP's position during future gas supply negotiations with the Dutch government. The President decided that SEP had not established serious and irreparable damage, on the basis that the national authorities are bound by the confidentiality rules contained in art 20 of Regulation 17/62[3].

1 Case 46/87R *Hoechst AG v EC Commission* [1987] ECR 1549, [1988] 4 CMLR 430 and Case 85/87R *Dow Chemical Nederland BV v EC Commission* [1987] ECR 4367, [1989] 4 CMLR 439.
2 Case T-39/90R [1990] ECR II-649. This was a conclusion not followed by the ECJ in the substantive proceedings: Case C-36/92P *SEP v EC Commission* [1994] ECR I-1911, ECJ.
3 See para **6.18**.

10.64
It is in principle open to a complainant who has commenced proceedings for the annulment of a Commission decision under Article 230 to apply for the suspension of the Commission's decision pending the outcome of the appeal[1]. This will, however, frequently involve removing, if only temporarily, the benefit of the decision from a third party and the Court is likely to be reluctant to do this[2].

1 See eg Joined Cases 160, 161/73R *Miles Druce and Co Ltd v EC Commission* [1973] ECR 1049, [1974] 1 CMLR 224 (application refused) and Joined Cases 160, 161, 170/73R II *Miles Druce and Co Ltd v EC Commission* [1974] ECR 281, [1974] 2 CMLR D17 (application granted).
2 See, eg Case 26/76R *Metro v EC Commission* [1976] ECR 1353, where the ECJ refused to suspend the Commission's decision granting exemption under Article 81(3) to SABA's selective distribution system; see also Case T-131/89R *Cosimex v EC Commission* [1990] ECR II-1, the first decision in a competition case by the Court of First Instance.

10.65
The Court will not usually entertain an application for interim relief in respect of a decision by the Commission which is anticipated but which, at the date of the application, has not yet been adopted[1]; the exception to this would be where the applicant can demonstrate that the future decision would immediately create rights for third parties and produce irreversible effects[2].

1 See, in the context of the Merger Control Regulation (Commission Regulation (EEC) 4064/89, OJ [1989] L 395/1), Case T-52/96 *Sogecable v EC Commission* [1996] ECR II-797.
2 Case T-395/94RII *Atlantic Container Line AB v EC Commission*, order of the President of the CFI [1995] ECR II-2893.

2 PROCEDURE

10.66
Applications for interim relief must be made in a separate document filed with the CFI, setting out the reasons for it and in particular the urgency of the case[1]. The case will usually, though not always, be heard by the President of the CFI sitting alone[2]. The decision of the CFI cannot be appealed, although parties can ask the President to revisit the matter in the event of a change of circumstances[3].

1 CFI Rules of Procedure, art 104(2).
2 EEC Treaty Protocol of the Statute of the Court of Justice of the EEC, Article 36 and CFI Rules of Procedure, art 106; this occurred, for example, in two of the first interim relief cases heard by the CFI: Case T-131/89R *Cosimex v EC Commission* [1990] ECR II-1 and Case T-23/90R *Peugeot v EC Commission* [1990] ECR II-195.
3 CFI Rules of Procedure, art 108.

F Article 234: References for a Preliminary Ruling

10.67

Under Article 234 (formerly Article 177) of the EC Treaty the ECJ has jurisdiction to give preliminary rulings concerning the interpretation of the Treaty, the validity and interpretation of acts of the institutions of the Community and the interpretation of the statutes of bodies established by an act of the Council of the European Union, where those statutes so provide[1]. Where any such question is raised before a national court of a Member State that court may request the ECJ to give a preliminary ruling if the national court considers that a decision on the question by the ECJ is necessary to enable it to give judgment. This is a matter of discretion on the part of the national court, except that if the issue is raised in a case pending before a national court against whose decisions there is no judicial remedy under national law, that court *must* bring the matter before the ECJ. There are a number of important competition law cases which have come before the ECJ by means of the Article 234 procedure[2].

1 As to Article 177 generally, see Collins *European Community Law in the United Kingdom* (4th edn, 1990) at pp 142–214; Arnull 'References to the European Court' (1990) 15 EL Rev 375–391.

2 Eg Cases 253/78 etc, *Procureur de la République v Giry and Guerlain* [1980] ECR 2327, [1981] 2 CMLR 99 (dealing with provisional validity); Case 170/83 *Hydrotherm Gerätebau GmbH v Compact* [1984] ECR 2999, [1985] 3 CMLR 224 (dealing with distribution agreements); Case 243/83 *Binon et Cie SA v Agence et Messageries de la Presse SA* [1985] ECR 2015, [1985] 3 CMLR 800 (dealing with distribution arrangements for newspapers and periodicals); Case 161/84 *Pronuptia de Paris GmbH v Pronuptia de Paris Irmgard Schillgalis* [1986] ECR 353, [1986] 1 CMLR 414 (dealing with franchise agreements); Case 27/87 *Erauw-Jacquery SprL v La Hesbignonne Société Co-opérative* [1988] ECR 1919, [1988] 4 CMLR 576 (dealing with licences of plant breeders' rights).

10.68

It is important for the national court to set out clearly the factual and legal context of the questions on which it seeks a preliminary ruling and to explain the factual assumptions on which the questions are based. The ECJ has made it clear[1] that these requirements are particularly important in competition law cases, where complex legal and factual issues arise and the Court will refuse to give a preliminary ruling if it considers the information supplied to it insufficient to enable it to do so[2].

1 Joined Cases C-320-322/90 *Telemarsicabruzzo v Circostel* [1993] ECR I-393, ECJ.

2 As it did in the *Telemarsicabruzzo* case, see n 1 above.

10.69

A court of final resort which would otherwise be bound to make reference under Article 234, third paragraph is not bound to do so if the point of law involved is clear. The leading judgment of the ECJ on this issue is *CILFIT Srl v Ministry of Health*[1], which identifies two situations in which the obligation under Article 234, third paragraph does not arise, even though a question of Community law is involved. The first is where the question is 'materially identical' with a question previously ruled on by the Court. The second is where 'the correct application of Community law may be so obvious as to leave no scope for any reasonable doubt as to the manner in which the question raised is to be resolved'[2]. However, the ECJ specifically drew national courts' attention to the fact that Community legislation is drafted in several languages and that the process of interpretation involves a comparison of the texts. A national court should therefore take great care before concluding that the law is clear. This warning is reflected in the House of Lords judgment in *Henn and Darby v DPP*[3], a case under Article 28 (formerly Article 30) of the EC Treaty.

1 Case 283/81 [1982] ECR 3415, [1983] 1 CMLR 472.
2 [1982] ECR 3415 at 3430, [1983] 1 CMLR 472 at 491.
3 [1981] AC 850, [1980] 2 All ER 166.

G Article 288: Actions for Damages against the Community

10.70
Under Article 288 (formerly Article 215), second paragraph of the EC Treaty, the Community is required, in accordance with the general principles of the laws of the Member States, to make good any damage caused by its institutions or by its servants in the performance of their duties[1]. An example of a case in the competition law field in which the ECJ awarded damages against the European Commission is the celebrated *Stanley Adams* case[2].

1 See generally Collins *European Community law in the United Kingdom* (4th edn, 1990) at pp 282–288.
2 Cases 145/83, 53/84 *Adams v EC Commission* [1986] QB 138, [1985] ECR 3539, see para **11.13**.

H Costs

10.71
The position regarding costs is set out in the Rules of Procedure of, respectively, the ECJ and the CFI. This is summarised at paras **10.105** (ECJ) and **10.91** (CFI).

I The Court of First Instance

1 BACKGROUND

10.72
The workload of the ECJ rose steadily during the 1980s, increasing the number of cases pending at any one time and considerably lengthening the duration of individual proceedings. By 1988, for example, the average length of time taken to obtain a preliminary ruling under Article 234[1] of the

EC Treaty was approximately eighteen months, compared with about nine months in 1980. The average length of direct action proceedings was even longer. The number of proceedings commenced before the Court will inevitably rise over time, due to factors such as the increasing awareness of European Community law, the gradual enlargement of the Community by the accession of new Member States and the growing number of directives emanating from the Community institutions, particularly in the context of the completion of the Community's internal market.

1 See paras **10.67–10.69**.

10.73

Although the ECJ from time to time introduced various procedural changes designed to speed up proceedings (for example, through the greater use of chambers as opposed to hearings before the full Court), these developments did not provide a solution to the problem. The need to establish an additional tribunal to take some of the burden away from the ECJ was considered as long ago as the mid-1970s when it was suggested that the numerous cases involving disputes between the Community institutions and their staff should be heard by a separate administrative tribunal rather than by the ECJ itself. In 1978 the ECJ proposed that not only staff cases but other categories of case, including competition cases, should be transferred to a new tribunal. However, no action was taken at that time, not least because such proposals required amendments to be made to the EEC, ECSC and Euratom Treaties. The matter was again raised in 1985 during the discussions which took place regarding Treaty amendments designed to improve the working of the European institutions. These led to the adoption of the Single European Act[1], which was signed in Luxembourg on 17 February 1986 and came into force, following ratification by the Member States, on 1 July 1987. This inserted a new Article in the Treaty of Rome, Article 168*a* (now Article 225)(and corresponding wording in the ECSC[2] and Euratom[3] Treaties), enabling the EC Council to establish the CFI.

1 OJ [1987] L 169/1.
2 Article 32*d*.
3 Article 140*a*.

10.74

Article 225 of the EC Treaty provided that, at the request of the ECJ and following consultation with the Commission and the European Parliament, the Council may, acting unanimously, attach to the ECJ a court with jurisdiction to hear and determine at first instance (with a right of appeal to the ECJ on points of law) certain classes of action or proceedings brought by natural or legal persons. Article 225 specifically provided that the new court would not be competent to hear actions brought by Member States or by Community institutions or questions referred from national courts for a preliminary ruling under Article 234. The Single European Act also added a new second paragraph to Article 245 (formerly Article 188) of the EC Treaty, empowering the Council to amend the provisions of Title III of the Statute of the ECJ, dealing with procedure. The ECJ duly submitted a proposal for the establishment of the CFI in 1987 and on 24 October 1988 the Council adopted a decision pursuant to Article 225, establishing the CFI[1].

1 Council Decision 88/591/ECSC, EEC, Euratom: published (in corrected form) OJ [1989] C 215/1, [1989] 3 CMLR 458.

2 JURISDICTION

10.75

Article 225 empowered the Council to give broad jurisdiction to the CFI to hear classes of action or proceeding brought by natural or legal persons. The only actions which Article 225 expressly excluded were those brought by Member States or by Community institutions (for example, proceedings under Article 226 (formerly Article 169) of the EC Treaty) or questions referred by a national court for a preliminary ruling under Article 234[1]. The Council's 1988 Decision[2] conferred on the CFI jurisdiction to hear four categories of case[3], namely:

(*a*) disputes between the Communities and their servants (so-called staff cases);
(*b*) actions for annulment or actions for failure to act brought against the Commission by undertakings or associations of undertakings concerning individual acts relating to the application of Articles 50 and 57 to 66 of the ECSC Treaty (dealing with levies, production quotas, agreements and concentrations);
(*c*) actions brought against an institution of the Communities by natural or legal persons pursuant to the second paragraph of Article 230 (action for annulment) and the third paragraph of Article 232 (action for failure to act) of the EC Treaty in relation to the implementation of the competition rules applicable to undertakings;
(*d*) damages claims brought by natural or legal persons against Community institutions where the damage suffered is alleged to have been caused through an act or failure to act which is the subject of any of the three categories identified above.

Its jurisdiction was extended in 1993[4] to cover all actions brought by natural or legal persons under Article 230 and Article 232 (with the exception of dumping and subsidy cases, where this extension will require a further decision by the Council).

1 See paras **10.67–10.69**.
2 Council Decision 88/591/ECSC, EEC, Euratom: published (in corrected form) OJ [1989] C 215/1, [1989] 3 CMLR 458.
3 Article 3.
4 See para **10.02**.

10.76

In relation to those categories of case identified at para **10.75**, the first instance jurisdiction of the CFI is exclusive; that is to say, the ECJ does not have discretion as to whether or not to pass a particular case falling into these categories to the CFI—the CFI automatically has exclusive jurisdiction (subject to appeal to the ECJ[1]). This was illustrated by the ECJ's order in *Asia Motors France v EC Commission*[2]. The applicants claimed that the Commission should have taken action against the French government and a number of Japanese automobile manufacturers under Articles 28 and 81 of the EC Treaty. The ECJ rejected the Article 28 element of the application as inadmissible and referred the Article 81 element to the CFI.

1 See para **10.92** ff.
2 OJ [1990] C 166/12.

10.77

Prior to the establishment of the CFI, the ECJ delivered judgment in a number of major cases arising out of Commission decisions under Articles 81 and 82: for example (to name but a few), the *Nungesser*[1]; *AM & S*[2]; *Philip Morris*[3] and *Woodpulp*[4] cases. As these were actions brought on appeal from Commission decisions, first instance jurisdiction in such cases would, if they were brought today, lie with the CFI. Conversely, other major ECJ judgments under Articles 81 and 82 have arisen out of references from national courts under Article 234 of the Treaty: for example, the *Perfumes*[5]; *Hydrotherm*[6]; *Binon*[7]; *Pronuptia*[8], *Erauw-Jacquery*[9] and *Oscar Bronner*[10] cases. These would not be heard by the CFI.

1 Case 258/78 *Nungesser v EC Commission* [1982] ECR 2015, [1983] 1 CMLR 278 (dealing with exclusive patent licences).
2 Case 155/79 *AM & S v EC Commission* [1982] ECR 1575, [1982] 2 CMLR 264 (dealing with legal privilege).
3 Cases 142, 156/84 *BAT and RJ Reynolds v EC Commission* [1986] ECR 1899, [1987] 2 CMLR 551 (dealing with the application of Article 81 to mergers).
4 Cases 89, 104, 114, 116–117, 125–129/85 *Ahlström v EC Commission* [1988] ECR 5193, [1988] 4 CMLR 901 (dealing with the extra-territorial application of Article 81).
5 Cases 253/78 etc, *Procureur de la République v Giry and Guerlain* [1980] ECR 2327, [1981] 2 CMLR 99 (dealing with provisional validity).
6 Case 170/83 *Hydrotherm Gerätebau GmbH v Compact* [1984] ECR 2999, [1985] 3 CMLR 224 (dealing with distribution agreements).
7 Case 243/83 *Binon et Cie SA v Agence et Messageries de la Presse SA* [1985] ECR 2015, [1985] 3 CMLR 800 (dealing with distribution arrangements for newspapers and periodicals).
8 Case 161/84 *Pronuptia de Paris GmbH v Pronuptia de Paris Irmgard Schillgalis* [1986] ECR 353, [1986] 1 CMLR 414 (dealing with franchise agreements).
9 Case 27/87 *Erauw-Jacquery Sprl v La Hesbignonne Société Co-opérative* [1988] 4 CMLR 576 (dealing with licences of plant breeders' rights).
10 Case C-7/97 *Oscar Bronner v Mediaprint* [1998] ECR I-7791.

10.78

Article 3(1) of the EC Council's 1988 Decision[1] conferring jurisdiction on the CFI expressly refers to Articles 230[2] and 232[3] of the EC Treaty (dealing respectively with actions for annulment and actions for failure to act). In addition, art 4 of the Council Decision provides that Article 229[4] of the Treaty shall also apply to the CFI. This means that the CFI has unlimited jurisdiction to cancel, reduce or increase fines imposed by the Commission under Articles 81 and 82, as well as jurisdiction to annul the decision imposing the fine.

1 See para **10.75**.
2 See para **10.09** ff.
3 See para **10.48** ff.
4 See para **10.05** ff.

10.79
Jurisdiction over damages claims against Community institutions has been conferred on the CFI[1] where the claim relates to an act or failure to act falling within one of the other three categories in relation to which jurisdiction has been passed to the CFI. For example, a damages claim might be made in relation to a decision taken under Article 230 of the EC Treaty or a failure to act under Article 232.

1 Council Decision 88/591/ECSC, EEC, Euratom, art 3(2).

10.80
Under art 4 of Council Decision 88/591[1], Articles 242 and 243 of the EC Treaty apply to the CFI. This means that the CFI has power to suspend the application of an act contested in proceedings before it and to prescribe any necessary interim measures in any case before it. This can be of particular relevance in cases under Articles 81 and 82[2].

1 Establishing the CFI.
2 See para **10.57** ff.

3 COMPOSITION AND ORGANISATION

10.81
The CFI is made up of 15 members, 'whose independence is beyond doubt and who possess the ability required for appointment to judicial office'[1]. The first members were appointed with effect from 1 September 1989 by a decision of the representatives of the governments of the Member States of the European Communities[2]. Members are appointed for a term of six years but with partial renewal of membership taking place every three years[3]. The CFI is required to sit in Chambers of three or five judges[4].

1 EC Treaty, Article 168*a*(3).
2 Council Decision 89/452/EEC, Euratom, ECSC, OJ [1989] L 220/76.
3 See n 1 above.
4 Council Decision 88/591/ECSC, EEC, Euratom, art 2(4).

10.82
There was much debate prior to the establishment of the CFI as to whether or not it should have Advocates General (as does the ECJ). The ECJ itself thought not; the European Parliament and the EC Commission thought that it should. A compromise was eventually agreed, whereby under art 2(3) of Council Decision 88/591 the members of the CFI may be called upon to perform the task of Advocate General. An Advocate General must be appointed if the CFI decides that the case needs to be heard in plenary session[1].

1 CFI Rules of Procedure, art 17, OJ [1991] L 136/1 (as amended).

4 COMMENCEMENT OF OPERATION OF THE COURT OF FIRST INSTANCE

10.83
Under art 13 of Council Decision 88/591 the provision conferring jurisdiction on the CFI (art 3 of that Decision) entered into force on the day of

publication in the Official Journal of the European Communities of the ruling by the President of the ECJ that the CFI had been constituted in accordance with law. That ruling was published on 31 October 1989[1]. All proceedings commenced after that date and which fall within the jurisdiction of the CFI have to be brought before it. In addition, cases pending before the ECJ on 31 October 1989 but in which the preliminary report of the judge-rapporteur had not yet been presented were also referred to the CFI[2]. 151 cases were referred to the CFI under this provision. The first decision of the CFI in a competition case was an order of the President of the CFI on 6 December 1989 on an application for interim relief in *Cosiméx*[3].

1 OJ [1989] L 317/48.
2 Council Decision 88/591/ECSC, EEC, Euratom, art 14.
3 Case T-131/89R *Cosimex GmbH v EC Commission* [1990] ECR II-1.

5 PROCEDURE BEFORE THE COURT OF FIRST INSTANCE

10.84

As in the case of the ECJ, the procedure before the CFI is largely governed by the provisions of the Protocol on the Statute of the Court of Justice[1]. The CFI was required to establish its own rules of procedure in agreement with the ECJ and with the unanimous approval of the Council[2]. Until that time, the rules of procedure of the ECJ[3] applied mutatis mutandis[4]. The CFI subsequently established its own rules[5], which came into force on 1 July 1991[6].

1 EC Treaty, Article 225(2) (ECSC Treaty, Article 32*d*(2); Euratom Treaty, Article 140*a*(2)).
2 EC Treaty, Article 225(4) (ECSC Treaty, Article 32*d*(4); Euratom Treaty, Article 140*a*(4)).
3 OJ [1982] C 39/1.
4 Council Decision 88/591/ECSC, EEC, Euratom, art 11.
5 These were published in the Official Journal of the European Communities on 30 May 1991, OJ [1991] L 136/1; see also the Instructions to the Registrar of the Court of First Instance, OJ [1994] L 78/32, [1994] 1 CMLR 821 and the advice for lawyers and agents regarding the written procedure before the Court of First Instance, drawn up by the Registrar, OJ [1994] C 120/16.
6 CFI Rules of Procedure, art 130.

10.85

A description of the detailed rules of procedure of the CFI and the ECJ is outside the scope of this work[1]. However, the following points should be noted.

1 For a detailed description see Millett *The Court of First Instance of the European Communities* (1990); see also Usher *European Court Practice* (1983), Lasok *The European Court of Justice: Practice and Procedure* (1994) and *Butterworths European Court Practice* (1993).

(1) Legal Representation

10.86

Parties to proceedings other than a Member State or a Community institution have to be represented by a lawyer entitled to practise before a court of a Member State[1]. However, university teachers who are nationals of a Member State in which they have a right of audience are treated for this purpose as lawyers entitled to practise before a court of a Member State[2]. At the hearing a party may address the CFI only through his agent, adviser or lawyer[3].

1 EEC Treaty Protocol on the Statute of the Court of Justice of the EEC, Article 17 (2nd para).
2 Ibid Article 17 (5th para).
3 See n 1 above, Article 18 (4th para) and Article 29.

(2) Two-Stage Procedure

10.87
Under the Protocol on the Statute of the Court of Justice of the EEC, procedure consists of two parts, namely a written and oral procedure. The procedure is primarily written. Proceedings are commenced by the lodging of a written application at the Registry of the CFI[1]. The defendant must lodge his defence within one month of service on him of the application[2]. It is possible for this time limit to be extended by the President of the CFI upon application (with reasons) made by the defendant[3]. Following service of the defence it is possible for the applicant to add to his case by serving a reply and for the defendant to then serve a rejoinder[4]. No new plea in law may be introduced during the course of proceedings unless it is based on matters of law or fact which come to light in the course of the written procedure[5]. Once pleadings have closed, the next stage is for the President of the CFI to fix a date on which the judge-rapporteur presents a preliminary report to the Court. This is not a public document.

1 EEC Treaty Protocol on the Statute of the Court of Justice of the EEC, Article 19 (1st para).
2 CFI Rules of Procedure, art 46(1).
3 Ibid art 46(3).
4 See n 2 above, art 47(1).
5 See n 2 above, art 48(2); also Cases T-68/89, 77, 78/89 *Società Italiano Vetro SpA v EC Commission* [1992] 5 CMLR 302 at para 82.

10.88
The CFI has power to make a very broad range of enquiry of its own. For example, it has power to require the parties to produce all relevant documents and information[1]. It may also commission reports from expert third parties[2] and obtain oral testimony from witnesses and experts[3] (although this is rare).

1 EEC Treaty Protocol on the Statute of the Court of Justice of the EEC, Article 21.
2 Ibid Article 22.
3 CFI Rules of Procedure, arts 64–76.

10.89
Where a third party intervenes in proceedings (for example, a complainant who intervenes to support a Commission decision which is being appealed), art 116 of the CFI Rules of Procedure provides that the

intervener must receive a copy of every document served on the parties. However, the President of the Court may, on application by one of the parties, omit secret or confidential documents[1].

1 As in Case T-66/94 *Auditel v EC Commission* [1995] ECR II-239, CFI.

10.90

The two main elements of the oral procedure are the hearing of the parties and the hearing of the Advocate General's opinion (although it is not in every case before the CFI that there is likely to be an Advocate General[1]). Hearings are usually held in public unless the CFI decides otherwise[2]. If there is to be an Advocate General's opinion in a case before the CFI this is delivered after the hearing of the parties (unlike in the case of the ECJ, there is provision for the Advocate General to deliver his opinion in writing[3]). Oral hearings before the CFI are likely, as in the case of hearings before the ECJ, to be kept short. Notes for the guidance of counsel at oral hearings prepared by the ECJ in 1986 asks that counsel restrict the length of their address to 30 minutes.

1 See para **10.82**.
2 EEC Treaty Protocol on the Statute of the Court of Justice of the EEC, Article 28.
3 Ibid Article 46 (3rd para).

6 COSTS

10.91

The position on costs before the CFI is set out in arts 87–93 of its Rules of Procedure. These largely mirror the provisions set out in the ECJ's own Rules of Procedure (arts 69–75). The following points should be noted:

(1) The unsuccessful party must pay the other party's costs, provided they have been asked for in the pleadings; if several parties are unsuccessful the Court has to decide how the costs should be shared[1].
(2) If each party is partially successful and partially unsuccessful, the Court may order that costs be shared[2].
(3) Exceptionally, a successful party may have to pay costs which it has caused the other party to incur unreasonably or vexatiously[3].
(4) Intervening Member States and institutions bear their own costs; other interveners may be ordered to pay their own costs[4].
(5) If a party discontinues or withdraws from proceedings he will usually be ordered to pay the other party's costs, provided these were asked for in the pleadings[5].
(6) If costs are not claimed in the pleadings, the parties bear their own costs[6].
(7) The recoverable categories of costs are sums payable to witnesses and experts and expenses necessarily incurred, in particular travel and subsistence expenses and the remuneration of agents, advisers or lawyers[7].
(8) There is no appeal from a CFI ruling on costs[8].

1 CFI Rules of Procedure, art 87(2), OJ [1991] L 136/1.
2 Ibid art 87(3).

3 See n 1 above, art 87(3). Joined Cases 15 and 29/59 *Société Metallurgique de Knutange v High Authority* [1960] ECR 1; Cases 123/81 and 123/81R *Krupp Stahl AG v EC Commission* [1981] ECR 2391; Case 282/81 *Ragusa v EC Commission* [1983] ECR 1245; Case 125/80 *Arning v EC Commission* [1981] ECR 2539; and Case T-28/90 *Asia Motor France SA v EC Commission* [1992] 5 CMLR 431.
4 See n 1 above, art 87(4). The position regarding the costs of intervening Member States and institutions was initially different under the ECJ Rules of Procedure; for a case involving the transitional position, see Case T-23/90 *Peugeot v EC Commission* [1991] ECR II-653, [1993] 5 CMLR 540, CFI. The position under the ECJ Rules of Procedure has now been brought in line with the position under the CFI Rules of Procedure: see new art 69(4). The text of the ECJ Rules of Procedure was published in July 1991: OJ [1991] L 176/7. A codified version, incorporating subsequent amendments, was published in 1999: OJ [1999] C 65/1.
5 See n 1 above, art 87(5).
6 See n 1 above, art 87(5).
7 See n 1 above, art 91. In relation to lawyers' fees, see Case T-23/90 DEP *Peugeot v EC Commission* [1995] ECR II-2057.
8 See n 1 above, art 92.

7 APPEALS TO THE EUROPEAN COURT OF JUSTICE

10.92
Article 225(1)[1] of the EC Treaty provides for a right of appeal to the ECJ against a judgment of the CFI on points of law only. Article 7 of Council Decision 88/591[2] inserts new provisions into the Protocol on the Statute of the Court of Justice of the EEC, setting out detailed rules concerning such appeals[3].

1 Corresponding to ECSC Treaty, Article 32*d*(1); Euratom Treaty, Article 140*a*(1).
2 OJ [1989] C 215/1, [1989] 3 CMLR 458.
3 Articles 49–54.

(1) Matters which can be the Subject of an Appeal

10.93
Appeals can be brought against the following decisions of the CFI:

(*a*) final decisions, ie decisions which bring an end to the case before the CFI;
(*b*) decisions disposing of the substantive issues in part only (for example, in the *Woodpulp*[1] case the ECJ delivered judgment on the issue of extra-territoriality before going on to consider the substantive issues to which the case gave rise);
(*c*) decisions disposing of a procedural issue concerning a plea of lack of competence or inadmissibility;
(*d*) decisions of the CFI rejecting an application to intervene;
(*e*) decisions of the CFI made under Article 242 or 243[2], concerning interim relief.

1 Joined Cases C-89, 104, 114, 116–117, 125–129/85 *A Ahlström Oy v EC Commission* [1993] ECR I-1307.
2 EEC Treaty Protocol on the Statute of the Court of Justice of the EEC, Article 50.

(2) Grounds of Appeal

10.94
Under the EC Treaty, Article 225(1), appeal to the ECJ can only be on points of law. This is re-stated in Article 51 of the Protocol on the Statute of the ECJ, which goes on to identify the following specific grounds of appeal:

(*a*) lack of competence of the CFI;
(*b*) breach of procedure before the CFI which adversely affects the interests of the appellant;
(*c*) infringement of Community law by the CFI.

These follow closely the grounds on which an action for annulment of a decision by the Council or the Commission can be brought under Article 230 of the EC Treaty[1]. In *Hilti*[2], the ECJ stated that the appraisal by the CFI of the evidence put before it does not constitute (except where the clear sense of that evidence has been distorted by the CFI) a point of law which is subject, as such, to review by the ECJ. It is not the ECJ's role to substitute, on grounds of fairness, its own view of the appropriate level of fines, in place of the assessment of the CFI[3]. No new point of law (ie. one not articulated before the CFI) may be introduced in the course of ECJ proceedings unless it is based on matters of law or fact which come to light in the course of the procedure[4].

1 See para **10.09** ff.
2 Case C-53/92P *Hilti v EC Commission* [1994] ECR I-667 at 707–8; see too Joined Cases C-241 and 242/91P *RTE and ITP v EC Commission* [1995] ECR I-743.
3 Case C-310/93P *BPB Industries Plc and British Gypsum Ltd v EC Commission* [1995] ECR I-865, at para 34 and Case C-185/95P *Baustahlgewebe v EC Commission* [1998] ECR I-8417.
4 See, for example, Case C-279/95P *Langnese Iglo v EC Commission* [1998] ECR I-5609 at paras 54 and 55.

(3) Persons who can Appeal

10.95
The persons party to the proceedings before the CFI can appeal, as can any party who intervenes in the CFI proceedings. However, interveners other than the Member States and the Community institutions may only bring an appeal where the decision of the CFI directly affects them[1]. It is not open to an intervener to seek from the ECJ a form of order different from that sought at first instance[2]. Member States and the Community institutions can even intervene before the ECJ in cases in which they chose not to intervene in the same proceedings before the CFI[3].

1 EEC Treaty Protocol on the Statute of the Court of Justice of the EEC, Article 49 (2nd para).
2 ECJ Rules of Procedure, art 116; see also Case C-53/92P *Hilti AG v EC Commission* [1994] ECR I-667 at 709.
3 See n 1 above, Article 49 (3rd para).

(4) Time for Appeal

10.96
Appeals must be lodged within two months of the notification of the CFI decision[1], except that appeals against a decision of the CFI dismissing an application to intervene must be brought within two weeks of the notification of the decision[2].

1 EEC Treaty Protocol on the Statute of the Court of Justice of the EEC, Article 49 (1st para).
2 Ibid Article 50 (1st para).

(5) Effect of Appeal

10.97
If an appeal against a decision of the CFI is lodged with the ECJ, the appeal does not have suspensory effect (ie the CFI decision takes effect immediately)[1]. However, this is subject to Articles 242 and 243 of the EEC Treaty, under which the ECJ may, if it considers that circumstances so require, order suspension of the CFI decision and prescribe any necessary interim measures. The operation of Articles 242 and 243, in the context of appeals against decisions made by the Commission, is described at paras **10.57–10.66**. It can be expected that the ECJ will apply similar principles in the context of appeals against decisions of the CFI.

1 EEC Treaty Protocol on the Statute of the Court of Justice of the EEC, Article 53.

10.98
There is one exception to the principle that appeals to the ECJ do not have suspensory effect: decisions of the CFI declaring a Regulation void do not take effect until the expiry of the two-month period for bringing an appeal or, if an appeal is brought within that period, until the appeal is dismissed[1]. This will rarely apply in the context of Articles 81 and 82 because most acts likely to be the subject of action before the CFI will take the form of Commission decisions, rather than regulations.

1 EEC Treaty Protocol on the Statute of the Court of Justice of the EEC, Article 53.

(6) Powers of the European Court of Justice on Appeal

10.99
The effect of a successful appeal to the ECJ is that the latter must quash the decision of the CFI. In so doing, it has a discretion to decide whether to give final judgment in the matter, where the state of the proceedings so permits, or to refer the case back to the CFI for final judgment. If the case is referred back to the CFI that court is bound by the decision of the ECJ on points of law[1]. In the interests of efficient administration of justice it seems likely that, wherever possible, the ECJ will itself deliver final judgment. However, if complex issues of fact or mixed law and fact remain outstanding, the ECJ will almost certainly have no alternative but to refer the matter back to the CFI.

1 EEC Treaty Protocol on the Statute of the Court of Justice of the EEC, Article 54.

10.100
Member States or Community institutions have a right to appeal against a CFI decision even if they did not intervene in the proceedings before the CFI itself[1]. If such an appeal is brought and is successful the ECJ is empowered, if it considers this necessary, to state which of the effects of the CFI's decision are to be considered as definitive in respect of the parties to the litigation[2]. This would enable the ECJ, if it felt circumstances so required, to protect the parties from prejudice arising because the Member State/Community institution concerned had only decided to appeal at the ECJ stage of the proceedings.

1 See para **10.95**.
2 EEC Treaty Protocol on the Statute of the Court of Justice of the EEC, Article 54.

8 EUROPEAN COURT OF JUSTICE APPEAL PROCEDURE

10.101
The procedure of the ECJ in dealing with appeals from decisions of the CFI is governed by Article 52 of the Protocol on the Statute of the Court of Justice of the EEC and by the ECJ's Rules of Procedure, in particular arts 110 to 123[1]. The procedure is essentially the same as that applicable to direct actions brought before the CFI (for example, annulment actions brought directly under Article 230), but with the necessary modifications to take account of the fact that the hearing is by way of appeal.

1 Articles 110–123 of the Rules of Procedure of the ECJ were added on 7 June 1989: OJ [1989] L 241/1. The current ECJ Rules of Procedure were republished in the Official Journal of the European Communities in 1999: OJ [1999] C 65/9.

(1) Legal Representation

10.102
Parties other than a Member State or Community institution must be represented by a lawyer entitled to practise before a court of a Member State and for this purpose university teachers who have a right of audience under their own national law can appear before the ECJ[1]. Member States and Community institutions can be represented by an agent who does not have to be legally qualified[2].

1 EEC Treaty Protocol on the Statute of the Court of Justice of the EEC, Article 17 (5th para).
2 Ibid Article 17 (1st para).

(2) Written and Oral Procedure

10.103
Procedure before the ECJ on appeal from the CFI is, as in the case of direct actions brought before the ECJ, in principle both written and oral. However, the ECJ has a discretion to dispense with the oral procedure[1].

Actions are commenced by the lodging of an application at the Registry of the ECJ or at the Registry of the CFI[2]. This must set out, inter alia, the grounds on which the appeal is based and the arguments of law relied on[3]. The appeal must seek to quash, in whole or in part, the decision of the CFI and can only seek the same form of order as that sought before the CFI[4]. Anyone who is party to the proceedings before the CFI may lodge a response within two months after service on him of notice of the appeal—this time limit cannot be extended[5]. The response must set out, amongst other things, the grounds relied on and arguments of law raised[6]. The appeal and the response can only be supplemented by a reply and a rejoinder with the leave of the President of the ECJ[7].

1 EEC Treaty Protocol on the Statute of the Court of Justice of the EEC.
2 ECJ Rules of Procedure, art 111(1).
3 Ibid art 112(1)(c).
4 See n 2 above, art 113(1).
5 See n 2 above, art 115(1).
6 See n 2 above, art 115(2)(c).
7 See n 2 above, art 117(1).

10.104
Following the close of the pleadings, the ECJ may (after receiving the report of the judge-rapporteur, and after hearing the Advocate General and the parties) decide to dispense with the oral procedure unless one of the parties objects on the grounds that the written procedure did not enable him fully to defend his point of view[1].

1 ECJ Rules of Procedure, art 120.

(3) Costs

10.105
The ECJ itself makes the decision as to costs if it dismisses the appeal or decides that the appeal is well-founded and itself gives final judgment in the case (as opposed to referring the matter back to the CFI for final judgment)[1]. Except in staff cases, the ECJ's normal rules on costs[2] apply to appeals[3]. That is to say, if the successful party has claimed costs the losing party must be ordered to pay them; if each party succeeds as to part of the case and loses as to other parts the ECJ has a discretion to order the parties to bear their own costs (either in whole or in part). The ECJ's normal rules on costs[4] are very similar to those for the CFI described at para **10.91**.

1 ECJ Rules of Procedure, art 122.
2 Ibid arts 69–75.
3 See n 1 above, art 118.
4 See n 1 above, art 118.

Chapter 11 EC Law Principles of General Application

A Introduction

11.01
There are a number of principles of EC law of general application to which regard should be had by undertakings and their advisers when dealing with Article 81 or 82 of the EC Treaty. These general principles can apply in a variety of situations and it therefore seems appropriate for them to be brought together in one chapter. The following topics are covered in this chapter:

(1) *Confidentiality:* The matters which tend to be relevant in the context of investigations under Articles 81 and 82 almost invariably involve disclosure to the European Commission of sensitive business information (for example, sales figures and profitability in relation to a particular product line, market share estimates, capacity utilisation and so on). Accordingly, it is vital for undertakings to know what duties the Commission owes to them when dealing with such information; this can be as important to undertakings who lodge complaints with the Commission against other undertakings as to the undertakings complained of themselves.
(2) *Legal privilege:* It is important that an undertaking seeking legal advice on the application of Articles 81 and 82 should know whether or not communications with its legal advisers can be requested by the Commission and be used against it (for example, as evidence of the fact that the undertaking was aware that its conduct fell foul of the EC Treaty provisions).
(3) *The right to be heard:* It is a fundamental principle of EC law that an undertaking against which proceedings are brought under Articles 81 and 82 should be able to express its views on the allegations made against it before a decision is taken by the European Commission.
(4) *Fundamental human rights:* Although the Treaty makes no express reference to fundamental human rights, such rights do form part of EC law.
(5) *Legal certainty:* The principle of legal certainty requires that the application of a legal provision to a particular situation be predictable.
(6) *The principle of proportionality:* This is a principle of general application in EC law and, as such, applies in the field of Articles 81 and 82. In essence, it requires that any measure taken by an EC institution such as the Commission should not be excessive by reference to the purpose for which the measure is adopted.

(7) *Self-incrimination:* It is unclear on the face of the Treaty whether undertakings accused of conduct prohibited by Article 81 or 82 benefit from a privilege against self-incrimination. This issue was clarified in two judgments[1] of the ECJ.

1 Case 374/87 *Orkem v EC Commission* [1989] ECR 3283, [1991] 4 CMLR 502; Case 27/88 *Solvay & Cie v EC Commission* [1989] ECR 3355, [1991] 4 CMLR 502.

B Confidentiality

1 BACKGROUND

11.02
During the course of any investigation undertaken by the European Commission it is likely to obtain information, much of it of a confidential nature, from a variety of sources. The proprietors of such confidential information have legitimate grounds for expecting that such confidentiality be respected. As will be seen below, both the EC Treaty itself and the regulations implementing Articles 81 and 82 recognise this. However, there is an inevitable tension between the need to respect the confidentiality of business information and the need to respect the rights of defence of an undertaking accused of violating Articles 81 and 82, with the possible consequence that that undertaking could be heavily fined and its conduct prohibited. Those rights of defence require the undertaking to know the basis of the allegations made against it, in order to enable it to respond. A balance has to be struck and the way in which that balance has been struck to date by the ECJ and the Commission is described in the following paragraphs.

11.03
Article 287 (formerly Article 214) of the EC Treaty prohibits the disclosure by members of the institutions of the Community, the members of committees and the officials and other servants of the Community of 'information of the kind covered by the obligation of professional secrecy, in particular information about undertakings, their business relations or their cost components'. That Treaty provision is of general application in EC law. In the context of Articles 81 and 82, art 20(2) of Regulation 17/62[1] (the general implementing regulation in relation to those two Articles) provides that:

> 'Without prejudice to the provisions of Articles 19 and 21 [of Regulation 17/62], the Commission . . . will not disclose information acquired by [it] as a result of the application of this Regulation and of the kind covered by the obligation of professional secrecy'.

Similarly, art 19(3) of Regulation 17/62 provides that the publication of proposed decisions under art 21 shall have regard to the legitimate interest of undertakings in the protection of their business secrets.

1 Council Regulation (EEC) 17/62, OJ Sp Ed [1959–62] p 87.

11.04
Article 20(2) of Regulation 17/62 is expressly stated to be without prejudice to the provisions of arts 19 and 21. Article 19(1) provides that, before the Commission takes certain decisions (for example, a decision requiring an infringement to be terminated or imposing a fine), it must give the undertakings concerned the opportunity of being heard on the matters to which the Commission has taken objection. This illustrates the tension referred to at para **11.02**. Before considering how this tension has been resolved by the ECJ and the Commission it is first necessary to consider what information is covered by the non-disclosure obligation.

2 INFORMATION TO WHICH THE OBLIGATION OF NON-DISCLOSURE APPLIES

11.05
Both Article 287 of the EC Treaty and art 20(2) of Regulation 17/62 refer to information of the kind covered by the obligation of professional secrecy. On the other hand, art 19(3) of Regulation 17/62 refers to business secrets (as does art 9(3) of Regulation 99/63[1] in the context of hearings). The ECJ has held that business secrets are in a special category[2]. The ECJ has not yet, however, stated what information it regards as being of the kind covered by the obligation of professional secrecy. It is likely that if and when it does have to address that issue it will have regard to the position under the laws of the various Member States[3].

1 Commission Regulation (EEC) 99/63, OJ Sp Ed [1963–64] p 47.
2 See para **11.07**.
3 As it did, for example, when considering the position in relation to legal privilege (see para **11.14** ff) and self-incrimination (see para **11.51**).

11.06
A summary of the legal position in the various Member States regarding professional secrecy is set out in the Edward Report prepared by the Consultative Committee of the Bars and Law Societies of the European Community in 1975[1]. It would seem clear that the notion of information covered by the obligation of professional secrecy is broader than the concept of a business secret and this is indeed inherent in the judgment of the ECJ in *AKZO*[2] considered below[3]. Confidential technical information and know-how is therefore probably covered. Indeed, it may well extend to all information other than that which is in the public domain.

1 'The professional secret, confidentiality, and legal professional privilege in the nine Member States of the European Community' (1975).
2 Case 53/85 *AKZO Chemie BV v EC Commission* [1986] ECR 1965, [1987] 1 CMLR 231.
3 See para **11.07**.

3 BUSINESS SECRETS

11.07
In the *AKZO*[1] case, the ECJ considered the position regarding disclosure of business secrets. The Commission had issued a Statement of Objections

against AKZO and had sent a copy of it to the complainant, ECS. The latter then asked the Commission to provide it with copies of the annexes referred to in the Statement of Objections, in order to enable it to exercise its right to be heard, as provided for in art 19(2) of Regulation 17/62[2]. Following an exchange of correspondence between the Commission and each of ECS and AKZO, the Commission duly disclosed a number of documents to ECS. This disclosure was subsequently challenged by AKZO before the ECJ. The ECJ cited both arts 19(3) and 21 of Regulation 17/62. Although these were not strictly applicable because they dealt with the publication of notices of decisions by the Commission, the ECJ noted that both articles required the Commission to have regard to the legitimate interest of undertakings in the protection of their business secrets. It regarded those articles as the 'exposition of a general principle', from which it followed that 'a third party who has submitted a complaint may not in any circumstances be given access to documents containing business secrets'. The ECJ's reason for this conclusion was that otherwise an undertaking might be inspired to lodge a complaint with the Commission solely in order to gain access to its competitors' business secrets.

1 Case 53/85 *AKZO Chemie BV v EC Commission* [1986] ECR 1965, [1987] 1 CMLR 231.
2 Council Regulation (EEC) 17/62, OJ Sp Ed [1959–62] p 87.

11.08

The ECJ held that, although it is for the Commission to assess whether or not a particular document contains business secrets, the Commission must take a number of steps before disclosing the information in question:

(*a*) it must provide the undertaking concerned (in that case, AKZO) with an opportunity to express its views;
(*b*) it must notify that undertaking of the reasons for its decision that a document does not contain business secrets; and
(*c*) it must give the undertaking concerned an opportunity to bring an action for review[1] *before* implementing its decision.

The Commission had not complied with this third requirement and the decision was therefore void, there being no need because of this failure by the Commission to consider whether the documents did in fact contain business secrets. It has been suggested by one Commission official[2] that the procedural steps laid down by the ECJ may enable a 'fractious defendant' to delay the administrative procedure and that, in order to avoid this, the Commission may prefer in future cases to do without the complainant's input on the evidence.

1 As to judicial review of Commission decisions, see Chapter 10.
2 Joshua 'Information in EEC Competition Law Procedures' [1986] EL Rev 409 at 422.

11.09

In *Postbank*[1], the Commission had authorised the use in national court proceedings of a version of the Statement of Objections which it had previously forwarded to the complainant in parallel administrative proceedings commenced by the Commission. The CFI held that Article 287 of the EC Treaty and art 20(2) of Regulation 17/62[2] required the Commission to ensure that the entitlement of the undertakings concerned to the protection of business secrets was not undermined by or during the transmission of the documents to the national courts. The Court held that the Commission should have followed the procedure laid down by the ECJ in the *Akzo*[3] case.

1 Case T-353/94 *Postbank NV v EC Commission* [1996] ECR II-921.
2 Council Regulation 17/62, OJ Sp Ed [1959–62] p 87.
3 Case 53/85 *Akzo Chemie BV v EC Commission* [1996] ECR 1965, [1987] 1 CMLR 231.

11.10
One situation in which the ECJ (now the Court of First Instance (CFI)) can be confronted head-on by the issue of confidentiality is where a third party intervenes in annulment proceedings brought against a Commission decision under Article 230 of the EC Treaty[1]. Article 116(2) of the Rules of Procedure of the CFI provides that the intervener is to receive a copy of every document served on the parties but that the CFI President may exclude 'secret or confidential documents'. This provision was applied in the *Hilti*[2] case[3]. In relation to those documents for which the CFI upheld the applicant's request for confidential treatment the court ordered the Registrar to serve a non-confidential version on the interveners. It dismissed the applicant's request that the court make it clear to the interveners that the documents disclosed to them should not be used for any purpose other than in connection with the proceedings—the court said that its Rules of Procedure did not contain any provision on which such a direction could be based.

1 As to interventions in the context of Article 173 proceedings, see paras **10.43–10.45**.
2 Case T-30/89A *Hilti v EC Commission* [1990] ECR II-163.
3 In fact, the provision applied was art 93(4) of the ECJ's Rules of Procedure, because the CFI's own Rules had not yet been adopted. Article 93(4) is in the same terms as art 116(2) of the CFI Rules.

4 THE POSITION OF DEFENDANT UNDERTAKINGS

11.11
The Commission may reach the decision in a particular case, having regard to Article 287 of the EC Treaty and to the relevant provisions of Regulation 17/62[1], that it is unable to disclose particular information of a confidential nature to an undertaking against which it has commenced proceedings under Articles 81 and 82 (and indeed, by analogy with the judgment of the ECJ in *AKZO*[2], if the information in question constitutes business secrets it will be bound not to disclose that information). The corollary of this, however, is that the Commission cannot, in making a decision adverse to a particular undertaking, rely on information which it has not disclosed to that undertaking. For example, in *Hoffmann-La Roche v EC Commission*[3] the ECJ said that the Commission could not use, to the detriment of the undertakings involved:

> 'facts, circumstances or documents which it cannot in its view disclose if such a refusal of disclosure adversely affects that undertaking's opportunity to make known effectively its views on the truth or implications of those circumstances on those documents or again on the conclusion drawn by the Commission from them'[4].

In *AEG-Telefunken*[5] the ECJ decided that the Commission had been wrong to place reliance, in reaching its final decision, on a document which it had not released to the defendant undertaking on the grounds of professional secrecy.

1 See paras **11.03–11.04**.
2 Case 53/85 *AKZO Chemie BV v EC Commission* [1986] ECR 1965, [1987] 1 CMLR 231.
3 Case 85/76 *Hoffmann-La Roche v EC Commission* [1979] ECR 461, [1979] 3 CMLR 211.
4 Ibid at point 14.
5 Case 107/82 *AEG-Telefunken v EC Commission* [1983] ECR 3151, [1984] 3 CMLR 325.

5 ACCESS TO COMMISSION FILE

11.12
The extent to which an undertaking against which proceedings are brought by the Commission under Articles 81 and 82 has a right of access to the Commission's file is considered elsewhere in this work[1].

1 See paras **7.27–7.44**.

6 RIGHT TO CLAIM DAMAGES FOR WRONGFUL DISCLOSURE

11.13
The ECJ held in the celebrated *Stanley Adams*[1] case that if the Commission receives information provided to it subject to a request for confidentiality it must comply with that request and if it fails to do so it can be liable in damages to the party affected under Article 288 of the EC Treaty. The ECJ held that the Commission officials involved in the case had negligently breached the obligation of professional secrecy laid down in Article 287 of the EC Treaty and art 20 of Council Regulation 17/62. The ECJ held that Mr Adams had also been negligent and that he had contributed significantly to the damage which he suffered. It apportioned responsibility equally between the two parties. Following the judgment in the *Stanley Adams*[2] case, the Commission issued internal instructions in order to try to ensure that such a situation did not arise again[3].

1 Cases 145/83, 53/84 *Stanley Adams v EC Commission* [1985] ECR 3539, [1986] 1 CMLR 506.
2 See n 1 above.
3 15th Report on Competition Policy (1985), paras 50 and 51; see further para **5.22**.

C Legal Privilege

1 INTRODUCTION

11.14
There is no provision of the EC Treaty, nor of Council Regulation 17/62 (implementing Articles 81 and 82 of the EC Treaty), which specifically

recognises any legal protection (ie protection from disclosure) of written communications between lawyer and client. The national laws of the various Member States do afford some protection to such communications, although its scope and the criteria for applying it vary[1]. In some cases the protection is based principally on the recognition of the nature of the legal profession itself, whilst other systems focus on the requirement that the rights of the defence must be respected.

1 As regards the position in the United Kingdom under the Competition Act 1998, see para **15.151** ff.

11.15

The position so far as Articles 81 and 82 are concerned was considered by the ECJ in 1982 in the leading case of *AM & S Europe Ltd v EC Commission*[1]. In that case, AM & S had instituted proceedings to have part of a Commission decision declared void. The part in question required the company to produce for examination by officers of the Commission charged with carrying out an investigation a number of documents for which the company had claimed legal privilege. The ECJ received evidence from a number of Member States and also from the Consultative Committee of the Bars and Law Societies of the European Community and the Opinion of the Advocate General sets out a convenient summary of the position under the national laws of the various Member States. Viewed against that background, the ECJ held that Regulation 17/62 must be interpreted as protecting the confidentiality of written communications between lawyer and client, subject to two important conditions, namely that:

(*a*) such communications are made for the purposes and in the interests of the client's rights of defence;
(*b*) they must emanate from independent lawyers, that is to say lawyers who are not bound to the client by the relationship of employment.

These two conditions are considered in turn below.

1 Case 155/79 [1982] ECR 1575, [1982] 2 CMLR 264.

2 'FOR THE PURPOSES AND IN THE INTERESTS OF THE CLIENT'S RIGHTS OF DEFENCE'

(1) The European Court of Justice's Ruling

11.16

The ECJ decided that privilege applies to all written communications exchanged after the initiation of the administrative procedure[1] under Regulation 17/62, possibly leading to a decision on the application of Articles 81 and 82 or to a decision imposing a pecuniary sanction on the undertaking concerned. It also held, however, that it must be possible to extend privilege to earlier written communications which have a relationship to the subject matter of that procedure. On the facts of the case, the communications in question had been drawn up during the period preceding, and immediately following, the accession of the United Kingdom to the Community and there was a gap of some six years between the date those communications were exchanged and the initiation of the procedure. Nevertheless, the ECJ decided that they were protected from disclosure, on the basis that they had a relationship to the subject matter of the procedure.

1 With regard to the meaning of the phrase 'initiation of a procedure', see para **7.08**.

11.17
It would seem therefore that legal advice given, for example, in relation to a particular agreement can be privileged even if proceedings in relation to that agreement are only commenced by the Commission some time afterwards. The position is perhaps not entirely free from doubt, in view of the specific language which the ECJ chose to use. Whilst it said that protection must be recognised as covering communications exchanged after the initiation of the administrative procedure, it was only prepared to say that it must 'also be possible' to extend it to earlier communications having a relationship to the subject-matter of the procedure. However, bearing in mind the age of the communications which, on the facts of the case, the ECJ was prepared to hold were the subject of privilege, there is a strong argument for construing the ECJ's judgment broadly on this particular point.

(2) Open Issues

11.18
The ECJ did not expressly hold that the communication between lawyers and clients must be made in confidence to benefit from privilege. It has been suggested by a Commission official[1] that this is implicit in the ECJ's judgment and that leaving the relevant document in an 'open file', or passing a copy to someone outside the company, might involve a loss of protection. Whether or not this is the case, the prudent course for any company receiving legal advice on competition law matters is to keep copies of such advice in a separate file.

1 Joshua 'Information in EEC Competition Law Procedures' (1986) EL Rev 409 at 424.

11.19
The same official has also suggested[1] that the protection is lost if the advice is not given in good faith ie if it is given to facilitate a breach of Community law. However, there may well be a fine line between advice which facilitates breach of the law and advice which enables an undertaking to conduct its business at the frontiers of what is legitimate; moreover, it will not always be clear whether or not particular conduct constitutes a breach of law, given the complex economic issues which are frequently involved.

1 Joshua 'Information in EEC Competition Law Procedures' (1986) EL Rev 409 at 424.

3 COMMUNICATIONS WITH INDEPENDENT LAWYERS

11.20
The ECJ limited the scope of privilege to communications with an independent lawyer, that is to say one who is not bound to his client by a relationship of employment. This was based, in the words of the ECJ, 'on a conception of the lawyer's role as collaborating in the administration of justice by the courts and as being required to provide, in full independence, and in the overriding interests of that cause, such legal assistance as the client needs'[1]. A further limitation imposed by the ECJ is that the lawyer must be entitled to practise his profession in one of the Member States. The ECJ's judgment therefore leaves outside the scope of privilege communications with two important categories of lawyer, namely the in-house lawyer and the lawyer qualified to practise in third countries but not in a Member State of the Community (irrespective of whether or not the lawyer is based within the Community).

1 Case 155/79 *AM & S Europe Ltd v EC Commission* [1982] ECR 1575, [1982] 2 CMLR 264 at para 24.

(1) In-house Lawyers

11.21
In confining the scope of privilege to independent lawyers, the ECJ has excluded from protection communications between an in-house lawyer and his colleagues. In *VW*[1] the Commission copied and took account of in-house legal department documentation relying on the judgment in *AM & S*. The CFI has, however, clarified one area of uncertainty, namely the status of internal documents (generated by either an in-house lawyer or indeed any other employee) which merely report the advice of independent lawyers. In *Hilti*[2] it held that the privilege of written communications between lawyer and client must be regarded as extending also to internal notes which are confined to reporting the text or context of such external advice.

1 Commission Decision (98/273/EC) OJ [1998] L 124/60 at para 199. See too Commission Decision (88/589/EC) OJ [1988] L 19/22.
2 Case T-30/89A *Hilti v EC Commission* [1990] ECR II-163.

11.22
The lack of legal privilege for communications with in-house lawyers is regrettable. In-house legal departments play an increasingly important role in ensuring compliance with EC and national competition law. If the 'modernisation' of Articles 81 and 82 referred to in para **3.02** proceeds, self-assessment by companies as to whether their conduct complies with EU competition rules is likely to become even more important than it is today, as the modernisation proposals will remove the incentive for precautionary notifications by the Commission with a view to seeking exemption under Article 81(3). If, as the modernisation proposals envisage, Article 81(3)

becomes directly applicable by national courts and authorities, the role of the in-house lawyer in ensuring compliance with the competition rules will increase still further.

11.23
The issue is not a straightforward one because the position of in-house lawyers is not the same in all EC member states. For example, not all in-house lawyers are members of their Law Society/Bar equivalents and are not therefore subject to a professional code of ethics. Nevertheless, the current position is unsatisfactory. It may be that the modernisation proposals referred to in paragraph **11.22** themselves provide an opportunity for amendment to be made to Council Regulation 17/62[1]. Indeed, such a move was made in April 1999 when an amendment to Regulation 17/62 was proposed in the European Parliament. That proposal was made in the context of the Commission's reform of the treatment of vertical agreements. The European Council rejected it as not being relevant to the reform of the law on vertical agreements.

1 Council Regulation (EEC) 17/62, OJ Sp Ed [1959-62] p 87.

11.24
The only alternative is for the European Court at some stage to reverse its ruling on the specific issue in the *AM & S* case[1]. There is precedent for the European Court departing from previous precedent[2]. Moreover, it is arguable that a subsequent judgment of the CFI[3] (admittedly in an entirely different context) has opened up the possibility of the court reversing *AM & S*. In the case in point, the CFI ordered that a group of Danish citizens should not have access to the advice given in writing to the European Council by its Legal Service (ie employed lawyers). The argument of the Council, accepted by the CFI, was that if documents discussing the legal position of the Council were to be disclosed, open debate and exchange of views within the institutions of the Community would be inhibited. The CFI specifically rejected the argument that access should be given because the Council's lawyers were employees, rather than members of an independent bar.

1 Case 155/79 *AM&S Europe Ltd v EC Commission* [1982] ECR 1575.
2 Case C-10/89 *SA CNL–SUCAL NV v HAG* [1990] ECR I-3711.
3 Case T-610/97R *Hanne Norup Carlsen v Council* [1998] ECR II-485.

(2) Non-Community Lawyers

11.25
The ECJ's judgment in *AM & S*[1] also excludes from protection communications with lawyers qualified in non-Member States of the Community (whether or not the lawyer is based in the Community). Mindful of the difficulties to which this gives rise, the Commission announced shortly after the ECJ's judgment that it would recommend to the Council of the European Union that bilateral negotiations be opened with countries such as the USA, with a view to achieving reciprocal protection for

communications for independent lawyers admitted to practise in those countries. Nothing has, however, materialised to date.

1 See para **11.15**.

4 PROCEDURE TO BE FOLLOWED

11.26

Having decided that there was a category of documents which could benefit from legal privilege, the ECJ in the *AM & S*[1] case had to consider the issue of how the question of whether or not a particular document was privileged should be determined in any given case. The Commission had argued that it should be the arbiter; others had argued that a third party arbitrator or a national court should resolve the issue. The ECJ rejected these arguments, holding that it should be the final arbiter, on an appeal from a decision of the Commission.

1 See para **11.15**.

11.27

The precise procedure to be followed was laid down by the ECJ. The undertaking concerned should provide the Commission inspector with 'relevant material' of a kind which enables him to satisfy himself that the documents in question satisfy the conditions necessary for privilege to attach (ie that they are from or to an independent lawyer and came into existence for the purpose and in the interests of the client's rights of defence). The undertaking is not, however, bound to reveal the contents of the documents to the Commission inspector. If the Commission is not satisfied that the conditions are met, it can take a decision under art 14(3) of Regulation 17/62[1], requiring the document to be produced or requiring further evidence to establish that privilege exists. That decision can then be challenged by the undertaking and proceedings brought under Article 230 of the EC Treaty[2]. Concern over the delay that this may cause is counter-balanced by the fact that the bringing of proceedings under Article 230 does not cause the Commission's decision to be automatically suspended[3]: it is for the undertaking concerned to apply to the ECJ for suspension by means of interim measures under Articles 242 and 243 of the EC Treaty[4]. Such an application can usually be dealt with fairly quickly.

1 Council Regulation (EEC) 17/62, OJ Sp Ed [1959–62] p 87. See para **6.36** ff.
2 See para **10.09** ff.
3 See para **10.57**.
4 See para **10.57** ff.

11.28

In practice, it should usually be relatively easy for the Commission inspector to satisfy himself whether or not the document in question is from or to an independent lawyer. For example, he could be shown a masked version of a letter of advice, revealing only the letterhead of the lawyer concerned. It might be more difficult for the inspector to be readily satisfied that the document was made for the purpose and in the interests of the rights of defence of his client. This would certainly be the case if a restrictive interpretation was given to that requirement. The ECJ in the *AM & S*[1] case itself appears to have interpreted that condition fairly broadly and major difficulties do not tend to arise in practice. The decision of the CFI in *Hilti*[2] may, however, introduce practical difficulties for the Commission: by extending privilege to internal documents summarising external legal advice, and thereby increasing the number of privileged documents, it is likely to lead to greater dispute between the Commission and the undertaking under investigation as to whether a particular document is privileged.

1 Case 155/79 *AM & S Europe Ltd v EC Commission* [1982] ECR 1575, [1982] 2 CMLR 264; see paras **11.16–11.17**.
2 Case T-30/89A *Hilti v EC Commission* [1990] ECR II-163: see para **11.21**.

5 WHOSE PRIVILEGE?

11.29
The question arises as to whom the protection belongs (ie the lawyer or the client). This is relevant in determining who has power to waive privilege. The ECJ indicated in *AM & S*[1] that the privilege is that of the client, not the lawyer, and it is therefore the client who is able to waive it. This gives rise to the question whether privilege can be waived inadvertently. For example, during the course of an inspection of documents the Commission inspector may be given a file of papers, some of which may include privileged communications. It is submitted that the better view is that privilege cannot be waived inadvertently, although it must be a question of fact whether in any particular case disclosure is or is not inadvertent.

1 Case 155/79 *AM & S Europe Ltd v EC Commission* [1982] ECR 1575, [1982] 2 CMLR 264.

11.30
The best course, if Commission inspectors arrive to conduct an inspection under art 14 of Regulation 17/62, is to ensure that no files are handed over until the documents contained in them are checked by the company or its lawyer, to ensure that all privileged communications are removed. If the company's lawyer is on hand this should be relatively easy. If, however, a lawyer is not available (and the Commission does not have to delay the investigation for more than a short time in order to wait for a lawyer to arrive[1]), the undertaking should do its best to identify those documents which it thinks might be privileged. Some undertakings keep legal advice in separate files so as to reduce the risk of inadvertent disclosure to a Commission inspector.

1 See paras **6.69–6.72**.

D The Right to be Heard

11.31
The right to be heard is a fundamental principle of EC law, particularly where sanctions can be imposed (as in the case of Articles 81 and 82 of the EC Treaty). This right is specifically enshrined in Regulation 17/62[1], the principal regulation implementing Articles 81 and 82. For example, art 19(1) of Regulation 17/62 provides that, before taking certain decisions against undertakings, the Commission must give the undertakings concerned the opportunity of being heard on the matters to which the Commission has taken objection. Similarly, art 2(2) of Regulation 2842/98[2] (the hearing regulation) stipulates that the Commission can only deal in its decisions with objections raised against undertakings in respect of which they have been afforded the opportunity of making known their views.

1 Council Regulation (EEC) 17/62, OJ Sp Ed [1959–62] p 87.
2 Commission Regulation (EC) 2842/98 OJ [1998] L 354/18.

11.32
The *Transocean Marine Paint*[1] case demonstrates that the right to be heard is a general principle of EC law and does not require to be embodied in a specific legislative provision. The ECJ there held that Regulation 99/63 (the predecessor to Regulation 2842/98) 'applies the general rule that a person whose interests are perceptibly affected by a decision taken by a public authority must be given the opportunity to make his point of view known'[2]. Accordingly, although the Regulation does not specifically give a right to be heard to an undertaking on which conditions are to be imposed in relation to an individual exemption under Article 81(3), the general principle nevertheless applied. The right to be heard is one of the principles of natural justice to which UK regulatory authorities are also subject when applying domestic competition law.

1 Case 17/74 *Transocean Marine Paint Association v EC Commission* [1974] ECR 1063, [1974] 2 CMLR 459.
2 [1974] ECR 1063 at para 15.

11.33
It should be borne in mind, however, that the Commission is free to take certain decisions in relation to Articles 81 and 82 without giving the undertaking concerned the opportunity to be heard. The most important decisions falling into this category are decisions by the Commission requiring information (under art 11 of Regulation 17/62[1]) and decisions ordering an investigation (under art 14 of Regulation 17/62[2]). It was argued in the *National Panasonic*[3] case that, notwithstanding the lack of any express reference to the right to be heard in the context of arts 11 and 14 of Regulation 17/62, the basic principle applied. The ECJ disagreed, holding that there was an important distinction between decisions taken at the investigatory stage and decisions holding that an infringement had occurred and/or imposing penalties. This distinction was recently confirmed by the ECJ in the *Hoechst*[4] and *Dow*[5] cases. However, the ECJ also made it clear in those cases that other rights of the defence had to be respected at all times

(including during investigations), referring specifically to the right to be legally represented and the privileged nature of correspondence between lawyer and client[6].

1 See para **6.12** ff.
2 See para **6.36** ff.
3 Case 136/79 *National Panasonic (UK) Ltd v EC Commission* [1980] ECR 2033, [1980] 3 CMLR 169.
4 Cases 46/87, 227/88 *Hoechst v EC Commission* [1989] ECR 2859.
5 Case 85/87 *Dow Benelux v EC Commission* [1989] ECR 3137 and Joined Cases 97–99/87 *Dow Chemical Iberica v EC Commission* [1989] ECR 3165.
6 See para **11.14** ff.

E Fundamental Human Rights

11.34

Although the EC Treaty makes no express reference to the protection of fundamental human rights, it is clear from a number of judgments of the ECJ that such rights do form part of EC law[1]. Indeed, the ECJ has also held[2] that it is entitled to have regard to international treaties concerning human rights. The most relevant of these is the European Convention for the Protection of Human Rights and Fundamental Freedoms[3]: although the Community itself is not a signatory to the Convention, each of the Member States is.

1 See eg Case 11/70 *Internationale Handelsgesellschaft v Einfuhr-und Vorratsstelle für Getreide und Futtermittel* [1970] ECR 1125, [1972] CMLR 255.
2 Case 4/73 *Nold KG v EC Commission* [1974] ECR 491, [1974] 2 CMLR 338.
3 4 November 1950.

11.35

The European Convention on Human Rights has been invoked in a number of actions for annulment of decisions by the European Commission under Articles 81 and 82. For example, in the *National Panasonic*[1] case it was argued that the Commission had violated the company's fundamental rights by ordering an on-the-spot investigation under art 14(3) of Regulation 17/62 without giving it prior warning. Specific reference was made to Article 8(1) of the Convention, under which 'everyone has the right to respect for his private and family life, his home and his correspondence'. The ECJ held that the right invoked by the company had not been violated. The ECJ reached a similar conclusion in the later *AKZO*[2], *Dow*[3] and *Hoechst*[4] cases.

1 Case 136/79 *National Panasonic (UK) Ltd v EC Commission* [1980] ECR 2033, [1980] 3 CMLR 169.
2 Case 5/85 *AKZO Chemie BV and AKZO Chemie UK Ltd v EC Commission* [1986] ECR 2585, [1987] 3 CMLR 716.
3 Case 85/87 *Dow Benelux v EC Commission* [1989] ECR 3137 and Joined Cases 97–99/87 *Dow Chemical Iberica v EC Commission* [1989] ECR 3165.
4 Cases 46/87, 227/88 *Hoechst v EC Commission* [1989] ECR 2859.

11.36

Another Article of the European Convention on Human Rights which is frequently invoked in cases under Articles 81 and 82 of the EC Treaty is

Article 6(1). This provides, in essence, that everyone has a right to a fair and public hearing within a reasonable time by an independent and impartial tribunal. Reliance on this Article was dismissed in both the *FEDETAB*[1] and *Pioneer*[2] cases, in which the ECJ decided that the Commission was not acting as a tribunal within the meaning of Article 6(1). This finding was affirmed in the *Enso Española*[3] case, in which the CFI held that a decision applying the Community rules cannot be unlawful merely because it was adopted under a system in which the Commission carried out both investigatory and decision-making functions. In that case, the applicants further argued that the power of review under Articles 229 and 230 was not a review by a court that has full jurisdiction, and does not cover all elements of the contested decision, as it does not include a review of the Commission's factual findings. The CFI rejected this argument and held that the requirement for effective judicial review of any Commission decision was a general principle of Community law and that this principle had not been infringed as the CFI was an independent and impartial court.

1 Cases 209–215, 218/78 *Heintz van Landewyck v EC Commission* [1980] ECR 3125, [1981] 3 CMLR 134.
2 Cases 100–103/80 *Musique Diffusion Française v EC Commission* [1983] ECR 1825, [1983] 3 CMLR 221.
3 Case T-348/94 *Enso Española SA v EC Commission* [1998] ECR II-1875, at paras 55–65.

11.37
In the *Shell*[1] case, the Commission's Directorate General for Competition had been reorganised during the administrative procedure leading up to the adoption of the Commission's decision[2], with the result that the same official acted as both investigator/inspector and examiner/rapporteur. The company argued that this meant that the guarantees of impartiality and fairness had disappeared. The CFI held[3] that this did not render the Commission's decision unlawful; the procedural guarantees provided for by Community law did not in its view require the Commission to adopt an internal organisation which precluded the same official from acting as investigator and rapporteur in the same case.

1 Case T-11/89 *Shell International Chemical Co Ltd v EC Commission* [1992] ECR II-757, CFI.
2 Commission Decision (86/398/EEC) *Polypropylene* OJ [1986] L 230/1, [1988] 4 CMLR 347.
3 Case T-11/89 *Shell*, n 1 above, at paras 31–40.

F Legal Certainty

1 GENERAL

11.38
The principle of legal certainty, which requires that the application of a law to a specific situation must be 'predictable'[1], is an important principle of EC law. It can, however, sometimes run into conflict with other fundamental principles. For example, in the context of Articles 81 and 82 of the EC

Treaty, it is important that no infringement of those provisions which comes to the attention of the European Commission should go unpunished. At the same time, an undertaking may be considered entitled to have the legal certainty of knowing that, after the effluxion of a particular period of time following the termination of the infringement in question, there is no further scope for the Commission to take action. The conflict between these two principles has been resolved, in the context of Articles 81 and 82, by Regulation 2988/74, which lays down certain limitation periods[2].

1 Schermers and Waelbroeck *Judicial Protection in the European Communities* (4th edn, 1987) p 46.
2 Council Regulation (EEC) 2988/74, OJ [1974] L 318/2. See para **9.96** ff.

11.39
A number of situations in which the principle of legal certainty has played a part in the context of EC competition law are set out below. These examples are not exhaustive.

2 PROVISIONAL VALIDITY

11.40
The doctrine of provisional validity is an example of the application of the principle of legal certainty. The doctrine has the effect that agreements in existence on 13 March 1962, the date on which Regulation 17/62[1] came into force, are to be given their full legal effect until the Commission takes a decision under Article 81(3). This avoids, in the context of these old agreements, the automatic nullity which flows from Article 81(2). In *Brasserie de Haecht*[2] the ECJ said that the general principle of certainty required that the court could only declare the agreement in question void after the Commission had taken a decision under Article 81(3)[3]. Until that time, the agreement could be enforced in national courts.

1 Council Regulation (EEC) 17/62, OJ Sp Ed [1959–62] p 87.
2 Case 48/72 *Brasserie de Haecht v Wilkin-Janssen* [1973] ECR 77, [1973] CMLR 287.
3 [1973] ECR 77 at para 9.

11.41
The fact that the principle of legal certainty can be made to give way to other principles of greater importance is shown by the fact that so-called 'new' agreements do not benefit from the doctrine of provisional validity[1].

1 See para **18.07**.

3 LIMITATION PERIODS

11.42
By their very nature, limitation periods serve to introduce legal certainty, in that they assure undertakings that they can no longer be subject to proceedings after the relevant period has expired. In the context of Articles 81 and 82, specific limitation periods were introduced in Council Regulation

2988/74[1]. The substance of that Regulation is discussed elsewhere in this work[2] but it should be noted that the recitals expressly state that it is necessary in the interests of legal certainty that the principle of limitation be introduced and that implementing rules be laid down. The introduction of this Regulation came about as a result of judgments of the ECJ[3] which held that, although the principle of legal certainty required a limitation period to be established, that was a matter for the Council of the European Union (in its role as legislator) rather than for the ECJ itself.

1 OJ [1974] L 319/1.
2 See para **9.96** ff.
3 Case 44/69 *Bucher v EC Commission* [1970] ECR 733 and Cases 48/69 *ICI v EC Commission* [1972] ECR 619, [1972] CMLR 557.

11.43
The judgment of the CFI in *Filtrona*[1] confirms the application of the principle of legal certainty in the context of time limits for the commencement of annulment proceedings under Article 230 of the EC Treaty. In that case the CFI held that, because the application had been lodged two days late, it was time barred. The CFI stated that, according to the settled case law[2] of the ECJ:

> '. . . the strict application of Community regulations on procedural time limits meets the requirement of certainty as to the law and the need to avoid any discrimination or arbitrary treatment in the administration of justice'[3].

1 Case T-125/89 *Filtrona Española v EC Commission* [1990] 4 CMLR 832.
2 Case 42/85 *Cockerill-Sambre v EC Commission* [1985] ECR 3749, [1987] 1 CMLR 325.
3 [1990] 4 CMLR 832 at 839.

4 NON-RETROACTIVITY

11.44
A further principle of Community law, and one which is really an aspect of the principle of legal certainty, is that of non-retroactivity. In the context of penal sanctions, the ECJ has held that the principle of non-retroactivity 'is one which is common to all the legal orders of the Member States and is enshrined in Article 7 of the European Convention for the Protection of Human Rights and Fundamental Freedoms as a fundamental right; it takes its place among the general principles of law whose observance is ensured by the Court of Justice'[1]. As in the case of other principles of Community law, the principle of non-retroactivity sometimes has to take second place to a principle of greater importance.

1 Case 63/83 *R v Kirk* [1984] ECR 2689 at 2718.

11.45
The measures taken by a Community institution can be retroactive in two ways. They can be 'truly' retroactive, in the sense that their effect is backdated. Alternatively, they can take immediate effect for the future, thereby applying to agreements already in existence at the date the measure is taken. The ECJ has held that, unless there are very good reasons,

regulations should not enter into force immediately as this would be in conflict with the principle of legal certainty[1]. Thus, most of the block exemptions adopted by the Commission under Article 81(3) apply three months (and occasionally six months[2]) after the date they are adopted. The EC Merger Regulation[3], was adopted in December 1989 but did not take effect until September 1990.

1 Case 17/67 *Neumann v Hauptzollamt Hof* [1967] ECR 441 at 456.
2 See, for example, Commission Regulation (EC) 2790/99 dealing with vertical agreements, OJ [1999] L 336/21.
3 Council Regulation (EEC) 4064/89, OJ [1989] L 395/1.

11.46
In addition, most block exemptions contain transitional provisions to allow undertakings time to bring their agreements into conformity with the relevant block exemption. The most striking example is perhaps provided by Regulation 1983/83[1] (dealing with exclusive distribution agreements), which replaced, and amended in certain significant respects, its predecessor, Regulation 67/67[2]. Regulation 1983/83 came into force on 1 July 1983. However, if an agreement was either in force on 1 July 1983 or entered into force between that date and 31 December 1983 and complied with Regulation 67/67, Article 81(1) did not apply to the agreement until 31 December 1986[3]. Regulation 1983/83 has itself since been replaced by Commission Regulation 2790/99[4], which also contains transitional provisions.

1 Commission Regulation (EEC) 1983/83, OJ [1973] L 173/1.
2 Commission Regulation (EEC) 67/67, OJ Sp Ed [1967] p 10.
3 See n 1 above, art 7.
4 OJ [1999] L 336/21.

5 LEGITIMATE EXPECTATIONS

11.47
The ECJ has held that the principle of the protection of legitimate expectations forms part of EC law[1]; that is to say, that Community institutions will not act contrary to expectations legitimately held by those affected by the action in question. In the context of Articles 81 and 82, this principle was cited by Advocate General Reischl in the *Perfumes* cases[2]. This was in the context of so-called 'comfort letters'[3], in which the Commission informs the undertakings concerned that it proposes to take no action in a particular case. Such letters are not binding on the Commission but the Advocate General was of the view that the Commission could not re-open its file unless new facts came to its attention or unless it became clear subsequently from a judgment of the ECJ that the Commission had been acting under a misapprehension as to the law. In the so-called *Ice-Cream* case[4], the CFI rejected an application that, by deciding that agreements which had previously been the subject of a comfort letter infringed Article 81, the Commission had breached the principle of the protection of legitimate expectations.

1 Case 112/77 *Töpfer* [1978] ECR 1019 at 1033.

2 Case 31/80 *L'Oréal v De Nieuwe AMCK* [1980] ECR 3775 at 3803, [1981] 2 CMLR 235 at 246.
3 See para **8.73** ff.
4 Case T-7/93 *Langnese-Iglo v EC Commission* [1995] ECR II-1533. See para **8.75**.

11.48
In the context of fines imposed by the Commission for infringements of Article 81 or 82, it is sometimes argued by applicants seeking to challenge the Commission's decision that a fine would be inappropriate because the undertaking had been entitled to place some reliance on a Commission notice. Strictly speaking, such notices have no legal force. Nevertheless, the ECJ was prepared in the *Sugar*[1] case to accept this argument in the context of the Commission's Notice on Commercial Agents. In the *Tetra Pak*[2] case the CFI rejected the invocation of the principle of legal certainty in the context of the inter-relationship between Article 82 and a block exemption under Article 81(3). The CFI accepted that one of the main purposes of block exemptions was to secure legal certainty for the parties to an agreement but held that this did not discharge undertakings from the obligation to comply with Article 82[3].

1 Cases 40–48 etc/73 *Suiker Unie v EC Commission* [1975] ECR 1663, [1976] 1 CMLR 295.
2 Case T-51/89 *Tetra Pak Rausing v EC Commission* [1991] 4 CMLR 334.
3 The principle of legal uncertainty was also unsuccessfully invoked in Case C-322/93P *Automobiles Peugeot SA v EC Commission* [1994] ECR I-2727.

G Proportionality

11.49
The principle of proportionality requires that the measure in question must not be excessive by reference to the purpose for which it is adopted[1]. The principle can be invoked in cases involving the imposition of penalties and is therefore sometimes prayed in aid in the context of European Commission decisions imposing fines under Article 81 or 82[2].

1 See eg in relation to the EC sugar market regime Case 181/84 *R v Intervention Board for Agricultural Produce, ex p E D & F Man (Sugar) Ltd* [1986] 2 All ER 115, [1985] ECR 2889, and in relation to the EC cereals market regime, Case 47/86 *Roquette Frères SA v ONIC* [1987] ECR 2889.
2 Eg Case 27/76 *United Brands v EC Commission* [1978] ECR 207, [1978] 1 CMLR 429 (at para 302); Cases 32/78, 36–82/78 *BMW v EC Commission* [1979] ECR 2435, [1980] 1 CMLR 370 (at para 47). In both cases the proportionality argument was readily dismissed by the ECJ on the facts.

11.50
There is no reason why this principle should not, however, be applied in other contexts in relation to Article 81 or 82. For example, it is an aspect to which the Commission should have regard in carrying out investigations under arts 11 and 14 of Regulation 17/62[1] and deciding whether to conduct an article 14 investigation by way of a 'dawn raid' or not[2]; nevertheless, it should be recognised that the ECJ is likely to be reluctant to interfere with the Commission's discretion in this regard. Indeed, in *National Panasonic*[3] the ECJ dismissed the argument that an article 14(3) decision could only be

taken without a prior article 14(2) request if the situation was very grave and involved the greatest urgency and the need for complete secrecy. The ECJ held that the Commission had a large measure of discretion in deciding whether to proceed immediately to an article 14(3) decision. In the context of art 11 the principle was unsuccessfully invoked before the CFI in the *SEP* case[4], although the Court did confirm that the principle of proportionality applied.

1 Council Regulation (EEC) 17/62, OJ Sp Ed [1959–62] p 87.
2 See para **6.40**.
3 Case 136/79 *National Panasonic (UK) Ltd v EC Commission* [1980] ECR 2033, [1980] 3 CMLR 169.
4 Case T-39/90 *SEP v EC Commission* [1991] ECR II-1497. Upheld by the ECJ in Case C-36/ 92P *SEP v EC Commission* [1994] ECR I-1911, ECJ.

11.51
The principle of proportionality was invoked in the *RTE* case[1]. The applicant argued that the Commission's decision[2] required it to grant a large number of intellectual property licences and to monitor compliance with the terms of them. This would entail a disproportionate burden in terms of cost and personnel for a relatively small organisation like RTE. The ECJ held that the applicant's argument was really an aspect of the same plea as that based on infringement of art 3(1) of Council Regulation 17/62[3]. The ECJ dismissed the applicant's claim.

1 Joined Cases C-241 and 242/91P *RTE and ITP v EC Commission* [1995] ECR I-743.
2 Commission Decision (89/205/EEC) *Magill TV Guide* OJ [1989] L 78/43, [1989] 4 CMLR 757.
3 See para **8.57**.

H Self-Incrimination

11.52
The extent to which undertakings accused of conduct prohibited by Articles 81 and 82 benefit from a privilege against self-incrimination is considered in Chapter 6[1].

1 See paras **6.74–6.76**.

Chapter 12 Enforcement by National Authorities

A Introduction

12.01
This Chapter considers the application of Articles 81 and 82 by the specialist competition authorities in the Member States. The starting point for consideration of this issue is Article 84 (formerly Article 88) of the EC Treaty, which provides:

> 'Until the entry into force of the provisions adopted in pursuance of Article 87 [now Article 83], the authorities in Member States shall rule on the admissibility of agreements, decisions and concerted practices and on abuse of a dominant position in the common market in accordance with the law of their country and with the provisions of Article 85 [now Article 81], in particular paragraph 3, and of Article 86 [now Article 82]'.

12.02
A number of points arise out of the wording of Article 84. Firstly, it appears to suggest that, once provisions have been adopted in pursuance of Article 83 (which has happened, notably in the form of Regulation 17[1]), the powers which it gives to the authorities of the Member States cease. This is not in fact the case. Regulation 17 itself provides (art 9(3)) that the authorities of the Member States remain competent to apply Articles 81(1) and 82 in accordance with Article 84, as long as the Commission has not itself initiated a procedure.

1 Commission Regulation (EEC) 17/62, OJ Sp Ed [1959–62] p 87.

12.03
Secondly, the jurisdiction conferred on the authorities of the Member States by virtue of Regulation 17, art 9(3) is not unlimited. It can be removed in any particular case once the Commission initiates a procedure[1]. In addition, art 9(3) does not refer to Article 81(3). This is because exemption granted pursuant to that provision remains the sole competence of the Commission[2].

1 See paras **7.09–7.10**.
2 Regulation 17/62, art 9(1).

B Which Authorities?

12.04
The ECJ made it clear in *BRT v SABAM*[1] that the authorities referred to in art 9(3) of Regulation 17 are those whose particular function is to apply

competition law (as opposed to the ordinary courts or tribunals, which acquire their jurisdiction to apply Articles 81 and 82 not from art 9(3) of Regulation 17 but from the direct effect of Articles 81 and 82[2]).

1 Case 127/73 [1974] ECR 51, [1974] 2 CMLR 238.
2 See para **18.02**.

12.05
In the United Kingdom, domestic competition law is administered by a variety of specialist bodies (in addition to the High Court and county court in England and Wales and the Court of Session in Scotland). These include the Office of Fair Trading, Competition Commission and Secretary of State for Trade and Industry.

C Practice to Date

12.06
The approach to the application of Articles 81 and 82 by the specialist national competition authorities varies within the EC. According to the Commission's Twenty-sixth Report on Competition Policy[1], only seven Member States (Belgium, France, Germany, Greece, Italy, Spain and Portugal) as yet have in their domestic legislation a legal basis for applying Articles 81 and 82. In 1994 the Commission presented the national competition authorities with a report[2] which identified three criteria to be applied in assessing which cases might be dealt with by a national authority rather than by the Commission. This reflects the Commission's keenness, through the doctrine of subsidiarity, to encourage national authorities/courts to deal with those cases which it does not believe have a Community interest. The three criteria which were identified were firstly, that the effects of the case must be located mainly within a single Member State (albeit that, if an agreement or practice implemented mainly in one Member State raises a question of Community interest, the Commission indicated that it would initiate proceedings on the basis of art 9(3) of Regulation 17/62, thereby removing the jurisdiction of the national authorities); secondly, that the case must involve infringements of Article 81(1) which probably do not satisfy the criteria of Article 81(3)[3]; and thirdly, that protection at national level must be effective, by which the Commission indicated that it meant not only that the national authority had adequate rules of substance and procedure but also the necessary human and material resources.

1 26th Report on Competition Policy, para 32.
2 24th Report on Competition Policy, para 42.
3 This reflects the fact that the Commission has sole competence to apply Article 81(3).

12.07
In 1997 the Commission published[1] a Notice on the application of Articles 81 and 82 by the national authorities. The thrust of the Notice is as follows:

(1) It invokes the principle of subsidiarity[2], stating that the involvement of national competition authorities in EC competition policy means that decisions can be taken as closely as possible to the citizen. The

draft states that the Commission is convinced that enhancing the role of national authorities will boost the effectiveness of Articles 81 and 82.

(2) National authorities should handle cases the effects of which are mainly felt in their territory and which appear unlikely to qualify for exemption under Article 81(3), unless the case displays a particular Community interest.

(3) Cases which display a particular Community interest, particularly from an economic or legal standpoint, will still have to be dealt with by the Commission (for example, cases involving a new point of law), as will cases involving alleged anti-competitive behaviour by public undertakings or undertakings to which a Member State has granted special or exclusive rights within the meaning of Article 86 (formerly Article 90) (such as the privatised utilities in the United Kingdom).

1 OJ [1997] C 313/3. This is the counterpart to the 1993 Notice on relations between the Commission and national courts.

2 This principle is enshrined in Article 5 (formerly Article 3*b*) of the EC Treaty.

12.08

The following points should be noted:

(1) The Notice expressly recognises that the Commission has exclusive powers, pursuant to Article 81(3), to declare the provisions of Article 81(1) inapplicable. It states that any restrictive practice that prima facie qualifies for exemption must therefore be examined by the Commission (rather than a national authority, which could not grant an exemption). On the other hand, the Notice contains a fairly lengthy section on what it refers to as 'dilatory notifications' ie a notification made by an undertaking threatened with an imminent (and adverse) decision by a national authority (the Notice also refers to notifications made with a view to preventing the imminent initiation of a national procedure which might result in an adverse decision). The Notice states that, if the Commission takes the view that such notification is chiefly aimed at suspending the national procedure, it will consider itself justified in not examining it as a matter of priority. It goes on to say that in such a case the national authority should ask the Commission for its provisional opinion on the likelihood of an exemption being granted (unless it was clear to the national authority, without input from the Commission, that the agreement or practice at issue could not be the subject of an individual exemption). It is questionable whether this is an appropriate application by the Commission of its duties and responsibilities under Article 81(3). It appears to be an attempt to reconcile the fact that, on the one hand, the Commission is keen to devolve to national authorities (and, indeed, national courts) application of Article 81 and, on the other, the fact that only the Commission has competence to grant an exemption under Article 81(3).

(2) The number of cases that will be genuinely national in nature (yet still have the requisite effect on trade between Member States) is likely to decrease, as the single market becomes an economic reality in an increasing number of sectors.

(3) Whilst the Notice does provide guidance as to the Commission's view on which cases should fall to be dealt with by national authorities and which by the Commission itself, it does little to advance the cause of legal certainty.

12.09
The Notice calls upon those Member States which have not already done so—which include the United Kingdom—to adopt legislation enabling their competition authorities to implement Articles 81 and 82. The pressure to do so is likely to increase.

12.10
Although there is no specific UK legislation conferring on the national authorities a legal basis for applying Articles 81 and 82, the Secretary of State did consider in 1991 whether arrangements for disseminating company news, following the introduction by the London Stock Exchange of its Regulatory News Service, constituted an abuse of a dominant position contrary to Article 82[1]. He concluded that the arrangements in question did infringe Article 82 but that the abuse could be remedied if the companies were free to pass announcements to other news vendors at the same time as they were given to the Exchange's company announcement office[2]. The Exchange subsequently introduced changes to this effect.

1 See para **18.04** .
2 DTI Press Notice, 31 October 1991.

12.11
In 1996 the UK government introduced[1] a limited application of Articles 81 and 82 by the relevant national authorities. This relates to matters in respect of which no implementing regulation has been made at a Community level under Article 83 of the EC Treaty, namely air transport services between EC Member States and non-EC Member States and secondly, international maritime and tramp vessel services.

1 EC Competition Law (Articles 88 and 89) Enforcement Regulations 1996, SI 1996/2199.

12.12
Regulation 3 of the 1996 Regulations[1] empowers the Secretary of State to request the Director General of Fair Trading to carry out a preliminary investigation, where it appears to the Secretary of State that the United Kingdom might have a duty to rule on whether an agreement or practice is prohibited by Article 81 or 82. Regulations 4 and 5 provide that the Secretary of State may, following such a preliminary investigation, decide to take no further action in respect of the agreement or practice or, in the case of an agreement, declare that the exemption provided for in Article 81(3) applies. Alternatively, he may decide to refer the matter to the Competition Commission for fuller investigation and report. Regulation 14 provides that the Secretary of State may accept enforceable undertakings from the persons concerned instead of making a reference to the CC. The Regulations make provision for the publication of decisions to take no further action or exemption declarations made by the Secretary of State

following a preliminary investigation and for the procedures to be followed with regard to the CC's investigation and report. Following a report by the CC which concludes that an agreement exists which falls within Article 81(1), the Secretary of State may declare an exemption or make an order for the purpose of terminating the infringement[2]. Where the CC concludes that an infringement of Article 82 has occurred, the Secretary of State may make an order for the purpose of terminating the infringement[3]. The Secretary of State may accept enforceable undertakings from the person(s) concerned, as an alternative to making an order[4].

1 SI 1996/2199.
2 Ibid regs 19 and 21(1) and (2).
3 SI 1996/2199, reg 21(3) and (4).
4 Ibid reg 22.

12.13
The 1996 Regulations[1] contain provisions for the enforcement of orders[2] and provide for an offence of filing false of misleading information[3] and for restricting the disclosure of information with respect to a particular business obtained except for permitted purposes[4]. Those provisions reflect parallel provisions contained in the Fair Trading Act 1973.

1 SI 1996/2199.
2 Ibid reg 24.
3 SI 1996/2199, reg 25.
4 Ibid reg 28.

Chapter 13 Introduction to Chapters 14–16

A Format of Chapters 14–16

13.01
The purpose of Chapters 14–16 is to describe the procedures for the enforcement of UK competition law by the relevant regulatory authorities. In contrast with the position under EC law, the procedure by which domestic UK law is enforced varies from statute to statute. This has the effect that different substantive issues are dealt with in different ways procedurally, and with different remedies available to the regulatory authorities, according to which statute applies to the particular agreement or conduct in question. With the repeal of the Restrictive Trade Practices Act 1976, the Resale Prices Act and the anti-competition practice provisions of the Competition Act 1980 and their replacement by the Competition Act 1998, the position has however, become less fragmented.

Chapters 14 to 16 deal with the following subjects:

Chapter 14: Fair Trading Act 1973

Chapter 15: Competition Act 1998

Chapter 16: Judicial Review

B Relationship with EC Law

13.02
Domestic UK competition law applies alongside EC competition law and both sets of law frequently apply to the same conduct or agreement. The principle that, in the event of an inconsistency, EC law prevails over the law of the United Kingdom[1], is as applicable in relation to competition law as it is in relation to other areas of law. However, it is not always straightforward in practice[2].

1 Case 6/64 *Costa v ENEL* [1964] ECR 585, [1964] CMLR 425; European Communities Act 1972, s 2(1).
2 See further *Butterworths Competition Law* Division I.

Chapter 14 Fair Trading Act 1973

A Introduction

14.01
In the context of this work, the relevant parts of the Fair Trading Act 1973 (FTA 1973) are Pts I, IV and V. Part I is a largely introductory section, dealing principally with definitional matters. Part IV deals with monopoly references and Pt V with merger references. The scope of this chapter is confined to the procedural aspects relating to monopoly references.

14.02
One or two preliminary points should be made at the outset. Control of the conduct of monopolists under the FTA 1973 is entirely administrative in nature. Investigations are carried out by the Competition Commission (CC), an administrative body whose nature and status is described in Division I and which inherited the functions of the former Monopolies and Mergers Commission[1]. The CC carries out such investigations following a reference made to it by either the Director General of Fair Trading (DGFT) or the Secretary of State for Trade and Industry. There is no role for the ordinary courts (except for the possibility of applying to the High Court for judicial review[2]and the possibility of action for breach of an order made or undertakings given following a CC report[3]). In 1995, the DGFT was given the power to recommend that the Secretary of State accept undertakings in lieu of the DGFT making a monopoly reference to the CC[4].

1 Competition Act 1998, s 45.
2 See Chapter 17.
3 See para **14.90**.
4 FTA 1973, s 56A introduced by the Deregulation and Contracting Out Act 1994. See further, para **14.28**.

14.03
Monopoly references to the CC are expressed to be in respect of a certain category of goods or services, rather than by reference to a particular company. The CC considers the existence or otherwise of a monopoly situation and identifies the person or persons in whose favour such a situation exists. CC reports derive their title from the goods or services involved, rather than the identity of the alleged monopolist(s)[1].

1 For example: *Beer* (1989) (Cm 651); *Artificial Lower Limbs* (1989) (Cm 594); *Opium Derivatives* (1989) (Cm 630); *Credit Card Services* (1989) (Cm 718); *Cross-Channel Car Ferry Services* (1989) (Cm 903); *Petrol* (1990) (Cm 972); *Soluble Coffee* (1991) (Cm 1459); *Razors and Razor Blades* (1991) (Cm 1472); *Fine Fragrances* (1993) (Cm 2380); *Films* (1994) (Cm 2673); *Video Games* (1995) (Cm 2781); *Milk* (1999) (Cm 4286); *Impulse Ice Cream* (2000) (Cm 4510); *New Cars* (April 2000) (Cm 4660).

14.04
The FTA 1973 provides for the investigation of so-called 'scale' and 'complex' monopolies. Scale monopolies arise where one firm has a share of supply of a given description of goods or services equal to or exceeding one quarter. Complex monopolies arise where one quarter of the supply is accounted for by several firms who act in a way that distorts competition, but not necessarily by colluding with each other. During the passage of the Competition Act 1998 through Parliament, there was considerable debate as to what effect that Act should have on the scale and complex monopoly provisions in the FTA 1973, bearing in mind that the CA 1998 introduced a prohibition of abuse of a dominant position[1]. The question which arose was whether it was appropriate to retain the scale and complex monopoly provisions respectively.

1 See para **15.06**.

14.05
Where there has been an infringement of the Chapter II prohibition, the DGFT has the power to impose a fine under the CA 1998[1] and to direct the cessation of the prohibited conduct[2]. Such directions cannot include a structural remedy (ie an order of divestment). There may, however, be circumstances where divestment would be a suitable remedy and accordingly the Government decided to retain the scale monopoly provisions contained in the FTA 1973: the power of divestment is among the powers available to the Secretary of State under the FTA 1973, Sch 8, Pt II. The Government stated during the passage of the 1998 Act through Parliament that the use of the scale monopoly provisions would, however, be rare and that they would 'essentially become reserve powers to deal with situations where the problem is market structure rather than abuse'[3]. In his Major Provisions Guidelines[4], the DGFT states that the scale monopoly provisions are intended for dealing with the situation where a prior infringement of the prohibitions in the Competition Act has already been proved but where the Director General believes that there is a real prospect of further abuse by the same company. The structural remedies available under the scale monopoly powers may be the only effective means of preventing those further abuses. Those Guidelines also note, however, that in the 'special circumstances' of the utility sectors (the difficulty of establishing competition) the full use of the scale monopoly provisions is retained – ie there is no need for a prior infringement of the CA 1998[5].

1 CA 1998, s 36.
2 CA 1998, s 33.
3 HL Committee, 13 November 1997, col 300 (Lord Simon).
4 Para 13.4.
5 Para 13.5. See also DGFT Guidelines 'Concurrent Application to Regulated Industries', para 4.8.

14.06
The Government gave as its principal reason for retaining the complex monopoly provisions contained in the FTA 1973 the need to control situations of competitive failure in an industry where neither the Chapter I prohibition nor the Chapter II prohibition might apply[1]. In addition, the

retention of the complex market provisions probably made it easier for the Government to decide to take most vertical agreements outside the scope of the Chapter I prohibition.

1 HL Report Stage, 19 February 1998, col 351; 'The Fair Trading Act complex monopoly provisions may enable the authorities to deal with problems that fall outside the Chapter I and Chapter II prohibition, particularly where there is parallel behaviour by companies in the market but no actual agreement' (Lord Simon).

14.07
The DGFT made two monopoly references in 1998:

(*a*) the supply of raw cows' milk;
(*b*) the supply of impulse ice cream.

The corresponding number of monopoly references in the years 1988–1997 was as follows[1]:

1988 — Four;
1989 — Seven;
1990 — Seven;
1991 — Three;
1992 — Eight;
1993 — Seven;
1994 — Six;
1995 — Nine;
1996 — Three;
1997 — One.

1 Source: *Annual Reports of the Director General of Fair Trading* 1988–1998.

B General Functions of the Director General of Fair Trading

14.08
Under the FTA 1973, s 2, the DGFT has the following general duties:

(*a*) to keep under review the carrying on of commercial activities in the UK relating to the supply of goods and services to consumers in the UK, and to collect information with respect to such activities, with a view to his becoming aware of practices which may adversely affect the economic interests of consumers in the UK;
(*b*) to receive and collate evidence available to him with respect to such activities and which appears to him to be evidence of practices which may adversely affect the interests of consumers in the UK (whether they are economic interests or interests with respect to health, safety or other matters);
(*c*) to keep under review the carrying on of commercial activities in the UK, and to collect information with respect to those activities, with a view to his becoming aware of monopoly situations or uncompetitive practices;

(*d*) to give information and assistance to the Secretary of State with respect to any of the above-mentioned matters;
(*e*) to make recommendations to the Secretary of State as to any action which in the opinion of the DGFT should be taken in relation to any of the matters in respect of which the DGFT has any such duties.

The DGFT has described the way in which he performs this function as follows[1]:

> 'The Office carries out this function in two ways. First, it monitors the economic performance of industries to identify areas where there may be monopolies and monopoly abuse. It pays particular attention to the economic performance of larger firms, taking account of the degree of import penetration, and information on price levels and movements, profits and market behaviour. Secondly, it takes note of complaints and other representations received from industry and the public'.

1 *Annual Report of the Director General of Fair Trading* 1989 p 34. This passage usually appears in each Annual Report.

C Specific Powers of Investigation of the Director General of Fair Trading in Relation to Monopoly Situations

14.09
The DGFT's duty to gather certain kinds of information, described at para **14.08**, is facilitated in the context of monopoly situations by s 44 of the FTA 1973. In order to exercise his powers under s 44 he must be satisfied that there are grounds for believing that:

(*a*) a monopoly situation may exist; and
(*b*) he would not be precluded from making a reference to the MMC with respect to the existence or possible existence of that situation: under the FTA 1973, s 50(2) the DGFT is not entitled to make a monopoly reference in relation to the supply of certain goods or services, namely those set out in Pt I of Sch 5, and Pt I of Sch 7, to the FTA 1973[1].

1 The scheduled goods and services are: gas supplies through pipes to tariff customers, the carriage of passengers by road in Northern Ireland, the carriage of goods or passengers by rail, postal services, raw cane or sugar beet, hops, port facilities, air navigation services, international carriage by air (other than charter flights), the provision by programme contractors of programmes for transmission and the provision of a licensed cable programme service.

1 MONOPOLY SITUATION

14.10
Assuming that the DGFT has grounds for believing that the conditions referred to in the preceding paragraph are satisfied, he may (in relation to any monopoly situation) require certain kinds of information and documents from specified categories of person for the purpose of deciding

whether to make a monopoly reference or to make a proposal under s 56A[1] for the Secretary of State to accept undertakings[2]. The categories of person are: any person who supplies or produces goods of the relevant description in the UK; any person to whom such goods are supplied in the UK; any person who supplies services of the relevant description in the UK; or any person to whom such services are supplied[3]. The information/documents which the DGFT may require to be produced under s 44 are as follows:

(1) Any specified documents, or any document which falls within a specified category, which are in a person's custody or under his control and which are 'relevant'[4]. For this purpose, a document is relevant if it is relevant to a decision whether to make a monopoly reference or whether to make a proposal under s 56A for the Secretary of State to accept undertakings[5]. The powers conferred by s 44 are exercised in relation to the document for the purpose of assisting the DGFT in determining whether to take that decision; a document includes information recorded in any form[6].
(2) Specified estimates, forecasts or returns, or other information[7]. In relation to information recorded otherwise than in legible form, the power to require its production includes power to require production of it in legible form, so far as the means to do so are within the custody or under the control of the person on whom the requirement is imposed[8].

1 See para **14.28**.
2 FTA 1973, s 44(1) and (1A).
3 FTA 1973, s 44(3).
4 FTA 1973, s 44(2)(*a*).
5 See para **14.28**.
6 FTA 1973, s 44(8)(*b*).
7 FTA 1973, s 44(2)(*b*).
8 FTA 1973, s 44(8)(*c*).

14.11
The DGFT must exercise the power to request information or documents referred to at para **14.10** by written notice served on the person on whom the requirement is imposed[1]. The power to require a person to produce a document includes power to take copies of it or extracts from it and to require the person notified, or any person who is a present or past officer of his or is or was at any time employed by him, to provide an explanation of the document. If the document is not produced, the person notified may be required to state, to the best of his knowledge and belief, where it is[2].

1 FTA 1973, s 44(4).
2 FTA 1973, s 44(5).

14.12
The DGFT may also enter the premises used by a person of the type referred to at para **14.10** for business purposes and require any person on the premises to produce any documents on the premises which are in his custody or under his control and which are relevant[1] and require any person on the premises to give him such an explanation of the documents as he may require.

1 FTA 1973, s 44(2)(c); for the meaning of 'relevant' and 'document' see para **14.10**.

14.13
These powers were strengthened by the Competition Act 1998 and broadly mirror the powers of investigation conferred on the DGFT when exercising his functions under that Act. However, it should be noted that there is no power under the FTA 1973 to enter premises with a warrant using reasonable force[1].

1 This power does exist under the CA 1998; see para **15.145**.

14.14
Nothing in s 44 of the FTA 1973 compels any person to produce any document which he could not be compelled to produce in civil proceedings before the High Court (or, in Scotland, the Court of Session) or to give any information which he could not be compelled to give in evidence in such proceedings[1].

1 FTA 1973, s 44(6).

D Offences in Connection with the Investigatory Powers of the Director General of Fair Trading

14.15
Any person who furnishes information to the DGFT which he knows to be false in a material particular, or recklessly furnishes information which is false or misleading in a material particular, is guilty of an offence[1] and liable, on summary conviction, to a fine not exceeding £2,000 and, on conviction on indictment, to imprisonment for a term not exceeding two years or to a fine or both[2]. If such an offence is committed by a body corporate, any director, manager, secretary or similar officer who is proved to have consented to or connived in the commission of the offence is also guilty[3]. Similarly, it is also an offence for a person to furnish information to a third party, knowing it to be materially false or misleading (or recklessly, in circumstances in which it is in fact materially false or misleading) and knowing that it is to be used for the purpose of furnishing information to the DGFT[4]. If, for example, false information is knowingly provided by a company under investigation to its legal adviser, who in turn knowingly passes it on to the DGFT, the company, its directors and the legal advisers are all potentially liable. These provisions also apply in relation to the furnishing of information to the Secretary of State and the CC[5].

1 FTA 1973, s 93B(1), inserted by the Companies Act 1989. As to the level of the fine, see Magistrates' Courts Act 1980, s 32.
2 FTA 1973, s 93B(3), inserted by the Companies Act 1989.
3 FTA 1973, s 132(1).
4 FTA 1973, s 93B(2), inserted by the Companies Act 1989.
5 See para **14.42**.

14.16
Certain additional offences were introduced into the FTA 1973 by the Competition Act 1998. Under s 46(4) of the FTA 1973 any person who

refuses or wilfully neglects to comply with the requirement to provide information or documents under s 44(2)[1] is guilty of an offence and liable, on summary conviction, to a fine not exceeding [the prescribed sum] or, on conviction or indictment, to imprisonment for a term not exceeding two years (or to a fine or both). It is a defence for a person charged with an offence in respect of a requirement to produce a document to prove that the document was not in his possession or under his control and that it was not reasonably practicable for him to comply with the requirement[2]. Where a person is charged with an offence in respect of a requirement to provide an explanation of a document or to state where a document is to be found, it is a defence for him to prove that he had a reasonable excuse for failing to comply with the requirement[3].

1 See para **14.10**.
2 FTA 1973, s 46(5).
3 FTA 1973, s 46(6).

14.17
A person who intentionally obstructs the DGFT in the exercise of his powers under s 44 is guilty of an offence and liable, on summary conviction, to a fine not exceeding [the prescribed sum] or, on conviction on indictment, to a fine[1]. A person who wilfully alters, suppresses or destroys any document which he has been required to produce under s 44(2)[2] is guilty of an offence and is liable, on summary conviction to a fine not exceeding [the prescribed sum] or, on conviction or indictment, to imprisonment for a term not exceeding two years (or to a fine or both)[3].

1 FTA 1973, s 46 (7).
2 See para **14.10**.
3 FTA 1973, s 46(8).

14.18
If an offence under FTA 1973, s 46 is committed by a body corporate, any director, manager, secretary or similar officer who is proved to have consented to or connived in the commission of an offence is also guilty[1].

1 FTA 1973, s 132(1).

E The Making of a Monopoly Reference to the Competition Commission

1 REFERENCE BY THE DIRECTOR GENERAL OF FAIR TRADING

14.19
The DGFT may make a monopoly reference to the CC where it appears to him that a monopoly situation exists or may exist in relation to the supply of goods or services of any description in or the export of goods of any description from the UK[1]. He is precluded, however, from making a reference in relation to certain matters[2]: these relate to the supply of goods or

services of any description specified in Pt I of Sch 5, or Pt I of Sch 7, to the FTA 1973[3]. The DGFT is required, in deciding whether to make a monopoly reference, to have regard to any directions which may have been issued by the Secretary of State[4] with regard to the order of priority for bringing any particular category of goods or services under review; no such directions are in existence at the present time.

1 FTA 1973, s 50(1).
2 FTA 1973, s 50(2).
3 See para **14.09**.
4 Under the FTA 1973, s 12.

14.20
When making a monopoly reference to the CC, the DGFT is required to send a copy of it to the Secretary of State. He must also arrange for the reference to be published in full in the London, Edinburgh and Belfast Gazettes and is required to arrange for it to be published in such other manner as he may think most suitable for bringing it to the attention of persons who, in his opinion, would be affected by it[1]. In practice, details of monopoly references are published in a number of national newspapers and relevant trade journals.

1 FTA 1973, s 53(1).

14.21
The Secretary of State has power, within a period of 14 days from the day on which the reference is first published in the Gazette, to direct the CC not to proceed with the reference[1]. This power has rarely, if ever, been invoked. If he does so, his direction must be published in the same way as the reference itself was published[2].

1 FTA 1973, s 50(6).
2 Ibid s 53(2).

14.22
If the DGFT is minded to make a particular reference, he sends a letter to the company or companies which he believes may be in a monopoly institution, notifying them of his intention to make a reference and enclosing a draft of it. The companies involved are invited to comment. In addition to putting forward reasons why they consider a reference inappropriate this gives them the opportunity to comment on the proposed definition of the relevant market.

2 REFERENCE BY THE SECRETARY OF STATE

14.23
The powers of the Secretary of State to make a monopoly reference are set out in the FTA 1973, s 51 and are broadly similar to the powers of the DGFT under s 50 of that Act. As far as matters falling within Pt I of Sch 5, or Pt I of Sch 7, to the FTA 1973 are concerned[1], the Secretary of State may not make a reference except jointly with the government minister who has

functions directly relating to the supply of the relevant goods or services[2].

1 These include matters such as goods supplied to tariff customers, mail, certain transport services and various agricultural matters. The provisions of these Schedules vary from time to time. For example, the DGFT can now refer charter flights: Monopoly References (Alteration of Exclusions) Order 1981, SI 1984/1887; also the supply of gas to industrial customers: Gas Act 1986.
2 FTA 1973, s 51(2).

3 FORM OF THE REFERENCE

14.24
The monopoly reference itself is a brief document. Section 47(1) of the FTA 1973 states that it should:

(*a*) specify the description of goods or services to which it relates;
(*b*) in the case of a reference relating to goods, specify whether it relates to the supply of goods in the UK or to the export of goods from the UK or both; and
(*c*) if the CC's consideration is to be limited to part of the UK, state the part of the UK concerned.

In terms of scope of the inquiry to be conducted by the CC, a monopoly reference can take one of two forms: it can either be limited to the facts[1] or not be limited to the facts[2]. The essential difference is that a monopoly reference not limited to the facts (which is by far the more common) requires the CC to investigate and report not only on the existence of a monopoly situation but also on the question whether any of the facts found by the MMC operate, or may be expected to operate, against the public interest. A monopoly reference limited to the facts merely requires the CC to investigate and report on the question whether a monopoly situation exists and, if so, whether: (*a*) the person in whose favour it operates is taking any steps to exploit or maintain the monopoly situation; and/or (*b*) whether any action or omission of that person is attributable to the existence of the monopoly situation.

1 FTA 1973, s 48; these are extremely rare. An example was *Wallpaper* HCP (1963–64) 59.
2 FTA 1973, s 49.

14.25
In the case of a monopoly reference not limited to the facts, the reference may direct the CC to consider, in the context of the public interest analysis, one or more specified matters. A non-exhaustive list of such specified matters is provided in the FTA 1973, s 49(3), namely prices charged or recommended, refusal to supply goods or services and discrimination in relation to the supply of goods or services[1].

1 References limited in this way are rare. However, examples include the *Chlordiazepoxide and Diazepam* reference HCP (1972–73) 197 where the MMC was asked to consider if Hoffmann- la Roche's prices were excessive; *Contraceptive Sheaths (2)* (1982) (Cmnd 8689), where the MMC was asked to consider if excessive profits were being earned; and *Specialist Advertising Services* (1988) (Cm 280), where the MMC was asked to consider the refusal to supply advertising services to persons who wished to place advertisements containing price information in magazines intended for campers, climbers and walkers.

4 VARIATION OF THE REFERENCE

14.26
The DGFT may at any time vary a reference made by him; similarly, the Secretary of State may vary a reference which he himself has made[1]. A reference limited to the facts may be varied so as to become one which is not limited to the facts[2]; however, a reference originally not limited to the facts may not be varied so as to become one limited to the facts[3]. If it is the DGFT who is varying a monopoly reference, the Secretary of State may (as in the case of the original reference) direct the CC not to give effect to the variation, provided that he does so within 14 days of the date on which the variation is first published in the Gazette[4].

1 FTA 1973, s 52(1).
2 See eg *Copper and Copper Alloys* HCP (1954–55) 56.
3 FTA 1973, s 52(2).
4 Ibid s 52(4).

5 TIME LIMIT FOR COMPETITION COMMISSION REPORT

14.27
Every monopoly reference must specify a period within which the CC is required to report on the reference and, if it fails to do so, the reference ceases to have any further effect and no action may be taken in relation to it[1]. The Secretary of State (but not the DGFT) may extend the time limit for a report on a reference on one or more occasions (where the reference was made by the Secretary of State jointly or with one or more other Ministers, the extension must also be jointly given)[2]. In the four monopoly references made by the DGFT in 1989[3], the periods of time given to the CC were all fairly short, ranging from four to nine months. The cases in which the CC delivered a report to the Secretary of State in 1989 illustrate the variations in the length of time it can take the CC to report on a monopoly reference, depending on the complexity of the issues and the size of the industry under investigation. At one extreme, the investigation into the *Supply of Cross-Channel Car Ferry Services*[4] was completed in four months. This contrasts with the two and a half year investigation into the *Supply of Beer*[5] and the two year investigation into the *Supply of Credit Card Services*[6].

1 FTA 1973, s 55(1).
2 Ibid s 52(2).
3 See para **14.07**.
4 Cm 903, report published December 1989.
5 Cm 651, report published March 1989.
6 Cm 718, report published August 1989.

6 UNDERTAKINGS IN LIEU OF A MONOPOLY REFERENCE

14.28
Since the beginning of 1995 the DGFT has had power to propose that the Secretary of State accept undertakings in lieu of the DGFT making a

monopoly reference[1]. He can make such a proposal where:

(*a*) he considers that a monopoly situation exists and that there are facts relating to that situation which may operate against the public interest;
(*b*) he intends, unless undertakings in lieu are accepted, to make a monopoly reference[2];
(*c*) and he considers that the undertakings which he has in mind would be sufficient to deal with such of the relevant adverse effects of the monopoly situation as he thinks need to be dealt with.

The proposal to the Secretary of State must include a statement of the terms of the proposed undertakings and the persons by whom they are proposed to be given, a statement of the facts relating to the monopoly situation which the DGFT considers may operate against the public interest and a statement of the effects identified by the DGFT as the relevant adverse affects of the monopoly situation.

1 FTA 1973, s 56A, introduced by the Deregulation and Contracting Out Act 1994.
2 Not being a monopoly reference limited to the facts, as to which see para **14.24**.

14.29
The DGFT may only make a proposal for undertakings in lieu of a reference under s 56A of the FTA 1973 if he has published a notice setting out certain matters, inviting representations within a stipulated period, and has duly considered those representations. The matters which have to be included in such a notice are: the identity of the person(s) in whose favour the DGFT considers the monopoly situation exists; the terms of the proposed monopoly reference; the facts relating to the monopoly situation which the DGFT considers may operate against the public interest; the effects identified by the DGFT as the particular effects, adverse to the public interest, which the facts relating to the monopoly situation may have; the terms of the undertakings which he is considering proposing that the Secretary of State accept in lieu of a monopoly reference; and the identity of the persons by whom the potential undertakings would be given[1]. In publishing this notice, the DGFT is required to have regard to the need for excluding, as far as practicable, (i) any matter which relates to the private affairs of an individual where publication of that matter would, or might, seriously and prejudicially affect the interests of that individual and (ii) any matter which relates to the affairs of a particular body of persons (whether corporate or unincorporate) where publication of that matter would or might seriously and prejudicially affect the interests of that body, unless in the DGFT's opinion inclusion of that matter is necessary for the purposes of the notice[2].

1 FTA 1973, s 56B.
2 FTA 1973, s 56C. This mirrors the corresponding provision regarding information which is excisable from monopoly reports by the CC: see para **14.59**.

14.30
If the Secretary of State accepts the DGFT's undertakings proposal[1], no monopoly reference may be made in the same, or substantially the same, terms as those published by the DGFT under s 56B (ie those published by

him preparatory to making the undertakings proposal) within a period of 12 months from the date of acceptance of those undertakings[2]. This does not, however, prevent a reference being made if the DGFT considers that any of the undertakings has been breached, or needs to be varied or superseded, and has given notice of that fact to the person responsible for giving the undertakings[3].

1 Either in the form proposed or with such modifications as the Secretary of State thinks fit: FTA 1973, s 56D(4).
2 FTA 1973, s 56D(1).
3 FTA 1973, s 56D(2).

14.31
The DGFT is required to keep the carrying out of a section 56A undertaking under review and from time to time to consider whether, by reason of any change of circumstances, the undertaking is no longer appropriate and either one or more of the parties to it can be released from it, or it needs to be varied or to be superseded by a new undertaking. If he concludes that there should be a release or variation of an undertaking, or that an undertaking should be superseded, he is required to give the Secretary of State advice to that effect[1], proposing the terms of variation or, as the case may be, the new undertaking[2]. The Secretary of State can only accept a new undertaking in place of an existing s 56A undertaking, or release or variation thereof, after considering the DGFT's advice on the subject[3].

1 FTA 1973, s 56E(2).
2 FTA 1973, s 56E(3).
3 FTA 1973, s 56F(1).

F Procedure before the Competition Commission

14.32
The CC may determine its own procedure for carrying out any investigation[1]. This encompasses, inter alia, the extent to which persons may be present or be heard (either by themselves or by their representatives), cross-examine witnesses or otherwise take part in the investigation, as well as the extent to which the CC's sittings are to be held in public. The CC is, however, required to take into consideration any representations made by persons appearing to have a substantial interest in the subject matter of the reference, and in general to permit any such person or body to be heard orally by the CC itself or by a member of it[2]. The CC has produced its own booklet[3], summarising the nature of its work and how it conducts its inquiries. In June 1991, the CC published the first five of a new series of fact sheets, designed to provide a short factual description of the CC and its work. It hopes to update these regularly.

1 FTA 1973, s 81(2).
2 Ibid s 81(1).
3 *The Role of the Commission* (3rd edn, January 1990).

14.33
In July 1999, the CC published a consultation document, in which it sought views on how it could increase the transparency of its procedures. This followed certain experiments with openness which the CC had already undertaken. These two developments followed the Government's Green Paper *A Fair Deal for Consumers – Modernising the Framework for Utility Regulation*, published in March 1998[1]. In that document, the Government had encouraged greater openness in the CC's procedure when dealing with licence modifications under various statutes in the regulated utility sectors[2].

1 Cm 3898.
2 For example, electricity, gas, telecommunications and water.

14.34
The experiments which the CC has undertaken recently have included the following:

(*a*) in a number of monopoly and merger enquiries, it has during the course of its enquiries published the public interest issues[1] which it has identified, thereby allowing third parties the opportunity to comment;
(*b*) in several enquiries, it has published the hypothetical remedies[2] which it is considering, again to allow third parties to comment;
(*c*) in one case[3], it held a joint hearing of the main and principal third parties; and
(*d*) in one other case[4] (in 1999) it held its first ever public hearing.

1 See para **14.50**. This is now a standard practice.
2 See para **14.54**.
3 *Cellnet* and *Vodafone* (the so-called *Calls to Mobiles* inquiry).
4 The investigation into the supply of new motor cars in the UK: public hearing held in July 1999.

14.35
In its July 1999 consultation document, the CC proposed the following steps to add to its existing practice of putting out an open invitation (through its website and advertisements in national and trade press) to submit evidence at the outset of an investigation:

(*a*) publication of an outline timetable for each enquiry;
(*b*) requests to parties to an enquiry to provide written evidence in a form that would enable the non-confidential parts to be made publicly available (for example, by the use of confidential annexes);
(*c*) encouragement to parties to publish their non-confidential information;
(*d*) listing on the CC's website the names of those who provide evidence, together with details of how to request copies of evidence from those who are willing to make their evidence publicly available;
(*e*) publication of a statement of the issues under consideration and the options for remedying possible detriments;
(*f*) the holding of joint or public hearings where this would appear to assist the enquiry process (although in its consultation document, the CC expresses the view that joint hearings should be held only where the issues are exceptionally complex).

14.36
In principle, greater transparency is to be welcomed. However, it is not without its difficulties:

(1) As far as the publication of non-confidential elements and individual parties' submissions are concerned, the enquiry process is already very demanding in terms of the timetable to which both the CC and the relevant parties need to work (this is true particularly in merger cases, but also in monopoly cases). If parties also have to prepare their submissions in a way which makes publication of non-confidential elements easy, that will simply add to the burden on the parties.
(2) There is a risk that publication of the public interest issues which the CC is considering could be misinterpreted as suggesting that CC is likely to adopt a particular line of reasoning when in fact at that stage it still has an open mind on the issues. This is an even greater danger when it comes to publishing hypothetical remedies: the CC typically canvasses a wide range of hypothetical remedies, at a stage when it has not yet necessarily come to a final view on the public interest issues themselves, let alone what remedies would be appropriate to deal with any particular adverse public interest finding. As a result, there is a danger of expectations being fuelled by misleading press reporting; there is also a risk of the financial markets being misled.

1 CONSTITUTION

14.37
The CC has a full-time Chairman appointed by the Secretary of State for Trade and Industry, who also appoints the other, part-time, members. Not more than three members are appointed as deputy chairmen. There are currently 36 Commissioners, out of a statutory maximum of 50[1].

1 Under the FTA 1973, s 4(2), the MMC may have up to 25 regular members. This can be increased by the Secretary of State by order under the FTA 1973, s 4(3) and he last increased the number to 50 with effect from 21 July 1989: Monopolies and Mergers Commission (Increase in Membership) Order 1989, SI 1989/1240.

14.38
Schedule 3 to the FTA 1973 contains provisions regarding the constitution of the CC and performance of its functions. Paragraph 10(1) provides that the Chairman of the CC may assign an investigation to a group, made up of not less than three regular members[1]. Under para 19, the Chairman of the group has a casting vote[2]. In order for the Secretary of State's order-making power[3] to apply, a majority of two-thirds of a group must reach an adverse public interest finding[4]. Dissentients may attach a dissenting opinion[5].

1 The number was reduced from five to three in 1989: Monopolies and Mergers Commission (Performance of Functions) Order 1989, SI 1989/122.
2 The casting vote was exercised, in the context of the Competition Act 1980, in *The BBC and ITP Ltd* (1985) (Cmd 9614).
3 See paras **14.77**–**14.91**.
4 FTA 1973, Sch 3, para 16(2).
5 FTA 1973, s 82(3), (4). See eg the note of dissent in *The Supply of Beer* (1989) (Cm 651).

14.39
No member declaring a material interest in the subject matter of a particular inquiry participates in the group dealing with that inquiry. The chairman appoints one member of the group, normally himself or one of the deputy chairmen, to act as Chairman of the group.

14.40
The CC has a staff of about 110 officials, the senior of whom is the Secretary to the CC. Staff include civil servants on loan from government departments, as well as secondments from the business world including accountants, economists, etc. Where there is a technical aspect to a reference the CC may retain outside advisers.

2 GATHERING OF INFORMATION

14.41
Under the FTA 1973, s 85, the CC has power to require any person to attend to give evidence or to produce any relevant documents and to require information from any person carrying on business on similar terms to those applying in respect of civil proceedings[1], including the power to take evidence on oath[2]. No-one can be compelled to give any evidence or produce any document which he could not be compelled to give or produce in a court of law[3].

1 FTA 1973, s 85(1).
2 Ibid s 85(2).
3 FTA 1973, s 85(3).

14.42
Anyone who wilfully alters, suppresses or destroys any document which he has been required to produce[1] or provides any information to the MMC which he knows to be false in a material particular (or recklessly makes a statement which is false in a material particular) is guilty of an offence[2]: he is liable on summary conviction to a fine not exceeding £2,000 or, on conviction on indictment to imprisonment for a term not exceeding two years or a fine (or both)[3]. The same applies to a person who provides information to a third party, knowing that it is to be used for the purpose of providing information to the CC[4].

1 FTA 1973, s 85(6)(*a*).
2 FTA 1973, s 93B(1), inserted by the Companies Act 1989.
3 FTA 1973, s 93B(3), inserted by the Companies Act 1989.
4 FTA 1973, s 93B(2), inserted by the Companies Act 1989.

14.43
If a person refuses or fails to comply with a notice served on him by the CC[1], any of the Commissioners conducting the inquiry may certify that fact in writing to a court and the court may enquire into the case[2]. If, after hearing evidence from witnesses and any statement which may be offered in defence, the court is satisfied that the person in question had no reasonable excuse for refusing or failing to comply with the notice, it may punish that

person (or, in the case of a body corporate, any director or officer) in the same way as if that person had been guilty of contempt of court[3]. That is to say, fines, sequestration of assets, or even imprisonment could be imposed.

1 Ie a notice under the FTA 1973, s 85(1).
2 FTA 1973, s 85(7), inserted by the Companies Act 1989.
3 FTA 1973, s 85(7A), inserted by the Companies Act 1989.

14.44
However, it has been the CC's invariable practice not to use these powers, but to request rather than require co-operation from persons concerned. Accordingly, the proceedings of the CC are essentially informal, without rules of evidence applying to limit the matters to which the CC may give consideration.

3 HEARINGS

14.45
The CC invites persons whom it believes to be concerned or interested to submit written evidence or opinions and to attend hearings. Transcripts are maintained at hearings and made available to the party concerned. In the majority of cases where questioning might involve disclosure of confidential information, such hearings are held in private, with each party appearing separately, although the CC can hold public hearings as well and announced in 1999 that it intended to hold more public hearings than it had in the past. Parties often appear with their legal advisers (counsel or solicitors). The role of the legal adviser at such hearings is very different from that played in a court of law. The CC expects questions to be answered by the company's executives but is willing to allow the legal adviser to make short opening and closing remarks and deal with issues of law which arise. Hearings are conducted as an investigation by the CC and not in an adversarial manner. In general, parties attending a hearing will find it difficult to ask questions themselves or to have them answered, and usually it is impossible to gauge the CC's thinking on any particular issue.

4 QUESTIONNAIRES AND SURVEYS

14.46
The CC frequently seeks information about the market and the practices referred to it by means of questionnaires or surveys, and may also make inquiries of trade bodies or government departments maintaining statistics on the industry concerned. Questionnaires may be sent to individual companies seeking information as to their activities, for example as to pricing policies, trading practices, profitability, group structure, equity interests in, and perception of, competitors, formal or informal links or agreements with companies in the UK or abroad and membership of trade bodies. Specific inquiries may commonly relate to regional aspects, efficiency of operations, unutilised capacity and any unusual or poorly

documented aspects of the industry under investigation. Companies may be asked to provide documentary material including copies of their agreements, statements of their policies, descriptions of their plans for the future and detailed information as to historical trading results.

14.47
Questionnaires may also be sent to companies or individuals occupying less prominent positions in the market concerned, to customers of, or suppliers to, the companies centrally concerned with the reference and to competitors of those companies. Public advertisements are frequently placed to invite comment. Consumer organisations, trade unions, government departments, the OFT and the Department of Trade and Industry, together with other relevant government departments, may make or be asked to make submissions or provide information. Any of these groups may be requested to attend separate hearings with the CC.

5 STAGES OF AN INQUIRY

(1) Preliminary

14.48
The CC usually begins by writing to companies, trade associations or individuals which may potentially be concerned, advising them that an investigation has been commenced, and stating the names of the group of members dealing with the reference, together with short biographical details. The CC may also at this stage seek to identify and obtain descriptions of the industry from public or trade bodies or other organisations keeping relevant descriptive materials.

(2) Factual

14.49
As indicated above, the CC may send out a number of questionnaires and conduct a number of surveys. It may, for example, identify issues by means of an early questionnaire and seek to explore them more fully in later ones. Such questionnaires can require exhaustive research by the companies under investigation and indeed may request them to provide information which they do not retain for their own management purposes, or in the form requested. For example, the CC may wish companies to disaggregate their trading figures in specific ways with a view to making comparisons between different companies or different industries. At about the same time the CC's staff may visit the companies concerned and request further information or conduct specific investigations (for example, as to production efficiency) and the group of Commissioners themselves may visit some or all of the companies concerned. The CC is likely, after receipt of the completed questionnaires, to hold hearings to clarify the information obtained and to seek further factual information (so-called 'clarification hearings').

(3) Public Interest Letter

14.50
After completion of the factual stage, the CC's staff prepares and sends to each potential 'monopolist' the 'public interest letter'. This letter generally states that the Commission has come to a provisional conclusion that a monopoly situation exists and identifies the grounds for that conclusion and the parties in whose favour the monopoly situation is provisionally considered to exist.

14.51
The public interest letter usually contains a number of annexes. One sets out in full the reference, the provisional finding of monopoly (or complex monopoly) and the reasons for it, and lists the public interest issues which the CC believes may arise from the monopoly situation. The CC will generally at this stage endeavour to be over-inclusive rather than omit possible issues, since if an issue has not been raised here or, if necessary, in a supplementary public interest letter, the Commission will not use it to support its conclusions.

14.52
Another annex describes the factual material which the CC has collected, which may at this stage already be in the format in which it will appear in the final Report. A further annex may contain a summary of comments received from the companies under investigation, lobby groups, individuals and other persons making submissions. The public interest letter usually gives the companies under investigation about a month to prepare their answers to the letter, although it is common for this period to be extended. Public interest hearings will generally be held once the written responses have been received.

(4) Technical Material

14.53
Where technical or detailed accounting matters are considered to be relevant by the CC, it may issue technical addenda to the public interest letter and hold staff level meetings with companies or trade associations concerned in order to deal with this material, in particular to clarify the factual position.

(5) Remedies Letter

14.54
The CC will commonly send a list of possible remedies to various persons, expressed to be on a hypothetical basis, inviting their comments on them. Alternatively, or in addition, it may canvass remedies during public interest hearings. The CC may list many different and mutually exclusive possible remedies, without particular reference to the public interest detriments they

might be thought to remedy. Although the companies directly concerned may receive the full list, other interested parties may be sent a shortened list. Specific hearings may be held to discuss remedies with interested parties.

(6) Preparation of Report

14.55
The CC's practice is to return to persons whose views or evidence are to appear in the Report a draft of that section of the Report for comment. It will also ask them to identify any matters which they request not be published, as constituting business secrets, etc[1]. The CC may also send to companies or trade associations aggregated data and extracts of chapters descriptive of the industry, although it will not reveal its conclusions.

1 See paras **14.58–14.60**.

G The Competition Commission Report

1 GENERAL

14.56
If the reference was made by the DGFT, the CC report is made to the Secretary of State; in any other case, it is made to the minister or ministers by whom the reference was made[1]. The report is required to include definite conclusions on the questions comprised in the reference, together with an account of the reasons for those conclusions and such a survey of the general position with respect to the subject matter of the reference, and of the developments which have led to that position, as in the opinion of the CC are expedient for facilitating a proper understanding of those questions and of the conclusions[2]. A typical report begins with a summary of the CC's main conclusions and findings; it then describes in detail the history of the relevant companies and a description of the relevant market(s), analyses the methods of trading of the relevant companies, their prices, profits, etc, summarises the views of the alleged monopolists and of interested third parties and sets out the CC's conclusions. Reports vary considerably in length, running in some cases to up to 500 pages[3].

1 FTA 1973, s 54(1).
2 FTA 1973, s 54(2).
3 As in the case of the *Beer* (1989) (Cm 651) and *Petrol* (1990) (Cm 972) Reports.

14.57
If, on a monopoly reference not limited to the facts, the CC determines that a monopoly situation exists and that facts which have come to its attention operate, or may be expected to operate, against the public interest, the report must specify those facts and the effects adverse to the public interest. In such a case, the CC must also consider what action (if any) should be taken for the purpose of remedying or preventing the adverse effects and may, if it thinks fit, include in the report recommendations as to such

action[1]. In considering the public interest aspects, the CC is required to exclude consideration of the question whether the provisions of any agreement which is registrable under the Restrictive Trade Practices Act 1976 operate, or may be expected to operate, against the public interest (in so far as they are provisions by virtue of which the agreement is registrable)[2].

1 FTA 1973, s 54(3).
2 Ibid s 54(5).

2 CONFIDENTIALITY

14.58
Typically, a large amount of information is supplied by persons whose activities come within the purview of a monopoly reference. Much of this is highly sensitive business information. The issue of confidentiality is therefore frequently uppermost in the minds of the persons involved. Section 133(1) of the FTA 1973 provides that '. . . no information with respect to any particular business which has been obtained under or by virtue of the provisions . . . of this Act . . . shall, so long as that business continues to be carried on, be disclosed without the consent of the person for the time being carrying out that business'. However, this is subject to two important provisos:

(1) Section 133(1) does not apply to any disclosure of information which is made for the purposes of facilitating the performance of any functions of, inter alia, the DGFT and the CC[1].
(2) Section 133(1) does not limit the matters which may be included in, or made public as part of, a report of the CC[2].

1 FTA 1973, s 133(2).
2 Ibid s 133(4)(*a*).

14.59
Section 82(1) of the FTA 1973, however, provides that the CC must have regard to the need for excluding from its Report, where practicable, matters specific to the affairs of a company or other body of persons or of an individual where publication might seriously and prejudicially affect the interests of that body or individual unless in the CC's opinion inclusion is necessary for the purposes of the report. In practice, the CC does seek to preserve the confidentiality of sensitive commercial information, in so far as is commensurate with its overriding obligation to include in the report such information as is necessary in order to facilitate a proper understanding of its conclusions (in accordance with the FTA 1973, s 54(2)).

14.60
In addition, a party seeking to have certain confidential information excluded from the report in its *published* form has an opportunity to make representations to the Secretary of State to this effect, even if the CC has found it necessary to include this information in the report in the form in which it goes to him[1].

1 See para **14.62**.

3 PUBLICATION OF REPORT

14.61
The minister to whom a report on a monopoly reference is made by the CC used to be required to transmit a copy of the report to every person named in the report in whose favour a monopoly situation was found to exist at least twenty-four hours before it was laid before Parliament[1]. This requirement was removed by the Competition Act 1998, s 69.

1 FTA 1973, s 83(1A), inserted by the Competition Act 1980, s 22.

14.62
The minister must exclude from the published report:

(*a*) any matter the publication of which would in his view be against the public interest[1];
(*b*) any matter relating to the private affairs of an individual whose interests would, in the opinion of the minister, be seriously and prejudicially affected by publication[2]; or
(*c*) any matter relating specifically to the affairs of any person whose interests would, in the opinion of the minister, be seriously and prejudicially affected by publication[3].

Until 1994 the CC and the Secretary of State separately invited requests for information to be excluded from reports under their respective duties. However, in order to speed up publication, the DTI no longer separately asks companies to request excisions of matter which they believe should be excluded from the published version of the Report. Instead, the parties are asked to put all their requests (ie those falling both to the CC and the Secretary of State to consider) direct to the CC. Any requests which the CC are unable to accept are then forwarded to the DTI for consideration. It still, however, remains open to parties to send any such requests direct to the DTI.

1 FTA 1973, s 83(3).
2 FTA 1973, s 83(3A)(*a*), inserted by the Companies Act 1989, Sch 20, para 12.
3 FTA 1973, s 83(3A)(*b*), inserted by the Companies Act 1989, Sch 20, para 12.

H Action Following Competition Commission Report

1 FAVOURABLE REPORT

14.63
If the CC concludes that no monopoly situation exists or that a monopoly situation exists but that it does not operate against the public interest, no further action may be taken. Equally, however, there is no scope for the businesses burdened by the lengthy investigation leading up to such a conclusion to recoup any of the sizeable costs which they will have incurred in the process. It is always open to the DGFT or the Secretary of State to

make another reference at a later date and a number of industries have been investigated more than once[1]. However, this does not normally occur unless there is a material change of circumstances. Alternatively, the DGFT sometimes conducts his own inquiry some years after an CC report is published, in order to review developments since the CC investigation. The results of such inquiries are published[2].

1 Eg the petrol industry has been investigated by the CC on three occasions in the last 25 years, reports being published in 1968, 1979 and 1990; reports on the supply of beer were published in 1969 and 1989 and on the supply of contraceptive sheaths in 1975 and 1982. Most recently, the DGFT made a monopoly reference in May 1990 in relation to the supply of new motor car parts (the supply of such parts having been previously investigated (and an order made) in 1982) and in September 1990 he made a reference in relation to the supply of photocopiers (an industry investigated by the CC in 1976).

2 Eg the DGFT published a report on the distribution of newspapers and periodicals in 1986, following an MMC report (Cmnd 7214) on news wholesaling in 1978. In September 1990 the DGFT published a report concerning the price of petrol, little more than a year after the CC had completed its own detailed investigation, in which it had concluded that the market for petrol was competitive. The DGFT's supplementary investigation arose out of concern over price rises following the Iraqi invasion of Kuwait: 'Changes in the Price of Petrol in the United Kingdom following the invasion of Kuwait' DGFT Report, September 1990.

14.64

In the *Steel Wire Fencing* case[1], the CC concluded that the monopoly situation did not operate against the public interest. Accordingly, there was no statutory basis for any further action. However, in response to a Parliamentary question[2], the Minister for Corporate and Consumer Affairs attached importance to an assurance given by the company concerned to the CC regarding the supply of its products. Although such an assurance has no legal force, the implication of the minister's statement was that the provisions of the Competition Act 1980 (dealing with anti-competitive practices)[3] could be invoked if necessary.

1 *The Supply of Steel Wire Fencing* (1987) (Cm 79).

2 Set out in the *Annual Report of the Director General of Fair Trading* 1987 p 60.

3 This was specifically referred to in the DTI press release of 25 February 1987.

2 UNFAVOURABLE REPORT

14.65

If the CC concludes that there is a monopoly situation and that there are aspects of it, or of the way in which it is exercised, which operate, or may be expected to operate, against the public interest, the appropriate minister may (although he is not obliged to do so) make an order with a view to remedying or preventing the adverse effects identified in the CC's Report[1]. The Secretary of State proceeded immediately to the making of an order (ie without allowing the parties concerned to negotiate undertakings with the DGFT[2]) following the CC's reports into the *Supply of Travel Agency Services for Tour Operators*[3] and the *Supply of Beer*[4]. The order-making power was also invoked following the reports into the *Supply of Credit Card Services*[5], the *Supply of Electrical Contracting Services in London Exhibition Halls*[6] and the *Supply of New Cars*[7].

1 FTA 1973, s 56(2). As noted at para **14.38**, a CC conclusion must, however, be disregarded in the context of order-making powers if the conclusion is not that of at least two-thirds of the group of Commissioners.
2 See paras **14.68–14.76**.
3 Cm 9879, report published September 1986, leading to the Restriction on Agreements and Conduct (Tour Operators) Order 1987, SI 1987/1131.
4 Cm 651, report published March 1989, leading to the Supply of Beer (Loan Ties, Licensed Premises and Wholesale Prices) Order 1989, SI 1989/2258 and the Supply of Beer (Tied Estate) Order 1989, SI 1989/2390.
5 Cm 718, report published August 1989, leading to the Credit Cards (Merchant Acquisition) Order 1990, SI 1990/2158 and the Credit Cards (Price Discrimination) Order 1990, SI 1990/2158.
6 Cm 995, report published April 1990, leading to the Electrical Contracting (London Exhibition Halls) Order 1995, SI 1995/3299.
7 Cm 4660, report published April 1990, leading to the Supply of New Cars Order 2000, SI 2000/2088.

14.66
Alternatively, and more usually, the DGFT may be asked by the appropriate minister to consult the relevant parties with a view to obtaining satisfactory undertakings, again for the purpose of remedying or preventing the adverse effects specified in the Report[1]. There has however been an apparently greater willingness to resort to the order-making powers in recent years[2]. Paragraphs **14.68–14.91** consider first the obtaining of undertakings by the DGFT before going on to consider the order-making power which exists under the FTA 1973, s 56(2).

1 FTA 1973, s 88(1).
2 See eg the cases cited in nn 3–5 to para **14.65**.

14.67
Notwithstanding the exhaustive nature of CC inquiries, the Secretary of State will sometimes instigate a further period of consultation at the time he publishes the CC report, before deciding what remedies are appropriate or what precise form particular remedies should take. For example, in *National Newspapers*[1], a three-month consultation period was announced, in order to ascertain whether the industry was able to come forward with voluntary proposals in place of the type of order which he had announced he was minded to make. In *Video Games*[2] the Corporate Affairs Minister's announcement, when publishing the CC's report, gave no indication of the government's intended action. Instead, it announced a three-month period for consultation on the CC's key recommendations. This in effect meant a substantial re-visiting of the issues dealt with in the CC's report.

1 *The Supply of National Newspapers* (1993) (Cm 2422); see further, para **14.89**.
2 *The Supply of Video Games* (1995) (Cm 2781); see also DTI Press Notice, 9 March 1995.

(1) Undertakings Obtained by the Director General of Fair Trading

(a) General

14.68
Under the FTA 1973, s 86(1), every CC report on a monopoly reference is passed by the CC to the DGFT and the minister (or ministers) to whom

such report is made are required to take account of any advice given to him (or them) by the DGFT with respect to the report. The only situation in which the CC is directed not to pass a copy of its report to the DGFT is where the reference was made by a minister or ministers and, by virtue of the FTA 1973, s 50, could not have been made by the DGFT[1].

1 See para **14.09**.

14.69

Where, as is the usual case, a copy of the CC's report is passed to the DGFT under s 86 of the FTA 1973, it is the DGFT's duty, if requested by the appropriate minister or ministers to do so, to consult the relevant parties with a view to obtaining from them undertakings to take action indicated in the request made to the DGFT as being action requisite for the purpose of remedying or preventing the adverse effects specified in the report[1]. Undertakings are given to the appropriate minister. For example, in April 1988 the Department ofTrade and Industry issued a press notice[2], announcing that Staveley Industries plc (British Salt) had given undertakings following publication of an CC report[3] nearly two years previously. Over two years elapsed between publication of an MMC report into the supply, maintenance and repair of postal franking machines[4] and the press notice announcing that satisfactory undertakings had been negotiated[5]. In another case in 1988[6], undertakings were given eight months after publication of the CC report. Where undertakings are given, the minister to whom they are given is under a duty to arrange for them to be published[7]. In a more recent case, involving Bryant & May Limited, undertakings were given in July 1992, only four months after the relevant CC report was published[8].

1 FTA 1973, s 88(1).
2 The text of the press notice is set out in the *Annual Report of the Director General of Fair Trading* 1988 pp 75–76.
3 *The Supply ofWhite Salt* (Cmnd 9778) published June 1986.
4 *The Supply, Maintenance and Repair of Postal Franking Machines* (Cm 9747) published March 1986.
5 The text of the press notice appears in the *Annual Report of the Director General of Fair Trading* 1988 pp 77–78.
6 *The Supply of Pest Control Services* (Cm 302) published February 1988; the text of the undertakings is set out in the *Annual Report of the Director General of Fair Trading* 1988 pp 78–79.
7 FTA 1973, s 88(2A), inserted by the Companies Act 1989.
8 *The Supply of Matches and Disposable Lighters within the UK for retail sale* (Cm 1854) (1992). The undertakings were published with an OFT Press Release on 28 August 1992.

14.70

If the DGFT seeks to obtain undertakings and either:

(*a*) he is satisfied that no such undertakings are likely to be given; or
(*b*) having allowed a reasonable period of time to elapse, he is satisfied that no such undertakings have been given

the DGFT is required to advise the minister[1] (which would usually include advice concerning the appropriateness of the exercise of order-making powers by the minister[2]).

1 FTA 1973, s 88(3).
2 See paras **14.77–14.91**.

14.71
If undertakings are negotiated, they are usually expressed to be without any time limit. However, the DGFT is under a duty to keep them under review and to consider whether, by reason of any change of circumstances, they need to be varied or superseded by a new undertaking; he is also required to notify the appropriate minister or ministers if it appears to him that the undertakings have not been or are not being fulfilled[1]. In October 1987 the Kellogg Company was released[2] from undertakings given following a CC Report in 1973[3]. These required the company to supply the DGFT with information on the profitability of its domestic sales of breakfast cereals. They were replaced by an assurance that the company would provide any information the DGFT might need in the future to review the breakfast cereals market or Kellogg's position in that market. In June 1992, undertakings previously given by Staveley Industries plc and a subsidiary in relation to the supply of White Salt were varied[4]. These undertakings were originally given in 1988, following a 1986 CC Report[5].

1 FTA 1973, s 88(4): see paras **14.72–14.74**.
2 *Annual Report of the Director General of Fair Trading* 1988 p 35. Kodak and six other companies were released in 1992 from undertakings given following a CC Report in 1966.
3 *The Supply of Ready Cooked Breakfast Cereal Foods* HCP (1972–73) 2.
4 See para **14.76**.
5 *The Supply of White Salt* (Cmnd 9778).

14.72
In January 1994 the DGFT announced[1] that he had begun a systematic review of the large number of undertakings which have been given in the past after investigation under the competition legislation. In April 1994 he published[2] a register of undertakings and orders in force under the FTA 1973. He also announced that he would consider in all future cases whether new undertakings can be time-limited.

1 OFT Press Release, 27 January 1994.
2 *Register of Undertakings and Orders under the Competition Act 1980 and the Monopoly Provisions of the Fair Trading Act 1973*, published by the OFT in April 1994, republished in April 1996.

(b) Breach of undertakings

14.73
Until recently, the only remedy in the event that such undertakings were subsequently broken was for the Secretary of State to exercise his order-making powers[1], breach of such order being capable of enforcement by civil proceedings by the Crown for an injunction or any other appropriate relief[2]. The undertakings were not as such enforceable[3].

1 See paras **14.77–14.91**. In one case in 1990, Pitney Bowes plc acknowledged that it was in breach of an undertaking given following a CC report in 1986. The company apologised for the breach and took steps to avoid its recurrence. The Secretary of State accepted the DGFT's advice that no further action was needed unless a further breach occurred: OFT Press Release, 11 June 1990.
2 FTA 1973, s 93(2).
3 See eg *Fogg v Esso Petroleum Ltd* (6 April 1990, unreported); also *R v Monopolies and Mergers Commission, ex p Air Europe* (1988) 4 BCC 182.

14.74
However, the Companies Act 1989[1] has introduced the possibility of direct enforcement of undertakings given to the Secretary of State, as if the obligations had been imposed by order. Breach of undertakings is not a criminal offence but they may be enforced by the Crown, or any other person[2], bringing civil proceedings to obtain an injunction or court order. Breach of a court order giving effect to undertakings would be a civil contempt of court for which there are severe penalties including fines, sequestration of assets and imprisonment.

1 FTA 1973, s 93A, inserted by the Companies Act 1989.
2 As far as action by persons other than the Crown is concerned, see paras **21.23–21.25.**

(c) Monitoring of undertakings

14.75
Under the FTA 1973, s 88, the DGFT has a duty to keep the performance of undertakings under review and:

(*a*) from time to time to consider whether, as a result of any change of circumstances, undertakings need to be varied or superseded; and
(*b*) if it appears that undertakings have not been or are not being fulfilled, or need to be varied or superseded, to give appropriate advice to the Secretary of State.

If undertakings are not being performed, the DGFT might advise the Secretary of State that new undertakings should be obtained. These would have to be agreed by the party concerned and cannot be imposed. However, if a party which had already given undertakings refused to give new or additional undertakings which the DGFT considered necessary, the Secretary of State would be able to exercise his order-making powers[1].

1 See paras **14.77–14.91**.

14.76
Under the FTA 1973, s 88, where there is a change of circumstances, the DGFT may advise that undertakings should be varied even if the existing undertakings are being fulfilled. The cases in which this has arisen to date have almost invariably related to relaxation of existing undertakings[1] but there is no reason in theory why the DGFT should not recommend that a more stringent undertaking should be obtained. In *White Salt* the Secretary of State for Trade and Industry in 1992 accepted[2] a revision of undertakings designed to limit the price of white salt given by Staveley Industries plc and its subsidiary British Salt Limited, following the report by the CC on *The Supply of White Salt* published in 1986[3]. Under the original undertakings, the maximum permitted level of British Salt's prices for white salt was determined by increases in a weighted index of production costs less an annual abatement of one percentage point. The base of the index was 31 January 1985. Since that time, the company's prices had been substantially below the level permitted. To reflect this, the revised undertakings now include an abatement of two percentage points and the index has been rebased to 31 January 1992. If the party concerned refused to vary its

undertaking, the Secretary of State would be able to exercise his order-making powers. However, he would still have to confine himself to taking such action as he considered necessary to remedy the adverse effects specified in the original CC Report.

1 As in the *Kellogg* case, referred to at para **14.71**. In another case undertakings given following the CC's report in 1968 (*The Supply of Electric Lamps*) were released in March 1991 because the market was more competitive: DTI press notice, 4 March 1991. Rank Xerox was released in 1991 from undertakings given in 1978; this release followed a favourable report by the CC in *Indirect Electrostatic Photocopyers* (Cm 1693) (1991). The DGFT refused in March 1992 to accede to a request by the Peninsular and Oriental Steam Navigation Company to be released from undertakings concerning the operation of cross- channel ferry services: DTI press notice, 11 March 1992.
2 DTI press notice, 11 June 1992.
3 *The Supply of White Salt in the United Kingdom* (Cmnd 9778) (1986).

(2) Order-Making Powers

(a) General

14.77
If the DGFT is unsuccessful in negotiating satisfactory undertakings or if the minister considers that undertakings would not be appropriate, the appropriate minister may by order made by statutory instrument take the action effects specified in the CC's Report[1]; such action can take the form of one or more of the powers specified in Pts I and II of Sch 8 to the FTA 1973. Although, as will be seen at para **14.82**, the order-making powers set out in Sch 8 are wide-ranging, he may only exercise such powers in order to remedy or prevent the adverse effects specified in the CC's report[2]. The minister must take account[3] of any recommendations by the CC and any advice given by the DGFT under s 88 of the FTA 1973[4], although he is not obliged to follow such recommendations or advice[5]. In order to assist in deciding whether to make an order, the Secretary of State may appoint an inspector to carry out a potentially wide-ranging investigation[6]. This power has not in practice been invoked.

1 FTA 1973, s 56(1), and (2). In March 1992 the Secretary of State for Trade and Industry announced his intention to exercise this power following the MMC's report in *The Supply of Razors and Razor Blades* (1991) (Cm 1472): DTI press notice, 11 March 1992.
2 FTA 1973, s 56(2).
3 FTA 1973, s 56(3).
4 See para **14.68**.
5 For examples of cases in which the minister chose to depart from such recommendations, see para **14.88**.
6 FTA 1973, s 92.

(b) Interim orders

14.78
If in any case the Secretary of State makes, has made or has under consideration the making of an order ('the principal order') exercising his Schedule 8 powers, he has the power to make an interim order under s 89 of the FTA 1973. An interim order may:

(*a*) prohibit or restrict the doing of things which might impede the operation or making of the principal order;
(*b*) impose on any person concerned obligations as to the carrying on of any activities or the safeguarding of assets;
(*c*) require any person to furnish such information to the DGFT as the Secretary of State may specify;
(*d*) provide for the carrying on of any activities or the safeguarding of any assets by a particular person or in a particular way[1].

Such orders are extremely rare. However, the power was recently exercised following the CC's report in *The Supply of Razors and Razor Blades*[2]: DTI press notice of 21 March 1991[3].

1 FTA 1973, s 89(3).
2 (1991) (Cm 1472).
3 The interim orders were subsequently revoked because the need for a principal order fell away: DTI press notice, 8 July 1993.

(*c*) *Procedure*

14.79
Before making an order which exercises any of the powers specified in Pt I of Sch 8 (this covers the vast bulk of his powers, with the principal exception of orders for the division of a business), the minister proposing to make the order is required to publish a notice stating his intention to do so, indicating the nature of the provisions to be embodied in the order and inviting interested parties to make written representations before a specified date (being not less than 30 days from the date of publication of the notice)[1]. Such an order is theoretically subject to annulment in pursuance of a resolution of either House of Parliament[2].

1 FTA 1973, s 91(2).
2 FTA 1973, s 134(1).

14.80
The procedure for adopting orders exercising any of the powers specified in Pt II of Sch 8 to the FTA 1973 is different (as will be seen at para **14.82**, Pt II deals with the division of a business). In such a case, no order can be made unless a draft of it has been laid before Parliament and approved by resolution of each House of Parliament. Under Sch 9 to the FTA 1973 the Secretary of State must publish in the London, Edinburgh and Belfast Gazettes a notice of his intention to lay a draft of the order before Parliament (it must also be published in two or more national, daily newspapers) and he is not permitted to lay a draft of the order before Parliament for a further period of 42 days. The notice must indicate the nature of the provisions which are to be embodied in the order and invite interested parties to submit written representations. The power of subsequent annulment of an order in pursuance of a resolution of either House of Parliament[1] accordingly does not apply in this case.

1 See para **14.79**.

(d) Persons who may be the subject of an order

14.81

Under the FTA 1973, s 90(2), an order declaring anything to be unlawful can declare it to be unlawful either for all persons or for certain persons specified in the order. On the face of it, this provides virtually unlimited jurisdiction. However, two constraints should be noted. Firstly, an order can only be made in relation to the conduct of a person outside the UK if that person is either a citizen of the UK and Colonies, a body corporate incorporated under the law of any part of the UK or a person carrying on business in the UK[1]. Secondly, as noted at para **14.77**, the order-making powers can only be exercised for the purpose of remedying or preventing the adverse effects specified in the CC's report[2].

1 FTA 1973, s 90(3). The issue of extra-territoriality will be dealt with in Division XII to be published with Issue 1.
2 FTA 1973, s 56(2).

(e) Powers available under Parts I and II of Schedule 8 to the Fair Trading Act 1973

14.82

The bulk of the order-making powers are set out in Pt I. The majority of these give the Secretary of State power to declare certain conduct unlawful; only three of them enable him to require the persons subject to the order to take action or refrain from taking action. Part I gives the relevant minister power to:

(*a*) preclude the making or execution of any agreement[1];
(*b*) prohibit a refusal to supply[2];
(*c*) prohibit a tie-in[3];
(*d*) prohibit price discrimination[4];
(*e*) prohibit the giving of any preference to any person[5];
(*f*) require a person to adhere to published list prices[6];
(*g*) require publication of price lists[7];
(*h*) regulate the prices to be charged[8];
(*i*) prohibit the recommendation of resale prices[9];
(*j*) prohibit the acquisition of any other business[10];
(*k*) prohibit or restrict the exercise of any right to vote exercisable by the holding of any shares, stocks or securities[11].

Part II of Sch 8 confers the power to require the division of a business[12] and to deal with a number of incidental matters, including:

(*a*) the transfer of property, rights, liabilities and obligations;
(*b*) the adjustment of contracts;
(*c*) the creation, allotment, surrender or cancellation of shares; and
(*d*) the termination or winding up of any company.

1 FTA 1973, Sch 8, paras 1–3.
2 FTA 1973, Sch 8, para 4.
3 FTA 1973, Sch 8, para 5.
4 FTA 1973, Sch 8, para 6.

5 FTA 1973, Sch 8, para 7.
6 FTA 1973, Sch 8, para 8.
7 FTA 1973, Sch 8, para 9.
8 FTA 1973, Sch 8, para 10.
9 FTA 1973, Sch 8, para 11.
10 FTA 1973, Sch 8, para 12.
11 FTA 1973, Sch 8, para 12C, inserted by the Companies Act 1989.
12 FTA 1973, Sch 8, para 14.

14.83

Section 90(5) of the FTA 1973[1] places a specific limitation on the Secretary of State's order-making power. It prevents him from cancelling or modifying conditions in licences of patents or registered designs by the proprietor of the patent or registered design. It also prevents him from requiring an entry to be made in the register of patents or the register of designs to the effect that licences under such a patent or design be available as of right. However, this is to some extent alleviated in the context of patents by s 51 of the Patents Act 1977[2] under which the Secretary of State may, following an adverse finding by the CC on a monopoly reference, apply to the Comptroller-General of Patents. The latter must consider whether the CC's findings include: (*a*) conditions in licences granted by a patent proprietor restricting the use of the invention by the licensee or the right of the proprietor to grant other licences; or (*b*) a refusal by the proprietor to grant licences on reasonable terms. If he concludes that the CC's findings do extend to such matters, he may by order cancel or modify any such condition or make an entry in the register making licences of the patent available as of right.

1 As substituted by the Companies Act 1989.
2 As substituted by the Copyright, Designs and Patents Act 1988.

14.84

One gap in Sch 8 to the FTA 1973, which emerged in two Competition Act cases[1], was the lack of any power to control copyright licences or to grant such licences as of right. This power has been added to those in Pt I of Sch 8 to the FTA 1973 by s 144 of the Copyright, Designs and Patents Act 1988.

1 *Ford Motor Co* (1985) (Cmd 9437); *The BBC and ITP Ltd* (1985) (Cmd 9614).

(f) Exercise of order-making powers in practice

14.85

The order-making powers available under Sch 8 are only rarely invoked. It is more usual for the Secretary of State to ask the DGFT to seek to obtain undertakings from the persons concerned[1]. Somewhat exceptionally, however, the order-making powers were invoked on three occasions in 1989/90[2]. The first of these was the Films (Exclusivity Agreements) Order 1989[3], which followed the CC's 1983 Report into the *Supply of Films for Exhibition in Cinemas*[4]. Negotiations with the film industry had taken place for several years after the report was published but ultimately the government decided to proceed by way of order. This prohibits the practice of 'barring', the system under which distributors and exhibitors decide which of two or more cinemas in a certain locality will exhibit a film first.

1 See paras **14.68–14.76**.
2 See also the Restriction on Agreements and Conduct (Tour Operators) Order 1987, SI 1987/ 1131, which followed the report on *Foreign Packaged Holidays* (1986) (Cm 9879); the Restriction on Conduct (Specialist Advertising Services) Order 1988, SI 1988/1017, which followed the report on *Specialist Advertising Services* (1988) (Cm 280), the Electrical Contracting (London Exhibition Halls) Order 1995, SI 1995/3299, which followed the report on *Electrical Contracting at London Exhibition Halls* (Cm 995) and the Supply of New Cars Order 2000, SI 2000/2088, which followed the report on *New Cars* (Cm 4660).
3 SI 1989/271.
4 Cmnd 8858.

14.86
The second occasion in 1989 in which the order-making powers were invoked followed the CC's Report into the *Supply of Beer*[1], in which it had found that a complex monopoly situation operated against the public interest. Two statutory instruments were approved by Parliament in December 1989. The first of these[2] requires all brewers to enable recipients of their loans to terminate them at not more than three months' notice without penalty, and to publish wholesale price lists for their beer, showing maximum prices for different categories of customer. The second of these[3] applies to brewers owning more than 2,000 licensed premises and requires them, by 1 November 1992, to cease to be brewers, or to reduce their estate to below 2,000 or to release from all product ties a number of their houses amounting to half the excess over 2,000; by 1 May 1990, to allow their tied tenants or recipients of their loans to choose at least one cask-conditioned beer from another supplier; and, also by 1 May 1990, to end all ties on wines, spirits, ciders, soft drinks and low alcohol and alcohol-free beers.

1 (1989) (Cm 651).
2 Supply of Beer (Loan Ties, Licensed Premises and Wholesale Premises) Order 1989, SI 1989/2258.
3 Supply of Beer (Tied Estate) Order 1989, SI 1989/2390.

14.87
The third case followed the CC's report on the *Credit Card Services*[1]. The CC had found that a scale monopoly existed in favour of Barclays Bank and a complex monopoly in favour of a number of other parties. It had recommended that two particular practices be abandoned, namely the 'no discrimination' rule (which requires traders to charge the same price for purchases made with Mastercard/Eurocard and Visa credit cards as for those paid for by other means) and certain practices preventing card issuers from acting as merchant acquirers from the date of their membership. The Secretary of State asked the DGFT to seek appropriate undertakings to implement these recommendations. However, these discussions were halted prematurely when Visa International Services Association commenced judicial review proceedings, challenging the legality of the CC's Report. These proceedings were unsuccessful and two statutory instruments which broadly put these recommendations into effect came into force on 28 February 1991[2].

1 (1989) (Cm 718).
2 Credit Cards (Merchant Acquisition) Order 1990, SI 1990/2158, and the Credit Cards (Price Discrimination) Order 1990, SI 1990/2159.

14.88
The *Beer* case demonstrates that, in deciding what order-making powers to invoke, the Secretary of State is not constrained by the recommendations of the CC (although he is obliged to take account of them[1]). In that case the remedies to which the government resorted (namely, the two statutory instruments referred to at para **14.86** and amendments to the Landlord and Tenant Act 1954) were very different from those recommended by the CC. An earlier case in which the Secretary of State took action different from that recommended by the CC followed the latter's report on the supply of *Chlordiazepoxide and Diazepam*[2]. The only limitation on the action which he can take is that it must remedy an adverse effect identified by the CC[3].

1 FTA 1973, s 56(3).
2 HCP (1972–73) 197; the relevant order is SI 1973/1093.
3 FTA 1973, s 56(2).

14.89
In *National Newspapers*[1] the Secretary of State decided to go further than was recommended by the CC in its Report. It had concluded that a particular monopoly situation operated against the public interest and made certain recommendations (which it acknowledged might have proved insufficient to remedy the adverse affects which it had identified). In his advice to the DTI the DGFT recommended a more fundamental remedy. This advice was accepted and in December 1993 the Corporate Affairs Minister announced that he intended to make an order imposing the stricter remedy[2]. Recognising that the changes which were proposed would have a significant impact on the market, the Minister announced a short period of consultation (three months) and indicated that, if during the consultation period, the industry came forward with voluntary proposals which would lead to a substantial increase in the level of competition, comparable to that which would be achieved by the proposed order, he would consider these as an alternative. He subsequently agreed to accept an industry code of practice, backed by voluntary undertakings[3].

1 *The Supply of National Newspapers* (Cm 2422) (1993).
2 DTI press notice, 9 December 1993.
3 Announcement by the Corporate Affairs Minister on 15 July 1994.

(g) Enforcement

14.90
Breach of an order is not a criminal offence[1]; however, the FTA 1973 specifically provides[2] that nothing in the Act limits any right of any person to bring civil proceedings in respect of contravention, or apprehended contravention, of any order. Moreover, it also provides[3] that compliance with such an order is enforceable by civil proceedings by the Crown for an injunction or any other appropriate relief. If the DGFT/Secretary of State

are satisfied that a particular breach is an isolated incident and against company policy, they may decide not to take enforcement measures[4].

1 FTA 1973, s 93(1).
2 FTA 1973, s 93(2).
3 Ibid.
4 As in one case following the beer orders referred to at para **14.86**; see OFT Press Release, 31 January 1991.

14.91

The FTA 1973 does not stipulate that anyone other than the Crown has a right to bring civil proceedings for breach of an order (it merely does not rule out the possibility). On the other hand, new s 93A(2)[1] does provide that, in relation to undertakings given in lieu of the making of an order, 'any person may bring civil proceedings in respect of a failure, or apprehended failure, of the responsible person to fulfil the undertaking, as if the obligations imposed by the undertaking on the responsible person had been imposed by an order to which s 90 of this Act applies'. This tends to strengthen the view that third party proceedings are, in principle, available both for breach of an order and breach of undertakings. As far as remedies are concerned, it would appear, in relation to injunctive relief, that a third party would need to show a special interest in the matter[2]. As to whether a damages action could be brought, the action would need to be by way of breach of statutory duty and it would be necessary for the court to decide whether Parliament intended that there should be a civil remedy; s 93A(2) suggests that it is intended that a remedy should be available. In the *Mid Kent*[3] case, Knox J held, in the context of undertakings[4] previously given) that breach of statutory duty and damage resulting therefrom were not of themselves enough to confer a private right of action on a prospective plaintiff, irrespective of whether the claim was for damages, injunction or a declaration. He held that, in the particular case in question, the statutory obligations which the undertakings were to be treated as creating were imposed to avoid particular detriment to the *public* interest identified by the MMC's report and not to avoid particular detriment to Mid Kent[5].

1 Inserted by the Companies Act 1989.
2 *Gouriet v Union of Post Office Workers* [1978] AC 435, [1977] 3 All ER 70, HL. See para **21.25**.
3 *Mid Kent Holdings plc v General Utilities plc* [1996] 3 All ER 132, [1997] 1 WLR 14.
4 The position should be the same in relation to orders.
5 See para **21.24**.

Chapter 15 Competition Act 1998

A Introduction

1 BACKGROUND TO THE ACT

15.01

Proposals for reform of UK competition law were put forward as long ago as 1989, when the Conservative Government published a White Paper, *Opening up Markets: New Policy on Restrictive Trade Practices*[1]. The White Paper proposals were confined to reform of the statutes dealing with restrictive trading agreements and resale price maintenance (respectively the Restrictive Trade Practices Act 1976 and the Resale Prices Act 1976).

1 Cm 727.

15.02

Following publication of the White Paper in 1989, the Conservative Government periodically restated its commitment to replacing the Restrictive Trade Practices Act 1976 with new legislation prohibiting anti-competitive agreements, when the parliamentary timetable permitted. In the event, it never found parliamentary time. As far as abuse of market power was concerned, the Conservative Government rejected the introduction of a prohibition system along the lines of Article 82 of the EC Treaty in favour of a more limited reform of existing UK law[1]. Again, however, no legislation was forthcoming.

1 *Abuse of Market Power: a Consultative Document on Possible Legislative Options* (Cm 2100).

15.03

In March 1996 the Government published a consultation document *Tackling Cartels and the Abuse of Market Power: implementing the Government's policy for competition law reform*[1]. This again advocated legislation modelled on EC Treaty, Article 81 to deal with restrictive agreements, but merely a strengthening of the existing law, rather than the adoption of a prohibition system based on EC Treaty, Article 82 in respect of abuses of market power. In August 1996, the Government published an explanatory document *Tackling Cartels and the Abuse of Market Power : A Draft Bill*[2], which not only set out the Government's proposals but also included a draft Bill. In the event, however, the Bill did not feature in the Queen's Speech in November 1996. Shortly afterwards, the Conservative Government lost the General Election in May 1997.

1 DTI, March 1996 (URN 96/760).
2 DTI, August 1996 (URN 96/905).

15.04
Following the election of the Labour Government in May 1997, the then Secretary of State for Trade and Industry, Margaret Beckett, introduced a Competition Bill in October 1997. This went considerably further than the previous Government's proposals, by including both a prohibition of restrictive agreements and abuse of dominant position, modelled in each case on Articles 81 and 82 of the EC Treaty. Following its passage through first the House of Lords and then the House of Commons, the Competition Bill received Royal Assent in 9 November 1998 and entered fully into force on 1 March 2000.

15.05
Parts of the Competition Bill were controversial and were extensively debated in Parliament. Some of the issues which gave rise to extensive debate were fairly general in nature (for example, the treatment of vertical agreements and the powers to be given to the various sectoral regulators). Others focussed on specific issues, for example the possible exclusion of pharmacies from the legislation and the issue of predatory pricing in the newspaper industry. Issues of interpretation are likely to arise on which it will be legitimate to refer to parliamentary debates, as recorded in Hansard[1], particularly to many of the statements of Lord Simon of Highbury, who introduced the Bill in the House of Lords.

1 Especially in the light of the judgment of the House of Lords in *Pepper v Hart* [1993] AC 593, on the admissibility of statements in parliamentary debates.

2 KEY FEATURES OF THE ACT

15.06
The following key features of the CA 1998 should be noted:

- it introduces a prohibition on agreements which prevent, restrict or distort competition within the United Kingdom. This is modelled on EC Treaty, Article 81;
- it introduces a prohibition of abuse of a dominant position which may affect trade within the United Kingdom. This is modelled on EC Treaty, Article 82;
- it requires that, so far as is possible (having regard to any relevant differences between the provisions concerned) questions arising under the Act in relation to competition are dealt with in a manner consistent with EC law;
- as a result, the Act moves away from the essentially form-based approach of its predecessor, the Restrictive Trade Practices Act 1976, introducing instead an approach based on considering the economic effects of the particular agreement or conduct;
- it confers on the Director General of Fair Trading (DGFT) greatly strengthened powers of investigation, modelled on those which the European Commission has in relation to breaches of EC Treaty, Articles 81 and 82;
- it gives the DGFT the power, inter alia, to impose fines of up to 10% of UK turnover;

— it gives concurrent powers to a number of sectoral regulators, namely those operating in the gas, electricity, railways, telecommunications and water industries;
— it repeals the Restrictive Trade Practices Act 1976, the Resale Prices Act 1976 and the provisions of the Competition Act 1980 dealing with anti-competitive practices;
— it does not, however, repeal the scale monopoly and complex monopoly provisions of the Fair Trading Act 1973, although it is the Government's intention[1] that (except in the regulated sectors) the scale monopoly provisions[2] should only be used as a control of last resort.

1 See para **14.05**.
2 See para **14.10**.

15.07
The CA 1998 makes certain changes to the scale monopoly and complex monopoly provisions of the Fair Trading Act 1973 and these are dealt with in para **14.10** ff. The CA 1998 also gives power to the High Court to issue a warrant for the DGFT to enter premises in connection with an investigation requested by the European Commission in the exercise of its powers under EC Treaty, Articles 81 and 82.

3 IMPACT OF THE HUMAN RIGHTS ACT 1998

15.08
The Human Rights Act 1998 (HRA 1998) received Royal Assent on the same day as the CA 1998. The HRA 1998 will require the CA 1998 to be applied in a way that is compatible with 'Convention rights' (ie rights arising under the European Convention on Protection of Human Rights and Fundamental Freedoms) and will make it unlawful for the UK competition authorities to act in a way that is incompatible with those rights. The HRA 1998 came fully into force on 2 October 2000.

The HRA is likely to have a significant impact on competition cases. For example:

— the requirement to respect the right to privacy (Article 8 of the Convention) is likely to be important in the context of investigations and so-called 'dawn raids';
— the undertakings against which proceedings are brought will be entitled to a fair trial pursuant to Article 6 of the Convention.

The case law of the European Court of Justice under Articles 81 and 82 is likely to guide the English courts in their application of the HRA 1998.

4 INSTITUTIONS

15.09
A feature of UK competition law is the number of institutions which have a role in its operation. This will remain the case under the CA 1998. The role of each of the institutions which have a function under the CA 1998 is

outlined below. One institution which does not have a role under the Act is the Restrictive Practices Court. With the repeal of the Restrictive Trade Practices Act 1976 from 1 March 2000, it will be abolished, with its only remaining role being to hear out cases still current on 1 March 2000.

(1) Director General of Fair Trading/Office of Fair Trading

15.10
The DGFT is in charge of the Office of Fair Trading (OFT). The OFT is divided into various divisions, one of which is the Competition Policy Division. This has been re-organised following the enactment of the CA 1998 into seven branches, modelled along the lines of the European Commission Directorate for Competition. The seven branches are:

(1) *Policy co-ordination*: Its role will be to ensure that all decisions under the CA 1998 are consistent, not only with each other but with EC rulings and precedents.
(2) *Mergers*: The CA 1998 leaves the current merger control provisions contained in the Fair Trading Act 1973 largely unaffected (except in relation to so-called ancillary restraints).
(3) *Cartel investigations*: This will investigate price-fixing and market sharing cases and will have enhanced powers to enter premises and take away evidence[1].
(4) *Sectoral branches*: There will be four, dealing respectively with:
    (i) media, sport and information industries;
    (ii) service industries;
    (iii) basic industries, energy and vehicles; and
    (iv) consumer goods.

1 See para **15.130** ff.

15.11
The DGFT plays a pivotal role in the structure set up under the CA 1998. His powers include:

— the power to issue individual exemptions from the so-called Chapter I prohibition (the prohibition modelled on Article 81 of the EC Treaty);
— the power to recommend to the Secretary of State the making of block exemption orders, exempting particular categories of agreement from the Chapter I prohibition;
— the giving of guidance on whether or not a particular agreement or conduct is likely to infringe the Chapter I prohibition or the Chapter II prohibition (the latter modelled on Article 82 of the EC Treaty);
— investigations into alleged infringements of the Chapter I prohibition or the Chapter II prohibition, including the power to require information/documents and to enter premises with or without a warrant;
— the making of decisions that the Chapter I or Chapter II prohibition has been infringed and the giving of directions to bring the infringement to an end;
— the giving of directions by way of interim measure;

— the imposition of financial penalties for the infringement of the Chapter I or Chapter II prohibition.

Each of these powers is considered later in this Chapter.

15.12
In recognition of the increased powers of the OFT, it made clear its intention to increase the number of staff working on competition regulation from 150 to 200[1].

1 *OFT opens for business on new competition law*, OFT Press Release, 27 November 1998.

(2) Competition Commission

15.13
The Competition Commission (CC) is a new institution established by the CA 1998 to take over the functions of the Monopolies and Mergers Commission[1]. The CC came into existence on 1 April 1999. The CC has jurisdiction to hear appeals from certain decisions taken by the DGFT[2]. Those appeals are to be determined by an appeal tribunal which will be under the control of the President of the Appeal Tribunals, a new post[3]. The first President of the Appeal Tribunal is Judge Christopher Bellamy QC, until recently a judge at the European Court of First Instance in Luxembourg.

1 CA 1998, s 45.
2 CA 1998, s 46.
3 CA 1998, s 48.

15.14
The role of the CC is considered in more detail in paras **15.210–15.251**.

15.15
Appeal lies from a decision of an appeal tribunal of the CC on a point of law or from any decision of an appeal tribunal as to the amount of a penalty. Appeal can only be made with leave. The court which hears such an appeal is the Court of Appeal (in relation to proceedings before a tribunal in England and Wales), the Court of Session (in relation to proceedings before a tribunal in Scotland) and the Court of Appeal in Northern Ireland (in relation to proceedings before a tribunal in Northern Ireland)[1].

1 CA 1998, s 49.

(3) High Court

15.16
As the Competition Bill went through Parliament, the Government stressed that third parties claiming to be damaged by agreements or conduct caught by the CA 1998 should be able to take private action[1]. There is in fact nothing on the face of the Act to suggest that the right of third party action is intended to form an important part of the scheme of the new legislation, on the grounds, it appears, that such a right exists under EC competition law and providing expressly for the right of private action might prevent

claimants from being able to invoke EC law principles[2]. Private actions for breach of the CA 1998 will be dealt with in the High Court. That is also the court which will hear any action in which voidness as a result of the CA 1998 is raised in litigation (as is the case in respect of alleged voidness under Articles 81 and 82 of the EC Treaty).

1 See, for example, HC 2R, 11 May 1998, col 35 (Margaret Beckett MP).
2 By virtue of CA 1998, s 60: see para **15.22** ff.

(4) Secretary of State and the DTI

15.17
The Secretary of State for Trade and Industry is responsible for the main CC appointments. He is also responsible for appointing the DGFT. He has no function in relation to the enforcement of the Chapter I and Chapter II prohibitions. He is, however, responsible for making block exemption orders[1], making the rules and regulations of the CC appeal tribunals, approving guidance given by the DGFT on penalties and any exclusions from the prohibitions and on co-ordination between the DGFT and the regulators who have concurrent jurisdiction.

1 See para **15.229** ff.

(5) The Sectoral Regulators

15.18
One of the notable features of the CA 1998 is that it accords jurisdiction to certain sectoral regulators concurrently with that of the DGFT[1]. The regulators concerned are:

— the Director General of Telecommunications;
— the Director General of Gas Supply;
— the Director General of Electricity Supply[2];
— the Director General of Water Services;
— the Rail Regulator;
— the Director General for Electricity Supply and Gas for Northern Ireland.

1 See para **15.255** ff.
2 This post and the post of Director General of Gas Supply are held by the same person, Callum McCarthy.

15.19
Appeal against their decisions in the exercise of their competition powers lies to the appeals tribunals of the CC (as is the case with decisions of the DGFT). However, the existing arrangements for references to the Monopolies and Mergers Commission in relation to the regulators' licensing functions continue, although they become references to the CC. A regulator's decision can therefore come up for review by different parts of the CC according to its origin (namely whether it is in relation to the exercise of his function under the specific legislation for the regulated sector concerned or under the general powers under the CA 1998).

5 RELEVANCE OF EC LAW PRINCIPLES

(1) Introduction

15.20
One of the main purposes of the CA 1998 is to bring domestic competition law in line with EC law. Accordingly, the Chapter I and Chapter II prohibitions are closely modelled on Articles 81 and 82 of the EC Treaty. There are, at the same time, subtle but important differences. Examples include the fact that the CA 1998 does not require an effect on trade between Member States, and a more lenient treatment of vertical agreements.

15.21
Consistency of application between domestic and EC law was one of the themes which ran through the parliamentary debates. For example, one of the reasons the Government gave for refusing to add an appreciability test to the notion of restriction of competition in the Chapter I prohibition was that this is already effectively read into the interpretation of Article 81 of the EC Treaty by European Court of Justice jurisprudence[1]. Accordingly, it was decided that the addition of a specific reference to 'appreciability' would impede, rather than enhance, consistent interpretation of the law.

1 See, for example, HL Report Stage, 9 February 1998, cols 884–888.

(2) Section 60

15.22
In order to ensure the development of jurisprudence under the CA 1998 in a manner which is consistent with corresponding EC law, the Government included s 60. This is likely to be a key provision in the Act and merits careful scrutiny.

15.23
Section 60(1) states the purpose of the section, which is unusual in itself in the context of UK legislation. The purpose is stated to be:

> 'to ensure that so far as is possible (having regard to any relevant differences between the provisions concerned), questions arising [under the Act] in relation to competition within the United Kingdom are dealt with in a manner which is consistent with the treatment of corresponding questions arising in Community law in relation to competition within the Community'.

15.24
The very language of s 60(1) emphasises that consistency of interpretation cannot be absolute. This is clear from the phrase 'so far as is possible' and from the specific reference to any relevant differences between the provisions concerned. As noted in para **15.20**, there are certain differences. One clear difference which might bring about a different legal conclusion is the focus under EC law on the objective of creating a single market, which has

greatly contributed to EC jurisprudence, particularly the law on parallel imports and attempts to limit such imports. That has led to the European Commission taking a very tough line in relation to export restrictions. It is by no means obvious that EU jurisprudence on that topic should flow through to the CA 1998.

15.25
Section 60(1) requires consistency (so far as possible) with regard to questions 'in relation to competition'. This clearly extends to substantive evaluation but it is less clear whether this language imports Community law in relation to procedural issues. This is an important question because much of the European Court's jurisprudence in the competition law field has focussed on procedural issues (notably the rights of defence).

15.26
It is clear from the Procedural Rules made by the DGFT[1] that it is not envisaged that the UK authorities will follow exactly the same procedures as the European Commission. On the other hand, during the passage of the Bill through the House of Lords, Lord Simon of Highbury on behalf of the Government indicated that general principles of Community law are to be imported, save where there is a relevant difference[2]. The principles which are clearly capable of being imported include the right to a hearing, the right to be informed of any matter which is to be relied on by the authorities, the right to obtain professional legal advice, proportionality and legitimate expectations.

1 These were required to be approved by the Secretary of State pursuant to CA 1998, s 51(5) and were approved by means of the Competition Act 1998 (Director's Rules) Order 2000, SI 2000/293 to which they are attached as a Schedule.
2 HL Committee, 25 November 1997, cols 960–963.

15.27
Section 60(1) refers to consistency of interpretation of corresponding questions arising in Community law, irrespective of the court which has opined on the Community law issue. On the face of it, this requires the DGFT, CC or court dealing with a case under the CA 1998 to have regard not only to the jurisprudence of the European Court of Justice but also to Community law jurisprudence of other UK courts and indeed potentially of courts in other member states. Courts in the UK are already becoming accustomed to having cases cited from other jurisdictions (such as Australia and the United States) and this provision may accelerate that process in relation to the courts of other EC Member States.

15.28
Section 60(2) fleshes out the purpose stated in s 60(1). It provides that at any time when a court determines a question arising in respect of the Chapter I and Chapter II prohibitions, it must act, so far as is compatible with the express provisions of the Act, with a view to securing that there is no inconsistency between the principles applied, and decisions reached, by the court and the principles laid down by the EC Treaty and the ECJ when determining any corresponding question arising in Community law.

15.29

The following points should be noted in relation to that provision:

(1) The term 'court' means any court or tribunal[1] and therefore includes the DGFT, the CC and the sectoral regulators when exercising concurrent jurisdiction under the Act.

(2) It refers to the principles laid down by the Treaty but not on the face of it to the principles laid down in regulations adopted pursuant to the Treaty. It does not therefore appear to be the case that the whole of Regulation 17/62 (the principal procedural regulation relating to EC Treaty, Articles 81 and 82[2]), is imported into UK law. That is certainly the view of the DGFT[3].

(3) Section 60(2) only refers to the jurisprudence of the ECJ and does not therefore on its face require consistency of treatment with Community law jurisprudence emanating from courts of other member states (contrast here the apparently broader language in s 60(1)).

(4) The term 'decision' is defined[4] to include a decision as to the civil liability of an undertaking for harm caused by its infringement of Community law. This is one of the provisions which the Government relies on in asserting that the CA 1998 creates civil liability (with the potential, inter alia, for a damages claim)[5].

(5) Finally, s 60(3) requires the UK authorities to have regard to any relevant decision or statement of the Commission. The term 'decision or statement of the Commission' could cover a very wide range of acts, from a fully reasoned decision, published in the Official Journal to press releases or remarks made by a Commission official in his official capacity. Section 60(3) does not state what weight should be given to each of these, merely that regard should be had to them. One assumes that the authorities will give far greater weight to certain decisions or statements than others and no doubt regard will be had to the context in which the statement was made. In its 'Major Provisions' Guidelines[6] the OFT states at para 6.2 that the DGFT's view is that s 60(3) is limited to statements which have the authority of the European Commission as a whole, such as decisions under Articles 81 or 82 and statements about policy approach in its annual Competition Policy Report.

1 CA 1998, s 60(5).
2 Council Regulation (EEC) 17/62, OJ Sp Ed [1959–62] p 87.
3 As expressed in the consultation document which he put out with a draft of the Director's Rules (since approved by the Secretary of State pursuant to CA 1998, s 51(5)): see para **15.26**.
4 CA 1998, s 60(6).
5 HL ZR, 30 October 1997, col 1148.
6 OFT 400 (March 1999).

15.30

The so-called 'comfort letters'[1] used by the Commission to close Article 81 proceedings without a formal decision clearly fall within the category of 'statement' and regard must presumably be had to these. Many such comfort letters close the Commission's proceedings without necessarily making it clear whether the reason for this is because it is not perceived that there is an appreciable effect on competition or because it is felt that there is an insufficient effect on trade between Member States. A closing of the European Commission file on the basis of the latter is not, of course, going to be of assistance to the UK authorities because they are not required to find an effect on trade between Member States. It is to be hoped that the European Commission may look at the terminology used in its comfort letters with a view to ensuring that they provide maximum assistance to the national courts and authorities. At the end of the day, of course, they are not legally binding and they will at most be of persuasive authority from the point of view of the UK authorities.

1 See para **8.72** ff.

(3) Article 234 References

15.31
Article 234 of the EC Treaty (formerly Article 177) provides an important mechanism for ensuring consistent interpretation of the EC Treaty across the Community, by enabling national courts to refer questions to the ECJ for a preliminary ruling. The ECJ issues binding (rather than merely advisory) judgments, although they are not dispositive of the individual case in question because it is for the relevant national court to apply the principle laid down by the ECJ to the facts of the specific case.

15.32
The question arises as to whether it would be open for a court in the UK to make a reference under Article 234 in respect of an interpretation of the CA 1998, in circumstances where it is clear on the face of the statute (notably in s 60) that it is the intention of the UK legislature that questions arising under the CA 1998 are dealt with in a manner which is consistent with the treatment of corresponding questions under Community law. If it is open for an Article 234 reference to be made in this way, the subsidiary question which arises is as to which UK courts/authorities are able to make such a reference: see para **15.36**.

15.33
As far as the issue of principle is concerned, the following aspects should be noted:

(1) One could expect that the ECJ (which is already an overworked institution) would be loath to be drawn into interpretation of national law issues.
(2) The CA 1998 is not in all respects a direct parallel of Articles 81 and 82 of the EC Treaty. For example, there is no need under the CA 1998 to demonstrate an effect on trade between Member States; also, the UK government has taken a more liberal approach to vertical agreements than is likely to be taken under the new EC block exemption for vertical agreements.
(3) Conversely, it would be undesirable from an EC law perspective for national laws which are clearly modelled on their EC law counterparts to be interpreted in widely divergent ways.

15.34
It is clear that the UK Government intends that it should be possible for a reference to be made to the ECJ under the CA 1998[1]. It seems reasonably clear from ECJ jurisprudence that this will indeed be possible. In the *Kleinwort Benson* case[2] the ECJ declined to give a preliminary ruling on a question of interpretation of the Civil Jurisdiction and Judgments Act 1982. In that case, however, the domestic court only had an obligation 'to have regard to the Court's case law'. There was no obligation to apply it. In the later *Leur-Bloem* case[3] the ECJ expressed the view that it had jurisdiction under Article 177 (now Article 234) where the national legislature:

> '... has chosen to apply the same treatment to purely internal situations and to those governed by the [relevant EC Directive], so that it has aligned its domestic legislation to Community law'.

The position under the CA 1998 is a closer analogy to *the Leur-Bloem* case than to the *Kleinwort Benson* case.

1 Statement of Lord Simon, HL Committee, 25 November 1997, col 975.
2 Case C-346/93 *Kleinwort Benson v City of Glasgow District Council* [1995] ECR I-615.
3 Case C-28/95 *Leur-Bloem v Inspecteur der Belastingsdienst* [1997] ECR I-4161 at para 34.

15.35
The subsequent *Bronner* case[1] appears to make the position clearer still. In that case, the Austrian Court was applying domestic law. Although that law was not written in the same terms as Article 82 of the EC Treaty, the Austrian court felt that an interpretation of Article 82 would assist it in reaching its decision (on the basis that it would violate EC law for it to interpret its own law in a manner which would be inconsistent with EC law). The ECJ accepted the reference, stating that :

> '... a request from a national court may be rejected only if it is quite obvious that the interpretation of Community law... bears no relation to the actual facts of the case or to the subject matter of the main action'.

1 Case C-7/97 *Oscar Bronner GmbH v Mediaprint Zeitungs und Zeitsschriftenverlag* [1999] 4 CLMR 112.

15.36
Assuming that there is scope for references to be made under Article 234, the question then arises as to which court/tribunal can make such a reference. Clearly the list includes the Court of Appeal and the House of Lords (as bodies hearing appeals from the CC); also the High Court, trying a civil action. This leaves the question as to whether the CC or the DGFT may themselves make Article 234 references. ECJ jurisprudence indicates that the body in question must have been called upon to give judgments in proceedings which require a judicial decision to be made and which it is under a legal duty to try[1]. It would appear that the CC's appeal tribunals would meet these tests and be able to make such a reference. However, it appears likely that the DGFT (and, by definition, the sectoral regulators[2]) would not be eligible, first, on the basis that their procedures are likely to be too far removed from those of a conventional court and second, because their decisions will be administrative rather than judicial in nature.

1 See Case C-54/96 *Dorsch Consult Ingenieurgesellschaft v Bundesbaugesellschaft Berlin* [1997] ECR I-4961 and Case C-111/94 *Job Centre* [1995] ECR I-3361.
2 They have concurrent power with the DGFT: see para **15.255** ff.

6 TRANSITIONAL ARRANGEMENTS

15.37
The transitional provisions of the CA 1998 are contained in Sch 13, which takes effect subject to s 74(2) of the Act. They are succinctly summarised in the OFT's 'Transitional Arrangements' Guidelines[1].

1 OFT 406 (March 1999).

15.38
The transitional provisions had two principal purposes. First, they provided a means by which the control of agreements under the Restrictive Trade Practices Act 1976 and the Resale Prices Act 1976 to the new Chapter I prohibition could be alleviated, allowing undertakings time to adapt and adjust. Second, they allowed a period of time to prepare for the introduction of the new Chapter II prohibition. The transitional scheme therefore delayed the entering into force of the Chapter I and Chapter II prohibitions until 1 March 2000 and provided certain additional transitional periods for existing agreements. There was no additional transitional period for the Chapter II prohibition, which therefore took effect on that date. There are special provisions for agreements which are currently subject to proceedings of the Restrictive Practices Court and for certain agreements in the regulated utility sectors. The CA 1998 is not retrospective in its effect[1].

1 HC SC G, 16 June 1998, col 448 (Nigel Griffiths MP).

15.39
The transitional arrangements are extremely complex. Further detail on those arrangements can be found in *Butterworths Competition Law*, Division I.

B Notifications

1 INTRODUCTION

15.40
As in the case of EC Treaty, Article 81, the Act prohibits agreements to which it applies but provides for the possibility of exemption from the prohibition. In order for an agreement to qualify for an exemption, it must:

(*a*) contribute to improving production or distribution or promoting technical or economic progress, while allowing consumers a fair share of the resulting benefit; and (*b*) must not impose on the undertakings concerned restrictions which are not indispensable for the attainment of those objectives, or afford the undertakings concerned the possibility of eliminating competition in respect of a substantial part of the products in question[1].

Accordingly, it enables parties to an agreement to notify it to the DGFT for the purpose of ascertaining whether it infringes the Chapter I prohibition and, if so, whether it merits an exemption from the prohibition. There is similarly scope for parties to notify conduct for the purpose of ascertaining whether it infringes the Chapter II prohibition. As in the case of EC Treaty, Article 82, there is, however, no scope for obtaining an exemption from the Chapter II prohibition. The Act provides for two types of notification, one for guidance and one for a decision. These are considered in turn below, in respect of the Chapter I prohibition and the Chapter II prohibition. Paras **15.86–15.102** describe the procedure to be followed in respect of an application for guidance or a decision.

1 CA 1998, ss 4 and 9.

15.41
The transitional arrangements under the CA 1998 contained provision for applications to be made for 'early guidance' prior to 1 March 2000 in respect of agreements entered into after the enactment of the Act (9 November 1998) but prior to 1 March 2000[1]. Any guidance so given has effect from 1 March 2000 as if given under s 15[2].

1 CA 1998, Sch 7(1).
2 CA 1998, Sch 7(4).

15.42
Individual exemptions, obtained following notification to the DGFT, should be distinguished from block exemption orders and parallel exemptions, neither of which require notification. These are considered in turn below.

(1) Block Exemption Orders

15.43
Under the CA 1998, s 6, if agreements which fall within a particular category of agreement are, in the DGFT's opinion, likely to be agreements which meet the exemption criteria set out in s 9 (see para **15.40**), he may recommend that the Secretary of State make a block exemption order, exempting the category of agreement in question from the Chapter I prohibition. A block exemption order may impose conditions or obligations subject to which the exemption is to have effect. The concept is similar to the concept of block exemption from the prohibition contained in EC Treaty, Article 81(1). Bearing in mind the number of block exemptions in existence under Article 81, there are likely to be very few block exemption orders made under the CA 1998. At present, there are none. A block exemption order will not exempt an agreement from the scope of the

Chapter II prohibition (this mirrors the position at the EC level in respect of EC Treaty, Article 82).

15.44

Before making a recommendation for a block exemption order to the Secretary of State, the DGFT must publish details of his proposed recommendation and consider any representations about it which are made to him[1]. If, subsequently, the DGFT concludes that it is appropriate to vary or revoke a block exemption order he may make a recommendation to that effect to the Secretary of State[2]. In a case where the Secretary of State wishes to exercise his power to vary or revoke a block exemption order (but in circumstances where there has been no recommendation to that effect from the DGFT), the Secretary of State must first inform the DGFT of the proposed variation or revocation and take into account any comments made by him[3]. A block exemption order may provide for a block exemption to have effect from a date earlier than that on which the order is made[4].

1 CA 1998, s 8(1).
2 CA 1998, s 8(3).
3 CA 1998, s 8(5).
4 CA 1998, s 8(6).

15.45

A block exemption order may provide that a party to an agreement which does not qualify for the block exemption created by the order but which satisfies specified criteria may notify the DGFT with a view to benefiting from a so-called 'opposition procedure' (this mirrors a similar type of procedure which operates under EC Treaty, Article 81[1]). An agreement notified under a provision included in a block exemption order is to be treated as benefiting from the block exemption order unless the DGFT is opposed to its being so treated and gives notice in writing to the party concerned of his opposition before the end of a period specified in the block exemption order[2].

1 CA 1998, s 7(1). In relation to the opposition procedure under Article 81, EC Treaty, see para **4.63** ff.
2 CA 1998, s 7(2).

(2) Parallel Exemptions

15.46

An agreement is automatically exempt[1] from the Chapter I prohibition if it is exempt from the prohibition contained in EC Treaty, Article 81(1) by virtue of any of the following:

(1) A regulation adopted by the European Commission or by the Council of the European Union (eg a block exemption adopted at the EC level).
(2) It has been given exemption by the Commission (ie following notification of an exemption under EC Treaty, Article 81(3)). It should be noted, however, that parallel exemption does not apply in the case of a

so-called comfort letter[2], although the DGFT is required to have regard to such a comfort letter[3].

(3) It has been notified to the Commission under an opposition procedure[4] in respect of Article 81 and the time for opposing, or objecting to, the agreement has expired and the Commission has not opposed it (or the Commission has opposed, or objected to, the agreement but has withdrawn its opposition or objection). An agreement is also exempt from the Chapter I prohibition if it does not affect trade between Member States but otherwise falls within the category of agreement which is exempt from the prohibition in EC Treaty, Article 81(1), by virtue of a block exemption[5]. Exemptions under the Chapter I prohibition pursuant to s 10 are referred to as 'parallel exemptions'[6].

1 CA 1998, s 10(1).
2 See para **8.72** ff.
3 CA 1998, s60(3).
4 See para **4.63** ff.
5 CA 1998, s 10(2).
6 CA 1998, s 10(3).

15.47

A parallel exemption takes effect on the day on which the relevant exemption from the Article 81 prohibition takes effect or (in the case of a parallel exemption operating in circumstances where there is no effect on trade between Member States) would take effect if the agreement in question affected trade between Member States; it ceases to have effect either if the relevant exemption ceases to have effect or if it is cancelled by the DGFT[1]. The CA 1998, s 10(5) provides that, in such circumstances and manner as may be specified in rules made by the DGFT, he may:

(*a*) impose conditions or obligations subject to which a parallel exemption is to have effect;
(*b*) vary or remove any such condition or obligation;
(*c*) impose one or more additional conditions or obligations; and
(*d*) cancel the exemption.

This is a somewhat controversial provision because the effect of it is that an agreement could be caught by the Chapter I prohibition in circumstances where it benefits from either an individual or block exemption at the EC level. This is less problematic in relation to those agreements which benefit from a parallel exemption but where there is no effect on trade between Member States; in that situation there is no clash between the position under the Act and the position under EC law. However, where that is not the case, it is debatable whether EC law allows the DGFT to impose stricter conditions than those imposed under Article 81(3) (the EC Treaty provision which allows for exemptions – individual or block – from the Article 81(3) prohibition). The position is not wholly clear as a matter of EC law[2] and may well in due course be the subject of a reference to the European Court under Article 234, EC Treaty.

1 CA 1998, s 10(4).
2 See *Butterworths Competition Law*, Division I.

15.48
In this context it is, however, interesting to note that the new European Commission block exemption in respect of vertical agreements[1] specifically provides in Article 7 that where, in any particular case, a vertical agreement to which the exemption applies has effects incompatible with the conditions laid down in Article 81(3), EC Treaty in the territory of a member state, or in a part thereof, which has all the characteristics of a distinct geographic market, the competent authority of that member state may withdraw the benefit of application of the regulation in respect of that territory. This produces the rather curious result that an agreement could benefit from the block exemption in certain EC member states but not others.

1 Commission Regulation (EC) 2790/1999, OJ [1999] L 336/21.

2 REASONS FOR NOTIFICATION

(1) General

15.49
The reasons for notification of an agreement under the CA 1998 are essentially the same as those for notifying under EC Treaty, Article 81[1]:

— first, it is only if notification is made that the DGFT can consider granting an individual exemption from the Chapter I prohibition;
— second, notification immunises the parties to an agreement from penalties under the Chapter I prohibition: see para **15.51**.

As an alternative to seeking an individual exemption, a party to an agreement may notify it to the DGFT in order to obtain guidance as to whether or not the agreement in question is likely to infringe the Chapter I prohibition and, if so, whether it is likely to be exempt from that prohibition. It is perhaps ironic that just at the time when the United Kingdom, after many years' delay, introduces a system modelled on that operated at the EC level the European Commission is actively considering, under its 'modernisation'[2] proposals, a radical overhaul of the EC system, including giving national authorities and courts the power directly to apply Article 81(3) (the provision on the basis of which exemption from the prohibition in Article 81(1), EC Treaty is obtained).

1 See para **4.01** ff.
2 See para **3.02**.

15.50
Notification of conduct does not immunise the party or parties involved in that conduct from penalties under the Chapter II prohibition. It is only the giving of guidance to the effect that the Chapter II prohibition is unlikely to be infringed, or the making of a decision that the Chapter II prohibition is not infringed, which have that effect[1].

1 See paras **15.82** and **15.85**.

15.51
If an agreement to which the Chapter I prohibition applies has been notified to the DGFT for a decision under CA 1998, s 14, no penalty can be imposed under Chapter I in respect of any infringement of the prohibition by the agreement which occurs during the period beginning with the date on which notification is made and ending with such date as may be specified in a notice in writing given to the applicant by the DGFT when the application is determined[1]. The date specified cannot be earlier than the date on which notice is given[2]. There is a similar protection from penalties in respect of agreements which are the subject of notification for guidance under s 13[3]. In both cases, immunity from penalties can be removed by a decision of the DGFT following a preliminary investigation[4].

1 CA 1998, s 14(4).
2 CA 1998, s 14(5).
3 CA 1998, s 13(4).
4 See para **15.62**.

15.52
If, following notification for a decision under s 14, the DGFT decides that an agreement has not infringed the Chapter I prohibition, no penalty can be imposed in respect of that agreement under Chapter I[1]. However, that immunity from penalties can be removed if:

(1) The DGFT takes action in respect of the agreement in circumstances where he has reasonable grounds for believing that there has been a material change of circumstances since he gave his decision or he has a reasonable suspicion that the information on which he has based his decision was incomplete, false or misleading in a material particular; and
(2) He considers that it is likely that the agreement will infringe the Chapter I prohibition; and
(3) He gives notice in writing to the party on whose application the decision was made that he is removing the immunity as from a date specified in his notice[2]. Moreover, if the DGFT has a reasonable suspicion that information on which he based the decision and which has been provided to him by a party to the agreement was incomplete, false or misleading in a material particular, the date specified in such a notice may be earlier than the date on which the notice is given[3].

1 CA 1998, s 16(3).
2 CA 1998, s 16(4).
3 CA 1998, s 16(5).

15.53
If an agreement is notified for guidance under Chapter I and the DGFT gives guidance that:

(*a*) it is unlikely to infringe the Chapter I prohibition (regardless of whether or not it is exempt);
(*b*) it is likely to be exempt under a block exemption, a parallel exemption or a s 11 exemption; or
(*c*) he would be likely to grant the agreement an individual exemption if asked to do so;

the DGFT may not impose any penalty under Chapter I in respect of that agreement[1]. However, that immunity from penalties may be removed by the DGFT in the following circumstances:

(*a*) he takes action with respect to the agreement in one of the circumstances referred to in para **15.54** below; and
(*b*) he considers it likely that the agreement will infringe the prohibition; and
(*c*) he gives notice in writing to the party on whose application the guidance was given that he is removing the immunity as from the date specified in his notice[2].

1 CA 1998, s 15(3).
2 CA 1998, s 15(4).

15.54
The circumstances referred to in para **15.53** above are:

(*a*) where the DGFT has reasonable grounds for believing that there has been a material change of circumstance since he gave his guidance; or
(*b*) where he has a reasonable suspicion that the information on which he based his guidance was incomplete, false or misleading in a material particular; or
(*c*) where one of the parties to the agreement applies to him for a decision under s14 with respect to the agreement; or
(*d*) a complaint about the agreement has been made by a person who is not a party to the agreement[1].

1 CA 1998, s 15(2).

15.55
If the DGFT has a reasonable suspicion that information on which he based his guidance and which was provided to him by a party to the agreement was incomplete, false or misleading in a material particular, the date specified in the notice referred to in para **15.53** above may be earlier than the date on which the notice is given[1].

1 CA 1998, s 15(5).

(2) Notification to the DGFT or the European Commission?

15.56
Many agreements are likely to be caught by both the Chapter I prohibition and Article 81 of the EC Treaty. The question which arises is whether such agreements should be notified to the DGFT, to the European Commission or to both. The DGFT has made it clear that he considers that notifications to both himself and to the European Commission are undesirable in terms of the compliance cost for undertakings and the duplication of effort by the competition authorities; he has also made it clear that he considers that the European Commission is the more appropriate authority to whom notification should be made if the agreement is caught by Article 81[1]. There are a number of reasons for this view and these are summarised in para **15.57**. In

addition, the DGFT is clearly keen to avoid being inundated by notifications following the coming into force of the CA 1998 and this is one means by which to try to keep down the number of notifications made to him. Indeed, in its booklet 'Is Notification Necessary'[2] the OFT expresses the view that few cases will genuinely need to be notified and strongly discourages undertakings from notifying on a fail-safe basis.

1 DGFT Guideline *The Chapter I Prohibition*, para 7.1.
2 Published August 2000.

15.57
There are several advantages to notifying agreements to the European Commission under EC Treaty, Article 81 rather than to the DGFT under the Chapter I prohibition:

(1) Only the Commission has the power to grant an exemption from the prohibition in EC Treaty, Article 81(1). Such an exemption automatically exempts the agreement from the scope of the Chapter I prohibition[1]. This is known as a 'parallel exemption'[2]. The converse is not, however, true, ie. exemption from the Chapter I prohibition does not preclude the application of Article 81(1).
(2) An Article 81(1) exemption has effect in all the EC Member States, whereas exemption by the DGFT has effect only in the United Kingdom.
(3) The DGFT may not impose a penalty under the Chapter I prohibition if the agreement in question has been notified to the European Commission and the Commission has not yet determined the matter[3]. The same is not true in reverse. If the Commission withdraws the benefit of provisional immunity from penalties under Article 81 in respect of the agreement before making its final determination, the immunity under the Chapter I prohibition automatically ceases on the same date[4]. The reference to provisional immunity from penalties is a reference to immunity from fines pursuant to Article 15(5)(a) of Council Regulation (EEC) 17/62[5]: see the Competition Act 1998 (Provisional Immunity from Penalties) Regulations 1999[6].

1 CA 1998, s 10(1)(*b*).
2 See para **15.46**.
3 CA 1998, s 41(2).
4 CA 1998, s 41(3).
5 See para **4.05**.
6 SI 1999/2281.

15.58
There is, however, an element of inflexibility in relation to notifications to the European Commission, in that the Commission does not have the power to grant retroactive exemption in all cases[1]. This means that parties to an agreement may consider it commercially necessary to notify the Commission as early as possible. The DGFT, on the other hand, does have the power to grant retroactive exemption in all cases[2].

1 See para **4.34**.
2 CA 1998, s 4(5).

15.59
As noted in para **15.56**, the DGFT has actively discouraged the making of dual notifications, ie to both himself and the European Commission. However, where dual notifications are made the DGFT has indicated[1] that his officials will liaise closely with those of the European Commission in order to determine which authority should assess the agreement. Where the Commission chooses to deal with the agreement (either by formal decision or by informal means) the DGFT is likely to take no action until the Commission has completed its assessment. An exemption decision under Article 81(3) will automatically exempt the agreement from the Chapter I prohibition[2]. In those (much more frequent) cases where closure of the Commission's procedure takes place by informal means, the DGFT has indicated[3] that as a general rule he will follow the Commission's assessment of the agreement and will consult the Commission before departing from it. However, if the Commission's procedure has closed on the basis that the agreement in question does not have an appreciable effect on inter-state trade that clearly leaves the way open for the DGFT to analyse whether the agreement has restrictive effects which affect trade within the United Kingdom.

1 DGFT Guideline *The Chapter I Prohibition*, para 7.9.
2 See para **15.57**.
3 DGFT Guideline *The Chapter I Prohibition*, para 7.9.

3 NOTIFICATION FOR GUIDANCE UNDER CHAPTER I

15.60
A party to an agreement may apply to the DGFT for guidance as to the application of the Chapter I prohibition. This is done by a notification under the CA 1998, s 13. On an application under s 13, the DGFT may (but is not obliged to) give the applicant guidance as to whether or not in his view the agreement is likely to infringe it[1]. If he concludes that it is, his guidance may indicate whether the agreement is likely to benefit from a block exemption, a parallel exemption or a s 11 exemption, or whether he would be likely to grant the agreement an individual exemption if asked to do so[2]. If he decides an application for guidance, the DGFT must state the facts on which it is based and the reasons for it[3]. If he exercises his discretion not to give guidance, he must give written notice of the fact to the applicant[4] and repay the fee which the applicant has paid[5].

1 CA 1998, s 13(2).
2 CA 1998, s 13(3).
3 *Director's Rules*, para 10.
4 Ibid.
5 *Director's Rules*, para 6(6)(b). As to the payment of fees, see para **15.103**.

15.61
A party to an agreement who makes an application for guidance must take all reasonable steps to notify all other parties to the agreement of whom he

is aware that the application has been made and that it is an application for guidance[1]. Notification must be in the specified manner.

1 CA 1998, Sch 5, para 2.

15.62

If, after a preliminary investigation of an application for guidance, the DGFT considers that it is likely that the agreement concerned will infringe the Chapter I prohibition and that it would not be appropriate to grant the agreement an individual exemption he may make a provisional decision; if he does so, the DGFT must notify the applicant in writing of that decision[1] and provide an account of the facts on which he based his decision[2]. The effect of such a decision is that the immunity from penalties under s 13(4)[3] is disapplied[4]. That disapplication is retrospective; ie the immunity is treated as never having existed.

1 CA 1998, Sch 5, para 3.
2 *Director's Rules*, para 9(2).
3 See para **15.51**.
4 CA 1998, Sch 5, para 3(2)(*b*).

15.63

When making a provisional decision, the DGFT must follow such procedures as may be specified; a provisional decision does not affect the final determination of an application[1].

1 CA 1998, Sch 5, para 3(4), (5).

4 EFFECT OF GUIDANCE UNDER CHAPTER I

15.64

If the DGFT gives guidance that:

(*a*) an agreement is not likely to infringe the Chapter I prohibition (regardless of whether or not it is exempt);
(*b*) the agreement is likely to be exempt under a block exemption, a parallel exemption or a s 11 exemption; or
(*c*) he would be likely to grant the agreement an individual exemption if asked to do so;

he may take no further action under the Chapter I prohibition with respect to that agreement unless:

(*a*) he has reasonable grounds for believing that there has been a material change of circumstance since he gave his guidance; or
(*b*) he has a reasonable suspicion that the information on which he based his guidance was incomplete, false or misleading in a material particular; or
(*c*) one of the parties to the agreement applies to him for a decision under s 14 with respect to the agreement; or
(*d*) a complaint about the agreement has been made to him by a person who is not a party to the agreement[1].

If, having given such guidance, he intends to take further action, he must consult the person to whom he gave the guidance[2].

1 CA 1998, s 15(2).
2 *Director's Rules*, para 11.

5 NOTIFICATION FOR A DECISION UNDER CHAPTER I

15.65
Under CA 1998, s 14 a party to an agreement may notify the DGFT with a view to obtaining a decision. On receipt of such an application, the DGFT may make a decision as to whether the Chapter I prohibition has been infringed and, if it has not been infringed, whether that is because of the effect of an exclusion or because the agreement is exempt from the prohibition[1]. The application may include a request for the agreement to which it relates to be granted an individual exemption[2].

1 CA 1998, s 14(2).
2 CA 1998, s 14(3).

15.66
As in the case of an application for guidance, an applicant for a decision must take all reasonable steps to notify all other parties to the agreement of whom he is aware that the application has been made and that it is an application for a decision[1]. If, after a preliminary investigation of an application, the DGFT considers that it is likely that the agreement concerned will infringe the Chapter I prohibition and that it would not be appropriate to grant the agreement an individual exemption he may make a provisional decision; if he intends to do so, he must first consult the applicant (and other parties to the agreement) [2] and, having decided to do so, he must notify the applicant in writing[3] and provide an account of the facts on which he based his decision and his reasons for it[4]. The effect of a provisional decision is that the immunity from penalties which results from an application for a decision (see para **15.51**) is disapplied retrospectively[5].

1 CA 1998, Sch 5, para 2.
2 *Director's Rules*, para 9(1).
3 CA 1998, Sch 5, para 3(1)(2).
4 *Director's Rules*, para 9(2).
5 CA 1998, Sch 5, para 3(2).

15.67
When making a provisional decision, the DGFT must follow such procedures as may be specified[1]. A provisional decision does not affect the final determination of an application[2].

1 CA 1998, Sch 5, para 3(3).
2 CA 1998, Sch 5, para 3(4).

15.68
The DGFT is required to arrange for the application for a decision to be published in such a way as he thinks most suitable for bringing it to the

attention of those likely to be affected by it, unless he is satisfied that it will be sufficient for him to seek information from one or more particular persons other than the applicant[1]. In determining the application, the DGFT is required to take into account any representations made to him by persons other than the applicant[2]. On an application under s 14:

— if the DGFT proposes to grant an exemption subject to conditions or obligations[3], he *must* consult the applicant, specifying the proposed conditions or obligations;
— if he proposes to grant an exemption, whether or not subject to conditions or obligations, he *must* consult the public; and
— if he proposes to make a decision that the Chapter I prohibition has not been infringed, he *may* consult the public[4] (similarly, if, on an application under s 22 for conduct to be considered, the DGFT proposes to make a decision that the Chapter II prohibition has not been infringed, he *may* consult the public[5]).

1 CA 1998, Sch 5, para 5(2).
2 CA 1998, Sch 5, para 5(3).
3 See para **15.73**.
4 *Director's Rules*, para 12.
5 Ibid.

15.69
If the DGFT determines an application for a decision he must publish his decision, together with his reasons for making it, in such manner as may be specified[1].

1 CA 1998, Sch 5, para 6.

15.70
Where the DGFT delays in making a decision, a person aggrieved by the delay may apply to court for a ruling that there has been undue delay on the part of the DGFT in determining the application. The court may give such directions to the DGFT as it considers appropriate for securing that the application is determined without unnecessary further delay[1].

1 CA 1998, Sch 5, para 7.

15.71
Although CA 1998, s 14(2) provides for the making of decisions by the DGFT, he is under no statutory duty to reach a decision and it appears likely that the OFT will adopt the practice of the European Commission, closing many of its cases by means of so-called 'comfort letters'[1]. By analogy with the practice of the European Commission under Article 81 of the EC Treaty, these will be non-binding letters used to close the OFT's file without the making of a formal decision. The non-binding nature of such letters means that they do not deliver the legal certainty of a decision. It remains to be seen whether an applicant for whom it is vital to obtain the legal certainty provided by a decision could apply to court under para 7 of Sch 5, CA 1998 for its application to be determined by decision rather than comfort letter. That paragraph applies if the court is satisfied, on the application of a person aggrieved by the failure of a the DGFT to determine an

application for a decision, that there has been undue delay on the part of the DGFT in determining the application.

1 For comfort letters at the EC level, see para **8.72** ff.

(1) Type of Decision which may be Taken

15.72

On an application for a decision, the DGFT may decide that the Chapter I prohibition has been infringed and that if it has not been infringed, whether that is because of the effect of an exclusion[1] or because the agreement is exempt from the prohibition[2].

1 As to exclusions generally, see *Butterworths Competition Law*, Division I.
2 CA 1998, s 14(2).

15.73

Where an exemption is granted, it may be granted subject to such conditions or obligations as the DGFT considers is appropriate to impose and has effect for such period as the DGFT considers appropriate[1]. The period must be specified in the grant of the exemption[2]. Accordingly, as in the case of exemptions under Article 81(3) of the EC Treaty, exemptions from the Chapter I prohibition cannot be indefinite. If the DGFT proposes to grant an exemption subject to conditions or obligations he must consult the applicant and the public, specifying the proposed conditions or obligations[3].

1 CA 1998, s 4(3).
2 CA 1998 s 4(4).
3 *Director's Rules*, para 12(1)(*a*).

(2) Application for Extension of an Individual Exemption

15.74

Under CA 1998, s 4(6), it is open to the beneficiary of an individual exemption to apply to the DGFT to have the period of the exemption extended. If so, it must submit a new Form N to the DGFT[1]. Such an application must be submitted not more than twelve months and not less than three months before the expiry of the exemption. If the DGFT proposes to grant the application, he must consult the public[2]. Once he makes a decision as to whether or not to grant the application, the DGFT must give written notice thereof to the applicant and publish the decision, specifying, if appropriate, the period of extension granted[3].

1 *Director's Rules*, para 19(1); for details in respect of Form N, see para **15.86** ff.
2 *Director's Rules*, para 19(2).
3 *Director's Rules*, para 19(4).

(3) Cancellation of an Individual Exemption

15.75

If the DGFT has reasonable grounds for believing that there has been a material change of circumstance since he granted an individual exemption, he may by notice in writing take one of the following steps:

— cancel the exemption;
— vary or remove any conditions or obligations; or
— impose one or more additional conditions or obligations[1].

He may also take any of those steps if he has a reasonable suspicion that the information on which he based his decision to grant an individual exemption (principally likely to be the contents of Form N, the notification form) was incomplete, false or misleading in a material particular[2]. Similarly, failure to comply with an obligation allows the DGFT to take any of those three steps[3].

1 CA 1998, s 5(1).
2 CA 1998, s 5(2).
3 CA 1998, s 5(4).

15.76
Where the DGFT proposes to take any of the steps referred to in para **15.75**, he must first consult the public and the person to whom notice of the decision to grant the exemption was given[1]. If he decides to take any of those steps, having first consulted, he must give notice of his decision in writing to the person to whom notice of the decision to grant the exemption was originally given, stating the facts on which he bases his decision and his reasons for it, and must publish the decision[2].

1 *Director's Rules*, para 20(1).
2 *Director's Rules*, para 20(2).

15.77
Breach of a condition contained in an exemption decision has the effect of cancelling the exemption[1]. Failure to comply with an obligation contained in an exemption decision allows the DGFT, by notice in writing, to take any of the steps referred to in para **15.75**.

1 CA 1998, s 5(3).

6 EFFECT OF A DECISION UNDER CHAPTER I

15.78
If the DGFT makes a decision that an agreement has not infringed the Chapter I prohibition he may take no further action under Chapter I with respect to the agreement unless:

(*a*) he has reasonable grounds for believing that there has been a material change of circumstance since he gave his decision; or
(*b*) he has a reasonable suspicion that the information on which he based his decision was incomplete, false or misleading in a material particular[1].

1 CA 1998, s 16(2).

15.79
It should be noted that a complaint made about the agreement by a third party does not constitute grounds for the DGFT to re-open matters. This is in contrast to the position where he has given guidance in response to an

application for guidance. The reason for the distinction is that guidance applications are dealt with without the matter becoming public and therefore without the opportunity for third party comments.

15.80
A decision by the DGFT that an agreement has not infringed the Chapter I prohibition provides immunity from penalties in respect of that agreement[1].

1 CA 1998, s 16(3).

7 NOTIFICATION FOR GUIDANCE UNDER CHAPTER II

15.81
A person may apply to the DGFT for guidance on the application of the Chapter II prohibition by means of a notification under CA 1998, s 21. A similar procedure is followed as in respect of a guidance application under s 13 in respect of the Chapter I prohibition[1].There are, however, several important differences:

— the provisions in s 13 regarding exemption are not mirrored in s 21 as there is no scope for an exemption from the Chapter II prohibition;
— a guidance application under Chapter II does not provide any immunity from penalties.

Guidance applications in respect of the Chapter II prohibition are likely to be infrequent, for the same reasons as in the case of applications for a decision.

1 See para **15.60** ff.

8 EFFECT OF GUIDANCE UNDER CHAPTER II

15.82
The effect of guidance that conduct is unlikely to infringe the Chapter II prohibition is essentially the same as for guidance that an agreement does not infringe the Chapter I prohibition or is likely to be exempt from that prohibition[1].

1 See para **15.64**.

9 NOTIFICATION FOR A DECISION UNDER CHAPTER II

15.83
The procedure to be followed[1] in respect of notification for a decision under Chapter II is broadly the same as in respect of Chapter I. However, notification for a decision under Chapter II does not have the effect of

immunising the notified party from penalties, unlike the position in respect of a notification under Chapter I[2].

1 CA 1998, s 22 and Sch 6.
2 See para **15.51**.

15.84
Notifications for a decision under Chapter II are in practice likely to be infrequent (this mirrors the position in relation to applications for negative clearance under Article 82 of the EC Treaty). This is for two principal reasons: first, as noted in para **15.50** notification for a decision under Chapter II does not have the effect of immunising the notified party from penalties; second, there is no possibility of an exemption for abuse of a dominant position: conduct by a dominant undertaking is either abusive or it is not.

10 EFFECT OF A DECISION UNDER CHAPTER II

15.85
The effect of a decision that conduct does not infringe Chapter II prohibition[1] is the same as a corresponding decision under Chapter I[2].

1 CA 1998, s 24.
2 See para **15.78**.

11 PROCEDURE TO BE FOLLOWED IN RESPECT OF AN APPLICATION FOR GUIDANCE OR A DECISION

(1) Form N

15.86
An application under s 13 (for guidance in respect of the Chapter I prohibition), s 14 (for a decision in respect of the Chapter I prohibition), s 21 (for guidance in respect of the Chapter II prohibition) and s 22 (for a decision in respect of the Chapter II prohibition) has to be made in accordance with the Rules of the DGFT[1]. The Director's Rules provide that a person who wishes to apply under any of those sections must submit Form N to him[2]. A copy of Form N is an Annex to the Rules of the DGFT. A copy is also available on the OFT website at http./www.oft.gov.uk.

1 CA 1998, Sch 5, para 2 and Sch 6, para 2.
2 *Director's Rules*, para 1.

15.87
The same notification form, known as Form N, will be used for guidance applications and applications for decisions. Although it is described as a form, the notes which accompany it make it clear that it is essentially a check-list of the information which must be supplied to the DGFT. The form is similar in scope to Form A/B, the form used for notifications under

Articles 81 and 82 of the EC Treaty[1]. Form N does not, however, require information regarding the effect of the agreement or conduct in question on trade between Member States because that is not relevant to substantive analysis under the Chapter I or Chapter II prohibitions. If a dual notification is being made to the DGFT and the European Commission[2], parties may choose to send three copies of the completed Form A/B, plus supporting documents, along with Form N, so as to enable them simply to cross-refer to information in Form A/B and merely address the UK-specific information required by Form N[3]. The DGFT has published *Guidance Notes on Completing Form N*[4].

1 See para **4.36** ff.
2 Dual notifications are being discouraged by the DGFT: see para **15.56**.
3 *OFT's Major Provisions Guidelines*, para 7.11 (OFT 400 (March 1999)).
4 OFT 431 (March 2000).

15.88
Applications for guidance or a decision should be sent to the DGFT at the following address: Co-ordination Unit CB3, The Office of Fair Trading, Fleetbank House, 2-6 Salisbury Square, London, EC4Y 8JX.

15.89
The principal information required by Form N is as follows:

(1) The identity of the undertaking(s) submitting the notification. If one undertaking (for example, a solicitor) is submitting the Form on behalf of another undertaking, proof of the former's authority to act must be provided.
(2) The goods or services involved must be fully described, along with the relevant Standard Industrial Classification Code, if known.
(3) The purpose of the notification (ie whether it is being made under Chapter I, Chapter II or both) and whether it is an application for guidance or a decision.
(4) If it is an application for a decision under Chapter I, whether an individual exemption is requested. It can be expected that many applications for a decision under Chapter I will be in the alternative (ie requesting either a decision that the agreement in question does not fall within the Chapter I prohibition or, if it does, that it merits an individual exemption).
(5) In respect of a notification under Chapter I, why the agreement in question is considered not to be caught by EC Treaty, Article 81 (this reflects the DGFT's view that, when an arrangement is also caught by Article 81 of the EC Treaty, the European Commission is the more appropriate authority to whom notification should be made (see para **15.56**).
(6) Whether the agreement or conduct is the subject of a notification to any other national competition authority.
(7) Whether the agreement or conduct being notified relates to any of the sectors in respect of which another UK regulator has concurrent jurisdiction (see para **15.255** ff).
(8) A description of the relevant product and geographic markets and, for

each of the parties to the agreement (where it is an agreement which is being notified), a list of all undertakings belonging to the same group as each of the parties and which are active in the same relevant product market or a market neighbouring the relevant product market.

(9) Market share information for each of the last three calendar or financial years (for each of the parties and their main competitors and five main customers, along with contact details).

(10) Information regarding market entry and potential competition in the relevant product and geographic markets.

(11) Reasons why the DGFT should conclude that the agreement or conduct in question is not covered by the Chapter I or Chapter II prohibition (as the case may be).

(12) In the case of an application for an exemption from the Chapter I prohibition, an explanation of why an exemption should be granted.

15.90

Two copies of Form N, in addition to the original, must be submitted to the DGFT[1]. In addition, if, in the applicant's opinion, a regulator, or more than one regulator, has or may have concurrent jurisdiction with the DGFT[2], one extra copy of Form N must be submitted to the DGFT for each such regulator. Where the notification relates to a standard contract, the number expected to be concluded should be stated.

1 *Director's Rules*, para 3.
2 In relation to concurrency generally, see para **15.255**.

15.91

Form N also requires a copy of the most recent in-house long-term market studies assessing or analysing the relevant markets, including any commissioned by the undertakings concerned from outside consultants. In addition, references to any external studies of the relevant product market(s) should be provided, along with a copy of any such study (where possible).

(2) Treatment of Confidential Information

15.92

If the notifying party/parties regard any information provided as confidential, it should be clearly identified as such and placed in a separate Annex, with an explanation as to why the information should be regarded as confidential.

(3) Role of Sectoral Regulators

15.93

As noted in para **15.18**, various sectoral regulators have jurisdiction, concurrently with the DGFT, under the CA 1998. Form N requires the notifying party/parties to indicate whether the arrangement or conduct being notified relates to any of the sectors in respect of which a regulator has concurrent jurisdiction, namely:

- — commercial activities connected with telecommunications;
- — the shipping, conveyance or supply of gas and activities ancillary thereto;
- — commercial activities connected with the generation, transmission or supply of electricity;
- — commercial activities connected with the supply of water or securing the supply of water or the provision or securing of sewerage services;
- — commercial activities connected with the generation, transmission or supply of electricity in Northern Ireland;
- — the conveyance, storage or supply of gas in Northern Ireland;
- — the supply of railway services.

15.94
If any of the sectors listed in para **15.93** are involved, one further copy of Form N and attachments should be provided to the DGFT for each relevant regulator who may have concurrent jurisdiction[1]. The DGFT's Guidance Notes on completing Form N[2] state that it would also be helpful if an additional copy of the Form was sent directly to the relevant regulator. However, the Guidance Notes also make it clear that failure to send an additional copy to or for the relevant regulator will not render the application incomplete (though it may cause delay in the initial allocation of the application).

1 *Director's Rules*, para 3.
2 OFT 431, March 2000.

(4) Other Procedural Aspects

Requirement for notification to be correct and complete

15.95
Paragraph 4(1) of the Director's Rules states that the information submitted as Form N must be correct and complete. For these purposes, information which is false or misleading will be treated as incorrect or incomplete. However, para 4(3) indicates that the DGFT may dispense with the obligation to submit any particular information (or document) if he considers that such information (or document) is unnecessary for the examination of the case. If the DGFT determines that the information submitted as Form N is incomplete in a material respect he is required to inform the applicant in writing within one month of receipt of Form N and payment of the prescribed fee[1].

1 *Director's Rules*, para 5(3).

Requirement to keep the notification up to date

15.96
Material changes in the facts contained in an application of which the applicant knows, or ought reasonably to know, must be communicated to the

DGFT (or, if another sectoral regulator is exercising jurisdiction, to that other sectoral regulator)[1].

1 *Director's Rules*, para 4(4).

Effective date of notification

15.97
An application takes effect on the date on which it is received by the DGFT along with payment of the prescribed fee[1]. However, if the DGFT decides that the information submitted as Form N is incomplete in a material respect, the application takes effect on the date on which the complete information is received by the DGFT[2]. Applications will not be effective unless the relevant fee is paid[3].

1 *Director's Rules*, para 5(1).
2 *Director's Rules*, para 5(3).
3 See para **15.103**.

Number of copies required

15.98
Form N must be supplied in original version plus two copies, together with either an original or certified copy, plus two further copies, of any relevant agreement and annexes. If the applicant believes that one or more other regulators has or may have concurrent jurisdiction with the DGFT, one extra copy of the information submitted as Form N must be supplied to the DGFT[1].

1 *Director's Rules*, para 3.

Informing other parties of the notification

15.99
A party to an agreement who makes an application in respect of the Chapter I prohibition must take all reasonable steps to notify all other parties to the agreement of whom he is aware that the application has been made and as to whether it is for guidance or a decision[1]. The same applies to an application in respect of conduct under Chapter II[2]. Such notification is required to be written and given within seven working days of the date on which the applicant receives acknowledgement of receipt of this application from the DGFT and the applicant is required to provide to the DGFT a copy of the notification made to the other parties[3]. The notes to Form N recognise that, in exceptional cases, it may not be practicable to inform all non-notifying parties to the notified agreement or conduct that it has been notified, for example, a standard from agreement concluded with a large number of undertakings.

1 CA 1998, Sch 5, para 2(2).
2 CA 1998, Sch 6, para 2(2).
3 *Director's Rules*, para 7.

Public register

15.100
The Director's Rules provide[1] that he will maintain a register on which will be entered, in respect of every application for a decision (but not guidance), a summary of the nature and objectives of the agreement or conduct in question and an indication of the outcome of the application. The register is open to public inspection at the OFT and on an OFT website. However, the actual text of agreements will not be placed on the register for public inspection, in contrast with the position which prevailed under the RTPA 1976.

1 Para 8.

Timetable

15.101
The Director's Rules do not set out any timetable for dealing with applications for guidance or a decision. At the time the DGFT published the Rules in draft he indicated that it was his intention to publish non-binding administrative timetables for dealing with applications.

Fees

15.102
The CA 1998, s 53 provides that the DGFT may charge fees for notifications. Under the Director's Rules[1] there is a fee of £5,000 for examining an agreement under s13 or considering conduct under s 21 (applications for guidance). A fee of £13,000 is payable for examining an agreement under s 14 or considering conduct under s 22 (applications for a decision). Payment can be made either by cheque or by the Bank Automated Clearing System (BACS)[2]. Applications for guidance or a decision will not become effective until the relevant fee has been paid. According to the preamble to the Rules when they were published in draft, the fees are 'based on the principle of full economic cost recovery'. The DGFT expressly rejected the idea of reduced fees for small and medium sized businesses, on the grounds that there is no direct correlation between the complexity of issues raised in an application for guidance or a decision and the size of the undertakings concerned. By way of contrast with the proposed fee-paying regime under the CA 1998, no fee is payable in respect of notifications under EC Treaty, Articles 81 and 82. The idea of a fee-paying regime for notifications is consistent with the clearly stated desire of the DGFT to keep the number of notifications which he receives to a minimum. Whether, however, it is reasonable that, in a regime based on the principle of prohibition but with scope for exemption following notification, fees of this size should be charged is debatable.

1 Para 6.
2 OFT Guidance Notes on Completing Form N (OFT 431, March 2000).

15.103
The fee is repayable in the following circumstances[1]:

(*a*) if the DGFT returns the information submitted as Form N to the applicant as being non-compliant[2]; or
(*b*) if the DGFT determines the application by exercising his discretion not to give guidance or make a decision.

1 *Director's Rules*, para 6(6).
2 *Director's Rules*, para 5(6).

C Complaints

1 INTRODUCTION

15.104
The bringing of complaints in relation to alleged anti-competitive agreements or abusive conduct will be a key feature of the regime established under the CA 1998. In the run-up to March 2000, when the Act came fully into force, the OFT undertook a programme designed to make businesses, big and small, aware of the scope of the new legislation and the penalties which can be imposed under it. Part of this was clearly designed to ensure that potential infringers were made aware of the investigative powers and remedies available to the authorities under the new Act. Part, however, was designed to ensure that those who may be potential victims of anti-competitive agreements/behaviour were aware of the greater opportunities for recourse which are now available to them. The Act certainly holds out the prospect of much speedier and more effective relief for persons who believe they are suffering from the anti-competitive behaviour of others. It remains to be seen how effective these remedies will be in practice.

15.105
Against that background, it is perhaps somewhat surprising that there is so little said about the rights of complainants in the CA 1998 itself. This mirrors the lack of specific provisions in the Act regarding the rights of those claiming to have been damaged by the anti-competitive agreements/conduct of others to claim damages[1].

1 See para **15.16**.

15.106
The remainder of this section seeks to piece together from various sources in the Act a picture of the rights of complainants under the CA 1998. Complaints may be made to the DGFT or to the appropriate sectoral regulator (where relevant). Paragraph 8.1 of the DGFT's 'Major Provisions' Guidelines[1] states that when a complaint falls within the concurrent jurisdiction of a regulator, it will usually be dealt with by that regulator, rather than the DGFT.

1 OFT 400 (March 1999).

2 WHO MAY COMPLAIN?

15.107
The CA 1998 does not stipulate who is entitled to complain to the DGFT. This contrasts with the position under EC law: Regulation 17/62[1] provides that natural or legal persons claiming a 'legitimate interest' are entitled to make an application to the European Commission for a finding of infringement under Articles 81 or 82 of the EC Treaty and a decision requiring that infringement to be brought to an end.

1 Council Regulation (EEC) 17/62, OJ SpEd 1959–62 p 87. See para **5.03** ff.

15.108
The ECJ and the European Commission have, through decisions taken over a number of years, established certain classes of complainant who clearly have a legitimate interest. The question arises as to whether the CA 1998 s 60 applies in this situation. As noted in para **15.23**, the purpose of that section is to ensure that, so far as possible, questions arising under the CA 1998 are dealt with in a manner which is consistent with the treatment of corresponding questions arising in Community law. The question of the locus standi of someone as complainant is essentially a procedural rather than a substantive one and, as noted in para **15.25**, it is arguable that s 60 mandates simply substantive, as opposed to procedural, consistency. However, in the absence of any specific coverage of this issue in the CA 1998 itself, recourse is likely to be had to EC law jurisprudence on this subject.

3 FORM AND CONTENTS OF COMPLAINT

15.109
There is no specified form to complete to make a complaint; however, guidance about the information likely to be required is available from the OFT and each of the sectoral regulators[1]. The relevant Guidelines of the DGFT[2] state that information should be given as to whether, for example, the complainant is a competitor or customer of the undertaking complained about or a final consumer, together with an explanation of the reasons for and details of the complaint. The Guidelines make it clear that information should, if possible, be provided about the market concerned; eg its annual value and the undertakings involved in it, together with information about their market shares and details of any recent independent studies of the market. The aim from the complainant's point of view should be to make the complaint look as professional, complete and authoritative as possible. If the complainant is seeking interim measures[3], this should be made clear.

1 *The DGFT's Major Provisions Guidelines*, para 8 (OFT 400, March 1999).
2 *The DGFT's Major Provisions Guidelines*, para 8.2.
3 See para **15.170** ff.

4 TIMING OF COMPLAINT

15.110
As in the case of Articles 81 and 82 of the EC Treaty[1], there is no stipulated time period within which a complaint should be made. However, if the complainant seeks the adoption by the DGFT of interim measures, it is vital that the complaint be made speedily[2].

1 See para **5.09**.
2 See para **15.115**.

5 CONSIDERATIONS TO BE TAKEN INTO ACCOUNT WHEN DECIDING WHETHER TO FILE A COMPLAINT OR BRING COURT PROCEEDINGS

(1) Introduction

15.111
A person who believes he is suffering damage as a result of an agreement or conduct in violation of Articles 81 or 82 of the EC Treaty has two basic options. He can either file a complaint with the European Commission or commence proceedings in a national court of a Member State[1]. The position under the CA 1998 is intended to be similar: a person who considers he is suffering damage as a result of an infringement of the Chapter I or Chapter II prohibitions can either complain to the DGFT or commence proceedings in the High Court. The CA 1998 is not in fact explicit about the right to make such a civil claim but there is no doubt that the Government intends that this right should exist, as it does under EC law[2].

1 See para **5.10** ff.
2 See, for example, HC 2R 11 May 1998, col 35 (Margaret Beckett MP, then Secretary of State for Trade and Industry).

(2) General Considerations

15.112
It is too early to assess the relative effectiveness of a complaint to the DGFT as compared with a private law action. However, the principal advantages of complaining to the DGFT are likely to be:

(1) This route is likely to be cheaper for the complainant; if the DGFT can be persuaded to take the matter up he and his staff will be responsible for handling the case.
(2) The investigatory powers of the DGFT[1] are more likely to yield valuable evidence than the discovery process under English law.
(3) The defendant in proceedings in a national court in the United Kingdom will probably be able to invoke a privilege against self-incrimination[2]. The protection against self-incrimination afforded to an undertaking investigated by the European Commission under EC law is substantially weaker[3] and, if regard is had to that jurisprudence under

the CA 1998, this is likely also to be the case in respect of investigations by the DGFT.

(4) Whereas the claimant in proceedings before a court will have to establish a causal nexus between the loss which it has suffered and the alleged infringement of the Chapter I or II prohibitions, the DGFT is not so constrained.

1 See para **15.130** ff.
2 Civil Evidence Act 1968, s 14; see also *Rio Tinto Zinc v Westinghouse Electric Corpn* [1978] AC 547.
3 See paras **6.74–6.76**.

15.113
The principal advantages of commencing court proceedings are:

(1) The court can almost certainly award damages[1], the DGFT cannot.
(2) It is always open to the claimant to abandon his claim, albeit at the risk of being liable for a portion of the defendant's costs; conversely, if the DGFT decides to take up a complaint filed with it the complainant loses control over matters.
(3) Domestic courts in the United Kingdom are able to grant injunctions ex parte (ie without prior notice to the defendant). It is clear under the CA 1998 that, before the DGFT adopts interim measures, he must give written notice to the person whom he proposes to make subject to the direction and give that person an opportunity to make representations[2].
(4) The DGFT does not have the power to award legal costs to a successful complainant.
(5) The claimant may wish to assert other causes of action in relation to an alleged violation of the Chapter I or Chapter II prohibitions (for example, a claim based on other domestic claims, such as breach of contract, or based in the alternative on Articles 81 or 82 of the EC Treaty). Whereas all these causes of action can be asserted in the High Court, the DGFT is empowered to deal only with claims based on the Chapter I and Chapter II prohibitions.

1 See para **15.111**.
2 CA 1998, s 35(3).

15.114
If an injured party decides to take the complaint route, a further decision which it has to take is whether to complain to the DGFT (under the CA 1998) or to the European Commission (under Articles 81 or 82 of the EC Treaty). If the subject-matter of the complaint has a clear European dimension (for example, a cartel operating at an international level), a complaint to the Commission is likely to be the better route, not least because its powers of investigation[1] extend to the whole of the EU, whereas the OFT's investigatory powers are confined to the United Kingdom. However, in those cases which are more national in nature, it is likely that a complaint to the OFT will be the better route: it can frequently be difficult to persuade the Commission to take up a complaint, whereas the OFT is likely to be a more enthusiastic recipient of those complaints (at least those which have some substance) which have a primarily UK focus.

1 See para **6.01** ff.

(3) Interim Measures v Interlocutory Relief

15.115
In addition to the general considerations outlined at paras **15.112–15.113**, there are a number of specific points which need to be borne in mind where the potential complainant/claimant is suffering damage which requires a speedy remedy (for example, as a result of a refusal to supply by a dominant undertaking). Here the respective merits of a complaint to the DGFT, seeking interim measures[1], and an application to the High Court for interlocutory relief need to be considered. Factors to be borne in mind include:

(1) The availability of ex parte relief from a court, a remedy which is not available to the DGFT[2].
(2) The fact that the standard of proof of the alleged infringement required by the DGFT (reasonable suspicion of an infringement[3]) is rather stricter than the test applicable under English law (there must be a serious question to be tried[4]).
(3) The need under s 35(2) to establish serious, irreparable damage (or the need for action to protect the public interest) before the DGFT can take action.
(4) In both situations, there is a need to apply promptly.
(5) An English court will usually order a party in favour of whom interlocutory relief is granted to give a cross-undertaking in damages. There is nothing in the CA 1998 which addresses this specific issue in the context of an interim measures award by the DGFT.
(6) It is possible that the DGFT may take the view, on any application for interim measures, that the matter should be dealt with by the High Court (under Articles 81 and 82 of the EC Treaty, the European Commission routinely considers whether the case should be dealt with by the domestic courts[5]).
(7) It is likely to be the case, as in the case of European Commission proceedings[6], that the process leading up to the adoption of interim measures by the DGFT will take longer than that for an interlocutory injunction application.

1 See para **15.170**.
2 See para **15.173**.
3 CA 1998, s 35(1).
4 See *American Cyanamid Co v Ethicon Ltd* [1975] AC 396, [1975] 1 All ER 504, HL and subsequent case law.
5 See para **5.18**.
6 Ibid.

6 RIGHTS OF COMPLAINANT

(1) DGFT's Duty to Investigate?

15.116
There is nothing in the CA 1998, the Director's Rules or Guidelines issued by him to indicate what, if any, duty the DGFT has to investigate a complaint. The DGFT has stated[1] that he may:

> '. . . pursue the complaint or he may consider that the complaint does not reveal a possible breach of either of the prohibitions. If he intends to take no further action he will inform the complainant as soon as possible and then the matter will be closed or re-directed to another body if appropriate'.

Under Articles 81 and 82 of the EC Treaty, the ECJ has developed jurisprudence regarding the European Commission's duty to investigate complaints[2] and it remains to be seen whether that jurisprudence will be applied under the CA 1998[3]. If not, then the only remedy which would be available to the complainant would be to bring a judicial review action, which in practice is likely to be very difficult[4]. A refusal to pursue a complaint is not one of the decisions appealable to the Competition Commission[5].

1 The 'Major Provisions' Guidelines, para 8.3.
2 See para **5.19**.
3 Pursuant to CA 1998, s 60: see para **15.12** ff.
4 See para **15.252**.
5 See para **15.215**.

(2) Confidential Information

15.117
The treatment of confidential information provided by a complainant to a regulator is a notoriously difficult issue[1]. The position under the CA 1998 appears to be as follows.

1 See, in respect of Articles 81 and 82 of the EC Treaty, para **5.20** ff.

15.118
Sections 55 and 56 of the CA 1998 contain certain qualified restrictions regarding the disclosure of information obtained by the DGFT (or any regulator having concurrent powers) under or as a result of any provision of the Act. Those provisions do not, however, apply to information afforded voluntarily to the DGFT by a complainant.

15.119
Confidentiality is likely to be of concern to a complainant in two respects:

— the complainant may provide the DGFT with information which it regards as commercially sensitive;
— the very identity of the complainant may be a matter of some sensitivity, because the complainant may fear repercussions were the undertaking complained against to learn the identity of the complainant.

15.120
As far as the first of these issues is concerned, the prudent course is for a complainant to put commercially sensitive information in a separate Annex of its complaint. Paragraph 27 of the Director's Rules requires a third party (such as a complainant) providing the DGFT with information which it regards as confidential to set the confidential information out in a separate Annex marked as such and with an explanation as to why it should be

treated as such. Paragraph 30 of the Director's Rules defines information as confidential if it is either commercial information the disclosure of which would, or might, significantly harm the legitimate business interests of the undertaking to which it relates or information relating to the private affairs of an individual, the disclosure of which would, or might, significantly harm his interests.

15.121

Rule 27 goes on to provide that the DGFT must, if he proposes to disclose any of the information contained in the confidential Annex, give the person who provided the information written notice of the proposed action and a reasonable opportunity to make representations to him, if it is practicable to so. This provides only very modest comfort to a complainant and this relative lack of protection of a complainant's interests may deter some potential complainants from coming forward.

15.122

As far as the identity of the complainant itself is concerned, the DGFT's 'Major Provisions' Guidelines[1] state that it may be necessary to divulge the source of the complaint in order to provide the undertaking complained against with full details of the agreement or conduct about which the complaint has been made and in order to verify these details. The Guidelines note that a complainant may not want to be identified to the undertaking complained about and states that this should be made clear to the DGFT. The Guidelines do not, however, indicate what the DGFT would do if the complainant maintained its request for anonymity but the DGFT felt that it could only pursue the complaint by divulging the complainant's identity. It remains to be seen whether the ECJ judgment in the celebrated *Stanley Adams* case[2] will be applied: in that case, the ECJ held that where a person supplies information to the Commission voluntarily, accompanied by a specific request that his/its identity be kept secret, the Commission must comply with that condition. Following that judgment, the Commission issued internal instructions as to how its officials should deal with such information[3].

1 (OFT 400, March 2000), para 8.4.
2 Case 145/83, 53/84 *Adams v EC Commission* [1986] QB 138, [1985] ECR 3539.
3 See para **5.22**.

(3) Right of the Complainant to be Heard

15.123

There is jurisprudence under Articles 81 and 82 of the EC Treaty regarding the complainant's right to be heard[1]. There is nothing in the CA 1998 itself, or in the Director's Rules, regarding this issue. One can expect that complainants will demand similar rights to those which they have in relation to complaints made under Articles 81 and 82.

1 See para **5.23** ff.

(4) Rejection of Complaint

15.124
A complaint may be rejected in one of three ways:

- by simply being allowed to gather dust (ie inaction rather than an actual rejection);
- by means of a formal rejection of the complaint; or
- by means of a positive decision in favour of the agreement/conduct complained about (following a notification by the party/parties to the agreement/conduct in question), thereby amounting to an implicit rejection of the complaint.

15.125
As far as the first of these is concerned (which, assuming the DGFT adopts good administrative practice, one hopes will not arise), the position is as set out in para **15.217**. As far as the second of these is concerned, there is nothing on the face of the CA 1998 to suggest that the complainant has any recourse against a decision formally rejecting a complaint. This should be contrasted with the position under the jurisprudence of the ECJ in respect of complaints under Articles 81 and 82 and it remains to be seen whether that jurisprudence will have any application under the CA 1998. This appears unlikely, given the fact that the grounds of appeal to the CC are expressly set out in the CA 1998[1].

1 CA 1998, s 46.

15.126
It may be that the agreement or conduct complained of is the subject of a notification for a decision[1] by one or more of the parties to the agreement or persons involved in the conduct in question. In such circumstances, the DGFT is obliged[2] to arrange for the application to be published 'in such a way as he thinks most suitable for bringing it to the attention of those likely to be affected by it', unless he is satisfied that it would be sufficient for him to seek information from one or more particular persons other than the applicant. He is also obliged[3], in determining the application, to take account of third party representations. Paragraph 8 of the Director's Rules states that he will maintain a register on which will be entered, in respect of every application for a decision, a summary of the nature and objectives of the agreement or conduct in question (together with an indication of the outcome of the application). This register will be open to public inspection at the OFT's offices and also on a website to be established.

1 CA 1998, s 14 (agreements) and s 22 (conduct).
2 CA 1998, s 12(2)(b) and Sch 5, para 5 (agreements) and s 20(2)(b) and Sch 6, para 5 (conduct).
3 CA 1998, Sch 5, para 5(3) (agreements) and Sch 6, para 5(3) (conduct).

15.127
The Director's Rules indicate[1] that if he proposes to grant an exemption from the Chapter I prohibition he will 'consult the public'; if, however, he proposes to make a decision that the Chapter I prohibition has not been

infringed he may but has not committed to doing so[2]. Where he is proposing to make a decision that the Chapter II prohibition has not been infringed, again he may consult the public[3].

1 Para 12(1)(*a*).
2 Para 12(1)(*b*).
3 Para 12(2).

15.128
If the DGFT decides that there has been no infringement of the Chapter I or Chapter II prohibition, or that an exemption should be granted from the Chapter I prohibition (with or without conditions or obligations attached), the complainant may apply to the DGFT, asking him to withdraw or vary that decision[1]. The application must be made in writing within one month of publication of the decision and must be reasoned[2]. The DGFT may decide that the complainant does not have a sufficient interest or that the application has not shown sufficient reason to withdraw or vary the decision[3]. In both situations, the applicant can appeal the DGFT's decision (ie not to withdraw or vary) to the CC[4]. The making of an application does not have a suspensive effect in relation to the decision in question[5].

1 CA 1998, s 47(1).
2 CA 1998, s 47(2) and *Directors Rules*, para 28.
3 CA 1998, s 47(3) and (4).
4 CA 1998, s 47(6).
5 CA 1998, s 47(7).

(5) The Complainant and Defamation

15.129
By analogy with the Court of Appeal decision in *Hasselblad*[1] in the context of Article 81 and 82 proceedings, it should not be possible for a person to bring defamation proceedings against a complainant who has supplied evidence to the DGFT in support of a complaint.

1 *Hasselblad (GB) Ltd v Orbinson* [1985] QB 475, [1985] 1 All ER 173, [1984] 3 CLMR 679; see para **5.34**.

D Investigations by the DGFT

1 INTRODUCTION

15.130
A feature of UK competition law prior to the CA 1998 was the relatively weak powers of investigation which it gave to the DGFT. These were in stark contrast to the powers of investigation of the European Commission in relation to Articles 81 and 82 of the EC Treaty[1].

1 See para **6.01**ff.

15.131
Sections 25–29 of the CA 1998 give the DGFT greatly enhanced powers of investigation, specifically:

— the power to require the production of specified documents or specified information;
— the power to enter premises without a warrant; and
— the power to enter and search premises with a warrant.

These are backed up by criminal sanctions.

2 POWER TO INVESTIGATE

15.132
Section 25 of the CA 1998 provides that the DGFT may conduct an investigation if there are 'reasonable grounds' for suspecting that the Chapter I prohibition or the Chapter II prohibition has been infringed. This provides greater scope for the DGFT to exercise his investigative powers than was the case under the RTPA 1976. Under s 36 of that Act, the DGFT had to have 'reasonable cause' to believe that the proposed addressee was or might be a party to an agreement caught by that Act. In the *WH Smith* case[1] it was held that the DGFT had to be able to establish that there was a strong prima facie case as to the existence of an agreement caught by the RTPA 1976. The requirement merely for 'reasonable suspicion' is a lower threshold test.

1 *Registrar of Restrictive Trading Agreements v W H Smith & Son Ltd* [1969] 3 All ER 1065, LR 7 RP 122 CA.

15.133
It is only if the DGFT has reasonable grounds for suspecting an infringement of either the Chapter I or Chapter II prohibition that he can proceed to use his investigative powers. Examples of information which could amount to reasonable grounds include a complaint, statements from employees or ex-employees and press reports. It is likely that the provision will be given a broad interpretation.

15.134
The DGFT's 'Powers of Investigation' Guidelines state that the DGFT may seek to obtain information through informal inquiries rather than through the formal investigative powers set out in the Act[1]. Undertakings will frequently wish to co-operate with such informal inquiries rather than force him to consider his formal powers. However, he cannot compel an undertaking to respond to an informal inquiry which is not backed by his statutory powers.

1 (OFT 404, March 1999), para 2.3.

3 REQUESTS FOR INFORMATION/DOCUMENTS

15.135
Where the DGFT has reasonable grounds for suspecting an infringement of the Chapter I or Chapter II prohibition he may require any person to

produce to him a specified document, or to provide him with specified information, which he considers relates to any matter relevant to the investigation[1]. This broadly corresponds to an Article 11 request by the European Commission under Council Regulation 17/62[2].

1 CA 1998, s 26.
2 See para **6.02** ff.

15.136
The following points should be noted:

(1) This power must be exercised by a notice in writing which indicates the subject-matter and purpose of the investigation and the nature of the criminal offences related to non-compliance[1].
(2) Any person can be the recipient of such a notice; the most likely addressee would be the person or persons suspected of committing an infringement but a notice could also be sent to others, such as a complainant or a customer, supplier or competitor of the person(s) being investigated.
(3) To constitute a 'specified' document, it must be specified, or described, in the notice or fall within a category of documents so specified or described[2].
(4) The DGFT may specify the time within which the document is to be produced or the information provided[3]; where a document is required, the DGFT has the power to take copies of it. He is also empowered to require the person producing the document (or any person who is a past or present officer of that person, or is or was at any time employed by him) to provide an explanation of the document[4]. A person required to provide an explanation of a document my be accompanied by a legal adviser[5].
(5) If the document in question is not produced, the person to whom the notice is addressed can be required to state, to the best of his knowledge and belief, where it is[6].
(6) The term 'document' includes information recorded in any form[7]. It could therefore include records held on computer.

1 See para **15.157**.
2 CA 1998, s 26(4).
3 CA 1998, s 26(5).
4 CA 1998, s 26(6)(*a*)(ii).
5 *Director's Rules*, para 13(3).
6 CA 1998, s 26(6)(*a*).
7 CA 1998, s 59(1).

15.137
The power to require documents or information provided for in s 26 operates entirely independently of the power to enter premises provided for in ss 27 and 28[1]. Accordingly, the s 26 power could be used either on its own or prior to or after exercise of the powers under ss 27 and 28. There is also in principle no reason why one person should not be the subject of more than one s 26 notice over a period of time.

1 See para **15.138** ff.

4 POWER TO ENTER PREMISES

15.138
The CA 1998 gives the DGFT two sets of powers to enter premises, one without a warrant and one with a warrant. These are considered in turn below. The power to enter without a warrant corresponds in broad terms to the provisions of Article 14 of Council Regulation 17/62 (investigations by the European Commission)[1]. Force cannot be used by the DGFT's investigating officers when entering without a warrant. However, in those circumstances where they are empowered to enter with a warrant 'reasonable force' may be used.

1 See paras **6.27**–**6.73**.

(1) Without a Warrant

Circumstances in which the power can be used

15.139
As in the case of the power to request specified documents or information, the power to enter premises only applies if the DGFT has reasonable grounds for suspecting an infringement of the Chapter I or Chapter II prohibition. An investigating officer can only enter premises pursuant to s 27 if he has given the occupier of the premises at least two working days' prior written notice of the intended entry[1]. However, this requirement does not apply if the DGFT has a reasonable suspicion that the premises are, or have been, occupied by a party to an agreement being investigated in respect of the Chapter I prohibition or conduct being investigated in respect of the Chapter II prohibition; similarly, if the investigating officer has taken all steps that are reasonably practicable to give notice but has not been able to do so[2].

1 CA 1998, s 27(2)(*a*).
2 CA 1998, s 27(3).

Procedure to be followed

15.140
Where the investigating officer is seeking to enter premises after the giving of two prior working days' notice, that notice must indicate the subject-matter and purpose of the investigation and indicate the criminal offences to which non-compliance could give rise[1]. Where entry is sought in circumstances in which two prior working days' notice is not given[2], the investigating officer must produce evidence of his authorisation and a document which indicates the subject-matter and purpose of the investigation and indicates the criminal offences which can flow from non-compliance.

1 CA 1998, s 27(2).
2 CA 1998, s 27(4).

15.141
The DGFT's Powers of Investigation Guidelines state that an investigating officer will hand over a document which sets out his powers and states that the occupier of the premises may request that its legal adviser be present[1].

1 (OFT 404, March 1999), para 4.9. See para **15.144**.

Powers of the investigating officer

15.142
Under s 27(5), an investigating officer entering premises pursuant to s 27 may:

— take with him such equipment as appears to be necessary (this might, for example, include portable computer or tape-recording equipment);
— require any person[1] on the premises to produce any document which he considers relates to any matter relevant to the investigation and, if such a document is produced, to provide an explanation of it;
— require any person to state, to the best of his knowledge and belief, where any such document is to be found;
— take copies of, or extracts from any document which is produced;
— require any information held on a computer and which is accessible from the premises (and which the investigating officer considers relates to any matter relevant to the investigation) to be produced in a form in which it can be taken away and in which it is visible and legible.

1 In this context, the word 'person' presumably means an individual, rather than an undertaking. There is no express restriction as to who the person needs to be; it could therefore include, for example, secretaries and IT personnel: see HL Committee, 17 November 1997, col 391 (Lord Simon).

15.143
It should be noted that for the purposes of s 27 the term 'premises' includes any vehicle (for example, a company car) but does not include domestic premises unless they are also used in connection with the affairs of an undertaking or documents relating to the affairs of an undertaking are kept there[1].

1 CA 1998, s 59(1).

Right of access to legal advice

15.144
The CA 1998 is silent regarding the extent to which a person whose premises are entered pursuant to s 27 has the right to access to legal advice. However, this issue is addressed in the Director's Rules[1], para 13 of which states that an investigating officer will grant a request of the occupier of premises to allow 'a reasonable time' for the occupier's legal advisor to arrive at the premises before the investigation continues, if the officer considers it reasonable in the circumstances to do so and if he is satisfied that such conditions as he considers it appropriate to impose in granting the

occupier's request are, or will be, complied with. Paragraph 13 somewhat opaquely provides that 'a reasonable time' is such period as the officer considers is reasonable in the circumstances. Paragraph 4.10 of the DGFT's Powers of Investigation Guidelines indicates that the DGFT's practice in this regard 'will go no further' than the practice of the European Commission when determining how long to wait for legal advisers to arrive. The following points should be noted:

(1) The position under EC law[2] is that European Commission investigating officials will typically wait up to (but no longer than) an hour for legal advisers to arrive. They would not, however, be willing to delay the investigation for the arrival of external legal advisers if the company has in-house legal advisers available[3].
(2) The sort of conditions which the DGFT's investigating officers might impose as a condition for delaying the investigation pending the arrival of legal advisers could include the sealing of cabinets, keeping business records in the same state and place as when the investigating officers arrived, suspending external e-mail and allowing the investigating officers to enter and remain in occupation of offices of their choice[4].

1 These Rules form a Schedule to the Competition Act 1998 (Director's Rules) Order 2000, SI 2000/293.
2 See para **6.73**.
3 *OFT's Powers of Investigation Guidelines*, para 4.11 (OFT 404, March 1999).
4 Ibid.

(2) With a Warrant

Circumstances in which the power can be used

15.145
The DGFT can apply to a judge to issue a warrant enabling a named investigating officer (and accompanying officers) to enter premises in three situations[1]:

(*a*) where the judge is satisfied that there are reasonable grounds for suspecting that there are on any premises documents, the production of which has been required under ss 26 or 27 and which have not been produced as required;
(*b*) where the judge is satisfied that there are reasonable grounds for suspecting that there are on any premises documents which the DGFT has power under s 26 to require to be produced and if the documents were required to be produced, they would not be produced but would be concealed, removed, tampered with or destroyed; or
(*c*) where the judge is satisfied that an investigating officer has attempted to enter premises in the exercise of his powers under s 27 but has been unable to do so and that there are reasonable grounds for suspecting that there are on the premises documents, the production of which could have been required under that section.

1 CA 1998, s 28.

15.146
It can be seen from para **15.145** that the only situation in which a warrant can be obtained to carry out an on-site investigation without an attempt first being made to use the powers provided for in ss 26 or 27 (power to request documents/information and power to enter premises without a warrant) is where there are reasonable grounds for suspecting that there are documents on the premises which could be required to be provided under the s 26 powers but, if they were so required, would be concealed, removed, tampered with or destroyed.

Procedure to be followed

15.147
A warrant issued under s 28 must indicate the subject-matter and purpose of the investigation and the nature of the criminal offences which can arise from non-co-operation[1]. A warrant issued under s 28 is valid for a period of one month from the date of issuance[2]. As in the case of entry under s 27 an investigating officer can take with him such equipment as appears to him to be necessary (for example, computer equipment or tape-recording equipment)[3]. However, this provision would also allow him to take with him equipment to make a forcible entry[4]. This is one of the important practical differences between entry with and without a warrant.

1 CA 1998, s 29(1).
2 CA 1998, s 28(6).
3 CA 1998, s 28(4).
4 Such as equipment to break locks: see *OFT's Powers of Investigation Guidelines*, para 5.5 (OFT 404, March 1999).

15.148
If the premises in question are unoccupied the investigating officer must, before executing the warrant, take such steps as are reasonable in all the circumstances to inform the occupier of the intended entry and, if the occupier is informed, afford him or his legal or other representative a reasonable opportunity to be present when the warrant is executed[1]. If the named officer is unable to inform the occupier of the intended entry he must, when executing the warrant, leave a copy of it in a prominent place on the premises[2]. On leaving premises which he has entered by virtue of warrant issued under s 28, the investigating officer must, if the premises are unoccupied or the occupier is temporarily absent, leave them as effectively secured as he found them[3].

1 CA 1998, s 29(3).
2 CA 1998, s 29(4).
3 CA 1998, s 29(5).

Powers of the investigating officer

15.149
A warrant issued under s 28 authorises a named officer of the DGFT (plus accompanying officers):

(1) To enter the specified premises, 'using such force as is reasonably necessary for the purpose'. Force cannot be used against the person[1].
(2) To search the premises and take copies of, or extracts from, any document appearing to be of a kind in respect of which the application for a warrant was granted. The officer is entitled to search offices, desks and filing cabinets etc.
(3) To take possession of any documents appearing to be of the relevant kind if such action appears to be necessary for preserving the documents or preventing interference with them or if it is not reasonably practicable to take copies of the documents on the premises. Unlike in the case of entry without a warrant, originals of documents may therefore be taken.
(4) To require any person to provide an explanation of any document appearing to be of the relevant kind or to state, to the best of his knowledge and belief, where it may be found.
(5) To require information held in a computer and accessible from the premises and which the named officer considers relates to any matter relevant to the investigation to be produced in a form which can be taken away and in which it is visible and legible[2].

1 *OFT's Powers of Investigation Guidelines*, para 5.4 (OFT 404, March 1999).
2 CA 1998, s 28(2).

Right of access to legal advice

15.150
The position is the same as in relation to the power to enter premises without a warrant[1].

1 See para **15.144**.

5 GENERAL LIMITATIONS ON INVESTIGATORY POWERS

(1) Privileged Communications

15.151
Under s 30, a person cannot be required, under any of the DGFT's investigative powers, to produce or disclose a privileged communication. This is defined[1] to mean a communication between a professional legal adviser and his client or made in connection with, or in contemplation of legal proceedings for the purposes of those proceedings, which (in either case) in proceedings in the High Court would be protected from disclosure on grounds of legal professional privilege.

1 CA 1998, s 30(2).

15.152
UK courts interpret[1] the term 'professional legal adviser' as including in-house lawyers as well as lawyers in private practice. Accordingly, the scope for legal privilege afforded under the CA 1998 is broader than that afforded

under the jurisprudence under the ECJ in the context of Article 81 and Article 82 investigations[2].

1 See 13 *Halsbury's Laws* (4th edn) paras 71–85.
2 See para **11.14**.

(2) Defence Against Self-incrimination

15.153
Paragraph 6.3 of the DGFT's Powers of Investigation Guidelines[1] states clearly that the defence against self-incrimination which has been recognised under EC jurisprudence[2] will apply. Paragraph 6.3 refers in this context specifically to s 60 of the CA 1998[3], albeit that this is a procedural rather than a substantive issue. As a result, the DGFT (or investigating officers) can require an undertaking to provide specific documents or specified information, including explanations of documents, but cannot compel the provision of answers which might involve an admission on its part of the existence of an infringement of either the Chapter I or Chapter II prohibitions. He may, however, request documents or information relating to facts (for example, whether a particular meeting took place and, if so, when it took place and who was present at it).

1 (OFT 404, March 1999).
2 See Case 374/87 *Orkem v EC Commission* [1989] ECR 3283; see also para **11.51**.
3 See para **15.22** ff.

(3) Confidential Documents

15.154
Documents or information whose disclosure is required under ss 26–28 may well contain highly sensitive business information. That does not provide a basis for the refusal to provide such information. However, the CA 1998 does place some restrictions on the onward disclosure of that information. The general principle is that no information which has been obtained pursuant to the provisions in ss 26–28 and relates to the affairs of any individual or to any particular business of an undertaking is to be disclosed during the lifetime of that individual or while that business continues unless consent to disclosure has been obtained from the person from whom the information was initially obtained and, if different, the individual to whose affairs the information relates or the person for the time being carrying on the business to which the information relates[1].

1 CA 1998, s 55(1), (2).

15.155
This general principle is, however, subject to a number of significant qualifications; in particular, the non-disclosure obligation does not apply to a disclosure made for the purpose of facilitating the performance of the DGFT's functions. Where the DGFT is considering whether to disclose any information acquired by him pursuant to ss 26–28, he is required to have

regard to the need for excluding, so far as is practicable, information the disclosure of which would in his opinion be contrary to the public interest[1]. He is also required to have regard to the need for excluding, so far as is practicable, commercial information the disclosure of which would, or might, in his opinion significantly harm the legitimate business interests of the undertaking to which it relates (or information relating to the private affairs of an individual the disclosure of which would, or might, in his opinion, significantly harm his interests) and the extent to which the disclosure is necessary for the purposes for which the Secretary of State or the DGFT is proposing to make the disclosure[2]. This effectively requires a balancing of these conflicting factors.

1 CA 1998, s 56(2).
2 CA 1998, s 56(3).

6 CRIMINAL SANCTIONS

15.156
The CA 1998 introduces a number of criminal offences in respect of failure by a person to comply with requirements imposed on him under ss 26, 27 or 28. It is not unusual for UK statutes to back up their enforcement powers with criminal sanctions. However, in doing so, the CA 1998 introduces criminal sanctions in circumstances where there is no similar scope for the imposition of criminal sanctions by the European Commission in exercise of its powers pursuant to Articles 81 and 82 of the EC Treaty.

(1) The Offences Themselves

15.157
The CA 1998 introduces the following specific offences (subject to the defences outlined in para **15.159**):

(*a*) a person is guilty of an offence[1] if he fails to comply with a requirement imposed on him under ss 26, 27 or 28[2];
(*b*) a person is guilty of an offence if he intentionally obstructs an officer acting in the exercise of his powers under s 27 or a warrant issued under s 28[3];
(*c*) a person is guilty of an offence if, having been required to produce a document under ss 26, 27 or 28 he intentionally or recklessly destroys or otherwise disposes of it, falsifies it or conceals it, or he causes or permits its destruction, disposal, falsification or concealment[4];
(*d*) it is an offence for a person to provide the DGFT with information which is false or misleading in a material particular, in circumstances where the person providing it knows that it is or is reckless as to whether it is; similarly, where a person provides such information to another person (for example, its legal adviser), knowing that the information is to be used for the purpose of providing information to the DGFT in connection with the exercise of any of his powers under the Act[5].

1 CA 1998, s 42(1).
2 See para **15.135** ff.
3 CA 1998, s 42(5) and (7).
4 CA 1998, s 43(1).
5 CA 1998, s 44(1) and (2).

15.158

If any such offence as is described in para **15.157** committed by a body corporate is proved to have been committed with the consent or connivance of an officer, or to be attributable to any neglect on his part, the officer as well as the body corporate is guilty of the offence and liable to be proceeded against[1]. For this purpose, the term 'officer' means a director, manager, secretary or other similar officer of the body, or a person brought in to act in any such capacity[2].

1 CA 1998, s 72(2).
2 CA 1998, s 72(3).

(2) Defences

15.159

There are various defences to charges brought pursuant to ss 42–44:

— if a person is charged under s 42 in respect of a requirement to produce a document, it is a defence for him to prove that the document was not in his possession or under his control and that it was not reasonably practicable for him to comply with the requirement[1];

— if a person is charged with an offence under s 42 in respect of a requirement to provide information or an explanation of a document, or to state where a document is to be found, it is a defence for him to prove that he had a reasonable excuse for failing to comply with the requirement[2];

— failure to comply with a requirement imposed under ss 26 or 27 is not an offence if the person imposing the requirement has failed to act in accordance with that section[3].

1 CA 1998, s 42(2).
2 CA 1998, s 42(3).
3 CA 1998, s 42(4).

(3) Sanctions

15.160

Offences will be tried either summarily in the Magistrates Court (or Sheriff Court in Scotland) or, in the case of more serious offences, on indictment in the Crown Court (or the High Court of the Justiciary in Scotland). A person liable on summary conviction for any of the offences outlined in para **15.157** is liable to a fine not exceeding the statutory maximum (currently £5,000). In respect of conviction or indictment for failing to comply with a requirement imposed under ss 26, 27 or 28, the person guilty of the offence is liable to a fine of unlimited amount. In respect of the other offences (intentional obstruction of an officer acting in the exercise of his powers under s 27 or under a warrant issued under s 28, destroying or falsifying documents and providing false or misleading information–see para **15.157** above) the maximum penalty is imprisonment for a term exceeding two years, or a fine (of unlimited amount), or both.

E Enforcement

1 INTRODUCTION

15.161
The DGFT has a number of powerful remedies at his disposal to enforce compliance with the Chapter I and Chapter II prohibitions:

— he may give directions designed to bring the infringement to an end;
— he may in certain circumstances give interim measures directions; and
— he may impose financial penalties.

These enforcement powers are considered in turn below. They represent a very considerable strengthening of the powers available to the DGFT compared to those available under the previous legislation (principally the RTPA 1976).

15.162
It is clearly intended[1] that the CA 1998 should create the right to bring private actions. Indeed, the DGFT has stated[2] that third parties who consider they have suffered loss as a result of an unlawful agreement have a claim for damages in the courts. In this context, a decision taken by the DGFT may have a significant bearing on the outcome of a subsequent private action arising out of the same alleged infringement. This is because of s 58, which provides that, unless a court directs otherwise, a finding of fact made by the DGFT in the course of determining an application for a decision under s 14 or s 22[3], or conducting an investigation under s 25[4], and which is relevant to an issue arising in Chapter I or Chapter II proceedings not brought by him, is binding on the parties.

1 See para **15.16**.
2 *OFT's Guidelines The Chapter I Prohibition*, para 6.5 (OFT 401, March 1999).
3 See paras **15.65** ff and **15.83** ff.
4 See para **15.132**.

2 DIRECTIONS

(1) Introduction

15.163
If the DGFT proposes to make a decision that the Chapter I or Chapter II prohibition has been infringed, he must give written notice to the applicant

(when there has been a notification), any other person who the DGFT is aware is a party to the agreement or conduct and any such person where there has been no notification. That notice must state the reasons for the decision and the action he proposes to take; the DGFT must also:

- provide the recipients of such a notice with an opportunity to make written and oral representations; and
- if requested, provide an opportunity to inspect the DGFT's file (excluding confidential documents and internal DGFT documents)[1].

For this purpose, the term internal document includes documents produced within the office of the DGFT (or another regulator), correspondence between the DGFT and another regulator (or between regulators) and correspondence between the DGFT (or another regulator) and a Government department or another authority (which clearly could include the European Commission or another national competition authority)[2]. If the DGFT subsequently makes a decision regarding the issue of infringement, he must notify the same category of persons of the decision, the facts on which it is based and his reasoning and publish the decision without delay[3].

1 *Director's Rules*, para 14.
2 Ibid, para 30(1)(f).
3 Ibid, para 15.

(2) In Relation to Agreements

15.164
Under s 32 of the CA 1998, if the DGFT has made a decision that an agreement infringes the Chapter I prohibition, he may give to such person or persons as he considers appropriate such directions as he considers appropriate to bring the infringement to an end. Section 32(3) specifically provides that a direction may include provision requiring the parties to the agreement to modify it or requiring them to terminate it. This does not purport to be an exhaustive list of the remedial action which he may take.

15.165
It should be noted that directions can be given to any person whom the DGFT considers appropriate. Most obviously, this would include the parties to the agreement in question. However, it could also extend to parents, affiliates or private individuals with the ability to influence or procure actions by the infringing persons[1].

1 See *OFT's Enforcement Guidelines*, para 2.2 (OFT 407, March 1999).

(3) In Relation to Conduct

15.166
Section 33 contains corresponding provisions regarding directions in relation to conduct. Section 33(3) provides that such directions may, in

particular, include provision requiring the person concerned to modify the conduct in question or requiring him to cease that conduct altogether.

15.167
Directions under ss 32 or 33 could not require divestment of all or part of a business: such structural remedies would only be appropriate following a monopoly investigation under the provisions of the FTA 1973[1].

1 See para **14.01** ff.

(4) Enforcement Directions

15.168
Under s 34 of the CA 1998, if a person fails, without reasonable excuse, to comply with a direction under ss 32 or 33 the DGFT may apply to the court for an order requiring compliance. Such a court order may provide for all of the costs of, or incidental to, the application for the order to be borne by the person in default or any officer of an undertaking who was responsible for the default[1]. Breach of such an order would be contempt of court, punishable by fines or imprisonment, at the court's discretion[2].

1 CA 1998, s 34(2)
2 *OFT's Enforcement Guidelines*, para 2.9 (OFT 407, March 1999).

(5) Procedure

15.169
Any direction given by the DGFT will set out the facts on which it is based and the reasons for it and will be published.

1 *Director's Rules*, paras 15 and 17.

3 INTERIM MEASURES

15.170
A powerful new tool available to the DGFT is the ability to make an interim measures direction under s 35 of the CA 1998. One of the complaints frequently levelled at UK competition law prior to the CA 1998 was that there was very little scope for the DGFT to take swift action even in respect of manifest violations of the RTPA 1976. A person suffering damage from an anti-competitive agreement or anti-competitive conduct has the choice under the new Act of seeking to persuade the DGFT to make an interim measures direction or applying to the High Court for interlocutory relief. The relative advantages and disadvantages of each are considered in para **15.115**.

15.171
In order for the DGFT to be able to make an interim measures direction the following conditions must be satisfied:

- the DGFT must have 'reasonable suspicion' that either the Chapter I prohibition or Chapter II prohibition has been infringed but he has not completed his investigation into the matter;
- the DGFT must consider that it is necessary for him to act as a matter of urgency for the purpose of either preventing serious, irreparable damage to a particular person or category of person or of protecting the public interest.

15.172

It is somewhat strange that the DGFT may make an interim measures direction on 'public interest' grounds, whereas his power to make a final decision under the Chapter I and Chapter II prohibitions is based on damage to competition. The term 'public interest' is not defined in the CA 1998[1]. However, during the Parliamentary debates on the Bill, the Government said that, in accordance with EC principles of proportionality, the DGFT's interim measures should not exceed what was necessary to achieve the proposed objective (which, one assumes, must somehow link the interim measures direction to the objective of any final decision)[2].

1 The definition does exist in FTA 1973, s 84, but only for the purposes of that Act.
2 HL Report Stage, 19 February 1998, col 356 (Lord Simon).

15.173

Before giving an interim measures direction, the DGFT must give written notice to the person(s) to whom he proposes to give the direction and give that person(s) an opportunity to make representations[1]. Such a notice must indicate the nature of the direction which the DGFT is proposing to give and his reasons[2]. The DGFT must allow the person receiving the notice an opportunity to make representations to him and that person may request a meeting to make oral representations[3]. He may also ask to inspect the DGFT's file relating to the proposed direction (excluding confidential information and the DGFT's internal documents[4]). It appears that the DGFT envisages a rather less formal process than applies under the equivalent EC regime[5]. It remains to be seen if that proves to be the case. An interim measures direction only has effect until such time as the DGFT has completed his investigation, at which time it may be replaced (if appropriate) by a direction under ss 32 or 33[6].

1 CA 1998, s 35(3).
2 CA 1998, s 35(4).
3 *OFT's Enforcement Guidelines*, para 3.10 (OFT 407, March 1999).
4 *Director's Rules*, para 18. As to the meaning of the term 'internal document', see para **15.163**.
5 See para **7.27** ff.
6 CA 1998, s 35(5).

15.174

Interim measures directions are enforceable in the same way as final directions under ss 32 and 33[1]. They are appealable to the Competition Commission[2] but appeal does not automatically cause the effect of the directions to be suspended.

1 CA 1998, s 35(7).
2 CA 1998, s 46(3). See para **15.201**

15.175
The interim measures powers of the DGFT are broadly similar to those of the European Commission under Articles 81 and 82 of the EC Treaty[1]. However, the OFT's 'Enforcement' Guidelines[2] suggest that the burden of proof in EC law is too high to make the use of interim measures effective and that they will feature to a greater extent under the CA 1998. We must wait to see whether that is borne out in practice.

1 See para **8.05** ff.
2 OFT 407 (March 1999).

4 PENALTIES

(1) Circumstances in which a Penalty may be Imposed

15.176
The DGFT may impose a penalty on an undertaking found to have infringed the Chapter 1 prohibition or the Chapter II prohibition but only if he is satisfied that the infringement was committed intentionally or negligently[1]. This is subject to limited immunity for so-called small agreements and conduct of minor significance[2].

1 CA 1998, s 36(1)–(3).
2 See para **15.201**.

15.177
The requirement that an infringement be committed intentionally or negligently mirrors the corresponding principle in Council Regulation 17/62/EEC in respect of Articles 81 and 82 of the EC Treaty[1]. This followed debate[2] in Parliament as to whether specific reference to intention or negligence was required, given the provisions of s 60[3] of the CA 1998. The better view is that s 60 does not import the provisions of Council Regulation 17/62. The DGFT is likely to find that an infringement has been committed negligently when an undertaking knew or ought to have known that its actions would result in infringement[4].

1 See para **9.16**.
2 HL consideration of Commons' Amendments, 20 October 1998, cols 1373–1376 (Lord McIntosh).
3 See para **15.22** ff.
4 *DGFT's Enforcement Guidelines*, para 4.9.

15.178
Notice of a penalty imposed under s 36 must be given in writing and must specify the date before which the penalty is required to be paid[1]. That date must not be earlier than the end of the period within which appeal against the notice may be brought under s 46[2]. It is likely that payment will be required within three months from the date of the notice[3]. When the DGFT requires payment of a penalty, he must inform the person in writing of the facts on which he bases the penalty and his reasons for requiring that person to pay it[4]. All sums received by the DGFT under s 36 are paid into the Consolidated Fund[5].

1 CA 1998, s 36(6)
2 CA 1998, s 36(7).
3 *OFT's Enforcement Guidelines*, para 4.41 (OFT 407, March 1999) .
4 *Director's Rules*, para 17(2).
5 CA 1998, s 36(9).

(2) Upper Limit for Penalties

15.179

Under s 36(8) of the CA 1998 no penalty fixed by the DGFT under s 36 may exceed 10% of the turnover of the undertaking. The statute is silent as to whether this is worldwide turnover or UK turnover. During the passage of the Bill through Parliament the Government confirmed that reference to turnover is to turnover arising in the UK[1]. This differs from the position which applies in respect of Articles 81 and 82 of the EC Treaty under Council Regulation 17/62[2]. Turnover is to be determined in accordance with provisions specified by order of the Secretary of State[3]. The Order[4] reflects the principle that, for the purpose of calculating the upper limit for penalties, turnover should be limited to UK turnover. It also reflects a policy decision announced in August 1999 that, for the purpose of the upper limit, turnover should be calculated in respect of the period of the infringement, up to a maximum of three years[5]. This latter approach was not foreshadowed during the passage of the Competition Act through Parliament and contrasts with the position under the EC Treaty, Articles 81 and 82, where the upper limit is limited to turnover in the preceding business year. The policy approach adopted in the UK effectively means that the upper limit is 30% of annual turnover in the UK.

1 HC SC G, 16 June 1998, col 454 (Nigel Griffiths MP).
2 Council Regulation 17/62/EEC/OJ L13, 21.2.62, p 204(s) edn 1959–62 p 87.
3 CA 1998, s 36(8).
4 The Competition Act 1998 (Determination of Turnover for Penalties) Order 2000, SI 2000/309.
5 *Tough Penalties for Anti-Competitive Practices*, DTI Press Release, 9 August 1999.

15.180

Specifically, the Order provides that the 10% of turnover limit for penalties is calculated by reference to 'the period of the infringement', namely:

- — the period between the dates on which an infringement of the Chapter I or the Chapter II prohibition is determined to have begun and ended; or
- — where such a period is less than *twelve months*, the period of twelve months ending on the date in the decision on which the infringement of the Chapter I or the Chapter II prohibition is determined to have ended; or
- — where such a period exceeds *three years*, the period of three years ending on the date of the decision on which the infringement is determined to have ended for the purposes of that decision.

15.181

The UK Government has rejected the idea that, for the purpose of calculating the upper limit, turnover should be limited to that on the market in which the infringement is taking place. In reaching that view, the Government has noted that the DGFT's guidance on penalties[1] will take this factor into account in any event when deciding what level of penalty to impose. In this respect, the position is the same as under Articles 81 and 82, EC Treaty[2].

1 See para **15.183**ff.
2 See para **9.38**.

15.182
The Order contains detailed accounting provisions whereby turnover is to be calculated, modelled on Article 5 of the EC Merger Regulation (4069/89). There are special provisions in relation to credit institutions, financial institutions and insurance undertakings. It is unclear why the Government feels it to be essential to have detailed rules for calculating turnover for the purpose of ascertaining the maximum level of fine which may be imposed. There is no definition of turnover in Article 15 of Council Regulation 17/62, the corresponding EC provision. Where an association of undertakings is the subject of a penalty, the turnover of that association is the aggregate turnover of the undertakings that are members of the association[1]. This corresponds with the position in respect of EC Treaty, Articles 81 and 82[2]. In terms of deciding whether turnover is generated in the United Kingdom, para 5(2) of the Order provides that, in determining where goods are sold or services provided, the turnover is to be attributed to the place where the customer is located when purchasing the goods or services.

1 The Competition Act 1998 (Determination of Turnover for Penalties) Order 2000, SI 2000/309, para 7.
2 See para **9.38**.

(3) Likely Approach of DGFT to Level of Penalties

15.183
The OFT's Enforcement Guidelines indicate that the DGFT intends to use his powers to impose penalties to the extent necessary to deter as well as to punish infringement[1]. The deterrent is not aimed solely at the undertaking the subject of the decision but at other undertakings who might be considering similar action[2]. Factors which he will take into account include the duration and gravity of the infringement and the degree of intention or negligence. Under s 38 of the CA 1998, the DGFT is required to prepare and publish guidance on the appropriate level of any penalty. Such guidance must first be approved by the Secretary of State. The DGFT may alter his guidance at any time but must publish it as altered (again with the approval of the Secretary of State[3]). The DGFT must have regard to this guidance when setting penalties[4]. He published draft Guidance in August 1999 and this was formalised[5] on the coming into force of the Act, having been approved by the Secretary of State in January 2000.

1 OFT 407 (March 1999), para 4.2.
2 Ibid.
3 CA 1998, s 38(2), (3). Para 4.32.

4 CA 1998, s 38(8).
5 OFT 423, March 2000.

Basic approach

15.184
The DGFT's Guidance states that his policy objectives are to impose penalties in infringing undertakings and to ensure that the threat of penalties will deter undertakings from engaging in anti-competitive practices. He has stated[1] that he intends to impose financial penalties which are severe, in particular in respect of agreements between undertakings which fix prices or share markets and other 'cartel' activities (defined for the purpose of the Guidance as agreements which involve price-fixing, bid rigging, the establishment of output restrictions or quotas and/or market sharing or market dividing).

1 Para 2.

15.185
Having stated those objectives, the Guidance goes on (*a*) to set out the steps that the DGFT will follow when calculating the amount of a penalty and (*b*) to provide a policy which will encourage 'whistleblowers' to come forward and reveal the existence and activities of a cartel, by granting such whistleblowers lenient treatment. These two aspects are considered in turn below.

15.186
The DGFT's Guidance contemplates a five-step approach to the calculation of financial penalties[1]:

(*a*) step 1—calculation of the starting point by applying a percentage determined by the nature of the infringement to the 'relevant turnover' of the undertaking;
(*b*) step 2—adjustment for duration;
(*c*) step 3—adjustment for other factors;
(*d*) step 4—adjustment for further aggravating or mitigating factors; and
(*e*) step 5—adjustment if the maximum penalty of 10% of the turnover of the undertaking is exceeded and to avoid double jeopardy.

1 Para 3.1.

15.187
In respect of step 1 (starting point), the DGFT will apply a percentage rate to the 'relevant turnover' of the undertaking, up to a maximum of 10%. For this purpose, the relevant turnover is the turnover of the undertaking in the relevant product market and geographic market affected by the infringement in the last financial year. The Guidance states that the starting point for penalties for price-fixing or market-sharing agreements and other cartel activities, and conduct which infringes the Chapter II prohibition and has or is likely to have a significant impact on the competitive process, is likely to be at or near 10% of the 'relevant turnover'[1] The damage caused to third parties and consumers as a result of the infringement will also be considered.

1 Para 4.

15.188
In respect of step 2 (adjustment for duration), penalties for infringements which last for more than one year may be multiplied by a number equal to or less than the number of years of the infringement (infringements lasting for only part of a year will be treated as lasting for a full year for these purposes)[1].

1 *DGFT's Guidance*, para 5 (OFT 423, March 2000).

15.189
At step 3, the penalty figure reached after the calculations in steps 1 and 2 may be adjusted, as appropriate to achieve the policy objectives (eg deterrent effect) and to take into account factors such as the estimated actual gain from the infringement[1]. Somewhat ominously, para 6.2 of the Guidance states that the step 3 adjustment may result in a substantial uplift of the financial penalty calculated under steps 1 and 2.

1 Para 6.

15.190
At step 4, the amount of the financial penalty reached through a combination of steps 1–3 may be increased by reference to aggravating factors or decreased by reference to mitigating factors. Amongst the aggravating factors cited are the role of the undertaking as a ring-leader, the involvement of the directors or senior management, retaliatory measures taken against other undertakings aimed at ensuring the continuation of the infringement, continuing the infringement after the start of the investigation and repeated infringements of the same type by the same undertaking or undertakings in the same group. Mitigating factors include where the undertaking has acted under severe duress or pressure, genuine uncertainty as to whether the agreement or conduct constituted an infringement, the existence of adequate steps to ensure compliance with the Act[1], the fact that infringement has been negligent rather than intentional and co-operation which enables the enforcement process to be concluded more effectively and/or speedily than would otherwise be the case, over and above that expected of any undertaking[2].

1 See para **2.02** ff in relation to compliance programmes. The Guidance refers to the Office of Fair Trading training booklet 'How your business can achieve compliance – A guide to achieving compliance with the Competition Act 1998' (OFT 424, August 1999).
2 *DGFT Guidance on penalties*, para 7.

15.191
In relation to compliance programmes, the OFT's Enforcement Guidelines state[1] that, in order for such a programme to lead to a reduced penalty:

— it must be actively implemented;
— it must have the visible and continuing support of, and be observed by, senior management;
— there must be appropriate compliance policies and procedures in place;
— there must be active and ongoing training for employees whose activities may be 'touched by competition law'; and

— the programme must be evaluated and formal audits carried out at regular intervals.

1 (OFT 407, March 2000), para 4.35.

15.192

Step 5 involves ensuring that the penalty calculated according to steps 1–4 does not in any event exceed 10% of the turnover of the undertaking (calculated in the way set out in para **15.179** ff)[1]. In addition, para 8.3 of the Guidance notes that, if a penalty or fine has been imposed by the European Commission, or by a court or other body in a member state in respect of an agreement or conduct, the DGFT must take that penalty or fine into account when setting the amount of the penalty in relation to that agreement or conduct[2].

1 *DGFT Guidance on Penalties*, para 8.
2 See para **15.199**.

Whistleblowing

15.193

A whole section of the Guidance on penalties is dedicated to the subject of lenient treatment for whistleblowers. This largely mirrors the position adopted by the European Commission in its notice on the subject[1] but with certain differences. The DGFT has also been strongly influenced by the whistleblowing policy under US anti-trust law[2].

1 See Commission Notice on the non-imposition or reduction of fines in cartel cases [1996] C207/4 and para **9.42**.
2 See *The Competition Act 1998 and EC Jurisprudence* by John Bridgeman, Director General of Fair Trading, PEBL Vol I, Issue 3 (December 1999), in which he notes that the OFT decided to follow the US approach because of its undoubted success, cartels being reported there at the rate of around two a month.

15.194

Where an undertaking participating in a cartel is the first to come forward to provide evidence of the existence and activities of that cartel, and fulfils certain requirements, it will benefit from total immunity from financial penalties in respect of that infringement. If the undertaking in question is the first to come forward *before* an investigation has commenced, it must, if it is to benefit from total immunity, satisfy the following conditions[1]:

— it must be the first to provide the DGFT with evidence of the existence and activities of the cartel;
— it must provide the DGFT with all the information, documents and evidence available to it regarding the existence and activities of the cartel;
— it must maintain continuous and complete co-operation throughout the investigation;
— it must not have compelled another undertaking to take part in the cartel and not have acted as the instigator or played the leading role in the illegal activity; and

— it must refrain from further participation in the illegal activity from the time it discloses the cartel[1].

This is slightly more generous than the position under the corresponding European Commission Notice, which states that an undertaking which fulfils all these criteria will benefit from a reduction of 'at least 75% of the fine or even from total exemption from the fine'.

1 *DGFT Guidance on penalties*, para 9.3.2.

15.195

If an undertaking is the first to provide the DGFT with evidence of the existence and activities of a cartel before written notice of a proposed infringement decision is given (but *after* an investigation has commenced) it will benefit from total immunity from penalties provided the conditions listed in para **15.194** are satisfied, but subject to the caveat that the DGFT must be satisfied that the undertaking should benefit from immunity, taking into account the stage at which the undertaking comes forward, and whether or not at that stage the DGFT has sufficient evidence to make an infringement decision. The grant of immunity is therefore discretionary. Again, this is expressed in slightly more generous terms than is the position under the European Commission Notice on the same subject: that provides that in these circumstances undertakings will benefit from a reduction of between 50% and 75% of the fine which would otherwise be imposed.

15.196

Where an undertaking provides evidence of the existence and activities of a cartel before written notice of a proposed infringement decision is given, but is not the first to come forward or does not meet all the requirements listed in para **15.194**, it will be granted a reduction in the amount of financial penalty that would otherwise be imposed of up to 50%, but only if the following conditions are met:

— the undertaking must provide the DGFT with all the information, documents and evidence available to it regarding the existence and activities of the cartel;
— it must maintain continuous and complete co-operation throughout the investigation;
— it must refrain from further participation in the illegal activity from the time it discloses the cartel.

15.197

There is a statement at the end of the Guidance on penalties which is designed to reassure an undertaking which comes forward with evidence of a cartel about the possible disclosure of its identity as a whistleblower. Para 9.7 states that the DGFT will endeavour, where possible, to keep the identity of the undertaking as a whistleblower confidential throughout the course of the investigation.

15.198

There is one additional provision which is contained in the Guidance but which does not appear in the European Commission Notice. This provision offers an additional reduction to a penalty imposed on an undertaking in respect of an infringement in one market if the undertaking concerned discloses information concerning a cartel in another market. The undertaking will receive total immunity with regard to the latter provided the conditions for total immunity are satisfied, together with a reduction in penalties which is additional to the reduction that it would have received for its co-operation in relation to the infringements relating to the first market. This concept has been borrowed from US antitrust enforcement policy.

Double jeopardy

15.199
Under s 38(9) of the CA 1998, if a penalty or a fine has been imposed by the European Commission, or by a court or other body in another Member State, in respect of an agreement or conduct, the DGFT (or the tribunal or the appropriate court) must take that penalty or fine into account when setting the amount of a penalty in relation to that agreement or conduct[1]. This raises an interesting question in circumstances where one agreement has effects in a number of Member States. The fact that the DGFT is only required to take the imposition of a fine or penalty by the Commission or another Member State authority into account (rather than requiring set-off as a matter of course) means that the DGFT will have a margin of discretion in deciding whether to reduce a penalty or fine which he otherwise would have imposed (and if so by how much) because of the imposition of the final penalty by the Commission or another Member State authority. A damages award is not, however, a factor which the Act requires to be taken into account.

1 This is explicitly recognised in the DGFT's *Guidance on Penalties*, para 8.3: see para **15.192**.

(4) Recovery of Penalties

15.200
If the specified date in a penalty notice is passed and the period during which an appeal against the imposition, or amount, of the penalty may be made has expired without an appeal having been made (or such an appeal has been made and determined), the DGFT may recover from the undertaking, as a civil debt, any amount payable under the penalty notice which remains outstanding[1].

1 CA 1998, s 37.

(5) Immunity in Respect of 'Small Agreements'

15.201
A party to a so-called 'small agreement' is immune from the imposition of penalties in respect of that agreement by virtue of s 39(3) of the CA 1998. However, the DGFT may withdraw that immunity if, following an

investigation into the agreement, he considers that it is likely to infringe the Chapter I prohibition[1]. The DGFT must give to each of the parties in respect of which immunity is withdrawn written notice of his decision to withdraw that immunity[2]. Such withdrawal can only take effect from a date after the date on which the decision is made (ie prospectively)[3].

1 CA 1998, s 39(4).
2 CA 1998, s 39(5).
3 CA 1998, s 39(7).

15.202
A small agreement is defined by s 39(1) to mean an agreement which falls within a category prescribed for the purposes of the section but which is not a price-fixing agreement. Section 39(9) defines a price-fixing agreement as one which has as its object or effect, or one of its objects or effects, restricting the freedom of a party to the agreement to determine the price to be charged (otherwise than as between that party and another party to the agreement) for the product, service or other matter to which the agreement relates. Section 39(2) of the CA 1998 provides that the criteria by reference to which such a category is to be prescribed may include the combined turnover of the parties to the agreement and the share of the market affected by the agreement. The Secretary of State prescribed the category of small agreement in Regulations which came into force on 1 March 2000[1]. The category is made up of agreements between undertakings, the combined applicable turnover of which for the business year ending in the calendar year preceding one during which the infringement occurred will exceed £20 million.

1 Competition Act 1998 (Small Agreements and Conduct of Minor Significance) Regulations 2000, SI 2000/262, para 3.

15.203
The power to impose penalties under s 36 of the CA 1998 is also disapplied if the DGFT is satisfied that the undertaking concerned acted on the reasonable assumption that s 39 gave it immunity in respect of the agreement[1].

1 CA 1998, s 36(4).

15.204
The immunity is only from penalties. The sanctions of voidness and possible third party action are still applicable.

(6) Immunity in Respect of 'Conduct of Minor Significance'

15.205
Similar principles to those set out in s 39 of the CA 1998 apply under s 40 to so-called 'conduct of minor significance'. That is defined as conduct which falls within the category prescribed for the purposes of the section. The prescribed conduct is conduct by an undertaking, the applicable turnover of which for the business year ending in the calendar year

preceding one during which the infringement occurred does not exceed £50 million[1].

1 The Competition Act 1998 (Small Agreements and Conduct of Minor Significance) Regulations 2000, SI 2000/262, para 4.

(7) Immunity in Other Cases

Following notification for guidance/a decision

15.206
If an agreement to which the Chapter I prohibition applies has been notified to the DGFT for guidance under s 13 or a decision under s 14, no penalty can be imposed under Chapter I in respect of the period beginning on the date of notification and a date specified in writing in a decision of the DGFT; notification of conduct does not, however, immunise the parties from penalties under the Chapter II prohibition[1].

1 See further para **15.50**.

Following notification to the European Commission

15.207
A penalty may not be imposed for infringement of the Chapter I prohibition during the period after notification to the European Commission seeking exemption under EC Treaty, Article 81(3) [1], but before the Commission determines the matter. However, if the Commission withdraws the benefit of provisional immunity from penalties[2] with respect to the agreement, immunity from penalties under the Chapter I prohibition also ceases.

1 See para **15.57**.
2 Under Article 15(6) of Council Regulation 17/62. See para **8.29** ff.

(8) Tax Deductibility of Penalties

15.208
The OFT's Enforcement Guidelines state[1] the Inland Revenue view as being that penalties under the Act will not be tax deductible. They are 'losses not connected with or arising out of the trade' and so are not deductible by virtue of s 74(1)(e) of the Income and Corporation Taxes Act 1998.

1 OFT 407 (March 1999), para 4.13, citing *IRC v Alexander von Glen & Co Ltd* (1920) 12 TC 232, CA.

(9) Limitation Period

15.209
It is unclear as to what, if any, limitation period applies in relation to the penalty regime. In respect of fines imposed under EC Treaty, Articles 81

and 82, the period after which the Commission can no longer impose fines is expressly provided for[1]. It is questionable whether or not s 60[2] of the CA 1998 has the effect of importing that regime. One thing is clear, namely that fines cannot be imposed for the period prior to 1 March 2000, the date of coming into force of the bulk of the CA 1998.

1 Under Council Regulation (EEC) 2988/74, OJ [1974] L319/1.
2 See para **15.22** ff.

F Appeals from Decisions of the DGFT: Role of the Competition Commission

1 FUNCTIONS OF COMPETITION COMMISSION

15.210
Section 45(1) of the CA 1998 establishes the Competition Commission (CC), which is to have such functions as are conferred on it by or as a result of the CA 1998.

15.211
Its principal functions are as follows:

- it hears appeals from certain decisions of the DGFT made under the CA 1998 in respect of the Chapter I and Chapter II prohibitions;
- the functions of the Monopolies and Mergers Commission (MMC) are transferred to the CC, with the MMC itself being dissolved[1].

1 CA 1998, s 45(3).

15.212
The functions of the MCC transferred to the CC are referred to in the CA 1998 as 'general functions'[1]. These are considered elsewhere in this Division[2].

1 CA 1998, Sch 7, para 1.
2 See para **14.19** ff.

2 MEMBERSHIP OF COMPETITION COMMISSION

15.213
The CC consists of:

(*a*) members appointed by the Secretary of State to form a panel for the purposes of its functions in relation to appeals in the CA 1998;
(*b*) members appointed by the Secretary of State to form a panel for the purposes of the CC's general functions;
(*c*) members appointed from the panel maintained by the Secretary of State in connection with newspaper merger references; and
(*d*) members appointed by the Secretary of State under or by virtue of provisions of the Water Industry Act 1991, the Electricity Act 1989, the

Telecommunications Act 1984 and the Electricity (Northern Ireland) Order 1992[1].

A person who is appointed as a member of a kind mentioned in (*a*)–(*c*) may also be appointed as a member of either of both of the other kinds mentioned in those paragraphs[2]. Persons appointed under para (*a*) are known as appeal panel members[3].

1 CA 1998, Sch 7, para 2(1).
2 CA 1998, Sch 7, para 2(3).
3 CA 1998, Sch 7, para 1.

15.214
The Secretary of State is required to appoint one of the appeal panel members to preside over the discharge of the CC's functions in relation to appeals; that person is known as the President of the Competition Commission Appeal Tribunals. The President must be a barrister or solicitor (or, in Scotland, Advocate) of at least ten years' standing and must appear to the Secretary of State to have appropriate experience and knowledge of competition law and practice[1]. Before appointing the President, the Secretary of State must consult the Lord Chancellor or Lord Advocate, as he considers appropriate[2]. The first such President is Judge Christopher Bellamy QC, previously judge at the Court of First Instance in Luxembourg.

1 CA 1998, Sch 7, para 4(3).
2 CA 1998, Sch 7, para 4(4).

3 DECISIONS WHICH ARE APPEALABLE

15.215
The following decisions by the DGFT are appealable to the CC by a party to an agreement in respect of which that decision has been made (or a person in respect of whose conduct that decision has been made)[1]:

(*a*) a decision as to whether the Chapter I prohibition has been infringed;
(*b*) a decision as to whether the Chapter II prohibition has been infringed;
(*c*) a decision as to whether to grant an individual exemption;
(*d*) in respect of an individual exemption, a decision as to whether to impose any condition or obligation (and, if so, what condition or obligation), as to the duration of the exemption and as to the starting date of the exemption;
(*e*) a decision whether to extend the period for which an individual exemption has effect and, if so, the length of that extension;
(*f*) a decision cancelling an exemption;
(*g*) a decision as to the imposition of any penalty under s 36 or as to the amount of that penalty;
(*h*) a decision withdrawing or varying any of the decisions listed in (*a*)–(*f*) above following an application by a third party;
(*i*) a direction under ss 32 or 33, requiring an infringement of the Chapter I or Chapter II prohibition to be brought to an end; and
(*j*) an interim measures direction given under s 35[2].

Except in the case of an appeal against the imposition, or the amount, of a penalty, the making of an appeal to the CC does not suspend the effect of the decision to which the appeal relates[3].

1 CA 1998, s 46.
2 See para **15.170** ff.
3 CA 1998, s 46(4).

15.216
Under the CA 1998, s 46(3), the Secretary of State may prescribe additional decisions which are available to the CC. The following additional decisions have been prescribed as decisions for the purpose of s 46:

(*a*) a decision of the DGFT imposing conditions or obligations subject to which parallel exemption is to have effect, or varying or removing any such conditions or obligations[1]; and
(*b*) a decision of the DGFT under the CA 1998, s 14[2] that the Chapter I prohibition would be infringed if it applied to the agreement the subject of the notification.

1 Competition Act 1998 (Notification of Excluded Agreements and Appealable Decisions) Regulations 2000, SI 2000/263, para 10; See, in relation to such decisions, para **15.47**.
2 Ibid.

15.217
It is interesting to note the decisions of the DGFT which are not subject to appeal under s 46. They include:

— a decision not to pursue a complaint;
— a decision to start an investigation[1];
— a decision requiring documents to be produced[2] or authorising entry into premises[3];
— an application for a judge's warrant[4];
— a decision imposing or varying conditions or obligations on block exemption[5];
— a notice removing immunity from penalties from an agreement previously found not to infringe[6];
— a provisional decision removing provisional immunity from penalties on notification[7];
— the giving or withholding of guidance[8].

1 See para **15.132**.
2 See para **15.135**.
3 See para **15.138**.
4 See para **15.145**.
5 CA 1998, s 6(6).
6 See para **15.52**.
7 See para **15.62**.
8 See para **15.60**.

15.218
The approach of listing decisions which are appealable (and therefore by omission those which are not) is in contrast with the EC law position, under which any decision that alters the legal position of an undertaking, provided it definitively lays down the authority's position, is appealable[1]. Decisions of

the DGFT which are not appealable may still form the basis of judicial review applications[2]. Moreover, applicants may seek to invoke procedural irregularities when challenging those decisions which are appealable.

1 See para **10.10** ff.
2 See para **15.252** ff.

4 PERSONS WHO MAY APPEAL

15.219

As noted in para **15.215** a party to an agreement in respect of which the DGFT has made a decision may appeal to the CC; as may a person in respect of whose conduct the DGFT has made a decision[1].

1 CA 1998, s 46(1)(2).

15.220

There is, in addition, scope for third party appeals. Under s 47, a third party may apply to the DGFT asking him to withdraw or vary a decision falling within any of the categories listed in *(a)*–*(f)* in para **15.215**. The application must be made in writing within one month of publication of the decision and give the applicant's reasons for considering that the relevant decision should be withdrawn or varied (as the case may be)[1]. If the DGFT decides either:

— that the applicant does not have a sufficient interest in the relevant decision; or
— that the application does not show sufficient reason why he should withdraw or vary the relevant decision he must notify the applicant of his decision[2]. The applicant may appeal to the CC against such a decision[3]. If the DGFT decides to proceed with the application, he must do so in accordance with such procedure as may be specified in rules under s 51[4]. The making of a third party application does not suspend the effect of the relevant decision[5].

1 CA 1998, s 47(1), (2) and *Director's Rules*, para 28.
2 CA 1998, s 47(3), (4)
3 CA 1998, s 47(6).
4 CA 1998, s 47(5).
5 CA 1998, s 47(7).

5 PROCEDURE

15.221

Schedule 8 of the CA 1998 sets out some basic provisions regarding appeals to a CC appeal tribunal. An appeal must be made by sending a notice of appeal to the CC within the specified period[1]. The notice of appeal must set out the grounds of appeal in sufficient detail to indicate under which provision of the Act the appeal is brought, to what extent the appellant contends that the decision against, or with respect to which, the appeal is brought was based on an error of fact or was wrong in law and to what extent (if any) the appellant is appealing against the DGFT's exercise of his discretion in making the disputed decision[2].

1 CA 1998, Sch 8, para 2(1). As to the specified period, see para **15.230**.
2 CA 1998, Sch 8, para 2(2).

15.222
The appeal tribunal has a range of powers at its disposal[1]. It may:

— confirm or set aside the decision, in all or part;
— remit the matter to the DGFT;
— impose or revoke, or vary the amount of, a penalty;
— grant or cancel an individual exemption or vary any conditions or obligations imposed in relation to the exemption by the DGFT;
— give such directions, or take such other steps, as the DGFT could himself have given or taken; or
— make any other decision which the DGFT could himself have made.

1 CA 1998, Sch 8, para 3(2).

15.223
The tribunal must determine the appeal 'on the merits' by reference to the grounds of appeal set out in the notice of appeal[1]. It appears therefore to be contemplated that the tribunal will in effect hear and decide the case de novo. However, according to the DGFT[2], the appeal tribunal will not carry out investigative work; if substantial new evidence comes to light at the appeal stage, the case will be referred back to the DGFT.

1 CA 1998, Sch 8, para 3(1).
2 *OFT's Major Provisions Guidelines*, para 14.5 (OFT 400, March 1999).

15.224
A tribunal's decision may be taken on a majority basis and the decision must state whether it was unanimous or taken by a majority[1]. The decision must also be recorded in a document which contains a statement of the reasons for the decision[2]. The President must make such arrangements for the publication of the tribunal's decision as he considers appropriate[3].

1 CA 1998, Sch 8, para 4(1).
2 CA 1998, Sch 8, para 4(2).
3 CA 1998, Sch 8, para 4(4).

15.225
The CA 1998, s 48(2) provides that the Secretary of State may make rules with respect to appeals and appeals tribunals, having first consulted the President of the Competition Commission Appeal Tribunals, the Council on Tribunals[1] and such other persons as he considers appropriate. Part II of Sch 8 provides an illustrative but non-exhaustive[2] list of the matters such rules may cover, in particular:

— the period within which an appeal must be brought;
— the form of the notice of appeal and the information to be contained in it;
— the carrying out of a preliminary consideration of proceedings (so-called 'pre-hearing review');

- provisions regarding the conduct of hearings, the persons entitled to represent the parties and the evidence which may be required or admitted in proceedings before the tribunal;
- provisions requiring persons to attend to give evidence and produce documents and give evidence and for authorising the administration of oaths to witnesses; and orders regarding the disclosure of documents and the appointment of experts. It is also envisaged that there may be rules under which a party who has brought an appeal may not withdraw it without the leave of the tribunal.

1 Tribunal and Inquiries Act 1992, s 8 and Sch 1, as amended by Sch 12, para 15 of the CA 1998.
2 CA 1998, s 48(4).

15.226
It is also envisaged that there may be rules which enable the tribunal to make an interim order granting, on an interim basis, any remedy which the tribunal would have power to grant in its final decision; it is specifically provided that such an interim order may suspend the effects of a decision made by the DGFT or vary the conditions or obligations attached to an exemption[1]. It is also envisaged that rules may make provision giving the tribunal powers similar to those given to the DGFT by s 35, namely the ability to make an interim measures direction[2].

1 CA 1998, Sch 8, para 13.
2 See para **15.170** ff.

15.227
The Secretary of State published draft Rules, the Competition Commission Tribunal Rules 1999 ('the draft Rules'), in November 1999. The Rules came into force on 1 March 2000[1]. In the preamble to the draft rules the following general points were made, which indicate the way in which the Government intends the appeal process should work:

(1) The point was made that, under the Act, cases are to be decided on the merits, by reference to the grounds of appeal set out in the Notice of Appeal[2]. The preamble stated that procedural irregularities will be taken into account 'if they are relevant to the merits of the case'. We must wait to see how frequently appeals invoke alleged procedural irregularity and how the appeal tribunal deals with such claims. In the EC context, many appeals of Article 81 and Article 82 cases involve alleged procedural irregularity of one form or another.
(2) It is intended that the tribunal's procedures should promote the objectives of fairness and consistency; thoroughness and rigour; transparency; and timeliness and efficiency. These objectives do not necessarily all pull in the same direction (for example, thoroughness and rigour may not be wholly compatible with timeliness and efficiency).
(3) The preamble stated that effective and active case management should lie at the heart of the process, stating that 'the essence of this approach is that the tribunal should seek to manage the focus and presentation of the appeal, as opposed to leaving these things largely to the parties to

decide'. The principal objectives of case management which were stated in the preamble include the elimination of peripheral points wherever possible and minimising a relevant argument in evidence. Emphasis is to be placed on written as opposed to oral procedures, minimising the matters to be dealt with at the oral hearing (this is consistent with the approach taken by the European Court of First Instance[3]).

(4) Whilst the preamble noted that active case management is the way the civil justice system is itself moving (under the Civil Procedure Rules 1998 adopted following Lord Woolf's Report), it indicates that the intention is to base the tribunal Rules on the rules of procedure of the European Court of First Instance, with some adaptation.

(5) It is intended to provide for an early reference to the ECJ where this would enable the matter to be disposed of more expeditiously overall.

(6) In drawing up the draft Rules, the Government assumed that the Human Rights Act 1998[4] was already in force and that the Rules would need therefore to comply with the European Convention on Human Rights. The Government believes that the Rules will allow the tribunal and hence the regime as a whole to operate in compliance with the Convention.

1 Competition Commission Appeal Tribunal Rules 2000, SI 2000/261.
2 CA 1998, Sch 8, para 3(1).
3 See para **10.87**.
4 See para **15.08**.

15.228
Paragraphs **15.229–15.249** summarise the key features of the Rules. The Notice of Appeal referred to in Schedule 8 of the Act is referred to in the Rules as 'an application', the person making the appeal as 'the applicant' and the person who made the disputed decision as 'the respondent'.

(1) Commencement of Proceedings

15.229
In proceedings before the tribunal, a party may be represented by a qualified lawyer having right of audience before a court in the United Kingdom, or by any other person allowed by the tribunal to appear on his behalf[1].

1 *Tribunal Rules*, para 5.

15.230
An appeal to the CC must be made not later than two months after the date upon which the applicant was notified of the disputed decision[1]. That time limit may not be extended unless the tribunal is satisfied that the circumstances are 'exceptional'[2]. The application must contain, inter alia, a brief statement of the facts, a summary of the principal grounds for contesting the decision, a succinct presentation of the arguments supporting each of those grounds, the relief sought and a schedule listing all the documents annexed to the application[3]. The notice of appeal must indicate to what extent (if any) the applicant contends that the decision the subject of the appeal was based on an error of fact or was wrong in law and to what extent

(if any) the applicant is appealing against the DGFT's exercise of his discretion in making the disputed decision[4].

1 *Tribunal Rules*, para 6(2).
2 *Tribunal Rules*, para 6(3).
3 *Tribunal Rules*, para 6(5).
4 CA 1998, Sch 8, para 2(2).

15.231
The Tribunal may require the application to be put in order if it considers that it does not contain the information referred to in Rule 6 (see para **15.230**), or is materially incomplete, or is 'unduly prolix or lacking in clarity'[1].

1 *Tribunal Rules*, para 7.

15.232
The Tribunal has power to strike out an application at any stage in the proceedings if it considers that the application discloses no valid ground of appeal, if it is satisfied that the applicant has habitually, consistently and without reasonable grounds instituted vexatious proceedings or if the application does not comply with Rule 5 in a substantial respect and the applicant has not remedied the defect, despite having been required to do so[1].

1 *Tribunal Rules*, para 8.

15.233
An application may only be amended with leave of the tribunal and leave may be granted on such terms as it thinks fit; a wholly new ground for contesting the decision may not be added unless such ground is based on matters of law or fact which have come to light since the application was made, or the circumstances are exceptional[1].

1 *Tribunal Rules*, para 9.

15.234
Similarly, an application may only be withdrawn with the leave of the tribunal (or if there has not yet been a hearing, the President alone), again on such terms as it thinks fit; if an application is withdrawn, a fresh application may not be brought in relation to the decision which was the subject of the application which has been withdrawn[1].

1 *Tribunal Rules*, para 10.

(2) Response to the Application

15.235
It is the responsibility of the tribunal (through its Registrars) to send a copy of the application to the respondent who made the disputed decision (this may be the DGFT or a sectoral regulator)[1]. The respondent must file its defence not later than six weeks, or such further time as the tribunal may allow, after the date on which the respondent received a copy of the application[2]. The defence must contain the arguments of fact and law upon which the respondent will rely in opposing the application, any relief sought

by the respondent and the schedule listing all the documents annexed to the defence[3]. If the tribunal considers that the defence does not contain the information required, or is materially incomplete, or is unduly prolix or lacking in clarity, it may give such directions as may be necessary to ensure that the defence is put in order[4]. It is the responsibility of the tribunal's registrar to send a copy of the defence to the applicant[5].

1 *Tribunal Rules*, para 11.
2 *Tribunal Rules*, para 12(1).
3 *Tribunal Rules*, para 12(3).
4 *Tribunal Rules*, para 12(6).
5 *Tribunal Rules*, para 12(7).

(3) Intervention, Consolidation and Location of Proceedings

15.236
The Registrar of the tribunal is required to publish notice of an application in the London, Edinburgh and Belfast Gazettes and in any other manner as the President of the Competition Commission Appeal Tribunals may think fit[1]. The notice must state, inter alia, the name of the applicant, the disputed decision, the particulars of the relief sought, a summary of the principal grounds relied on and a statement indicating that any person who considers that he has sufficient interest may apply, within one month of publication of the Notice[2], to intervene in the proceedings.

1 *Tribunal Rules*, para 13(1).
2 *Tribunal Rules*, para 13(2).

15.237
A person who considers that he has 'sufficient interest' in the outcome of any proceedings may apply to the tribunal to intervene, within one month of the date upon which the notice of the application is published; notice of the application to intervene must be given to the other parties to the proceedings with a request for their observations on the application[1]. The application must contain a concise statement of the matters in issue in the proceedings which affect the person making the application, the name of the party whose position the person making the request intends to support and a succinct presentation of the reasons for making the application[2]. If the tribunal is satisfied, having taken into account the observations of the parties, that the intervening party has a sufficient interest it may admit the intervention on such terms and conditions as it thinks fit[3].

1 *Tribunal Rules*, paras 14(1) and (2).
2 *Tribunal Rules*, para 14(5).
3 *Tribunal Rules*, para 14(6).

15.238
If two or more applications have been made in respect of the same matter, or which involve the same issues, the tribunal may, on the application of a party or of its own motion, order that the applications or any particular issue or matter raised in the application be consolidated or heard together[1].

1 *Tribunal Rules*, para 15.

15.239
The tribunal is required, as soon as practicable, to determine the part of the United Kingdom in which the proceedings are to take place, having regard to the part of the United Kingdom where:

(*a*) the applicant is habitually resident or has his principal place of business;
(*b*) the majority of the parties are habitually resident or have their principal places of business;
(*c*) any agreement, decision or concerted practice to which the disputed decision relates was made or implemented or intended to be implemented;
(*d*) any conduct to which the disputed decision relates took place; and
(*e*) having regard to the convenience of any witness[1].

1 *Tribunal Rules*, para 16.

(4) Preparation for Deciding the Application

15.240
The tribunal is empowered, at any time, to give such directions as it thinks fit to secure the just, expeditious and economical conduct of the proceedings[1]. These directions may include, inter alia, a setting of time limits to be observed in the conduct of the oral hearing, a requirement that the parties file additional pleadings, a requirement that persons attend to give evidence or produce documents, a determination as to the evidence which may be required or admitted in proceedings before the tribunal and the extent to which it shall be oral or written, a requirement for the disclosure of documents or classes of documents, the appointment and instruction of experts, whether by the tribunal or by the parties, and for the award of costs or expenses[2].

1 *Tribunal Rules*, para 17(1).
2 *Tribunal Rules*, para 17(2).

15.241
The tribunal may put questions to the parties, invite written or oral submissions on certain aspects of the proceedings, ask the parties for information or documents and summon the parties or their representatives to meetings[1].

1 *Tribunal Rules*, para 17(3).

15.242
The Tribunal Rules contemplate the holding of a pre-hearing review, to be held in private, the purpose of which shall be to ensure the efficient conduct of the proceedings, to determine the points on which the parties must present further argument or which call for further evidence to be produced, to clarify the forms of orders sought by the parties, their pleas in law and arguments on the points at issue between them, to ensure that as much agreement can be reached as possible between the parties about the matters in issue and to facilitate the settlement of the proceedings[1].

1 *Tribunal Rules*, para 18.

15.243
The tribunal may receive evidence of any fact which appears to it to be relevant, whether or not the evidence was available to the respondent when the disputed decision was taken and is not bound by any enactment or rule of law relating to the admissibility of evidence in proceedings before courts of law[1]. The tribunal may require any witness to give evidence on oath or affirmation of it in writing by way of affidavit[2]. Witnesses may be summoned to attend hearings of the tribunal and to answer any questions or produce any documents or other material which relate to any matter in question in the proceedings[3].

1 *Tribunal Rules*, para 20(2).
2 *Tribunal Rules*, para 20(3).
3 *Tribunal Rules*, para 20(4).

(5) The Hearing Itself

15.244
The draft Tribunal Rules provide that hearings of the tribunal are to be in public except where the tribunal is satisfied that it will be considering information at the hearing which is, in its opinion, confidential information of the kind to which s 56 of the CA 1998 applies[1].

1 *Tribunal Rules*, para 23.

(6) Decision of the Tribunal

15.245
The decision of the tribunal must be delivered in public[1]. The tribunal may make an award of costs payable by one party to another in respect of the whole or part of the proceedings[2].

1 *Tribunal Rules*, para 25(1).
2 *Tribunal Rules*, para 26(1).

15.246
If all the parties agree the terms on which to settle all or any part of the proceedings, they may apply to the tribunal for a consent order[1]. The application for a consent order must include a draft form of the consent order and 'consent order impact statement', which is to provide an explanation of the draft order, the circumstances giving rise to it, the relief to be obtained if the order is made and the anticipated effects on competition of that relief[2]. If the tribunal considers that the proposed consent order may have a significant effect on competition it must publish a notice in the London, Edinburgh and Belfast Gazettes, and in such other manner as the tribunal may direct[3]. Any person may send his comments upon an application for a consent order within one month of the date upon which the notice was published[4]. After hearing the parties and considering the comments of third parties, the tribunal may make the consent order in the terms requested, may impose any new or varied terms or may refuse to make any order at all[5].

1 *Tribunal Rules*, para 28(1).
2 *Tribunal Rules*, para 28(2) and (3).
3 *Tribunal Rules*, para 28(4).
4 *Tribunal Rules*, para 28(6).
5 *Tribunal Rules*, para 28(9).

(7) References to the European Court

15.247
The tribunal may, of its own motion at any stage in the proceedings or on the application by a party before or at the oral hearing, make an order requesting a preliminary ruling of the European Court, in which case the proceedings are to be stayed until the preliminary ruling has been given (unless the tribunal orders otherwise)[1].

1 *Tribunal Rules*, para 31.

(8) Interim Orders and Measures

15.248
As noted in para **15.215**, the making of an appeal to the CC does not suspend the effect of the decision to which the appeal relates, unless it is an appeal against the imposition, or the amount, of a penalty[1]. However, the tribunal may make an order suspending the effect of the disputed decision in whole or in part or varying any or all of the conditions or obligations attached to an exemption granted by the DGFT[2]. In addition, the tribunal may make an order granting on an interim basis any remedy which the tribunal would have the power to grant in its final decision[3]. In exercising its interim order making power, the tribunal may take account of all relevant circumstances, including the urgency of the matter, the effect on the applicant if the interim application is not granted and the effect on competition if the interim application is granted[4].

1 CA 1998, s 46(4).
2 *Tribunal Rules*, para 32.
3 *Tribunal Rules*, para 32(1).
4 *Tribunal Rules*, para 32(4).

15.249
On receiving an interim application, the tribunal's Registrar must send a copy to all the other parties to the proceedings, informing them of the date by which they must submit written or oral observations to the tribunal[1]. The tribunal must then fix a date for the hearing of the application for interim relief[2]. If the urgency of the case requires, the tribunal is empowered to grant the interim application before the observations of the other parties have been submitted[3].

1 *Tribunal Rules*, para 32(8).
2 *Tribunal Rules*, para 32(9).
3 *Tribunal Rules*, para 32(10).

6 APPEALS FROM DECISIONS OF THE COMPETITION COMMISSION

15.250
There is scope for appeals from decisions of an appeal tribunal on one or other of two grounds. First, appeal may be made on a point of law; second, appeal may be made from any decision of an appeal tribunal as to the amount of a penalty[1]. Appeal lies to the Court of Appeal (where the tribunal is in England and Wales), the Court of Session (where the tribunal is in Scotland) and the Court of Appeal in Northern Ireland (where the tribunal is in Northern Ireland)[2]. Appeal may only be made with leave of the tribunal in question or of the appropriate court[3]. An application to the tribunal may be made orally at any hearing at which the decision which is the subject of the proposed appeal is delivered by the tribunal, or in writing to the Registrar of the tribunal within 28 days of the notification of that decision. An application for leave to appeal made in writing must state the grounds on which the applicant intends to rely in his appeal[4]. Where the application for leave to appeal is made in writing, the tribunal must decide on the basis of the application and, unless it considers that special circumstances render a hearing desirable, in the absence of the parties[5].

1 CA 1998, s 49(1).
2 CA 1998, s 49(4).
3 CA 1998, s 49(2).
4 *Tribunal Rules*, para 29.
5 *Tribunal Rules*, para 30.

15.251
Appeal may be made at the instance either of a party (namely a person who is a party to the proceedings in which the decision was made) or of a person who has a 'sufficient interest' in the matter[1].

1 CA 1998, s 49(2).

G Role of Judicial Review under the Competition Act 1998

15.252
It remains to be seen what role judicial review will play in relation to the new Act, given the role which will be played by the CC. Up to now, judicial review has been the only means of controlling the decisions of the competition authorities. Judicial review does not involve a substantive appeal on the merits of the case but in essence involves a challenge to their rationality, legality and procedural fairness. Challenges to the decisions of UK competition authorities by way of judicial review have not met with great success[1].

1 See para **16.01** ff.

15.253
There is nothing in the CA 1998 which purports to eliminate the ability to challenge a decision of the DGFT by way of judicial review. Indeed, in the House of Lords, Lord Simon stated:

'... we are doing nothing in the Bill to prevent the application of the normal rules of judicial review. Therefore, the lawfulness of decisions may be tested in the courts'[1].

1 HL Report Stage, 19 February 1998, col 381.

15.254
That having been said, we must wait to see how the residual right to apply for judicial review and the right of appeal to the CC will mesh together. The following points should be borne in mind:

(1) It is a general principle that only in exceptional circumstances will leave to bring judicial review proceedings be granted if a statutory right of appeal exists[1]. Accordingly, where there is a clear right of appeal to the CC it may be expected that a judicial review application will fail.
(2) However, as noted in para **15.217**, there are a number of situations in which there is no right of appeal to the CC. In relation to those matters, there is in principle no reason why a judicial review application could not be brought.
(3) This leaves open the question, to which there is at yet no clear answer, as to how the CC will interpret its appeal function. One can certainly expect that it will seek to review the substantive merits of a decision taken by the DGFT. However, experience of proceedings before the CFI and ECJ suggests that many cases will be appealed to the CC on essentially procedural grounds (for example, taking into account inadmissible evidence, refusal to grant an oral hearing, inadequate access to the DGFT's file etc). If the CC shows itself willing to hear cases appealed on those grounds, then one could expect that judicial review applications based on the same grounds would fail. If, on the other hand, the CC decides not to admit essentially procedural appeals, then one can expect greater emphasis on judicial review. It is only when the first decisions start being taken under the new Act that we shall know how these issues will be decided.

1 *Harley Development Inc v IRC* [1996] 1 WLR 727, 746C; see too *R v Secretary of State for the Home Department, ex p Capti-Mehmet* [1997] COD 61.

H Enforcement of the Competition Act in the Regulated Sectors

1 INTRODUCTION

15.255
One of the most controversial issues during the passage of the Competition Bill through Parliament was whether the so-called 'sectoral regulators' should have jurisdiction, concurrently with the DGFT, under the Act. The regulators concerned are those listed in para **15.257**. Amongst the issues to which concurrency gives rise are the following:

— the question how exercise of the Competition Act powers will mesh with the powers and duties which the various sectoral regulators have under the industry-specific legislation which they administer;
— the risk that a proliferation of regulators exercising the powers created under the Act will lead to the Act being applied differently in different sectors of the economy; and
— the danger of double jeopardy, with the risk that the same issue could be investigated by the DGFT and the relevant sectoral regulator; indeed, for multi-utilities there is even a theoretical risk of treble jeopardy.

15.256
The Government rejected the arguments which were put to it against giving the sectoral regulators concurrent jurisdiction with that of the DGFT and it remains to be seen whether the risks referred to in para **15.255** will arise in practice. Certainly, it is clear that the Government and the regulators themselves are mindful of the risks and regulations, and guidelines are in the course of finalisation which are designed to eliminate or at least minimise those risks.

2 WHICH REGULATORS HAVE CONCURRENT JURISDICTION?

15.257
The following regulators have jurisdiction concurrent with that of the DGFT under the CA 1998[1]:

— the Director General or Telecommunications;
— the Director General of Electricity Supply;
— the Director General of Gas Supply[2];
— the Director General of Electricity Supply for Northern Ireland;
— the Director General of Water Services;
— the Rail Regulator; and
— the Director General of Gas for Northern Ireland.

1 CA 1998, s 54(1) and CA 1998, Sch 10, para 1.
2 This post and the post of Director General of Electricity Supply are both held by the same person, Callum McCarthy.

15.258
The regulators referred to in para **15.257** may apply the competition powers under the CA 1998 to the sectors for which they are each responsible. Specifically, this means that:

(1) The Director General of Telecommunications may exercise concurrent powers in relation to agreements caught by the Chapter I prohibition and conduct caught by the Chapter II prohibition which relate to 'commercial activities connected with telecommunications'[1].
(2) The Director General of Gas Supply may apply the same powers in relation to 'the shipping, conveyance or supply of gas and activities ancillary thereto'[2].

(3) The Director General of Electricity Supply has the same powers in relation to 'commercial activities connected with the generation, transmission or supply of electricity'[3].

(4) The same applies to the Director General of Electricity Supply for Northern Ireland[4].

(5) The Director General of Water Supply has the same powers in relation to 'commercial activities connected with the supply (or securing of supply) of water or of sewerage services'[5]. However, his jurisdiction is limited to England and Wales, reflecting his jurisdiction under the Water Industry Act 1991. The DGFT has sole jurisdiction elsewhere in the United Kingdom.

(6) The Rail Regulator has the same powers in respect of the supply of railway services[6].

1 A phrase defined in the Telecommunications Act 1994, s 4(3).
2 Gas Act 1986, ss 5(1) and 36A(4), as amended.
3 Electricity Act 1989, s 43, as amended.
4 CA 1998, Sch 10, para 7.
5 Water Industry Act 1991, s 31, as amended.
6 Railways Act 1993, ss 4 and 67, as amended by the CA 1998, Sch 10, para 6.

15.259

There are certain specific limitations on the Rail Regulator's power, notably in respect of agreements under which train operators are given rights to use the rail network, stations and light maintenance depots and in respect of the channel tunnel rail link[1].

1 Railway Act 1993 s 22(6A) and 6(B).

3 BASIC ELEMENTS OF CONCURRENCY

15.260

The sectoral regulators have the following functions under the CA 1998 concurrently with the DGFT:

- considering notifications for a decision or guidance[1];
- granting exemptions;
- receiving complaints;
- imposing interim measures;
- carrying out enquiries and investigations;
- imposing penalties;
- issuing advice and information on the application of the CA 1998 in the relevant sector[2].

1 However, only the DGFT can accept applications for guidance and notifications: see para **15.261**.
2 See, for example, the Director General of Telecommunications' Guidelines *Application of the Competition Act in the Telecommunications Sector* and the Director General of Water Services' Guidelines *Application in the Water and Sewerage Sectors.*

15.261

Notifications for a decision or guidance can only be made to the DGFT[1]. If the matter falls within one of the industry sectors identified in para **15.258**, an additional copy of the notification form (Form N) should be provided to the relevant sectoral regulator (although it should be noted that failure to send an additional copy of the form to or for the sectoral regulator does not render the notification incomplete). The OFT's guidelines 'Concurrent Application to Regulated Industries' states[2] that applicants will be told as soon as practicable who is dealing with the case (ie the DGFT or the relevant sectoral regulator), and if the case is subsequently transferred to another regulator or the DGFT.

1 *Director's Rules*, para 1. See also the Competition Act 1998 (Concurrency) Regulations 2000, SI 2000/260, para 4.
2 OFT 405 (March 1999), paras 3.3 and 3.4.

15.262
Complaints, on the other hand, may be made either to the DGFT or to the relevant regulator. As to how complaints will be handled as between the DGFT and the sectoral regulators, see para **15.265** ff.

15.263
The making of rules, directions and guidance as to penalties is reserved to the DGFT but he must consult the regulators if their sectors are affected[1].

1 CA 1998, s 38(7).

15.264
The Act gives the Secretary of State power[1] to make regulations with a view to co-ordinating the concurrent application of the Act by the DGFT and the various sectoral regulators. The Secretary of State has made such regulations, which came into force on 1 March 2000[2].

1 CA 1998, s 54(4).
2 See para **15.265**.

4 CO-ORDINATION OF ACTIVITY BETWEEN THE DGFT AND THE SECTORAL REGULATORS

15.265
Section 54(4) enables the Secretary of State to make regulations for the purpose of co-ordinating the performance of functions under the CA 1998 which are exercisable by the DGFT or any of the sectoral regulators. Such Regulations have now been adopted[1]. These provide as follows:

(1) In order to determine which regulator has jurisdiction in a given case, the DGFT may send to any other regulator details of any application for guidance or a decision[2] which he receives and one regulator may send to another regulator details of any information he receives that an infringement of the Chapter I or Chapter II prohibition may have taken place[3].
(2) If the DGFT considers that another regulator has or may have concurrent jurisdiction in relation to an agreement or conduct in respect of which an application for guidance or a decision has been submitted he must send a copy of the information submitted in that application to

that regulator and inform the applicant in writing that he has done so[4]. If one regulator proposes to exercise jurisdiction in a case not the subject of application for guidance or a decision and that regulator considers that another regulator has or may have concurrent jurisdiction in relation to that case, he must inform that other regulator in writing of his intention to exercise jurisdiction[5]. In either of these cases, the DGFT and the relevant regulator(s) must agree who is to exercise jurisdiction; in the case of an application for guidance or a decision, the applicant must be notified once a decision has been taken as to which regulator will have jurisdiction[6].

(3) If the relevant regulators are not able to reach agreement as to who is to take jurisdiction, the DGFT must inform the Secretary of State and the Secretary of State is to be required to make a decision as to which regulator should have jurisdiction, taking account of representations made by the regulators themselves[7].

(4) Where two or more regulators may have concurrent jurisdiction in relation to a case, neither shall exercise jurisdiction in relation to that case before agreement has been reached as to who is to have jurisdiction (or a determination made by the Secretary of State where the regulators have been unable to reach agreement amongst themselves)[8]; once agreement has been reached on jurisdiction (or a determination made by the Secretary of State), no other regulator may exercise jurisdiction under the Act in relation to the case in question[9]. However, one regulator may agree to transfer a case to another regulator who has concurrent jurisdiction and, where this happens in the case of an application for guidance or a decision, the transferring regulator must inform the applicant in writing[10]. Notification is also to be made to the undertaking in question in relation to those cases which are not the subject of an application for guidance or a decision (for example, an infringement proceeding following a complaint).

(5) The Regulations provide for one regulator to appoint an officer of another regulator to act as his officer in relation to an individual case[11].

1 The Competition Act 1998 (Concurrency) Regulations 2000, SI 2000/260.
2 See para **15.261**.
3 Regulations, para 3.
4 Regulations, para 5(1). See para **15.261**.
5 Regulations, para 5(2).
6 Regulations, para 5(3) and (4).
7 Regulations, para 6; the Secretary of State must make his decision within eight working days.
8 Regulations, para 7(1).
9 Regulations, para 7(2).
10 Regulations, para 8(2).
11 Regulations, para 9.

15.266

The OFT's Guidelines 'Concurrent Application to Regulated Industries' make it clear that, in general, an agreement or conduct which falls within the industry sector of a regulator who has concurrent jurisdiction under the CA 1998 will be dealt with by that regulator[1]. However, the Guidelines make it clear that this will not be a binding rule and they list certain factors which will be considered in determining which of the DGFT or a sectoral regulator should deal with a particular case, namely the sectoral knowledge of a regulator, any previous contacts between the parties or complainants and the regulator or with the DGFT, and any recent experience in dealing with any of the undertakings or similar issues which may be involved in the proceedings.

1 OFT 405 (March 1999), para 3.1.

5 INTERFACE BETWEEN THE COMPETITION ACT AND THE SECTOR-SPECIFIC LEGISLATION

15.267

In some circumstances, a particular agreement or practice may fall within the scope of a regulator's sector-specific legislation as well as within the prohibitions contained within the CA 1998. For example, a regulated company may operate under a licence which prevents it from showing undue preference to, or undue discrimination against, a class of persons[1]. In some circumstances, sector-specific legislation requires a regulator to enforce a licence condition. However, it may be more effective or more efficient to use the powers available under the CA 1998. Accordingly, the Act amends the sector-specific legislation to provide that a regulator's duty to take licence enforcement action does not apply where he is satisfied that, in a particular case, it would be more appropriate to proceed under the Act.

1 OFT Guidelines *Concurrent Application to Regulated Industries*, para 4.2 (OFT 405, March 1999).

15.268

It is in principle open to a sectoral regulator to begin an investigation under the CA 1998 and then to decide mid-process to switch over to use the enforcement powers in the sector-specific statute. This creates an imbalance from the point of view of due process: the DGFT and the sectoral regulators have very considerable investigative powers under the CA 1998[1] but their decision-making is subject to appeal to the Competition Commission[2]. Review under the sector-specific legislation is much more limited.

1 See para **15.130** ff.
2 See para **15.215** ff.

6 ENSURING CONSISTENCY OF DECISION-MAKING

15.269

It is clearly vital that, if concurrent jurisdiction is to work successfully in practice, mechanisms are put in place in order to ensure consistency of decision-making. The DGFT and each sectoral regulator are represented on a Concurrency Working Party, which was formed in 1997. It is intended[1] that the Working Party will continue in operation after implementation of the Act to deal with certain key issues:

— information about complaints received and investigations in progress or contemplated will be shared to ascertain whether there is concurrent jurisdiction;
— information about cases in progress, including matters of general policy and the way in which the Act is interpreted and applied will also be shared, with a view to ensuring consistency in decision-making;
— the Working Party will provide a forum within which the regulators will agree (or seek to agree) who is to have concurrent jurisdiction in any given case;
— the Working Party will keep under review the concurrency guidelines themselves.

1 OFT's Guidelines *Concurrent Application to Regulated Industries*, para 3.8 (OFT 405, March 1999).

7 CONFIDENTIALITY

15.270
As noted in para **15.154**, the CA 1998 imposes certain limits on the disclosure of information obtained by the DGFT or one of the sectoral regulators under the Act. However, as also noted in para **15.155** there are certain situations in which disclosure is permitted and these include disclosure for the purpose of facilitating the performance by one of the regulators of their functions under the sector-specific legislation[1]. This means that information obtained by one of the sectoral regulators following a complaint made under the CA 1998 may be used by that regulator for the performance of one of his functions under the sector-specific legislation relating to that regulator.

1 CA 1998, s 55(3)(*a*)(i) and Sch 11.

Chapter 16 Judicial Review: UK

A Introduction

16.01

As has been explained at paras **1.03–1.07**, UK competition law is applied by a number of bodies, in particular the Director General of Fair Trading (DGFT), the Competition Commission (CC) and the Secretary of State for Trade and Industry[1]. The acts and decisions of these bodies are in principle capable of being challenged in the High Court[2] by means of a claim for judicial review. Such claims are dealt with by procedures laid down in the Supreme Court Act 1981 and Ord 54 of the Civil Procedure Rules. Certain decisions of the DGFT under the CA 1998 are susceptible to appeal to the Competition Commission[3] but others are not[4]. It remains to be seen what role judicial review will play in relation to those decisions of the DGFT taken under the CA 1998 and which are not appealable to the Competition Commission[5].

1 The CC has inherited the functions of the Monopolies and Mergers Commission (MMC). In addition, there are a number of 'specialist' bodies established by the statutes which have provided for the privatisation of various industries: eg OFTEL (regulating the telecommunications industry), OFGEM (regulating the gas and electricity industries) and OFWAT (regulating the water industry).
2 In England and Wales; the Court of Session in Scotland.
3 See para **15.215**.
4 See para **15.217**.
5 See para **15.252**.

16.02

The law relating to judicial review has developed rapidly in recent years and applies to the acts and decisions of bodies as diverse as the Commission for Racial Equality and the Civil Aviation Authority. It is not the purpose of this chapter to provide a comprehensive analysis of the law and practice relating to applications for judicial review[1]. Rather, this chapter is confined to considering the scope for application of judicial review to the decisions of the UK competition authorities. In order to do this it is, however, necessary to provide a summary of the grounds on which judicial review can be sought and the procedures which apply. As will be seen during the course of this chapter, the scope for successful challenge against the decisions of the competition authorities is limited, not least because of the broad degree of discretion with which the authorities are vested[2].

1 The principal works covering the topic include: Wade *Administrative Law* (7th edn, 1994); de Smith *Judicial Review of Administrative Action* (6th edn, 1998); Craig *Administrative Law* (4th edn, 1999); and Aldous & Alder *Applications for Judicial Review* (2nd edn, 1993).
2 See para **16.55**.

B Circumstances in which Judicial Review may be Granted

16.03
The principal grounds on which judicial review can be applied for are set out below.

1 ULTRA VIRES

16.04
If an administrative body takes action for which it has no statutory authority, that action is in principle susceptible to judicial review as being ultra vires. If, for example, a proposed merger is referred to the CC under the Fair Trading Act 1973 (FTA 1973), s 75 and it concludes that it would not operate against the public interest, the Secretary of State has no power to block the merger (or permit it subject only to conditions) and any attempt to do so would be ultra vires. This should be contrasted with the position where the CC concludes that a merger may be expected to operate against the public interest: in that case, the Secretary of State has power to block the merger, to allow it subject to certain conditions or to allow it unconditionally. In *R v Secretary of State for Trade, ex p Anderson Strathclyde*[1], the target of a take-over bid failed in its attempt to persuade the High Court to overturn the minister's decision to allow a proposed merger in circumstances where the MMC had recommended that it be blocked.

1 [1983] 2 All ER 233: see paras **16.21–16.22**.

2 ERROR OF LAW

16.05
If an administrative body misdirects itself on a question of law the decision which it reaches on the basis of that erroneous interpretation can be the subject of an application for judicial review. The error of law must be on the face of the record, although this requirement is interpreted broadly. A case in which error of law was alleged (unsuccessfully) followed the report of the MMC under the monopoly provisions of the FTA 1973[1] in *The Supply of Credit Card Services*[2]. Visa International Service Association instituted judicial review proceedings at the end of 1989 claiming, inter alia, that the MMC had made certain errors of law in relation to the provisions of the FTA 1973 dealing with so-called 'complex monopoly situations'. Visa's claims were dismissed by the High Court[3], whose decision was subsequently upheld by the Court of Appeal. In another case, the High Court overturned an MMC Report on the basis that the MMC had misconstrued the phrase 'a substantial part of the United Kingdom' in the FTA 1973, s 64(3) in the context of a local bus merger[4]. Although this decision was upheld by the Court of Appeal, it was subsequently overturned by the House of Lords[5]. More recently, the High Court ruled that the DGFT was

not entitled, by virtue of s 6(2) of the Competition Act 1980, to include in a reference to the MMC under s 5 of the Act any course of conduct which he had not already described as anti-competitive in a report under s 3 of the Act[6]. The DGFT decided not to appeal against that judgment but rather to vary the reference made to the MMC[7].

1 For a description of the substantive application of the monopoly provisions of the FTA 1973, see Chapter 15.
2 (1989) (Cm 718).
3 *R v Monopolies and Mergers Commission, ex p Visa International Service Association* [1991] COD 29; aftd [1991] CCLR 13, CA.
4 *R v Monopolies and Mergers Commission, ex p South Yorkshire Transport Ltd* [1993] 1 WLR 23: see paras **16.42, 16.43**.
5 *R v Monopolies and Mergers Commission, ex p South Yorkshire Transport Ltd* [1993] 1 WLR 23; see paras **16.42, 16.43**.
6 *R v Director General of Fair Trading, ex p Southdown Motor Services Ltd,* (1993) Times, 18 January.
7 OFT Press Release, 12 January 1993.

16.06
Mindful of the possibility of legal proceedings, it is not unusual for the MMC (now the CC), in particular, to obtain outside legal advice on the interpretation of particular statutory provisions. Examples in the field of mergers include its reports on the proposed acquisition of *C Walker & Sons (Holdings) Ltd by British Steel plc*[1] and the proposed merger of the *Colne Valley Water Co and Rickmansworth Water Co with water enterprises carried on by General Utilities PLC*[2]. Although the obtaining of such advice naturally does not immunise it from the possibility of an application for judicial review, it assists in demonstrating that the MMC has acted reasonably; the onus is on the person(s) claiming to be adversely affected by its findings to commence legal proceedings.

1 Cm 1028, April 1990.
2 Cm 1029, April 1990.

16.07
It is not always easy to determine whether a particular finding is one of law or one of fact and degree. If the latter, it is likely to be considerably more difficult to overturn as the courts are extremely reluctant to interfere with findings of fact. An example of the fine borderline which can exist is provided by the Court of Appeal's decision in *R v Monopolies and Mergers Commission, ex p Argyll Group plc*[1]. There, the Distillers Company had been the subject of rival bids by Argyll and Guinness. The first bid by Guinness had been referred to the MMC, following which Guinness made certain amendments to its proposal (involving the disposal, in the event that the bid was successful, of a number of distilleries operated by Guinness and Distillers). In the light of this, Guinness persuaded the MMC chairman that it had abandoned the 'arrangements such as are mentioned in the reference' within the meaning of the FTA 1973, s 75(5) and that he should accordingly request the Secretary of State to lay the reference aside. The revised bid arrangements were not referred to the MMC and Guinness was ultimately successful in its bid for Distillers.

1 [1986] 2 All ER 257, [1986] 1 WLR 763.

16.08
Argyll argued that the chairman of the MMC had misdirected himself as to the proper meaning of s 75(5) of the FTA 1973, contending that Guinness had not abandoned the arrangements mentioned in the original reference. In the Court of Appeal Sir John Donaldson, having dismissed Argyll's contention, went on to say that:

> '. . . just as it is not for us to review the chairman's factual conclusion that the merger proposal, the subject matter of the reference, had been abandoned, that being a matter of fact and degree for him . . . so it is not for the Secretary of State to review his conclusion'[1].

1 [1986] 1 WLR 763 at 771.

3 NATURAL JUSTICE

16.09
The rules of natural justice constitute, essentially, a duty to act fairly. They tend to be regarded as being made up of two rules: that the decision-making body should not be biased through having an interest in the matter in question (*nemo judex in causa sua*) and that it should afford each party affected by its ultimate decision a fair hearing (*audi alteram partem*). Each of these is considered in turn below.

(1) No Bias

16.10
If the members of an administrative body have a personal or financial interest in the outcome of a proceeding before that body, the rules of natural justice require them to refrain from participating in the decision-making process. The categories of 'interest' which might lead a particular person to be biased are not closed and great care is usually taken to ensure that the potential for bias is not allowed to arise. For example, in two merger cases (*Charter Consolidated/Anderson Strathclyde*[1] and *Guinness/Distillers*[2]), the minister in question in each case delegated the decision-making role to a junior minister because the former had a financial interest in the outcome of the proposed bids.

1 Cmnd 8771, December 1982.
2 (1986).

(2) Right to a Fair Hearing

16.11
The right to a fair hearing is essentially the right of a person directly affected by the decision in question to be heard and to be given an opportunity to comment on the matters on which the decision-making body may rely. Failure to adhere to this principle provides a basis for judicial review[1]. The category of administrative body to which this principle applies has

tended to be broadened in recent years. It is clear that it applies to those bodies responsible for administering UK competition law. Thus, in *Secretary of State for Trade and Industry v Hoffmann–La Roche & Co AG*[2], Lord Diplock accepted that:

> 'It is the duty of the Commissioners to observe the rules of natural justice in the course of their investigation—which means no more than that they must act fairly by giving to the person whose activities are being investigated a reasonable opportunity to put forward facts and arguments in justification of its conduct of these activities before they reach a conclusion which may affect him adversely'[3].

1 As in *Ridge v Baldwin* [1964] AC 40, [1963] 2 All ER 66 (dismissal of a chief constable by a police authority on the basis of allegations not put to him).
2 [1975] AC 295, [1974] 2 All ER 1128.
3 [1975] AC 295 at 368, [1974] 3 WLR 104 at 133–4.

16.12

The CC is mindful of the need to ensure that the parties principally involved in any inquiry conducted by it have an opportunity to comment on issues on which it may ultimately wish to make a finding (although it studiously avoids providing one party with extracts of another party's evidence or, in most cases, even a full summary of evidence). The difficulty which any party would have in successfully challenging a CC report on the basis of alleged breach of this rule of natural justice is shown by the *Matthew Brown* case[1]. There Matthew Brown plc was the subject of a takeover bid by Scottish & Newcastle Breweries plc. This bid was referred to the MMC, which concluded that the proposed merger would not operate against the public interest. Matthew Brown sought judicial review of the MMC's report, arguing that there had been manifest unfairness in that the report included conclusions based on certain materials submitted to the MMC by Scottish & Newcastle which had not been put to Matthew Brown for comment. In dismissing the application, Macpherson J held that:

> 'The timetable and conduct of the case by the Commission must be looked at as a whole. It is wrong, in my judgment, to seek to impose on the Commission any such uniform requirement that every piece of material put before the Commission which may in any way influence its report must go to all parties or even to the opposing main participants in the bid . . . the concept of fairness is itself flexible and should not be subject to the court laying down rules or steps which have to be followed. The question in each case is whether the Commission has adopted a procedure so unfair that no reasonable Commission or group would have adopted it, so that it can be said to have acted with manifest unfairness. Provided each party has its mind brought to bear on the relevant issues it is not in my judgment for the court to lay down rules as to how each group should act in any particular inquiry'[2].

In the subsequent *Stagecoach*[3] case, Collins J adopted a slightly less stringent test, namely one of fairness, than that adopted in *Matthew Brown.*

1 *R v Monopolies and Mergers Commission, ex p Matthew Brown plc* [1987] 1 All ER 463, [1987] 1 WLR 1235; see also *R v Monopolies and Mergers Commission, ex p Air Europe Ltd* (1988) 4 BCC 182.
2 [1987] 1 WLR 1235 at 1242.
3 *R v Monopolies and Mergers Commission, ex p Stagecoach Holdings plc* (5 July 1996, unreported).

4 REASONABLENESS

16.13

The decision of a public authority is liable to be quashed in judicial review proceedings if the court concludes that the decision is such that no authority properly directing itself on the relevant law and acting reasonably could have reached it (ie the decision lacked rationality). This is the so-called *Wednesbury* principle[1]. It should be noted that the test is not whether the decision itself is reasonable but whether a reasonable tribunal could have come to that decision. The test is easily stated but it can frequently be far from clear in any given case as to which side of the reasonableness line a particular decision falls. It is, however, very unlikely that this ground for invoking judicial review could be successfully invoked in the context of decisions by the UK competition authorities, given the very broad discretion which they enjoy under the relevant legislation[2].

1 A principle which derives its name from *Associated Provincial Picture Houses Ltd v Wednesbury Corpn* [1948] 1 KB 223, [1947] 2 All ER 680, HL.

2 See eg the decision of the House of Lords in *Lonrho plc v Secretary of State for Trade and Industry* [1989] 2 All ER 609, subnom *R v Secretary of State for Trade and Industry, ex p Lonrho plc* [1989] 1 WLR 525: see paras **16.34–16.36**. See too *R v Monopolies and Mergers Commission, ex p NHBC* (1994) Independent, 20 January.

16.14

In considering whether a particular administrative decision is rational the courts have on occasion in recent years considered whether the remedy adopted has been disproportionate to the mischief at which it is aimed[1]. Although the scope for invoking an alleged lack of proportionality is, as in the case of other grounds for seeking judicial review, likely to be limited in the context of UK competition law, its developing role in the context of judicial review is intriguing because of the possibility that English law will be influenced in this area by EC law: as noted in Chapter 11, the principle of proportionality is an established element of EC law.

1 See eg *R v Barnsley Metropolitan Borough Council, ex p Hook* [1976] 1 WLR 1052 at 1057, 1063, CA; also *R v Secretary of State for Transport, ex p Pegasus Holidays (London) Ltd* [1988] 1 WLR 990 at 1001 and *R v Brent London Borough Council, ex p Assegai* (1987) Times, 18 June.

16.15

Whether proportionality will continue to be just one element of the consideration whether a decision is unreasonable or develop as an independent ground for challenge remains to be seen. It is a basic principle of administrative law that in judicial review cases the courts have a supervisory function and are not exercising an appellate jurisdiction. There is likely therefore to be some judicial concern[1] that if proportionality develops as a separate ground for review rather than remain as an element of the reasonableness test, the courts could depart from a purely supervisory role and begin to substitute their own judgment.

1 See, eg the judgment of Lord Donaldson in the Court of Appeal in *R v Secretary of State for the Home Department, ex p Brind* [1991] 1 AC, [1990] 1 All ER 469. The House of Lords upheld the Court of Appeal's judgment although it did not rule out the possible future development of the law in that respect [1991] 1 All ER 720.

5 DISCRETION

16.16
Even if a case is susceptible to judicial review on the basis that it falls into one of the categories set out above, the court is not bound to grant it; rather it has a discretion to do so. For example, in a case in the competition law field, *R v Monopolies and Mergers Commission, ex p Argyll Group plc*[1], the Court of Appeal exercised its discretion and declined to grant judicial review, because of the needs of good public administration[2].

1 [1986] 2 All ER 257, [1986] 1 WLR 763.
2 See paras **16.55–16.57**.

C Prospects for a Successful Application for Judicial Review in the Competition Law Field

1 CASE LAW TO DATE

16.17
There are so far only a few reported judgments on applications for judicial review of decisions by UK competition authorities, most of which involve the CC or its predecessor (the MMC). Of those a number arose out of contested take-overs which had been referred to it under the merger control provisions of the FTA 1973. Paragraphs **16.18–16.49** summarise the findings in the principal cases to date; paras **16.50–16.57** then attempt to draw certain conclusions in the light of those decisions and the more general trends in judicial review cases in recent years.

(1) Hoffmann–La Roche[1]

16.18
Facts: In *Hoffmann–La Roche*[1] *v Secretary of State for Trade and Industry* the MMC had conducted a monopoly inquiry into the level of profits made by certain drug companies. In the light of its finding that the determination of price levels of certain drugs by Roche Products operated against the public interest, the Secretary of State laid before Parliament statutory orders directing the appellants to reduce their prices and one of these was duly approved by both Houses of Parliament. The appellants informed the Secretary of State that they would not obey the order and brought proceedings against him, claiming that the procedures adopted by the MMC had been contrary to the rules of natural justice and that the order was ultra vires and invalid; in turn, the Secretary of State brought proceedings for an injunction restraining the appellants from charging any prices in excess of those specified in the order.

1 [1975] AC 295, [1974] 2 All ER 1128.

16.19
The court's judgment: The case principally centred around whether, in return for being granted an interim injunction, the Secretary of State was obliged to give an undertaking in damages in order to compensate the appellants if at the trial of the action the order was held to be invalid. The House of Lords ruled that, in a case where the Crown sought by injunction to enforce what was prima facie the law of the land (as opposed to proprietary rights), the person against whom it was sought was required to show very good reason why the Crown should be required to give a cross-undertaking in damages. In reaching a view on this, all the circumstances should be taken into account and, on the facts of the case, the House of Lords held that the Secretary of State was entitled to the injunction which he sought without being required to give such an undertaking.

16.20
Although the House of Lords was not required to reach a conclusion on the merits of the appellants' case that the rules of natural justice had been breached, the strength (or otherwise) of that case was a relevant factor in deciding whether or not the Crown should give an undertaking in damages; indeed, it appears from the judgment of Lord Diplock that the majority of their Lordships believed that an undertaking in damages should only be required if the appellants had succeeded in showing a strong prima facie case that the order sought to be enforced by the injunction was ultra vires and it is clear that he believed that they had failed to do so. He accepted, however, that it was indeed the duty of the Commissioners to observe the rules of natural justice in the course of their investigation which he took to mean 'no more than that they must act fairly by giving to the person whose activities are being investigated a reasonable opportunity to put forward facts and arguments in justification of his conduct of these activities before they reach a conclusion which may affect him adversely'[1].

1 [1975] AC 295 at 368, [1974] 3 WLR 104 at 134.

(2) Anderson Strathclyde[1]

16.21
Facts: The applicant was subject to a take-over bid by Charter Consolidated plc, which was referred to the MMC. The MMC concluded (by a majority of four to two) that it might be expected to operate against the public interest and recommended that it be blocked. This recommendation was based principally on the adverse effects on management and labour relations which the MMC believed would occur, rather than any direct effect on competition. The minister decided that it was speculative to conclude that the merger might harm the public interest and decided not to block it. The applicant challenged this decision on two grounds:

(*a*) that the minister was bound as a matter of law to accept the MMC's recommendation—his only discretion was in deciding the appropriate remedy;

(*b*) that the minister had taken into account irrelevant considerations in reaching his decision.

1 *R v Secretary of State for Trade, ex p Anderson Strathclyde* [1983] 2 All ER 233.

16.22

The court's judgment: The applicant failed on both issues. As far as the first is concerned, the court had little difficulty on the language of the statute[1] in concluding that the minister had a broad discretion to accept or reject the MMC's recommendation. On the second issue, the minister's reasons for departing from the MMC's recommendation were set out in a short press release. The applicant argued that these showed that he had misinterpreted the MMC's findings and accordingly had taken account of matters that he should not. The court disagreed, noting, in particular, that the minister was entitled to have regard to the views of the two dissenting members of the MMC:

> '. . . it was a matter for the Minister, in his unfettered discretion, to choose between those two views, taking into account any other matters . . . He preferred the view of the minority. Whether he was right or wrong about that is a matter of political judgment, and not a matter of law'[2].

1 FTA 1973, ss 73(2) and 73(3).
2 [1983] 2 All ER 233 at 243.

(3) Argyll[1]

16.23

Facts: This case arose out of rival bids by Argyll and Guinness to take over the Distillers Company. Guinness's initial bid was referred to the Monopolies and Mergers Commission for investigation. Before the investigation commenced, Guinness informed the Commission's chairman that it had decided to amend its proposed bid by disposing, in the event that the bid was successful, of certain distilleries operated by Guinness and Distillers. The MMC chairman considered that this meant that Guinness had abandoned the arrangements mentioned in the reference within the meaning of the FTA 1973, s 75(5) and that he should accordingly request the Secretary of State to lay the reference aside. The Secretary of State duly did so and decided not to refer the revised bid to the MMC.

1 *R v Monopolies and Mergers Commission, ex p Argyll Group plc* [1986] 2 All ER 257, [1986] 1 WLR 763, CA.

16.24

As minority shareholders in Distillers, Argyll sought judicial review of the decision that the proposal had been abandoned and the Secretary of State's consent to the laying aside of the reference. The issue also arose whether, under the Fair Trading Act 1973, the chairman of the Commission had power, acting on his own, to take the decision that Guinness had abandoned its original merger proposal or whether this was something which could only be done by a properly constituted group of members of the MMC.

16.25
The court's judgment: On the main issue of construction of the FTA 1973, s 75(5) the Court of Appeal held that it was a question of fact and degree whether any new arrangements subsequently put forward were sufficiently different from Guinness's original arrangements that it could be said that the proposed arrangements had been abandoned. This was, in the words of Sir John Donaldson, 'supremely a matter for the Commission'. As far as the power of the chairman of the MMC to take this decision on his own was concerned, the Court of Appeal accepted that he did not have any independent authority to do so but nevertheless went on to hold that a properly constituted group of members of the MMC would have reached the same conclusion as he had. Taking into account the needs of good public administration[1], the court exercised its discretion and refused to grant judicial review.

1 See paras **16.55–16.57**.

(4) Elders[1]

16.26
Facts: The *Elders*[1] case arose out of its bid for Allied-Lyons plc, which had been referred to the MMC. During the course of the investigation, Elders supplied the MMC with confidential details of the financial arrangements which would form the basis of its bid in the event that it were permitted to proceed. Under the FTA 1973, s 133[2] the MMC is under a duty not to disclose information obtained by it without the consent of the person to whose business it relates, unless such disclosure is necessary for the purpose of facilitating the performance of its functions. The MMC had concluded that, in order to enable it to perform its functions under the Act, it was necessary for Allied-Lyons to be able to comment on the information and accordingly the MMC notified Elders that it intended to disclose the information concerned to Allied-Lyons. Elders applied for judicial review of the MMC's decision.

1 *R v Monopolies and Mergers Commission, ex p Elders IXL Ltd* [1987] 1 All ER 451, [1987] 1 WLR 1221.
2 For a discussion of the FTA 1973, s 133, see para **14.58**.

16.27
The court's judgment: Elders' application was based on two grounds: firstly, that the MMC had been guilty of a procedural impropriety in that the decision to disclose was a decision which was unfair to Elders, and secondly, that disclosure would contravene the Fair Trading Act 1973, s 133(1) and could not be justified under the exception contained in s 133(2)(*a*) of that Act. There was, however, no suggestion that the MMC had acted irrationally. As far as the first ground was concerned, the judge accepted that each of the companies was entitled to be treated fairly. However, the judge emphasised that the considerations of fairness arose in the course of a statutory investigation as to what was or was not in the public interest and he concluded that the MMC had been 'correct in subordinating a perceived detriment to Elders to their judgment of how best to perform their statutory function'. In saying this, he emphasised that there was no suggestion of irrationality or bad faith on the part of the MMC.

16.28
As far as the second ground was concerned, Elders argued that the court had to determine whether, viewed objectively, the exception in s 133(2)(*a*) of the FTA 1973 was satisfied. The judge rejected this argument on the basis that the subsection did not require the court to consider whether disclosure in fact facilitated the carrying out of the MMC's statutory functions but merely whether disclosure was made 'for the purpose of' so facilitating. He was satisfied on the evidence that this indeed was the MMC's intention and again he stressed the fact that the formation of that intention had neither been irrational nor made in bad faith.

(5) Matthew Brown[1]

16.29
Facts: This case arose out of a bid by Scottish & Newcastle Breweries plc for Matthew Brown, which was referred to the MMC for investigation. During the course of the investigation, Scottish & Newcastle had supplemented its original evidence regarding the effect the merger might have on competition in a particular part of the UK. The MMC ultimately concluded that the proposed merger would not operate against the public interest and Matthew Brown sought judicial review to have the report set aside. The substance of the additional Scottish & Newcastle evidence had not been put to Matthew Brown for comment and it argued that the MMC had acted in a way which was manifestly unfair, because the report included conclusions based on that additional material.

1 *R v Monopolies and Mergers Commission, ex p Matthew Brown plc* [1987] 1 All ER 463, [1987] 1 WLR 1235.

16.30
The court's judgment: In dismissing the application for judicial review, the High Court held that the question in such a case was whether the MMC had adopted a procedure so unfair that no reasonable MMC group would have adopted it. The court was satisfied that the whole question of concentration in the part of the UK market covered in Scottish & Newcastle's further evidence was fully in the minds of the MMC and both companies concerned. In the subsequent *Stagecoach*[1] case, the High Court departed from the test adopted in the *Matthew Brown* case, ruling that the appropriate test was not one of 'Wednesbury unreasonableness' but simply one of fairness (likely to be a less stringent test).

1 *R v Monopolies and Mergers Commission, ex p Stagecoach Holdings plc* (5 July 1996, unreported): see para **16.46**.

(6) Air Europe[1]

16.31
Facts: During the course of its consideration in 1987 of the proposed merger between British Airways and British Caledonian, the MMC took account of certain assurances offered by British Airways during the inquiry

and decided that the merger would not operate against the public interest; it is clear from the MMC's report that these assurances played an important part in its decision. Air Europe argued strongly to the MMC that the proposed merger should not be allowed to proceed. Air Europe applied for judicial review, seeking an order of certiorari to quash the report of the MMC. There were two principal grounds for its application, namely illegality and procedural impropriety. As far as illegality was concerned, Air Europe argued that the MMC had acted ultra vires in taking into account the assurances given by British Airways during the course of the MMC's enquiry when determining whether the proposed merger may be expected to operate against the public interest. The alleged procedural impropriety was that the MMC had acted unfairly in failing to invite Air Europe to comment on the British Airways assurances.

1 *R v Monopolies and Mergers Commission, ex p Air Europe Ltd* (1988) 4 BCC 182.

16.32

The court's judgment: As far as the alleged illegality was concerned, Air Europe's argument was based on the premise that the MMC should report on the basis of the proposals as they stood at the date of the reference. It accepted that the MMC could refer to the British Airways assurances in its report and, if appropriate, recommend that undertakings along the lines of those assurances be given for the purpose of remedying any adverse affects of the merger. Rejecting the Air Europe argument, the High Court held that it would be artificial to require the MMC to report on the original proposal and, in so doing, to ignore the assurances offered.

16.33

As far as the alleged procedural impropriety was concerned, Air Europe argued that the MMC had breached the rules of natural justice by not inviting Air Europe to comment on the assurances offered by British Airways. Air Europe's contention was rejected relatively swiftly, on the basis that it had made it clear in its submissions to the MMC that it saw no purpose in limited safeguards; nothing would suffice except a radical re-appraisal of the entire air licensing system.

(7) Lonrho[1]

16.34

Facts: This case arose out of the long-running battle for control of House of Fraser plc, the owner of a large number of department stores including Harrods. In 1985 the Secretary of State for Trade and Industry announced that he had decided not to refer the proposed acquisition by Al Fayed Investment & Trust (UK) plc to the MMC. Evidence subsequently came to light which suggested that there were material facts which had not been known by the Secretary of State at the time he had made his decision not to refer the proposed acquisition. Under the FTA 1973, s 64(4)(*b*), the Secretary of State has power to make a reference if it appears to him that new material facts about the merger have come to light and if he makes the reference within six months of the emergence of those facts. Acting on the advice of the Director General of Fair Trading, the Secretary of State decided in 1988 that the new facts which had emerged did not justify a reference. In accordance with his usual practice, the Secretary of State did not give any reasons for the decision not to refer. That decision was challenged by Lonrho, which had for several year's itself been attempting to obtain a controlling interest in Harrods.

1 *Lonrho plc v Secretary of State for Trade and Industry* [1989] 2 All ER 609, sub nom *R v Secretary of State for Trade and Industry, ex p Lonrho plc* [1989] 1 WLR 525, HL.

16.35

The court's judgment: The House of Lords held that the Fair Trading Act 1973 imposed no duty upon the Secretary of State to make a reference in any given case; rather he had a discretion to do so. It was held that Lonrho had failed to show that no reasonable Secretary of State could have failed to make a reference. As far as the absence of reasons was concerned, it was held that this did not of itself provide any support for the suggested irrationality of the decision reached by the Secretary of State. The only relevance of an absence of reasons was that, if all other evidence suggested that the Secretary of State had no rational reason for reaching the decision which he did, he could not complain if a court did indeed draw this inference.

16.36

Lord Keith, giving the judgment of the House of Lords, made the following general statement in relation to the role of the courts when reviewing ministerial decisions:

> 'The judgments of the Divisional Court [which had found in favour of Lonrho] illustrate the danger of judges wrongly, though unconsciously, substituting their own views for the views of the decision-maker who alone is charged and authorised by Parliament to exercise a discretion. The question is not whether the Secretary of State came to a correct solution or to a conclusion which meets with the approval of the Divisional Court but whether the discretion was properly exercised'[1].

In a recent article[2] Sir Gordon Borrie, QC, Director General of Fair Trading, welcomed that statement, indicating that he hoped the judgment of the House of Lords in the *Lonrho* case would mark the beginning of a period of measured judicial restraint.

1 [1989] 1 WLR 525 at 535: this statement was made in the context of the Secretary of State's decision to delay publication of a review of an inspector's report regarding the acquisition of House of Fraser plc by Al Fayed Investment and Trust (UK) plc, rather than the decision not to refer the acquisition to the MMC; however, the statement would appear to be one of general application; see too, in other contexts, *Chief Constable of the North Wales Police v Evans* [1982] 1 WLR 1155 at 1160 (Lord Hailsham).
2 'The Regulation of Public and Private Power' (1989) PL 552.

16.37

A further twist in the battle for control of House of Fraser plc is provided by the High Court's decision in *Lonrho plc v Tebbit*[1]. Lonrho's bid for the company in 1979 had been referred to the MMC, following which Lonrho had given the DTI undertakings not to acquire 30% or more of the equity share capital of House of Fraser plc. Several years later a new bid was made by Lonrho for the company and was again referred to the MMC. This time (in February 1984) the MMC reported that a take-over by Lonrho would not operate against the public interest. Several weeks later a third party made a rival bid for House of Fraser (which was not referred[2]) and Lonrho renewed an earlier application to be released as a matter of urgency from its previous undertaking to the DTI. By the time the DTI released Lonrho from the undertaking, the third party had already acquired control of House of Fraser.

1 *Lonrho plc v Tebbit* [1991] 4 All ER 973; upheld by the Court of Appeal [1992] 4 All ER 280.
2 This decision was unsuccessfully challenged by Lonrho: see paras **16.34–16.36**.

16.38
Once the MMC had made its second report, the Secretary of State for Trade and Industry had no power to make any new order (or seek any further undertaking in lieu thereof) to restrict Lonrho's ability to bid. However, the Fair Trading Act 1973 was completely silent as to what was to happen to an existing undertaking where a fresh report concluded that the merger was no longer against the public interest. Lonrho argued that there must be an implied obligation to release an undertaking which was no longer justified, giving rise to a duty of care owed to it by the Secretary of State under private law. The Secretary of State denied this, arguing that any implied obligation was a matter of public law and did not give rise to private law rights. The High Court refused to accept that Lonrho's claim disclosed no reasonable cause of action and therefore decided not to strike out the claim. It held that the matter should be decided at full trial, including the question whether the release of the undertaking was a policy decision rather than merely an operational decision.

(8) Visa[1]

16.39
Facts: This case arose out of an investigation by the MMC into the alleged existence of a monopoly situation in the United Kingdom in the supply of credit card services. The MMC concluded[2] that Visa's requirement that (*a*) traders not impose a surcharge on transactions when a Visa card was used, and (*b*) its members be required to issue a stipulated number of cards before they could become 'merchant acquirers' was contrary to the public interest. The Secretary of State accepted these findings and decided to make orders that agreements containing such restrictions were unlawful[3].

1 *R v Monopolies and Mergers Commission, ex p Visa International Services Association* [1991] CCLR 13, CA.
2 *The Supply of Credit Card Services* (1989) (Cm 718).
3 The order-making procedure was interrupted by the judicial proceedings but was subsequently completed: see para **14.87**.

16.40
The court's judgment: Visa sought judicial review of the MMC's report and also of the decisions of the Secretary of State made following the report. A

declaration was sought that, in a number of different respects, the MMC had erred in law in reaching its conclusions and making recommendations. The relief sought against the Secretary of State was by way of declaration that, in accepting those recommendations, he had acted ultra vires and his decision was void and/or of no effect. At first instance, the judge ruled[1] that the MMC had not erred in law either in relation to the 'no discrimination rule' or the 'merchant acquirer rule'. A separate issue which was raised was whether the MMC had erred in law in concluding that it had jurisdiction over Visa because the latter had a place of business in the United Kingdom. On this issue the judge found that the MMC had indeed erred in law. However, this error would only have been of importance if the MMC was not otherwise entitled to take Visa into consideration and he held that there was a separate basis on which this could be done; accordingly, the error of law could not impugn the report.

1 [1991] COD 29.

16.41

The judge's general approach to the MMC's report is particularly noteworthy. Although he said that it was not disputed that the MMC's findings, and any actions taken thereafter by either the DGFT or the Secretary of State, were amenable to judicial review on conventional public law principles, he went on to say that:

> 'The [MMC] Report must not be read as if it were a statute or a judgment. It should be read in a generous not restrictive way and the Court should be slow to disable the MMC from recommending action considered to be in the public interest or to prevent the Secretary of State from acting thereon unless any perceived errors of law are both material and substantial'.

The Court of Appeal rejected Visa's appeal against the judge's decision and refused leave to appeal to the House of Lords[1].

1 Judgment dated 4 October 1990 (not yet reported).

(9) South Yorkshire Transport[1]

16.42

Facts: This case arose out of the acquisition by South Yorkshire Transport of a number of local bus businesses in the Sheffield area, as a result of which the company's share of the Sheffield bus market rose from about 73% to 87%. The acquisitions were referred to the MMC which concluded that they could be expected to operate against the public interest[2]. The Secretary of State accepted this conclusion and ordered the company to sell the four businesses concerned. In order to enable the MMC to have jurisdiction, it was necessary for it to find that the Sheffield bus market constituted 'a substantial part of the United Kingdom'[3]. The company applied for judicial review.

1 *R v Monopolies and Mergers Commission, ex p South Yorkshire Transport Ltd* [1992] 1 All ER 257, CA, overturned on appeal by the House of Lords, [1993] 1 WLR 23.
2 (1990) (Cm 1166).
3 FTA 1973, s 64(3).

16.43
The court's judgment: The basis of South Yorkshire Transport's case was that the Sheffield area did not constitute 'a substantial part of the United Kingdom' within the meaning of the FTA 1973, s 64(3) and that the MMC did not therefore have jurisdiction; on this basis the Secretary of State was not entitled to order disposal of the businesses acquired. The High Court upheld the applicant's case[1], holding that the Sheffield area, representing about 4% of national bus services, could not be described as substantial. However, the decision was overturned by the House of Lords, which held that on their true construction the words 'a substantial part of the United Kingdom' connoted any part of such size, character and importance as to make it worth consideration for the purposes of the Act, that the MMC had not mis-directed itself and that it had in the circumstances rightly concluded that the reference area was sufficiently worthy of consideration[2]. Giving the judgment of the House, Lord Mustill indicated that, once the MMC had correctly established the criteria for interpreting the word 'substantial' in the context in which it was used, the courts should only interfere with the MMC's application of those criteria 'if the decision is so aberrant that it cannot be classed as rational'[3].

1 By a majority of two to one, the Court of Appeal upheld the High Court ruling: *R v Monopolies and Mergers Commission ex p South Yorkshire Transport Ltd* [1992] 1 All ER 257.
2 [1993] 1 WLR 23.
3 Ibid at p 32.

(10) Southdown Motor Services[1]

16.44
Facts: This case arose out of an investigation by the DGFT under the anti-competitive practice provisions of the Competition Act 1980[2]. Following his own investigation and report, the DGFT had decided to make a reference to the MMC concerning the operation of bus services in the Bognor Regis area. In fact, the DGFT's report had been concerned essentially with Southdown's conduct of two particular bus services. The company claimed that the reference to the MMC was phrased too broadly, in that it extended to courses of conduct which the DGFT had not described as anti-competitive. It accordingly applied for judicial review.

1 *R v Director General of Fair Trading, ex p Southdown Motor Services Ltd* (1993) Times, 18 January.
2 Since repealed by the Competition Act 1998.

16.45
The court's judgment: Section 6(2) of the CA 1980 provides that the DGFT may not specify as the subject of investigation by the MMC any course of conduct which is not described in his own report. Counsel for the DGFT argued that his report had dealt generally with courses of conduct by Southdown in the Bognor Regis area and argued that though not all of these had been described as anti-competitive this was not an essential prerequisite of s 6(2), which did not expressly restrict references to the

MMC to courses of conduct which the DGFT had found to be anti-competitive. The judge dismissed this argument, holding that it was difficult to see how there could be a reference under s 6(2) which did not concern an anti-competitive course of conduct. The judge therefore held that the reference, in specifying as a course of conduct the charging of uneconomic fares in connection with bus services *generally* in the Bognor Regis area, was unlawful. The DGFT decided not to appeal against this judgment and instead varied the terms of reference to the MMC under the provisions of s 6(6) of the CA 1980[1].

1 OFT Press Release, 12 January 1993.

(11) Stagecoach Holdings[1]

16.46

Facts: This case involved two applications by Stagecoach for judicial review of decisions of the MMC in reports presented to Parliament in March and April 1995 respectively. In each case the MMC decided that a merger situation had been created which might be expected to operate against the public interest and made recommendations to the Secretary of State accordingly. The company claimed that there had been material unfairness in the procedure which the MMC had adopted and that this constituted a procedural inpropriety. Stagecoach argued that it was never told the views of certain third parties and had no chance to deal with them or, more particularly, to try to show that they were unreliable.

1 *R v Monopolies and Mergers Commission, ex p Stagecoach Holdings plc* (5 July 1996, unreported).

16.47

The court's judgment: It was argued on behalf of the MMC that the court should only intervene if satisfied that the MMC has acted irrationally. Counsel for the MMC cited the decision in the *Matthew Brown* case[1]. In that case, it had been held that the question in each case was whether the MMC had adopted a procedure so unfair that no reasonable Commission or group could have adopted it, so that it can be said to have acted with manifest unfairness. The judge in the *Stagecoach*[2] case disagreed. He held, citing the *Guinness*[3] case, that the matter had to be decided, not on grounds of 'Wednesbury unreasonableness'[4], but in accordance with the principles of fair procedure which had been developed over the years, and of which the courts are the author and sole judge; ie in essence the rules of natural justice. This test is likely to be easier for a party in the position of Stagecoach to satisfy, although the judge still accepted that the court should be slow to intervene. On the facts of the case, Stagecoach's application was dismissed.

1 *R v Monopolies and Mergers Commission, ex p Matthew Brown plc* [1987] 1 All ER 463, [1987] 1 WLR 1235; see para **16.29** ff.
2 See para **16.46**.
3 *R v Takeover Panel, ex p Guinness plc* [1990] 1 QB 146.
4 A principle derived from *Associated Provincial Picture Houses Ltd v Wednesbury Corpn* [1948] 1 KB 223, [1947] 2 All ER 680.

(12) Thomson Holidays

16.48
Facts: In *Thomson Holidays*[1], the Secretary of State had made an order[2] following a report of the MMC[3] relating to the supply of tour operators' services and travel agents' services. Thomson argued that certain elements of the Order were ultra vires, discriminatory and 'Wednesbury unreasonable'.

1 *R v Secretary of State for Trade and Industry, ex p Thomson Holidays Ltd* (2000) Times, 12 January, CA.
2 The Foreign Package Holiday (Tour Operators and Travel Agents) Order 1998, SI 1998/1945.
3 *Foreign Package Holidays* (Cm 3813).

16.49
The court's judgment: In holding in favour of Thomson, the Court of Appeal ruled that certain parts of the Order were ultra vires, the FTA 1973, s 56(3). The Secretary of State argued that she was entitled to remedy the 'adverse effects' found by the MMC, not limited by the matrix of facts the MMC had held gave rise to those effects. The Court held that such an approach would give the Secretary of State so wide-ranging a function that it could not possibly be intended by the regime laid out in the FTA 1973. This judgment is the first successful legal challenge to an order following an MMC (now Competition Commission) report and represents an important reining in of ministerial power.

2 SCOPE FOR JUDICIAL REVIEW OF DECISIONS/ ACTS OF THE COMPETITION AUTHORITIES IN THE LIGHT OF THE CASES TO DATE

16.50
Judicial review of administrative action was described (not in the context of competition law but in a general context) by Sir Gordon (now Lord) Borrie (during his tenure as DGFT) as a 'growth industry'[1]. In saying this, he cited the following statistics: in 1974 there were 160 applications for leave to seek judicial review; by 1989 this figure had grown to 1,229 applications. The increasing willingness on the part of private citizens to challenge the decisions of administrative bodies has been matched in recent years by the willingness of the courts to extend the categories of administrative body which are susceptible to judicial review[2].

1 'The Regulation of Public and Private Power' 1989 PL 552.
2 Eg the Panel on Take-overs and Mergers: *R v Panel on Take-overs and Mergers, ex p Datafin plc* [1987] QB 815, [1987] 1 All ER 564, CA; Lloyd's: *R v Committee of Lloyd's, ex p Posgate* [1983] CLY 2001; the self-regulatory organisations recognised by the Securities and Investments Board: *R v Financial Intermediaries, Managers and Brokers Regulatory Association, ex p Cochrane* [1991] BCLC 106; the Advertising Standards Authority: *R v Advertising Standards Authority Ltd, ex p Insurance Service plc* (1989) 133 Sol Jo 1545.

16.51
It is beyond doubt, as is demonstrated by the judgments summarised at paras **16.18–16.49**, that the various bodies responsible for administering

UK competition law are susceptible to judicial review. However, those judgments make it clear that it is only in rare cases that the courts will be prepared to overturn decisions or acts of the DGFT, the CC or the Secretary of State. There are several reasons for this.

16.52

First and foremost, this is an area of law in which Parliament has invested the regulators with an extremely broad degree of discretion. For example, the DGFT has a discretion whether to investigate a particular practice or conduct and, if it does, it has a further discretion to decide whether or not to refer the matter for fuller investigation by the CC; the CC in turn has a broad discretion under the Fair Trading Act 1973 to determine whether or not particular conduct or a particular merger may be expected to operate against the public interest (and indeed the public interest test itself is all-embracing). Moreover, competition policy lies at the crossroads between law and economics and one can expect the courts to be reluctant to second-guess the decisions of the regulators.

16.53

Even when one moves away from the broad area of discretion to other grounds of possible review, such as error of law on the face of the record and breach of the principles of natural justice, the prospects for successful challenge are slim. As far as a challenge based on error of law is concerned, the reason for this is largely because there is only limited scope for erroneous statutory interpretation. The *Argyll*[1] and *Elders*[2] cases are examples of challenges based on alleged errors of law (both of which failed), but such cases are likely to be rare. The more recent *Visa*[3] case involved an alleged error of law. Visa's application was rejected and, as noted above[4], the judge at first instance held that the courts should be slow to disable the MMC (now the CC) from recommending action considered to be in the public interest unless errors of law are both material and substantial. This indicates that because the CC and the Secretary of State are guardians of the public interest, the courts are likely to be particularly reluctant to intervene. Although the High Court was prepared to intervene in the *South Yorkshire Transport*[5] case, its judgment was overturned on appeal by the House of Lords[6]. The *Southdown Motor Services*[7] case is the one decision to date in which a DGFT decision was successfully challenged (there the DGFT decided not to appeal).

1 *R v Monopolies and Mergers Commission, ex p Argyll Group plc* [1986] 2 All ER 257, [1986] 1 WLR 763.
2 *R v Monopolies and Mergers Commission, ex p Elders IXL Ltd* [1987] 1 All ER 451, [1987] 1 WLR 1221.
3 *R v Monopolies and Mergers Commission, ex p Visa International Service Association* [1991] CCLR 13. See also *R v Monopolies and Mergers Commission, ex p NHBC* (1994) Independent, 20 January on the interpretation of a particular section in the monopoly provisions of the Fair Trading Act 1973. The application for judicial review failed.
4 See para **16.41**.
5 See paras **16.42, 16.43**.
6 [1993] 1 WLR 23.
7 *R v Director General of Fair Trading, ex p Southdown Motor Services Ltd* (1993) Times, 18 January.

16.54
As far as natural justice is concerned, the *Elders*[1], *Matthew Brown*[2] and *Stagecoach*[3] cases make it clear that the courts are likely to be most reluctant to intervene in the way in which the CC conducts itself (although the *Stagecoach* decision supports a less stringent test than, for example, *Matthew Brown*). Nevertheless, parties and their advisers appearing before the CC should be vigilant to ensure that it does keep within the bounds of natural justice.

1 *R v Monopolies and Mergers Commission, ex p Elders IXL Ltd* [1987] 1 All ER 451, [1987] 1 WLR 1221.
2 *R v Monopolies and Mergers Commission, ex p Matthew Brown plc* [1987] 1 All ER 463, [1987] 1 WLR 1235.
3 *R v Monopolies and Mergers Commission, ex p Stagecoach Holdings plc* (5 July 1996, unreported).

16.55
Finally, a word should be said about the exercise of the court's discretion. Even if a case falls into one of the categories where judicial review will lie, the court is not bound to grant it; rather it has a discretion to do so. In this context, the Master of the Rolls, giving the principal judgment of the Court of Appeal in the *Argyll*[1] case, said the courts have to approach their duties with a 'proper awareness of the needs of public administration'. Without seeking to catalogue them all, he mentioned a few which he believed to be relevant in that case:

(*a*) good public administration is concerned with substance rather than form;
(*b*) good public administration is concerned with speed of decision, particularly in the financial field;
(*c*) good public administration requires a proper consideration of the public interest: in that context, he described the Secretary of State as the guardian of the public interest;
(*d*) good public administration requires a proper consideration of the legitimate interests of individual citizens but in judging the relevance of an interest, however legitimate, regard has to be had to the purpose of the administrative process concerned;
(*e*) lastly, good public administration requires decisiveness and finality, unless there are compelling reasons to the contrary: accordingly, in the *Argyll*[2] case itself account had to be taken of the probability that stock market transactions had probably been done in reliance on the validity of the decisions which were the subject of challenge.

1 *R v Monopolies and Mergers Commission, ex p Argyll Group plc* [1986] 2 All ER 257, [1986] 1 WLR 763.
2 Ibid.

16.56
Taking those factors into account, the Court of Appeal refused to grant judicial review, even though it found that the chairman of the MMC did not have legal authority to act as he had done: the Court of Appeal was satisfied

that a properly constituted group of Commissioners would have reached the same conclusion as the chairman had done.

16.57
The view that good administration requires decisiveness and finality, particularly in the context of decisions having a bearing on the financial markets, was restated by the Master of the Rolls in the *Datafin*[1] case in the context of the Panel on Take-overs and Mergers. There the Court of Appeal held that the Panel was a judicially reviewable body but the applicant's claims were dismissed. The Master of the Rolls expressed the firm view that 'in the light of the special nature of the Panel, its functions, the market in which it is operating, the time scales which are inherent in that market and the need to safeguard the position of third parties, who may be numbered in thousands, all of whom are entitled to continue to trade upon an assumption of the validity of the Panel's rules and decisions, unless and until they are quashed by the court, I should expect the relationship between the Panel and the court to be historic rather than contemporaneous'. That is to say, the court should allow contemporaneous decisions to take their course and should confine its intervention to the making of declaratory orders designed to prevent a future error by the Panel. This concern over the impact of judicial intervention in relation to bodies making decisions affecting the financial markets is of greater relevance to the Panel than to any of the competition law bodies. Nevertheless, it is an aspect which should be borne in mind in the context of CC investigations in relation to proposed mergers, particularly as the Master of the Rolls' comments in *Datafin*[2] echo his own statements regarding good administration in the *Argyll*[3] case.

1 *R v Panel on Take-overs and Mergers, ex p Datafin plc* [1987] QB 815, [1987] 1 All ER 564, CA.
2 Ibid.
3 *R v Monopolies and Mergers Commission, ex p Argyll Group plc* [1986] 2 All ER 257, [1986] 1 WLR 763.

D Types of Relief Available in Judicial Review Proceedings

16.58
There are five main types of relief which may be sought in judicial review proceedings, namely:

(*a*) a quashing order (formerly known as certiorari);
(*b*) a prohibiting order (formerly known as prohibition);
(*c*) a mandatory order (formerly known as mandamus);
(*d*) declaration or injunction;
(*e*) claim for damages (though only if along with another claim for relief[1]).

Each of these is briefly considered in turn below.

1 Civil Procedure Rules (CPR) 54.3(2).

1 QUASHING ORDER

16.59
This is an order that the decision of a particular body be quashed. This is the principal remedy which was sought in the *Anderson Strathclyde*[1] and *Matthew Brown*[2] cases.

1 *R v Secretary of State for Trade, ex p Anderson Strathclyde* [1983] 2 All ER 233: see para **16.21**.
2 *R v Monopolies and Mergers Commission, ex p Matthew Brown plc* [1987] 1 All ER 463, [1987] 1 WLR 1235: see para **16.29**.

2 PROHIBITING ORDER

16.60
This is an order restraining a body from acting outside its jurisdiction. For example, in the *Elders*[1] case, Elders sought, amongst other things, an order of prohibition, restraining disclosure by the MMC of certain confidential financial information.

1 *R v Monopolies and Mergers Commission, ex p Elders IXL Ltd* [1987] 1 All ER 451, [1987] 1 WLR 1221: see para **16.26**.

3 MANDATORY ORDER

16.61
This is an order requiring a body to carry out its judicial or other public duty, ie to take a positive step. This was sought in the *Lonrho*[1] case, in which Lonrho sought an order requiring the Secretary of State to refer to the MMC the acquisition by Al Fayed Investment and Trust (UK) plc of House of Fraser plc.

1 *Lonrho plc v Secretary of State for Trade and Industry* [1989] 2 All ER 609, sub nom *R v Secretary of State for Trade and Industry, ex p Lonrho plc* [1989] 1 WLR 525, HL: see para **16.34**.

4 DECLARATION OR INJUNCTION

16.62
It is open to a party seeking judicial review to apply for a declaration or an injunction.

It should be noted that the House of Lords decided in the *Factortame*[1] case that Ord 53, r 1(2) (the predecessor of CPR 54) should not be construed as conferring jurisdiction to grant injunctions against the Crown in judicial review proceedings (in that case the proceedings were against the Secretary of State for Transport). In the same case, in which the House of Lords sought a preliminary ruling under Article 234 of the EC Treaty, the European Court of Justice has now ruled[2] that the English courts do have power to suspend an Act of Parliament alleged to be in breach of EC law, ie injunctive relief *can* be sought against the Crown if the basis of the applicant's case against the Crown is that it is acting in breach of EC law. It is quite conceivable that such a case could arise in the competition law field, particularly as the UK authorities have shown a tendency recently to investigate business conduct which is the subject of directly applicable EC law[3]. The Court of Appeal has subsequently held that the courts have jurisdiction to order a stay of the implementation of the decision under challenge pending determination on the application for judicial review[4].

1 *R v Secretary of State for Transport, ex p Factortame Ltd* [1990] 2 AC 85, [1989] 2 All ER 692.

2 [1990] 3 CMLR 867. See Barav 'Enforcement of Community Rights in the National Courts: the Case for Jurisdiction to grant Interim Relief' (1989) 26 CML Rev 369–390.

3 Eg MMC Report on the *Supply of Beer* (1989) (Cm 651) and Commission Regulation (EEC) 1984/83, OJ [1983] L 173/5; also MMC inquiry into the *Supply of New Motor Cars and Parts* (referred to the MMC in May 1990) and Commission Regulation (EEC) 123/85, OJ [1985] L 15/16.

4 *R v Secretary of State for Education and Science, ex p Avon County Council* [1991] 1 QB 558, [1991] 1 All ER 282, CA.

5 DAMAGES

16.63

The court has power to award damages on a claim for judicial review if the claimant has included a claim for damages and if the court is satisfied that, had the claim for damages been made in an action begun by the claimant at the time of making his claim, he could have been awarded damages.

16.64

There is nothing to stop a claimant seeking more than one of these remedies. For example, in the *Elders*[1] case, Elders sought an order of certiorari to quash the decision by the MMC to disclose certain confidential financial information to the company whose takeover it was investigating, a declaration that the Commission was under no duty to disclose such information and that such a disclosure would constitute a breach of the Fair Trading Act 1973 and an order of prohibition restraining disclosure.

1 *R v Monopolies and Mergers Commission, ex p Elders IXL Ltd* [1987] 1 All ER 451, [1987] 1 WLR 1221.

E Procedure for Applying for Judicial Review

16.65

The procedure governing claims for judicial review is largely set out in the Civil Procedure Rules 1998 Pt 54. The principal procedural aspects are, in outline, as follows.

1 TWO STAGE PROCESS

16.66

A claim for judicial review must be made in two stages. Firstly, under CPR 54, the leave of the court must be obtained and only if it is granted will the court proceed to hear the substantive claim for judicial review. The purpose of the two-stage procedure is in order to enable the courts to eliminate frivolous or vexatious applications at an early stage; leave should accordingly be granted if the court believes that there is an arguable case for granting the relief claimed[1]. It is open to the judge to grant leave to apply for judicial review without holding a hearing, ie based solely on the papers filed with the court.

1 *IRC v National Federation of Self Employed and Small Businesses* [1982] AC 617 at 642 and 644, HL.

2 DELAY IN APPLYING FOR RELIEF

16.67

A claim for judicial review must be made promptly and in any event within three months from the date when grounds for the claim first arose[1]. The Court of Appeal has held that even if an application for leave is made within the three-month period this does not necessarily mean that it has been made promptly[2]. Accordingly, the claimant may need to seek an extension of time even in circumstances where the application is made within the three-month period.

1 CPR 54.5(1).

2 *R v Stratford-on-Avon District Council, ex p Jackson* [1985] 3 All ER 769, [1985] 1 WLR 1319.

Chapter 17 Private Enforcement of EC Competition Law in National Courts: Introduction

A General

17.01

Some provisions of the EC Treaty produce direct effects, such that they can be relied upon by natural or legal persons in national courts of the Member States. It is well established that Articles 81 and 82 fall into the category of provisions which have direct effect. The leading case on this is *BRT v SABAM*[1], in which the European Court of Justice (ECJ) said[2] that:

> 'As the prohibitions of Articles 85(1) and 86 [now Articles 81(1) and 82] tend by their very nature to produce direct effects in relations between individuals, these Articles create direct rights in respect of the individuals concerned which the national courts must safeguard'.

1 Case 127/73 [1974] ECR 51, [1974] 2 CMLR 238. See too Case T-51/89 *Tetra Pak Rausing SA v EC Commission* [1991] 4 CMLR 334 at para 42 and Case C-234/89 *Delimitis v Henninger Bräu* [1991] ECR I-935, [1991] 4 CMLR 329 at para 45.

2 [1974] ECR 51 at 62.

17.02

This principle has been incorporated into UK law by the provisions of the European Communities Act 1972. Section 2(1) of that Act provides that:

> 'All such rights, powers, liabilities, obligations and restrictions from time to time created or arising by or under the Treaties[1], and all such remedies and procedures from time to time provided for by or under the Treaties, as in accordance with the Treaties are without further enactment to be given legal effect or used in the United Kingdom shall be recognised and available in law, and be enforced, allowed and followed accordingly …'

Section 3(1) of the European Communities Act 1972 provides that, in any legal proceedings, questions as to the meaning or effect of any of the Treaties must be treated as questions of law and (if they are not referred to the ECJ[2]), be determined as such in accordance with the principles laid down by the ECJ.

1 The term 'Treaties' in this context includes the EC, ECSC and Euratom Treaties, the Accession Treaties, the Single European Act, Treaties with third countries entered into by the Communities and other ancillary treaties: European Communities Act 1972, s 1(1), as amended.

2 Eg under the EC Treaty, Article 234.

17.03
In the leading case under English law regarding the application of Article 82, *Garden Cottage Foods Ltd v Milk Marketing Board*[1], Lord Diplock in the House of Lords delivered the following ringing affirmation of the principle enunciated in *BRT v SABAM*:

> 'This Article [Article 82] of the Treaty of Rome was held by the European Court of Justice in [*BRT v SABAM*] to produce direct effects in relations between individuals and to create direct rights in respect of the individuals concerned which the national courts must protect. This decision of the European Court of Justice as to the effect of Article 86 [now Article 82] is one which section 3(1) of the European Communities Act 1972 requires your Lordships to follow. The rights which the Article confers upon citizens in the United Kingdom accordingly fall within section 2(1) of the Act. They are without further enactment to be given legal effect in the United Kingdom and enforced accordingly'.

1 [1984] AC 130, [1983] 2 All ER 770.

17.04
One of the most important principles of Community law is that, in the event of conflict between Community law and the national law of a Member State, Community law prevails[1]. That principle is one which must, by virtue of the European Communities Act 1972, s 2(1), be recognised and to which effect must be given by courts in the United Kingdom. The effect of these principles when applied together is that Articles 81 and 82 take precedence over conflicting principles of national law so that, for example, the provisions of an agreement otherwise enforceable as a matter of English law can be rendered null and void by virtue of Article 81(2).

1 Case 6/64 *Costa v ENEL* [1964] ECR 585, [1964] CMLR 425.

17.05
It is not infrequently the case that a particular agreement or course of conduct falls within the ambit of Articles 81 and/or 82 and at the same time is subject to applicable national competition law. Various permutations are possible: in any given case, national law may be stricter than Community law, the two may be equally strict, or Community law may be stricter than national law[1].

1 See *Butterworths Competition Law*, Division I, Chapter 4.

B Interplay between the European Commission's Enforcement of Articles 81 and 82 and their Enforcement in National Courts

17.06
As national courts are also empowered to apply Articles 81 and 82, one and the same agreement or course of conduct may become the subject matter of a European Commission investigation and at the same time (or at an earlier or later date) come before a national court, giving rise to the possibility of conflicting decisions. This raises a number of jurisdictional issues which are considered in Chapter 18.

17.07
At the present time the enforcement of Articles 81 and 82 is still in practice primarily in the hands of the European Commission, as opposed to the national courts of Member States. This contrasts with the position which exists in the United States of America, where private law suits brought in the federal courts play a major part in the enforcement of the anti-trust laws[1]. The imbalance between enforcement by the Commission on the one hand, and the application of Articles 81 and 82 in national courts on the other, is something which has been a concern to the Commission for some time, not least because its resources are stretched to the limit. In its Thirteenth Report on Competition Policy (1983) the Commission noted that there was a 'widespread misconception among members of the public in Europe that only the Commission can enforce Articles 85 and 86 [now Articles 81 and 82]'[2]. It indicated that it was studying how to encourage actions before national courts. In its Fifteenth Report on Competition Policy (1985) the Commission stated[3] that it had established as a priority reinforcing the role which national courts play in the enforcement of Articles 81 and 82. In that Report, it identified a number of factors which lay behind its desire to encourage application of Articles 81 and 82 in national courts. These were:

(*a*) more frequent application at national level would increase the awareness of Community citizens as to the scope and meaning of these two provisions; this would lead to a greater respect for them;
(*b*) de-centralised application would provide a quick and efficient way of bringing to an end infringements and providing legal security;
(*c*) de-centralised application would mean that the Commission's workload would no longer include cases which did not pose any particularly complicated or novel legal or economic issues, leaving it better able to deal with the complex cases[4].

1 This owes much to the availability of treble damages under the Sherman Act 1890, s 7 and the Clayton Act 1914, s 4.
2 At para 217.
3 At para 38.
4 15th Report on Competition Policy, para 39.

17.08
The Commission took this issue a stage further in early 1993 with its adoption of a Notice on co-operation between national courts and the Commission in applying Articles 81 and 82 of the EC Treaty[1]. During the course of consultation leading up to the adoption of this Notice, the Commission's view that it is entitled to establish priorities in deciding how to utilise its finite resources received support from the CFI in its judgment in *Automec*[2].

1 OJ [1993] C 39/6. The Notice does not apply to the transport sector or to the competition rules laid down in the ECSC Treaty: ibid, para 45. A parallel Notice regarding the relationship between the EFTA Surveillance Authority and national courts in respect of Articles 53 and 54 of the EEA Agreement was published in 1995: OJ [1995] C 112/7.
2 Case T-24/90 *Automec v EC Commission* [1992] 5 CMLR 431.

17.09
In its 1993 Notice the Commission states that:

> 'The administrative resources at the Commission's disposal to perform its tasks are necessarily limited and cannot be used to deal with all the cases brought to its attention. The Commission is therefore obliged, in general, to take all organisational measures necessary for the performance of its tasks and, in particular, to establish priorities'[1].

It goes on to indicate that it intends to concentrate on matters having 'particular political, economical or legal significance for the Community', stating that complaints which lack these features should be handled by national courts or national authorities[2]. If the complainant can secure adequate protection of his rights before a national court, the Commission considers that there would not normally be sufficient Community interest to justify it dealing with the matter[3]. The Commission's desire to focus on cases of particular economic or legal significance is understandable. However, it gives rise to a number of potential difficulties:

- small cases sometimes raise significant legal issues and it is not always easy to identify them in advance;
- it would be a matter of concern if, as seems inevitable, the effect of the Commission's policy is to restrict access by small and medium-sized undertakings for which the cost of bringing national court proceedings may be prohibitive;
- greater application of Articles 81 and 82 will almost certainly give rise to more Article 234 cases[4], thereby imposing other burdens on the Commission, not to mention the ECJ;
- an increased role for national courts will highlight the different procedural position in each Member State.

1 Notice on co-operation between national courts and the Commission in applying Articles 81 and 82 of the EEC Treaty, para 13.
2 Ibid para 14.
3 See n 1 above, para 15.
4 In relation to Article 234 generally, see para **18.25**.

17.10

In its 1993 Notice, the Commission invites national courts to seek from the Commission information which may assist those courts in applying Articles 81 and 82. The Notice specifically refers to information of a procedural nature designed to enable a court to ascertain whether a certain case is pending before the Commission and, if so, its likely timescale, guidance on points of law and information regarding factual data (statistics, market studies and economic analyses). In doing so the Notice specifically recognises that the Commission must comply with Article 287 of the EC Treaty and art 20 of Regulation 17/62[1] (concerning information of a confidential nature). In 1999 the Commission answered five questions or groups of questions put by national courts pursuant to the 1993 Notice[2].

1 Council Regulation 17/62, OJ Sp Ed [1959–62] p 87.
2 29th Report on Competition Policy, p 17.

17.11

In *Automec*[1] the CFI examined the Commission's obligations when it receives a complaint under art 3 of Regulation 17/62[2]. The Court held that:

> '... for an institution performing a public-service task, the power to take all the organisational measures necessary for the fulfilment of that task, including settling priorities in the framework laid down by law, where those priorities have not been settled by the legislature, is an inherent part of the administration. This must apply particularly where an authority has been given a supervisory and regulatory function as general and extensive as that assigned to the Commission in the field of competition. Therefore the fact that the Commission allocates different degrees of priority to the matters referred to it in the field of competition is compatible with its obligations under Community law'[3].

The CFI stated that its role is to verify whether the Commission has given proper reasons for closing the file on a complaint on the basis of its power to accord different degrees of priority to different matters. The CFI declared that, as an administrative body, the Commission must act in the public interest. This meant that it was legitimate for the Commission to refer to the Community interest in order for it to decide its priorities. However, it made it clear that the Commission could not simply cite the Community interest in a vacuum; it must set out the legal and factual considerations which had led it to conclude that there is insufficient Community interest in the particular case in point[4]. The CFI identified a number of factors to which the Commission had to have particular regard, namely the importance of the alleged infringement to the functioning of the Common Market; the probability of being able to establish the existence of the infringement; and the extent of the investigative measures necessary in order to fulfil successfully its task of ensuring compliance with Articles 81 and 82.

1 Case T-24/90 *Automec v EC Commission* [1992] 5 CMLR 431.
2 Council Regulation (EEC) 17/62, OJ Sp Ed [1959–62] p 87.
3 See n 1 above, para 77.
4 See n 1 above, para 85.

17.12

One aspect which weighed heavily with both the Commission and the CFI in the *Automec*[1] case was the fact that the contractual interpretation of the distribution arrangements in question was already before the Italian courts and there was no reason why the Article 81 aspects should not be brought before the national courts as well. However, the judgment is relied on heavily in the Commission's 1993 Notice[2] and the principles laid down by the CFI are of more general application. This was borne out in *Ladbroke Racing Ltd v EC Commission*[3], where no parallel national court proceedings were taking place and the CFI held that the Commission was not entitled to conclude that Articles 81 and 82 did not apply without first completing its examination of the compatibility of the national legislation with Community law.

1 Case T-24/90 *Automec v EC Commission* [1992] 5 CMLR 431.
2 Notice on co-operation between national courts and the Commission in applying Articles 81 and 82 of the EEC Treaty, OJ [1993] C 39/6.
3 Case T-548/93 [1996] 4 CMLR 549.

17.13

There remain a number of significant obstacles to the greater application of Articles 81 and 82 in national courts. Firstly, in any given case there will be both advantages and disadvantages from the point of view of the potential claimant/complainant. Various considerations which should be borne in mind in deciding whether to file a complaint with the Commission or commence proceedings in a national court are considered in Chapters 1–16. Secondly, the remedies available and the procedures to be followed in national courts are at the present time matters of national, rather than Community, law. In its Fifteenth Report on Competition Policy (1985), the Commission noted[1] that substantial differences existed between Member States as to the availability of injunctions and the approach to the question of damages. It concluded that it would be undesirable for this to lead to the competition rules being applied with varying degrees of effectiveness in different parts of the Community. One possibility would be for the Council of the European Union, acting on a proposal from the Commission, to adopt a directive under Article 83 of the Treaty, harmonising the laws of Member States in relation to the application of Articles 81 and 82. In its Fifteenth Report, the Commission indicated that it was too early to judge whether any steps of this kind were necessary but it is likely that this issue will re-surface during the course of the next few years. The Commission's Notice on co-operation between national courts and the Commission in applying Articles 81 and 82 of the EC Treaty makes no reference to harmonisation in this field. Bearing in mind that such harmonisation would probably have to deal with procedural matters (such as admissibility of evidence, privilege against self-incrimination and so on), the Commission may well regard this area as a legal minefield which it would prefer to avoid. The 1993 House of Lords Select Committee Report on the enforcement of the competition rules states that in the longer term it would be desirable to harmonise national remedies, particularly with regard to damages, injunctions and interim measures[2].

1 At para 41.
2 House of Lords Select Committee Session 1993–1994 *Enforcement of Commission Competition Rules*, para 137.

17.14

One important factor which acts as a deterrent to the bringing of national proceedings, at least in cases where the agreement in question has been notified[1] to the Commission, is that only the Commission can grant individual exemptions under Article 81(3). In a radical and controversial White Paper published in 1999[2] the Commission has proposed that it should no longer have a monopoly over the grant of individual exemptions under Article 81(3) and that both national courts and national competition authorities should have that power. Under this proposal, there would no longer be a need for a system of notification in order to apply Article 81(3). Instead, Article 81 would be capable of being applied as a whole by national courts and authorities. This proposal raises a number of difficult issues. If it is adopted, it would greatly change the way in which Article 81 is applied in national courts.

1 As to notification generally, see Chapter 4.
2 *White Paper on Modernisation of the Rules implementing Articles 81 and 82 of the EC Treaty*, Commission Programme 99/027 (April 1999).

Chapter 18 Jurisdiction

A Basic Jurisdiction of National Courts to Apply Articles 81 and 82

18.01

With a few important exceptions, details of which are set out below, the national courts of Member States have jurisdiction to apply Articles 81 and 82 of the EC Treaty, notwithstanding that the European Commission itself has jurisdiction. Indeed, as has been noted in Chapter 17, the Commission has actively encouraged private litigants to exercise their rights under Articles 81 and 82 in the national courts.

18.02

Articles 81 and 82 can in principle be applied in two different kinds of court or tribunal, that is to say either in a court or tribunal whose particular function is to apply competition law or in the ordinary courts or tribunals (such as the High Court in England and Wales and the Court of Session in Scotland). The authority of the ordinary courts or tribunals to apply Articles 81 and 82 derives from their direct effect, as laid down by the ECJ in *BRT v SABAM*[1], whereas courts or tribunals whose particular task is to apply domestic competition law derive their competence from Article 84 of the EC Treaty. This distinction is relevant in the context of jurisdiction because of art 9(3) of Council Regulation 17/62, which provides as follows:

> 'As long as the Commission has not initiated any procedure under Articles 2, 3 or 6 [of Regulation 17/62][2], the authorities of the Member States shall remain competent to apply Article 85(1) [now Article 81(1)] and Article 86 [now Article 82] in accordance with Article 88 [now Article 84] of the Treaty'.

The meaning of the term 'initiation of a procedure' is considered in Chapters 1–16. At first sight it would appear that art 9(3) of Regulation 17/62 would preclude *any* court or tribunal in a Member State from applying Articles 81 and 82 once the Commission has itself initiated a procedure. However, the ECJ gave a narrower meaning to art 9(3) in its judgment in *BRT v SABAM*[3]; it placed considerable emphasis on the reference to Article 84, from which the specialist competition law courts and tribunals derive their competence to apply Articles 81 and 82, and accordingly held that art 9(3) did *not* deprive the ordinary courts and tribunals of their competence even where the Commission has initiated a procedure. The ECJ's rationale was essentially that:

> 'To deny, by virtue of ... article 9, the national courts' jurisdiction to afford this safeguard would mean depriving individuals of rights which they hold under the Treaty itself'[4].

1 Case 127/73 [1974] ECR 51, [1974] 2 CMLR 238.
2 Ie with a view to granting negative clearance, ordering termination of an infringement or granting an exemption.
3 See n 1 above.
4 [1974] ECR 51 at 63; confirmed by the ECJ in Joined Cases 209–213/84 *Ministère Public v Asjes* [1986] ECR 1425, [1986] 3 CMLR 173.

18.03
The extent to which ordinary courts or tribunals (as opposed to specialist ones) apply domestic competition law varies from Member State to Member State. The position as far as the UK is concerned is that domestic competition law is administered by both the ordinary courts and by certain specialised regulatory bodies, namely the Office of Fair Trading and the Competition Commission. The ordinary courts (such as the High Court in England and Wales) have jurisdiction to apply the Competition Act 1998. However, these non-specialist courts could not be said to be 'especially entrusted' with the task of applying domestic legislation on competition (the term used by the ECJ in *BRT v SABAM*[1]). Accordingly, the fact that the European Commission may have initiated a procedure in a given case does not prevent the High Court in England and Wales (and other non-specialist courts such as the Court of Session in Scotland and the county court in England and Wales) from applying Articles 81 and 82.

1 Case 127/73 [1974] ECR 51, [1974] 2 CMLR 238.

18.04
In 1991 the Secretary of State considered a complaint by Reuters that the arrangements for disseminating company news, following the introduction by the London Stock Exchange of its Regulatory News Service, constituted an abuse of a dominant position contrary to Article 82 of the Treaty of Rome. This followed a report by the Director General of Fair Trading to the Secretary of State that these rules were anti-competitive as a matter of United Kingdom law[1]. The Secretary of State concluded that the arrangements in question infringed Article 82 but that the abuse would be remedied if companies were free to pass announcements to other news vendors at the same time as they were given to the Exchange's company announcements office[2]. The Exchange subsequently introduced changes to this effect. This is a rare example of the application of Articles 81 or 82 by a body charged with a special role under United Kingdom domestic competition law[3].

1 Pursuant to provisions of the Financial Services Act 1986.
2 DTI press notice, 31 October 1991.
3 See, more generally on this issue, paras **12.01–12.13**.

B Situations in which Jurisdiction of National Courts is Qualified or Removed

18.05
There are a number of situations in which the jurisdiction of national courts to apply Articles 81 and 82 is either circumscribed or removed altogether. The situations in which this arises are set out below (at paras **18.06–18.24**).

1 DOCTRINE OF PROVISIONAL VALIDITY IN RELATION TO ARTICLE 81

(1) General

18.06
The doctrine of provisional validity, a doctrine created by the ECJ[1], is a somewhat elusive one and one which gave rise to a number of commentaries in the early 1970s[2]. A fundamental distinction is drawn in this context between 'old agreements' on the one hand and 'new agreements' on the other. Old agreements are ones which came into force before 13 March 1962, the date on which Regulation 17/62 entered into force. New agreements are those made after that time; there is, however, a third category, namely 'accession agreements': these are agreements which were in existence on the various accession dates which have so far occurred[3] and which were only brought within the scope of Article 81 by virtue of the accession of one or more Member States on that date.

1 Case 48/72 *Brasserie de Haecht v Wilkin-Janssen* [1973] ECR 77, [1973] CMLR 287; Case 59/77 *De Bloos v Bouyer* [1977] ECR 2359, [1978] 1 CMLR 511. See, more recently, Case C-234/89 *Delimitis v Henninger Bräu* [1991] 4 CMLR 329 at para 48.
2 Eg Vogelaar and Guy 'The Second Brasserie de Haecht Case: a Delphic Oracle' (1973) 22 ICLQ 648; Wertheimer 'The Haecht II Judgment and its Repercussions' (1973) CML Rev 386; Dashwood 'A New Look at Provisional Validity': [1974] CLJ 116; Gijlstra and Murphy 'EEC Competition Law after the Brasserie de Haecht and SABAM cases' [1974] LIEI 2.
3 See para **4.26**.

18.07
The position, as far as the doctrine of provisional validity is concerned, of each of these three categories of agreement is as follows:

(1) *Old Agreements*: If these were duly notified within the appropriate time limit under Regulation 17/62 (ie by 1 November 1962)[1], or were exempt from notification by virtue of art 4(2) of that Regulation[2], they must be given their full legal effect until such time as the European Commission takes a decision in application of Article 81(3): *Brasserie de Haecht v Wilkin-Janssen*[3] and *De Bloos v Bouyer*[4]. The practical effect of this is that in such circumstances a national court cannot apply Article 81(2) to render such an agreement, or part thereof, void unless and until the Commission reaches a decision under Article 81(3) (which may never happen)[5].
(2) *New Agreements*: The doctrine of provisional validity enunciated in the *Brasserie de Haecht*[6] and *De Bloos*[7] cases does *not* apply to new agreements. That is to say, a national court *can* give full effect to Article 81(1) and render such an agreement null and void under Article 81(2). Having said that, practical difficulties can arise in such circumstances, particularly if there is a possibility that a national court could hold such an agreement null and void under Article 81(1), only for the Commission subsequently to grant an individual exemption in relation to that agreement (usually retrospectively) under Article 81(3). The way in which this problem is likely to be resolved in practice is described at paras **18.13–18.24**.

(3) *Accession Agreements*: The ECJ has not so far had to determine whether the doctrine of provisional validity applies to accession agreements. It probably does by way of analogy. Certainly, this was the view expressed by the Commission in its Third Report on Competition Policy (1973)[8]. This was also the view of one High Court judge before whom this issue came to be considered[9].

1 See para **4.24**.
2 See para **4.11** ff.
3 Case 48/72 [1973] ECR 77, [1973] CMLR 287.
4 Case 59/77 [1977] ECR 2359, [1978] 1 CMLR 511; see too Commission Notice on co-operation between national courts and the Commission in applying Articles 81 and 82 of the EEC Treaty, OJ [1993] C 39/6.
5 See also Case C-39/96 *KVB v Free Record Shop BV* [1997] ECR I-2303.
6 See n 3 above.
7 See n 4 above.
8 At para 5(a).
9 Bridge J in *Esso Petroleum Co Ltd v Kingswood Motors (Addlestone) Ltd* [1974] QB 142 at 154.

18.08
The practical reason for developing the doctrine of provisional validity was to confer legal certainty in relation to agreements which initially fell outside the EC Treaty provisions (by pre-dating the Treaty itself or Regulation 17/62) but which were subsequently found to be within it. The significance of the doctrine will naturally diminish over time as more and more old agreements are terminated or expire. However, the doctrine still has some life in it, particularly if it does apply to accession agreements.

(2) Loss of Provisional Validity

18.09
Provisional validity comes to an end if and when the Commission grants a decision in application of Article 81(3), whether this be a decision granting or refusing exemption. Moreover, the ECJ held in one of the *Perfumes* cases[1] that provisional validity may also be lost in circumstances where the Commission informs the parties that it is closing its file by means of a comfort letter[2]. In that case the Commission had indicated that the agreement in question did not appear to fall within Article 81(1) (and accordingly Article 81(3) would not come into play). In view of this, the ECJ took the view that it was highly unlikely that the Commission would ever take a formal exemption decision; as a result the possibility of exemption being made retroactive (to the date of notification) was theoretical and therefore the rationale for continued provisional validity no longer applied. Some comfort letters do not, however, indicate why the Commission does not intend to pursue a particular matter further and in such circumstances provisional validity may not be affected[3].

1 Case 99/79 *Lancôme v Etos* [1980] ECR 2511, [1981] 2 CMLR 164; see too Commission Notice on co-operation between national courts and the Commission in applying Articles 81 and 82 of the EEC Treaty, OJ [1993] C 39/6, para 31.
2 As to comfort letters, see generally para **8.72** ff.
3 See Kerse *EEC Antitrust Procedure* (3rd edn, 1994) p 364.

18.10
The ECJ made it clear in the *KVB*[1] case that an agreement which benefits from provisional validity only continues to do so for as long as its terms remain unchanged or, in the event of amendments, if these do not have the effect of reinforcing or extending its restrictive effects.

1 Case C-39/96 *KVB v Free Record Shop BV* [1997] ECR I-2303.

2 INDIVIDUAL AND BLOCK EXEMPTIONS

18.11
Under art 9(1) of Regulation 17/62, only the European Commission (subject to review by the ECJ) has power to grant individual exemptions pursuant to Article 81(3). However, national courts do have power to determine whether an agreement falls within a block exemption[1]. In *Delimitis*[2] the ECJ made it clear that a national court can only apply a block exemption if the agreement in question conforms with it in every respect. Although a national court cannot itself grant an individual exemption under Article 81(3), it will, if called upon to enforce an agreement which has been notified to the Commission, need to give some consideration to whether or not the agreement is likely to be exempted by the Commission—this is relevant in the context of deciding whether or not the proceedings should be stayed pending a Commission decision[3]. In *Tetra Pak*[4] the CFI confirmed that the power of national courts to apply Article 82 is not limited by the fact that the practice in question has been granted exemption under Article 81(3).

1 Case 59/77 *De Bloos v Bouyer* [1977] ECR 2359, [1978] 1 CMLR 511; Case 170/83 *Hydrotherm v Compact* [1984] ECR 2999, [1985] 3 CMLR 224. For a case where this occurred, see *Cutsforth v Mansfield Inns Ltd* [1986] 1 All ER 577, [1986] 1 WLR 558.
2 Case C-234/89 *Delimitis v Henninger Bräu* [1991] ECR I-935, [1991] 4 CMLR 329 at para 55.
3 See para **18.13** ff.
4 Case T-51/89 *Tetra Pak Rausing SA v EC Commission* [1991] 4 CMLR 334.

3 SPECIAL SECTORS

18.12
In certain sectors special rules apply. The extent to which national courts have jurisdiction in relation to these is outside the scope of this work.

1 For coverage of this topic, see *Butterworths Competition Law*, Division IX.

4 STAY OF PROCEEDINGS PENDING COMMISSION DECISION

18.13
In view of the fact that national courts and the European Commission have concurrent jurisdiction in relation to Articles 81 and 82, there can be a very real risk of conflict between the decisions reached by the two bodies. For

example, a national court may be called upon to resolve a contractual dispute between two parties to an agreement, in circumstances where the agreement has been submitted to the Commission by way of an application for negative clearance and/or notification for an individual exemption, but the Commission has not yet reached a decision (indeed, it may not even have begun to consider the case). In such circumstances, there is a risk that the national court will hold the agreement (or part of it) null and void pursuant to Article 81(2) and that the Commission will subsequently grant an individual exemption (which, by way of exacerbating the conflict, is likely to be made retrospective to the date on which the agreement was originally notified[1]).

1 This is not invariably the case: see paras **8.35–8.36**.

18.14

The ECJ made it clear in the *Brasserie de Haecht*[1] and *BRT v SABAM*[2] cases that in such circumstances the national court has the option to stay the proceedings before it pending a decision by the Commission. In those cases, the ECJ gave the following guidance: although the national court should feel free to stay its proceedings (pending the outcome of the Commission's action) if it considers it necessary on the grounds of legal certainty, the court should generally allow the proceedings before it to continue if it considers that either:

(*a*) the behaviour or agreement in dispute is clearly not capable of having an appreciable effect on competition or trade between Member States; or

(*b*) there is no doubt of the incompatibility of that behaviour/agreement with Article 81/82[3].

1 Case 48/72 *Brasserie de Haecht v Wilkin-Janssen* [1973] ECR 77 at 87, [1973] CMLR 287 at 302 (in respect of Article 85).

2 Case 127/73 *BRT v SABAM* [1974] ECR 51 at 63, [1974] 2 CMLR 238 (in respect of Article 86).

3 See now also Case C-234/89 *Delimitis v Henninger Bräu* [1991] ECR I-935, [1991] 4 CMLR 329 at paras 49–52. On the issue of when proceedings should be stayed, see Greaves 'Concurrent Jurisdiction in EEC Competition Law: when should a National Court stay proceedings?' [1987] ECLR 256.

18.15

In *MTV Europe*[1], the plaintiff sought damages for alleged breach of Articles 81 and 82. In parallel, it was pursuing a complaint in relation to the same matters with the European Commission. The defendants sought a complete stay of the High Court proceedings pending final determination of the plaintiff's complaint by the Commission (including any appeal to the CFI or ECJ). The High Court ordered a partial stay, in the sense that the action should not be set down for trial until one month after the Commission's decision but that in the meantime all preparations for trial should proceed. This decision was upheld by the Court of Appeal. The Court of Appeal's judgment was subsequently followed in *Philips Electronics v Ingman*[2].

1 *MTV Europe v BMG Records (UK) Ltd* [1997] 1 CMLR 867, CA.

2 [1998] 2 CMLR 839. For another example of a stay being granted, see *Williams v Welsh Rugby Union* [1999] Eu LR 195.

18.16
The Commission's 1993 Notice on co-operation between national courts and the Commission in applying Articles 81 and 82 of the EEC Treaty[1] identities a number of situations which can arise (this was prepared after the judgment of the ECJ in *Delimitis*[2]). The Notice identifies the following situations:

(1) If the national court concludes that the agreement or conduct in question does not fall within Article 81(1) or Article 82, it should pursue its proceedings on the basis of that finding. This is so even if the agreement has been notified to the Commission and the latter has not yet reached a decision[3].

(2) If the national court concludes that an agreement falls within Article 81(1), it must then consider whether it is capable of being exempted under Article 81(3) by the Commission. If the agreement has not been notified to the Commission pursuant to Regulation 17/62[4], exemption under Article 81(3) is ruled out (subject to the provisions of art 4(2) of Regulation 17/62[5]). The prohibition laid down in Article 81(1), and the nullity flowing from Article 81(2), therefore operates[6]. However, it is necessary in such a case for a national court to consider whether the agreement in question falls within the scope of a block exemption regulation, in which case individual exemption is not necessary[7]. It has been clearly established by the ECJ[8] that a national court has power to determine whether an agreement falls within a block exemption. However, in its judgment in *Delimitis*[9] the ECJ made it clear that a national court can only apply a block exemption if the agreement in question conforms with it in every respect.

(3) The most complicated situation contemplated by the Notice is where an agreement is caught by Article 81(1) and has been notified to the Commission. The problem here is that, under art 9(1) of Regulation 17/62[4], only the Commission has power to grant individual exemptions pursuant to Article 81(3). The concurrency of jurisdiction between national courts and the Commission is, to that extent, only partial. A number of situations can arise and these are described in para **18.17**.

1 OJ [1993] C 39/6.
2 Case C-234/89 *Delimitis v Henninger Bräu* [1991] ECR I-935, [1991] 4 CMLR 329.
3 Notice, para 23. See also Case C-250/92 *Gøttrup-Klim v Dansk Landbrugs Grovvareselskab Amba* [1994] ECR I-5641, at para 58.
4 Council Regulation (EEC) 17/62, OJ Sp Ed [1959–62] p 87.
5 See para **4.11** ff.
6 Notice, para 28.
7 Ibid para 26.
8 Case 170/83 *Hydrotherm Gerätebau GmbH v Andreoli* [1984] ECR 2999, [1985] 3 CMLR 224.
9 See n 2 above.

18.17
Where an agreement is caught by Article 81(1) and has been notified to the Commission, a number of different situations can arise:

(1) If the Commission has already granted exemption from the prohibition laid down in Article 81(1), the national court is bound by that decision, giving full force to the agreement/practice in question[1].

(2) The Commission may have issued a so-called 'comfort letter'[2]. Such letters can take a number of forms. The type of comfort letter under consideration here is one which expressly or impliedly indicates that the agreement in question is caught by Article 81(1) but states that it appears to fulfil the conditions of Article 81(3). Many more notifications are concluded by means of a comfort letter than terminate with a Commission decision[3]. An earlier draft of the Notice indicated that, where the Commission has issued a comfort letter, the national court could treat the agreement as valid between the parties. This suggestion was tantamount to allowing a national court to apply Article 81(3) in a positive way. In *Delimitis*[4], the judgment in which was handed down after the first draft of the Notice had been prepared, the ECJ specifically stated[5] that a national court could not, by virtue of Article 81(3), declare Article 81(1) to be inapplicable. The Notice as adopted merely states that national courts may take account of these letters as factual elements[6].

(3) The Notice states[7] that if a national court concludes that an individual exemption is not possible, it should apply the prohibition and nullity rule laid down in Article 81(1) and (2). This is broadly consistent with *Delimitis*[4] and earlier case law[8]. If, on the other hand, the national court believes that it is possible that the Commission would regard the agreement as meriting exemption, it really has little option but to suspend the national proceedings[9]. The Notice suggests[10] that in this situation the national court may inform the Commission and ask the latter to give it a provisional opinion. If such an opinion indicates that exemption is unlikely, the draft Notice suggests that the national court should resume its proceedings and prohibit the agreement[10].

1 Notice, para 25.
2 As to comfort letters, see generally para **8.72** ff.
3 See para **8.72**.
4 Case C-234/89 *Delimitis v Henninger Bräu* [1991] ECR I-935, [1991] 4 CMLR 329.
5 See n 4 above, at para 55.
6 Notice, para 25; see *Inntrepreneur Estates Ltd v Mason* [1993] 2 CMLR 293.
7 Ibid para 30.
8 Case 48/72 *Brasserie de Haecht SA v Wilkin-Janssen* [1973] ECR 77, [1973] CMLR 287 and Case 127/73 *BRT v SABAM* [1974] ECR 51, [1974] 2 CMLR 238.
9 The Notice states (para 30) that the national court should suspend its proceedings.
10 Notice, para 38. For an example of this process in action, see the Commission's decision in *SCK/FNK* OJ [1994] L 117/30, at paras 14 and 15.

18.18
In *Delimitis*[1] the ECJ suggested that the national court might ask the Commission how far the proceedings before it have got and what is the probability of the Commission coming to a formal decision. In fact, it is difficult to see that a national court could order a stay without making such a request—it would really need to know that there is a likelihood of a formal decision being issued in due course before it could justify a stay. If, in its reply, the Commission indicates that it does intend to take a formal decision but that this may take some considerable time, the national court is inevitably placed in an extremely difficult position. Recourse to the ECJ does not provide a solution in a case where the issue is whether or not an

agreement qualifies for an exemption under Article 81(3); this is a matter on which the Commission must first reach a view which is then subject to possible appeal to the ECJ. In the Notice[2], the Commission states that it will endeavour to give priority to requests from national courts in proceedings which have been stayed in this way, particularly if the outcome of civil litigation depends on it. More generally, the Notice states[3] that before applying Article 81(1) or Article 82, national courts should feel free to ask the Commission for its opinion on the appropriate interpretation of Community law[4]. In this context, earlier drafts of the Notice surprisingly made no reference to the Article 234 procedure[5], whereby preliminary rulings can be obtained from the ECJ regarding the interpretation of Articles 81(1) and 82. In its final form, the Notice does refer to Article 234[6].

1 Case C-234/89 *Delimitis v Henninger Bräu* [1991] ECR I-935, [1991] 4 CMLR 329.
2 Notice, para 37.
3 Ibid para 38.
4 The Commission's 24th Report on Competition Policy, para 50 cites an example of such a request from a Master of the Queen's Bench Division of the High Court.
5 See paras **10.67–10.69**.
6 Notice, para 39.

18.19
However, some difficult issues arise. Firstly, this proposed co-operation between national courts and the Commission is subject to any limits placed by national courts' rules of procedure. The admissibility in evidence by English Courts of informal interpretative opinions from the Commission must be highly questionable. This is particularly so bearing in mind that the information received by the Commission may be based on, for example, uncorroborated statements by third parties, not susceptible to cross-examination. Moreover, as soon as such a procedure was set in motion, the parties to proceedings might well set about vociferous lobbying of the Commission to influence the views expressed to the national court, a process which English judges might view with mistrust. Secondly, there is the question of the Commission's obligations of professional secrecy under Regulation 17/62[1]. Article 20(1) of the Regulation provides that information acquired as a result of the application of arts 11–14 (the provisions empowering the Commission to request information and undertake investigations[2]) is to be used 'only for the purpose of the relevant request or investigation'. More generally, art 20(2) of Regulation 17/62 provides that the Commission must not disclose information acquired as a result of the application of the Regulation and of the kind covered by the obligation of professional secrecy[3].

1 Council Regulation (EEC) 17/62, OJ Sp Ed [1959–62] p 87.
2 See Chapter 6.
3 See para **11.05**.

18.20
In the *Spanish Banks* case, the Spanish Tribunal for the Defence of Competition asked the ECJ, under a reference pursuant to Article 234 of the EC Treaty, whether the national authority responsible for the application in a Member State of Articles 81 and 82 could use information

obtained by the Commission pursuant to Regulation 17/62 in national proceedings[1]. The ECJ held that the effect of Article 287 of the EC Treaty[2], coupled with art 20 of Regulation 17/62, was that the national authority could not use information obtained by the Commission under arts 11–14 of Regulation 17/62, or information contained in notifications under arts 2, 4 or 5 of that Regulation, as a means of proof in the enforcement of either national or EC competition law. The Commission had argued that national authorities should be able to use such information in the enforcement of EC competition law but not national competition law (no doubt in the hope of increasing the enforcement of EC competition law by national courts/authorities[3]). The Court did, however, indicate[4] that such information could be taken into account by the national authorities in deciding whether to open their own procedure.

1 Case C-67/91 *Direccion General de Defensa de la Competencia v Associacion Espanola de Banca Privada* [1992] ECR I-4785.
2 See para **11.03**.
3 See paras **17.07**–**17.08**.
4 See n 1 above, para 39.

18.21

In *Postbank*[1], parallel proceedings were running before both the Commission and a national court. The Commission sent to the complainant (which was also a party in the national proceedings) a copy of the Statement of Objections which it had prepared and authorised the production and use of that document in the national proceedings. This decision was challenged and interim measures sought under Articles 242 and 243 of the EC Treaty[2], seeking suspension of the operation of the Commission's decision (on the grounds that the document in question was to be formally included in the national court proceedings within a few weeks). The President of the CFI ruled in favour of the applicant and the Court subsequently annulled the Commission's decision on the ground that it had not given the applicant an opportunity to state its view on the production of the document in question[3].

1 Case T-353/94R *Postbank v EC Commission* [1994] ECR II-1141.
2 As to Articles 242 and 243 generally, see paras **10.57**–**10.66**.
3 Case T-353/94 *Postbank v EC Commission* [1996] All ER (EC) 817; see also para **4.53**.

18.22

In *British Leyland Motor Corpn Ltd v Wyatt Interpart*[1], a case in which the defendant had invoked Article 82 by way of defence to an action for copyright infringement and had also filed a complaint against the plaintiffs with the European Commission, the court granted a stay at the request of the defendant, on condition that it pursued the proceedings before the Commission 'with due diligence'. Conversely, in the *Club* case[2] the Brussels Commercial Court was prepared to take a robust view and refused to grant a stay, holding that the mere possibility that an exemption might be forthcoming was not an adequate reason for granting a stay.

1 [1979] 3 CMLR 79.
2 *Club NV v Elsevier-Sequoia NV* [1980] 3 CMLR 258.

18.23
In one case[1] the Commission issued a declaratory decision under Regulation 17/62, art 3[2] in order to assist a national court (in that case a Dutch court) which had granted a stay of proceedings.

1 Commission Decision (88/491/EEC) *Bloemenveilingen Aalsmeer* OJ [1988] L 262/27, [1989] 4 CMLR 500.
2 See para **8.62**.

18.24
As a matter of English law, proceedings will not be struck out for want of prosecution if this is due to the fact that the parties are awaiting a decision by the Commission[1].

1 *Aero Zipp Fasteners Ltd v YKK Fasteners (UK) Ltd* [1978] 2 CMLR 88.

C Article 234 Proceedings

18.25
In a case where a national court is in doubt as to the correct interpretation of Article 81 or 82 (or any of the secondary legislation made thereunder, such as an applicable block exemption), it is open to it to refer one or more questions to the ECJ in Luxembourg under Article 234 of the EC Treaty[1]. If the court in question is one against whose decision there is no judicial remedy under national law, it *must* bring the matter before the ECJ[2]. However, under the 'acte clair' principle a court of final resort is not obliged to make an Article 234 reference when the point of law is not in doubt[3].

1 As to Article 234 generally, see Collins *European Community Law in the United Kingdom* (4th edn, 1990) pp 142–214 and Arnull 'References to the European Court' (1990) 15 EL Rev 375–391.
2 Article 234, 3rd para.
3 Case 283/81 *CILFIT Srl v Ministry of Health* [1982] ECR 3415, [1983] 1 CMLR 472; see para **10.69**.

18.26
A number of leading judgments of the ECJ in relation to Articles 81 and 82 have been delivered in cases referred to it under Article 234[1].

1 Eg Cases 253/78, 1–3/79 *Procureur v Giry and Guerlain* [1980] ECR 2327, [1981] 2 CMLR 99 (dealing with provisional validity); Case 170/83 *Hydrotherm v Compact* [1984] ECR 2999, [1985] 3 CMLR 224 (dealing with distribution agreements); Case 243/83 *Binon et Cie SA v Agence et Messageries de la Presse SA* [1985] ECR 2015, [1985] 3 CMLR 800 (dealing with distribution arrangements for newspapers and periodicals); Case 161/84 *Pronuptia de Paris GmbH v Pronuptia de Paris Irmgard Schillgalis* [1986] ECR 353, [1986] 1 CMLR 414 (dealing with franchise agreements); Case 27/87 *Erauw-Jacquery SprL v La Hesbignonne Société Co- opérative* [1988] ECR 1919, [1988] 4 CMLR 576 (dealing with licences of plant breeders' rights); Case C-7/97 *Oscar Bronner v Mediaprint Zeitungsundzeitschriften-verlag* [1998] ECR I-7791.

D Nature of the Cause of Action for Breach of Articles 81 and 82

18.27
In order to bring a case under English law the plaintiff must establish a cause of action. In the context of Articles 81 and 82, the English courts have contemplated two possible causes of action:

(*a*) the so-called 'new torts or wrongs', a phrase coined by Lord Denning in *Application des Gaz v Falks Veritas Ltd*[1];
(*b*) breach of statutory duty.

These are considered in turn below.

1 [1974] Ch 381, [1974] 3 All ER 51, CA.

1 THE NEW TORTS OR WRONGS

18.28
In the *Application des Gaz*[1] case, Lord Denning said:

> 'Articles 85 and 86 [now Articles 81 and 82] are part of our law. They create new torts or wrongs. Their names are "undue restriction of competition within the Common Market" and "abuse of a dominant position within the Common Market". Any infringement of those Articles can be dealt with by our English courts. It is for our courts to find the facts, to apply the law and to use the remedies which we have available'.

However, judicial doubt has subsequently been cast on the notion that Articles 81 and 82 created new torts or wrongs, for example by Roskill LJ in *Valor International Ltd v Application des Gaz SA*[2]. In the light of the House of Lords' decision in the *Garden Cottage* case[3] regarding the alternative cause of action, breach of statutory duty[4], it seems unlikely that one needs to go so far as to regard Articles 81 and 82 as creating new torts or wrongs.

1 [1974] Ch 381, [1974] 3 All ER 51, CA.
2 [1978] 3 CMLR 87 at 100, CA.
3 *Garden Cottage Foods Ltd v Milk Marketing Board* [1984] AC 130, [1983] 2 All ER 770.
4 See paras **18.29**, **18.30**.

2 BREACH OF STATUTORY DUTY

18.29
If a statute imposes a duty and a person breaches that duty, third parties who have suffered damage as a result can sometimes sue that person for breach of statutory duty. Some statutes expressly provide for this remedy: for example, the Restrictive Trade Practices Act 1976, s 35(2)[1]. Others do not, but depending on a number of factors, may nevertheless be such as to give rise to a cause of action for breach of statutory duty[2].

1 Now repealed by the Competition Act 1998.

2 As to the basic principles involved in relation to actions for breach of statutory duty, see *Clerk & Lindsell on Torts* (16th edn, 1989) ch 14; *Street on Torts* (8th edn, 1988) ch 22; *Salmond & Heuston on the Law of Torts* (19th edn, 1987) ch 10; Stanton *Breach of Statutory Duty in Tort* (1986).

18.30

In giving the leading judgment of the House of Lords in *Garden Cottage Foods Ltd v Milk Marketing Board*[1], Lord Diplock said that:

> 'A breach of the duty imposed by Article 86 [now Article 82] not to abuse a dominant position in the Common Market or in a substantial part of it, can thus be categorised in English law as a breach of a statutory duty that is imposed not only for the purpose of promoting the general economic prosperity of the Common Market but also for the benefit of private individuals to whom loss or damage is caused by a breach of that duty'[2].

1 [1984] AC 130, [1983] 2 All ER 770.
2 [1984] AC 130 at 141, [1983] 2 All ER 770 at 775.

Chapter 19 Remedies

A Introduction

19.01

There are two quite distinct ways in which the issue of the compatibility (or otherwise) of a particular agreement or course of conduct with Articles 81 or 82 of the EC Treaty can come before a national court. First, a defendant in proceedings (either a party to the agreement in question or a third party) may seek to rely on one or both of these Treaty provisions by way of defence. For example, a claim by a licensor under a patent licence for non-payment of royalties may be met by a defence that the licence is void and unenforceable under Article 81[1]; alternatively, the owner of an intellectual property right, such as a copyright, may bring proceedings against a third party for copyright infringement and that third party may seek to pray in aid by way of defence Articles 81 and/or 82[2].

1 As in *Chemidus Wavin v TERI* [1978] 3 CMLR 514, CA.
2 As in *British Leyland Motor Corpn Ltd v Armstrong* [1984] 3 CMLR 102, CA; revsd [1986] AC 577, [1986] 1 All ER 850, HL.

19.02

The second way in which a litigant can bring Articles 81 and 82 before a national court is by way of a claim for an injunction and/or damages, ie a claim which seeks to use Articles 81 and 82 as a sword, rather than a shield (as occurred, for example, in the *Garden Cottage*[1] case).

1 *Garden Cottage Foods Ltd v Milk Marketing Board* [1984] AC 130, [1983] 2 All ER 770, HL.

19.03

It is probably fair to say that English case law regarding the use of Articles 81 and 82 as a shield (the so-called 'Euro-defence') is better developed than it is in relation to their use as a sword. However, there have been signs in recent years of an increasing tendency to bring proceedings before the English courts on the basis of alleged infringements of Articles 81 and 82 and this is a trend which is likely to continue, bringing with it, one hopes, much-needed clarification on a number of issues which are as yet unresolved.

B Reliance on Articles 81 and 82 by way of Defence

19.04

Consideration will be given separately in this section to the situation in which Articles 81 and 82 are relied upon by way of defence in:

(*a*) proceedings between the parties to an agreement;
(*b*) proceedings brought by third parties.

1 PROCEEDINGS BETWEEN THE PARTIES TO AN AGREEMENT

19.05
The basic principle is that agreements which are prohibited under Article 81(1) are automatically void (and therefore unenforceable): Article 81(2). Although Article 82 contains no provision corresponding to Article 81(2), agreements which infringe it should in principle also be unenforceable (there is nothing to prevent the entry into and operation of an agreement constituting an infringement of both Article 81 and, if one of the parties is in a dominant position, Article 82[1]).

1 As eg in Case 85/76 *Hoffmann-La Roche v EC Commission* [1979] ECR 461, [1979] 3 CMLR 211. See too Case 66/86 *Ahmed Saeed Flugreisen and Silver Line Reisebüro v Zentrale zur Bekämpfung Unlauteren Wettbewerbs eV* [1989] ECR 803, [1990] 4 CMLR 102.

19.06
The ECJ held as long ago as 1966, in the *STM*[1] case, that the voidness provided for in Article 81(2) only applies to those parts of an agreement which fall within Article 81(1) and not necessarily to the whole agreement. The voidness will only extend to the whole agreement if those parts which fall within Article 81(1) cannot be severed from the rest of the agreement. This was subsequently confirmed in the *Ciments et Betons* case[2]. In that case the ECJ also confirmed that the issue of severance is one of national rather than Community law[3]. This is far from satisfactory: it is not desirable that the extent of the voidness resulting from the application of Article 81(2) should vary in identical cases, depending on the governing national law.

1 Case 56/65 *Société Technique Miniere v Maschinenbau Ulm* [1966] ECR 235, [1966] CMLR 357.
2 Case 319/82 *Société de Vente de Ciments et Betons v Kerpen and Kerpen* [1983] ECR 4173, [1985] 1 CMLR 511.
3 See paras **19.07–19.10**.

19.07
An as yet unresolved issue concerns the status of agreements which fell outside Article 81(1) when they were entered into, because at that stage they did not have a significant effect on competition or inter-state trade, but which subsequently have become significant and have therefore outgrown the de minimis doctrine. There are various possibilities. One is that the agreement is rendered void ab initio; a second possibility is that it becomes unenforceable from the moment that Article 81(1) begins to apply to it; a third possibility is that it benefits from a form of provisional validity, being enforceable until the European Commission takes action in respect of it. The second possibility would seem the correct approach but it could present a national court with the invidious task of having to determine the precise point in time at which the agreement entered the domain of Article 81(1). Moreover, a similar situation could arise in reverse: an agreement is

appreciably restrictive of competition at the outset (and is therefore caught by Article 81) but subsequently ceases to have such an effect.

19.08
In *Passmore v Morland plc*[1] the Court of Appeal ruled that an agreement could move from voidness to validity (and potentially back again) according to its effect on the market. Chadwick LJ said that an agreement which is not caught by Article 81(1) at the time when it is entered into (because it does not have the effect of preventing, restricting or distorting competition) may subsequently, and as a result of a change in those circumstances, come within the scope of the prohibition. He went on to say that the reverse must also be true. He dismissed the argument that the principle of legal certainty required that a provision, once tainted by Article 81(1), should remain tainted forever. The House of Lords refused leave to appeal in this case.

1 [1999] 3 All ER 1005, [1999] 1 CMLR 1129.

(1) Severance

19.09
The doctrine of severance is one which is recognised under English law. This doctrine includes the so-called 'blue pencil' rule, under which parts of a restrictive covenant which infringe a particular rule of law can, in principle, be severed from the rest of the covenant, provided that the court does not need to re-write the covenant in order to achieve this effect[1]. If, however, the effect of severance is to alter entirely the scope and intention of the agreement, a court is likely to refuse to do so[2].

1 *Goldsoll v Goldman* [1915] 1 Ch 292, CA.
2 *Attwood v Lamont* [1920] 3 KB 571, CA.

19.10
The leading English case on severance under Article 81(1) is *Chemidus Wavin v TERI*[1]. In that case the plaintiff licensor under a patent licence sued the licensee for non-payment of minimum royalties. The defendant asserted by way of defence that the agreement infringed Article 81(1). The Court of Appeal upheld the decision of the judge at first instance, namely that, irrespective of whether certain provisions of the agreement did indeed infringe Article 81(1), those provisions could be excised from the rest of the agreement and accordingly Article 81(1) did not provide a valid defence to the claim for payment of royalties. The Court of Appeal left open the question of whether the exercise being performed was, strictly speaking, one of severance; in fact, it tended towards the view that the exercise was not one of severance in the sense in which English courts were accustomed to using the term. Rather, the position was, according to the words of Buckley LJ, that:

> 'In applying Article 85 [now Article 81] to an English contract, one may well have to consider whether, after the excisions required by the Article of the Treaty have been made from the contract, the contract could be said to fail for lack of consideration or on any other ground, or whether the contract would be so

changed in its character as not to be the sort of contract that the parties intended to enter into at all'[2].

1 [1978] 3 CMLR 514.
2 Ibid at 520.

19.11
Whether the exercise is one of severance or not is perhaps something of an exercise in semantics[1]. Either way, the effect of the judgment in the *Chemidus Wavin*[2] case is that those clauses of an agreement which remain after any provisions which infringe Article 81(1) have been removed will be enforceable unless:

(*a*) either the contract could be said to fail for lack of consideration (or on any other ground); or
(*b*) the contract would be so changed in its character as not to be the sort of contract that the parties intended to enter into at all.

This means that each case will necessarily turn on its own facts; in the *Chemidus Wavin*[3] case itself the licensee had received the benefit of the patents and the court therefore appears to have taken the view that there was accordingly valid consideration for the payment of royalties and that the removal of the void provisions did not change the contract out of all recognition. The potential impact of Article 81, coupled with the doctrine of severance, is something which parties to a proposed agreement should bear in mind before entering into it. For example, two companies may negotiate an exclusive licence of certain intellectual property rights in return for a particular royalty (a level which the licensee might not have been willing to pay for a non-exclusive licence). The exclusivity may be null and void under Article 81(1) but under the doctrine of severance it may be possible to cut out the offending part, effectively rendering the licence non-exclusive (but at the same royalty rate).

1 It was treated as an act of severance in *Higgins v Marchant & Eliot Underwriting Ltd* [1996] 3 CMLR 349.
2 [1978] 3 CMLR 514, CA.
3 Ibid. For a subsequent case in which the issue of severance had to be considered in the context of Article 81, see the decision of M Barnes QC in *Inntrepeneur Estates Ltd v Mason* [1993] 2 CMLR 293, in which he severed the unlawful provision; see too *Inntrepreneur Estates v Boyes* [1993] 2 EGLR 112.

(2) Principal English Cases to Date

19.12
Among the principal English cases to date in which, in a dispute between the parties to an agreement, the alleged voidness of one or more provisions of the agreement has been considered are:

(1) *Dymond v GB Britton & Sons (Holdings) Ltd*[1]: That case involved a claim for unpaid royalties by a licensor under an exclusive patent licence. He proceeded under RSC Order 14 for summary judgment and would have succeeded if he had been able to demonstrate that the

defendant had no arguable defence. The defendant in fact argued that the agreement infringed Article 81(1). Although the judge was clearly sceptical about the validity of the defence, he felt obliged to hold that the defendant had at least an arguable defence and accordingly dismissed the plaintiff's claim for summary judgment.

(2) *Chemidus Wavin v TERI*[2]: This also involved a claim by a patentee against its licensee, this time for minimum royalties. As noted at para **19.10**, the patentee succeeded in its claim, notwithstanding the defendant's assertion that one or more provisions infringed Article 81(1), because the court felt able to excise the offending provisions.

(3) *Felixstowe Dock & Rly Co v British Docks Board*[3]: This involved a claim that an agreement for one party to take over the other amounted to the abuse of a dominant position, the defendant relying on the judgment of the ECJ in *Continental Can*[4] in its defence to the plaintiff's claim to enforce the contract. The court had no evidence to support the alleged dominance or abuse and the defence was therefore dismissed.

(4) In *Sirdar v les Fils de Louis Mulliez*[5] an injunction was sought to prevent the use of a trade mark, one of the grounds being that the defendant's action constituted breach of an agreement under which the defendant had agreed to use his mark only in France and the plaintiff his mark only in the United Kingdom. The plaintiff's case was rejected on other grounds but the court indicated that it saw no reason in principle to depart from an earlier decision[6] of the EC Commission which had held that the trade mark agreement was void under Article 81(1).

(5) *Potato Marketing Board v Robertsons*[7]: The Board sued for payment of a farming levy. The defendant relied in his defence on the assertion that the Board was abusing a dominant position. The court held that there was no evidence of dominance or of an abuse.

(6) *Potato Marketing Board v Drysdale*[8]: This was similar to the previous case; this time, the court concluded that the defendant's reliance on Article 82 gave rise to no triable issue because there was no effect on trade between Member States. Accordingly, there was no need to consider the issue of dominance or of abuse.

(7) *Kall Kwik Printing (UK) Ltd v Bell*[9]: The plaintiff operated a franchise system. Following its termination of the defendant's franchise agreement, the plaintiff sought an interlocutory injunction to enforce, inter alia, a restrictive covenant contained in the franchise agreement which prevented the defendant from engaging in any competing business within a certain geographic area for a period of 18 months following termination. The defendant argued that the provision in question was void and unenforceable by virtue of Article 81(1). The defendant drew the judge's attention to the fact that the block exemption which deals with franchise agreements[10] expressly permits such non-competition covenants only if they continue 'for a reasonable period which may not exceed one year'. The judge gave short shrift to this argument holding that 'Article 85[11] has nothing to do with this case and I can therefore ignore it … I therefore come back to the ordinary common law questions which are more comprehensible'.

(8) *Heathrow Airport Ltd v Alpha Airport Holdings (UK) Ltd*[12]: the plaintiff sought summary judgment on its claim for arrears of the rent of two

buildings and adjoining land at Heathrow Airport, occupied by a subsidiary of the defendant for the purpose of the supply of flight catering services to airlines. The defendant argued that it had an arguable defence that the rent was excessive, unfair and discriminatory and that there had been an abuse of dominant position contrary to Article 82. The question which arose was whether the defendant had shown there was an issue or question which ought to be tried. For the purposes of the application, the plaintiff accepted that it was arguable that it was in a dominant position. However, it was held that the defendant had failed to show that it had an arguable case that the demand for rent constituted an abuse of that dominant position or that the alleged abuse affected trade between Member States.

The case of *Holleran v Daniel Thwaites plc*[13] is an example of a case in which reliance on Article 81 was used partly by way of defence, partly by way of attack. The two plaintiffs, each tenants of public houses, had received notices to quit from Thwaites for refusing to enter into new tenancy agreements which it claimed (but they disputed) complied with Commission Regulation 1984/83 (the block exemption which at that time dealt with exclusive purchasing). They succeeded in obtaining an injunction against the brewer, restraining it from recovering possession of their premises pursuant to the notice to quit and also restraining it from issuing further notices to quit by reason of a failure to enter into a tenancy agreement infringing Article 81. The tenants effectively asserted their rights under Article 81 in an attacking manner from an essentially defensive position. In *Enterprise Inns v Carr*[14], one of a number of cases involving tied houses in the brewing industry, the judge rejected the defendant's Article 81 defence to the plaintiff's application for an injunction requiring the defendant to honour the tie.

1 [1976] 1 CMLR 133.
2 [1978] 3 CMLR 514, CA.
3 [1976] 2 CMLR 655, CA.
4 Case 6/72 *Europemballage Corpn and Continental Can v EC Commission* [1973] ECR 215, [1973] CMLR 199.
5 [1975] 1 CMLR 378.
6 Commission Decision (75/297/EEC) *Sirdar/Phildar* OJ [1975] L 125/27, [1975] 1 CMLR D93.
7 [1983] 1 CMLR 93.
8 [1986] 3 CMLR 331, CA.
9 [1994] FSR 674.
10 Commission Regulation (EEC) 4087/88.
11 Now Article 81.
12 Judgment of Lawrence Collins QC, 18 December 1997.
13 [1989] 2 CMLR 917.
14 Judgment dated 14 February 1997.

19.13

Although the cases referred to at para **19.12** do not provide any particularly clear picture of the likely attitude of an English court to a so-called Euro-defence relied on in proceedings between two parties to an agreement, one general point can be made. The courts are likely to approach the defence with a degree of scepticism and it is up to the defendant, in seeking to rely on Articles 81 and 82, to provide real evidence to back up his claim. This comes out even more clearly in those cases in which a Euro-defence has been used in proceedings brought by third parties[1].

1 See para **19.17**.

(3) Recovery of Monies Previously Paid

19.14
It is a basic principle of English law that a party to an illegal agreement cannot recover monies paid, or property transferred, under it[1]. Agreements which violate Article 81(1) or Article 82 are unlawful and it would seem that this basic principle should apply to such agreements. The Court of Appeal held in the *Gibbs Mew* case[2] that an agreement caught by Article 81(1) is illegal, rather than merely void, with the result that the parties to an agreement which infringes Article 81 cannot bring an action in tort or in restitution for compensation for any harm suffered.

1 See Goff and Jones *Law of Restitution* (5th edn, 1998) ch 24. In relation to restitution generally, see Jones 'Recovery of Benefits Conferred under Contractual Obligations Prohibited by Article 85 or 86 of the Treaty of Rome' LQR 112 (1996), 606–631.
2 *Gibbs Mew Plc v Gemmell* [1998] Eu LR 588.

19.15
There are, however, several points which should be noted. Firstly, if after the offending provision has been severed[1], the provision under which the monies have been paid (or goods transferred) still stands, it is probably not necessary to invoke the principle referred to at para **19.14**: the provision for payment/transfer of goods would not be tainted with the illegality. For example, in *Chemidus Wavin v TERI*[2] the plaintiff succeeded in claiming unpaid royalties, notwithstanding the presence in the licence agreement of provisions caught by Article 81(1); it must follow that in such a case royalties already paid could not be recovered by the licensee. Secondly, there are likely to be cases (particularly under Article 82) in which the parties are not in pari delicto. For example, an undertaking might have abused its dominant position by charging excessive prices. In such a case a court might be prepared to allow the 'abused' party to recover the 'excess' element of the price. That this would be the case in an Article 82 context is suggested by the *GT-Link* case[3] which concerned state liability but which laid down a principle which is capable of application beyond that specific context.

1 See paras **19.09–19.11**.
2 [1978] 3 CMLR 514, CA.
3 Case C-242/95 *GT-Link A/S v De Danske Statsbaner* [1997] ECR I-4349, [1997] 5 CMLR 601.

2 PROCEEDINGS BROUGHT BY THIRD PARTIES

19.16
The extent to which a person against whom proceedings are brought by a third party can rely by way of defence on Articles 81 or 82 has so far arisen

principally in cases in which the plaintiff is seeking to take action for the alleged infringement of an intellectual property right. This issue has usually been considered[1] in the context of the claimant's attempt to demonstrate that the defence (or at least that part relying on Articles 81 and 82) raises no good ground for defending the action and should accordingly be struck out[2].

1 See, eg *ICI v Berk Pharmaceuticals* [1981] 2 CMLR 91; *Lansing Bagnall v Buccaneer Lift Parts* [1984] 1 CMLR 224, CA; *Ransburg-GEMA AG v Electrostatic Plant Systems* [1989] 2 CMLR 712.

2 Under RSC Ord 18, r 19.

19.17

The present position reached by the English courts is that Articles 81 and 82 do, in principle, provide the basis for a defence to an action brought by a third party; however, there must be a genuine nexus between the relief which the plaintiff is seeking and the alleged contravention of Articles 81 or 82. This was confirmed in the case of *Ransburg-GEMA AG v Electrostatic Plant Systems*[1], in which the plaintiffs sued the defendants for infringement of copyright in drawings relating to electrostatic powder coating equipment. The defendants raised 'Euro-defences' based on Articles 30 and 82. Aldous J said that:

> 'For there to be a defence under Article 86 [now Article 82], it must be pleaded that the plaintiff is in a dominant position and that the relief claimed would involve an abuse of that dominant position affecting trade between Member States. If such is pleaded properly and proved, the court is precluded from granting the relief [sought by the plaintiff], because to do so would produce a result which could be contrary to the Treaty ... it is quite clear that to succeed the defendants must plead that an act amounts to an abuse and properly allege and particularise how that act falls within Article 86'[2].

The cases of *ICI v Berk Pharmaceuticals*[3], on the one hand, and *British Leyland v T I Silencers*[4] and *Lansing Bagnall v Buccaneer Lift Parts*[5] on the other are illustrative of the operation of this dividing line. In the *ICI*[6] case, the plaintiffs sued the defendants for passing off and the court held that the mere fact that the plaintiffs might or might not be imposing unfair selling prices on their customers did not mean that the defendants were thereby 'set free from any liability to the plaintiffs if they, the defendants, commit the tort of passing off (or, indeed, any other tort) against them'[7]. Conversely, in the *T I Silencers*[8] case a Euro-defence was allowed to stand in circumstances in which it was claimed that infringement proceedings were being threatened in order to coerce the defendant into entering into a licence agreement which arguably infringed Articles 81 and 82. In the *Lansing Bagnall*[9] case, the defence was that the plaintiff was dominant by virtue of its monopoly right to supply spare parts and the infringement proceedings in relation to those spare parts was itself abusive.

1 [1989] 2 CMLR 712; see too *Chiron Corpn v Murex Diagnostics Ltd (No 2)* [1994] 1 CMLR 410.

2 At paras 10 and 29.

3 [1981] 2 CMLR 91.

4 [1981] 2 CMLR 75, CA.

5 [1984] 1 CMLR 224, CA.

6 See n 4 above.
7 [1981] 2 CMLR 91 at 97.
8 See n 4 above.
9 See n 5 above.

19.18
The Court of Appeal in the *Lansing Bagnall*[1] case distinguished the *ICI*[2] case on the ground that the latter involved an action for passing-off rather than a copyright action. This distinction is somewhat artificial; the real issue (as demonstrated in the more recent *Ransburg*[3] case) should be whether there is a nexus between the actions of the plaintiffs and the alleged breaches of Articles 81 and 82. It should, however, be noted that in *Pitney Bowes Inc v Francotyp-Postalia GmbH*[4] Hoffmann J accepted that it might be possible to differentiate patents; the argument being that national law already has a code under which compulsory licences can be imposed upon patentees who abuse or fail to exploit their rights (Patents Act 1977, ss 48–53) and that it is not therefore necessary to invoke Article 82. This is an issue which would almost certainly have to be referred to the ECJ under Article 234 of the EC Treaty[5].

1 [1984] 1 CMLR 224.
2 [1981] 2 CMLR 91.
3 *Ransburg-GEMA AS v Electrostatic Plant Systems* [1989] 2 CMLR 712.
4 [1990] 3 CMLR 466.
5 See paras **10.67–10.69**.

19.19
In *Pitney Bowes*[1] the High Court ruled that threats by a dominant undertaking to bring legal proceedings for breach of patent rights, even if made in bad faith, cannot constitute an abuse of a dominant position under Article 82, but might amount to the independent tort of malicious prosecution.

1 *Pitney Bowes v Francotyp-Postalia GmbH* [1990] 3 CMLR 466.

19.20
The difficulties which a defendant will face in establishing the necessary nexus, at least in a case where the plaintiff is seeking to enforce an intellectual property right, have been increased by the decision of the ECJ in *AB Volvo v Eric Veng*[1]. That case involved an Article 234 reference from the High Court. Volvo were the proprietors of a registered design in respect of car wings and were seeking to enforce it against the defendants. The latter contended that the plaintiffs' action was in breach of Article 82 as they were refusing to licence the defendants upon reasonable terms. The ECJ held that a refusal to grant a licence (whether or not on reasonable terms) cannot *in itself* constitute an abuse of a dominant position. In order for the refusal to amount to an abuse within the meaning of Article 82 there has to be an additional element in the conduct of the dominant undertaking (for example, the arbitrary refusal to supply spare parts only to certain persons, in casu independent repairers, the fixing of prices for spare parts at an unfair level or a decision no longer to produce spare parts for a particular

model even though many cars of that model are still in circulation). The decision of the ECJ in the *Volvo*[2] case was relied upon by Aldous J in the *Ransburg*[3] case referred to above. There the judge examined each of the individual paragraphs of the defence and held that none of them provided an arguable defence. For example, the defendant pleaded that the plaintiffs' refusal to sell spare parts to them amounted to an abuse of a dominant position. The comment of Aldous J on this was that Article 82 did not have the effect that all refusals to supply spare parts were wrongful and therefore something more than the mere refusal to supply had to be pleaded and particularised. In this context he went on to say that:

> 'If the defendants wished to allege that enforcement of the plaintiff's copyright would be an abuse within Article 86 [now Article 82] because of some arbitrary refusal to supply, then they should plead it properly with adequate particulars as to the refusal to supply and how the relief sought would involve an abuse within Article 86'[4].

1 Case 238/87 *AB Volvo v Erik Veng* [1988] ECR 6211, [1989] 4 CMLR 122.
2 See n 1 above.
3 [1989] 2 CMLR 712. It was also cited in *Pitney Bowes Inc v Francotyp-Postalia GmbH* [1990] 3 CMLR 466. See also *Chiron Corpn v Organon Teknika Ltd* [1992] 3 CMLR 813 at 823, again a judgment of Aldous J.
4 Ibid at para 19.

19.21

The message is clear. Any defendant wishing to raise Article 81 or 82 in his defence (be it in the context of an attempt by the plaintiff to enforce an intellectual property right, or any other context) must plead and particularise his case very precisely. In particular, his defence (and any further and better particulars thereof) should reveal not only an arguable infringement by the plaintiff of Articles 81 and/or 82 but should also demonstrate a real nexus between the plaintiff's actions and the alleged breaches of Article 81 or 82.

19.22

The Court of Appeal's judgment in the *Lloyd's*[1] case illustrates the effectiveness of Article 81(1) in national proceedings. In that case, the judge had ordered the trial of certain preliminary issues, including a number of EC law issues. The two defendants had, as 'names' of Lloyd's, incurred substantial liabilities, which they had failed to discharge. Lloyd's accordingly paid monies out of its Central Fund in order to discharge those liabilities. It brought its action under a particular byelaw and was seeking reimbursement from the two defendants. The preliminary issues included whether any of the functions of Lloyd's constituted activities subject to, inter alia, Article 81 of the EC Treaty and whether certain byelaws and decisions of Lloyd's constituted violations of Article 81. In reversing the judgment at first instance, the Court of Appeal concluded that, in the absence of further evidence, it could not as a preliminary matter rule out the Article 81 arguments. It therefore held that the defendants had at least an arguable Article 81 case (albeit one which subsequently failed).

1 *Society of Lloyd's v Clementson (No 2)* [1996] CLC 1590.

C Articles 81 and 82 as a Sword

1 SUMMARY OF CURRENT POSITION

19.23
The extent to which Articles 81 and 82 can be used as a sword giving rise to a cause of action in its own right, and the remedies available to a plaintiff who makes out his case, is gradually receiving judicial clarification, although there are still a number of issues in respect of which the position is not yet clear. In parallel, of course, the courts in other Member States are wrestling with the same issues in the context of their own national law and there remains the possibility that at some stage in the future the European Commission will decide that there is no alternative but for it to put forward proposals with a view to achieving some degree of uniformity in the application of Articles 81 and 82 in national courts[1].

1 See para **17.08**. As to the use of Articles 81 and 82 as a sword, see Picanol 'Remedies in National Law for Breach of Articles 85 and 86 of the EEC Treaty: A Review' [1982] 2 LIEI 1; Temple Lang 'EEC Competition Actions in Member States' Courts–Claims for Damages, Declarations and Injunctions for Breach of Community Antitrust Law' Fordham Corporate Law Inst 1984; Steiner 'How to make the Action suit the Case: Domestic Remedies for Breach of EEC Law' (1987) 12 EL Rev 102.

19.24
In summary, the present position under English law is as follows:

(1) Infringements of Articles 81 and 82 can be the subject of applications for injunctive relief at the suit of an injured party, the onus being on that party (as in the case of any other application for injunctive relief) to satisfy the basic conditions which need to be satisfied if a court is to exercise this discretionary remedy[1];
(2) It is almost, though not absolutely, certain that a remedy in damages is available to a party who can establish that he has suffered loss as a result of a breach of Article 81 or 82[2]. However, the English courts have come to the view that a party to a contract cannot claim damages against the other party on the basis that the contract infringes Article 81, because they are 'in pari delicto'[3].

1 See para **19.26** ff.
2 See para **19.31** ff.
3 See para **19.37**.

2 BASIC GROUND RULES

19.25
As has been indicated earlier[1], Articles 81 and 82 produce direct effects in relations between individuals and, as such, create direct rights in respect of the individuals concerned which national courts must safeguard[2]. National courts in turn are in principle free to decide how these rights should be safeguarded[3]. However, this is subject to two important qualifications. Firstly, the ECJ has made it clear that the remedies available for enforcing rights

arising under Community law must be no less extensive than the rights available for the enforcement of similar rights arising under national law[4]. Secondly, as far as procedural aspects are concerned, the ECJ has said[5] that:

> 'It is for the domestic legal system of each Member State to designate the courts having jurisdiction and determine the procedural conditions governing actions at law intended to safeguard the rights which derive from the direct effect of Community law, it being understood that such conditions cannot be less favourable than those relating to similar actions of a domestic nature and that under no circumstances may they be so adapted as to make it impossible in practice to exercise the rights which the national courts have a duty to protect ...'

1 See paras **17.01–17.03**.
2 Case 127/73 *BRT v SABAM* [1974] ECR 51, [1974] 2 CMLR 238.
3 Case 33/76 *Rewe v Landwirtschaftskammer Saarland* [1976] ECR 1989, [1977] 1 CMLR 533; Case 45/76 *Comet v Produktschap voor Siergewassen* [1976] ECR 2043, [1977] 1 CMLR 533.
4 Case 158/80 *Rewe v Hauptzollamt Kiel* [1981] ECR 1805, [1982] 1 CMLR 449.
5 Case 826/79 *Amministrazione delle Finanze dello Stato v MIRECO* [1980] ECR 2559.

3 INJUNCTIVE RELIEF

19.26
It is clear from the judgment of the House of Lords in *Garden Cottage Foods Ltd v Milk Marketing Board*[1] that injunctive relief on an interlocutory basis (ie pending full trial) is available to restrain a breach of Article 82. It is, of course, necessary for the plaintiff to satisfy the court that the normal conditions for the granting of interlocutory relief are satisfied, that is to say the conditions laid down by the House of Lords in *American Cyanamid Co v Ethicon Ltd*[2]. In particular, the plaintiff must demonstrate to the satisfaction of the court that damages would not be an adequate remedy[3] (as to the availability of damages for breach of Articles 81 and 82, see paras **19.31** ff). This is likely to be a difficult hurdle in practice for a plaintiff to overcome, as was the case in *Garden Cottage*[4] itself; this is a factor which any potential plaintiff should consider in deciding whether its interests are best served by commencing proceedings in an English court or filing a complaint with the European Commission[5]. In that case, the plaintiffs had for two years been purchasing substantial quantities of bulk butter from the defendants. However, supplies were subsequently terminated, following the defendants' decision to supply bulk butter only to four named distributors (not including the plaintiffs). The plaintiffs sought an injunction restraining the defendants from withholding supplies of butter contrary to Article 82 and applied for an interlocutory injunction. On appeal, the House of Lords held (with one dissenting voice, that of Lord Wilberforce) that it was clearly arguable that a remedy in damages would be available to the plaintiffs to compensate for any loss and there were no grounds for interfering with the view of the judge at first instance that damages would provide the plaintiffs with an adequate remedy.

1 [1984] AC 130, [1983] 2 All ER 770.
2 [1975] AC 396, [1975] 1 All ER 504.
3 An application for interlocutory relief failed on this ground in *Chelmkarm Motors Ltd v Esso Petroleum Co Ltd* [1979] 1 CMLR 73.

4 See n 1 above.
5 As to the relative merits of a complaint and proceedings in a national court, see paras **5.10–5.18**.

19.27

Whilst the difficulties of satisfying the conditions laid down in the *American Cyanamid*[1] case are considerable, they are not insurmountable. For example, in the case of *Budgett v British Sugar*[2], the High Court was prepared to grant an injunction restraining the defendant from refusing to accept orders from the plaintiff, a sugar merchant, in order to enable it to continue supplies to its regular customers. Similarly, in the dispute between *ECS* and *AKZO*, during the course of which ECS applied for interim measures from the EC Commission[3], it appears that ECS obtained an ex parte injunction restraining AKZO from reducing its selling prices in breach of Article 82. In contrast, the Scottish Outer House refused, during the course of the battle in 1986 to acquire the Distillers Company, to grant an application for an interim interdict (the Scottish law equivalent of an interim injunction) on the basis of Article 82 to prevent the merger of Distillers and Guinness; the court decided that there was no prima facie case and in any event the balance of convenience favoured Guinness and Distillers[4]. A more recent case in which the plaintiff failed to obtain injunctive relief for alleged breach of Article 82 is *Leyland Daf Ltd v Automotive Products plc*[5]; in that case the Court of Appeal was satisfied that the withholding of further supplies to an insolvent company until goods already supplied had been paid for was not an abuse of a dominant position; see too *Megaphone International Ltd v British Telecommunications plc*[6] and *Fyffes plc v Chiquita Brands International*[7].

1 [1975] AC 396, [1975] 1 All ER 504, HL.
2 This case has not been fully reported but a note of it prepared by Professor Korah appears in (1979) EL Rev at p 417.
3 See para **8.28**.
4 *Argyll Group v Distillers* [1986] 1 CMLR 764.
5 [1994] 1 BCLC 245.
6 (28 February 1989, unreported).
7 [1993] FSR 83. In that case, the plaintiffs had made a complaint to the European Commission in parallel to the High Court proceedings. The Commission had issued a statement of objections but had not issued a final decision. The court decided that, although there was an arguable Article 81 case, the balance of convenience was against granting an injunction.

19.28

Although the *Garden Cottage*[1] case was necessarily limited by its facts to a consideration of Article 82, there is no reason in principle why any distinction should be drawn, in the context of the availability of injunctive relief, between Articles 81 and 82. Indeed, in *Cutsforth v Mansfield Inns*[2] the plaintiffs, who were suppliers of juke boxes and other amusement machines, obtained an interim injunction restraining the defendant brewer from excluding the plaintiffs from the brewer's tied houses. Similarly, in *Holleran v Daniel Thwaites plc*[3] the High Court granted an interim injunction sought by the plaintiffs, tenants of two tied houses owned by the defendant. The plaintiffs had refused to enter into the defendant's new standard form tenancy agreement which it believed complied with Regulation 1984/83 (the exclusive purchasing block exemption in force at the time) but which they felt did not. The defendant issued the plaintiffs with notices to quit and they in turn commenced proceedings seeking, inter alia, an interim injunction restraining the defendant from enforcing or giving effect to the notices to quit and from recovering possession of the premises pursuant to the notices to quit. The court held that it was strongly arguable that the agreement did not satisfy the provisions of Regulation 1984/83, that it was proper to enjoin exercise of the defendant's contractual rights and that the balance of convenience lay in favour of granting the interim injunction.

1 [1984] AC 130, [1983] 2 All ER 770, HL.
2 [1986] 1 All ER 577, [1986] 1 CMLR 1.
3 [1989] 2 CMLR 917.

19.29

An illustration of the way in which Articles 81 and 82 can be prayed in aid in an English court by a target company in a hostile bid situation is provided by the proceedings commenced by Plessey in December 1988 against two companies, the General Electric Company (GEC) and Siemens, who had mounted a joint bid for Plessey. In that case, Plessey claimed that the proposed joint offer by GEC and Siemens would be made pursuant to an agreement which infringed Article 81 and accordingly Plessey sought an injunction restraining them (and others) from, inter alia, acquiring or offering to acquire, whether conditionally or otherwise, any of the share capital of Plessey and otherwise carrying out or acting in furtherance of any agreement or concerted practice involving any two or more of them. In addition to this injunctive relief, Plessey claimed damages for breach of statutory duty under Articles 81 and 82. During the first brief hearing, which was ex parte (ie without the participation of the defendants), Plessey successfully obtained an injunction. During the inter partes hearing a few days later the High Court ruled that, although Plessey had an arguable case for its assertion that the underlying agreement between GEC and Siemens contravened Article 81, the balance of convenience was against granting an injunction[1]. One factor which particularly influenced the court was that the matter was being examined concurrently by the European Commission, GEC and Siemens having notified (or proposing shortly to notify) the arrangement to the Commission. The judge found it inconceivable that GEC and Siemens would proceed with their planned post-acquisition restructuring of Plessey until they had received the Commission's blessing and accordingly Plessey's contention that it would be 'swallowed up' and 'dismembered' was unrealistic.

1 (20 December 1988, unreported).

19.30

All the cases referred to at paras **19.26–19.29** were concerned with the question whether *interim* injunctive relief should be granted to the plaintiff, pending full trial (although in cases where the plaintiff is successful in his application for interim relief this is frequently determinative of the matter, the defendant not taking the case to full trial). However, there appears to be no reason in principle why a permanent injunction should not also be granted at full trial if circumstances justify it.

4 DAMAGES

19.31

In the *Garden Cottage* case[1], the House of Lords expressed the view, by a majority of four to one, that if (as it found to be the case) contravention of Article 82 gave rise to a cause of action in English law, that cause of action entitled the plaintiff to a remedy in damages. To hold otherwise would, in the words of Lord Diplock, involve the invention of a 'cause of action with characteristics that are wholly novel as respects the remedies that it attracts'[2]. Lord Wilberforce was a lone voice in considering that the availability of an action in damages was uncertain. He felt that the House of Lords should not, during the course of interlocutory proceedings in which the availability or otherwise of damages had not been fully argued, 'decide difficult questions of law which call for detailed argument and mature considerations'[3].

1 *Garden Cottage Foods Ltd v Milk Marketing Board* [1984] AC 130, [1983] 2 All ER 770.
2 [1984] AC 130 at 144.
3 [1984] AC 130 at 152.

19.32

The views of their Lordships regarding damages in the *Garden Cottage* case[1] were subsequently considered by the Court of Appeal in *Bourgoin SA v Ministry of Agriculture, Fisheries and Food*[2]. That case involved a claim for damages not for breach of Article 81 or 82 but for breach of Article 28 (dealing with free movement of goods). The Court of Appeal drew a basic distinction between Articles 28 and 82, concluding that the former gave rise to public law obligations whilst the latter gave rise to private law obligations. On this basis, it concluded that damages were not available for breach of Article 28[3], the only remedy being the public law remedy of judicial review. In so doing, however, the Court of Appeal endorsed the view of the majority in the *Garden Cottage* case[4] regarding the availability of damages for breach of Article 82, Parker LJ stating at one point that:

> 'That [ie *Garden Cottage*] is clear authority that a private law action for breach of Article 86[5] against an undertaking sounds in damages'[6].

1 [1984] AC 130, [1983] 2 All ER 770, HL.
2 [1986] QB 716, [1985] 3 All ER 585.
3 Or at least that damages were not available for breach of Article 28 simpliciter; in that case the court found that the minister's action constituted the separate tort of misfeasance in public office.
4 See n 1 above.
5 Now Article 82.
6 [1986] QB 716 at 787, [1985] 3 All ER 585 at 631.

19.33

There is therefore weighty judicial authority for the view that damages are available under English law for breaches of Articles 81 and 82. On the other hand, the House of Lords' decision in *Garden Cottage*[1] was an appeal from the grant of an interlocutory injunction and (as Lord Wilberforce himself noted in his dissenting judgment) full argument on the point had not therefore been heard. Moreover, the *Bourgoin*[2] case involved Article 28, not

Articles 81 and 82, and therefore the views of the Court of Appeal, whilst certainly persuasive, are not binding, being merely obiter dicta. Damages have not as yet been awarded by an English (or Scottish) court in any reported case in respect of a breach of Article 81 or 82, although a number of cases have been settled out of court on payment of monetary sums.

1 [1984] AC 130, [1983] 2 All ER 770.
2 [1986] QB 716, [1985] 3 All ER 585.

19.34
It is submitted that the better view, and one for which English judicial authority is in support, is that damages are, in principle, available for breach of Articles 81 and 82. However, there are a considerable number of procedural aspects which in practice will make it difficult for a plaintiff bringing an action on the basis of either Article 81 or Article 82 to succeed in recovering damages. These procedural difficulties are considered in Chapter 20.

19.35
The ECJ's judgment in *Francovich*[1] moves closer towards a Community law principle that a remedy in damages should be available for all infringements of those Treaty provisions which have direct effect (which include Articles 81 and 82[2]). Moreover, the ECJ's judgment in *Factortame*[3] emphasises the importance of ensuring that the remedies made available by national law provide an *effective means* for individuals to exercise their Community law rights[4]. Advocate General van Gerven provides an excellent summary of the case law to date in his opinion in *Banks v British Coal Corpn*[5], concluding that 'as a result of its obligation to ensure that Community law is fully effective and to protect the rights thereby conferred on individuals, the national court is under an obligation to award damages for loss sustained by an undertaking as a result of the breach by another undertaking of a directly effective provision of Community competition law'.

1 Joined Cases C-6, 9/90 *Francovich and Bonifaci v Italy*, [1991] ECR I-5357, [1993] 2 CMLR 66. See also Maitland-Walker 'A step closer to a Definitive Ruling on a Right in Damages for Breach of the EC Competition Rules' [1992] 1 ECLR 3 and Hoskins 'Garden Cottage Revisited: the Availability of Damages in the National Courts for Breaches of the EC Competition Rules' [1992] 6 ECLR 257.
2 See para **17.01**.
3 Case C-213/89 *Factortame* [1990] ECR I-2433 at para 19.
4 Although neither the *Francovich* nor *Factortame* cases were competition cases, there would seem no reason why the principles which they lay down should not be regarded as of general application.
5 Case C-128/92 [1994] ECR I-1209, at 1243–1251. *Banks* was a case involving provisions of the ECSC Treaty, but in considering those provisions the Advocate General reviewed the ECJ case law on the corresponding provisions.

19.36
In the *Irish Aerospace*[1] case a claim for damages for alleged violation of Article 82 was dismissed by the High Court as disclosing no cause of action. The reason for the decision had nothing to do with whether or not damages were, in principle, available for a breach of Article 82 but was based instead on the fact that the defendants (the Civil Aviation Authority and the European Organisation for the Safety of Air Navigation) were

essentially regulatory bodies and did not pursue activities of an economic or commercial nature. It is interesting to note that the judge cited two earlier decisions of the Brussels Appeal Court in which the same conclusion had been reached in relation to one of the defendants in the present case.

1 *Irish Aerospace (Belgium) NV v European Organisation for the Safety of Air Navigation* [1992] 1 Lloyd's Rep 383.

19.37

Assuming damages are in principle available for breach of Articles 81 and 82, the question arises as to whether or not damages are available as between two contracting parties. That is to say, can contracting party A claim damages against contracting party B on the ground that the agreement breaches Article 81, thereby causing him financial loss? The Court of Appeal ruled in the *Gibbs Mew* case[1] (admittedly obiter as it concluded on the facts that there was no infringement of Article 81(1)) that contracting party A cannot claim damages in such circumstances, because he and contracting party B are in pari delicto. This issue has since been made the subject of a reference to the ECJ under Article 234, EC Treaty[2].

1 [1998] Eu LR 588.
2 *Crehan v Courage (and associated cases)* [1999] Eu LR Rep 834.

Chapter 20 Procedural Issues

A Introduction

20.01
Any party to proceedings in an English court who wishes to invoke Article 81 or 82 of the EC Treaty (whether as a shield or as a sword) faces a range of procedural difficulties. Whilst none of these are insurmountable, they are aspects which merit careful consideration before proceeding with the claim, or the defence, as the case may be.

B Specific Procedural Issues

20.02
Paragraphs **20.03–20.22** identify some of the more important procedural issues which arise in relation to Articles 81 and 82. Some of these are not confined to the application of these Articles but are nevertheless considered here because they are likely to be particularly relevant in relation to claims or defences mounted on the basis of either Article.

1 ESTABLISHING THE BREACH OF DUTY

20.03
Under English case law to date, the most likely basis for action under Articles 81 and 82 is that breach of them constitutes a breach of statutory duty[1]. It would be necessary for a plaintiff mounting a claim on the basis of either Article to satisfy the usual requirements for establishing a breach of duty under English law[2]. For example, because a statutory duty is imposed to prevent some particular form of harm, it is usually necessary for the plaintiff to establish that the loss which he has suffered was within the scope of injury contemplated[3].

1 *Garden Cottage Foods v Milk Marketing Board* [1984] AC 130, [1983] 2 All ER 770, HL; see para **18.30**.
2 See, generally, *Clerk and Lindsell on Torts* (17th edn, 1995); *Street on Torts* (10th edn, 1999); *Salmond & Heuston on the Law of Torts* (21st edn, 1996).
3 *Gorris v Scott* (1874) LR 9 Exch 125; in that case a statutory order required that those parts of a ship occupied by animals be divided into pens. The order was violated, causing the plaintiff's sheep to be washed overboard. The plaintiff failed in his claim because the purpose of the order was to prevent the spread of disease.

2 NEED FOR SUFFICIENT NEXUS

20.04
The High Court decision in *Ransburg-GEMA AG v Electrostatic Plant Systems*[1], to which reference has already been made[2], makes it clear that where a defendant seeks to rely upon Article 81 or 82 by way of defence he must show a genuine nexus between the actions of the plaintiff on the one hand and the alleged breaches of Articles 81 and 82. A defendant in such circumstances should anticipate that the court will scrutinise very closely the defendant's case, as set out in the defence itself and any further and better particulars which are subsequently served, as happened in the *Ransburg*[3] case itself. If the court is not satisfied that there is such a nexus, the Euro-defence is likely to be struck out, as in *ICI v Berk Pharmaceuticals Ltd*[4].

1 [1989] 2 CMLR 712. See too *Higgins v Marchant & Eliot Underwriting Ltd* [1996] 3 CMLR 349.
2 See para **19.17**.
3 See n 1 above.
4 [1981] 2 CMLR 91.

20.05
The need to establish a nexus, or causal connection, is no less important where the plaintiff is seeking to rely on Article 81 or 82 as a sword, rather than by way of defence. If he is to succeed in a claim for damages, for example, he will need to establish that the loss which he has suffered is directly attributable to the alleged breaches of Articles 81 and 82.

3 BURDEN OF PROOF

20.06
The burden of proving that the agreement or conduct in question is in breach of Article 81 or 82 lies on the party claiming that to be the case[1]. In *Shearson Lehman Hutton Inc v Maclaine Watson & Co Ltd*[2], a case which arose out of the collapse of the International Tin Council, Webster J in the High Court noted that, even though the standard of proof in civil proceedings was a balance of probabilities, there were various degrees of proof. He went on to hold that, because an infringement of Article 81 (and presumably the same would apply in his view in relation to Article 82) carried with it a liability to penalties and fines he would apply the standard of a 'high degree of probability', though less than the standard of proof in criminal matters (proof beyond reasonable doubt)[3]. This is open to some doubt, particularly in view of the Community law principle[4] that remedies must be capable of being resorted to under conditions not less favourable than those applicable to the enforcement of a similar right of a domestic nature.

1 *Potato Marketing Board v Robertsons* [1983] 1 CMLR 93 at 98.
2 [1989] 3 CMLR 429.
3 This decision was cited, but not followed, by the Irish High Court in *Masterfoods Ltd T/A Mars Ireland v HB Ice Cream Ltd* [1992] 3 CMLR 830 at 873.
4 See para **19.25**.

20.07
In the *George Michael*[1] case the judge applied the normal civil law standard of proof, without formally ruling on Sony's claim that a higher standard of proof applied. That case illustrates very well the need to satisfy the court that all the elements of Article 81 (or Article 82, as the case may be), are made out, and to adduce the necessary evidence, even when applying the ordinary level of proof. The case involved not only claims based on Article 81 but also on common law restraint of trade and the plaintiff relied on the same evidence in relation to both claims. The judge made it clear that in his view it was 'unfortunate' that the Article 81 issue had not been specifically addressed in evidence. He did not consider that he had heard evidence which made out the necessary effect on trade between Member States in the market concerned (that for recording services).

1 *Panayiotou v Sony Music Entertainment (UK) Ltd* [1994] Ch 142, [1994] 1 All ER 755.

4 QUANTIFICATION OF DAMAGES

20.08
There is as yet no English case law on the question how damages should be calculated in a case brought under Article 81 or 82. This is an aspect which is likely to give rise to a number of difficult issues. For example, if a customer of a raw material believes that he has suffered loss because of market-sharing arrangements operated by all the Community suppliers of that raw material he will need to establish, inter alia, by what amount the prices which he has paid have been higher as a result. Similarly, if he has passed on the higher prices to his own customers it may be that he will not be able to establish any loss: it remains to be seen whether such a 'passing-on' defence will be accepted by the courts. It is also an open issue whether there will be scope for an award of exemplary damages[1].

1 On the subject of exemplary damages generally, see *Clerk & Lindsell on Torts* (17th edn, 1995) pp 1497–1503; *Street on Torts* (10th edn, 1999) pp 527–530; *Salmond & Heuston on the Law of Torts* (21st edn, 1996) pp 503–506.

5 DISCOVERY AND SELF-INCRIMINATION

20.09
The House of Lords held in *Westinghouse Uranium Contract Litigation*[1] that a party can claim privilege from discovery and disclosure of documents by invoking the Civil Evidence Act 1968, s 14, on the grounds that to do so might incriminate him and make him vulnerable to the imposition of a fine by the European Commission for breach of Article 81 or 82. If a party wishes to take this point and claim privilege the procedure which should be followed is that he should make and produce his list of documents in the ordinary way and then object to their production[2]. If a defendant invokes Article 81 or 82 but the plaintiff prevents essential facts being put before the national court by claiming privilege against self-incrimination, the court is likely to have to stay the proceedings before it, pending a decision by the Commission[3].

1 *Rio Tinto Zinc v Westinghouse Electric Corpn* [1978] AC 547, [1978] 1 All ER 434.
2 *British Leyland v T I Silencers* [1980] 1 CMLR 598.
3 As in *British Leyland v Wyatt Interpart* [1979] 3 CMLR 79.

20.10

Under English law, a solicitor who, in the course of discovery in an action, obtains possession of copies of documents belonging to his client's adversary gives an implied undertaking to the court not to use that material nor to allow it to be used for any purpose other than the proper conduct of that action on behalf of his client[1]. This undertaking can be released or modified by the court in 'appropriate circumstances'. Against this background, the High Court was asked in the *Apple* case[2] to relieve the applicant from this implied undertaking so as to enable it to put certain documents obtained on discovery before the Commission (the issues which were being litigated in the High Court were also being examined by the Commission in parallel proceedings). The High Court considered that it was desirable that each tribunal should have the opportunity of evaluating the same evidence and accordingly the application for release from the implied undertaking was granted. This release was made subject to the condition that the plaintiffs should draw the attention of the Commission to the fact that the relevant documents contained business secrets or other material to which the obligation of professional secrecy might apply[3].

1 *Crest Homes plc v Marks* [1987] AC 829 at 853; see also *Harman v Secretary of State for the Home Department* [1983] 1 AC 280, [1982] 1 All ER 532.
2 *Apple Corpn Ltd v Apple Computer Inc* [1992] 1 CMLR 969.
3 As to the relevance of business secrets and professional secrecy in Commission proceedings, see paras **11.02–11.13**.

20.11

The *Westinghouse*[1] and *Apple*[2] cases now need to be read in the light of the ECJ's judgment in *Otto v Postbank*[3]. In that case, the defendant in proceedings in a Dutch court argued that the Dutch rules of procedure were incompatible with Community law, in so far as they compelled it to produce incriminatory evidence. The defendant relied on the ECJ's judgment in *Orkem*[4], in which the Court had held that the European Commission could not, in the context of proceedings commenced by it pursuant to Regulation 17[5], compel the undertaking concerned to provide it with answers which might involve an admission of the infringement which it was incumbent on the Commission to prove[6].

1 *Rio Tinto Zinc Corpn v Westinghouse Electric Corpn* [1978] AC 547, [1978] 1 All ER 434.
2 *Apple Corpn Ltd v Apple Computer Inc* [1992] 1 CMLR 969.
3 Case C-60/92 [1993] ECR I-5683.
4 Case 374/87 *Orkem v EC Commission* [1989] ECR 3283, [1991] 4 CMLR 502.
5 Council Regulation (EEC) 17/62, OJ Sp Ed [1959–62] p 87.
6 See paras **6.74–6.75**.

20.12

In *Otto*[1] the ECJ held that, because the Dutch proceedings concerned exclusively the private relationship between individuals and could not lead to the imposition of a penalty by a public authority, Community law did *not* require that a party should have the option of refusing of give answers which might admit the existence of an infringement; it was a matter to be governed by national law. One of the arguments made, unsuccessfully, by the defendant in *Otto*[1] was that the incriminatory evidence in question might well be brought to the attention of the Commission. The ECJ accepted this but indicated that the Commission could not use such information as a means of evidence of an infringement of Article 81 or 82, or indeed as evidence justifying the initiation of an inquiry. There is clearly a parallel here with the ECJ's earlier judgment in the *Spanish Banks* case[2], in which it held that the national authorities could not use information obtained by the Commission under Regulation 17[3] as a means of proof in the enforcement of EC (or national) competition law (although it did hold that such information could be taken into account by the national authorities in deciding whether to open their own procedure)[4].

1 Case C-60/92 *Otto BV v Postbank NV* [1993] ECR I-5683.
2 Case C-67/91 *Dirección General de Défensa de la Competencia v Associación Espanola de Banca Privada*, [1992] ECR I-4785, ECJ.
3 Council Regulation (EEC) 17/62, OJ Sp Ed [1959–62] p 87.
4 See para **18.20**.

6 GATHERING OF EVIDENCE

20.13
Where the conduct (or agreement) which is alleged to contravene Article 81 or 82 involves undertakings located in various Member States (for example, the operation of an international cartel), there will be significant difficulties in collecting evidence, both of a practical nature and because of the need to comply with whatever may be the local legal requirements in the Member States concerned. In such cases, there may be a strong argument in favour of the person who is considering mounting a claim filing a complaint with the Commission, leaving the latter to exercise its considerable investigative powers under arts 11 and 14 of Council Regulation 17/62[1].

1 See para **6.01** ff.

20.14
This is not to suggest that Articles 81 and 82 are, at a stroke, rendered virtually toothless as far as proceedings in national courts are concerned, merely because of the difficulties of gathering evidence. Moreover, the broad application of Articles 81 and 82 (and, in particular, the broad interpretation of the requirement for an effect on trade between Member States) means that there is considerable scope for the application of Articles 81 and 82 in cases involving parties in one Member State where the conduct or agreement in question is, on the face of it, of a 'local nature'[1].

1 See, eg *Cutsforth v Mansfield Inns* [1986] 1 All ER 577, [1986] 1 WLR 558 (involving the supply of amusement machines to public houses in the Humberside area); *Holleran v Daniel Thwaites plc* [1989] 2 CMLR 917 (involving tenancy agreements in relation to two tied houses in Lancashire).

7 CHOICE OF WHERE TO SUE

20.15
Under the Convention on Jurisdiction and the Enforcement of Judgments in Civil and Commercial Matters[1] a defendant domiciled[2] in a Contracting State may be sued there, even if the tort in question was not committed there; if there are a number of defendants, domiciled in different Contracting States, the action may be brought in any of those States[3]. In addition, under Article 5(3) of the Convention the action may instead be brought in the State where the tort occurred. Under Article 26 of the Convention a judgment given in one Contracting State must be recognised in any others, with certain limited exceptions[4]. A plaintiff contemplating bringing proceedings under Articles 81 and 82 may therefore have some scope for forum-shopping; where this is the case, careful thought should be given to the advantages and disadvantages of the various possible fora (from the point of view of remedies available, location of relevant evidence, language of the proceedings, procedural hurdles and so on).

1 The so-called Brussels Convention 1968, enacted into UK law by the Civil Jurisdiction and Judgments Act 1982, which came fully into force on 1 January 1987.
2 Domicile is determined in accordance with Articles 52 and 53 of the Convention on Jurisdiction and the Enforcement of Judgments in Civil and Commercial Matters; see also the Civil Jurisdiction and Judgments Act 1982, ss 41 and 42.
3 Convention on Jurisdiction and the Enforcement of Judgments in Civil and Commercial Matters, Article 6(1).
4 See n 3 above, Articles 27 and 28.

8 SERVICE OUT OF THE JURISDICTION

20.16
It should be borne in mind that it is sometimes necessary to obtain the leave of an English court in order to serve process out of the jurisdiction. The procedure whereby leave is applied for is set out in RSC Ord 11. However, as a result of the United Kingdom's accession to the Brussels Convention[1], it is no longer necessary to seek leave in cases in which the court has jurisdiction by virtue of the Civil Jurisdiction and Judgments Act 1982[2] (which implemented the Convention), that is to say where the defendant is domiciled in a Contracting State[3].

1 Convention on Jurisdiction and the Enforcement of Judgments in Civil and Commercial Matters 1968.
2 The Civil Jurisdiction and Judgments Act 1982 came into force on 1 January 1987.
3 See para **20.15**.

9 PARTICIPATION OF THE EUROPEAN COMMISSION

20.17
The European Commission may apply to the Court of Appeal under RSC Ord 59, r 8 that notice of appeal in a particular case be served upon it, enabling it to address arguments to the court. This procedure has been

successfully invoked in one reported case to date, *Hasselblad v Orbinson*[1], in which Counsel for the Commission appeared as amicus curiae to assist the Court of Appeal in understanding the workings of the Commission and the operation of Council Regulation 17/62[2]. The Commission was not, however, joined as a party to the proceedings as such: in order for a person to be joined as a party there must be an issue between that person and someone already a party, in respect of which some remedy or relief could be claimed[3]. The Court of Appeal only gives a direction under Ord 59, r 8 where there is good reason for doing so and the participation of the Commission in this way in national proceedings is likely to be the exception rather than the rule.

1 [1985] QB 475, [1984] 3 CMLR 679.
2 The principal Regulation under which the Commission exercises its powers under Articles 81 and 82.
3 *Re I G Farbenindustrie AG's Agreement* [1944] Ch 41, CA; *Spelling Goldberg Productions v BPC Publishing Ltd* [1981] RPC 280, CA.

20.18
In the Commission's 1993 Notice[1] on the application of the EC competition rules by national courts, the section on co-operation between the Commission and the courts[2] identifies the following principal means by which the Commission can assist a national court (none of them involving active participation by the Commission in the national proceedings):

— the national court may ask for information of a procedural nature to enable it to discover whether a particular case is pending before the Commission and, if so, the stage which it has reached;
— the Notice invites national courts to consult the Commission on points of law, although it points out that the answers given by the Commission are not binding and that this type of consultation is without prejudice to a national court's right to refer questions to the ECJ under Article 177 of the EC Treaty[3];
— national courts are invited to seek information from the Commission regarding factual data (statistics, market studies and economic analysis), subject to the Commission's duty not to disclose information of a confidential nature[4].

1 OJ [1993] C 39/6.
2 See ibid paras 33–44.
3 See para **10.67** ff.
4 As to which, see para **11.02** ff.

10 RELEVANCE OF PRIOR COMMISSION/COURT DECISION

20.19
Where the Commission has determined that a particular undertaking has violated Article 81 or 82, one or more third parties may seek to claim damages in a national court in respect of that illegal activity. The difficult question that arises is the extent to which the Commission's decision is binding before the national court. At the stage at which the matter comes

before the national court, the Commission's decision may or may not have been the subject of an appeal to the CFI and/or the ECJ.

20.20
The traditional view under English law rules on hearsay is that the contents of competition reports are not admissible as evidence of the facts stated therein. In *Macarthy v Unichem*[1] it was held that reports of the UK Monopolies and Mergers Commission constituted hearsay evidence and were therefore not admissible under the Civil Evidence Act 1968. Subsequently, the Law Commission in its report on the Hearsay Rule in Civil Proceedings[2] recommended that the general exclusion of hearsay evidence should be abolished and that hearsay evidence should be admissible, albeit that there should be safeguards built into the legislation. This recommendation was enacted into the Civil Evidence Act 1995. In *Iberian v BPB*[3], Mr Justice Laddie had to determine whether the findings of the Commission, the CFI and the ECJ were admissible in and binding on parties to English proceedings. In that case, the plaintiff was seeking damages from the defendants. The Commission had previously found the defendants to be in breach of Article 82 and that finding had been upheld on appeal by both the CFI and the ECJ. The judge held that (whether expressed in terms of res judicata or abuse of process) it would be contrary to public policy to allow persons who have been involved in competition proceedings in Europe to deny in a national court the correctness of the decision reached in those proceedings.

1 *Macarthy plc v Unichem Ltd* (24 November 1989, unreported).
2 Cm 2321, September 1993.
3 [1996] 2 CMLR 601.

11 ARBITRATION

20.21
In *Eco Swiss v Benetton*[1] the ECJ had to consider the application of Article 81 in the context of arbitration proceedings. In that case, an arbitrator had awarded damages for wrongful (as a matter of national law) termination of a trademark licence agreement which infringed Article 81. Benetton sought to prevent the enforcement of the award of damages, arguing that this would involve enforcement of an agreement which infringed EC competition law. Dutch law allows challenge to an arbitral award only on grounds of public policy. The Dutch Supreme Court referred to the ECJ the question whether EC law required the Dutch courts to consider the alleged infringement of EC competition law as a matter of public policy. The ECJ held that it did.

1 Case C-126/97 [1999] 2 All ER (Comm) 44.

12 JUDICIAL REVIEW

20.22
The Court of Appeal has held that, because Articles 81 and 82 give rise to private rights of action, it is not appropriate for them to be the subject of the

judicial review procedure under RSC Ord 53[1] (this is in contrast with the position in relation to Article 28 of the EC Treaty, dealing with free movement of goods[2]). In *R v Ministry of Agriculture, Fisheries and Food, ex p Dairy Trade Federation Ltd*[3], the applicant sought leave to apply for judicial review relating to a decision to approve the scheme for the re-organisation of the arrangements for the marketing of milk submitted by the Milk Marketing Board. The applicant represented the interests of purchasers of raw milk in the United Kingdom. It was argued that the respondents had breached, inter alia, Articles 81 and 82 of the EC Treaty, in approving the scheme pursuant to which Milk Marque (a voluntary producer co-operative society, which was the successor to the Milk Marketing Board) was able to abuse its dominant position. The application was rejected on a number of grounds, in particular the fact that the applicant had failed to apply for judicial review promptly. In addition, the court considered, in the context of how to exercise its discretion in deciding whether to grant leave for judicial review, the alternative remedies which were available. It concluded that the real complaint of the Federation was that Milk Marque was abusing its dominant position. This, it concluded, could be remedied by one of three alternative routes:

— a private civil law action by the Federation against Milk Marque in the High Court for breach of Article 82;
— a complaint under Article 82 to the European Commission in relation to Milk Marque's conduct;
— a request to the Director General of Fair Trading that he refer the matter to the Monopolies and Mergers Commission under the monopoly provisions of the Fair Trading Act 1973[4].

1 *An Bord Bainne v Milk Marketing Board* [1984] 1 CMLR 519; on appeal [1984] 2 CMLR 584, CA.
2 *Bourgoin SA v Ministry of Agriculture, Fisheries and Food* [1986] QB 716, [1985] 3 All ER 585.
3 [1995] CoD 3.
4 FTA 1973, s 50.

Chapter 21 Private Enforcement of UK Competition Law in National Courts

A Introduction

21.01
United Kingdom competition policy is traditionally focused predominantly on public rather than private enforcement. Prior to the Competition Act 1998 scope for enforcement by private individuals/companies was more limited than is the case in relation to Articles 81 and 82. For example, the principal statute dealing with restrictive trading agreements, the Restrictive Trade Practices Act 1976 (RTPA 1976), only afforded a private right of action (for breach of statutory duty) in the event that the parties to a registrable agreement failed to furnish particulars of it to the Office of Fair Trading (OFT)[1]. That is to say, the private right of action was dependent upon the formalistic issue of registration, rather than the substance of the agreement. If particulars were duly furnished, no such action could be brought, even if the agreement restricted competition significantly. In such a case enforcement was a matter exclusively for the Director General of Fair Trading (DGFT), who was empowered to refer the agreement to the Restrictive Practices Court[2]. Although the Resale Prices Act 1976[3] did enable an action for breach of statutory duty to be brought in relation to prohibited collective or individual resale price maintenance, instances of resale price maintenance was relatively rare and private actions for damages even rarer; accordingly, as in the case of the RTPA 1976, enforcement was largely in the hands of the DGFT. The Fair Trading Act 1973 (FTA 1973) and the Competition Act 1980 (CA 1980) provided very little scope for private enforcement.

1 RTPA 1976, s 35(2): see para **21.16** ff.
2 RTPA 1976, s 1(2).
3 Resale Prices Act 1976, s 25(3).

21.02
It is probably fair to say that the paucity of reported cases involving the application of any of the statutes referred to in the preceding paragraph also owes much to an attitude of mind on the part of litigants and potential litigants. It is widely believed that the enforcement of these statutes is a matter for the regulatory authorities. As a result, whilst a large number of complaints are filed with the DGFT each year, the number of private lawsuits involving any of these statutes as either a shield or a sword is very small.

21.03
This position is likely to change with the enactment of the Competition Act 1998. As the Competition Bill went through Parliament, the Government stressed that third parties who were claiming to be damaged by agreements or conduct caught by that Act should be able to take private action[1]. There is in fact nothing on the face of the Act to suggest that the right of third party action is intended to form an important part of the scheme of the new legislation, on the grounds, it appears, that such a right exists under EC competition law and providing expressly for the right of private action might prevent claimants from being able to invoke EC law principles[2]. Private actions for breach of the Act will be dealt with in the High Court; that is also the Court which would hear any action in which voidness as a result of the Act is raised in litigation (as is the case in respect of alleged voidness under Articles 81 and 82 of the EC Treaty).

1 See, for example, HC 2 R , 11 May 1998, col 35 (Margaret Beckett MP).
2 By virtue of the Competition Act 1998, s 60: see para **15.22** ff.

21.04
The remainder of this chapter sets out the present scope for private enforcement of UK competition law (both statutory and under the common law restraint of trade doctrine) through the courts. It deals in turn with the use of such law as (*a*) a shield and (*b*) a sword. Although the RTPA 1976 has been repealed by the CA 1998, there is scope for private enforcement in respect of agreements entered into prior to its repeal and to which the RTPA 1976 applied.

B UK Competition Law as a Shield

1 COMPETITION ACT 1998

21.05
Under the CA 1998, s 2(4), an agreement caught by the Chapter I prohibition is void. It would be open to a defendant to invoke s 2(4) in the same way as would be open to it to do so in relation to an agreement caught by Article 81 of the EC Treaty. The same should also be true in relation to conduct which is caught by the Chapter II prohibition[1], in the same way as is possible in relation to abuse of a dominant position under Article 82 of the EC Treaty.

1 CA 1998, s 18.

21.06
It is still too early to know the extent to which CA 1998 will be invoked by way of a defence to actions either brought by contracting parties or by third parties. It can be expected that similar issues will arise as have arisen in cases in which Articles 81 and 82 have been invoked by way of defence[1].

1 See para **19.04** ff.

2 RESTRICTIVE TRADE PRACTICES ACT 1976—AGREEMENTS WHICH HAVE NOT BEEN FURNISHED TO DIRECTOR GENERAL OF FAIR TRADING

21.07

As far as the RTPA 1976, s 35 is concerned, the position is in principle straightforward. If the parties failed to furnish particulars of a registrable agreement to the OFT within the statutory time limit, the restrictions in question are void and unenforceable, irrespective of their merits or relative insignificance: because the system laid down under the RTPA 1976 was form- and registration-based, failure to register was in and of itself the determining factor. The failure to furnish particulars of a registrable agreement can therefore be a powerful weapon in the hands of a defendant. There are, however, relatively few reported cases in which such a failure has in fact been invoked by way of defence. Now that the RTPA 1976 has been repealed (with effect from 1 March 2000), the scope to invoke the RTPA 1976 by way of defence will clearly diminish in time. However, its potential application should continue to be born in mind in relation to agreements entered into prior to that date.

21.08

Topliss Showers Ltd v Gessey & Son[1] is an example of a case in which the defendant was successful in invoking s 35 of the RTPA 1976 by way of defence to an action for breach of contract. Following a dispute between a manufacturer and a marketer of shower valves the two companies entered into a settlement agreement containing a number of restrictions imposed on each party. Under the agreement most of the restrictions were only to take effect for a relatively short period of time. The terms of the settlement were not furnished to the OFT. One of the parties subsequently commenced legal action, claiming damages and injunctive relief for alleged breaches of the settlement agreement and the defendant (in addition to denying the allegations) argued that the relevant restrictions were void and unenforceable due to the failure to register. The judge found in favour of the defendant: having concluded that the agreement was registrable under the RTPA 1976 but had not been furnished, the consequences set out in the RTPA 1976, s 35 were, he said, 'bound to follow'. The judge made it clear that he reached his conclusion without enthusiasm, viewing the defence as technical and artificial in view of the fact that the restrictions had only been accepted for a short period. Nevertheless, this case serves to emphasise that it is the failure or otherwise to furnish particulars which is crucial—if there has been such a failure, the reasonableness, significance or duration of the restrictions is of no relevance. The judge also dismissed the plaintiff's argument that the defendant was estopped from relying on any failure to furnish because it had accepted the benefits of the terms of settlement. He stated that:

> 'Where registration is a statutory requirement imposed as a matter of public policy I do not see that it would be right for the court to allow a party to rely on an estoppel to avoid the consequences of non-registration'[2].

1 [1982] ICR 501. See also *Associated Dairies Ltd v Baines* [1995] ICR 296.
2 [1982] ICR 501 at 518.

21.09

In *Storrie Estate Agency Ltd v Adams*[1] the Scottish Outer House held that the restrictions in a service agreement were void and unenforceable as a result of a failure to furnish particulars, in circumstances where the service agreement was part of an overall arrangement for the purchase of a business[2].

1 1989 SLT 305; see also *Sterling Financial Services Ltd v Johnston* 1990 SLT 111, Scottish Outer House and *Snushalls Team Ltd and Prudential Property Services Ltd v Marcus*, judgment dated 21 March 1990 (unreported).
2 Two statutory instruments (one relating to goods agreements and one to services agreements) made after the *Storrie* case (see n 1 above) subsequently removed the obligation to furnish particulars from many agreements for the sale of a business.

21.10

A case in which the RTPA 1976, s 35 was unsuccessfully invoked is *Academy Sound and Vision Ltd v WEA Records Ltd*[1]. On this occasion the defendant's reliance on s 35 was dismissed because the court concluded that the copyright agreement in question satisfied the provisions of para 5A of Sch 3 to the RTPA 1976 and accordingly was exempt from registration. Similarly, in *MD Foods plc v Baines*[2] the House of Lords stated that the agreement in question was not registrable because the part which was not covered by s 9(3) fell within para 2(*b*) of Sch 3 to the RTPA 1976.

1 [1983] ICR 586. Another case in which the defence of non-registration was raised is *Vernon v Universal Pulp Containers* [1980] FSR 179; the issue was raised in the context of interlocutory proceedings; the court took the view that the defence was arguable and found that the balance of convenience favoured the defendants.
2 [1997] 1 All ER 833.

21.11

Where s 35 of the RTPA 1976 applied, the agreement was expressed to be void 'in respect of all restrictions accepted'[1]. The RTPA 1976 was silent as to the status of other provisions of the agreement. It would seem in principle that the doctrine of severance should apply, as it does in the case of restrictive provisions caught by Article 81 of the EC Treaty[2]. Accordingly, the rest of the agreement should be enforceable unless the offending elements cannot be successfully severed and/or severance causes the agreement to be altered out of all recognition.

1 RTPA 1976, s 35(1)(*a*).
2 See para **19.09** ff.

21.12

On its plain wording, s 35(1)(*a*) of the RTPA 1976 rendered all restrictions void. Under the RTPA 1976, s 43(1) the term 'restriction' was defined to include 'a negative obligation, whether express or implied and whether absolute or not'. However, the question arises whether the voidness in fact applied only to those provisions by virtue of which an agreement is registrable. The distinction is not purely academic, because there were certain restrictions which the RTPA 1976 allowed to be disregarded for the purpose of determining registrability. Moreover, on a literal reading of s 43(1) the term 'restriction' could be taken to extend to obligations not even covered by s 6 or 11 of the RTPA 1976. The predecessor to the RTPA 1976, s 35, s 7 of the Restrictive Trade Practices Act 1968, only rendered 'relevant' restrictions void. These were defined in s 14 of the 1968 Act as ones by virtue of which an agreement was registrable. Section 35 of the RTPA 1976 abandoned the reference to relevant restrictions but it is unclear whether this was intended to have a substantive effect on the operation of the RTPA 1976.

21.13
In the *Harper and Tunstall* case[1] counsel for the DGFT was prepared to concede that s 35 of the RTPA 1976 only applied to restrictions by virtue of which the agreement was subject to registration. However, the point did not have to be decided. In a later unreported case[2], Mackinnon J adopted the same approach in the context of a staff-poaching provision contained in a sale of business agreement and related service agreement. He appears to have reached the view which he did on the basis that the provision in question was not a restriction of the type covered by s 11 of the RTPA 1976 and therefore had 'nothing to do with the mischief at which the Act was aimed', rather than on the basis that it was a section 11 restriction but one which fell to be disregarded under the RTPA 1976, s 18(6)[3].

1 *Re Agreements relating to the supply of Diazo Copying Materials, Machines and Ancillary Equipment* [1984] ICR 429.
2 *Snushalls Team Ltd and Prudential Property Services Ltd v Marcus* (21 March 1990, unreported); for a contrary interpretation of the RTPA 1976, s 35, see the Law Society's Gazette, 22 August 1990, pp 23–24.
3 RTPA 1976, s 18(6) provided that, in determining registrability, no account should be taken of restrictions which relate to the workers to be employed.

21.14
Although the interpretation of Mackinnon J in the *Snushalls*[1] case does fly in the face of the apparently plain wording of the statute, it is submitted that it is the correct one. However, in view of the fact that he reached his decision on the basis that the provision was not a section 11 restriction, rather than on the basis of the RTPA 1976, s 18(6), it technically left open the question whether a restriction to which a provision such as s 18(6) applies is rendered void by the RTPA 1976, s 35. It is submitted not.

1 See para **21.13**, n 2.

C UK Competition Law as a Sword

1 GENERAL

21.15
The two principal UK competition law statutes, namely the Competition Act 1998 and the Fair Trading Act 1973, provide some scope for private enforcement through the courts. They do so in different ways and each is

considered in turn below. First, brief consideration is given to the position in respect of agreements which were caught by the Restrictive Trade Practices Act 1976 prior to its repeal on 1 March 2000.

2 RESTRICTIVE TRADE PRACTICES ACT 1976

21.16
Section 35(1)(*b*) of the RTPA 1976 made it unlawful for any person who carried on business within the United Kingdom and who was party to an agreement which was registrable, but particulars of which were not furnished in time, to give effect to, or enforce or purport to enforce, the agreement in respect of any restrictions or information provisions. Section 35(2) went on to provide that the obligation to comply with that subsection was a duty owed to any person who may be affected by a contravention and any breach of that duty was actionable. This was subject to the usual defences applying to actions for breach of statutory duty[1].

1 On the subject of breach of statutory duty generally, see *Clerk & Lindsell on Torts* (17th edn, 1995) ch 11; *Street on Torts* (10th edn, 1999) ch 21; *Salmond & Heuston on the Law of Torts* (21st edn, 1996) ch 10.

21.17
Actions for breach of statutory duty under s 35(2) of the RTPA 1976 were commenced in the High Court (or the county court if the sum claimed is sufficiently small). In such proceedings, reliance may be placed[1] upon any findings of fact and law which are made in proceedings brought before the RPC by the DGFT under the RTPA 1976, s 35(3). Only a party carrying on business in the United Kingdom could be sued[2].

1 RTPA 1976, s 35(7).
2 RTPA 1976, s 35(1)(*b*).

21.18
There is, however, no reported case under the RTPA 1976, s 35(2), although a number of cases have been settled out of court. One of the principal difficulties which a plaintiff was likely to face, and on which evidence arising from s 35(3) proceedings was unlikely to assist him, was the assessment of the quantum of damages[1]. It would frequently also be difficult to establish to the satisfaction of the court a nexus between the plaintiff's loss and the restrictive agreement[2]. One of the most commonly cited examples of an out-of-court settlement of an action brought under the RTPA 1976, s 35(2), involved the Post Office. The case involved suppliers of insulated electric wires and cables who had allegedly colluded in relation to supplies to the Post Office. These arrangements came to light during the course of a Monopolies and Mergers Commission inquiry under the Fair Trading Act 1973. The Post Office commenced proceedings under s 35(2) and a settlement was eventually reached involving a payment to the Post Office (by way of adjustment to prices previously charged to it) of some £9 million[3].

1 For similar difficulties in relation to Articles 81 and 82, see para **20.08**.
2 For similar difficulties in relation to Articles 81 and 82, see paras **20.04**, **20.05**.
3 *Annual Report of the Director General of Fair Trading* 1979 p 37.

21.19

The RTPA 1976 was repealed with effect from 1 March 2000. However, it is submitted that if a claimant could show loss arising from a breach of statutory duty committed prior to repeal, he has a potential cause of action in respect of the period up to the date of repeal (subject to the relevant limitation period).

3 ORDERS AND UNDERTAKINGS UNDER THE FAIR TRADING ACT 1973

21.20

The scope for private enforcement of the monopoly and merger provisions of the FTA 1973 is limited. This is a natural consequence of the fact that the provisions in question do not prohibit particular conduct by monopolists or particular anti-competitive practices[1]. Rather, the FTA 1973 sets out circumstances in which particular conduct or practices can be investigated by the DGFT in the first instance, and subsequently by the Competition Commission, in order to establish whether a particular merger situation, or the facts relating to a particular monopoly situation, operate or may be expected to operate against the public interest. Until such time, the conduct/practice in question is entirely lawful.

1 Compare the position in relation to Articles 81 and 82 of the EC Treaty.

21.21

If particular conduct by a monopolist is found to be against the public interest, the FTA 1973 enables the Secretary of State to make orders designed to remedy the adverse public interest effects[1]. It is only after such an order comes into force that conduct in violation of the order gives rise to potential action by the Secretary of State himself or by third parties. The scope for action by third parties is set out at paras **21.23** ff.

1 See para **14.77** ff.

21.22

The FTA 1973 specifically contemplates the possibility of the party whose conduct has been the subject of an adverse public interest finding by the Competition Commission giving undertakings to the Secretary of State as to its future conduct, in lieu of an order[1]. Until recently, such undertakings were not enforceable by the Secretary of State[2] or by third parties; the only remedy was for the Secretary of State to make an order which would be enforceable. In practice, the majority of cases tend to be settled by undertakings rather than by formal orders and the statutory framework therefore contained something of a lacuna. This has now been rectified by the Companies Act 1989, which has added a new provision to the FTA 1973[3] under which undertakings are now enforceable. The present position in relation to the enforceability of undertakings by third parties is set out at para **21.25**.

1 FTA 1973, s 88: see para **14.68**.
2 See para **14.73**.
3 FTA 1973, s 93A.

(1) Enforceability of Orders by Third Parties

21.23
Orders made by the Secretary of State under the FTA 1973 are enforceable by civil proceedings by the Crown for an injunction (interdict in Scotland) or other 'appropriate relief'[1]. Breach of such an order does not constitute a criminal offence[2]. If the Crown were to obtain an injunction which was subsequently breached, this would amount to contempt of court which could be punished by imprisonment.

1 FTA 1973, s 93(2).
2 FTA 1973, s 93(1).

21.24
As far as action by third parties is concerned, the FTA 1973, s 93(2) provides that nothing elsewhere in the section limits the right of any person to bring civil proceedings in respect of a contravention or apprehended contravention of any such order. However, this does not necessarily mean that such rights do in fact exist. In *Mid Kent Holdings v General Utilities*[1], the plaintiff sought a declaration that the defendant was in breach of undertakings previously given by it to the Secretary of State following a merger inquiry conducted by the Monopolies and Mergers Commission—now the Competition Commission—(although the case concerned an undertaking[2] to the Secretary of State, rather than an order made by him, the same principles should apply in both cases). Mr Justice Knox held that the FTA 1973 did not confer on a private person a right of action to enforce such undertakings. The question whether Mid Kent had such a right had to be determined by reference to general law principles. Under those principles, a breach of statutory duty and damage resulting therefrom were not of themselves enough to confer a private right of action on a prospective plaintiff, irrespective of whether the claim was for damages, injunction or a declaration. The judge held that, in the particular case in question, the statutory obligations which the undertakings were to be treated as creating were imposed to avoid particular detriment to the *public* interest identified by the MMC's report, and not to avoid particular detriment to Mid Kent. This case establishes that the question whether a private party can bring an action to enforce undertakings given to the Secretary of State (and it would seem an order made by the Secretary of State) must be determined on a case-by-case basis, having regard to the nature and purpose of the particular undertakings/order.

1 *Mid Kent Holdings plc v General Utilities plc* [1996] 3 All ER 132.
2 See para **21.25**.

(2) Enforceability of Undertakings by Third Parties

21.25
Until recently, the only remedy in the event that undertakings were subsequently broken was for the Secretary of State to exercise his order-making powers under the FTA 1973[1]. The FTA 1973, s 93A(2), introduced by the

Companies Act 1989, now makes it possible for the Crown or for third parties to take action in relation to the breach of undertakings accepted by the Secretary of State under:

(*a*) FTA 1973, s 75G (undertakings in relation to a proposed merger, in lieu of a reference to the Monopolies and Mergers Commission (MMC));

(*b*) FTA 1973, s 88[2] (undertakings following a report by the MMC in relation to a merger situation or a monopoly situation).

Section 93A(2) of the FTA 1973 provides that:

> 'Any person may bring civil proceedings in respect of any failure, or apprehended failure, of the responsible person to fulfil the undertakings, as if the obligations imposed by the undertakings on the responsible person had been imposed by an order to which section 90 of this Act applies'.

Section 93A(2) is on the face of it expressed in more positive terms than s 93(2) itself (the subsection dealing with enforcement of orders). However, it would seem from the *Mid Kent* case[3] that the same principles apply in either case. This is logical.

1 See *Fogg v Esso Petroleum Ltd* (6 April 1990, unreported); also, *R v Monopolies and Mergers Commission, ex p Air Europe* (1988) 4 BCC 182.
2 See para **14.69** ff.
3 *Mid Kent Holdings plc v General Utilities plc* [1996] 3 All ER 132, see para **21.24**.

4 COMPETITION ACT 1998

21.26
As noted in para **21.03** during the passage of the Competition Act 1998 through Parliament, the Government made it clear that third parties who were claiming to be damaged by agreements or conduct caught by the Act should be able to take private action[1]. There is in fact nothing on the face of the CA 1998 to suggest that the right of third party action is intended to form an important part of the scheme of the new legislation, on the grounds, it appears, that such a right exists under EC competition law and providing expressly for the right of private action might prevent claimants from being able to invoke EC law principles[2].

1 See, for example, 2 HC Official Report (6th series), col 35 (11 May 1998, per Margaret Beckett MP).
2 By virtue of the Competition Act 1998, s 60: See para **15.22**.

21.27
One provision of the CA 1998 which is consistent with the right of private action (and which would indeed facilitate such action) is s 58. That provides that a finding of fact made by the DGFT in the course of dealing with a notified agreement or notified conduct, or conducting an investigation under s 25[1], which is relevant to an issue arising in 'Part I of proceedings' is binding on the parties if the time for bringing an appeal in respect of the finding has expired without the bringing of an appeal or if the decision of an appeal tribunal on such an appeal has confirmed the finding. For this purpose, 'Part I proceedings' means proceedings in respect of an alleged

infringement of either the Chapter I prohibition (restrictive agreements) or the Chapter II prohibition (abuse of dominant position) but which are brought otherwise than by the DGFT.

1 See para **15.132**.

Index

All references are to paragraph numbers

All references are to paragraph numbers

All references are to paragraph numbers

All references are to paragraph numbers

All references are to paragraph numbers

All references are to paragraph numbers

All references are to paragraph numbers

All references are to paragraph numbers

All references are to paragraph numbers